SALADS

Favorite Recipes of Home Economic Teachers

Too good to be forgotten...

2,000 Favorite Recipes

SALADS

Favorite Recipes of Home Economic Teachers

FRP
P. O. Box 305142
Nashville, Tennessee 37230
1-800-358-0560

ISBN: 978-0-87197-537-9

Cover and chapter opener design by Rikki Odgen Campbell/pixiedesign, llc

Printed in China

Other books in this series:

DESSERTS

MEATS

CASSEROLES

VEGETABLES

To order this and many other award-winning cookbooks, visit www.cookbookmarketplace.com or call 1-800-269-6839.

Revised slightly from the version published in 1965.

TABLE OF CONTENTS

MAKE THE RIGHT CHOICE BECAUSE . . .

salads are always in good taste. Without them, many meals would be incomplete. Salads offer variety, food values and often that bit of color needed to perk up an otherwise drab menu.

The uses of salads are almost as varied as the kinds of salads from which to choose. Most frequently, salads are served in medium-size portions as accompaniments to meals and are light rather than heavy. Small bits of tart fruit or seafood arranged on a bed of greens are appetite teasers and are often used as the first course of a meal.

Hearty salads — those that contain meat, poultry or seafood with fresh raw or cooked vegetables — are a meal in themselves and are used as main dishes. Cheese and eggs also make good bases for tasty main dishes.

Sweet salads are sometimes served as desserts and are used for special occasions.

A good rule of thumb to remember when choosing a salad is that light rather than heavy, rich salads go better with hearty meals. Tart salads are especially good with seafoods. Hot or hearty salads make good main dishes and fruit salads may be used as appetizers, desserts or meat accompaniments.

SECRETS OF A SUCCESSFUL SALAD MAKER

Choose pleasing combinations of ingredients with contrasts in color, texture, form and flavor. Experiment with color, but use only foods with pleasing color combinations that do not clash.

Experiment with soft and firm food textures. Try fruits and vegetables mixed for a different and delightful taste treat.

Prepare ingredients carefully. Use only clean chilled, crisp greens. When using fruits, drain thoroughly on absorbent paper. Drain vegetables in a sieve.

Cut or tear foods into pieces that are large enough to tell what they are, yet small enough to handle easily. Avoid cutting salad greens. Cutting tends to make them wilt faster.

Keep hot salads hot, not lukewarm, and cold salads icy cold.

Use the correct dressing. Don't drown salads. Too much dressing will make salads limp, soggy and unattractive. A small amount of dressing adds just the right flavor. Add dressings at the last possible moment. If salads stand in their dressings too long, they tend to lose their crispness and are unattractive.

Prepare salads just before serving for a fresh, crisp look and taste. Serve on chilled plates.

Toss salads lightly to prevent bruising and discoloration. Don't over-mix.

Arrange salads attractively, but avoid a fixed, rigid look. Make sure the greens don't extend over the edge of the plate. Never crowd a large salad on a too-small plate.

Garnish salads attractively, but don't use too much garnish.

Serve salads daily, but aim for variety.

TENDER, LOVING CARE . . .

is what a wooden salad bowl deserves and needs. A salad bowl is almost essential when it comes to making a good salad. The harder the wood, the better the bowl because hard wood does not absorb too much of the liquid dressing. But no matter how hard the wood, salad bowls deserve special attention.

Never soak wooden bowls or salad servers in water. Rinse them quickly in clear lukewarm water after using. Rinse in cold water. Wipe completely dry and store in a dry place. In time garlic, dressings and other flavorings will season the bowl.

SALAD GREENS . . . THE START OF IT ALL

Almost every salad creation starts with greens, whether they be mixed in the salad or used as beds. Often the wide selection of greens from which to choose is overlooked.

In addition to the familiar standbys, head or leaf lettuce, other plants such as romaine, endive, water cress, chicory and escarole provide an added attraction to salads.

Uncooked green vegetable leaves are fine for salads and beds, too. Spinach, kale, celery leaves, beet and turnip tops, Swiss chard and dandelion greens are rich in vitamins and have a zesty tang. Any of these may be used mixed for a green salad or as beds for other types of salads.

To make sure that the bed is eaten, sprinkle it with dressing before the salad is arranged on top. Keep the bed small and never let the greens extend over the edge of the plate.

BIBB LETTUCE is a small, crisp, cup-shaped lettuce with a distinct color and flavor. The leaves are a deep rich green that blend to a whitish green toward the core.

BOSTON LETTUCE is loosely headed with oily feeling leaves. It is not especially crisp. The outer leaves are a deep dark green and the inner leaves shade to almost white. It is very perishable and should be used the day it is purchased.

ICEBERG LETTUCE is the best known and most available lettuce on the market. Heads are firm, heavy and crisp textured. The cores are small. Leaves are medium green on the outside and shade to pale green in the center.

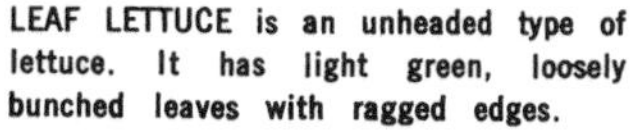

LEAF LETTUCE is an unheaded type of lettuce. It has light green, loosely bunched leaves with ragged edges.

CHICORY OR CURLY ENDIVE has a large head with long, ragged leaves. It has a slightly bitter flavor.

CHINESE OR CELERY CABBAGE has a long, oval head that is firm, fresh and well blanched.

ESCAROLE has large, broad leaves that shade from deep green on the outside to butter yellow in the center. Its edges look ruffled. It is sturdy and crisp and has a slightly bitter flavor.

FRENCH OR BELGIAN ENDIVE is light green, almost white. Its head is compact, 5 to 6 inches long. It has a slightly bitter taste.

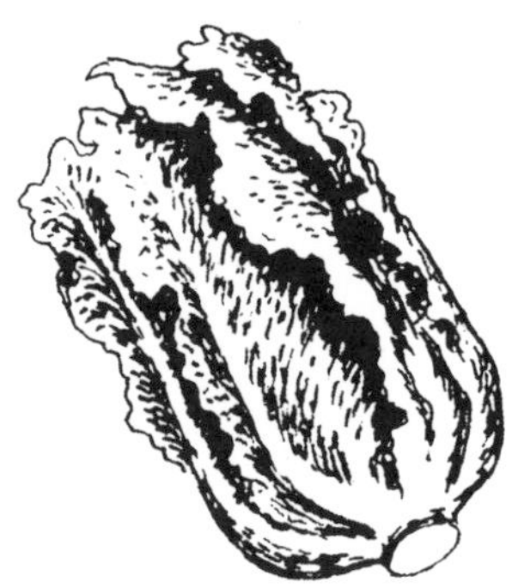

ROMAINE OR COS is lettuce with an enlongated head and stiff leaves. The leaves are coarse but sweet. They keep well. The dark outer leaves shade to almost white at the root end. The lighter inner leaves are particularly tender and flavorable.

SPINACH LEAVES are slightly tart and tangy.

WATER CRESS is an aquatic plant sold in bunches. The leaves are small, oval and mildly pungent.

In general, all greens should be young and crisp, clean, green and tender. Avoid greens with leaves that are yellow or withered or that have rusty red streaks or spots. These discolorations are harmless, but make unattractive salads.

Remember when choosing greens that the darker salad vegetables offer larger amounts of vitamins A and C, and are richer in iron than the paler ones.

Select crisp lettuce such as iceberg that is firm and heavy for its size. If it is to be used for cups, choose lettuce with a loose head. Leaf lettuce should have pale green leaves and a firm core.

Select chicory, endive and escarole that have a few dark, tough outer leaves. The inner leaves are more likely to stay crisp longer and have a better flavor.

Spinach should have dark, small tender leaves. A good sign of toughness is coarse stems.

When selecting celery, make sure that the stalks are solid and thick, yet brittle enough to snap easily. Stalks that are medium in length are usually best. Avoid celery with cracked stalks and brown dry tops. Test the stalk to see if it is firm by gently pressing it.

PREPARING GREENS FOR SALADS

A salad is good only if the greens are fresh and crisp instead of wilted and watery.

Rinse greens carefully under cool running water to remove any outside grit. Remove discolored, wilted leaves. Remove tough outer leaves. If they are unbruised, shred them for use in sandwiches and as salad beds. These outer leaves, although they aren't as tender as the inner ones, are especially rich in vitamins and minerals.

To rid greens of bugs, add 4 tablespoons of salt to each gallon of water. Rinse well. Shake off excess water or drain well. Place in refrigerator to crisp.

Just before making the salad, remove the greens from the crisper and finish washing them.

Iceberg lettuce—cut out the core with a sharp knife to separate the leaves. Hold the lettuce with cored side up under running water. Run cold water into the core opening. The leaves will separate. Shake off excess water. Dry thoroughly.

Romaine, endive, escarole, leaf lettuce, etc.—separate leaf by leaf and wash well. Dry thoroughly.

Chicory, young spinach—wash in several changes of water to remove all grit. Dry well.

Water cress, parsley, mint—open and pick over bunch to remove all dead and tough stems. Wash thoroughly under cold running water. Drain well and store loosely—separate from other salad greens—with stem down in a covered jar in the refrigerator.

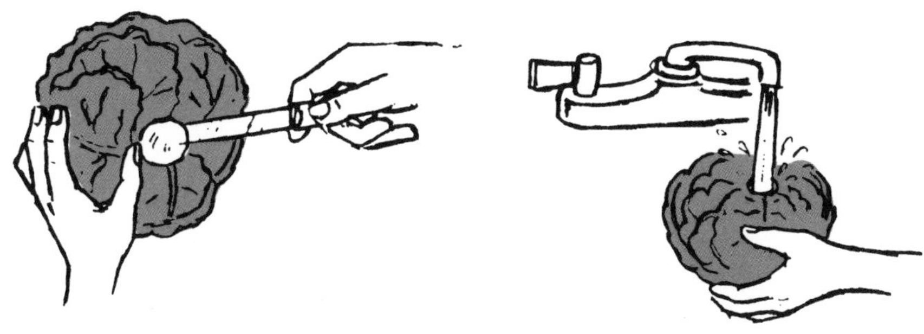

DRYING GREENS

Drying greens is very important. This job must be done very gently because some greens are tender and will bruise easily. Shake off excess water after washing. Spread the greens out on a fresh clean tea towel or paper towel. Roll up loosely and put into the refrigerator until it is time to prepare the salad.

DRESSING A SALAD

Salad dressings are like the icing on a cake—the varieties are almost endless. And just as icings add that extra taste appeal to cakes, dressings do the same for salads.

If a salad looks attractive, it's no problem to get guests to take that first bite. But it's the dressing that makes the salad disappear.

Never soak or drown a salad in dressing. Too much dressing will result in a soggy, limp product. Add dressings just before serving for a better salad flavor and crisp texture.

CHOOSING A DRESSING

There is no definite rule that declares what dressing must be used with a particular salad. But there are guideposts to follow.

Tangy French dressings are used to marinate vegetables and to toss with greens. Use tart or sweet dressings for fruit salads.

Mayonnaise and salad dressing combinations enhance meat, seafood, egg and molded salads.

Cooked dressings just naturally go with greens and vegetables.

Sour cream dressings add zip to fruit and vegetable salads.

DRESSING DICTIONARY

FRENCH DRESSING is a mixture of oil, vinegar and seasonings. Clear French dressing separates and must be thoroughly shaken before it is used. Creamy French dressings are homogenized and will stay mixed.

MAYONNAISE is smooth and creamy. It is made by beating oil very slowly into seasoned vinegar and egg. It is mildly flavored and can be used with additional seasonings.

COOKED DRESSING has a cooked white sauce and egg base. It is fluffy, creamy and has a zippy flavor.

SALAD DRESSING is a rich, smooth blend of mayonnaise and cooked dressing.

Fine salad oil is essential to good dressings. Choose either corn, cottonseed, olive, peanut or soy oil, or a blend of these. Never use mineral oil, it may rob the body of important vitamins.

Lemon juice gives a tangy accent to dressings. Fresh, canned or frozen, it not only adds zip and tartness, but vitamin C as well. Use lemon juice interchangeably with vinegar.

Vinegar comes in many exciting flavors. Choose from one of or several of these:

CIDER—*Is a good all-purpose vinegar for salads and dressings.*

MALT—*Has a rich flavor gives added zest to dressings.*

TARRAGON—*Has a herb fragrance which is wonderful in salads and dressings.*

WINE—*Is made from select table wines. It adds zest to dressings.*

BASIL, HERB AND SPICE OR MIXED HERB—*Is used lightly in salad dressings or on cooked greens, slaw.*

GARLIC WINE—*Is used instead of garlic in salads and dressings.*

MOLDING A MASTERPIECE

Stars, crescents, bunnies, fish, ring—all of these special molds are available for making congealed salads in fancy shapes. Rounds, square, oval and oblong molds may also be found on the market.

One of the most popular of these is the ring mold because the center may be filled with fruits, jelly, vegetables, cheese or a bowl of dressing, which makes it versatile.

Don't overlook the possibility of using the most common utensils in your kitchen for molding salads. Custard cups, muffin pans, cake tins, ice cube trays, empty coffee cans and even paper cups, make effective molds.

To mold a perfect salad follow these simple rules:

To avoid diluting the gelatin mixture, drain frozen or canned fruits thoroughly before adding, or substitute syrup from the fruits as a part of the liquid for added flavor.

Let gelatin set until it is the consistency of unbeaten egg whites before adding fruits and vegetables. If they are added to the gelatin mixture before it sets, they will settle to the bottom of the mold.

Carefully fold the fruits and vegetables into the thickened gelatin to distribute them evenly.

To mold different flavors or colors in layers, let each layer set before adding the next one.

For a stay-put garnish in a molded salad, arrange the design, such as a ring of cucumber slices, on a layer or partially set gelatin. Chill, pour another layer over the design. Chill.

To keep the bubbles in a carbonated beverage that is used as the liquid in a gelatin salad, pour the beverage down the side of the bowl. Stir with an up and down motion.

For success in molding and unmolding a layered or ribbon salad use heavy duty aluminum foil. Tear off long strips of the foil and cross them in the bottom of a loaf pan, leaving strips extending out of the pan. Mold salad layers according to recipe directions. When salad is congealed, lift the foil strips to loosen the firm gelatin. Unmold very carefully and peel off foil.

This unusual recipe makes an attractive centerpiece for salad plates or ring-molded salads.

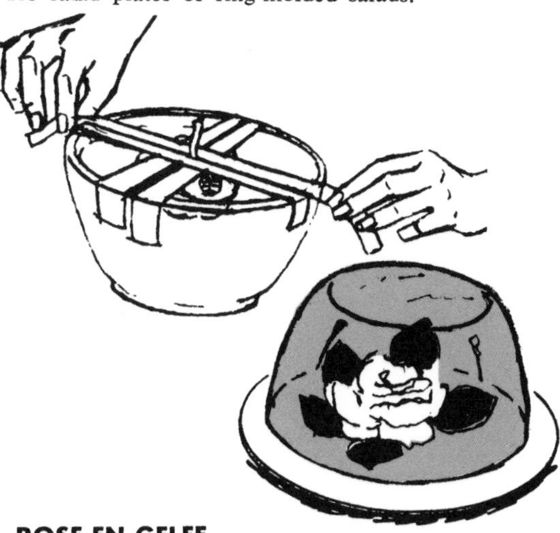

ROSE EN GELEE

1 partially opened rose or artificial flower
2 envelopes unflavored gelatin
⅔ c. sugar
2 c. boiling water
1 c. cold water

Mix gelatin and sugar. Add boiling water; stir until gelatin dissolves. Add cold water; cool. Invert flower in the center of a 1-quart bowl. Clip stem so it extends just above rim of bowl. To hold flower in place, secure tightly with 4 pieces of tape placed across top of bowl, each on one side of stem. Carefully pour in gelatin. If desired, insert a few leaves. Chill until set. Remove tape and clip stem. Unmold and place right side up in center of salad plate.

Leanna Boline, Paola H. S.
Paola, Kansas

CHILLING TO THE RIGHT CONSISTENCY

Different recipes will call for different degrees of chilling the gelatin mixture.

When a recipe calls for a mixture chilled to "slightly thicker than unbeaten egg whites," it means that the gelatin will dribble unevenly from a spoon when chilled to the proper degree of coldness.

For whipped cream mixtures, the gelatin mixture should be chilled so it is thick enough to mound slightly when dropped from a spoon.

Gelatin mixtures will pour from a spoon in an unbroken stream when it is "chilled to unbeaten egg white consistency." This is the consistency usually required for simple gels and chiffons.

Gelatin mixtures require from two to four hours to set in the refrigerator. They will congeal faster if they are in small individual molds.

For a quick chill, place gelatin mixture in freezer compartment for ten minutes. Or set the bowl in ice water and stir the mixture until it starts to thicken. If mixture becomes too solid, remelt over boiling water.

FROZEN SALADS

A boon to the hurried homemaker is the salad which can be frozen. It may be prepared days in advance of serving time and still be fresh and delicious.

Salads which freeze best are those with a base of cream cheese, cottage cheese or whipped cream. Those which contain large amounts of mayonnaise or salad dressing tend to separate if frozen.

In general, salads which are frozen in refrigerator ice trays are best suited for freezing.

Be sure that salads that are to be frozen and left in the freezer for any length of time are packaged in moisture-vaporproof containers.

Limit storage time for frozen salads. Don't store them in the freezer for more than three months.

Frozen salads are generally better if they are served before they are completely thawed.

UNMOLDING GELATIN SALADS

Dip mold in warm, but not hot, water to the depth of the gelatin. Loosen around the edge with the tip of a paring knife.

Rinse the serving dish with cold water. Don't dry the plate so the gelatin will slide easily if it needs to be centered on the plate.

Place the serving dish on top of the mold and turn upside down. Shake gently, holding serving dish tightly to the mold. Remove mold carefully.

If the gelatin does not unmold rapidly, repeat the process.

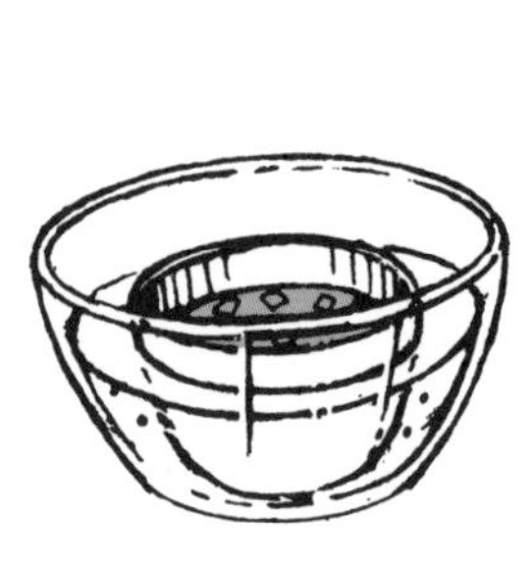

Selecting Fruits for Salads

FRUIT	HOW TO SELECT	STORAGE
APPLES	Avoid those that are soft to the touch or that have shriveled skin.	Keep in cool place. Can be refrigerated.
BANANAS	Should be plump and firm with a bright yellow skin, or, when fully ripe, flecked with brown. Avoid those that are green-tipped.	Store at room temperature. Refrigerator storage stops ripening, impairs flavor.
BERRIES	Should be bright, clean, plump, fully colored and fragrant. Avoid over ripe, soft berries with leaking juice.	Very perishable. Pick over carefully and spread out before refrigerating. Wash just before using. Use as soon as possible.
CITRUS FRUITS	Choose those that are firm and heavy for their size, with fine-textured skins. Avoid those that have a puffy skin (except loose-skinned tangerines.)	Store in a cool, dark, dry place, or refrigerate.
CHERRIES	Choose those that are plump, firm, bright and have stems attached. Stain will indicate if they are over ripe.	Wash and store in refrigerator.
GRAPES	Should be plump, with fresh good color and firmly attached stems. If stems are brittle, bunches will "shatter" easily.	Store in refrigerator for as short a time as possible.
MELONS	Should have fragrant aroma, be unbruised. A ripe melon will be soft near the stem and will give a little. Thump watermelons. If they give a hollow, not dull,, thudding sound, they are ripe.	Store at 70°F. to ripen. Refrigerate before serving.
PEACHES	Should be plump, firm, smooth-skinned and of good color (whitish or yellowish with a reddish blush). Avoid those that are shriveled or very green.	Very perishable. Handle gently and refrigerate.
PEARS	Should be smooth-surfaced, fragrant, well-shaped. Firm to fairly firm, but not hard. Avoid those that are rotted or bruised at stem or blossom end.	Store in a cool, dry, dark spot. If hard, ripen at room temperature.
PINEAPPLE	Should be fragrant, dark orange-yellow in color, heavy to feel. Avoid those with discolored areas or soft, watery spots. To test for ripeness, pull one of the leaves at the top. It should pull out easily.	Keep in cool place.
PLUMS	Choose plump, dark ones that are soft but not mushy. Avoid if shriveled or brownish.	Keep in refrigerator.

PREPARING FRUITS FOR SALADS

MELON BALLS—

Use melon ball tool, or scoop out fruit with ½ teaspoon measuring spoon.

CITRUS FRUITS—

The 'round and 'round method—Cut the peel away in a continuing spiral with a slight sawing motion. Don't remove the white inner portion which clings naturally to the "meat." It is rich in vitamins and minerals.

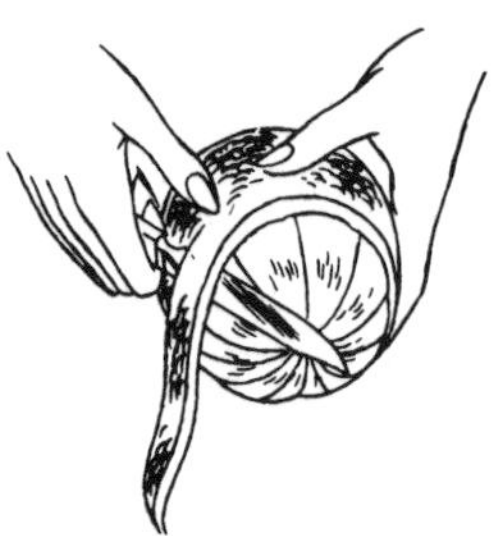

Basketball method—With a sharp knife slice off the stem end of the fruit. Score the peel with a knife so that it looks like the sections on the outside of a basketball. Don't cut down into the "meat." Pull the peel away with your fingers, again leaving the white inner skin which clings to the "meat."

Cartwheels—Use them peeled for salads, unpeeled for garnishes. Slice fruit crosswise in desired thickness. For halfwheels, cut cartwheels in two parts.

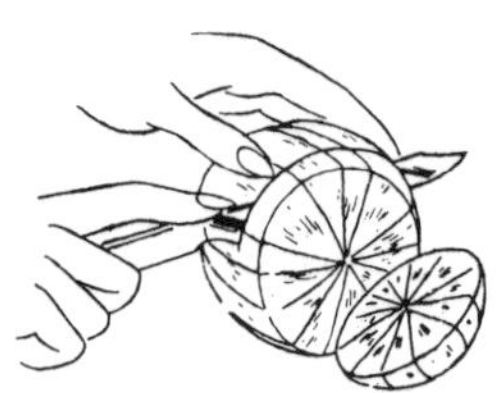

Sections—Peel fruit. Cut sections halfway between segment walls so that the membrane is in the center of the "meat."

Segments—Peel fruit, gently separate into natural divisions.

Shells—Score fruit around middle with knife point; peel away from fruit with spoon handle. Edges can be notched with scissors.

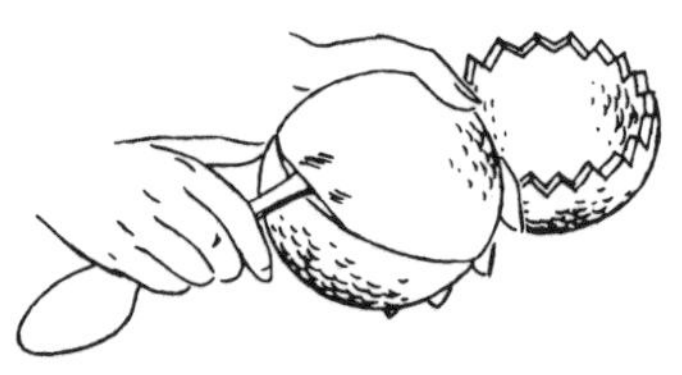

Swirling Fringe Edge—Cut top edge at angle with sharp knife after fruit sections have been cut out.

FANCY BASKETS—

Cut ¼-inch wide strip around top of orange or grapefruit half, leaving 1 inch on each side uncut. Cut down through membrane to free strips.

A-Bow—Cut the ¼-inch strip as above. Cut each strip at center and fold back. Fasten with toothpicks.

B-Handles—Pull together at top the two ¼-inch strips, without further cutting. Fasten with picks.

C-Spiral—Cut each strip near attached end, roll tightly and fasten with picks.

To prevent fruit, other than citrus from discoloring, slice fruit with a stainless steel knife at the last moment. Or, sprinkle with lemon juice, powdered ascorbic or citric acid preparations and store in refrigerator until time to serve.

A New Idea... Orange Chunks with Dips

Cartwheels for Ambrosia

Jiffy Salad Guide

VEGETABLES

START WITH	COMBINE WITH	SERVE WITH
Shredded cabbage	Chopped onion Thinly sliced carrots	Olive French Dressing
Shredded cabbage	Chopped green pepper Chopped pimiento	Garlic French Dressing Dash Tabasco
Shredded cabbage	Drained pineapple chunks	Fluffy Cream Dressing with extra salt, to taste
Shredded cabbage	Salted peanuts	French Dressing
Shredded cabbage	Chopped celery Chopped parsley	Thousand Island French Dressing
Shredded cabbage	Unpared red apples, diced Nut meats, broken	Cooked Mayonnaise, with extra salt, to taste
Shredded cabbage	Minced green pepper Minced onion	Celery Seed French Dressing
Tomatoes, cut into eighths	Chopped onion Capers	Celery Seed French Dressing
Tomatoes, sliced	Sliced cucumber	Garlic French Dressing
Tomatoes, cut in very thin vertical slices	Minced parsley Minced green onions Freshly ground black pepper	1-Minute French Dressing
Tomatoes, cut into eighths	Head lettuce, broken into bite-size pieces	Onion French Dressing
Tomatoes, sliced	Avocado, pared and cut into strips	French Dressing
Tomatoes, sliced	Cottage cheese	Chive French Dressing

Jiffy Salad Guide Continued

VEGETABLES

START WITH	COMBINE WITH	SERVE WITH
Tomatoes, centers removed	Diced cooked chicken	Creamy French Dressing
Cucumber, sliced	Green onions, sliced or Sweet onion, sliced	French Dressing
Cucumber, sliced	Sliced tomatoes	Garlic French Dressing
Cucumber, sliced	Sliced radishes Green pepper strips	Onion French Dressing
Cucumber, chopped	Chopped onion Hearts of lettuce	Creamy French Dressing
Cucumber, with center removed	Fill cucumber with seasoned cream cheese. Slice and arrange on lettuce	French Dressing
Cucumber, sliced	Sliced onions Lettuce chunks Tomato wedges	French Dressing

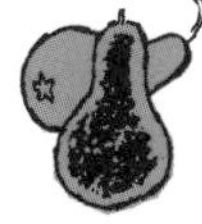

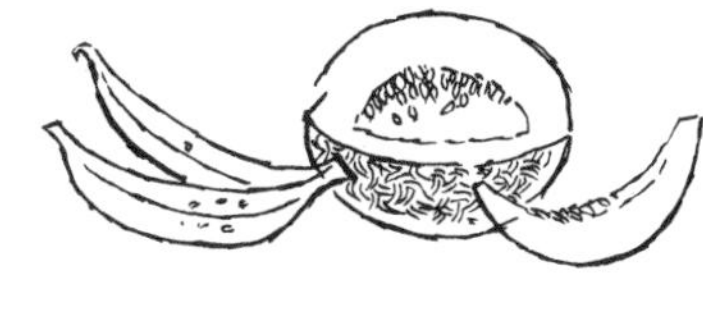

FRUIT

START WITH	COMBINE WITH	SERVE WITH
Red apples, sliced	Spread apple slices with cream cheese	French Dressing
Red apples, sliced	Grapefruit sections	Fruit Dressing
Apple wedges, cooked in cinnamon candy syrup	Avocado, pared and sliced	French Dressing
Diced apples	Halved raw cranberries. Diced celery	Creamy French Dressing

Jiffy Salad Guide Continued

FRUIT

START WITH	COMBINE WITH	SERVE WITH
Diced apples	Diced celery Orange sections	Mayonnaise
Diced apples	Chopped celery Nuts Seeded Tokay grapes	French Dressing
Crushed pineapple	Chopped cucumber Lettuce	Mayonnaise
Pineapple chunks (fresh or canned)	Sliced bananas Diced celery	Cooked Dressing
Pineapple chunks (fresh or canned)	Melon balls	Mint French Dressing
Sliced pineapple (fresh or canned)	Cream cheese Chopped nuts	French Dressing
Sliced pineapple (fresh or canned)	Grapefruit sections Orange sections	Fruit Dressing
Sliced pineapple (fresh or canned)	Prunes, stuffed with cream cheese	French Dressing
Sliced pineapple (fresh or canned)	Peach halves Cottage cheese	Creamy French Dressing
Bananas, sliced	Red apples, sliced	Fruit Dressing
Bananas, sliced	Shredded cabbage	Mayonnaise with prepared mustard added
Bananas, sliced	Grapefruit sections Orange sections	Honey French Dressing
Bananas, sliced	Pineapple slices Red berries	French Dressing
Bananas, sliced lengthwise	Spread with peanut butter, press together. Slice crosswise. Sprinkle with chopped salted peanuts.	Creamy French Dressing

Salad Making Terms and Definitions

BEAT—*To make a mixture smooth or to introduce air by using a brisk, regular motion that lifts the mixture over and over*

BLANCH—*To parboil in water for a minute, or to pour boiling water over food and then drain it almost immediately*

BLEND—*To thoroughly mix two or more ingredients*

CHILL—*To refrigerate until thoroughly cold*

CHOP—*To cut into pieces with a sharp knife*

CREAM—*To work one or more foods until mixture is soft and creamy*

CUT—*To divide food materials with a knife or scissors*

DICE—*To cut into cubes*

FLAKE—*To break into small pieces*

FOLD—*To combine by using two motions, cutting vertically through the mixture and turning over and over by sliding the implement across the bottom of the mixing bowl with each turn*

GARNISH—*To decorate. Ex: to decorate a fish salad with hard-cooked eggs or parsley*

GRATE—*To cut food into minute bits by rubbing on a grater*

GRIND—*To cut food into tiny particles by putting through a grinder*

MARINATE—*To let food stand in a marinade—usually an oil-acid mixture such as French dressing*

MINCE—*To cut or chop into very small pieces*

MIX—*To combine ingredients in any way that evenly distributes them*

PARE—*To cut off the outside covering*

PEEL—*To strip off the outside covering*

SCALD—*To heat milk to just below the boiling point*

SHRED—*To cut finely with a knife or sharp instrument*

SLIVER—*To slice into long, thin strips*

STIR—*To mix food materials with a circular motion for the purpose of blending or securing uniform consistency*

TEAR—*To break or tear into bite-size pieces*

TOSS—*To lightly blend food ingredients*

WHIP—*To beat rapidly to produce expansion due to the incorporation of air as applied to cream, egg and gelatin dishes*

HERB, SPICE, CHEESE, AND BLEND CHART

Never Store Seasonings Above or Near the Stove. Keep Them Tightly Covered. When Seasonings Lose Their Delicate Aroma Replace Them.

HERBS:	USE WITH
BASIL	Tomato salads, fresh tomato slices
CARAWAY	Coleslaw, beet salads
DILL SEED	Coleslaw, potato salad
MARJORAM	French dressing, fresh tomato slices, meat salads
OREGANO	Potato or tuna salads
ROSEMARY	French dressing or mayonnaise for chicken or potato salads
SAVORY	Tossed salads
THYME	French dressing marinade for diced chicken

SPICES:	USE WITH
ALLSPICE	Fruit salads, fruit salad dressings
CINNAMON	Tomatoes, cottage cheese garnishes
GINGER	Pear salads
MACE	Whipped cream dressings for fruit salads
MUSTARD	Mixed with water for commercial mayonnaise or French dressing
PAPRIKA	Add to oil and vinegar for additional color
CAYENNE PEPPER	Salad dressings, meat, fish and vegetable salads

BLENDS:	USE WITH
SEASONING SALT	Substitute for salt in oil and vinegar dressings
ITALIAN DRESSING	French dressing, tossed green salads
APPLE PIE SPICE	Waldorf salad
CURRY POWDER	French dressing for chicken salad
SALAD LIFT	Add to oil and vinegar for French dressing or stir into prepared salad dressing
PICKLING SPICE	Beet salads
HERB SEASONING	Sliced cucumbers, sliced tomatoes, French dressing

CHEESE CHART

CHEESE	USE WITH
AMERICAN CHEDDAR	Tossed salads, dressings, appetizers
BLEU (BLUE)	Tossed salads, dressings, appetizer spreads
BRICK	Salads, appetizers
CAMEMBERT	Fruit salads, appetizer spreads
COTTAGE	Fruit, vegetable salads
CREAM	Fruit, vegetable salads, dressings, appetizer spreads
GORGONZOLA	Salads, dressings
GOUDA	Appetizers
MUENSTER	Raw vegetable appetizers
PROVOLONE	Appetizers
ROQUEFORT	Dressings, appetizers
RICOTTA	Salads, appetizers
SWISS	Fruit, vegetable salads

SALAD CALORIE CHART

	Amount	Calories
CHEESE		
Blue Mold (Roquefort type)	1 oz.	105
Cheddar or American:		
Ungrated	1 1-in. cube	70
Grated	1 cup	455
Cheddar, process	1 oz.	105
Cheese foods, Cheddar	1 oz.	28
Cottage cheese (from skim milk):		
Creamed	1 oz.	30
Creamed	1 cup	240
Uncreamed	1 oz.	25
Uncreamed	1 cup	195
Cream cheese	1 oz.	105
Cream cheese	1 T	55
Swiss	1 oz.	105
MEAT, POULTRY, FISH, SHELLFISH, RELATED PRODUCTS		
Bacon, broiled or fried crisp	2 slices	95
Chicken, cooked:		
Flesh and skin, broiled	3 oz. without bone	185
Canned, boneless	3 oz.	170
Pork, cured, cooked:		
Ham, smoked, lean and fat	3 oz.	290
Luncheon meat:		
Cooked ham, sliced	2 oz.	170
Canned, spiced or unspiced	2 oz.	165
Crab meat, canned or cooked	3 oz.	90
Salmon, pink, canned	3 oz.	120
Shrimp, canned, meat only	3 oz.	110
Tuna, canned in oil, drained, solids	3 oz.	170
NUTS, PEANUTS, RELATED PRODUCTS		
Almonds, shelled	1 cup	850
Brazil nuts, broken pieces	1 cup	905
Cashew nuts, roasted	1 cup	770
Coconut:		
Fresh, shredded	1 cup	330
Dried, shredded, sweetened	1 cup	345
Peanuts, roasted, shelled:		
Halves	1 cup	840
Chopped	1 T	50
Peanut butter	1 T	90
Pecans:		
Halves	1 cup	740
Chopped	1 T	50
Walnuts, shelled:		
Black or native, chopped	1 cup	790
English or Persian:		
Halves	1 cup	650
Chopped	1 T	50
VEGETABLES AND VEGETABLE PRODUCTS		
Beans:		
Lima, immature, cooked	1 cup	150
Snap, green: Cooked in small amount of water	1 cup	25
Canned, solids and liquids	1 cup	45
Beets, cooked, diced	1 c.	70
Cabbage:		
Raw:		
Finely shredded	1 c.	25
Cole slaw	1 c.	100
Cooked	1 c.	40

SALAD CALORIE CHART — Continued

	Amount	Calories
Cabbage, celery or Chinese:		
Raw, leaves and stem, 1-inch pieces	1 c.	15
Cooked	1 c.	25
Carrots:		
Raw:		
Whole, 5½ x 1 in. (25 thin strips)	1 carrot	20
Grated	1 c.	45
Cooked, diced	1 c.	45
Cauliflower, cooked, flower buds	1 c.	30
Celery, raw:		
Stalk, large outer 8 x 1½ in. at root end	1 stalk	5
Pieces, diced	1 c.	20
Cucumbers, 10-oz., 7½ x 2 in.:		
Raw, pared	1 cucumber	25
Raw, pared, center slice, ⅛-in. thick	6 slices	5
Endive, curly (including escarole)	2 oz.	10
Lettuce, headed, raw:		
Head, loose leaf, 4-in. diameter	1 head	30
Head, compact, 4¾-in. diameter, 1 lb.	1 head	70
Leaves	2 large or 4 small	5
Mushrooms, canned, solids and liquid	1 c.	30
Onions:		
Mature:		
Raw, 2½-in. diameter	1 onion	50
Cooked	1 c.	80
Young, green, small, without tops	6 onions	25
Parsley, raw, chopped	1 T.	1
Peas, green:		
Cooked	1 c.	110
Canned, solids and liquids	1 c.	170
Canned, strained	1 oz.	10
Peppers, sweet; Raw, medium, about 6 per lb.:		
Green pod without stem and seeds	1 pod	15
Red pod without stem and seeds	1 pod	20
Canned, pimentoes, medium	1 pod	10
Potatoes, medium, about 3 per lb.; Boiled		
Peeled after boiling	1 potato	105
Peeled before boiling	1 potato	90
Potato chips, medium 2-in. diameter	10 chips	110
Radishes, raw, small, without tops	4 radishes	10
Sauerkraut, canned, drained, solids	1 c.	30
Tomatoes:		
Raw, medium 2 x 2½-in. diameter, about 3 per lb.	1 tomato	30
Tomato juice, canned	1 c.	50
Tomato catsup	1 T.	15
FRUIT AND FRUIT PRODUCTS		
Apples, raw, medium 2½-in. diameter, about 3 per lb.	1 apple	70
Apple juice, fresh or canned	1 c.	125
Applesauce, canned:		
Sweetened	1 c.	185
Unsweetened	1 c.	100
Apricots:		
Raw, about 12 per lb.	3 apricots	55
Canned, in heavy syrup: Halves and syrup	1 c.	220
Dried:		
Uncooked, 40 halves, small	1 c.	390
Cooked, unsweetened, fruit and liquid	1 c.	240
Avocados, raw:		
California varieties, 10 oz., 3⅓ x 4¼-in., peeled, pitted	½ avocado	185

SALAD CALORIE CHART — Continued

	Amount	Calories
Florida varieties, 13 oz., 4 x 3 in., peeled, pitted	½ avocado	160
½-inch cubes	1 c.	195
Bananas, raw, 6 x 1½ inch, about per lb.	1 banana	85
Blackberries, raw	1 c.	85
Blueberries, raw	1 c.	85
Cantaloups, raw, medium, 5-in. diameter, about 1⅔ lb.	½ melon	40
Cherries:		
Raw, sour, sweet, hybrid	1 c.	65
Canned, sour, red, pitted	1 c.	105
Cranberry sauce, sweetened, canned or cooked	1 c.	550
Cranberry juice cocktail, canned	1 c.	140
Dates, "fresh" and dried, pitted, cut	1 c.	505
Figs:		
Raw, small 1½ in. diameter, about 12 per lb.	3 figs	90
Dried, large, 2 x 1 inch	1 fig	60
Fruit cocktail, canned in heavy syrup, solids and liquids	1 c.	195
Grapefruit:		
Raw, medium 4¼ in. diameter		
White	½ grapefruit	50
Pink or red	½ grapefruit	55
Raw, sections, White	1 c.	75
Grapefruit juice:		
Fresh	1 c.	95
Canned:		
Unsweetened	1 c.	100
Sweetened	1 c.	130
Grapes, raw:		
American type (slip skin)	1 c.	70
European type (adherent skin)	1 c.	100
Grape juice, bottled	1 c.	165
Lemons, raw, medium, 2⅕ in. diameter	1 lemon	20
Lemon juice:		
Fresh	1 c.	60
Fresh	1 T.	5
Canned, unsweetened	1 c.	60
Lemonade concentrate, frozen, sweetened		
Undiluted, 6-fluid oz. can	1 can	430
Water added	1 c.	110
Lime juice:		
Fresh	1 c.	65
Canned	1 c.	65
Oranges, raw:		
Navel, California (winter), 2⅘ in. diameter	1 orange	60
Other varieties, 3 in. diameter	1 orange	70
Orange juice:		
Fresh:		
California Valencia, summer	1 c.	120
Florida varieties:		
Early and midseason	1 c.	100
Late season	1 c.	110
Canned, unsweetened	1 c.	120
Frozen concentrate:		
Undiluted 6-fluid oz. can	1 can	330
Water added	1 c.	110
Orange and grapefruit juice:		
Frozen concentrate:		
Undiluted 6-fluid oz. can	1 can	330
Water added	1 c.	110
Papayas, raw, ½-in. cubes	1 c.	70

SALAD CALORIE CHART — Continued

	Amount	Calories
Peaches:		
Raw:		
Whole, medium, 2-in. diameter, about 4 per pound	1 peach	35
Sliced	1 c.	65
Canned, yellow-fleshed, solids and liquids	1 c.	65
Syrup pack, heavy, halves or slices	1 c.	200
Dried:		
Uncooked	1 c.	420
Cooked, unsweetened, 10-12 halves and 6 T. liquid	1 c.	220
Frozen:		
Carton, 12 oz.	1 carton	265
Can, 16 oz.	1 can	355
Peach nectar, canned	1 c.	115
Pears:		
Raw, 3 x 2½ in.-diameter	1 pear	100
Canned, solids and liquids, heavy syrup pack, halves or slices	1 c.	195
Pear nectar, canned	1 c.	130
Pineapple:		
Raw, diced	1 c.	75
Canned, syrup pack, solids and liquid:		
Crushed	1 c.	205
Sliced, slices and juice	2 Small or 1 large slice and 2 T. juice	95
Pineapple juice, canned	1 c.	120
Plums, all except prunes:		
Raw, 2-in. diameter, about 2 oz.	1 plum	30
Canned, syrup pack (Italian prunes), plums and juice	1 c.	185
Prunes, dried:		
Medium, 50-60 per lb.:		
Uncooked	4 prunes	70
Cooked, unsweetened, 17-18 prunes and ⅓ c. liquid	1 c.	305
Canned, strained	1 oz.	25
Prune juice, canned	1 c.	170
Raisins, dried	1 c.	460
Raspberries, red:		
Raw	1 c.	70
Frozen, 10-oz. carton	1 carton	280
Strawberries:		
Red, capped	1 c.	55
Frozen, 10-oz. carton	1 carton	300
Frozen, 16-oz. can	1 can	485
Tangerines, raw, medium, 2½-inch diameter, about 4 per lb.	1 tangerine	40
Tangerine juice:		
Canned, unsweetened	1 c.	105
Frozen concentrate:		
Undiluted, 6-fluid oz. can	1 can	340
Water added	1 c.	115
Watermelon, raw, 4 x 8-in. wedge	1 wedge	120
FATS AND OILS		
Oils, salad or cooking:		
Corn	1 T.	125
Cottonseed	1 T.	125
Olive	1 T.	125
Soybean	1 T.	125
Salad dressings:		
Bleu cheese	1 T.	90
Commercial, plain, mayonnaise type	1 T.	60
French	1 T.	60
Home-cooked, boiled	1 T.	30
Mayonnaise	1 T.	110
Thousand Island	1 T.	75

APPETIZERS

As their name implies, appetizers are appetite-teasers. Their main function is not to satisfy hunger, but to whet the appetite. Good appetizers should strike an expectant note for the meal that is to follow.

Appetizers, which are usually finger foods, must be attractive to see, as well as tangy and tantalizing to the taste buds.

When planning appetizers, keep in mind the meal that is to follow. If the dinner is to be rich and heavy, avoid serving appetizers that are rich and filling. Choose instead, crisp, fresh appetizers such as raw vegetables with a sour cream dunk sauce. If the meal is to be light, heavier and more filling appetizers may be served.

Never serve appetizers made with the same foods that are to be included in the meal. For example, don't serve seafood appetizers if seafood is included on the dinner menu.

Hot or cold, take your choice. Appetizers may be served either way. Be sure that those to be served cold are crisp and cold, not lukewarm, melted and wilted. Hot appetizers should be piping hot.

WHEN AND WHERE TO SERVE APPETIZERS

Appetizers are always served before the main course and are either passed around or served buffet-style.

There are no set rules governing where appetizers must be served. Some prefer to serve them outside on the patio if weather conditions are favorable. Still others like to serve them in the living room. If appetizers are served at the dining table, they usually replace the soup course.

Since most appetizers are eaten with the fingers, it is not always necessary to provide forks. Do make sure that napkins are within easy reach and that there is a convenient place to set glasses and plates. Always keep appetizers small enough to handle easily.

SERVING WITH A FLAIR

All foods taste better if they are attractive to look at, and appetizers are no exception. Hollowed shells of fruits such as melons, pineapple and grapefruit make attractive and unusual serving dishes. Appetizers are appealing when arranged attractively on trays, bread boards, serving platters or in baskets.

Surround dips with mounds of chips and crackers. Serve seafood appetizers from beds of shredded ice.

Provide alcohol lamps so guests can toast their own tiny meat appetizers or sandwiches. Keep appetizers hot in chafing dishes and let guests help themselves.

APPETIZER TERMS

ANCHOVY—*A small, smoked, herring-like fish packed in oil and canned. Very salty and pungent.*

ANCHOVY PASTE—*A paste made of anchovies.*

ASPIC—*Jellied broth used to make cold vegetable, meat or fish molds.*

CANAPES—*Small pieces of fried or toasted bread spread or garnished with seasoned toppings.*

CAVIAR—*The roe of sturgeon. Very expensive.*

RED CAVIAR—*Salmon roe, less expensive.*

COMPOTE—*A mixture of fresh or cooked fruits.*

CROUTONS—*Small toasted bread cubes.*

DEVILED—*Combined with sharp seasonings and cooked with a crumb topping. Or crumbled, cooked and served with a sharp sauce.*

HORS D'OEUVRE—*Appetizers served with cocktails or before dinner.*

FOIE GRAS—*Preserved goose liver.*

PATE—*Paste usually made of poultry, seafood or meat. Used as spreads for canapes or crackers or cut into thin slices and served with a garnish.*

PATE DE FOIE GRAS—*A pate made with goose livers. Sometimes made with chicken livers.*

PUREE—*Usually vegetables or fruits which have been put through a sieve or food milk to form a smooth paste.*

SPANISH OLIVES—*Green olives stuffed with pimento.*

TRUFFLES—*A dark, rich fungus which grows underground in some parts of Europe. Used in some pates. Very expensive.*

THE FINISHING TOUCH

A garnish has two functions—to decorate a salad and to add to its taste.

A garnish is not the center of attraction and should be kept small. The garnish should provide contrast and added interest to a salad, but should never be gaudy.

Never over-garnish a salad, especially if it is served buffet-style. Guests may end up with no salad, just garnishes.

Choose salad plates carefully. The dish, as well as the salad and its garnish, is important in the attractiveness of the salad. Always leave some plate showing to provide a frame for the salad.

Use your imagination when arranging a salad on a plate. Often the way a salad is placed on the serving plate is all the garnish that's needed.

CHOOSING A GARNISH

Type of Salad . . . Garnish

TOSSED GREEN . . . Apples; artichoke bottoms; avocado; bacon; cheese; meat; eggs; citrus fruit; grapes; olives; radishes; seafood; cold, cooked vegetables; croutons; nuts.

TOSSED VEGETABLE . . . Anchovies; bacon; Bleu cheese; capers; eggs; grated lemon rind; nuts; pickle relish; sardines; dill pickles; pimento.

POULTRY . . . Asparagus tips; avocado; cranberry jelly; fruit; olives; nuts; water cress; dill; mint; parsley.

FRUIT . . . Cheese; cheese spreads; nuts.

MEAT, SEAFOODS . . . Fruit; cheese; cucumbers; olives; tomatoes; pickles; mushrooms.

DRESS UP FOOD

CELERY CURLS—

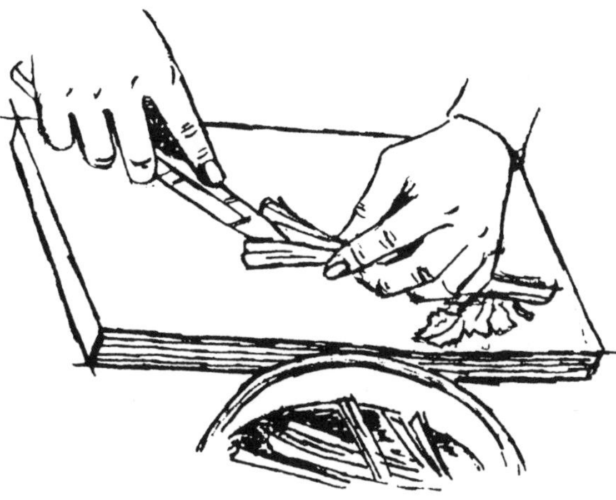

Cut celery stalks in short pieces. Slice ends in narrow lengthwise strips. Both ends may be slit if desired. Place cut celery in ice water.

CARROT CURLS—

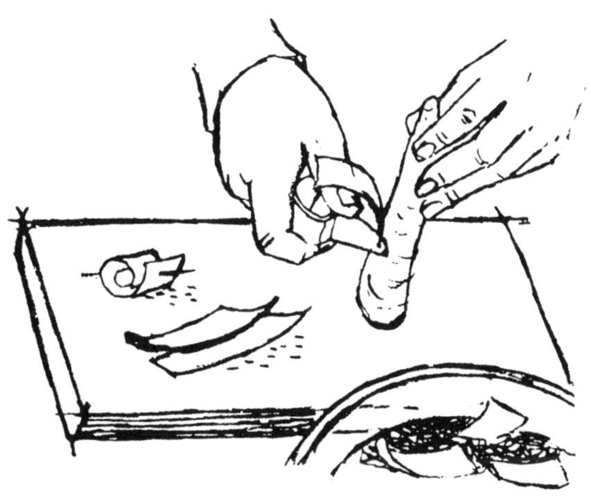

Scrape raw carrots to remove tough outer skin. Use potato peeler to make thin strips down the length of the carrot. Roll up strips, secure with toothpicks and place in ice water until crisp and curled.

SCORED OR FLUTED CUCUMBER—

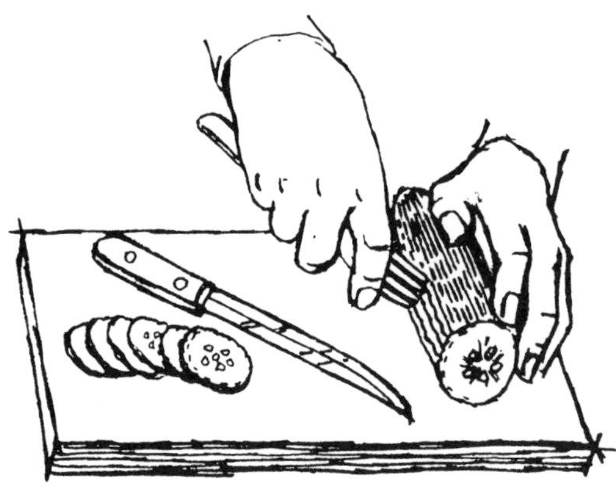

Cut off end of the cucumber. Peel if the cucumber is tough. Leave young cucumber unpeeled for added color. Pull the tines of a fork firmly down the length of the cucumber into thin slices. Chill in the refrigerator.

TOMATO FLOWERS—

Using a sharp knife, cut the tomato into wedges, making sure that it is not cut completely through. Lightly spread wedges apart.

RADISH ROSES—

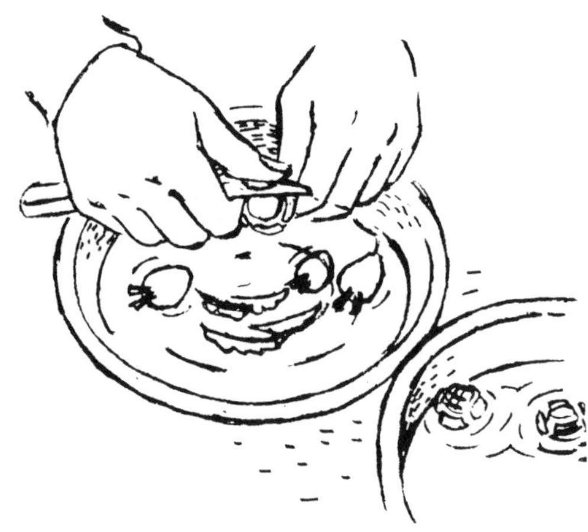

Using a sharp knife, cut off the radish root. Leave some of the stem and leaves. Thinly slice around the radish from stem to the root end. Place in ice water. Do not try to separate or spread the petals apart. The ice water will cause them to bloom.

ORANGE, LEMON, GRAPEFRUIT FLOWERS

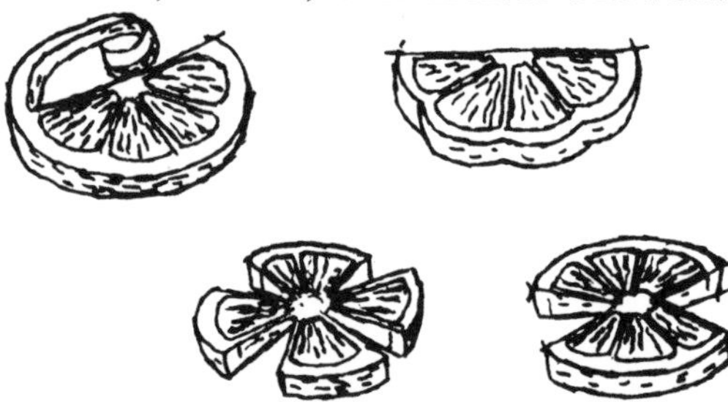

—Cut unpeeled fruit into eighths, slicing almost to the bottom. Spread wedges gently apart.

ORANGE, LEMON, GRAPEFRUIT TWISTS—

Cut unpeeled fruit into thin slices. Cut through one side of the peel. Twist.

Appetizers

CHEESE BALL

Number of Servings — 10-15

1 small glass Vera sharp cheese
¼ lb. Bleu cheese
4 3-oz. pkg. cream cheese
1 t. red pepper
1 T. Worcestershire sauce
¼ t. salt
Grated garlic
1 c. pecans, chopped
1 c. fresh parsley, finely chopped

Let cheeses reach room temperature. Mix together. Use small amount of cream if necessary to mix cheeses well. Add salt, pepper, garlic, Worcestershire sauce and ½ cup pecans. Spread remaining pecans and parsley on a large sheet of waxed paper. Shape cheese into a ball and roll in pecan-parsley mixture. Refrigerate overnight. Serve with cocktail crackers.

Frieda C. Black, Walterboro H. S.
Walterboro, South Carolina

MYSTERY CHEESE BALLS

Number of Servings — 3 Balls

1½ lb. American cheese
6 5-oz. jars Bleu cheese
2 t. Worcestershire sauce
2 t. onion juice
½ t. garlic salt
½ c. nuts, chopped
½ c. parsley, chopped

Have cheeses at room temperature. Put American cheese in electric mixer and soften. Add Bleu cheese, one jar at a time, blending well. Add onion juice, Worcestershire sauce and garlic salt. Chill. Form into 3 balls about the size of your fist; refrigerate. Roll in nuts and parsley. Wrap in foil; refrigerate. Cheese balls will keep a month.

Mrs. Shirley Andersen, Dalton H. S.
Dalton, Nebraska

CHEESE BALL

Number of Servings — 25-30

6 oz. Roquefort cheese, softened
10 oz. sharp cheese spread, softened
10 oz. cream cheese, softened
2 T. onion, grated
1 t. Worcestershire sauce
1 c. pecans, ground
½ c. parsley, finely chopped

Combine cheeses, onion and Worcestershire sauce. Blend well. Stir in ½ cup pecans and ¼ cup parsley. Shape mixture into ball. Place in bowl lined with waxed paper. Chill overnight. About ½ hour before serving roll ball in mixture of remaining pecans and parsley.

Mrs. Jean H. Teale, Bentleyville-Ellsworth
Area Joint H.S.
Ellsworth, Pennsylvania

CHEESE BALL

Number of Servings — 10

1 4-oz. jar Roquefort cheese spread
2 4-oz. jars Old English cheese spread
2 T. catsup
1 t. Worcestershire sauce
1 drop Tabasco sauce

Combine all ingredients. Form into a ball. Refrigerate. Roll the ball in parsley or pecans if desired. (May be used as a pretzel dip).

Miss Roberta Bosch, Mandan Jr. H.S.
Mandan, North Dakota

BLEU CHEESE BALL

Number of Servings — 6

½ clove garlic
1 lb. cream cheese
¼ lb. Bleu cheese
1 T. Worcestershire sauce
1 dash Tabasco sauce
Brazil nuts, sliced

Blend cheeses and sauces in bowl which has been rubbed with garlic. Form mixture into a ball and roll in sliced nuts. Serve with crackers or chips.

Mrs. Clarice J. Hubbard, Mitchell Jr. H.S.
Mitchell, South Dakota

MYSTERY CHEESE BALL SPREAD

Number of Servings — 2 Cups

3 5 oz. pkgs. Bleu cheese spread
½ 8 oz. pkg. cream cheese
1 t. onion, finely chopped
1 t. Worcestershire sauce
½ c. walnuts, chopped
2 T. parsley, chopped

Blend cheeses, onion and Worcestershire sauce; chill overnight. Shape into a ball; roll in walnuts and parsley. Or serve as a spread for crackers.

Cowen Morgenstern, Hamden H.S.
Hamden, Ohio

PARTY CHEESE BALL

Number of Servings — 40

½ c. walnuts, chopped
3-5 oz. Bleu cheese
1 8-oz. pkg. cream cheese
¼ t. garlic salt
1 T. green pepper, minced
1 T. pimento, minced

Heat oven to 350°F. Spread walnuts in a shallow pan and toast for 8-10 minutes or until golden. Stir occasionally. Blend cheeses; stir in garlic salt, pimento and green pepper. Chill until firm. Shape into a ball; roll in toasted walnuts. Chill until serving time. Serve with assorted crackers.

Mrs. Ethel B. Douglas, Kaplan H. S.
Kaplan, Louisiana

CHEESE BALL PICK-ME-UPS

Number of Servings — 7½ Dozen

1 8-oz. pkg. cream cheese
1 4-oz. pkg. Bleu cheese
1 5-oz. jar Old English cheese
1 6-oz. roll smoked cheese
1 t. Ac'cent
Dash of salt
¼ t. garlic powder or 1 clove garlic, crushed
1 T. Worcestershire sauce
⅛ t. Tabasco sauce
1 c. parsley, finely snipped
1 c. pecans, finely chopped
Pretzel sticks

Have cheeses at room temperature. Blend well with Ac'cent, salt, garlic and sauces. Add ⅓ cup parsley and ½ cup pecans; blend. Chill cheese mixture until it is easy to handle. Form into tiny balls about 1 inch in diameter and roll in reserved parsley-nut mixture. Refrigerate. Cheese balls will keep for several days. Insert a pretzel stick in each cheese ball just before serving.

Mrs. Lura Lee Davis, Reagan Junior H. S.
Sweetwater, Texas

CHEESE LOAF

Number of Servings — 4½ Cups

1 lb. sharp process American cheese
1 8-oz. pkg. cream cheese
1 4-oz. pkg. Bleu cheese
1 6-oz. roll smoke-flavored cheese food
2 T. prepared horseradish
1 T. prepared mustard
1 T. onion salt
1 clove garlic, grated
2 T. parsley, chopped

Let cheese soften at room temperature. With electric mixer, combine all ingredients except parsley. Shape into a loaf; keep chilled until about an hour before serving time. Let loaf reach room temperature before serving. Sprinkle with parsley.

Mrs. Jean P. Driver, Fort Defiance H. S.
Fort Defiance, Virginia

CHEESE LOG

1 lge. pkg. cream cheese
1 jar Old English cheese
¼ t. garlic salt
½ t. Worcestershire sauce
1 c. nuts, chopped or 1 c. parsley, minced

Combine cheeses, garlic salt and Worcestershire sauce with a fork until well blended. Shape cheese mixture into roll or ball; roll in nuts or parsley. Refrigerate. Serve with snack crackers.

Kathleen Kniola, New Buffalo Area Schools
New Buffalo, Michigan

FROZEN LOG

Number of Servings — 1 Loaf

½ lb. yellow sharp cheese
8 slices uncooked bacon
½ t. Worcestershire sauce
2 small onions
1 t. dry mustard
2 t. mayonnaise

Put all ingredients through a food chopper. Mix well. Roll into a log the size of a 50 cent piece. Freeze. When ready to serve, slice and place on bread rounds, crackers, or split English muffins. Broil until browned. Serve with a salad.

Mrs. Mary Evans, MacArthur H. S.
San Antonio, Texas

PECAN-CHEESE MOLD

Number of Servings — 25

1 lge. glass cheddar cheese spread
1 small pkg. cream cheese
½ t. Worcestershire sauce
6 or 8 stuffed olives, chopped
1 c. pecans, chopped

Let all ingredients reach room temperature. Thoroughly blend cheeses; add Worcestershire sauce and olives. Form into balls and roll in pecans. Chill. Serve with crackers. Make several days before serving so pecans will permeate cheese.

Dorothy Jean Keller, Cobden Unit School
Cobden, Illinois

CHEESE ROLL

Number of Servings — 6-8

1 6-oz. pkg. cream cheese
1 lb. sharp cheese
1 c. nuts (pecans)
1 clove garlic
Mayonnaise
Chili powder

Grind cheese, garlic, nuts and cream cheese. Blend with hands. Add mayonnaise to soften. Shape and roll in chili powder. Chill.

Mrs. Betty Tipton, Everman H. S.
Everman, Texas

CHEESE ROLL

½ lb. American cheese, grated
6 3-oz. pkgs. cream cheese, softened
2 t. onion, grated
2 t. Worcestershire sauce
1 sliver of garlic, crushed
¼ c. pecans or walnuts, finely chopped

Mix cheeses with an electric mixer. Blend. Add onion, Worcestershire sauce and garlic; mix well. Grease mold with butter; sprinkle the nuts over the inside of mold. Carefully pour cheese mixture into mold. Chill for several hours. Serve with crisp crackers around the cheese mixture.

Mrs. Frances Dailey, Greensburg Salem Sr. H.S.
Greensburg, Pennsylvania

PAPRIKA CHEESE ROLL

½ lb. Old English cheese, cut up
½ lb. Velveeta cheese
1 clove garlic
2 T. mayonnaise
1 t. mustard
1 t. horseradish
Paprika

Soften cheeses over hot water. Add seasonings; mix well. Place cheese mixture on waxed paper which has been generously sprinkled with paprika; form into a roll. Wrap cheese roll in waxed paper and chill. Slice thin and serve with assorted crackers.

Mrs. Ruby Beto, Indian School
Flandreau, South Dakota

CHEESE PUMPKINS

Number of Servings — 24

1 lb. mild cheese, grated
½ t. onion salt
½ t. garlic salt
½ t. paprika
Mayonnaise
½ c. cracker meal
Cloves

Combine cheese, onion salt, paprika and garlic salt. Add enough mayonnaise to moisten. Form mixture into balls of desired size. Roll in cracker meal. Flatten each ball slightly and make creases in "pumpkins" with back of table knife. Top with cloves. Refrigerate.

Mrs. Annie Glenn Templeton, Boonshill School
Petersburg, Tennessee

TARTELETTES AU FROMAGE (Cheese Tarts)

Number of Servings — 12

2 c. light cream
3 eggs
1 c. Swiss cheese, grated
⅔ c. cooked ham, diced
1 T. butter, melted
12 partially baked tart shells
Cayenne pepper to taste
Salt to taste
Pepper to taste

Combine eggs and cream; beat. Add salt, pepper and cayenne pepper; strain. Add the cheese and butter. Put a spoonful of ham in the bottom of each tart shell. Fill shell with the custard mixture. Bake at 350°F. 15 minutes or until the custard is set. Serve warm.

Mary Lou Thomas, Wauseon H. S.
Wauseon, Ohio

ROQUEFORT ROLLS

Number of Servings — 16 to 20 Rolls

2 3-oz. pkg. cream cheese
⅛ lb. Roquefort cheese
2 T. celery, finely chopped
1 T. onion, finely chopped
Dash of cayenne pepper
Salad dressing
1½ c. California walnut meats, finely chopped

Blend cream and Roquefort cheeses. Add celery, onion, cayenne, and salad dressing. Form in tiny rolls (or balls if preferred). Roll in nut meats and chill.

Mrs. Jo Frances Weimar, Alto H. S.
Alto, Texas

THREE-WAY CHEESE TREAT

Basic Cheese Base:
1½ lb. cream cheese
1½ lb. cheddar cheese, grated
¼ c. milk

Blend cheeses and milk. Divide mixture into 3 portions to be used as base for Caraway loaf, Anchovy loaf and Coffee loaf.

Caraway Loaf:

4 T. caraway seed
1 T. horseradish
1 T. Worcestershire sauce

Thoroughly blend ingredients with ⅓ of the basic cheese base. Shape into a long loaf. Chill 4 hours or until firm. Slice; serve on Corn Thins.

Anchovy Loaf:

2 oz. anchovy paste

Thoroughly blend anchovy paste with ⅓ of the basic cheese base. Shape into long loaf; chill 4 hours. Slice and serve on Triangle Thins.

Coffee Loaf:

1 T. instant coffee
2 T. sugar

Thoroughly blend coffee and sugar with remaining ⅓ of the basic cheese base. Shape into long loaf. Chill until firm. Slice; serve on Wheat Thins.

Ann Williams, Angier H. S.
Angier, North Carolina

DRIED BEEF SPREAD

Number of Servings — 8-10

1 jar chipped dried beef
1 8-oz. pkg. cream cheese
1 t. horseradish
1 t. prepared mustard
1 T. salad dressing

Cream the cheese. Shred the dried beef by hand. Combine all ingredients with cheese; mix thoroughly. Serve as an appetizer on crackers or potato chips or use as sandwich filling.

Gertrude E. Swartz, Avondale Senior H. S.
Auburn Heights, Michigan

ALBUQUERQUE DIP

Number of Servings — 6

1 qt. cottage cheese
¼ c. milk
1 pkg. onion soup mix

Mix all ingredients in blender or with electric mixer until cheese is smooth.

Mabel Moorhouse, Belen H. S.
Belen, New Mexico

ALWAYS A FAVORITE DIP

Number of Servings — 6-8

Dip Base:
1 8-oz. pkg. cream cheese
¼ c. canned milk
1 T. lemon juice
1 T. onion flakes or minced onion
Dash of paprika

Soften cream cheese. Add milk; blend. Add lemon juice and blend. Add onion and paprika.

Variations:

1 can smoked clams or oysters
1 c. pimento cheese
½-1 c. small shrimp
¼ c. carrots, grated
¼ c. green pepper, grated

Add any one of the above ingredients to the dip base. Blend well.

Mrs. Elsie Strum Hutchinson,
Duncan U. Fletcher H. S.
Jacksonville Beach, Florida

ANCHOVY DIP

1 8-oz. pkg. cream cheese
2 T. cream
2 t. grated onion
½ t. celery seeds
1 T. lemon juice
2 t. anchovy paste

With an electric mixer soften the cream cheese until it is smooth. Beat in other ingredients. Beat until fluffy.

Mrs. Flo Brame, Lake Air Jr. High
Waco, Texas

AVOCADO-ROQUEFORT DIP

Number of Servings — 8

1 pt. sour cream
1 ripe avocado, mashed
¼ lb. Roquefort cheese, cubed
1 t. Worcestershire sauce

Fold sour cream into avocado. Add cheese and Worcestershire sauce. Serve with chips.

Mrs. Hazel C. Jacobsen, Highland H. S.
Ault, Colorado

GREEN GODDESS DIP (Avocado)

Number of Servings — 2½ Cups

1 soft, ripe avocado
1 c. sour cream
½ c. parsley, finely chopped
¼ c. green onions, finely chopped
½ t. salt
½ t. seasoning salt
¼ c. mayonnaise

Mash avocado well, add sour cream and mayonnaise and mix well. Add salt and seasoning salt and mix well. Fold in chopped parsley and chopped green onions. Served cold with chips or crackers.

Mrs. Marie Lovil, McLeod H. S.
McLeod, Texas

GUACAMOLE

Number of Servings — 6

2 avocados
Salt, lemon juice
Grated onion
1 tomato, peeled and chopped
3 canned peeled green chili peppers, chopped or
a few drops of Tabasco sauce
1 clove of garlic

Mash avocados with salt, lemon juice and grated onion to taste. Add tomato and peppers or Tabasco sauce. Heap in a bowl that has been rubbed with garlic. Serve with toasted tortillas or corn chips.

Eva Hernandez, Belen H.S.
Belen, New Mexico

GUACAMOLE DIP OR SALAD

Number of Servings — 4

1 avocado
½ c. tomatoes, diced
1 T. onions, diced
½ t. garlic salt
1 T. lemon juice or vinegar
½ c. green chili sauce
salt and pepper to taste

Cream avocado; add remaining ingredients. Serve as a dip or as individual servings on lettuce.

Joan Killgore, Gallup H. S.
Gallup, New Mexico

CATALINA DIP

Number of Servings — 4

1 3-oz. pkg. cream cheese
½ c. Catalina dressing
¼ t. salt

Soften cream cheese with fork. Stir in dressing until dip is light and fluffy. Add salt, and stir. Serve with corn or potato chips or crackers.

Martha Wooton, West Hopkins H. S.
Nebo, Kentucky

BACON AND SOUR CREAM DIP

Number of Servings — 3 Cups

1 8-oz. cream cheese
3 T. chives, finely cut
1 c. sour cream
1 t. horseradish
Dash of garlic salt
Dash of cayenne
4 strips cooked bacon, crumbled
2 strips bacon, cooked crisp

Soften cheese at room temperature. Blend together cheese, chives, sour cream, horseradish, salt, and cayenne. Mix with crumbled bacon. Top with remaining 2 strips crisp bacon.

Mrs. Esther Cain, Brodhead H. S.
Brodhead, Wisconsin

CARROT DIP

3 medium carrots
3 medium dill pickles
1 small jar pimento
2 green peppers
1 small onion
3 hard cooked eggs, chopped
Salt and pepper to taste
Mayonnaise

Grind together carrots, pickles, pimento, peppers and onion. Drain on paper towels or cheese cloth. Add eggs, salt and pepper and enough mayonnaise to hold mixture together.

Mrs. Jane Wisdom, Hillsboro H. S.
Hillsboro, Illinois

BLEU CHEESE DIP

Number of Servings — 10-15

3 oz. cream cheese
2 oz. Bleu cheese
½ t. Worcestershire sauce
⅓ c. cream
1 t. chives, chopped
Paprika

Blend all ingredients except paprika. Pour into serving bowl. Sprinkle with paprika. Serve with chips or vegetable strips.

Mrs. Charles Streeter, Wamego Rural H. S.
Wamego, Kansas

HOT CHEESE DIP

Number of Servings — 2 Cups

2 lb. processed cheese
1 can tomatoes with chili peppers

Combine ingredients; place over low heat until cheese melts. Serve hot or cold with chips.

Mrs. Velma Ethridge, Hambrick Junior H. S.
Houston, Texas

JALAPENO CHEESE DIP

Number of Servings — 2 Pints

1 medium onion, finely chopped
1 medium green bell pepper, finely chopped
1 pod garlic, finely chopped
4 Jalapeno peppers
2 lb. Velveeta cheese, cut up
1 pt. cottage cheese
2 T. flour
2 T. margarine
¾ c. cream

Mix flour and cream in double boiler. Add margarine and cheeses; melt. Add remaining ingredients and simmer 10 to 15 minutes or until thick, stirring occasionally. If desired, serve warm as a dip or as a spread for crackers and sandwiches.

Mrs. Martha J. Barr, Fluvanna H. S.
Fluvanna, Texas

ROQUEFORT CHEESE DIP

Number of Servings — 1¼ Cups

3 t. evaporated milk
1 c. cottage cheese
1 onion, thinly sliced
1 t. Worcestershire sauce
3 oz. Roquefort cheese, crumbled

Combine all ingredients in order given. Blend until smooth. Serve with crackers.

Eva Jane Schwartz, Gettysburg Area Sr. H. S.
Gettysburg, Pennsylvania

SMOKY CHEESE DIP

Number of Servings — 1½ Cups

2 3-oz. pkg. cream cheese
1 6-oz. roll smoky cheese
1 small clove garlic, minced
⅓ c. pineapple juice
¼ t. Tobasco sauce
1 t. Worcestershire sauce

Put all ingredients in blender, and blend about 20 seconds or until smooth. Chill and serve.

Mrs. Glenda Ballinger, Kirkman Technical H. S.
Chattanooga, Tennessee

COCKTAIL SPREAD OR DIP

Number of Servings — 36 + Crackers

2 pkg. cream cheese
1 T. water
2½ t. Beau Monde seasoning salt
2 t. fine chopped dried parsley

Mix ingredients and refrigerate severals hours before serving.

Elaine M. McCoy, Cle Elum H. S.
Cle Elum, Washington

CHICKEN-CHEESE DIP OR SPREAD

Number of Servings — 2 Cups

1 8-oz. pkg. cream cheese
¾ c. cooked chicken, finely ground
¼ c. olives, ground
2 t. onion, grated
1 c. celery, grated
1 t. Worcestershire sauce
Mayonnaise

Mix ingredients in order with enough mayonnaise to moisten.

Chicken Substitutions:

Ground dates, figs, raisins or crushed, drained pineapple or
¼ c. mashed Bleu cheese and ¼ c. sour cream or
½ c. ground ham and 2 hard cooked eggs, finely diced

Shirley Mae Griffiths, Wilson Borough H. S.
Easton, Pennsylvania

CLAM DIP

Number of Servings — 20

¾ block margarine, melted
2 8-oz. pkg. cream cheese
Dash of hot sauce
1 t. Worcestershire sauce
1 c. clams, drained
1½ c. mushroom soup

Combine all ingredients with melted margarine. Slowly heat but do not boil. Serve hot with chips or crackers. If mixture becomes to thick add more melted margarine.

Mrs. Mildred F. Gauthier, Cottonport H. S.
Cottonport, Louisiana

CHILI SAUCE OR DIP

Number of Servings — 5 Pints

12 lge. tomatoes
1 red pepper
1 green pepper
4 onions
2 T. salt
Cream cheese
1 t. ginger
1 t. cloves
1 t. cinnamon
3 c. sugar
3 c. vinegar
4 apples, finely chopped

Cook all ingredients except apples and cream cheese for at least 2 hours or longer if a thicker sauce is desired. Add apples and cook 30 minutes longer. If a sweeter dip is desired, amount of vinegar used may be reduced. Blend with cream cheese for use as a chip dip or cracker spread.

Mrs. Carol Paynter, Mineral Point H. S.
Mineral Point, Wisconsin

CLAM DIP

Number of Servings — 12

1 8-oz. pkg. cream cheese
3-4 T. mayonnaise
¼ c. celery, finely diced
2 T. canned pimento, drained and finely cut
1 t. horseradish
1 small can clams, drained
Salt to taste
1 t. onion, grated or onion juice

Cream the cream cheese and mayonnaise. Add remaining ingredients. Serve with chips or crackers.

Mrs. Jane Golden, New Caney H. S.
New Caney, Texas

CLAM-CHEESE DIP

Number of Servings — 1 Pint

1 7-7½-oz. can minced clams
2 3-oz. pkg. cream cheese
¼ t. salt
2 t. onion, grated
1 t. Worcestershire sauce
3 drops Tabasco sauce
1 t. parsley, chopped
2 t. lemon juice

Drain clams; reserve liquid. Soften cheese at room temperature. Combine all ingredients except liquid; blend into a paste. Add liquid, 1 tablespoon at a time, beating after each addition until desired consistency is reached. Chill.

Mrs. Irene B. Knudsen, Del Norte H. S.
Crescent City, California

COPONATINI

Number of Servings — 50

2 medium eggplants, cubed
1 can tomato sauce
1 lge. onion, finely chopped
2 celery stalks, finely chopped
1 clove garlic, finely chopped
10 green olives, quartered
3 T. cooking oil
1 t. vinegar
Sugar and salt to taste
1 T. salt

Soak eggplants in 1 tablespoon salt for about 30 minutes. Squeeze out lightly. Cook in hot oil until tender; add tomato sauce. Saute onion, celery, garlic and olives in a small amount of oil; add vinegar. Mix all ingredients together with sugar and salt and cook until flavors are blended. Serve on crackers or with meats.

Mrs. Ted Trotter, Independence H. S.
Independence, Louisiana

CUCUMBER DIP

1 8-oz. pkg. cream cheese
¼-½ c. unpeeled cucumber, shredded and drained
¼ t. Worcestershire sauce
Dash of garlic salt

Combine cream cheese and cucumber; blend until smooth. Add Worcestershire sauce and garlic salt; mix well. Serve with potato chips.

Mrs. Grace E. Kukuk, Negaunee H. S.
Negaunee, Michigan

CUCUMBER DIP

Number of Servings — ¾ Cup

1 3 oz. pkg. cream cheese
2 T. finely chopped onion
½ c. finely chopped cucumber
Light cream
Salt
Cucumber slices

Combine cheese, onion, and cucumber. Add enough cream to make cheese mixture of dipping consistency. Add salt to taste. Garnish with unpeeled cucumber slices.

Mrs. Karen Williams, Eagle Bend H. S.
Eagle Bend, Minnesota

CRAB DIP

1 lge. pkg. cream cheese
3 T. mayonnaise
1 lge. clove garlic
2 T. grated onion
1 t. Worcestershire sauce
1 can crab, drained

Cream the cheese and mayonnaise together, add grated onion. Press garlic through press and add to mixture. Mix in Worcestershire sauce, and crab (drained). Chill a few hours before serving. Serve with dipper potato chips.

Cathy O'Farrell, St. Helens Sr. H. S.
St. Helens, Oregon

HOT CRAB DIP

Number of Servings — 12-15

3 T. melted butter
3 T. flour
½ t. salt
1½ c. milk
1 T. Worcestershire sauce
½ t. Tabasco sauce
¼ t. black pepper
¼ t. dry mustard
½ t. dried parsley
1 lb. crab meat
3 T. cooking sherry

Combine butter, flour and milk to make a sauce. Add all remaining ingredients except cooking sherry. Just before serving, add sherry. Serve in a chafing dish with melba toast squares or cocktail crackers.

Leona Woodling, Churchland H. S.
Chesapeake, Virginia

CRAB-CHEESE DIP

Number of Servings — 1½ Cups

1 8-oz. pkg. cream cheese
⅓-¼ c. light cream or milk
2 t. lemon juice
1-1½ t. Worcestershire sauce
1 clove garlic
Salt and pepper to taste
1 6½ or 7½-oz. can crab or 1 c. flaked crab meat

Blend cream cheese and gradually add light cream. Beat smooth. Add lemon juice, Worcestershire sauce, minced garlic, salt and pepper. Remove bony bits from one 6½ or 7½-ounce can (1 cup) crab meat, drained. Snip meat in fine pieces and stir into creamed mixture. Chill.

This recipe submitted by the following teachers:

Mrs. Sally Hildebrand, Enumclaw H. S.
Enumclaw, Washington

Mrs. Florence R. Newman, Westdale Junior H. S.
Baton Rouge, Louisiana

DIET DIP

1 pt. cottage cheese
1 envelope French onion soup mix
1 T. lemon juice
Few drops Tabasco sauce (optional)

Cream cottage cheese with electric mixer or in blender. Add remaining ingredients. Cover and chill for several hours to soften the onion bits. Serve with crackers, fresh vegetables, or potato chips.

Nelle G. Tramp, Merino H. S.
Merino, Colorado

DILL DIP

⅔ c. mayonnaise
⅔ c. sour cream
1 T. green onion, shredded
1 T. parsley, whole
1 t. dill weed
1 t. Beau Monde seasoning

Mix all ingredients. Set aside for several hours so flavors will blend. (Note: Do not use fresh onions and parsley. Use those found on the spice shelf.)

Mrs. Joan Ragan, San Ramon H. S.
Danville, California

DIP MIX

Number of Servings — 2½ Cups

1 small garlic bud
4 onions and tops, finely chopped
2 T. dry parsley
Salt and pepper to taste
1 c. sour cream
1 c. mayonnaise
1 pkg. Bleu cheese, cut up

With mixer, combine all ingredients except cheese. Fold in cheese or mix lightly with electric mixer.

Mrs. Loren Davis, Lake Preston H. S.
Lake Preston, South Dakota

GARLIC DIP

1 3-oz. pkg. cream cheese
1 t. Worcestershire sauce
¼ t. pepper
1 t. tomato catsup
½ t. instant garlic powder
⅛ t. salt
Evaporated milk

Combine all ingredients except the milk. Blend with electric mixer, adding milk gradually until mixture has consistency desired. Served with potato chips as a dip or as an appetizer with crackers.

Mrs. Betty Lou Archambault, Merrimack H. S.
Merrimack, New Hampshire

DEVILED HAM DIP

Number of Servings — 1⅔ Cups

1 4½ oz. can deviled ham
1 8 oz. pkg. cream cheese
½ c. egg, chopped
Pepper
Stuffed olives, sliced
Milk, cream or mayonnaise

Combine ham, cream cheese and egg. Add pepper to taste. Thin mixture with milk, cream or mayonnaise. Garnish with olive slices.

Veronica Iva Peters, Blaine Jr.-Sr. H. S.
Blaine, Washington

FROSTED DEVILED HAM

Number of Servings — 10

2 4½-oz. can deviled ham
1 T. onion, minced
1 8-oz. pkg. cream cheese
¼ c. sour cream
2½ t. sharp mustard

Mix deviled ham and onion together. Mound mixture on a plate. Mix remaining ingredients together. Frost ham mound with cream cheese mixture. Refrigerate overnight. Serve with chips or crackers or use as a sandwich spread.

Joyce Titus, New Knoxville H. S.
New Knoxville, Ohio

ZIPPY DEVILED HAM DIP

Number of Servings — 1 Cup

1 2½ oz. can deviled ham
3 oz. pkg. cream cheese
1 T. onion, grated
¾ t. Worcestershire sauce
½ t. horseradish
¼ c. salad dressing

Combine all ingredients; cream well. If it is too thick, add a little milk.

Mrs. Cleta Salyers, Malvern Community High
Malvern, Iowa

HOMAS BI THINEH (Lebanese Appetizer)

Number of Servings — 12

1 19-oz. can garbanzos, well drained
1 t. salt
1 clove garlic, crushed
½ c. olive or salad oil
1 T. lemon juice
Chopped parsley
Paprika

Put peas, salt and garlic into a blender and mash thoroughly. Add oil, a little at a time until mixture is the consistency of soft mashed potatoes. Add lemon juice. Garnish with parsley and paprika. Serve with crisp crackers.

Mrs. Jeanne Bundi, Van Buren School
Van Buren, Ohio

LIVER DIP

1 pkg. chicken livers or ½ lb. calves liver
2 lge. onions
5 hard cooked eggs
1 c. mayonnaise
1 c. butter

Fry liver and onions in butter. Put liver, onions and hard eggs thru food chopper. Add mayonnaise; stir.

Catherine S. Bradley, Hopewell Senior H. S.
Aliquippa, Pennsylvania

LULU PASTE

2 eggs, slightly beaten
3 T. sugar
3 T. vinegar
¼ t. salt
¼ t. pepper
2 pkg. cream cheese
1 T. onion, chopped
2 T. pepper, chopped

Combine eggs, vinegar, sugar, salt and pepper. Cook over low heat until thick. Cool. Add cream cheese, onion and pepper. Serve on crackers or bread.

This recipe submitted by the following teachers:

Ruth McLaughlin, New London H. S.
New London, Ohio

Mrs. Ruth G. Reeder, Southwestern Jr.-Sr. H. S.
Hanover, Pennsylvania

MOCK OYSTER ROCKEFELLER

Number of Servings — 25-30

1 onion, finely chopped
Margarine
1 lge. can mushrooms, drained and finely chopped
1 can cream of mushroom soup
1 pkg. broccoli, chopped and cooked
1 roll garlic cheese
Hot sauce to taste

Saute onion in margarine; add other ingredients. Serve hot on crackers.

Mrs. Lucille Gelpi, Hahnville H. S.
Hahnville, Louisiana

HOT MUSHROOM DIP

Number of Servings — 2 Cups

1 lb. fresh mushrooms
1 clove garlic, crushed
2 T. butter
1 small onion, grated
¼ t. Ac'cent
⅛ t. mustard
½ t. soy sauce
⅛ t. paprika
1 T. flour
1 c. sour cream
⅛ t. salt
⅛ t. pepper

Brown mushrooms, garlic and onion in butter. Combine Ac'cent, mustard, soy sauce, paprika, salt, pepper and flour with a little cream to make a paste, add to mushrooms. Blend in remaining cream; stir over low heat until thickened. Do not boil. Serve with crackers or chips.

Annie Lillian Brewton, Escambia H. S.
Pensacola, Florida

ONION-DILL DIP

Number of Servings — 8

1 8-oz. pkg. cream cheese
¼ c. cream
2 t. onion, grated
½ t. prepared mustard
1 t. dill seed
2 t. Worcestershire sauce
1 T. lemon juice

Blend cream cheese with cream until smooth. Add remaining ingredients; stir well. Serve with celery and carrot sticks.

Mrs. Rochelle Heider, Brillion H. S.
Brillion, Wisconsin

ONION SOUP DIP

Number of Servings — 3½ Cups

½ pt. sour cream
1 pt. cottage cheese
½ c. mayonnaise
1 pkg. onion soup mix
2 T. chopped parsley

Combine sour cream and cottage cheese. Add mayonnaise and mix well. Add onion soup mix and parsley. Blend. Chill and serve with crackers, Melba toast, or potato chips.

Mrs. Eleanor Zbornik, Arlington H. S.
Arlington, Iowa

SMOKED OYSTER DIP

1 8-oz. pkg. cream cheese
¼ c. light cream or milk
2 t. lemon juice
1 t. Worcestershire sauce
Salt and pepper
1 T. onion, grated
1 flat can smoked oysters, drained and chopped

Beat together all ingredients except oysters. Add oysters; chill.

Mrs. Marguerite McGinness, Danbury H. S.
Danbury, Texas

SHRIMP DIP

Number of Servings — 15-20

1 can broken shrimp, washed and drained
1 c. sour cream
⅓ c. mayonnaise
1 t. onion juice
2 T. Beau Monde
¼ t. paprika
¼ t. horseradish

Combine all ingredients; mix well. Chill several hours to season. Serve with crackers. Note: Beau Monde is found on the spice shelf in specialty stores.

Mrs. Imogene Ford Abernathie, Williamsville H. S.
Williamsville, Illinois

SHRIMP DIP

Number of Servings — 1 Pint

1 can Frozen Shrimp Soup
4 slices cheddar cheese
1 roll nippy cheese
½ t. Worcestershire sauce
1 t. fresh lemon juice

Place all ingredients in a heavy sauce pan. Cover and heat over low heat until cheese is melted. Stir until smooth. Serve warm with crackers, chips or raw cauliflower pieces.

Mrs. Gerald Evarts, Honesdale H. S.
Honesdale, Pennsylvania

SHRIMP-ONION DIP

½ pt. sour cream
½ pkg. dry onion soup mix
1 small can canned shrimp
2 T. sweet pickle, chopped
1 t. sweet pickle juice

Combine ingredients; chill. Serve with potato chips.

Mrs. Shirley Hodges, Avenal H. S.
Avenal, California

SHRIMP DIP

Number of Servings — 8-10

3 lb. cooked, cleaned shrimp
1 c. mayonnaise
2 hard-cooked eggs, finely chopped
6-8 chopped stuffed green olives
1 T. chopped green pepper
1 minced garlic clove
1 T. anchovy paste
1 t. Worcestershire sauce
1 t. dry mustard
Salt - (To taste)
Freshly ground pepper

Mix all ingredients together and chill for an hour. Will keep well for several weeks.

Mrs. Marion Stier, Farmington, H. S.
Farmington, Minnesota

SPAGHETTI SAUCE DIP

1 pt. sour cream
1 pkg. dry spaghetti sauce mix

Blend cream and spaghetti mix. Serve with corn or potato chips.

Mrs. Nancy W. Piner, Smyrna Consolidated School
Smyrna, North Carolina

CAPER SAUCE FOR COLD LOBSTER

Number of Servings — 12

½ c. mayonnaise
Few grains of salt
⅛ t. paprika
⅛ t. dry mustard
3 T. caper liquid
1 T. anchovy paste
½ c. small curd cottage cheese
⅓ c. milk
Whole capers

Blend cottage cheese in blender with milk until of consistency of whipped cream. Add remaining ingredients except capers. Blend 2 minutes on high speed. Pile in a bowl and chill. Garnish with whole capers. Cut lobster in bite size and insert each with toothpick. Serve on chipped ice centered with the sauce bowl.

Willie B. Barry, Martin H. S.
Laredo, Texas

CUCUMBER SAUCE

Number of Servings — 6

½ c. whipping cream, chilled
¼ t. salt
Few grains pepper
2 T. vinegar
1 cucumber, pared, chopped and drained

Whip cream; add salt and pepper. Gradually add vinegar. Fold in cucumber. Serve chilled.

Miss Clara Barrows, Groton H. S.
Groton, South Dakota

CUCUMBER SAUCE

Number of Servings — 1½ Cups

1 c. peeled cucumbers, finely chopped
½ t. salt
1 T. supar
1 T. cider vinegar
⅛ t. ground white pepper
½ c. heavy cream, whipped

Combine cucumbers and salt. Cover and refrigerate for at least an hour. Drain; add sugar, vinegar and white pepper. Fold in cream just before serving.

Mrs. Lou John, Clarissa H. S.
Clarissa, Minnesota

LOBSTER SAUCE

Number of Servings — 4

1 c. lobster meat
2 c. medium cream sauce
½ t. salt
⅛ t. pepper
1 t. Worcestershire sauce
2 T. cooking sherry

Combine lobster, salt, pepper, Worcestershire sauce, and sherry. Add cream sauce. Heat thoroughly. Serve with rolls or as a dip for toast.

Barbara A. West, Cradock H. S.
Portsmouth, Virginia

REMOULADE SAUCE

Number of Servings — 6-8

¼ c. vinegar
1½ T. prepared mustard
½ t. salt
¼ t. cayenne pepper
1½ t. paprika
Horseradish to taste
1 T. catsup
½ clove garlic, mashed to a paste
½ c. salad oil
¼ c. green onions and tops, finely minced
¼ c. celery, finely chopped

Combine vinegar, mustard, horseradish, salt, pepper, paprika, catsup and garlic. Mix well. Add salad oil; beat vigorously. Add green onions and celery. Pour over boiled seasoned shrimp and serve as a first course on a salad plate or in a cocktail glass, or serve as an appetizer in a bowl accompanied by shrimp stuck on toothpicks inserted in a snack holder.

Mrs. Evelyn B. Fontenot, Church Point H. S.
Church Point, Louisiana

GLAZE FOR HORS D'OEUVRES AND CANAPES

4 t. unflavored gelatin
⅓ c. cold water
1 c. boiling water or clear meat stock

Combine gelatin and cold water; let stand until thick. Pour boiling water or stock over gelatin-water mixture. Chill until mixture is consistency of unbeaten egg whites. Put hors d'oeuvers on cake rack with drip pan underneath. Pour glaze over hors d'oeuvres; remelt any glaze which drips off. If desired make glazed hors d'oeuvres a day in advance and store in refrigerator in waxed paper lined boxes.

Mrs. June Patchett, Young America H. S.
Metcalf, Illinois

DEVILED EGGS

Number of Servings — 6-12

6 hard cooked eggs
2 T. mayonnaise
1 t. prepared mustard
½ t. salt
¼ t. paprika
Dash of pepper
1 T. sweet pickles, chopped
1 T. stuffed olives, chopped

Slice eggs in half lengthwise with a wet knife. Remove yolks and mash with a fork. Add all other ingredients and mix well. Put yolk mixture into egg whites, heaping lightly. Garnish with a dash of paprika, additional olives, or a sprig of parsley. Chill before serving.

Mrs. D. J. Dear, Stringer H. S.
Bay Springs, Mississippi

CHEESE DEVILED EGGS

Number of Servings — 6

6 hard cooked eggs, chilled
½ c. cheese crackers, finely crushed
½ c. mayonnaise
1 t. prepared mustard
1 T. parsley, chopped
¼ t. salt
⅛ t. pepper
Paprika

Slice eggs in half lengthwise; remove yolks. Press yolks through a fine sieve. Add mustard parsley, salt, pepper, and half of the crumbs and mayonnaise. Blend. Refill centers of whites with yolk mixture. Press two halves together. Dip one end of each egg in remaining mayonnaise, then in crumbs. Sprinkle with paprika.

Barbara Widmyer, Conneaut Lake Area H. S.
Conneaut Lake, Pennsylvania

CHINESE EGG

Number of Servings — 12

12 hard cooked eggs
1 qt. boiling water
3 T. orange pekoe tea
1 t. anise seed
4 T. soy sauce
1½ T. salt

Shell eggs carefully so whites are not broken. Pour boiling water over tea; let steep for 5 minutes. Strain. Combine anise seed, soy sause and tea. Add whole eggs; simmer for 1 hour. Chill. These will keep covered and refrigerated.

Lucile B. McGehee, South West Dekalb
South Decatur, Georgia

CANTALOUPE SALAD COCKTAIL

Number of Servings — 4

1 cantaloupe
2 peaches, sliced
1 c. honeydew melon, cubed
1 c. seeded Tokay grapes, halved
¼ c. French fruit dressing

Cut cantaloupe lengthwise into 8 wedges; chill. Combine peaches, honeydew melon and grapes with dressing. Chill 1 hour. For each serving arrange 2 cantaloupe wedges to form oval or circle and fill centers with fruit mixture.

French Fruit Dressing:
Makes 1¾ cups
⅓ c. sugar
1 t. salt
1 t. paprika
¼ c. orange juice
2½ T. lemon juice
1 T. vinegar
1 c. salad oil
1 t. onion, grated

Combine ingredients in a bottle or jar; cover and shake thoroughly.

Lula Pettey, Russell County H. S.
Russell Springs, Kentucky

MOCK CHAMPAGNE

Number of Servings — 14

½ c. sugar
1 c. water
½ c. fresh orange juice, chilled
1 c. fresh grapefruit juice, chilled
1 qt. ginger ale, chilled

Combine sugar and water. Cook until syrupy. Chill. Add remaining ingredients. Pour over finely crushed ice. Serve immediately.

Mrs. Virginia Matulka, Wheeler County H. S.
Bartlett, Nebraska

MOCK PINK CHAMPAGNE

Number of Servings — 14 Cups

½ c. sugar
1½ c. water
2 c. cranberry juice
1 c. pineapple juice
½ c. orange juice
2 7-oz. bottles lemon-lime carbonated beverage

Boil sugar and water until sugar dissolves; cool. Stir in cranberry, pineapple, and orange juice. Chill. Just before serving add carbonated beverage.

Mrs. Deanna House, Monroe H. S.
Monroe, Wisconsin

COLA-COCKTAIL

Number of Servings — 4

2 pkg. dietetic raspberry gelatin
1 c. hot water
1 c. hot dietetic cola
1 8¼-oz. can artificially sweetened fruit cocktail, drained

Dissolve gelatin in hot water and cola. Chill until mixture reaches the consistency of jelly. Add fruit cocktail. Chill until firm.

Mrs. Sharron Lykke, S. F. Austin H. S.
Austin, Texas

CRANBERRY COCKTAILS

Number of Servings — 1

¼ c. cranberry cocktail juice
¼ c. 7-Up

Pour juice into a 4-oz. glass and chill. Just before serving add 7-Up. Glasses may be frosted, if desired.

Mrs. Carole Wright, Frazeysburg H. S.
Frazeysburg, Ohio

CRANBERRY PINK FLUFF

Number of Servings — 4

1 pkg. lemon flavored gelatin
1 c. hot water
1 c. cranberry juice cocktail
2 egg whites (beaten stiff but not dry)

Dissolve gelatin in hot water. Stir in cranberry juice. Chill until slightly thickened. Beat egg whites stiff, not dry. Gradually pour cranberry mixture over egg whites, beating until mixed and foamy. Pour into 4 individual sherbet glasses. Mixture will separate into a red and pink layer. Chill 4 hours.

Mrs. James Potter, Tomah H. S.
Tomah, Wisconsin

HOT SPICED CRANBERRY COCKTAIL

Number of Servings — 12

¾ c. brown sugar
1 c. water
¼ t. salt
¼ t. nutmeg
¼ t. cinnamon
2-4 drops oil of cloves
2 1-lb. cans cranberry sauce
3 c. water
1 qt. pineapple juice

Heat in a saucepan until near boiling the brown sugar, 1 cup water, salt, nutmeg and cinnamon. Beat the cranberry sauce with a rotary beater. Run through a sieve. Combine the remaining ingredients and add the heated mixture. Simmer for 5 minutes. (May be used as a punch.)

Ceceilia Patry, Phillipsburg H. S.
Phillipsburg, Kansas

FRUIT COCKTAIL

Number of Servings — 6

1 can frozen pineapple chunks
1 can Mandarin orange sections
1 pkg. frozen mixed fruit
2 T. orange curacao cordial

Mix fruits; keep chilled until ready to serve. Add curacao just before serving.

Mrs. Ada B. Dobson, Edison Junior H. S.
Macomb, Illinois

FROZEN FRUIT CUP

Number of Servings — 8

1 c. fruit cocktail or fruit, cut up
½ c. seedless grapes
½ c. watermelon balls
1 bottle ginger ale, chilled
Mint leaves

Mix fruits, place in ice cube tray. Pour ginger ale over fruit and freeze 1½ to 2 hours or until mixture is a mush. Serve in small sherbet glasses and garnish with mint leaves.

Abbie E. Nordstrom, Edmonds Sr. H. S.
Edmonds, Washington

HOLIDAY FRUIT CUP

Number of Servings — 14

2 grapefruit
6 oranges
1 N. 2 can crushed pineapple
1 8-oz. jar Maraschino cherries, finely cut

Remove juice and seeds from grapefruit and oranges. Do not strain juice. Add cherries and cherry juice to grapefruit—orange mixture. Add pineapple; chill about 8 hours to thoroughly blend flavors.

Mrs. M. Judelle Jones, Turlock H. S.
Turlock, California

OAHU FRAPPE

Number of Servings — 6

½ c. sugar
¾ c. water
¾ c. orange juice, strained
1½ c. unsweetened pineapple juice
Grated orange rind (optional)

Cook sugar and water for 5 minutes; cool slightly. Add juices; freeze to a mush. Serve in chilled sherbet glasses and garnish with grated orange rind.

This recipe submitted by the following teachers:

Mrs. James Hoppenstedt, Magnolia-Swaney H. S.
McNabb, Illinois

Mrs. Marilyn Tidwell, Cambridge H. S.
Cambridge, Idaho

FRUIT ICE

Juice of 3 lemons, strained
Juice of 3 oranges, strained
3 bananas, mashed
7-Up or Upper 10
3 c. water
2 c. sugar

Heat sugar and water together until sugar dissolves. Cool. Blend all ingredients except 7-Up and mint leaf. Put into ice cube trays; freeze. When mixture freezes to a slush stage, pour mixture into blender. Beat well. Return to trays; freeze until firm. Spoon into cups and pour 7-Up or upper 10 over it. Garnish with mint leaf.

Mrs. Patricia Davison, Bountiful H. S.
Bountiful, Utah

FRUIT KABOBS

Fresh or frozen melon balls
Whole strawberries
Pineapple chunks
Bananas
Skewers or toothpicks
½ Grapefruit

Use half of grapefruit (cut side down) on a plate or tray to arrange kabobs. Place fruit on skewers and stick into grapefruit. Makes attractive centerpieces for breakfast or brunch.

Mrs. Ralph Shipman, Paris H. S.
Paris, Texas

LIME PUNCH COCKTAIL

Number of Servings — 8 Quarts

2 lge. cans frozen lemonade
1 qt. ginger ale, chilled
3 pkgs. lime drink powder
1½ c. sugar (more or less as desired)
3 qts. water

Combine lemonade, drink powder, sugar and water. Refrigerate. Add ginger ale just before serving.

Betty Rogers, Wakefield H. S.
Wakefield, Nebraska

GRAPEFRUIT (Broiled)

Number of Servings — 2

1 grapefruit
2 T. brown sugar
2 Maraschino cherries

Cut grapefruit in half. Cut around each section and remove center. Sprinkle 1 tablespoon brown sugar on each half. Place a cherry in the center. Broil about 3 inches from heat until all the sugar melts and the edge of grapefruit turns a delicate brown. Serve immediately.

Mrs. Genevieve Snyder, Cocalico Union Sr. H. S.
Denver, Pennsylvania

GRAPE JUICE SUPREME

Number of Servings — 12

1 qt. bottled grape juice
1 lge. 7-Up
Lemon juice
Sugar
Vanilla ice cream, if desired

Pour a little lemon juice in flat shallow dish. Dip edges of juice glasses in juice about ⅛ inch. Dip the edge again in sugar. Place glasses thus fixed in freezer until ready for use. Just before serving time remove the glasses from freezer and fill with the grape juice and 7-Up that have been mixed together. A small spoonful of ice cream may be added if desired.

Mrs. L. E. Hansberger, Canton Sr. H. S.
Canton, Illinois

INDIAN PUNCH COCKTAIL

Number of Servings — 1 Gallon

4 lemons
1 pt. sugar
1 qt. water
1 c. strong tea
1 T. vanilla extract
1 T. almond extract
1 lge. bottle ginger ale

Remove juice from lemons. Boil sugar, water and lemon rind for 3 minutes. Cool. Add lemon juice, tea, vanilla and almond extracts. Immediately before serving add ginger ale and pour over chipped ice.

Mrs. Mary Jane Day, Lincoln Rural H. S.
Lincoln, Kansas

MINT COCKTAIL

Number of Servings — 5-6

1 No. 300 crushed pineapple, undrained
2 oranges, cut in bite size pieces
½ lb. dinner mints
3 bananas, cut in bite size pieces
3 peaches, cut in bite size pieces

Combine all ingredients. Refrigerate several hours.

Mrs. Mollie Keller, Havre H. S.
Havre, Montana

BACON BITS

Number of Servings — 20

20 slices bread
2 T. melted butter
2 egg whites
1 c. grated sharp cheese
⅔ c. chopped green pepper
1 t. chopped parsley
½ t. salt
Dash of pepper
3 slices bacon, finely chopped

With 2 inch cookie cutter, cut 20 bread rounds. Toast on one side under broiler. Brush untoasted sides with melted butter. Fold cheese into stiffly beaten egg whites, add green pepper, parsley, salt and pepper. Spoon mixture on buttered side of bread rounds. Sprinkle tops with finely chopped bacon. Broil 4 or 5 inches from heat for 10 minutes or until bacon browns and cheese melts.

June L. Schwar, Penn Manor Junior H. S.
Millersville, Pennsylvania

BACON 'N' ONION APPETIZER

Number of Servings — 10

½ lb. bacon
1 small jar cocktail onions
⅓ c. brown sugar

Cut bacon slices into thirds. Dip in brown sugar. Wrap bacon pieces with sugar side in around cocktail onion. Secure with toothpick. Broil about 2 minutes on each side. May be served hot.

Mrs. Jeanne Clark, Bentley H. S.
Flint, Michigan

BURNING BUSHES

Number of Servings — 15-20

1 3-oz. pkg. cream cheese
1 t. dehydrated minced onion
1 T. Worcestershire sauce
⅛ t. salt
Dash of black pepper
1 jar dried beef

Have ingredients at room temperature. Blend all ingredients except dried beef to form a smooth paste. Arrange thin slices of dried beef on bread board to form single five or six inch square layers. Pieces will have to overlap to form a continuous piece. Spread beef slices with cheese mixture and roll up as a jelly roll. Roll should be an inch or so in diameter. Wrap in moisture-vapor-proof paper and chill for several hours. Slice in ¾ inch slices. Serve on toothpicks.

Mrs. Paralee Coleman, Wellington H. S.
Wellington, Texas

BEEF-STUFFED MUSHROOMS

Number of Servings — 25

1½ lb. medium mushrooms
1 lb. lean ground beef
¼ c. mayonnaise
1 T. prepared mustard
½ t. sugar
1 T. onion, minced
1 T. parsley, chopped
2 t. salt

Remove stems from mushrooms; wash caps in salt water. Broil mushroom caps, rounded side down, for 3 minutes. Combine remaining ingredients; shape into balls which fit mushroom caps. Place balls in mushroom caps. Broil about 2 inches from heat for about 5-8 minutes. Serve piping hot.

Phyllis J. Hill, Paradise Valley H. S.
Phoenix, Arizona

CHICKEN LIVERS

Number of Servings — 8

1 box frozen chicken livers
1 lb. fine sliced lean bacon
1 box round toothpicks

Thaw chicken livers. Cut slice of bacon in half. Roll one half sliced bacon around each chicken liver. Secure with tooth pick. Broil until bacon is cooked on one side. Turn and broil on other side 6 to 8 minutes or until done. Serve at once.

Mrs. Geraldene Asell, Thomas Downey H. S.
Modesto, California

CHICKEN-NUT PUFFS

Number of Servings — 20-25

1½ c. cooked or canned chicken, drained and finely chopped
⅓ c. toasted almonds, chopped
1 c. canned or fresh chicken broth
½ c. salad oil or chicken fat
2 t. seasoned salt
⅛ t. cayenne
1 t. celery seed
1 T. parsley flakes
2 t. Worcestershire sauce
1 c. flour
4 eggs

Mix chicken and almonds together. Combine chicken broth, oil or fat, seasoned salt, cayenne, celery seed, parsley flakes and Worcestershire sauce. Bring to a boil. Add flour; cook over low heat, beating rapidly, until mixture leaves sides of pan and forms a smooth compact ball. Remove from heat; add eggs, one at a time. After each addition, beat with a spoon until mixture is shiny. Stir in chicken mixture. Drop ½ teaspoon of mixture at a time on greased baking sheet. Bake at 450°F. for 10 to 15 minutes. Serve hot.

Mrs. Mary A. Moore, Area IV Consultant
Stephenville, Texas

CHICKEN LIVER ROLLUPS

Number of Servings — 4

4 water chestnuts
4 fresh chicken livers
4 strips bacon

Roll chicken livers around chestnuts. Wrap with bacon strips; fasten with toothpicks. Broil until bacon is crisp.

Helena T. Martines, Gompers Junior H. S.
Los Angeles, California

CHICKEN SALAD PUFFS

Number of Servings — 4

½ c. water
¼ c. butter
½ c. sifted flour
2 eggs
2 c. cooked chicken, diced
1 c. celery, sliced
¾ c. olive chunks
⅓ c. mayonnaise
1 T. lemon juice
1 t. onion, grated
¼ t. Worcestershire sauce
⅛ t. black pepper
Salt to taste

Combine water and butter; heat to boiling. Add flour; stir over direct heat until mixture forms a ball that follows spoon around the pan. Remove from heat. Add unbeaten eggs one at a time; beat vigorously and until well blended after each addition. Drop in 4 mounds on ungreased baking sheet. Bake in preheated 400F oven, 45 to 50 minutes. Cool on wire rack. Combine chicken, celery and olives. Blend in remaining ingredients; mix lightly with chicken mixture. Split puffs and fill with chicken mixture.

Mrs. Rubye R. Hill, York Community H. S.
Thomson, Illinois

SPICY FRANKFURTER APPETIZERS

Number of Servings — 8-16

1 1½-oz. pkg. spaghetti sauce mix
1 8-oz. can tomato sauce
1½ c. water
2 T. salad oil
1-2 lb. frankfurters, cut in 1 inch pieces

Prepare spaghetti sauce mix according to package directions, using tomato sauce, water and salad oil. Refrigerate sauce and frankfurters until serving time. Heat frankfurters in sauce. Serve in casserole over candle warmer at table. Or heat and serve from chafing dish. Provide picks so guests can spear their own. Serve with chunks of French bread if desired.

Helen Smith, Galion Senior H. S.
Galion, Ohio

CRISPY HAM BITS

Number of Servings — 1 Cup

½ c. cooked ham, ground
¼ c. cheddar cheese, grated
¼ c. condensed tomato soup
1 T. onion, minced
¼ t. horseradish
¼ t. prepared mustard

Mix ingredients together in given order. Spread on crackers. Broil 3 inches away from heat for 3 to 5 minutes or until slightly brown. Serve hot.

Marcelle T. Montminy, Memorial H. S.
Manchester, New Hampshire

DEVILED HAM PUFFS

Number of Servings — 6

½ lb. pkg. cream cheese
1 t. onion juice
½ t. baking powder
1 egg yolk
Salt to taste
24 small bread rounds
2 2¼-oz. cans deviled ham

Blend cheese, onion juice, baking powder, egg yolk and salt together. Toast the bread rounds on one side. Spread the untoasted sides with deviled ham. Cover each with a mound of cheese mixture. Place on a cookie sheet and bake at 375°F for 10 to 12 minutes or until puffed and brown. Serve hot.

Mrs. Mary Eriksen, Brandywine Heights H. S.
Topton, Pennsylvania

HAPPY GOODIES

Number of Servings — 12

6 chicken livers, quartered
12 water chestnuts, cut in half
¼ c. soy sauce
1 T. Worcestershire sauce
2 T. water
¼ t. garlic powder
Bacon slices

Mix soy sauce, Worcestershire sauce, water and garlic powder in a pint jar; add livers and water chestnuts. Marinate at least two hours or overnight. Turn or shake jar occasionally to soak chestnuts and livers thoroughly. Remove from liquid. Wrap a piece of chicken liver and a slice of water chestnut with a slice of bacon. Secure with toothpick. Broil for 5 to 7 minutes, or until bacon is crisp.

Mrs. M. V. Highsmith, Horn Lake H. S.
Horn Lake, Mississippi

GRAPEFRUIT CONVERSATION PIECE

1 lge. firm grapefruit
Cocktail sausages

Cut a hole in one end of grapefruit just large enough to hold a sterno lamp. Place on a small platter and surround with real or artificial leaves. Thrust wooden picks through cocktail sausages and stick into the grapefruit. Let guests broil their own sausages over lamp.

Mrs. Carol Hawkins, Turlock H. S.
Turlock, California

QUICK KABOBS

Number of Servings — 60 Kabobs

1 can luncheon meat, cut in ½" squares
1 No. 2½ can sliced pineapple
1 medium bottle Maraschino cherries

Cut pineapple into six chunks per slice. Place meat, pineapple chunks and cherries on toothpicks.

Mrs. Emaline Miller, Orosi Union H. S.
Orosi, California

LIVER PASTE

Number of Servings — 50-75

1 round roll soft liverworst
2 hard cooked eggs
1 t. dried parsley
1 t. onion, chopped
¼ c. celery, finely chopped
2 T. mayonnaise

Blend liverworst and eggs together. Add remaining ingredients; blend well. Use as a spread on assorted crackers for appetizers.

Phyllis P. Nash, Conestoga Sr. H. S.
Berwyn, Pennsylvania

POULTRY MEAT BALLS

Number of Servings — 24

½ c. butter or margarine
8 slices very dry bread
2 lge. onions
2 cloves garlic (opt.)
6 c. cooked chicken or turkey, finely chopped
4 T. Worcestershire sauce
½ t. ground cardamon
2 t. salt
1 t. black pepper
¼ t. red pepper
2 T. flaked or fresh parsley, finely chopped
3 eggs, well beaten

Place bread, onions, and garlic in blender; blend until very fine. Saute bread mixture in butter or margarine until light brown. Remove from heat; blend in remaining ingredients. Shape into meat balls the size of a walnut. Fry in deep fat at 375°F. until golden brown.

Mrs. Danis Hilliard, Adams City H. S.
Adams City, Colorado

HOT SPICED MEAT BALLS

Meat Balls:
¾ lb. ground beef
¾ c. fine dry bread crumbs
1½ T. onion, minced
½ t. prepared horseradish
3 drops Tabasco sauce
2 eggs, beaten
¾ t. salt
½ t. pepper

Combine all ingredients; form into ¾-inch meat balls. Cook meat balls; pour off drippings.

Sauce:
¾ c. catsup
½ c. water
¼ c. vinegar
1 T. onion, minced
2 T. brown sugar
2 t. Worcestershire saucc
1 t. dry mustard
¼ t. pepper
1½ t. salt
3 drops Tabasco sauce

Mix all ingredients; pour over cooked meat balls. Cover and cook 10 minutes. Shake occasionally. Serve hot.

Shirley Seaney, El Paso H. S.
El Paso, Texas

SUNDAY NIGHT MEAT BALLS

Number of Servings — 8

¾ lb. ground beef
¾ c. bread crumbs
1½ T. onion, minced
3 drops Tabasco sauce
2 eggs, beaten
¾ t. salt
¼ lb. butter

Combine beef, bread crumbs, onion, Tabasco sauce, eggs and salt. Shape into small meat balls. Fry the balls in butter, turning often, until brown.

Sauce:
¾ c. catsup
½ c. water
¼ c. vinegar
2 T. brown sugar
1 t. dry mustard
1 T. onion, minced
2 t. Worcestershire sauce
1½ t. salt

Combine sauce ingredients; simmer 15 minutes. Pour sauce over browned meat balls and simmer 10 minutes longer. Keep warm in chafing dish.

Betty Goodhue Keeney, Gilbert Community H. S.
Gilbert, Iowa

SWEDISH MEAT BALL APPETIZERS

Number of Servings — 10-15

1 lb. round steak, finely ground
1 small onion, finely ground
½ lb. pork steak, finely ground
1 c. dry bread crumbs
1 c. milk
1 egg, beaten
1 t. salt
¼ t. allspice
¼ t. pepper

Have meats run through a fine grinder at least 3 times. Combine meat and onion. Soak bread crumbs in milk; add egg and seasonings. Mix thoroughly with meat-onion mixture. Form into small balls about the size of a large marble. Roll in flour and brown in hot fat. Shake the pan slightly as they brown to keep the balls round and evenly brown. Put in a casserole dish and bake about 30 minutes at 300°F. Spread out on absorbent paper. When cool place on picks for appetizers.

Mrs. Archie Strand, Chester H. S.
Chester, South Dakota

COCKTAIL WIENERS

Number of Servings — 10

¾ c. prepared mustard
1 c. currant jelly
8-10 Frankfurters

Mix mustard and jelly in chafing dish or double boiler. Diagonally slice frankfurters into bite-size pieces. Add to sauce and heat through.

Mrs. Loretta Walker, Foshay Jr. H. S.
Los Angeles, California

MEXICAN TOSTADAS TAPATIAS

Number of Servings — 30

30 tortillas
1 lb. frijole beans, mashed
½ lb. spicy sausage
⅓ c. sharp cheese, grated
3 avocados, cut in pieces
6 tomatoes, cut in pieces
2 onions, chopped
Canned green chili peppers in vinegar or jalapenas

Fry tortillas in oil until crisp. Brown sausage; add mashed beans; simmer, spread sausage-bean mixture on crisp tortillas. Spread cheese, onions, tomatoes, avocados and more cheese over the beans. Top with green pepper slivers.

Phyllis Christmann, Carrington H. S.
Carrington, North Dakota

APPETIZER PIZZA

Number of Servings — 8-10

4 English muffins
Butter
½ lb. ground beef or sausage
½ t. salt
1 T. minced dry onion
1 T. oregano leaves
⅓ lb. Muzzarella cheese, shredded

Saute meat in 1 teaspoon butter. Add salt and onion; cook until done. Split muffins; spread lightly with butter. Toast under broiler until lightly browned.

Sauce:

¼ 6-oz. can tomato paste
¼ c. water
⅓ t. salt
½ t. sugar

Combine sauce ingredients; spread mixture over muffin halves. Spoon meat mixture over sauce. Sprinkle with cheese; add oregano. Bake at 400°F. until cheese is melted. Cut in quarters and serve.

Carolyn Hutton, Edwardsville Junior H. S.
Edwardsville, Illinois

LITTLE PIZZAS (Teen's Choice)

Number of Servings — 10

1 pkg. sausage links
1 pkg. refrigerator biscuits
½ can tomato paste
Oregano
1 c. cheddar cheese, shredded

Roll each biscuit out to 4-inch diameter. Place on baking sheet; spread tomato paste over biscuits. Sprinkle with oregano. Add about 6 penny-size pieces of sausage to each biscuit; sprinkle with cheese. Bake in 450°F oven for 5 minutes. Serve hot.

Mrs. Diane M. Brown, Grayville H. S.
Grayville, Illinois

SAUSAGE CRESCENTS

Number of Servings — 16

1 can refrigerated crescent dinner rolls
16 brown n' serve sausages

Cut crescent triangles in half making two small triangles. Place a brown and serve sausage on each small triangle and roll up. Bake on an ungreased baking sheet for 10-13 minutes until golden brown at 375 degrees F.

Mrs. Harriet Gerou, Beaverton H. S.
Beaverton, Michigan

ANCHOVY SPREAD

Number of Servings — 20-25

1 small pkg. cream cheese
1 can flat anchovies, cut
½ medium Bermuda onion
½ c. sour cream
Dash of Worcestershire sauce

Mix all ingredients thoroughly with a fork. Serve as a spread for crackers. If a thinner consistency is desired for use as a dip, add more sour cream.

Mrs. George B. Carty, Tamassee D.A.R. School
Tamassee, South Carolina

BROILED CLAMS

Number of Servings — 4

12 medium-sized cherrystone or soft shell clams
Salt to taste
Cayenne pepper to taste
Paprika to taste
Green pepper, finely chopped
Red pimento, finely chopped
12 pieces bacon, cut the size of the clam
Lemon sections

Prepare a shallow baking pan with crumbled aluminum foil. Firmly arrange clams on foil to steady them while cooking. Season each clam with salt, paprika and cayenne pepper. Add a pinch of green pepper, pimento and bacon pieces. Place pan about 4 inches from broiler; broil until bacon is cooked. Remove bacon; place in a warm dish. Broil clams 5-6 minutes longer. Serve in shell. Garnish with bacon and lemon sections.

Ruth Adams, Claymont H. S.
Claymont, Delaware

SHRIMP CANAPES

Number of Servings — 12

18 shrimp
2 T. butter
1 hard cooked egg
1 T. parsley, finely chopped
¼ c. mayonnaise or French dressing
12 crisp crackers

Finely chop six shrimp; set aside remaining whole shrimp to chill. Force egg yolk through a sieve; set aside. Blend butter and chopped shrimp; spread on crackers. Dip reserved shrimp into mayonnaise or French dressing. Place on crackers. Sprinkle sieved egg yolks and chopped parsley over each cracker.

Nancy R. McGath, Fremont Sr. H. S.
Fremont, Nebraska

SHRIMP ARNAUD

¼ c. vinegar
¼ c. salad oil
¼ c. chili sauce
¼ t. garlic salt
1 t. prepared mustard
1 lb. shrimp, cooked

Blend vinegar, oil, chili sauce, garlic salt and mustard. Add shrimp and toss to coat with sauce. Marinate overnight. Insert a toothpick in each shrimp before serving.

Elizabeth Woodward, New London H. S.
New London, Ohio

PINEAPPLE SHRIMP (Luau Leis)

Number of Servings — 8

1 14-oz. can chunk pineapple, drained
2 T. soy sauce
2 T. lemon juice
1 T. salad oil
1 t. dry mustard
24 lge. cooked shrimp, de-veined
Macadamia nuts or peanuts, finely chopped
Flaked coconut

Drain pineapple. Blend together ¼ cup pineapple syrup, soy sauce, lemon juice, oil and mustard. Pour over shrimp; cover and let stand ½ hour. Soak 8 bamboo skewers in water. Alternate 3 shrimp and 4 pineapple chunks on each skewer. Brush on remaining marinade. Place on rack or in shallow pan. Broil 2 to 3 inches from heat, turning and basting until hot and lightly browned, 3 to 5 minutes. Sprinkle 4 skewers with nuts and 4 with coconut.

Mrs. MaryAnn Seidler, Colby H. S.
Colby, Wisconsin

BAKED STUFFED MUSHROOMS

Number of Servings — 12

24 lge. mushrooms
1 clove garlic, minced
¼ c. parsley, minced
¼ c. Swiss cheese, grated
Salt and pepper to taste
½ c. plus 2 T. bread crumbs
2 T. onion, minced
¼ c. sherry
Few drops lemon juice
3 T. butter

Wash mushrooms and remove stems, leaving caps intact. Sprinkle a few drops of lemon juice in each cap; set aside. Finely mince stems; saute in butter. Combine cheese, ½ cup bread crumbs, salt and pepper. Add parsley, garlic and onion. Add sherry. When minced stems are brown, add to stuffing mixture and stir thoroughly. Pile filling into mushroom caps; sprinkle with 2 tablespoons bread crumbs and dot with butter. Bake 15 minutes in 350°F. oven.

Mrs. Jo Anne Sandager, Stillwater Junior H. S.
Stillwater, Minnesota

HI-HAT MUSHROOMS IN WINE SAUCE

Number of Servings — 4-6

16 medium fresh mushrooms
½ lb. ground sausage
1 cup tomato sauce
1 c. white wine
½ clove garlic
⅛ t. oregano

Wash mushrooms; remove and chip stems. Add stems to sausage. Stuff the caps, rounding meat mixture into a high crown. Bake in 350°F. oven for 30 minutes. Mince garlic; mash to a pulp. Heat tomato sauce, wine, garlic and oregano in a chafing dish. When blended, add the mushrooms. Cover and let sauce bubble. Spear mushrooms with toothpicks and serve.

Mrs. Katheryn Chambers, Wayne City School
Wayne, Nebraska

HOT CRANBERRY PUNCH COCKTAIL

¾ c. brown sugar
1 c. water
¼ t. salt
½ t. cinnamon
½ t. allspice
¾ t. cloves
2 1-lb. cans cranberry jelly, crushed with fork
3 c. water
1 qt. pineapple juice
3 c. strong tea

Boil first 6 ingredients together for 1 minute. Add next 3 ingredients to hot syrup. Stir until jelly dissolves. Add tea. Punches better if prepared day before serving and reheated. Use a cinnamon stick in each glass for stirring.

Ruth Bergee, Centennial Sr. H. S.
Circle Pines, Minnesota

PEPPER APPETIZER

Number of Servings — 25

3 c. vinegar
1 c. salad oil
1 T. salt
12 green or red peppers
1 c. pickling onions, peeled

Wash peppers; remove seeds and centers and cut into serving pieces. Bring vinegar, oil and salt to a boil. Add a few peppers and onions at a time, turning in boiling liquid until peppers change color. Do not overcook, keep crisp. Cool and store in refrigerator if to be served within a few days. These peppers may also be canned if desired.

Odessa L. Carlson, Wakefield H. S.
Wakefield, Michigan

TOMATO-GEL APPETIZERS

Number of Servings — 6

2 c. tomato juice
½ t. salt
1 leaf of celery
Few grains cayenne
1 envelope gelatin
¼ c. cold water
1 T. lemon juice
1 T. onion juice
1 small bottle stuffed olives

Mix together and boil 10 minutes: Tomato juice salt, cayenne and celery leaf. Sprinkle gelatin on cold water and let stand five minutes: Add the hot mixture to the soaked gelatin. Stir until dissolved and add lemon juice and onion juice. Strain. Add Olives. Pour into Mold. Chill.

Marqet Condell, Snohomish H. S.
Snohomish, Washington

TOMATO COCKTAIL

4 c. tomato juice
1 c. water
½ c. sugar
1 c. celery, finely cut
1 T. salt
Pepper to taste
2 T. Worcestershire sauce
2 T. lemon juice

Cook all ingredients except lemon juice and Worcestershire sauce until celery is soft enough to strain through a colander. Add Worcestershire sauce and lemon juice. Cook two minutes longer.

Mrs. Vivian Petz, Northumberland Area School
Northumberland, Pennsylvania

HOMEMADE TOMATO JUICE

Number of Servings — 8-12

1 qt. canned tomatoes
3 c. cold water or liquids saved from cooking vegetables
Celery salt
Garlic salt
Onion salt
Accent
Salt
Sugar
Few drops Worcestershire sauce
Few drops lemon juice

Put tomatoes into food mill; add water or vegetable liquid. Press until only seeds remain. Season to taste. Chill.

Martha Jaquish Barocco, Northern Tioga School District
Elkland, Pennsylvania

Garnishes & Accompaniments

BANANA-COCONUT ROLLS

4 ripe bananas, peeled and cut in 1-inch cubes
½ pt. sour cream
1 t. lemon juice
1 T. honey
Coconut, flaked or toasted

Mix sour cream with lemon juice and honey. Coat banana cubes with sour cream mixture; roll bananas in coconut. Serve on toothpicks or bamboo skewers.

Sara Skandera, The Dallas Senior H. S.
The Dallas, Oregon

CARROT RELISH

3 medium to lge. carrots
1 lge. lemon, seeded
½ c. sugar (scant)

Finely grind carrots and lemon in a food chopper. Add sugar. Store in a jar in refrigerator for several hours or overnight to develop flavor. Serve with fish or meat salads.

Dorothy E. Kinsman, Ishpeming H. S.
Ishpeming, Michigan

ORANGE TEA BISCUITS

Number of Servings — 5

1 pkg. prepared dinner biscuits
½ small can frozen orange juice
20 sugar cubes

Preheat oven to 375°F. Soak sugar cubes in orange juice until well saturated. Place biscuits in greased 8 x 8 x 2 baking dish. Press two sugar cubes into center of each biscuit. Bake 10-12 minutes until orange syrup is golden brown.

Mrs. Ruth H. Methvin, Fall River H. S.
McArthur, California

STUFFED CELERY

Number of Servings — 15-30

2½ c. cheddar cheese, grated
2 T. mayonnaise
1 small clove of garlic, chopped fine
1 can pimento, chopped
1 bunch celery

Combine cheese, mayonnaise, garlic and pimento, mixing well. Clean celery stalks and remove some of the leaves from the outer stalks. Trim off very wide stalk ends. Cut long stalks into about 3 inch pieces, leaving the end leaves for trimming. Chill in ice water for an hour if time permits. Drain and fill centers.

Mrs. D. J. Dear, Stringer H. S.
Bay Springs, Mississippi

CHEESE COOKIES

Number of Servings — 9 Dozen

2 sticks butter or margarine
1 lb. sharp cheese, grated
2½ c. flour
1 t. salt
1 t. red pepper
1 c. nuts, chopped

Cream butter; add cheese. Sift together flour, salt, and pepper; add to cheese mixture. Work mixture with your hands if necessary. Add nuts; work them in. Shape mixture into rolls 1 inch in diameter. Wrap in waxed paper and chill overnight. Bake in 425°F. oven 10 minutes. Cool before removing from cookie sheet. Dough will keep in the refrigerator for many days or it may be frozen.

This recipe submitted by the following teachers:

Mrs. Arthur Deffebach, Ranger H. S.
Ranger, Texas

Mrs. Wanda Brian, Brock School
Weatherford, Texas

CHEESETTES

Number of Servings — 36

1 c. sifted flour
½ t. dry mustard
½ t. salt
¼ t. paprika
½ t. baking powder
½ c. butter or margarine
1 c. grated cheese, packed

Cream butter and cheese; mix in sifted dry ingredients. Form into small balls and mark with a fork or force through a cookie press. Bake at 375°F. for 10 minutes.

Mrs. Albertine P. McKellar, Rowland H. S.
Rowland, North Carolina

CHEESE CRUNCHIES

Number of Servings — 6-8

1 5-oz. glass Old English cheese
1 stick margarine
1 c. flour
Pinch of salt

Have cheese and margarine at room temperature. Cream margarine and cheese. Add flour and salt. Form mixture into little balls. Bake on ungreased cookie sheet in 350°F. oven until lightly brown. Remove and serve hot.

Mrs. Maurice Templeton, Junction City H. S.
Junction City, Arkansas

CHEESE PUFFS

Number of Servings — 30 Puffs

½ c. butter or margarine
1 c. sifted flour
2 c. cheese, shredded
½ t. paprika
¼ t. red pepper
½ t. salt

Cream butter or margarine. Add cheese; cream well. Add seasonings to flour and combine with the cheese mixture. Blend well. Shape into 1-inch balls. Freeze or chill thoroughly. Place on cookie sheet and bake at 350°F. for 15 minutes. Serve with salads.

Bessie Boyd, Huntsville H. S.
Huntsville, Texas

CHEESE DEVILS

Number of Servings — 4-6

¾ c. American cheese, grated
1 T. onion, minced
1 T. pimiento, minced (optional)
2 t. Worcestershire sauce
1 T. chili sauce
⅛ t. salt
Dash of cayenne pepper

Mix ingredients well; spread on crisp crackers. Put in hot oven or under broiler until cheese melts. Serve with salads or as an appetizer.

Phyllis A. May, Walter Johnson H. S.
Bethesda, Maryland

CHEESE-HAM NUGGETS

Number of Servings — 50

2 c. natural sharp cheese, grated
½ c. margarine
1¼ c. sifted flour
½ t. salt
1 t. paprika
50 ¼-inch cubes cooked ham

Blend cheese and margarine. Add dry ingredients and mix well. Wrap each ham cube in 1 teaspoon dough. Place on ungreased baking sheet. Bake at 400°F. for 15 minutes.

Carolyn Dyer, McKinney H. S.
McKinney, Texas

CHEESE-OLIVE BALLS

½ lb. sharp cheese
¼ c. butter or margarine
1½ c. flour
Dash of cayenne pepper
½ t. paprika
Green or ripe olives (ripe preferred)

Blend cheese and butter. Stir in flour that has been sifted with the cayenne pepper, and paprika. Mix well. Wrap 1 teaspoon of dough around 1 olive. Bake on ungreased cookie sheet 10 minutes at 400°F.

Mrs. Barbara H. Thompson, Tom Bean H. S.
Tom Bean, Texas

CHEESE-OLIVE PUFFS

Number of Servings — 48

½ c. margarine
2 c. sharp cheese, grated
1¼ c. flour
1 t. paprika
48 stuffed olives, drained

Blend margarine, cheese, flour and paprika. Chill dough and olives 20 minutes or longer. Mold ½ teaspoon of dough around dry olives. Flour hands if needed. Chill overnight. Bake at 400°F. for 10-12 minutes.

Barbara Lassiter, South Mecklenburg H. S.
Pineville, North Carolina

CHEESE-OLIVE NUGGETS

Number of Servings — 24-30 Nuggets

¼ lb. sharp cheese (1⅓ c)
¼ c. soft butter
¾ c. flour
⅛ t. salt
½ t. paprika
24-30 stuffed green olives, medium size

Grate cheese and cream with butter. Sift flour, salt and paprika into cheese-butter mixture. Mix to form dough. Shape around olives, using about one (1) teaspoon dough for each. Place on ungreased baking sheet and bake at 400°F. for 12 to 15 minutes or until light golden brown. Serve hot or cold.

NOTE: Nuggets may be covered with foil and refrigerated 4 to 5 hours before baking.

This recipe submitted by the following teachers:

Frances Blandford, State School for Girls
Gainesville, Texas

Mrs. Joel Ferrell, Brinkley H. S.
Brinkley, Arkansas

CHEESE SURPRISES

Number of Servings — 50

1 stick margarine
½ lb. sharp or mild cheese, grated
1½ c. flour
¼-½ t. Tabasco sauce
Dash of garlic salt
Small size stuffed olives or slices of Vienna sausages

Have butter and cheese at room temperature. Blend together with fingertips. Add flour gradually blending well. Add garlic salt and Tabasco and mix well. Break off small bits and flatten in palm of hand using just enough to wrap completely around an olive or slice of Vienna sausage. Bake on ungreased cookie sheet at 375°F. about 15 minutes or until lightly colored but not browned.

Ruth Stovall, State Supervisor Home Ec. Education
Montgomery, Alabama

IDIOT STICKS

Number of Servings — 25

1 loaf of day-old bread
Garlic powder, to taste
Grated cheese, to taste
Onion powder, to taste
¼ lb. butter, melted

Trim crusts from bread and brush with butter. Sprinkle with garlic powder, cheese and onion powder. Stack bread slices and cut into ¾-inch strips. Place in a single layer on a cookie sheet and bake for 3 to 4 minutes at 400°F.

Nina B. Moore, Sharpsville H. S.
Sharpsville, Indiana

CHEESE STRAWS

Number of Servings — 8

1 c. flour
¼ t. salt
⅛ t. cayenne pepper
¼ c. American cheese, grated
¼ c. butter or shortening
Cold water

Sift salt, pepper and flour together; add cheese and mix evenly. Cut in butter or shortening. Sprinkle in enough cold water to make a stiff dough. Roll to ⅛-inch thickness; cut into ½-inch x 5-inch strips. Place on baking sheet. Bake about 6 minutes at 450°F. Serve with a salad or vegetable juice cocktail.

Mrs. Helen Crone, Morton H. S.
Morton, Texas

CHEESE STRAWS

2 c. grated cheese
½ stick butter
1½ c. flour
1 t. baking powder
1 t. salt
¼ t. pepper
Cold water

Sift together dry ingredients. Add cheese and mix well. Cut in butter. Add enough water to blend. Roll ¼-inch thick. Cut into strips or press through cookie press into strips.

Mrs. Velm T. Strickland, Myrick H. S.
Laurel, Mississippi

EASY CHEESE WAFERS

Number of Servings — 50

2 c. mild cheese, grated
½ stick butter
1 c. flour
1 t. salt
¼ t. red pepper
¾ c. pecans, finely chopped

Cream butter. Sift flour with salt and red pepper; mix with pecans and cheese. Add butter. Shape mixture into two rolls; chill. Slice thin; place on cookie sheet and bake at 375°F. for 8-10 minutes.

Sarah Lou Cobb, Cherokee Junior H. S.
Orlando, Florida

CHEESE STRAWS

Number of Servings — 8

1 c. fresh bread crumbs
1 c. grated sharp cheddar cheese
⅔ c. flour
1 T. butter, melted
½ t. salt
⅛ t. white pepper
Dash of cayenne
2 T. milk

Mix crumbs, cheese, flour, melted butter, and seasonings. Add milk if needed. Roll or pat one fourth inch thick. Cut into trips, one fourth inch wide and about 4 inches long. Bake until lightly brown at 375°F.

This recipe submitted by the following teachers:

Mrs. Dimple W. Williams, Independence H. S.
Independence, Mississippi

Mrs. Dorothy W. Burd, Oldham County H. S.
LaGrange, Kentucky

GARLIC CHEESE STRAWS

Number of Servings — 2½ Dozen

½ c. shortening
1 c. sharp American cheese, shredded
3 T. parmesan cheese, grated
¾ t. garlic salt
1 c. sifted flour

Cream shortening; add cheeses. Beat well. Sift flour and garlic salt together; stir into the creamed mixture. Mix to a smooth dough. Force through a ¾ to 1-inch wide saw tooth flat attachment of cookie press. Press in 5-inch lengths on ungreased cookie sheet. Bake at 350°F. for 12 minutes. Let cool on sheet for a few minutes; remove carefully from cookie sheet.

Helen Janis Hale, Somerset H. S.
Somerset, Kentucky

DATE-FILLED CHEESE PASTRIES

Number of Servings — 8

½ c. butter
¼ lb. cheddar cheese, grated
1 c. flour
7 oz. dates, cut up
½ c. light brown sugar
¼ c. water

Cream butter and cheese with hands. Gradually add flour to make dough. Shape into smooth round, two rounds are better than one. Chill several hours or overnight. Combine dates, sugar, and water in saucepan. Cook over low heat stirring constantly until soft, about 5 minutes. Cool mixture. Slice chilled cheese dough about ⅛ inch thick, a few slices at a time. Spread dough with chilled date filling. Place another round on top. Bake at 352°F. for 15 to 18 minutes.

Flora Ward, Newville H. S.
Newville, Alabama

CHEESE PETITS FOURS

Number of Servings — 40-48

1 loaf bread, unsliced
¼ lb. butter or margarine
1 small glass Old English cheese
1 egg

Remove crust from bread. Cut loaf into 1-inch slices; quarter each slice. Combine butter, cheese and egg. Beat with mixer until mixture reaches a smooth spreading consistency. Spread cheese mixture on one side of the bread cubes. Place on a cookie sheet and bake 10-15 minutes at 350°F. (Petits fours may be frozen and then baked.)

Princess L. Egbert, Grants Pass Sr. H. S.
Grants Pass, Oregon

OLIVE AND CHEESE SNACK

Lge. green stuffed olives, cut in halves lengthwise
Swiss cheese, cut same size as olives
Narrow bacon strips, partially cooked
Ovals or 2" rounds of bread
Paprika

Place cut side of olives on pieces of cheese. Wrap with bacon. Place open end down on bread rounds or ovals. Bake at 450°F. for about 7 minutes or until bread is toasted. Sprinkle lightly with paprika and serve at once.

Mrs. Janet Iler, Avon H. S.
Avon, Illinois

CHEESE STRAWS

1 c. process cheese, shredded
3 T. butter
4½ T. milk
¾ c. flour
1½ c. fresh bread crumbs
Salt
Paprika
Cayenne

Blend cheese and butter; add milk. Mix flour, bread crumbs and seasonings to taste. Add to cheese mixture. Knead lightly until smooth. Roll out as pastry; cut into 6X½-inch strips. Bring the ends of ¼ of the strips together to form circles. Place all of the strips on greased baking sheet. Bake at 400°F for 10 minutes or until brown. Put 3 straws through each circle for serving.

Banita L. Standaert, Cashton H. S.
Cashton, Wisconsin

CREAM CHEESE AND CARROT BALLS

Number of Servings — 6

3 raw carrots
3 T. salad dressing
1 3-oz. pkg. cream cheese
3 t. lemon juice

Grate outer part of carrots; do not use hard inner core. Thoroughly mix cream cheese, salad dressing and lemon juice. When creamy, drop by teaspoonfuls into grated carrot. Roll mixture into balls. Chill. Garnish for green fruit salads.

Mrs. Peggy Draughn, Benton H. S.
Benton, Mississippi

CHEESE WAFERS

Number of Servings — 100 Wafers

¾ lb. sharp cheddar cheese, grated
¼ lb. butter
1 t. baking powder
1¾ c. sifted flour
1 t. salt
Dash of cayenne pepper
Dash of mustard

Cream cheese and butter. Add remaining ingredients and mix well with hands. Shape with cookie press. Cook 15 minutes at 350°F.

Mrs. Elizabeth S. Watson, Geo. R. Clark H. S.
Winchester, Kentucky

CREAM CHEESE PINEAPPLES

Number of Servings —6

1 8-oz. pkg. cream cheese
½ c. stuffed olives, thinly sliced
6 1½" sections celery, cut in thin strips

Divide cheese into 6 equal portions. Use a knife or spatula to mold each portion into the shape of a miniature pineapple. Chill. Gently press olive slices into cream cheese shapes. Insert celery pieces into top.

Marina Economos, Sandstone H. S.
Sandstone, Minnesota

CRANBERRY APPLE RELISH

4 c. cranberries
2 apples, pared and cored
2 oranges
1 lemon
2½ c. sugar

Put cranberries and apples through food chopper. Quarter whole oranges and lemon. Remove seeds, and put fruit through chopper. Add sugar and blend. Chill in refrigerator several hours before serving. Will keep well in the refrigerator several weeks.

Mrs. Frances Detmer, Weeping Water H. S.
Weeping Water, Nebraska

STUFFED DILL PICKLES

4 lge. dill pickles
1 3-oz. pkg. cream cheese
Cream
Worcestershire sauce
Crisp bacon bits or chopped pimento (opt.)

Cut off ends of pickles; remove centers with apple corer or potato peeler. Soften cheese with cream. Add Worcestershire sauce to taste and bacon or pimento if desired. Stuff pickles with cheese mixture. Chill 2-4 hours. Cut into ½-inch slices.

Mrs. Juanita Goss, Avoca H. S.
Avoca, Texas

CIDER RELISH

Number of Servings — 6-10

1 envelope unflavored gelatin
1½ c. cider
¼ c. sugar
½ c. raw carrots, ground
1 c. celery, chopped
½ c. raw cranberries, ground

Soften gelatin in ½ cup cider. Heat remaining cider but do not boil. Add sugar to hot cider. Pour over softened gelatin and stir until dissolved. Cool until slightly congealed. Add carrots, celery and cranberries. Pour into a 1-quart mold. Chill until firm. Serve as a relish or salad.

Mrs. Annette B. Tramm
Bradley-Bourbonnais Community H. S.
Bradley, Illinois

ROLLED WHEAT MUFFINS

Number of Servings — 12

1 c. rolled wheat
1 c. buttermilk
⅓ c. butter
½ c. brown sugar
1 egg
1 c. sifted enriched flour
1 t. salt
1 t. baking powder
½ t. soda

Soak rolled wheat in the buttermilk for one hour. Cream butter and sugar until light and fluffy. Add the egg and beat well. Add to milk and wheat mixture. Sift together the flour, baking powder, salt and soda. Add to the other mixture and stir just until dry ingredients are moistened. Drop the batter from a spoon into greased muffin pans, filling ⅔ full. Bake in hot oven (425°F.) 20 to 25 minutes or until muffins are a golden brown.

Mrs. Thelma L. Fowler, South Side H. S.
Counce, Tennessee

TOMATO ROSES

Number of Servings — 6

6 small tomatoes, peeled
1 8-oz. pkg. cream cheese
1 T. mayonnaise

Thoroughly mix cream cheese and mayonnaise. Use a teaspoon to form cream cheese mayonnaise petals around tomato to resemble a rose.

Dorothy Maltby, Muskegon Sr. H. S.
Muskegon, Michigan

PARTY MIX

1 stick margarine
½ t. garlic salt
½ t. onion salt
½ t. celery salt
1 t. Worcestershire sauce
2 t. soy sauce
4 c. cereal (such as Rice Chex and Cherrios)
1 c. mixed nuts

Place ingredients (except cereal and nuts) in 3-4 quart metal mixing bowl and place in 250°F. oven. Stir until mixed. Add cereal and mixed nuts. Stir from the bottom until mixed well. Return to oven. Heat 1 to 1½ hours stirring every 15 to 20 minutes. Cool and store in closed jar or can. These will keep several weeks if cooled well before storing in jar with tight top.

Mrs. Patricia H. Leete, Deep Creek H. S.
Chesapeake, Virginia

PICKLED PRUNES

Number of Servings — 12

12 lge. dried prunes
⅔ c. vinegar
⅓ c. juice from cooked prunes
½ c. granulated sugar
2 inches stick cinnamon
6 whole cloves
12 English walnut halves

Partially cook prunes as directed on box. Cool. Make a slit in the side of each prune. Remove the pit; insert a walnut. Press cut edges together. Combine vinegar, prune juice and sugar. Boil 5 minutes. Add cinnamon, cloves and prunes. Simmer until prunes are moderately soft. Cool. Remove from prunes liquid. Refrigerate until ready to use. Place one on each fruit salad or use as a garnish on a dinner or luncheon plate.

Lucile K. Lawson, Trinity County H. S.
Hayfork, California

BACON WRAPPED OLIVES

1 jar lge. stuffed olives
1 pkg. thinly sliced bacon

Cut each slice of bacon in half and wrap each olive with the ½ slice of bacon securing with a toothpick. Broil until bacon is crisp turning once during the broiling period.

Mrs. Shirley A. Randall, John Edwards H. S.
Port Edwards, Wisconsin

Dressings

CELERY SEED DRESSING

½ c. sugar
1 t. dry mustard
1 t. salt
1 t. or more onion, grated or onion juice (opt.)
¼ to ⅓ c. vinegar
⅔ to 1 c. salad oil
1 t. to 1 T. celery seed
1 t. paprika (opt.)

Mix sugar, mustard, salt and onion. Alternately add vinegar and oil a little at a time, beginning with vinegar. Beat well. Add celery seed. Cover and store in refrigerator. Serve on fruit or fresh vegetable salads.

This recipe submitted by the following teachers:

Mrs. Margaret Cepelka, Clarke County H. S.
Berryville, Virginia
Marlys Skarsvaag, Ulen H. S.
Ulen, Minnesota
Margaret Slonaker, Sulphur Springs H. S.
Jonesboro, Tennessee
Mrs. Mildred W. Tate, Henderson City H. S.
Henderson, Kentucky
Joyce P. Davis, Henderson County H. S.
Henderson, Kentucky
Opal Y. Mitchell, Carlisle County H. S.
Bardwell, Kentucky
Mrs. Vivian Hevelone, Chase County H. S.
Imperial, Nebraska
Bonnie Moore, Wiley H. S.
Wiley, Colorado

BETTY'S HONEY-CELERY SEED DRESSING

Number of Servings — 1½ Cups

¾ c. salad oil
2 T. cider vinegar
2 T. fresh lemon juice
1 t. salt
½ t. paprika
½ c. honey
¾ t. celery seed
½ t. grated lemon rind

Combine all ingredients in blender or jar. Blend or shake until thoroughly mixed. Chill. Shake before using. Make dressing at least one day before using for improved flavor.

Mrs. Betty Fraley Eggebraaten, Roosevelt H. S.
Minneapolis, Minnesota

OIL DRESSING

2 t. salt
2 t. paprika
2 t. dry mustard
2 t. celery seed
1 c. sugar
½ c. vinegar
2 T. onion, grated
2 c. warm salad oil

Mix all ingredients together adding oil last. Warm the dressing in a pan set in hot water. Beat until thick. Refrigerate.

Mrs. Patsy Sachse Edmunds, Crete-Monee H. S.
Crete, Illinois

SWEET ONION DRESSING

Number of Servings — 2 Cups

1 c. sugar
1 t. salt
1 t. paprika
¼ c. onion juice
½ t. mustard
½ c. cider vinegar
1¼ c. corn oil
1 T. celery seed

Dissolve first five ingredients in vinegar and boil one minute. Cool to luke warm; beat until thick. Gradually add oil, beating constantly. When stiff, fold in celery seed.

Mrs. Virginia Boyle, Ashland H. S.
Ashland, Illinois

HONEY DRESSING

1 c. salad oil
Juice of ½ small onion
1 c. sugar
¾ t. paprika
1 T. celery seed
½ t. salt
½ c. cider vinegar
¾ t. dry mustard

Mix sugar, salt and dry mustard; add vinegar and onion juice. Beat well with electric mixer. Gradually add oil, beating until mixture is thick and smooth. Stir in paprika and celery seed.

Mrs. R. Mushinski, Cambridge H. S.
Cambridge, Wisconsin

OIL SALAD DRESSING

1 c. sugar
½ c. vinegar
½ c. salad oil
1 t. celery seed
1 t. salt
1 t. onion, grated

Combine all ingredients; beat or stir well. Chill several hours. Serve over shredded cabbage or other green or vegetable salads.

Mary Alice Poland, Roberts Thawville H. S.
Roberts, Illinois

ONION SALAD DRESSING

1 c. salad oil
½ c. white vinegar
1 c. sugar
1 t. salt
1 t. dry mustard
1 medium onion, grated
1 t. celery seed

Combine oil, sugar, salt, mustard and onion. Beat with electric mixer set at high speed while slowly adding vinegar. Beat until smooth and thick. Add celery seed, stirring with a spoon until blended.

Mrs. Dianne Fynboh, Onamia H. S.
Onamia, Minnesota

CELERY SEED DRESSING

Number of Servings — 3 Pints

3 c. sugar
1 T. paprika
1 c. catsup
1 c. vinegar
1 T. salt
1 T. onion, grated or onion juice
3 c. salad oil
1 T. celery seed

Combine sugar, paprika, salt, onion or onion juice and catsup. Alternately, add oil and vinegar, beating well after each addition. Add celery seed. Use on vegetable salads.

Pearl E. Reuter, Fayetteville H. S.
Bedford, Indiana

BLEU CHEESE DRESSING

Number of Servings — 2 3/4 Cups

1½ c. salad oil
¼ c. water
¼ c. vinegar
¼ c. lemon juice
½ c. crumbled Bleu cheese
⅛ t. Worcestershire sauce
Dash of Tabasco sauce
⅛ t. black pepper, coarsely ground
Few grains cayenne pepper
¼ t. ground celery seed
¼ t. mustard
1 t. paprika
1 t. garlic salt
½ t. salt
1 t. onion salad

Mix ingredients together in quart jar. Stir to moisten dry ingredients. Cover tightly, and shake vigorously until thoroughly mixed. Store in Refrigerator. Shake before using.

Mrs. C. A. Fricke, Glendale H. S.
Glendale, Oregon

ROKA-BLEU CHEESE DRESSING

Number of Servings — 1 Pint

1 5-oz. jar Roka cheese spread
3 T. sour cream
2 T. mayonnaise
½ t. salt
½ t. peper
¼ t. onion salt
¼ t. garlic salt
½ t. paprika
Milk or cream
¼-⅓ c. Bleu cheese, crumbled

Combine Roka cheese spread, sour cream, mayonnaise and seasonings. Blend thoroughly. Thin with milk or cream to obtain desired consistency. Add bleu cheese.

Elizabeth L. Stephenson, Brighton Sr. H. S.
Brighton, Colorado

BLEU CHEESE DRESSING

Number of Servings — 30

1 qt. mayonnaise
1 triangle Bleu cheese
1 medium green pepper, grated
1 medium onion, grated
1 t. garlic salt
1 t. celery salt
½ t. onion salt

Mix cheese into the mayonnaise with a fork. Add pepper, onion, garlic, celery and onion salt.

Gladys Hetherton, Cascade, Montana

BLEU CHEESE DRESSING

Number of Servings — 5 Cups

1 qt. mayonnaise
1 t. garlic powder
1 3-oz. pkg. Bleu cheese
½ c. whipping cream
½ c. buttermilk

Beat all ingredients together until smooth. Cover and refrigerate.

Judith M. Unze, Appleton H. S.
Appleton, Minnesota

CREAM CHEESE DRESSING

Number of Servings — 6

1 8-oz. pkg. cream cheese, softened
⅛ t. salt
1 T. lemon juice
2-3 T. mayonnaise

Cream the cheese with an electric mixer. Add remaining ingredients; mix well. Serve on fruit halves or lettuce.

Mrs. Deanna Patin Roy, Fifth Ward H. S.
Marksville, Louisiana

ROQUEFORT OR BLEU CHEESE DRESSING

Number of Servings — 1 Quart

¼ lb. Roquefort or Bleu cheese
1 small onion, grated
Juice of 2 lemons
2 c. sour cream
½ c. mayonnaise
Salt and pepper

Break cheese into small pieces. Thoroughly blend remaining ingredients. Dressing will keep about 1 month in the refrigerator.

Diane Greaney, Oxnard H. S.
Oxnard, California

FANNY'S FRENCH OR ROQUEFORT CHEESE DRESSING

Number of Servings — 1 1/2 Pint

1 c. salad oil
¾ c. catsup
Juice of 1 lemon
¼ c. sugar
2 whole garlic buds
2 t. onion, grated
1 t. salt
1 t. paprika
¼ c. apple cider vinegar
1¼ c. mayonnaise
1 oz. Roquefort cheese, crumbled

Thoroughly blend all ingredients except mayonnaise and cheese. Let stand at least 2 hours. Just before serving add mayonnaise and cheese. Mix well.

Mrs. Betty Irelan, Grand Blanc H. S.
Grand Blanc, Michigan

BLEU CHEESE DRESSING

Number of Servings — 6

½ pt. sour cream
1¼ oz. pkg. Bleu cheese, crumbled
½ t. Worcestershire sauce
¼ t. dry mustard
Lge. pinch sweet basil
¼ t. garlic salt
¼ c. salad oil or buttermilk
1 t. lemon juice
⅛ t. coarse pepper
⅛ t. salt

Combine all ingredients. Mix well. Let stand for 24 hours.

Vera L. Snyder, Selah H. S.
Selah, Washington

ROQUEFORT-SOUR CREAM DRESSING

Number of Servings — 4 Cups

1 pt. mayonnaise
1½ c. sour cream
½ T. lemon juice
1½ T. vinegar
½ T. salt
½ T. Worcestershire sauce
1 t. onion juice
¼ t. black pepper
1 t. garlic powder
Dash of Tabasco sauce
2 lge. pkg. Roquefort cheese, crumbled

Beat all ingredients with electric mixer until well blended. Store in covered container in refrigerator.

Mrs. Garnet C. Jackson, Indio H. S.
Indio, California

SOUR CREAM WESTERN DRESSING

Number of Servings — 6-8

1 c. sour cream
1 c. ripe olives, finely chopped
2 t. sugar
2 t. lemon juice
¼ t. celery salt
⅛ t. salt
1 2-oz. pkg. Bleu cheese, crumbled

Mix ingredients in order listed and chill. Use over the following combination of vegetables: Wedges of celery, quarters of tomatoes, sliced cucumbers (skins on), green pepper rings and cauliflower flowerlets or your favorite tossed salad mixture.

Alice S. Clements, Indiana Joint Jr. H. S.
Indiana, Pennsylvania

BLEU CHEESE—SOUR CREAM DRESSING

½ c. sour cream
¼ t. salt
¼ t. dry mustard
1 c. buttermilk
1 c. mayonnaise
3 T. lemon juice
⅓ c. Bleu cheese, crumbled

Combine sour cream, salt, mustard, lemon juice, ½ c. buttermilk and mayonnaise. Add cheese and remaining buttermilk. Let stand 24 hours before using.

Mrs. Alvera Lewman, Chaffey H. S.
Ontario, California

ROQUEFORT DRESSING

1 qt. mayonnaise
1 small onion, ground
1 small green pepper, ground
1 clove garlic, ground
¼ lb. Roquefort cheese

Grind the onion, green pepper, and garlic. Add mayonnaise and mix well in blender or mix master. Add the cheese and mix a little more.

Mrs. Margaret Redman, Marquette Jr. H. S.
Marquette, Michigan

ROQUEFORT DRESSING

Number of Servings — 1 Quart

1 cup sour cream
2 c. mayonnaise
¼ c. wine vinegar
1 T. lemon juice
6 oz. Roquefort or Bleu cheese, crumbled
Dash of garlic salt

Blend lemon juice, cheese and vinegar. Add sour cream, mayonnaise and garlic salt. Blend well.

Mrs. Gene Taresh, East Nicolaus H. S.
East Nicolaus, California

PEARLY ROQUEFORT DRESSING

Number of Servings — 1 Quart

1 egg
1 c. salad oil
1 T. lemon juice
1 t. Worcestershire sauce
¼ t. garlic powder
¼ t. salt
Dash pepper
1 c. sour cream
1 4-oz. pkg. Roquefort cheese
1 3-oz. pkg. cream cheese

Beat together egg and salad oil. Add lemon juice, Worcestershire sauce, garlic powder, salt and pepper. Beat until well blended. Crumble cheeses into oil mixture with a fork; mix well. Fold in sour cream.

Mrs. Anthony G. Stone, Newell-Providence Community School
Newell, Iowa

QUICK ROQUEFORT DRESSING

Number of Servings — ⅔ Cup

½ c. French dressing
¼ c. crumbled Roquefort cheese

Combine French dressing and cheese in a jar shake well. Add salt and pepper to taste.

Audrey Rohrer, Belle Fourche H. S.
Belle Fourche, South Dakota

COOKED SALAD DRESSING

Number of Servings — 1 Pint

2 eggs
½ t. salt
¼ c. vinegar
¾ c. water
½ c. sugar
2 T. cornstarch
½ t. mustard

Beat eggs in small saucepan. Add other ingredients in order given, combining sugar and cornstarch. Cook over low heat stirring constantly until thick.

Mrs. Carol Brann, Jr.-Sr. H. S.
Mifflinburg, Pennsylvania

HELENA'S COOKED DRESSING

1 c. sugar
1 T. flour
1 t. mustard
1 t. salt
1 t. paprika
2 eggs
1 c. vinegar

Combine all ingredients. Cook in top of double boiler until thickened, stirring constantly. Cool; refrigerate. Use with meat, seafood or vegetable salads. Add whipped cream for use with fruit salads.

Mrs. Jean Cummings, Kingsford H. S.
Kingsford, Michigan

COOKED SALAD DRESSING

Number of Servings — 2½ Quarts

2 c. sugar
5 T. flour
1 t. salt
1 T. dry mustard
12 egg yolks, well beaten
5½ c. milk
1 c. butter or margarine
1½ c. cider vinegar

Mix dry ingredients. Combine with egg yolks, milk and butter. Bring to boil, stirring constantly while slowly adding vinegar. Dressing is less likely to curdle if all vinegar is added before butter has completely melted. Simmer for 5 minutes. Seal in jars. Delicious with apple or raw carrot and raisin salads.

Joyce Woods Kennedy, Knoch Jr.-Sr. H. S.
Saxonburg, Pennsylvania

COOKED SALAD DRESSING

8 egg yolks
½ t. dry mustard, dissolved in 1 T. boiling water
1 c. sugar
2 T. flour
½ t. salt
½ c. sour cream
1 c. hot vinegar

Beat egg yolks until light and lemon colored. Add mustard, sugar, flour, salt, and sour cream, beating constantly. Add hot vinegar. Cook in double boiler until thick. Remove from heat and beat well until creamy (use rotary beater or electric mixer). Use for potato, egg, or cabbage salad.

Mrs. LaVera Kraig, Monroe Jr. H. S.
Aberdeen, South Dakota

OLD SOUTHERN BUTTERMILK SALAD DRESSING

Number of Servings — 15

½ c. sugar
1 t. dry mustard
1 t. salt
¼ t. celery seed
1 T. flour
2 beaten eggs
½ c. vinegar
1 c. buttermilk
1 T. butter

Mix sugar, mustard, salt, celery seed and flour. Add vinegar, buttermilk and butter. Cook in double boiler until thickened. Pour thick mixture over beaten eggs. Return to double boiler; cook until mixture reaches a consistency of soft custard. Cool. Use with fruit salads or coleslaw.

Ruth C. Peabody, Sunnyside Junior H. S.
Sunnyside, Washington

GRANDMOTHER'S SALAD DRESSING

2 t. sugar or honey
1 t. salt
1 t. dry mustard
2 grains cayenne
2 T. flour
¾ c. water
1 egg, well beaten
2 T. butter, melted
¼ c. vinegar
Whipped cream or whipped evaporated milk

Combine dry ingredients; add egg. Mix thoroughly. Add water, butter and vinegar. Mix thoroughly. Cook over low heat until thick and smooth, stirring constantly. Cool. Thin with cream or milk before serving.

Mrs. Jane Greenman, Eau Claire Senior H. S.
Eau Claire, Michigan

POTATO SALAD DRESSING

Number of Servings — 1 Quart

5 eggs
1½ c. sugar
1 c. vinegar
1 c. sweet or sour cream
1 t. salt
2 T. prepared mustard
2 T. butter

Beat eggs in top of double boiler; add remaining ingredients and cook over water until mixture coats a spoon and becomes quite thick. Dressing may be used on potato salad by itself or mixed with an equal amount of commercial dressing.

Mrs. Lois Simmonds, DeSoto H. S.
De Soto, Wisconsin

FRENCH DRESSING

Number of Servings — 1 Pint

1 small onion, minced
2 T. cider vinegar
¾ c. sugar
½ c. water
2 T. tarragon vinegar
2 T. lemon juice
½ c. catsup
1 c. oil
1 t. salt
1 t. dry mustard
1 t. paprika
1 t. horseradish
1 t. Worcestershire sauce

Soak onion in vinegar. Boil sugar and water to soft ball stage. Remove onion from vinegar; combine remaining ingredients. Mix thoroughly with electric beater.

Mrs. Hugh M. French, A. C. Davis H. S.
Yakima, Washington

FRENCH DRESSING

Number of Servings — 20

½ c. catsup
¼ c. salad oil
¼ c. vinegar
¼ c. sugar
1 T. onion, minced
1 t. salt
1 t. paprika
½ t. garlic salt

Combine catsup, vinegar, sugar, onion, salt, paprika and garlic salt. Slowly add oil while beating at high speed. Shake dressing before using.

Carol J. Andersen, Sauk Rapids Public H. S.
Sauk Rapids, Minnesota

FRENCH DRESSING

Number of Servings — ¾ Quart

1 c. salad oil
½ c. vinegar
1 c. catsup
1 c. sugar
¼ c. onion, grated
Juice of one lemon
2 t. paprika
2 t. salt

Mix well with egg beater. Refrigerate.

Beverlee Brown, Miller Public School
Miller, South Dakota

FRENCH DRESSING

Number of Servings — 24-30

½ c. salad oil
¼ c. vinegar (weaken a little with water)
1 t. paprika
⅓ c. sugar
⅓ c. catsup
½ t. salt
1 T. lemon juice
⅓ onion, minced or 1-2 buds garlic, minced

Combine all ingredients and shake well.

Mrs. Corinne Brown, Story City Community H. S.
Story City, Iowa

FRENCH DRESSING

Number of Servings — 1 Cup

½ t. salt
½ t. paprika
½ t. dry mustard
1 t. sugar
¼ c. catsup
¼ c. cider or tarragon vinegar
½ c. salad oil.
½ t. Worcestershire sauce
1 t. minced onion

Combine all ingredients. Seasonings may be varied to taste.

Barbara Gioria, Bellows Falls H. S.
Bellows Falls, Vermont

FRENCH DRESSING

Number of Servings — 1 Pint

1 c. catsup
½ c. vinegar
¼ c. sugar
1 t. onion, grated
1 t. salt or celery salt
½ t. paprika
¼ c. water
Juice of ½ lemon
Pepper to taste
½ c. salad oil

Combine all ingredients except oil. Blend for 1 minute in electric blender set on high or medium speed. Reduce speed to low and slowly add oil. Blend thoroughly. Refrigerate. Shake well before using.

Mrs. Floramae Buhr, Bowler H. S.
Bowler, Wisconsin

FRENCH DRESSING

½ c. catsup
½ c. salad oil
¼ c. sugar
2 T. vinegar

Combine all ingredients; shake until sugar is dissolved. Refrigerate.

Loraine Burtch, Edison Jr. H. S.
Champaign, Illinois

FRENCH DRESSING

1 c. vegetable oil
½ c. vinegar
⅓ c. sugar
½ c. catsup
1 T. Worcestershire sauce
1 T. salt
1 small garlic
1 onion, finely cut

Combine ingredients in bottle or jar; cover and shake thoroughly.

Mrs. Lyla David, Benkelman H. S.
Benkelman, Nebraska

FRENCH DRESSING

1 c. salad oil
¾ c. sugar
1 c. catsup
1 t. salt
4 T. onion, grated
¼ c. vinegar
Juice of 1 lemon

Combine all ingredients and shake well.

Mrs. Darlene Freadkoff, Valley City Central H. S.
Valley City, North Dakota

FRENCH DRESSING

Number of Servings — 1 Pint

1 c. salad oil
½ c. white vinegar
1 c. sugar
½ medium onion, grated
1 t. salt
1 t. dry mustard
1 t. celery seed

Beat oil, sugar, vinegar, onion, salt and dry mustard with electric mixer until thick. Add celery seed; stir with a spoon. Refrigerate.

Audrey Gavin, Tracy H. S.
Tracy, Minnesota

FRENCH DRESSING

Number of Servings — 1 Pint

1 c. catsup
¾ c. salad oil
6 T. sugar
2 T. lemon juice
2 T. vinegar
¼ t. salt
¼ t. paprika
Dash of garlic powder

Beat all ingredients with electric mixer until thoroughly mixed. Refrigerate. Shake before using.

Mrs. Myrtle M. Joy, Meredosia-Chambersburg H. S
Meredosia, Illinois

FRENCH DRESSING

Number of Servings — 1 ½ Cups

½ c. catsup
½ c. salad oil
¼ c. vinegar
Juice of 1 lemon
1 T. onion, finely minced
¼ c. sugar
1 t. salt
1 t. paprika

Mix all ingredients. Shake well in tightly covered jar or blend for one minute in a blender. Use on tossed vegetable salad or fresh fruit salad.

Mrs. Floyd King, Malden H. S.
Malden, Illinois

FRENCH DRESSING

Number of Servings — 3 Cups

½ c. sugar
1 t. mustard
1 t. salt
⅛ t. paprika
½ c. vinegar
2 c. salad oil
½ c. catsup
Onion slices (Optional)

Mix sugar, salt, mustard and paprika. Alternately add vinegar and oil, beating constantly. Add catsup and beat until well mixed. If desired, add onion. Refrigerate.

Mrs. Ruth Lathrope, Wonewoc-Center H. S.
Wonewoc, Wisconsin

FAVORITE SALAD DRESSING

⅓ c. sugar
⅓ c. catsup
⅓ c. vinegar
⅓ c. salad oil

Combine ingredients in order given. Mix well.

Mary Jean Kearsley, Fruita Jr.-Sr. H. S.
Fruita, Colorado

FRENCH DRESSING

Number of Servings — 1 Quart

¾ c. salad oil
1 bottle catsup
1 bottle chili sauce
1 t. paprika
Salt to taste
¼ c. vinegar
¼ c. sugar
1 onion, grated
1 green pepper, diced

Method: Whip above at high speed.

Verlys M. Malme, Erskine School
Erskine, Minnesota

FRENCH DRESSING

Number of Servings — 1 Cup

½ c. salad oil
½ c. vinegar or lemon
1 t. paprika
1 t. sugar
1 t. salt
1 t. dry mustard
Cayenne to taste

Combine all ingredients in a jar. Cover and shake vigorously.

Julia Mason, Bonner Springs H. S.
Bonner Springs, Kansas

FRENCH DRESSING

Number of Servings — 1 Pint

1 c. vinegar
¾ c. oil
1 t. salt
2 t. dry or prepared mustard
½ c. sugar
1 t. paprika
1 clove garlic
1 T. onion, grated
¼ c. catsup or chili sauce

Combine all ingredients except catsup or chili sauce. Shake well. Add chili sauce or catsup. Remove garlic clove after 24 hours.

Mrs. Edith Osborne, Sonora Union H. S.
Sonora, California

FRENCH DRESSING

Number of Servings — 100

Garlic salt or garlic clove
1 c. vinegar
1⅔ c. oil
1 c. sugar
4 t. salt
1 t. pepper
1 t. paprika
¼ t. celery salt

Mix ingredients either by beating or shaking in a jar.

Mrs. Mary B. Pattberg, Housatonic Valley
Regional H. S.
Falls Village, Connecticut

FAVORITE FRENCH DRESSING

Number of Servings — 32

1 c. salad oil
⅔ c. catsup
¼ c. sugar
Juice of 1 to 2 lemon
1 t. Worcestershire sauce
1 t. dry mustard (opt.)
1 t. paprika
½ to 1 t. salt
½ c. vinegar
1 clove garlic (opt.)

Mix all ingredients except garlic and vinegar with a rotary beater. Add vinegar. If desired, float a clove of garlic on top of dressing.

This recipe submitted by the following teachers:

Mrs. Genevieve Pieretti
State Division of Vocational Education
Carson City, Nevada

Mrs. Lenda B. Edwards, Bennettsville H. S.
Bennettsville, South Carolina

FRENCH DRESSING

Number of Servings — 1 Quart

2 c. salad oil
1 c. vinegar
⅔ c. sugar
1 c. catsup
⅔ c. onion, grated
1 t. salt
1 T. paprika
1 clove garlic

Combine ingredients in order; shake well. Refrigerate. Dressing will keep for a month.

Mrs. Dorothy E. Puryear, Eureka Jr. H. S.
Eureka, California

DELICIOUS FRENCH DRESSING

1 c. vegetable oil
½ c. sugar
⅓ c. catsup
¼ c. vinegar
1 t. salt
1 t. paprika
1 T. onion juice or 1 small onion, grated

Combine all ingredients; mix with rotary beater. Dressing will be fairly thick and will not separate too much if thoroughly mixed.

Mrs. Lucy Roths, McLoughlin H. S.
Milton-Freewater, Oregon

DELUXE FRENCH DRESSING

1 c. oil
½ c. vinegar
½ c. sugar
2 T. chili sauce
2 T. onion, minced
½ t. pepper
1 t. salt
1 t. paprika

Beat all ingredients together. Dressing will keep for several months.

Margaret S. Yoder, Upper Perkiomen H. S.
East Greenville, Pennsylvania

FAVORITE SALAD DRESSING

Number of Servings — 6

1 c. salad oil
½ c. granulated sugar
⅔ c. vinegar, slightly weakened
½ c. catsup
1 t. salt
2 t. paprika
2 T. onion, minced

Mix ingredients in tightly covered quart jar. Shake well. Refrigerate. Reshake before using. Keeps well in refrigerator.

Mrs. Lois S. Gross, Black Creek Twp. H. S.
Rock Glen, Pennsylvania

FAVORITE FRENCH DRESSING

1 c. catsup
1 c. cooking oil
½ c. vinegar
1 t. paprika
1 c. sugar
1 small onion, grated
Garlic seasoning (Optional)

Combine all ingredients. Mix for 30 minutes with electric mixer set on slow speed. Ingredients may be combined in blender.

Mrs. Audrey Richards, Crivitz H. S.
Crivitz, Wisconsin

FRENCH CHEF'S FRENCH DRESSING

Number of Servings — 3½ Cups

1 c. water
1 c. sugar
2 garlic buds
1 c. catsup
⅔ c. vinegar
1 c. salad oil
1 T. prepared mustard
1 t. salt
½ t. pepper
½ t. paprika
2 or 3 drops Tabasco sauce
1 t. Worcestershire sauce

Cook water, sugar and garlic together until mixture thickens slightly and turns amber. Cool. Pour into quart jar or bottle with remaining ingredients. Shake well. For improved flavor, make several days in advance.

Helen M. Bell, South Junior H. S.
Grants Pass, Oregon

LOW-CALORIE FRENCH DRESSING

Number of Servings — 1 Cup

1 clove garlic, sliced
¼ c. vinegar
¾ t. salt
⅛ t. pepper
¼ t. paprika
2 t. sugar
½ c. tomato juice
2 T. water
2 T. salad oil

Add garlic to vinegar; let stand 20 minutes. Strain. Combine salt, pepper, paprika and sugar in a jar. Add tomato juice, water, vinegar, and oil. Cover and shake vigorously. Store in refrigerator. Shake again before using.

Ann Friends Huh, Caledonia H. S.
Caledonia, Minnesota

JERRY'S FAVORITE

Number of Servings —1 1/2 Quarts

3 c. vinegar
3 c. salad oil
3½ c. sugar
3 T. paprika
1 T. celery salt
1 T. onion salt
¼ t. garlic powder

Beat all ingredients with electric mixer until creamy. Refrigerate.

Edith Hansen, Mt. Pleasant Jr. H. S.
Mt. Pleasant, Michigan

JULIA'S SALAD DRESSING

⅔ c. sugar
1 c. salad oil
½ c. chili sauce or catsup
½ c. vinegar
1 t. salt
1 t. garlic salt
1 small onion, grated (more if desired)

Combine all ingredients in a quart jar; shake well. For improved flavor prepare dressing one day in advance. Keeps well.

Carol Steele, Powers-Spalding H. S.
Powers, Michigan

LIMESTONE FRENCH DRESSING

1 c. sugar
1 t. paprika
½ c. vinegar
1½ T. dry mustard
1 t. salt
¼ c. onion, grated
1 t. celery seed
½ c. catsup
1 c. salad oil

Combine sugar, paprika, vinegar, mustard and salt. Bring to a boil. Remove from heat. Slowly add remaining ingredients. Mix well.

Viola Kanten, Taylors Falls Public Schools
Taylors Falls, Minnesota

FRENCH DRESSING (Tomato Paste)

Number of Servings — 1 Quart

1 can tomato paste
1 c. salad oil
1 c. vinegar
2 T. Worcestershire sauce
1 T. prepared mustard
3 T. sugar
2 T. salt
1 small onion, grated
1 clove garlic, crushed

Combine ingredients in a quart jar. Shake well. Refrigerate for 24 hours before serving.

Ruth Richmond, Carthage-Troy H. S.
Coolville, Ohio

MARY'S SALAD DRESSING

¼ c. onions, chopped
2 t. sugar
2 t. salt
¼ t. pepper
¼ t. paprika
4 T. vinegar
4 T. catsup
⅔ c. salad oil

Combine all ingredients in order given. Shake well before serving.

Mrs. Jane Savidge Jefferis, Northern Burlington
County Regional H. S.
Columbus, New Jersey

MODIFIED FRENCH DRESSING

Number of Servings — 1 Quart

2 c. salad oil
⅔ c. catsup
1 small onion, grated or 1 pkg. prepared dry minced onion
2 t. salt
1-2 c. sugar
2 t. celery seed
⅔ c. vinegar

Beat first 5 ingredients with electric mixer for 20 minutes. Add celery seed and vinegar and beat until well mixed. Refrigerate.

Mrs. F. S. Longfellow, Scottland H. S.
Scottland, Illinois

STATE FAIR SALAD DRESSING

¼ t. dry mustard
¾ t. salt
¼ t. paprika
1½ T. sugar
1 T. catsup
¼ t. thick meat sauce
¼ c. lemon juice
½ c. salad oil

Mix ingredients in a jar and shake well. Chill. Serve over vegetable salads.

Verna J. Erickson, Hyre Junior H. S.
Akron, Ohio

TOSSED SALAD OIL DRESSING

Number of Servings — 1 Quart

1 c. salad oil
1 c. catsup
1 c. sugar
1 c. vinegar
¼ c. water
½ t. paprika
½ t. salt
1 large onion, sliced

Beat all ingredients except onion in order given with rotary beater. Add onion slices and let dressing stand for 30 minutes. Remove onion slices. Dressing will keep in the refrigerator for several months.

Mrs. Ruth Sloan, Ridgeville H. S.
North Ridgeville, Ohio

SALAD DRESSING

1 can tomato soup
¾ c. oil
¾ c. vinegar
Grated onion (opt.)
½ c. sugar (scant)

Combine all ingredients in a jar; shake well.

Imogene G. Johnson, Torrington H. S.
Torrington, Connecticut

FRENCH DRESSING

Number of Servings — 1 Quart

1 can tomato soup
1 t. dry mustard
1 c. sugar
½ t. garlic salt
1 t. paprika
¾ c. vegetable oil
½ c. wine vinegar
1 t. Worcestershire sauce

Mix all ingredients. Refrigerate.

Sandra Binder, New Athens Comm. H. S.
New Athens, Illinois

FRENCH DRESSING

Number of Servings — 1 Quart

1 c. salad oil
1 c. vinegar
1 T. sugar
1 can condensed tomato soup
1 t. salt
1 t. pepper
1 t. paprika
1 t. dry mustard
1 t. Worcestershire sauce

Combine all ingredients; blend with electric blender for 30 seconds.

Mrs. Esther Course, Santa Paula Union H. S.
Santa Paula, California

FRENCH DRESSING

Number of Servings — 1 Quart

1 t. powdered mustard
1 t. pepper
1 t. salt
1 t. celery seed
¾ c. sugar
¾ c. vinegar
1 10½-oz. can tomato soup
1 t. Worcestershire sauce
¾ c. salad oil
1 small whole onion or 1 clove garlic

Combine ingredients in order given in a quart jar; shake vigorously. Store in a covered jar in the refrigerator.

Mrs. Kareen Daby, Campbell H. S.
Campbell, Minnesota

FRENCH DRESSING

Number of Servings — 3 Cups

1 No. 10½-oz. can tomato soup
1 c. vinegar
½ c. oil
1 T. Worcestershire sauce
2 t. salt
½ t. paprika
½ t. pepper
1 t. dry mustard
¼ c. sugar
1 t. onion juice
1 clove garlic

Combine all ingredients together in a jar. Cover, and shake well. Chill. Shake again before serving.

Mrs. Cynthia Ebert, Ripon Sr. H. S.
Ripon, Wisconsin

FRENCH DRESSING

Number of Servings — 1 Quart

1 T. sugar
1 t. salt
1 t. dry mustard
1 t. paprika
1 10½-oz. can condensed tomato soup
1 c. vinegar
1 T. Worcestershire sauce
1 c. salad oil
1 clove garlic, grated
1 small onion, grated

Combine all ingredients in quart jar or bottle; cover and shake thoroughly.

Mrs. Luana Hutchings, Moapa Valley H. S.
Overton, Nevada

CREAMY FRENCH DRESSING

Number of Servings — 1 Quart

2 t. salt
½ t. black pepper
1 T. dry mustard
1 t. paprika
¼ c. sugar
1 3-oz. pkg. pectin powder
½ c. cider vinegar
1½ c. salad oil
1 T. Worcestershire sauce
1 T. scraped onion
1 can tomato soup
1 clove garlic

Combine all dry ingredients and sift three times. Combine soup and vinegar. Add onion and Worcestershire sauce; mix well. Add dry ingredients. Slowly add oil, beating constantly. Fill quart jar with dressing; add garlic. Dressing does not separate. Keeps indefinitely.

Suzanne Sanders,Burlington-Edison H. S.
Burlington, Washington

FRENCH DRESSING

¾ c. sugar
¾ c. salad oil
¾ c. vinegar
1 can tomato soup
1 T. onion, grated
1 t. salt
1 t. dry mustard
½ t. garlic powder (Optional)

Mix all ingredients together; shake well. Refrigerate until used.

Dennice M. Meyer, Escondido H. S.
Escondido, California

FRENCH DRESSING

Number of Servings — 1½ Pints

½ c. vinegar
1 T. mustard
1 t. salt
½ t. paprika
½ t. pepper
1 T. Worcestershire sauce
½ c. salad oil
¾ c. sugar
1 can tomato soup
1 small whole onion

Mix mustard and vinegar in quart jar. Add remaining ingredients in order given. Shake well. Dressing keeps well in the refrigerator.

Laura T. Russell, Claypool H. S.
Claypool, Indiana

HELEN'S DRESSING

1¼ c. of sugar
1 t. salt
½ t. dry mustard
½ t. paprika
1 small dry onion, finely chopped
½ green pepper, finely chopped
½ c. salad oil
1 can tomato soup
2 T. Worcestershire sauce

Combine all ingredients. Mix well. Let stand for several hours.

Helen Theriault Stover, Havermale Jr. H. S.
Spokane, Washington

TANGY SALAD DRESSING

Number of Servings — 6

½ c. salad oil
¼ c. vinegar
2 T. sugar
1 T. onion, chopped
½ c. tomato soup, undiluted

Combine all ingredients; shake well. Cover and refrigerate. Shake before using.

Mrs. Mary Yost, Warren H. S.
Vincent, Ohio

FAVORITE FRENCH DRESSING

Number of Servings — 1 Quart

1 c. vinegar
1 c. sugar
1 c. oil
1 t. salt
½ t. pepper
1 t. dry mustard
1 t. Worcestershire sauce
3 t. paprika
1 can condensed cream of tomato soup
1 onion, grated
1 clove garlic, grated

Mix all ingredients together and beat with rotary beater until well blended. Refrigerate. Dressing will keep for about a month.

Mrs. Charles Klarich, Granger H. S.
Granger, Washington.

FRUIT SALAD DRESSING

2 c. pineapple juice
1 6-oz. can concentrated orange juice
1 c. sugar
Juice of 1 lemon
3 T. flour
¼ c. honey

Mix all ingredients well. Bring to a boil over low heat. Cool.

Sandra Gill, Bruce H. S.
Bruce, Wisconsin

FRUIT SALAD DRESSING

Juice of 1 lemon
Juice of 1 orange
⅓ c. pineapple juice (about)
½ c. sugar
⅛ t. salt
3 eggs

Measure lemon and orange juice into measuring cup; add enough pineapple juice to make one cup liquid. Blend all ingredients in top of double boiler. Cook, stirring constantly, over simmering water about 10 minutes or until thickened. Cool; cover and refrigerate.

Jo Ann Kangas, Jr. H. S.
Virginia, Minnesota

PINEAPPLE SALAD DRESSING

Number of Servings — 8-10

1 T. cornstarch
¼ c. sugar
1 c. pineapple juice
1 egg, beaten until thick

Combine cornstarch and sugar. Add pineapple juice and beaten egg. Cook until thick in double boiler. Use on fruit salad.

Mrs. Ruth Dolsen, Walled Lake Senior H. S.
Walled Lake, Michigan

FRUIT SALAD DRESSING

Number of Servings — 10-15

½ c. sugar
1 T. flour
1 beaten egg yolk
1 c. pineapple juice
3 T. lemon juice
1 T. lemon rind, grated

Mix sugar and flour together. Add beaten egg yolk and fruit juices. Stir in lemon rind. Cook over medium heat until thick, stirring constantly. This keeps indefinitely in refrigerator. It is delicious used on fresh fruits; may also be used on fruit—cottage cheese salad.

Norma Oslund, Marshall Sr. H. S.
Marshall, Minnesota

PINEAPPLE DRESSING

Number of Servings — 2 Cups

⅓ c. sugar
4 t. cornstarch
¼ t. salt
1 c. unsweetened pineapple juice
¼ c. orange juice
1 to 2½ T. lemon juice to taste
2 eggs, beaten
2 3-oz. pkg. cream cheese, softened

Combine dry ingredients in saucepan; blend in fruit juices. Cook, stirring constantly until clear. Remove from heat and slowly stir into eggs. Return to saucepan and cook over low heat, stirring constantly, 3 to 5 minutes or until mixture thickens slightly. Cool 5 minutes. Beat in cream cheese until smooth. Chill.

This recipe submitted by the following teachers:

Carolyn Carpenter, Sam Houston H. S.
Arlington, Texas

Mrs. Frank E. Anderson, Owosso H. S.
Owosso, Michigan

PINEAPPLE DRESSING

Number of Servings — 2 Cups

¼ c. sugar
2 T. cornstarch
Dash of celery salt
¼ t. salt
1½ c. pineapple juice, unsweetened
4 egg yolks, slightly beaten
¼ c. lemon juice

Mix sugar, cornstarch, celery salt, and salt in top of double boiler. Stir in pineapple juice. Cook over boiling water, stirring constantly, until thick. Cover and cook 10 minutes, stirring occasionally. Stir a little of the cooked mixture into the slightly beaten egg yolks. Add to remaining hot mixture. Cook over hot water, stirring constantly, 3 minutes. Stir in lemon juice. Chill.

Variations:

Pineapple Cream Dressing: To the cool dressing add 1 cup of whipped cream.

Orange-Pineapple Dressing: Use ¾ cup each orange and pineapple juice.

Amelean Maud, Adena H. S.
Adena, Ohio

SWEET SALAD DRESSING

Number of Servings — 1½ Cups

1 c. sugar
½ c. water
¼ c. vinegar
2 eggs, beaten
Sweet or sour cream

Combine eggs, sugar, vinegar and water. Cook in double boiler until thick. Thin with cream before using. Serve over fruit salads.

Mrs. Dorothy Riley, Haxtun H. S.
Haxtun, Colorado

ARGYLE DRESSING

1 t. butter
1 t. salt
1 T. sugar
1 t. mustard
4 T. vinegar
4 egg yolks, beaten
8 marshmallows
1 c. whipped cream
1 c. nuts (opt.)

Cream butter, salt, and sugar. Add mustard (dissolved in small amount of the vinegar), egg yolks and remaining vinegar. Cook in double boiler. While hot add marshmallows. Chill. Fold in cream and nuts.

Hazel S. Wilkinson, Carroll H. S.
Ozark, Alabama

FRUIT SALAD DRESSING

½ c. lemon juice
2 eggs, beaten
¾ c. sugar
Whipped cream to taste

Mix lemon juice, eggs and sugar in small saucepan. Cook over low heat, stirring constantly, until mixture is consistency of custard. Cool and refrigerate in a covered dish. When ready to use in salad, mix the desired amount of whipped cream with lemon juice mixture. After the lemon and cream is mixed, it must be used the same day, it will not keep.

Mrs. Carl Ekstrom, New Carlisle H. S.
New Carlisle, Indiana

FRUIT SALAD DRESSING

Number of Servings — 2 Cups

⅓ c. butter
1 c. sugar
2 T. flour
1 c. sweetened pineapple juice
2 eggs
½ c. crushed pineapple, well drained
Toasted shredded coconut
Whipped cream (Optional)

Sift flour with sugar. Melt butter in saucepan. Remove from heat. Add flour—sugar mixture and stir rapidly until smooth. Bring pineapple juice to a boil. Add slowly to first mixture; stir well. Return to heat and boil until mixture is thick and clear, stirring constantly. Add eggs slowly to hot mixture, stirring rapidly. Let come to a boil. Remove from heat and add crushed pineapple. Cool; refrigerate. If desired, thin dressing with whipped cream. Serve on fruit sald garnished with toasted shredded coconut.

Grace Abrahamson, Wessington Springs College High School
Wessington Springs, South Dakota

FRUIT SALAD DRESSING

Number of Servings — 8-10

2 T. flour
6 T. sugar
1 egg, beaten
1 c. pineapple juice
3 T. lemon juice
½ pt. whipped cream

Mix flour and sugar in top of double boiler. Add egg; stir. Combine pineapple and lemon juice; stir into first mixture. Cook over hot water until thick and smooth, stirring constantly. Cool. Fold in whipped cream just before serving.

Emily Slamar Strahler, Pueblo H. S.
Tucson, Arizona

FAMOUS FRUIT SALAD DRESSING

Number of Servings — 2 Cups

⅓ c. sugar
1 t. flour
1 egg yolk
½ c. pineapple juice
2 T. lemon juice
1 t. celery seed
1 c. whipped cream

Combine sugar, flour, egg yolk, pineapple juice and lemon juice in a saucepan; stir until smooth. Cook over low heat until thickened, stirring constantly. Fold celery seed into whipped cream. Just before serving fold whipped cream into thickened mixture.

Mrs Carol G. Lewis, J. P. Knapp H. S.
Currituck, North Carolina

FRUIT SALAD DRESSING

Number of Servings — 18-24

1 pkg. vanilla pudding mix
1 16-oz. can fruit cocktail, drained
Milk
2 c. miniature marshmallows
1 pt. whipped cream

Prepare vanilla pudding according to package directions using juice from fruit cocktail plus enough milk to make 2 cups liquid. Fold in fruit cocktail and marshmallows. Cool. Add whipped cream before serving.

Mrs. Muriel Hyden, Appleton Sr. H. S.
Appleton, Minnesota

PINEAPPLE CREAM DRESSING

Number of Servings — 12

2 egg yolks
1 c. sugar mixed with ¼ c. flour
¼ c. lemon juice
1 c. pineapple juice
Dash of salt
1 c. heavy cream whipped
2 stiffly beaten egg whites

Beat egg yolks and gradually beat in sugar-flour mixture. Add fruit juice and salt. Cook in top of double boiler until mixture thickens. Cool. Fold in whipped cream and whipped egg whites.

Mary Prideaux Blackman, Blacklick Township H. S.
Twin Rocks, Pennsylvania

THREE-FRUIT SALAD DRESSING

Number of Servings — 3 Cups

½ c. sugar
2 T. cornstarch
¼ c. boiling water
3 T. lemon juice, strained
3 T. orange juice, strained
6 T. pineapple juice
2 eggs, beaten
1 c. whipped cream

Mix sugar and cornstarch in top of double boiler. Stir while adding boiling water and juices. Cover and cook about 15 minutes, stirring occasionally. Mixture will not thicken much. Add a small amount of the hot mixture to the eggs, stirring constantly. Add eggs to remaining mixture in double boiler. Cover and cook until thick. Cool. Refrigerate. When ready to serve, add whipped cream.

Agnes K. Van Oosten, Park County H. S.
Livingston, Montana

FRUIT SALAD DRESSING

Number of Servings — 6

1 egg, beaten
1/3 c. sugar
1/4 c. pineapple juice
3 T. lemon juice
1/2 c. whipped cream

Combine egg, sugar and fruit juices. Cook over hot water until mixture thickens. Stir constantly. Cool. Fold in whipped cream.

Helen Tussey, Sugar Valley Area
Loganton, Pennsylvania

AVOCADO-OLIVE DRESSING

Number of Servings — 6-8

1 medium avocado
1 4-oz. can ripe olives, sliced or chopped
1 c. mayonnaise

Peel avocado and remove seed. Mash until soft and smooth. Add drained olives and mayonnaise; mix well. Serve on cottage cheese and pineapple.

Mrs. Evelyn Lewis, Antelope Union H. S.
Wellton, Arizona

AVOCADO-DILL DRESSING

Number of Servings — 2 Cups

1 medium avocado, peeled and sliced
1/3 c. salad oil
1 T. sugar
4 T. lemon juice
1/2 t. salt
1 t. dill seed
1/2 c. water

Put all ingredients except 1/4 cup water in blender and blend for 2 minutes. Add remaining water. If dressing is too thick, add more water. Refrigerate. Serve on mixed fruit salads.

Mrs. E. Howard, Kent-Meridian Senior H. S.
Kent, Washington

COFFEE-FRUIT DRESSING

Number of Servings — 1 1/2 Cups

1 1/2 t. instant coffee
1/2 t. dry mustard
1/2 t. salt
1/4 c. butter, melted
2/3 c. sweetened condensed milk
1/4 c. lemon juice
1/3 c. pineapple juice
1 egg yolk

Blend coffee, mustard and salt; stir into melted butter. Combine milk, juices and yolk. Stir into butter mixture and beat until thick.

Mrs. Mary Jane Wilson, Woodland Junior H. S.
Fayetteville, Arkansas

CREAM DRESSING

Number of Servings — 6

1 3-oz. pkg. cream cheese
1/2 c. heavy cream
6 lge. marshmallows, quartered

Cream the cheese with the heavy cream. Add marshmallows; mix well. Let stand overnight. Beat well before serving.

Marval Klecker, Veroqua Sr. H. S.
Viroqua, Wisconsin

FRUIT SALAD DRESSING

Number of Servings — 1/2 Pint

1 onion (size of an egg)
1/2 c. sugar
1/2 t. dry mustard
1 c. oil
2 T. vinegar
1 t. celery salt
1/4 t. salt

Grate the onion; strain. Use juice only. Mix sugar and mustard. Slowly add oil and remaining ingredients. Put in a jar; shake well. Let stand before using.

Deirdre Williams, Crook County H. S.
Prineville, Oregon

GRAPEFRUIT SALAD DRESSING

1/3 c. sugar
1 t. salt
1/4 t. paprika
1/4 c. vinegar
1/4 c. salad oil
2 t. onion, grated
2 T. celery, minced
2 T. green pepper, minced
4 drops Worcestershire sauce

Combine all ingredients in jar; shake thoroughly. Serve on grapefruit, lettuce or cabbage salads.

Lorna Carswell, River Valley H. S.
Spring Green, Wisconsin

PEANUT BUTTER DRESSING

Number of Servings — 3/4 Cup

1/4 c. peanut butter
1/3 c. salad oil
1/4 c. vinegar
1/2 t. salt
5 t. sugar
1/2 t. prepared mustard
1/8 t. paprika

Beat all ingredients together until smooth. Serve on fruit salads.

This recipe submitted by the following teachers:

Pat Breidenbach, Elkton H. S.
Elkton, South Dakota

Marlene Jucht, Mitchell Senior H. S.
Mitchell, South Dakota

HONEY DRESSING

Number of Servings — 2 Cups

¼-⅔ c. sugar
1 t. dry mustard
1 t. paprika
1 t. celery seed
¼ t. salt
⅓ c. honey
⅓ c. vinegar
1 T. lemon juice
1 t. onion, grated
1 c. salad oil

Mix sugar, mustard, paprika, celery seed and salt. Add honey, vinegar, lemon juice and onion. Pour oil into mixture very slowly, beating constantly with rotary or electric mixer.

This recipe submitted by the following teachers:

Mrs. Alice Requa Smith, Sunrise Park Sr. H. S.
White Bear Lake, Minnesota

Gloria J. Meyers, McCaskey H. S.
Lancaster, Pennsylvania

HONEY-BANANA DRESSING

Number of Servings — 1 Cup

½ c. honey
2 T. mayonnaise
2 T. vegetable oil
1 banana, crushed

Mix all ingredients in blender or with beater. Chill. Serve on fruit salad.

Joleen Hartung, Edgerton Public School
Edgerton, Minnesota

HONEY-SPICE DRESSING

Number of Servings — 4

6 T. honey
3 T. lemon juice
1 t. ground ginger

Mix ingredients in a small dish. Stir well and refrigerate. Before using, stir again. Serve on fruit salads.

Mrs. Justine C. Irwin, Meeker H. S.
Meeker, Colorado

LEMONADE DRESSING

Number of Servings — 6

⅓ c. undiluted frozen lemonade concentrate
⅓ c. honey
⅓ c. salad oil
1 t. celery seed

Combine ingredients; beat with rotary beater until smooth. Serve with fruit salads.

Helene Fanberg, Whitehall H. S.
Whitehall, Michigan

RUBY RED DRESSING

Number of Servings — ¾ Cup

½ c. currant jelly
¼ c. vegetable oil
2 T. lemon juice
Dash of salt
Few drops onion juice

Beat jelly with fork until smooth. Add rest of ingredients and beat until smooth. Use on citrus fruits.

Agnes Falkowski, Southern Door H. S.
Brussels, Wisconsin

QUICK 'N' EASY DRESSING

1 c. corn oil
⅔ c. catsup
⅔ c. honey
¼ c. vinegar
2 T. onion, minced or dried

Combine all ingredients. Beat with an electric mixer until thick.

Mrs. Linda Knutson, Casselton H. S.
Casselton, North Dakota

GREEN MAYONNAISE

Number of Servings — 3 Cups

2 eggs
Juice of 1 lemon
1 t. vinegar
3 green onions
1 t. parsley
2 buttons garlic
¾ t. dry mustard
1¼ t. salt
1 pt. oil

Put all ingredients in blender except oil. Blend well. Add oil gradually; blending until desired consistency.

Lulu Smith, Jr. H. S.
Sand Springs, Oklahoma

SOY MAYONNAISE

Number of Servings — 2½ Cups

Mix in blender.

½ c. Soyalac
1 c. water

Add gradually.

1 c. oil
½ t. salt
Juice of 1 lemon

Season with onion, garlic or paprika.

Grace Smith, North Whitfield H. S.
Dalton, Georgia

LOW-CHOLESTEROL MAYONNAISE

Number of Servings — 1 Pint

¼ t. paprika
Dash of cayenne pepper
1 t. salt
½ t. dry mustard
2 egg yolks
2 T. vinegar
2 c. corn oil
2 T. lemon juice
1 T. hot water

Let eggs reach room temperature. Mix dry ingredients; add egg yolks and blend. Add vinegar and mix well. Add oil, 1 teaspoon at a time, beating with rotary beater or electric mixer set at high speed, until ¼ cup has been added. Add remaining oil in increasing amounts, alternating last ½ cup with lemon juice. Add an extra tablespoon of lemon juice to vary the flavor, if desired. Beat in hot water. This takes away oily appearance.

Barbara Waybourn, Patton Springs H. S.
Afton, Texas

MAYONNAISE (Cooked)

Number of Servings — 2 Cups

1 t. salt
1 t. dry mustard
1½ T. flour
3 T. sugar
2 eggs, beaten
1 c. sweet milk
½ c. vinegar
2 T. butter
¾ c. commercial mayonnaise

Mix salt, dry mustard, flour and sugar together. Combine eggs, milk and vinegar. Add liquid mixture to dry mixture; stir. Cook until thick. Remove from heat; add butter and mayonnaise. Stir.

Mrs. Emma Benner, Newport H. S.
Newport, Pennsylvania

QUICK MAYONNAISE DRESSING (Cooked)

2 egg yolks
2 T. vinegar
2 T. lemon juice
1 t. sugar
½ t. salt
½ t. mustard
¼ t. paprika
1 c. salad oil
⅓ c. flour
1 T. butter
1 c. cold water

Combine egg yolks and vinegar. Beat well. Add lemon juice, sugar, salt, mustard, paprika and salad oil. Combine remaining ingredients in a double boiler; cook until thick. Add hot mixture to egg-vinegar mixture. Beat until thick enough to hold shape.

Lillian Mattson, Moses Lake H. S.
Moses Lake, Washington

POPPY OR CELERY SEED DRESSING

Number of Servings — 1 ¾ Cups

1 t. salt
1 t. dry mustard
1 t. paprika
1 t. poppy or celery seed
3 T. sugar
⅓ c. vinegar
1 c. vegetable oil
1 T. onion, grated
¼ c. filbert nuts, chopped (For fruit salads)

Place all ingredients in a small bowl. Beat with rotary beater until blended and thickened. Place in covered container. Chill several hours. Shake before serving.

Mrs. Paula E. Compton, Custer County H. S.
Miles City, Montana

POPPY SEED DRESSING

Number of Servings — 1 ½ Cups

½-¾ c. sugar
1 t. dry mustard
1 t. salt
Onion juice or grated onion to taste
5 T. white vinegar
1 c. salad oil
1-1½ T. poppy seed
1½ T. lemon juice (opt. for cole slaw)

Mix sugar, mustard, salt, onion and 2 tablespoons of vinegar. Add salad oil slowly, beating constantly. Add remaining vinegar (lemon juice if used), and continue beating until dressing is thick. Stir in the poppy seed. Store in refrigerator. Serve with fruit salads, fruit gelatin molds, grapefruit-avocado combination, or cole slaw.

This recipe submitted by the following teachers:

Mrs. Ida Mae Niebuhr, Gonzales H. S.
Gonzales, Texas

Mrs. Ruby Maynard, Angleton H. S.
Angleton, Texas

Mrs. Ann Hohman, Juniata Valley H. S.
Alexandria, Pennsylvania

Mrs. J. E. Stover, Benjamin H. S.
Benjamin, Texas

Mrs. Martha Lou Long, McCamey H. S.
McCamey, Texas

POPPY SEED DRESSING

Number of Servings — 2 Cups

1 egg
¼ c. sugar
¼ c. lemon juice
1 T. poppy seed
1 t. dry mustard
½ t. paprika
½ t. salt
1½ c. salad oil
¼ c. honey
1 t. onion, grated

Measure first seven ingredients into mixing bowl. Gradually add salad oil, about ¼ cup at a time,

(Continued on next page)

beating constantly on high speed with mixer. Add honey and onion. Mix at medium speed. Refrigerate. Shake before using. Serve with chilled fruit.

Katharine Rigby, Miller H. S.
Hemlock, Ohio

RUSSIAN DRESSING

Number of Servings — 1 Pint

1 c. oil
½ c. sugar
⅓ c. catsup
1 t. steak sauce or Worcestershire sauce
¼ c. vinegar
1 medium onion, grated
½ t. salt
1 t. paprika
1 clove garlic

Mix all ingredients together; beat with an egg beater. Store in a jar in refrigerator.

Mrs. Don Dubbe, Sturgis H. S.
Sturgis, South Dakota

RUSSIAN DRESSING

1 c. mayonnaise
⅔ c. chili sauce
2 scallions, finely chopped
¼ green pepper, finely chopped
2 T. lemon juice

Mix all ingredients; chill at least an hour.

Peggy Rozell, Bagdad H. S.
Bagdad, Arizona

RUSSIAN DRESSING

1 c. water
1 c. sugar
Juice of 2 lemons
2 c. salad oil
1 c. catsup
2 t. Worcestershire sauce
2 T. onion, grated
1 t. celery salt
1 t. paprika
Pinch of red pepper

Boil water and sugar. Cool. Add remaining ingredients and mix thoroughly. Chill.

Carol Van Sickle, Wells Public Schools
Wells, Minnesota

THOUSAND ISLAND DRESSING

1 c. salad dressing or mayonnaise
⅓ c. chili sauce
2 hard cooked eggs, chopped
1 small green pepper, chopped
1 doz. stuffed olives, sliced
Few drops of onion juice

Combine all ingredients.

Mrs. Sara Carnahan, Wamego Rural H. S.
Wamego, Kansas

THOUSAND ISLAND DRESSING

4 c. mayonnaise
1 c. chili sauce
2 hard boiled eggs
½ c. sweet pickles, chopped
¼ c. green pepper, chopped

Combine ingredients in order listed. Chill and serve.

Mrs. Pam Fankhanel, Bemidji Senior H. S.
Bemidji, Minnesota

THOUSAND ISLAND DRESSING

Number of Servings — 1½ Cups

1 c. salad dressing
¼ c. chili sauce
2 hard cooked eggs, chopped
2 T. green pepper, chopped
2 T. celery, chopped
1½ T. onion, finely chopped
¼ c. stuffed green olives, chopped
½ t. salt
1 t. paprika
3 T. sugar

Combine all ingredients; mix well. Refrigerate.

Mrs. Thordis K. Danielson, New Rockford H. S.
New Rockford, North Dakota.

FRESH VEGETABLE THOUSAND ISLAND DRESSING

Number of Servings — 3½ Cups

½ c. mayonnaise
1 can condensed tomato soup
1 t. dry mustard
½ t. paprika
1 hard cooked egg, chopped
½ c. celery, chopped
1 lge. carrot, chopped
1 t. onion, minced
4 medium sweet pickles, chopped

Mix mayonnaise with soup; add remaining ingredients. Chill.

Betty Herrin, Albany H. S.
Albany, Texas

SLIM JIM THOUSAND ISLAND DRESSING

Number of Servings — 1¾ Cups

1 c. sour cream
¼ t. salt
¼ c. pickle relish
¼ c. chili sauce
1 T. green onion, minced
2 hard cooked eggs, finely chopped
1 T. pimento, chopped
Lemon juice

Lightly combine all ingredients except lemon juice. Add additional salt and lemon juice to taste. Chill thoroughly.

Mrs. Karen Davies, Evergreen Junior H. S.
Everett, Washington

THOUSAND ISLAND DRESSING

Number of Servings — 1 1/2 Cups

1 c. mayonnaise
½ t. salt
¼ t. pepper
Dash of cayenne
1 T. lemon juice
1 T. catsup
1 t. Worcestershire sauce
2 T. sweet pickles, chopped, or pickle relish
2 t. parsley, chopped
⅓ c. celery, finely chopped
1½ T. pimento, chopped
1 T. onion, finely chopped

Combine all ingredients. Mix well and chill. Serve on lettuce wedges.

Mrs. Barbara Hiller, Winnebago Community School
Winnebago, Minnesota

THOUSAND ISLAND DRESSING

Number of Servings — 1 Quart

3 egg yolks
2 c. corn oil
½ c. vinegar
½ bottle chili sauce
2 pimentos, chopped or ground
½ green pepper, chopped or ground
3 hard cooked eggs, chopped or ground
1 small bottle stuffed olives, chopped or ground
1 small onion, minced
Pinch of salt

Chill beater and bowl. Have all ingredients at room temperature. Beat egg yolks until light in color. Add oil, a drop at a time, and continue beating until mixture thickens. When mixture becomes thick, thin with small amount of vinegar. Continue until oil and vinegar are used. Add chili sauce, pimentos, peppers, eggs, olives onion and salt. Stir together. Chill in Refrigerator in covered jar.

Bernice W. Jager, Bird Island Public
Bird Island, Minnesota

THOUSAND ISLAND DRESSING

Number of Servings — 30-35

6 hard cooked eggs, chopped
¼ c. plus 2 T. olives, chopped
¼ c. sweet pickle relish
¼ c. chili sauce or catsup
½ qt. mayonnaise
1 small onion, grated

Mix all ingredients. Chill.

Mrs. Melvin Tavares, Kempton-Cabery, H. S.
Kempton, Illinois

BUSY-DAY SALAD DRESSING

Number of Servings — 24

1 c. mayonnaise
½ c. canned milk
½ c. any prepared French dressing or ¼ c. French dressing and ¼ c. Italian dressing

Blend mayonnaise and milk. Add and blend French dressing (red) or Italian dressing (white) or mixture of the two.

Mrs. R. L. Hutchinson, Duncan U. Fletcher H. S.
Jacksonville Beach, Florida

BUTTERMILK SALAD DRESSING

Number of Servings — 1 Pint

1 c. buttermilk
1 c. mayonnaise
2 T. paprika
Onion salt to taste

Combine all ingredients. Whip with an electric mixer.

Mrs. Mary Turner, Hagerman Municipal Schools
Hagerman, New Mexico

CABBAGE DRESSING

Number of Servings — 1 Pint

½ c. water
1 c. sugar
1 c. vinegar
1 t. celery seed
1 t. mustard seed

Combine all ingredients. Boil for 3 minutes. Refrigerate.

Sharron Mallin, Martin Hughes H. S.
Buhl, Minnesota

CATALINA DRESSING

Number of Servings — 1 Pint

¼ t. black pepper
¼ c. vinegar
½ c. catsup
1 small onion, grated
½ t. salt
½ c. sugar
1 c. salad oil

Using a rotary beater, mix all ingredients except oil in order listed. Gradually add oil while beating. Refrigerate.

Mrs. Ina Luadtke, Fisher H. S.
Fisher, Minnesota

CONDENSED MILK DRESSING

Number of Servings — 2 1/4 Cups

2 eggs
¾ c. vinegar
2-3 T. water
1 can condensed milk
½ t. prepared mustard

Beat eggs until thick. Add 1 tablespoon vinegar-water mixture to eggs and beat. Add 1 to 2 tablespoons milk; beat. Repeat additions of vinegar and milk, beating after each. Blend in mustard. Store, tightly covered, in refrigerator. Serve on tomato, chopped cabbage or fruit salad.

Thelma Huff, Pelahatchie Attendance Center
Pelahatchie, Mississippi

COLESLAW DRESSING

5 T. sugar
1 T. plus 1 t. flour
1 t. dry mustard
Pinch of salt
1 egg, beaten
¼ c. vinegar
¾ c. water
Butter size of walnut
1 c. salad dressing

Thoroughly mix sugar, flour, mustard, salt and egg; set aside. Combine vinegar, water and butter; bring to a boil. Add first mixture and cook for a few minutes. Remove from heat; beat well. Add salad dressing and beat again. Dressing will keep for several weeks in refrigerator.

Mrs. Barbara Hinegardner, Bel Air Junior H. S.
Bel Air, Maryland

CUCUMBER DRESSING

1 qt. mayonnaise
3 medium cucumbers
3 small onions
¼ c. lemon juice
¼ c. sugar
¼ t. green color
¼ t. Ac'cent
¼ t. garlic powder
2 T. Worcestershire sauce

Grind cucumbers and onions and drain well. Add sugar, lemon juice, and seasonings. Add color and mayonnaise. Stir until smooth.

Helen Hutchison, Regional Supervisor
Home Economics Education
Jackson, Tennessee

GREEN GODDESS SALAD DRESSING

½ pt. sour cream
½ can anchovy fillets
2 T. parsley, chopped
½ medium avocado
Freshly ground black pepper to taste
Salt to taste

Mash anchovies and avocado to a pulp. Add remaining ingredients and mix well. More anchovies may be added if desired.

Nita P. Lowery, South Mountain H. S.
Phoenix, Arizona

LIME CASTLE SALAD DRESSING

½ c. sugar
⅔ c. catsup
1 c. oil
½ c. white vinegar
1 t. vinegar
1 onion, grated
1½ t. salt

Combine sugar, catsup, oil and vinegars. Blend well. Add onion and salt; stir.

Mrs. Sue Dowler, Haltom H. S.
Fort Worth, Texas

ITALIAN SALAD DRESSING

Number of Servings — 6

¼ c. olive oil
2 T. lemon juice
1 t. lemon rind, grated
Salt to taste
½ t. oregano or thyme
1 clove garlic, minced
1 T. Parmesan cheese, grated
½ t. black pepper, freshly ground

Combine all ingredients; mix well. Chill. Mix again before using.

Angela D'Gerolamo, Riverdale H. S.
New Orleans, Louisiana

HUBBELL HOUSE SALAD DRESSING

Number of Servings — 1 Quart

1 c. mayonnaise
1 c. salad dressing
1 c. tartar sauce or sandwich spread
1 c. tomato soup
1 small onion, grated
4 sweet pickles, finely chopped
1 t. dry mustard
2 T. vinegar
2 T. chili sauce
2 T. sweet pickle juice

Blend salad dressing with mayonnaise. Add remaining ingredients; mix well.

Gladys Severance, Huron H. S.
Huron, South Dakota

LOW CALORIE DRESSING

Number of Servings — 2 Cups

1 c. cottage cheese
1 10½-oz. can condensed tomato soup
1 T. India or sweet pickle relish
1 T. lemon juice
Grated rind of 1 lemon (opt.)
Salad greens

Blend all ingredients except salad greens; chill. Stir well and serve over crisp salad greens. Two tablespoons dressing contains 25 calories.

Charlyene Deck, Exeter Union H. S.
Exeter, California

LOW-CALORIE SALAD DRESSING

Number of Servings — 4

½ c. unsalted tomato juice
2 T. lemon juice or vinegar
1 T. onion, chopped
1 T. parsley, chopped
1 t. fresh horseradish
1 T. green pepper

Combine all ingredients. Refrigerate. Use on salad greens, cucumber slices or raw vegetable mixtures. Dressing contains 7 calories per serving.

Mrs. Willye Pearl Mdodana
San Luis Obispo Junior H. S.
San Luis Obispo, California

McKEE SALAD DRESSING

Number of Servings — 1 Quart

2 8-oz. cans tomato sauce
⅓ c. lemon juice
1 c. salad oil
⅓ c. vinegar
2 garlic cloves, crushed
¼ t. garlic salt
½ t. thyme
½ t. parsley
½ t. rosemary
¼ t. basil
⅛ t. marjoram
⅛ t. bay leaf, crushed
½ c. sugar or sweeten to taste

Mix ingredients in a saucepan and bring to a boil. Remove from heat and beat with rotary beater. Use when cool. Flavor improves after being refrigerated for two days. Use an any vegetable salad.

Helen M. McKinley, Oxnard H. S.
Oxnard, California

GREEN SALAD DRESSING

Number of Servings — 1 Quart

1 c. white vinegar
1 c. white sugar
1 c. vegetable oil
1 T. prepared mustard
1 T. salt
1 T. Worcestershire (Optional)
1 small can pimentos
1 green sweet pepper
1 medium onion

Mix first six ingredients well. Grind together, pimentos, pepper and onion. Add vegetables to first mixture, let stand at least 3 hours in refrigerator. Will keep indefinitely if under refrigeration.

Mrs. Allen Mayhew, Greensburg Rural H. S.
Greensburg, Kansas

TOSSED GREEN SALAD DRESSING

Number of Servings — 2 Cups

2 T. anchovy paste
3 T. onion, chopped
1 T. lemon juice
1 small clove garlic
3 T. wine vinegar
⅓ c. parsley, chopped
⅓ c. milk
1 c. mayonnaise

Put ingredients into blender and mix until smooth. Dressing keeps indefinitely in closed container in refrigerator.

Leonora H. Gross, Stockton Unified School District
Stockton, California

HORSE-RADISH CREAM

1 c. whipping cream
1 t. sugar
⅛ t. salt
1 T. vinegar
4 T. prepared horse-radish, drained

Whip cream until stiff. Fold in remaining ingredients. Note (In our community this is served at public baked ham suppers)

Bernice E. Kirkeby, Willow Lake H. S.
Willow Lake, South Dakota.

MOM'S DRESSING

Number of Servings — 1 Cup

¾ c. mayonnaise
¼ c. vinegar
½ t. sugar
1 T. celery seed

Combine all ingredients until well-mixed. Serve over green tossed salad.

Mrs. Carolene Wood, Perkins H. S.
Perkins, Oklahoma

PENNSYLVANIA DUTCH DRESSING

Number of Servings — 4

2-3 slices of bacon
1 egg, beaten
2-4 T. vinegar
¼ c. sugar

Fry bacon until crisp; drain and crumble. If vinegar is strong, add enough water to make ¼ c. liquid. Combine egg, sugar and vinegar. Combine egg mixture and half of the bacon drippings. Cook over low heat until thickened. Serve over fresh leaf lettuce or spinach while still hot. Use bacon bits for garnish.

Mrs. Bertha Netzel, H. S.
Wittenberg, Wisconsin.

POTATO SALAD DRESSING

Number of Servings — 8

½ pt. whipping cream
1 T. mayonnaise
1 T. salad dressing
1 T. brown sugar
2 T. sweet pickle relish

Cream mayonnaise and salad dressing. Gradually add whipping cream. Add brown sugar and pickle relish and combine with salad.

Yvonne Elzinga, Payson H. S.
Payson, Utah

QUICK SALAD DRESSING

1 c. evaporated milk
2 T. vinegar
¼ c. sugar

Combine ingredients. Serve with fruit salads, slaws or tossed salads.

Mable Frary, Vian H. S.
Vian, Oklahoma

ROTISSERIE DRESSING

Number of Servings — 1 Pint

2-3 garlic cloves, minced
1 c. mayonnaise
¼ c. chili sauce
¼ c. catsup
1 t. Worcestershire sauce
¼-1 t. black pepper
½ c. salad oil
¼ t. Tabasco sauce
¼ t. paprika
1 small onion, grated
2 T. water or juice of 1 lemon plus 1 t. water
1 t. prepared mustard
Salt to taste

Mix ingredients well. Keep refrigerated.

This recipe submitted by the following teachers:

Mrs. Ruth J. Shaw, Umatilla H. S.
Umatilla, Florida

Elsie C. Smith, Utica H. S.
Utica, Mississippi

SEAFOOD SALAD DRESSING

2 c. mayonnaise
¼ c. catsup
¼ c. green onions, chopped
¼ c. dill pickles, chopped
2 hard cooked eggs, chopped
1 clove garlic (split and stuck on toothpick)
½ t. black pepper
1 can shrimp
1 can crab

Mix mayonnaise and catsup; fold in onion, pickle, egg and pepper. Add garlic. Cover and place in refrigerator for several hours. When ready to serve, remove garlic and fold in shrimp and crab. Pour over chopped lettuce, tomatoes and avocado or salad greens.

Mrs. Evelyn H. Duke, Caldwell H. S.
Columbia, Louisiana

SHRIMP LOUIS SALAD DRESSING

2 c. mayonnaise
½ c. chili sauce
¼ t. Ac'cent
2 t. sugar
Dash of white pepper
Juice of 1 lemon
⅓ c. India relish
2 boiled eggs, chopped

Mix all ingredients together. Chill well. Serve over green salad or boiled shrimp and lettuce and tomato.

Mrs. May Campbell, Orangefield H. S.
Orangefield, Texas

VINEGAR AND SPICE-FREE SALAD DRESSING

Number of Servings — 1 Pint

2 eggs
½ c. lemon juice
½ c. salad oil
1 can sweetened condensed milk
½ t. dry mustard (opt.)
½ t. salt

Beat eggs until foamy. Beat in remaining ingredients at low speed. Dressing will be quite thick. Store in covered jar.

Adele Lehnherr, Union H. S.
Juda, Wisconsin

ZIPPY VEGETABLE SALAD DRESSING

Number of Servings — 6

¼ c. honey
⅔ c. undiluted evaporated milk
¼ c. lemon juice
½ t. salt
½ t. dry mustard
1 t. paprika

Combine all ingredients. Beat until creamy smooth. Refrigerate until thick.

Mrs. Gwen Bayer, Summerville Union H. S.
Tuolumne, California

Egg Salad

EASTER EGG SALAD

Number of Servings — 4

1 T. salt
3 qt. boiling water
½ lb. elbow macaroni
½ c. salad dressing
2 T. French dressing
1 t. salt
3 drops Tabasco sauce
1 c. cooked kidney beans, drained
3 hard-cooked eggs, diced
¼ c. sweet pickles, chopped
Watercress

Combine 1 tablespoon salt, boiling water and macaroni. Cook for 8 minutes or until macaroni is tender; drain and rinse. Combine salad dressing, French dressing, 1 teaspoon salt and Tabasco sauce. Fold in kidney beans, eggs, pickles and macaroni. Serve on nests of watercress.

Mrs. Gloria J. Love, Cumberland Valley Sr. H. S.
Mechanicsburg, Pennsylvania

DEVILED EGG ASPIC SALAD

Number of Servings — 6

3 deviled eggs, sliced lengthwise
2 c. tomato juice
1 t. basil
1 T. onion, minced
1 T. celery, minced
1 T. green pepper, minced
1 3-oz. pkg. lemon gelatin
½ t. salt
2 T. chives or garlic vinegar

Combine tomato juice, basil, onion, green pepper and celery. Bring to a boil. Remove from heat; strain. Add gelatin, vinegar or chives and salt; stir until dissolved. Let set until mixture begins to congeal. Arrange eggs, cut side up, in a flat oblong bowl. Pour gelatin mixture over eggs. Chill until firm. When ready to serve, cut so the yellow and white side of egg is centered in aspic. If desired, serve with salad dressing or sour cream dressing.

Charlotte R. Turner, Hendersonville H. S.
Hendersonville, North Carolina

DEVILED EGG MOLD

Number of Servings — 6

1 envelope unflavored gelatin
½ c. water
1 t. salt
1-2 T. lemon juice or vinegar
¼ t. Worcestershire sauce
Cayenne pepper to taste (opt.)
¾ c. mayonnaise or salad dressing
1½ t. onion, grated
¼-½ c. green pepper, finely diced
¼ c. pimento, chopped
4 hard-cooked eggs, chopped
½ c. celery, finely chopped

Soften gelatin in cold water; place over hot water to melt. Remove from heat and add salt, lemon juice or vinegar, Worcestershire sauce and cayenne pepper if desired. Cool. Stir in mayonnaise or salad dressing. Fold in remaining ingredients. Turn into a 3-cup mold or individual molds. Chill until firm.

This recipe submitted by the following teachers:

Sister Mary Louise, Notre Dame H. S.
Clarksburg, West Virginia

Mrs. Ruth Dunn Jordan, Benjamin Russell H. S.
Alexander City, Alabama

Jane McMaster, Everett School
Winnsboro, South Carolina

EGG AND CHEESE SALAD

Number of Servings — 8

6 hard cooked eggs, mashed
¼ c. chives, chopped
¾ c. small curd cottage cheese
½ c. salad dressing
3 T. vinegar
1 T. white sugar
Salt and pepper to taste

Combine eggs, chives and cottage cheese. Mix salad dressing, vinegar, sugar, salt and pepper. Combine the 2 mixtures. Serve on lettuce as a salad or use as a sandwich spread.

Dorothy Tenniswood, New Troy H. S.
New Troy, Michigan

EGG NEST SALAD

Number of Servings — 6

6 hard-cooked eggs
⅛ t. salt
Dash of pepper
3 T. mayonnaise
6 crisp lettuce leaves, washed and drained
Paprika

Gently remove whole egg yolks; set aside. Cut the whites into small pieces with a fork. Add salt, pepper and mayonnaise to egg whites; mix. Place a rounded tablespoon of egg white mixture on lettuce leaf. Press mixture slightly with bowl of spoon for "nest" effect. Center egg yolk on nest. Garnish with paprika, if desired.

Wilma Keeler, Cadillac Senior H. S.
Cadillac, Michigan

EGG SALAD

Number of Servings — 8

4 hard cooked eggs, mashed
½ c. carrots, ground to a pulp
½ c. celery, ground to a pulp
Salt and pepper to taste
2 t. mayonnaise
Stuffed olives (opt.)

Mix all ingredients except olives and blend thoroughly. Garnish with sliced olives. Omit olives for use as a dip or spread.

Elizabeth Barclay, Seminole H. S.
Largo, Florida

EGG SALAD MOLD

Number of Servings — 8

1 envelope unflavored gelatin
½ c. cold water
½ c. boiling water
¾ c. mayonnaise
10 hard-cooked eggs
¼ c. stuffed olives, chopped
2 t. onion, grated
2 T. parsley, chopped
¼ c. celery, chopped
4 or 5 olives, sliced (garnish)
Salad greens

Soften gelatin in cold water; dissolve in boiling water. Cool. Add mayonnaise, 8 chopped eggs, olives, onion, parsley and celery. Mix lightly but thoroughly. Slice remaining eggs; arrange around sides and bottom of salad mold. Pour in part of gelatin mixture to hold slices in place. Chill until firm. Add remaining gelatin mixture. Chill until firm. Unmold on salad greens and press olive slices around sides. Serve cold.

Mrs. Grace B. Callaway, Greensboro H. S.
Greensboro, Georgia

EGG SALAD

Number of Servings — 4

6 hard-cooked eggs, chopped
½ c. celery, diced
¼ c. green pepper, diced
1 T. pimento, chopped
½ c. mayonnaise
½ t. salt
¼ t. black pepper

Combine all ingredients. Serve on lettuce. Garnish with additional pimento.

Winifred Blackwood, Hominy H. S.
Hominy, Oklahoma

FLUTED EGG SALAD

Number of Servings — 6

6 hard-cooked eggs
1 t. prepared mustard
3 T. relish spread
⅓ t. salt
Paprika
Mayonnaise

Flute eggs by cutting with end of knife in sawtooth fashion around egg, cutting through to yolk. Remove and mash egg yolks. Combine with other ingredients. Refill whites with egg yolk mixture. Place in nest of lettuce, using three halves per serving. Sprinkle with paprika; garnish with mayonnaise.

Mrs. Minnie Lou Honeycutt, Piedmont H. S.
Monroe, North Carolina

GLENNA'S EGG SALAD

6 hard-cook eggs, riced
1 pkg. lemon gelatin
1 c. hot water
1 t. prepared mustard
1 t. celery salt
½ t. paprika
½ t. salt
⅓ c. vinegar
⅓ c. mayonnaise

Dissolve gelatin in hot water. Add remaining ingredients; beat, cool. Serve on lettuce with additional mayonnaise.

Glenna A. Starbird, Oxford Hills H. S.
Norway, Maine

MOLDED EGG SALAD

Number of Servings — 6

8 hard-cooked eggs, coarsely chopped
1 c. celery, finely diced
¼ c. salad dressing
1 t. Worcestershire sauce
1 T lemon juice
1 t. scraped onion
Salt and pepper to taste
6 thick tomato slices
Salad greens
Paprika
Celery curls

Mix eggs, celery, dressing and all seasonings except paprika. Press into molds and chill. Unmold on tomato slices placed in a bed of salad greens. Sprinkle with paprika. Garnish with celery curls and additional seasoning if desired.

Zelda Leigh Powell, Mandeville H. S.
Mandeville, Louisiana

EGG MOLD

Number of Servings — 8

12 hard-cooked eggs, chopped
3 T. green peppers, chopped
2 T. sweet relish
½ c. celery, finely chopped
¾ c. mayonnaise
1 t. salt
1 envelope unflavored gelatin
⅓ c. cold water

Soften gelatin in cold water; place over hot water to melt. Mix eggs and peppers with the relish, celery and salt. Add gelatin to mayonnaise and pour into egg mixture. Mix well. Pour into a mold. Chill until firm. Serve on endive or lettuce.

Mary H. Sargent, North H. S.
Minneapolis, Minnesota

GRAHAM'S EGG SALAD

Number of Servings — 6

1 envelope unflavored gelatin
1 c. mayonnaise
6 hard-cooked eggs, sliced
½ c. celery, diced
⅓ c. olives, chopped
Tabasco sauce to taste
Dash of garlic salt
Salt to taste
¼ c. cold water

Soften gelatin in cold water; place over hot water to melt. Mix mayonnaise, celery, eggs, olives, salt, garlic salt and Tabasco. Add gelatin. Refrigerate several hours to set.

Mrs. Gavin G. Craig Jr., Alvaton H. S.
Alvaton, Kentucky

LETTUCE-HARD "BOILED" EGG SALAD

Number of Servings — 6

1 head lettuce torn in small pieces
1 small onion, chopped
2 hard-cooked eggs, chopped
4 pieces bacon, fried and crumbled
Mayonnaise
Salt and pepper to taste

Combine lettuce, onion, eggs, salt and pepper with enough mayonnaise to hold ingredients together. Top with bacon. Serve immediately.

Beth White, Goliad H. S.
Goliad, Texas

PENNSYLVANIA DUTCH RED BEET EGGS

Number of Servings — 8

5 medium red beets
1 c. vinegar
1 c. water
½ c. granulated sugar
1 t. salt
8 hard-cooked eggs

Boil beets until tender; remove skins and slice ½-inch thick. Mix vinegar, water, sugar and salt. Pour mixture over beets and refrigerate overnight. Next day remove half of beet slices and add whole shelled eggs. Refrigerate another day until eggs become rosy-red in color. Use sliced eggs as a salad garnish or serve with beets as a salad.

Lucy M. Bamberger, Eastern Lebanon County H. S.
Myerstown, Pennsylvania

SMOKED EGGS

Number of Servings — 6

6 hard-cooked eggs, hot
¼ c. vinegar
1¾ c. cold water
2 t. liquid smoke

Place eggs in a jar; add remaining ingredients. Cover and refrigerate for several hours. Eggs may be kept in liquid smoke as long as desired.

Doris H. Schlumpf, Durand Unified High
Durand, Wisconsin

STUFFED EGGS

Number of Servings — 6

6 hard-cooked eggs
Small cubes of ham, olives or pimento
3 T. butter, softened
1 t. Worcestershire sauce
2 T. mayonnaise
Salt and pepper to taste

Cut the eggs in half lengthwise; remove yolks. Force yolks through a fine sieve. Place a cube of ham, olive or pimento in each egg white. Combine yolks with remaining ingredients; beat until mixture is smooth. Force egg yolk mixture through a pastry tube. Decorate the egg whites with the yolk mixture as desired.

Mrs. Bethel Schmidt, Community High School
Vicksburg, Michigan

TASTY EGG SALAD

Number of Servings — 6

6 hard-cooked eggs, chopped
3 stalks celery, finely cut
1 medium onion, finely cut
½ c. cream cheese, cubed
1 lge. dill pickle, finely cut
½ c. salad dressing

Combine ingredients in order given. Blend well. Chill for 30 minutes before serving on lettuce.

Idella I. Alfson, Woonsocket School
Woonsocket, South Dakota

Frozen Fruit Salads

FROZEN CHEESE-BANANA-FRUIT SALAD

Number of Servings — 8

1 c. whipped cream
¼ c. mayonnaise
1 c. bananas, mashed
¼ c. orange juice
2 T. lemon juice
½ c. red, sour cherries
½ c. pears, diced
½ c. cream cheese
½ t. salt

Beat mayonnaise into whipped cream. Fold in bananas. Blend in remaining ingredients. Freeze. Serve with dressing.

DRESSING:
1 banana, mashed
½ c. sugar
1 t. lemon juice

Combine all ingredients; mix well.

Margaret E. Gilliland, Columbia H. S.
Columbia, Pennsylvania

FROZEN BANANA SALAD

Number of Servings — 8

1 3-oz. pkg. cream cheese, softened
½ c. mayonnaise
¼ c. sugar
3 T. lemon juice
⅓ c. nuts, chopped
⅓ c. coconut
¼ c. Maraschino cherries, chopped
2 c. bananas, sliced
⅔ c. evaporated milk, chilled

Blend cheese, mayonnaise, sugar and 2 tablespoons lemon juice. Stir in nuts, coconut and cherries. Add bananas. Whip milk until it holds a peak. Add remaining lemon juice; blend. Fold milk into cheese mixture. Freeze. Serve immediately after removing from freezer.

Charlotte Carter, Carpinteria H. S.
Carpinteria, California

FROZEN BANANA SALAD

Number of Servings — 10

1 T. lemon juice
½-1 t. salt
2 T. mayonnaise
½ c. nuts, chopped
2 3-oz. pkg. cream cheese, softened
2 T. crushed pineapple
½ c. Maraschino cherries, quartered
½ c. whipped cream
3 ripe bananas, cubed

Blend lemon juice, salt and mayonnaise; stir into cheese. Add pineapple, cherries and nuts. Fold in whipped cream. Add bananas. Freeze.

This recipe submitted by the following teachers:

Mrs. Betty Hastings, Cloverleaf Senior H. S.
Lodi, Ohio

Mrs. Sue Bevill, Winnfield H. S.
Winnfield, Louisiana

FROZEN BANANA-APRICOT SALAD

Number of Servings — 8-10

2 ⅔c. sugar
1 c. water
1 12-oz. pkg. frozen strawberries
1 c. crushed pineapple
4 bananas, sliced
4 c. apricot nectar
1 egg
Juice of 1 orange
Juice of 1 lemon
1 c. whipped cream

Boil 2 cups sugar and water until syrupy; add strawberries. Cool. Add bananas, pineapple and apricot nectar. Freeze. Combine ⅔ cup sugar, egg, orange and lemon juice. Cook until thick. Cool. Fold in whipped cream. Spread on top of frozen mixture. Freeze.

Charlene Swanson, Elwood H. S.
Elwood, Nebraska

FROZEN BANANA-FRUIT SALAD

Number of Servings — 8-10

2 3-oz. pkg. cream cheese
½-1 t. salt
2 T. salad dressing or mayonnaise
1-3 T. lemon juice
½ c. crushed pineapple, drained
2 c. ripe bananas, diced
½ c. marshmallows, diced (opt.)
1 c. whipped cream
½ c. Maraschino cherries, coarsely chopped
½ c. pecans or walnuts, coarsely chopped

Mash cheese; blend with salt, salad dressing and lemon juice. Mix well. Fold in pineapple, cherries, nuts, bananas and marshmallows if desired. Fold in whipped cream. Freeze until firm with refrigerator freezer control set at coldest setting.

This recipe submitted by the following teachers:

Mrs. Alice E. Blackburn, Southeast District
Supervisor, Home Economics Education
Montevallo, Alabama

Mrs. Josephine Rummler
Belding Area Schools
Belding, Michigan

FROZEN BANANA FRUIT SALAD

Number of Servings — 12

½ t. salt
1½-2 T. vinegar
1½ T. flour
1 egg (opt.)
¼ c. sugar
¾ c. pineapple juice
3 bananas, crushed
1 c. pineapple, diced
12 Maraschino cherries, chopped
1 c. pears, diced
1 c. whipped cream
Nuts, chopped

(Continued on next page)

Combine salt, vinegar, flour, sugar, pineapple juice and egg, if desired. Cook in double boiler until thick; cool. Add bananas, pineapple, cherries and pears. Fold in whipped cream. Pour into 2 trays; freeze. Garnish with nuts and additional whipped cream, if desired.

This recipe submitted by the following teachers:

Leona Ferch Smith, Sunnyside H. S.
Sunnyside, Washington

Thelma Wilkins, Cowpens H. S.
Cowpens, South Carolina

Frances Willis, Senior H. S.
Denison, Texas

Mrs. Mildred Sanders Williamson, Five Points H. S.
Five Points, Alabama

BANANA-SOUR CREAM JUBILEE

Number of Servings — 12

2 c. sour cream
¾ c. sugar
2 T. lemon juice
1 small can crushed pineapple
Salt to taste (opt.)
2-4 T. Maraschino cherries, chopped
½ c. miniature marshmallows (opt.)
1-2 bananas, crushed
¼-½ c. nuts, chopped

Combine all ingredients in order; mix. Pour into paper baking cups; freeze. Serve on lettuce. Garnish with additional Maraschino cherries or nuts, lemon twists, mint leaves, or orange slices.

This recipe submitted by the following teachers:

Mrs. Dorothy West, Littlefield H. S.
Littlefield, Texas

Mrs. Gail Patton, Hollywood Junior H. S.
Memphis, Tennessee

M. Elizabeth Brannon, Hillcrest H. S.
Simpsonville, South Carolina

Mrs. Brownie Whipple
Ballard Memorial H. S.
Barlow, Kentucky

Levern Gayman, San Luis Obispo Sr. H. S.
San Luis Obispo, California

BANANA-STRAWBERRY SALAD

Number of Servings — 12

30 lg. marshmallows, finely cut
1 No. 2½ can crushed pineapple
2 boxes frozen strawberries, undrained
3 bananas, cubed
1 pt. whipped cream

Combine marshmallows and pineapple; let stand overnight. Add remaining ingredients; mix well. Freeze.

Muriel Barnes, Bellingham H. S.
Bellingham, Minnesota

FROZEN FRUIT-CHEESE SALAD

Number of Servings — 16

1 3-oz. pkg. cream cheese
2 T. cream
2 T. lemon juice
⅛ t. salt
1 c. pineapple, diced
½ c. marshmallows, quartered
1 c. Maraschino cherries, quartered
1 banana, mashed
2 c. whipped cream
¾ c. mayonnaise

Mix cheese, cream, lemon juice and salt together until smooth. Add pineapple, cherries, banana and marshmallows. Combine cream and mayonnaise. Fold into fruit mixture. Pour into ice trays; freeze. Serve on lettuce.

Rachael A. Dix, Acting State Adviser
Future Homemakers of America
Montpelier, Vermont

FROZEN CRANBERRY SALAD

Number of Servings — 12

2 c. cranberries, ground
1 No. 2 can pineapple
1½ c. sugar
1½ c. miniature marshmallows
½ pt. whipped cream

Combine cranberries, pineapple, sugar and marshmallows. Chill for 30 minutes. Add whipped cream. Freeze.

Helen Baker, Owendale-Gagetown Area Schools
Owendale, Michigan

FROZEN CRANBERRY SALAD

Number of Servings — 6

1 1-lb. can cranberry sauce
1 8¾-oz. can crushed pineapple
1 c. miniature marshmallows
1 T. lemon juice
¼ c. whipped cream
¼ c. mayonnaise
¼ c. confectioner's sugar

Combine cranberry sauce, pineapple, marshmallow and lemon juice. Combine whipped cream, mayonnaise and sugar; spread over cranberry mixture. Freeze.

Mrs. Mary Campbell, Canton H. S.
Canton, Pennsylvania

FROZEN CRANBERRY SALAD

Number of Servings — 15

1 c. granulated sugar
2 c. apples, ground
2 c. miniature marshmallows
1 lb. fresh cranberries, ground
1 pt. whipped cream

Combine cranberries, marshmallows, sugar and apples; let stand for 30 minutes. Add whipped cream. Freeze.

Mrs. Frank Clark, Elmwood H. S.
Elmwood, Ill.

FROZEN CRANBERRY SALAD

Number of Servings — 12

1 lb. raw cranberries
3 apples, peeled
20 lg. marshmallows
1 c. nuts
1 c. sugar
1 c. whipped cream

Grind cranberries, apples and marshmallows together. Add nuts and sugar; let stand until sugar dissolves. Add whipped cream. Stir. Freeze. For a low-calorie salad, substitute liquid sweetener and 1 small package dessert topping mix for the sugar and whipped cream.

Mrs. Irma Dixon, Georgetown H. S.
Georgetown, Illinois

FROZEN CRANBERRY SALAD

Number of Servings —10

1 qt. cranberries, chopped
1¼ c. sugar
1 c. crushed pineapple, drained
1 lb. miniature marshmallows
1 c. whipped cream

Combine all ingredients; freeze.

Ira E. Grubl, Linton Public School
Linton, North Dakota

FROZEN CRANBERRY SALAD

Number of Servings — 12

4 c. whole cranberries
3 T. lemon juice
1 pt. whipped cream
1 c. walnuts, finely chopped

Blend cranberries and lemon juice. Spread cranberry mixture in a cake pan. Combine whipped cream and nuts. Spoon whipped cream mixture on top of the cranberries. Freeze.

Madeline Johnson, Pinehurst Junior High
Pinehurst, Idaho

FROZEN CRANBERRY SALAD

Number of Servings — 24

1 lb. cranberries, ground
2 c. nuts, chopped
2 c. sugar
6 Delicious apples, ground
1 lb. miniature marshmallows
1 pkg. dessert topping mix

Mix cranberries, apples, marshmallows and sugar. Refrigerate overnight. Whip dessert topping mix according to package directions; add nuts. Fold into chilled cranberry mixture. Freeze.

Blanche Burns, Strathmore H. S.
Strathmore, California

FROZEN CRANBERRY SALAD

Number of Servings — 12

1 qt. raw cranberries
2 c. raw apples
1 lb. marshmallows, quartered
1 c. sugar
½ c. nuts, chopped
2 c. whipped cream

Grind cranberries and apples together. Add marshmallows and sugar. Let stand at least 30 minutes or overnight. Mix nuts and whipped cream; add to cranberry mixture. Cover with foil. Freeze.

This recipe submitted by the following teachers:

Mrs. Marilyn Kane, Arlington H. S.
Arlington Heights, Illinois

Mrs. Patricia Larson, Milaca H. S.
Milaca, Minnesota

Barbara Gutz, Big Horn H. S.
Big Horn, Wyoming

WALNUT-CRANBERRY RIBBON LOAF

Number of Servings — 6-8

1 1-lb. can cranberry sauce
¾ c. apple, peeled, cored and grated
½ pt. whipped cream
¼ c. confectioner's sugar
1 t. vanilla
½ c. English walnuts or pecans, chopped

Crush cranberry sauce with fork; stir in apple. Pour into freezing tray. Mix whipped cream, sugar, vanilla and ⅓ cup nuts. Spoon over cranberry layer; sprinkle with remaining nuts. Freeze until firm.

Mrs. Barbara Power, Triad H. S.
North Lewisburg, Ohio

FROZEN CRANBERRY SALAD

Number of Servings — 8

1 can whole cranberries
1 can crushed pineapple
½ pt. sour cream
¼ c. pecans, chopped (Opt.)
Red food coloring

Combine all ingredients; mix thoroughly. Freeze.

Edith P. Kreidler, Berrien Springs H. S.
Berrien Springs, Michigan

FROZEN CRANBERRY SALAD

Number of Servings — 15

1 lb. cranberries, coarsely ground
2 c. sugar
20 marshmallows, finely cut
1 No. 2 can crushed pineapple, drained
½ c. nuts, chopped
1 c. whipped cream

Combine cranberries and sugar; let stand for 2 hours. Fold in remaining ingredients. Cover with foil; freeze.

Mrs. Luella Robb, Round Valley H. S.
Covelo, California

FROZEN CRANBERRY SALAD

Number of Servings — 6

1 No. 2 can crushed pineapple
1 lb. marshmallows, cut
1 lb. cranberries, ground
2 c. sugar
1 c. whipped cream

Combine pineapple and marshmallows; let stand overnight. Combine cranberries and sugar; let stand overnight. Combine mixtures; fold in whipped cream. Freeze.

June Stultz, Renton H. S.
Renton, Washington

FROZEN CRANBERRY SAUCE SALAD

Number of Servings — 10

1 16-oz. can cranberry sauce
2-3 T. lemon juice
1 c. whipped cream
¼ c. confectioner's sugar
¼ c. salad dressing or mayonnaise
1 c. toasted pecans, chopped

Mash cranberry sauce with a fork; add lemon juice and blend well. Put in freezing tray and chill. Combine remaining ingredients; pour over cranberry mixture. Freeze.

This recipe submitted by the following teachers:

Mrs. Jerry Barton, Matthews Junior H. S.
Lubbock, Texas

Mrs. Pauline I. Kuykendall, Kernersville Jr. H. S.
Kernersville, North Carolina

Mrs. Joanne M. Richards, North Bethesda Jr. H. S.
Bethesda, Maryland

Mrs. Stacie O. Houser, Sun Valley H. S.
Monroe, North Carolina

FROSTY CRANBERRY TIP-TOPS

Number of Servings — 6-8

1 1-lb. can cranberry sauce
2-3 T. lemon juice
1 c. whipped cream
1 3-o. pkg. cream cheese, whipped
¼ c. mayonnaise
¼ c. sifted confectioners' sugar
1 c. nuts, chopped, (Opt.)

Crush cranberry sauce with a fork; add lemon juice and blend well. Pour into small paper cup. Combine remaining ingredients; spread over cranberry mixture. Freeze.

This recipe submitted by the following teachers:

Mrs. Julian A. Raburn, Telfair County High
McRae, Georgia

Mrs. Ruth H. Sylvest, Broadmoor H. S.
Baton Rouge, Louisiana

Mrs. Allan P. Cobb, Mosinee H. S.
Mosinee, Wisconsin

FROZEN FRUIT SALAD

Number of Servings — 8-10

½ lb. miniature marshmallows
1 c. mayonnaise
3 c. fruit cocktail or other diced fruit
2 T. confectioner's sugar
1 T. unflavored gelatin
2 T. cold water
¼ lb. cheese, grated
1 c. whipped cream

Soak gelatin in cold water for 5 minutes; stir into mayonnaise. Mix in fruit, marshmallows and cheese. Mix sugar and whipped cream together; fold into fruit mixture. Pour into small ice trays. Freeze.

Suzanne H. Waldrop, Park City School
Park City, Kentucky

FROZEN FRUIT COCKTAIL SALAD

Number of Servings — 8

1 No. 2½ can fruit cocktail, drained
1 t. unflavored gelatin
3 T. lemon juice
1 3-oz. pkg. cream cheese
¼ c. mayonnaise
Dash of salt
⅔ c. whipping cream, chilled
½ c. sugar
½ c. nuts, chopped

Soften gelatin in lemon juice; dissolve over hot water. Blend cream cheese with mayonnaise and salt. Stir in gelatin. Whip cream until stiff, gradually adding sugar during last stages of beating. Fold in cheese mixture, nuts and fruit cocktail. Pour into refrigerator tray lined with wax paper. Freeze until firm.

Mrs. Minnie G. Burke, Los Gatos H. S.
Los Gatos, California

PINK SNOW SALAD

Number of Servings — 20

1 tall can evaporated milk, chilled
2 T. lemon juice
1 can fruit cocktail, drained
1 can peaches or 2 c. fresh peaches, sliced
¾ c. sugar
1 can pineapple chunks, drained
1 small bottle Maraschino cherries, drained
3 T. cherry juice
1 c. miniature marshmallows
½ c. pecans, chopped

Beat chilled milk until stiff with electric mixer set at high speed. Add lemon juice. Fold in remaining ingredients. Freeze.

Mrs. Sudie Mitchell Bell
Isola White Attendance Center
Isola, Mississippi

FROZEN FRUIT SALAD

Number of Servings — 6

2 eggs, separated
¾ c. sugar
6 Graham crackers, crushed
¼ c. coconut
1 c. fruit cocktail or 1 c. peaches, drained
¼ t. salt
2 c. whipped cream
1½ t. vanilla

Beat egg yolks; add sugar, cracker crumbs, coconut, fruit, salt and vanilla. Fold in whipped cream. Beat egg whites until they form a soft peak; fold into egg yolk mixture. Stir once or twice while salad is freezing.

Ruth Bosley, Leavenworth H. S.
Leavenworth, Indiana

FROZEN FRUIT SALAD

Number of Servings — 6

½ 3-oz. pkg. lime gelatin
¼ c. hot water
1 can fruit cocktail
1 c. whipped cream
3 T. salad dressing

Dissolve gelatin in hot water; add fruit cocktail. Freeze until mushy. Mix whipped cream and salad dressing; add to fruit cocktail mixture. Freeze until firm.

Mrs. Marilee Houg, Baldwin-Woodville H. S.
Baldwin, Wisconsin

FROZEN FRUIT SALAD

1 c. mayonnaise
1 lg. pkg. cream cheese
2 c. fruit cocktail, drained
1 c. pecan halves
1 pt. whipping cream, chilled
1 c. sugar

Whip cream; gradually add sugar. Mix Cream Cheese and mayonnaise. Add fruit cocktail and pecans; mix. Fold in whipped cream. Freeze.

Phyllis Pruett Smith, Brownstown Com. H. S.
Brownstown, Illinois

FROZEN FRUIT SALAD

Number of Servings — 10-12

2 3-oz. pkg. cream cheese
¾ c. mayonnaise
1 c. whipped cream
1 No. 2½ can fruit cocktail, drained
½ c. Maraschino cherries, drained and quartered
2½ c. marshmallows, diced

Soften cream cheese; blend with mayonnaise. Fold in remaining ingredients. Freeze until firm.

Ethel Larson, John R. Rogers H. S.
Spokane, Washington

FROZEN FRUIT SALAD

Number of Servings — 10-12

1 t. unflavored gelatin
2 T. lemon juice
1 3-oz. pkg. cream cheese
Pinch of salt
1 pkg. dessert topping mix
½ c. sugar
1 No. 2½ can fruit cocktail, drained
½ c. nuts
½ t. red food coloring (Opt.)

Soften gelatin in lemon juice; dissolve over hot water. Cream the cheese; add salt and gelatin mixture. Prepare dessert topping mix according to package directions; gradually adding sugar. Fold in fruit cocktail, cheese-gelatin mixture, nuts and food coloring, if desired. Pour into trays lined with waxed paper. Freeze.

Inez Dykstra, Lovington H. S.
Lovington, New Mexico

FROZEN FRUIT SALAD

Number of Servings — 10

2 cans fruit cocktail, drained
Juice from fruit cocktail
2 T. butter
2 T. flour
2 T. sugar
2 T. lemon juice
2 eggs, well beaten
1 c. whipped cream
16 marshmallows, finely cut

Melt butter in double boiler; add flour, fruit cocktail juice, sugar, lemon juice and eggs. Cook, stirring until smooth; cool. Add whipped cream, marshmallows and fruit cocktail. Freeze.

Mrs. Alma M. Scott, Marion H. S.
Marion, South Dakota

FROZEN FRUIT SALAD

Number of Servings — 10

2 eggs, beaten
5 T. lemon juice
5 T. sugar
2 T. butter
1 can diced pineapple, drained
1 lg. can fruit cocktail, drained
1 6-oz. bottle Maraschino cherries, drained
2 c. white cherries, halved
½ lb. marshmallows, chopped
1 c. whipped cream

Cook eggs, sugar and lemon juice over hot water, beating constantly until mixture is thick. Remove from heat; add butter and remaining ingredients. Freeze.

Mrs. Elizabeth Sweet, Mount Morris H. S.
Mount Morris, Illinois

FROZEN FRUIT SALAD

Number of Servings — 10

1 small can crushed pineapple, drained
3 T. flour (rounded)
½ c. sugar
1 egg, beaten
1 lg. pkg. cream cheese
1 lg. can fruit cocktail, drained
½ pt. whipped cream

Combine juice drained from pineapple with flour, sugar and egg; cook until thick, stirring constantly. Add cream cheese to hot mixture. Mix until smooth. Cool. Add pineapple and fruit cocktail; fold in whipped cream. Freeze.

Mrs. Virginia Smith, North H. S.
Evansville, Indiana

FROZEN FRUIT SALAD

Number of Servings — 15-20

1 No. 2 can crushed pineapple, drained
1 No. 2 or 2½ can fruit cocktail, drained
1 can Mandarin oranges
1 pt. small curd cottage cheese
10-oz. miniature marshmallows
1 pkg. dessert topping mix
½ c. mayonnaise

Blend fruit and marshmallows together. Add mayonnaise and cheese. Beat dessert topping mix; add to fruit mixture. Freeze.

Mrs. Helen E. Stanford, Union H. S.
Union, Oregon

QUICK FROZEN FRUIT SALAD

Number of Servings — 6-8

1 c. fruit cocktail, drained
¼ c. cherries, chopped
½ c. miniature marshmallows
½ c. fruit cocktail juice
1 T. lemon juice
1 t. confectioner's sugar
¼ c. nuts, chopped
1 c. dessert topping mix

Combine fruit cocktail, cherries and marshmallows. Stir in juices and sugar. Add nuts; mix well. Fold in dessert topping mix prepared according to package directions. Freeze until firm.

Dianne Warnock, Clay H. S.
Oregon, Ohio

FROZEN FRUIT MEDLEY

Number of Servings — 10

1 No. 2½ can fruit cocktail
1 pkg. lemon gelatin
1 c. hot water
2 T. lemon juice
2 3-oz. pkg. cream cheese, softened
¼ c. salad dressing
1½ c. miniature marshmallows
¼ c. Maraschino cherries, drained and quartered
1 pkg. dessert topping mix, whipped

Dissolve gelatin in hot water; add lemon juice. Combine cream cheese and salad dressing; heat until smooth. Add to gelatin mixture. Chill. Stir in marshmallows and fruit. Fold in dessert topping mix. Freeze.

Lois J. Smeltzer, Eastern Lebanon Co. H. S.
Myerstown, Pennsylvania

ROSY FRUIT COCKTAIL SLICES

Number of Servings — 10-12

2 3-oz. pkg. cream cheese
1 c. mayonnaise
1 c. whipped cream
1 No. 2½ can fruit cocktail, drained
½ c. Maraschino cherries, drained and quartered
2½ c. marshmallows, cut up
Few drops red food coloring or Maraschino cherry juice

Blend cheese with mayonnaise. Fold in remaining ingredients. Freeze until firm. Let thaw at room temperature for a few minutes before serving.

This recipe submitted by the following teachers:

Mrs. John Leischner, DeLand-Weldon H. S.
DeLand, Illinois

Mrs. Dixie E. Stafford, Charlotte H. S.
Charlotte, Texas

Mrs. Gail Atchison, East Grand Forks H. S.
East Grand Forks, Minnesota

FROZEN FRUIT-HONEY SALAD

Number of Servings — 6-8

2 T. sugar
1 T. flour
½ c. honey
1 egg
⅓ c. lemon juice
2 c. fruit cocktail, drained
1 c. bananas, sliced
⅓ c. orange slices, diced
¼ c. Maraschino or Bing cherries, pitted and quartered
1 c. whipped cream

Combine sugar, flour and honey. Bring to a boil; cook 1 minute, stirring constantly. Beat egg while gradually adding lemon juice. Add a small amount of the honey mixture to the egg; mix well. Return mixture to heat and bring to a boil, stirring constantly. Remove from heat; cool. Combine fruits; add to honey mixture. Fold in whipped cream. Freeze.

This recipe submitted by the following teachers:

Mrs. Georgia Balls, Highland H. S.
Pocatello, Idaho

Mrs. Charles W. Smith, South Junior H. S.
Rapid City, South Dakota

Frances Eldridge Central Senior H. S.
Clifton, Illinois

FROSTY PINK FROZEN FRUIT SALAD

Number of Servings — 9-12

2 3-oz. pkg. cream cheese
½-1 c. mayonnaise or salad dressing
1 No. 2½ can fruit cocktail, drained
½ c. Maraschino cherries, drained and quartered
2½ c. miniature marshmallows
1 c. whipped cream
Red food coloring or cherry juice (opt.)
1 c. nuts (opt.)

Soften cream cheese; blend with mayonnaise. Stir in fruit, marshmallows and nuts, if desired. Fold in whipped cream. Tint with few drops red food coloring or cherry juice, if desired. Freeze until firm.

This recipe submitted by the following teachers:

Charlotte Chafin, Nolan Junior H. S.
Killeen, Texas

Mrs. Jean Rascoe, Southern Junior H. S.
Owensboro, Kentucky

Mrs. Genevieve R. Hayes, Pikeville H. S.
Pikeville, Kentucky

Joyce Meek, Sugar Grove H. S.
Sugar Grove, Virginia

Rose Marie Hornbacher, Glen Ullin H. S.
Glen Ullin, North Dakota

Mrs. Estelle Boles Nickell, Morgan County H. S.
West Liberty, Kentucky

Helen Chase, Canby Public School
Canby, Minnesota

Barbara Campbell, Redmond Junior H. S.
Redmond, Washington

Mrs. W. L. Cope, Swansea H. S.
Swansea, South Carolina

Mrs. Grace Karhoff, Senior H. S.
Ottawa, Kansas

FROZEN MINT-PINEAPPLE SALAD

Number of Servings — 10-12

1 No. 2 can crushed pineapple, drained
1 c. miniature marshmallows
1 c. white cherries, drained and pitted
½ c. mayonnaise
2 T. lemon juice
1 c. whipped cream
¼ c. green Maraschino cherries, chopped
⅛ t. peppermint extract
Few drops green food coloring

Combine pineapple, marshmallows and white cherries. Beat mayonnaise, lemon juice and peppermint extract into whipped cream. Tint light green with food coloring. Fold in fruit mixture. Arrange Maraschino cherries in bottom of an oiled loaf pan. Carefully pour in salad. Freeze until firm.

Barbara Barker, Arlington H. S.
Arlington Heights, Illinois

FROZEN MINT SALAD

Number of Servings — 4

12 lg. marshmallows
1 T. pineapple juice
⅛ t. green food coloring
⅛ t. peppermint extract
1 c. crushed pineapple
¼ c. salad dressing
¼ c. whipped cream

Melt marshmallows in pineapple juice over low heat. Add food coloring and peppermint extract; cool. Add pineapple, salad dressing and whipped cream. Freeze until firm.

Mrs. Carolyn Arthur, Mayville H. S.
Mayville, Wisconsin

FROSTY MINT CUBES

Number of Servings — 8-10

1 No. 2 can crushed pineapple, drained
2 t. unflavored gelatin
½ c. mint jelly
Dash of salt
1 c. whipped cream
Green food coloring
Juice drained from pineapple

Soften gelatin in pineapple juice; add jelly and salt. Heat, stirring constantly until gelatin dissolves and jelly melts. If necessary, beat to blend in jelly. Add pineapple. Chill until mixture is thick and syrupy. Fold in whipped cream; tint with few drops of food coloring. Freeze until firm. Cut into cubes or slices to serve.

JoAnn L. Bedore, Grand Blanc H. S.
Grand Blanc, Michigan

FROZEN PEPPERMINT DESSERT-SALAD

Number of Servings — 20

1 No. 2 can crushed pineapple
1 pkg. strawberry gelatin
¼ c. cinnamon candies
1 10½-oz. pkg. miniature marshmallows
2 c. heavy cream
¼ lb. soft butter mints, crushed

Combine pineapple, gelatin powder, cinnamon candies and marshmallows; mix well. Chill overnight. The next day set refrigerator control at lowest temperature. Beat the cream, one cup at a time, in a chilled bowl with chilled beaters until cream piles softly. Pour cream and mints into chilled pineapple mixture. Fold together thoroughly and pour into refrigerator trays. Freeze 2 to 3 hours or until firm.

Ada Newell, Garden City Junior H. S.
Garden City, Kansas

APPLE-ORANGE FROST

Number of Servings — 12

1 No. 2 can applesauce
1 small can orange juice
2-3 T. lemon juice
3 egg whites, stiffly beaten
Artificial sweetener equivalent to 3 T. sugar

Combine applesauce, orange juice, lemon juice and sweetener. Fold in egg whites. Freeze until firm. Salad will keep from 2 to 4 weeks in freezer.

Mrs. Janet Krumme, Seymour Senior H. S.
Seymour, Indiana

FROZEN APPLE-PINEAPPLE SALAD

Number of Servings — 12

1 9-oz. can crushed pineapple, drained
2 eggs, beaten
½ c. sugar
¼ t. salt
½ c. mixed pineapple syrup and water
3 T. lemon juice
2 c. unpeeled apples, finely diced
½ c. celery, finely diced
1 c. whipped cream

Combine eggs, sugar, salt, lemon juice and syrup-water mixture. Cook over low heat, stirring constantly until thick. Chill. Fold in pineapple, apples, celery and whipped cream. Pour into a 2-quart refrigerator tray or salad mold; freeze.

Mrs. Barbara Deane, Sheridan Community H. S.
Hoxie, Kansas

FROZEN BERRY-ICE CREAM SALAD

1 qt. vanilla ice cream
½ c. mayonnaise
1 c. canned pineapple, drained
1 c. blueberries, drained
2 c. raspberries or strawberries

Soften ice cream; quickly blend in mayonnaise. Add fruit; mix. Freeze 2-3 hours or until firm.

Mrs. Violet Moseley, Avon Park H. S.
Avon Park, Florida

FROZEN FRUIT AND CHEESE SALAD

Number of Servings — 8

1 lg. pkg. cream cheese
1 c. heavy sour cream
2 T. lemon juice
⅛ t. salt
1 c. canned pineapple, diced
1 c. grapes, seeded
1 c. cherries, pitted
1 banana, sliced
1 c. whipped cream
¾ c. mayonnaise
½ c. marshmallows, quartered

Cream the cheese, sour cream, lemon juice and salt. Add fruits and whipped cream. Fold in mayonnaise and marshmallows; freeze.

Mrs. Lenore W. Shearer, Tuscarora Valley H. S.
Port Royal, Pennsylvania

FROZEN CHEESE SALAD

Number of Servings — 6

½ c. canned pineapple, chopped
3 T. green pepper, chopped
⅛ c. Maraschino cherries, chopped
⅛ c. nuts, chopped
¼ t. onion, grated
1 3-oz. pkg. cream cheese, mashed
½ c. mayonnaise
½ c. whipped cream
3 T. sugar

Stir mayonnaise into cream cheese. Add pineapple, pepper, cherries, nuts and onion. Mix in whipped cream sweetened with sugar. Freeze.

Mrs. D. E. Haugh, North Chicago H. S.
North Chicago, Illinois

DATE-CHEESE SALAD

Number of Servings — 8-10

1 small can evaporated milk, chilled
2 pkg. cream cheese, softened
½ c. pecans, chopped
½ c. almonds, slivered
1 c. dates, chopped
¼ c. lemon juice
½ c. mayonnaise
1 8½-oz. can crushed pineapple

Whip the milk; gradually add lemon juice as it begins to thicken. Blend cheese and mayonnaise together; blend into milk mixture. Fold in remaining ingredients. Freeze.

Carolyn Lutkemeier, Frankfort H. S.
Frankfort, Kentucky

COTTAGE CHEESE SALAD

Number of Servings — 12

2 c. small curd cottage cheese, sieved
1 c. sour cream
3 T. confectioner's sugar
¾ t. salt
1 c. pineapple tidbits, drained
1 c. orange, diced
1 c. cooked prunes, pitted and chopped
1 lge. banana, sliced
½ c. Maraschino cherries, drained and sliced
½ c. blanched almonds, chopped
1 c. sour cream
2 T. Maraschino cherry juice

Combine all ingredients except sour cream and cherry juice. Pour into trays that have been rinsed in cold water. Freeze. Let stand at room temperature for a few minutes before serving. Serve with a mixture of sour cream and cherry juice.

Mrs. Trudy Fulmer, Springfield H. S.
Springfield, South Carolina

FROZEN CHRISTMAS SALAD

Number of Servings — 10-12

1 8-o. pkg. cream cheese, softened
3/4 c. mayonnaise
1 No. 2 1/2 can apricots, drained and cut
1 No. 2 can pineapple tidbits, drained
6 green Maraschino cherries, chopped
6 red Maraschino cherries, chopped

Gradually add mayonnaise to cream cheese; beat until creamy. Add apricots. Stir in pineapple and cherries. Freeze.

Mrs. Marjorie P. Kibelbek,
Bethlehem-Center Junior H. S.
Brownsville, Pennsylvania

"DUNCAN AND HINDS" FROZEN FRUIT SALAD

Number of Servings — 50

12 t. unflavored gelatin
1/2 c. cold fruit juice
2 c. hot fruit juice
6 T. sugar
1 t. salt
1 c. mayonnaise
2 c. cream or evaporated milk, whipped
6 c. fresh or canned fruit, drained and diced

Soften gelatin in cold fruit juice; dissolve in hot fruit juice. Add sugar and salt; stir until dissolved. Chill until mixture begins to thicken. Beat mayonnaise gradually into whipped cream or milk. Fold in gelatin and fruit. Fill quart containers to within 1/2 inch of top; seal. Freeze; shaking vigorously twice during the first hour. May be stored for several months in freezer.

Mrs. Myrtle Duncan Brookshire
Johnson County H. S.
Mountain City, Tennessee

FROSTY FRUIT SALAD

Number of Servings — 6-8

1 orange, peeled and cubed
2/3 c. pineapple, diced
3/4 c. Royal Anne cherries, pitted and halved
1 banana, cubed
2 canned pear halves, diced
1/4 c. Maraschino cherries, diced
1/4 c. blanched almonds, chopped
1 pkg. cream cheese, softened
1/2 c. mayonnaise
1/2 c. whipped cream

Combine fruits and nuts. Cream the cheese; blend in mayonnaise. Add to fruit mixture; blend well. Fold in whipped cream. Pour into lightly oiled mold; freeze. After salad is frozen it may be removed from mold and wrapped for freezer storage.

This recipe submitted by the following teachers:

Effie G. Hoyle, Warwick H. S.
Newport News, Virginia

Mrs. Rose Marie Romero, Rio Grande H. S.
Albuquerque, New Mexico

FROSTY SALAD LOAF

Number of Servings — 8

1 8-o. pkg. cream cheese
1 c. sour cream
1/4 c. sugar
1/4 t. salt
1 1/2 c. fresh Bing cherries, pitted and halved
1 1-lb. can unpeeled apricot halves, drained and sliced or 1 1-lb. can sliced peaches, drained
1 9-o.z can crushed pineapple, drained
2 c. miniature marshmallows
Few drops red food coloring (Opt.)

Soften cheese at room temperature; beat until fluffy. Stir in sour cream, sugar and salt; add fruits and marshmallows. Add enough food coloring to make mixture a pale pink if desired. Pour into a loaf pan and freeze about 6 hours or overnight. To serve, remove from freezer and let stand a few minutes.

This recipe submitted by the following teachers:

Gladys Anderson, Mandan H. S.
Mandan, North Dakota

Mrs. Marion R. Hessler
Governor Mifflin Senior H. S.
Shillington, Pennsylvania

FROZEN FRUIT SALAD

Number of Servings — 10-12

3 3-oz. pkg. cream cheese
1 c. mayonnaise
1 pt. whipped cream
1 c. bananas or seeded white grapes, diced
1 c. crushed pineapple
1 c. Royal Ann cherries, pitted

Blend cheese and mayonnaise; add whipped cream and fruits. Freeze.

Bertha Keller Benthien,
Clermont Northeastern H. S.
Owensville, Ohio

FROZEN FRUIT SALAD

Number of Servings — 8

1 c. uncooked apricots, soaked, drained and quartered
1/2 c. strawberries, drained and sliced
1 c. peaches, drained and diced
1/2 c. seeded grapes, halved
1/2 c. pineapple, drained and diced
1 c. mayonnaise
1 t. unflavored gelatin
2 T. cold water
1/2 c. whipping cream
2 T. confectioners' sugar

Soak gelatin in cold water for 5 minutes; melt over hot water. Combine gelatin, fruits and mayonnaise; mix well. Let stand for a few minutes. Whip cream; add sugar. Add to fruit mixture. Mix well. Freeze until firm.

Mrs. Pearl Creese, Hopewell Jr. H. S.
Aliquippa, Pennsylvania

FROZEN FRUIT SALAD

Number of Servings — 8

½ T. unflavored gelatin
¼ c. cold water
¾ c. Royal Anne cherries, drained and halved
2 slices pineapple, drained and diced
½ c. Maraschino cherries, drained and sliced
1 11-oz. can Mandarin oranges, drained and diced
1 banana, diced
1 c. whipped cream
1 c. salad dressing

Soften gelatin in the cold water; dissolve over hot water. Cool. Add salad dressing. Fold in whipped cream and fruit. Freeze until firm.

Cecelia Butler, Clayton Jr. H. S.
Clayton, New Mexico

FROZEN SALAD

Number of Servings — 20

1 c. pineapple juice
2 T. flour
2 T. sugar
½ c. butter
1 egg
Pineapple
60 miniature marshmallows
8 Maraschino cherries, cut in eighths
Fresh or canned peaches
Fresh grapes
1 pt. whipped cream

Combine pineapple juice, flour, sugar, butter and egg; cook until thick. Add fruit and marshmallows. Cool, Fold in whipped cream. Freeze.

Mrs. Less Feichtinger, Minnetonka H. S.
Excelsior, Minnesota

FROZEN FRUIT SALAD

Number of Servings — 8-10

4 egg yolks
4 T. Tarragon vinegar
4 T. sugar
1 pt. whipped cream
1 c. pecans, chopped
1 small can pineapple
1 small bottle Maraschino cherries
½ lb. marshmallows
⅛ t. salt

Combine egg yolks, vinegar and sugar. Cook in double boiler until thick. Cool. Add whipped cream. Cut fruit, nuts and marshmallows into egg yolk mixture. Add salt; mix well. Cover with waxed paper; freeze.

Elizabeth McClure, Greencastle H. S.
Greencastle, Indiana

FROZEN FRUIT SALAD

Number of Servings — 8

1 envelope unflavored gelatin
¼ c. cold water
⅓ c. mayonnaise
1 c. whipped cream
1 c. canned pineapple chunks, drained
1 c. Mandarin orange sections, drained
1 c. peaches, drained
½ c. Maraschino cherries, dates or nuts, chopped (Opt.)

Soften gelatin in cold water; dissolve over hot water. Blend in mayonnaise and whipped cream. Fold in remaining ingredients. Freeze until firm.

Carol Logan, Saltsburg Joint H. S.
Saltsburg, Pennsylvania

FROZEN FRUIT SALAD

Number of Servings — 8

2 eggs, slightly beaten
½ c. sugar
⅛ t. salt
½ c. pineapple juice
¼ c. lemon juice
1 c. celery, chopped
½ c. pineapple, shredded
2 apples, finely chopped
1 c. whipped cream

Combine eggs, sugar, salt and juices; blend well. Cook in double boiler until thick. Cool. Fold in fruit. Fold fruit mixture into whipped cream. Freeze.

Mrs. Ruth Reich, Meyersdale Joint H. S.
Meyersdale, Pennsylvania

FROZEN FRUIT SALAD

Number of Servings — 8-10

1 8-oz. can Royal Anne cherries, drained
1 8-oz. can pineapple tidbits, drained
2 bananas, sliced
1 small bottle Maraschino cherries, drained
Few grains salt
1 T. mayonnaise
½ c. pineapple juice
1 T. lemon juice
3 T. Maraschino cherry juice
1 T. flour
2 T. pecans, chopped
1 jar whipped cream

Combine fruits; add juices. Thicken Maraschino cherry juice with flour; cook until thick. Cool; Add to fruit mixture. Add salt, mayonnaise, pecans and whipped cream. Freeze.

Louise Temple, Exeter H. S.
Exeter, New Hampshire

FROZEN FRENCH FRUIT SALAD

Number of Servings — 6

1 T. lemon juice
2 bananas, diced
¾ c. pineapple, diced
12 red Maraschino cherries, chopped
⅓ c. French dressing
1 c. whipped cream
½ c. mayonnaise
⅛ t. salt
2 T. confectioner's sugar

Pour lemon juice over bananas; add pineapple, cherries and French dressing. Chill for 2 hours. Drain. Fold whipped cream into mayonnaise; add salt and sugar. Fold in fruit mixture. Freeze—do not stir.

Mrs. Ray Sartor, Pine Grove School
Ripley, Mississippi

FROZEN FRUIT-DRESSING SALAD

Number of Servings — 12

Fruit Salad Dressing:
½ c. sugar
1 t. salt
3 T. flour
2 eggs
4 T. vinegar
1½ c. pineapple juice

Mix ingredients in order given. Stirring well. Cook over low heat until thick and smooth, stirring constantly. Chill. Makes about 2 cups.

3 ripe bananas, mashed
1 c. canned pineapple, diced
1 c. canned pears
12 Maraschino cherries, thinly sliced
1 c. fruit salad dressing
1 c. whipped cream

Combine bananas, pineapple, pears and cherries. Add fruit salad dressing and whipped cream. Freeze until firm.

Mrs. LaVerne Kennedy, Rotan Independent Schools
Rotan, Texas

FROZEN FRUIT-HONEY SALAD

Number of Servings — 6

1 4-oz. pkg. cream cheese
3 T. mayonnaise
2 T. honey
1 c. white cherries, pitted
3 pineapple slices, diced
½ pt. whipped cream

Mix cream cheese with mayonnaise; add honey. Mix well. Add cherries and pineapple; fold in whipped cream. Freeze. Serve plain or with whipped cream or pineapple-fruit dressing.

Beryl Cone, The Plains H. S.
The Plains, Ohio

FROZEN GOLDEN FRUIT SALAD

Number of Servings — 6

Golden Fruit Dressing:
1 T. butter
¼ c. orange juice
¼ c. pineapple juice
1 t. lemon juice
¼ c. sugar
3 egg yolks
½ c. whipped cream

Combine all ingredients, folding in whipped cream last.

½ c. oranges, drained and diced
⅓ c. pineapple, drained and diced
¾ c. Royal Anne cherries, pitted
¼ c. Maraschino cherries, drained
¾ c. bananas, diced
1 c. Golden Fruit dressing

Combine all ingredients; mix thoroughly. Freeze. May be kept in freezer for as long as 2 months.

Laura E. Sumner, Cobre H. S.
Bayard, New Mexico

FROZEN FRUIT-MALLOW SALAD

Number of Servings — 8-10

1 9-oz. can crushed pineapple
1 3-oz. pkg. cream cheese, softened
1 7-oz. bottle 7-Up or lemon-lime carbonated beverage
2-2½ c. frozen peaches, thawed, drained and diced
1 c. seedless grapes, halved
1 c. whipped cream
1½ c. miniature marshmallows

Blend pineapple into cheese. Stir in 7-Up or carbonated beverage. Mix fruit into the mixture. Freeze until partially thickened. Fold whipped cream and marshmallows into the cheese mixture. Freeze until firm. Let stand at room temperature for a few minutes before serving.

This recipe submitted by the following teachers:

Mrs. Ruth C. Stowe, Stephens County H. S.
Eastanollee, Georgia

Charline Webb, Gaylesville H. S.
Gaylesville, Alabama

FROZEN GRAPE-PINEAPPLE SALAD

Number of Servings — 6-8

2 3-oz. pkg. cream cheese, softened
2 T. mayonnaise
2 T. pineapple syrup
24 marshmallows, quartered
1 No. 2 can pineapple bits, drained
1 c. whipped cream
2 c. Tokay grapes, halved and seeded

Blend cream cheese with mayonnaise. Beat in pineapple syrup. Add marshmallows and pineapple. Fold in whipped cream and grapes. Pour into 1-quart tray. Freeze until firm.

Mrs. Beverly Soden, Wisner H. S.
Wisner, Nebraska

HOLIDAY ORANGE SALAD

Number of Servings — 8-10

2 pkg. orange gelatin
1 11-oz. can Mandarin oranges, drained
2 c. mixed Mandarin orange juice and water, heated
1 pt. orange sherbet

Dissolve gelatin in hot juice-water mixture. Immediately add sherbet; stir until melted. When mixture begins to congeal add oranges. Pour into a 2-quart ring mold. Chill until firm. Wrap in moisture-proof paper. Freeze. To serve, unwrap and thaw in refrigerator 3-4 hours or overnight. Unmold and fill center with Mandarin Orange-Fruit salad.

Mandarin Orange Fruit Salad:

1 11-oz. can Mandarin oranges, drained
1⅔ c. crushed pineapple or chunks
1 c. flaked coconut
1 c. sour cream
1 c. miniature marshmallows

Combine all ingredients. Chill several hours or overnight. Do not freeze.

Gudrun Harstad, Detroit Lakes Senior H. S.
Detroit Lakes, Minnesota

FROZEN SUMMER FRUIT SALAD

Number of Servings — 8

½ c. strawberries, sliced
½ c. pineapple, sliced
½ c. orange segments, diced
½ c. bananas, diced
2 t. lemon juice
1 t. unflavored gelatin
1 T. cold water
4 t. syrup or strained honey
⅔ c. whipped cream

Combine fruits and lemon juice; chill. Soften gelatin in cold water; dissolve over hot water. Add syrup and fruit mixture. Fold in whipped cream. Freeze.

This recipe submitted by the following teachers:

Geneva Robertson, Dobyno Bennett H. S.
Kingsport, Tennessee

Sister Mary Ambrose Sacred Heart H. S.
Salina, Kansas

HOLIDAY WREATH MOLD

Number of Servings — 10

2 3-oz. pkg. cream cheese
1 c. mayonnaise
1 c. heavy cream, whipped
½ c. red Maraschino cherries, quartered
½ c. green Maraschino cherries, quartered
2½ c. crushed pineapple, drained
½ c. walnuts, chopped
2½ c. marshmallows, diced

Combine cheese and mayonnaise; blend until smooth. Fold in whipped cream, fruit, nuts and marshmallows. Pour into 1-quart ring mold. Freeze until firm. Serve as dessert or salad.

This recipe submitted by the following teachers:

Roberta M. Pettersen, Long Prairie H. S.
Long Prairie, Minnesota

Mrs. Zula R. Rowland, Mackville School
Mackville, Kentucky

Mrs. Barbara Bradley, Rose Bud School
Rose Bud, Arkansas

MARSHMALLOW-LIMEADE FREEZE

Number of Servings — 6-8

2 eggs, slightly beaten
⅓ c. confectioner's sugar
¼ c. lime juice
⅛ t. salt
1 T. butter
2 c. miniature marshmallows
1 14-oz. can pineapple tidbits
1 16-oz. can peaches, drained
1 c. whipped cream
Green food coloring

Combine eggs, sugar, lime juice, salt, butter and marshmallows. Cook over low heat, stirring constantly, until thickened. Cool. Fold fruit, lime mixture and food coloring into whipped cream. Turn into a 5-cup mold or bowl; freeze. Remove salad from freezer and let reach room temperature about 30 minutes before serving.

Roberta Foth, Howard H. S.
Howard, Kansas

ORANGE-CREAM MOLD

Number of Servings — 12

½ c. hot water
1 c. pineapple juice
1 pkg. orange gelatin
1 8-oz. pkg. cream cheese
¼ c. orange juice
2 T. lemon juice

Combine hot water and pineapple juice; add gelatin. Stir until gelatin is dissolved. Combine gelatin mixture, cream cheese, orange and lemon juice. Blend well. Pour into paper lined muffin pan. Freeze until firm.

Mrs. Jean Still, Clover Park Vocational-Technical
Tacoma, Washington

FROZEN PEAR SALAD

Number of Servings — 10-12

1 pkg. lime or cherry gelatin
1¾ c. pear juice
Juice of ½ lemon
2 3-oz. pkg. cream cheese
1 No. 3 can pears, drained and diced
½ pt. whipped cream
½ c. almonds, slivered (opt.)

Heat pear juice. Add gelatin and dissolve. Add lemon juice and cream cheese; mix well. Chill. Add pears, nuts and whipped cream. Pour into 9 x 9 pan. Freeze; stirring once or twice.

Mrs. Ruth DeFriese, Young H. S.
Knoxville, Tennessee

FROZEN PINEAPPLE SALAD

Number of Servings — 8-10

2 egg yolks
2 T. vinegar
2 T. sugar
1 No. 2 can crushed pineapple
10-oz. marshmallows, cut in small pieces
1 c. whipped cream
Few drops green food coloring
½ c. almonds (Opt.)

Cook egg yolks, vinegar and sugar together over low heat until thick. Pour pineapple over marshmallows. Fold in cool egg yolk mixture and whipped cream. Add food coloring and nuts; Blend. Freeze.

Mrs. Ernest Sampson, Huron High School
Huron, South Dakota

FROZEN PINEAPPLE-ORANGE SALAD

Number of Servings — 8

1 c. pineapple juice
2 T. flour
¼-½ c. butter
⅛ c. sugar
Pinch of salt
1 egg, slightly beaten
2 T. lemon juice
4 slices pineapple, finely cut
2 oranges. finely cut
¼ c. nuts, chopped
10 marshmallows
8 Maraschino cherries
1 pt. whipped cream

Make a paste of flour and some of the pineapple juice. Gradually add remaining juice. Add butter, sugar and salt. Cook in top of double boiler for about 10 minutes. Add the egg and continue cooking for a few minutes longer, stirring constantly. Cool. Add lemon juice, pineapple, oranges, nuts, marshmallows and cherries; fold in whipped cream. Pour in refrigerator tray; freeze.

This recipe submitted by the following teachers:
Ruth Cooper Humphrey, Wheeler County H. S.
Alamo, Georgia
Mrs. Myrtle Halvorson, Simmons Junior H. S.
Aberdeen, South Dakota

RAISIN CARNIVAL SNOW

Number of Servings — 8-10

1 c. dark or golden raisins
1 11-oz. can Mandarin oranges, drained
1 9-oz. can pineapple tidbits, drained
1 8-oz. pkg. cream cheese
½ t. salt
2 t. vanilla
Juice from oranges and pineapple
½ t. almond extract
1 T. lemon juice
½ t. lemon rind, grated
2 c. miniature marshmallows
½ c. Maraschino cherries, halved
1 c. whipped cream
Red food coloring (opt.)

Combine raisins and juice from oranges and pineapple; heat to simmering. Remove from heat; cover and cool. Blend cream cheese until soft; beat in salt, vanilla, almond extract, lemon juice and rind. Blend in raisin mixture. Stir in fruits and marshmallows. Fold in whipped cream. Add food coloring if desired. Freeze.

Madelyn Thames Everett, Magee H. S.
Magee, Mississippi

PINK RASPBERRY SALAD

Number of Servings — 12

1 No. 2 can crushed pineapple
2 3-oz. pkg. raspberry gelatin
1 lg. can condensed milk, chilled and whipped
Nuts, chopped

Heat pineapple; add gelatin and stir until dissolved. Chill. Add whipped cream. Sprinkle with nuts. Freeze.

Mrs. Eleanor Finley, Rostraver Sr. H. S.
Belle Vernon, Pennsylvania

FROZEN PINEAPPLE SALAD

1 3-oz. pkg. cream cheese
¼ c. mayonnaise
2 T. lemon juice
15 marshmallows, quartered
1 c. pineapple, drained and diced
¼ c. dates, diced
1 c. whipped cream

Combine cheese and mayonnaise; mix until smooth. Add lemon juice, marshmallows, pineapple and dates. Fold in whipped cream. Freeze.

A. Dorothea Nevramon
Steele, North Dakota

PINEAPPLE-CREAM CHEESE FREEZE

Number of Servings — 6-8

1 small bottle Maraschino cherries, cut up
1½ c. miniature marshmallows
1 3-oz. pkg. cream cheese
1 small can crushed pineapple
1 can chilled evaporated milk, whipped

Combine cherries, marshmallows, cream cheese and pineapple. Fold in whipped milk. Freeze.

Mrs. Wilma Frick, Armijo H. S.
Fairfield, California

FROZEN PINEAPPLE-CHEESE SALAD

Number of Servings — 10

2 3-oz. pkg. cream cheese
1 c. mayonnaise
2 c. crushed pineapple, drained
3 T. confectioners' sugar
1 c. whipped cream

Beat cream cheese until soft; blend in mayonnaise. Add pineapple and sugar. Fold in whipped cream. Freeze.

Ruth Maud, South Lebanon H. S.
Lebanon, Pennsylvania

FROZEN PINEAPPLE-MARSHMALLOW SALAD

Number of Servings — 10-16

1 small can crushed pineapple
16 marshmallows, chopped
1 3-oz. pkg. cream cheese
¼ c. nuts, chopped
1 c. whipping cream
¼ c. salad dressing
1 T. confectioners' sugar

Mash cream cheese; add pineapple, marshmallows, and nuts. Whip cream with salad dressing and sugar until stiff. Add to cheese mixture. Freeze.

Mrs. Carol Stromaglio, Thornapple-Kellogg H. S.
Middleville, Michigan

FROZEN FRUIT DELIGHT

Number of Servings — 6

1 6-oz. pkg. cream cheese
1 c. mayonnaise
1 c. whipped cream
1 c. Maraschino cherries, diced
1 No. 2 can crushed pineapple, drained
2½ c. marshmallows, diced

Blend cheese with mayonnaise. Fold in remaining ingredients. Freeze.

Ruth M. Bearup, Silver H. S.
Silver City, New Mexico

FROZEN DELIGHT

Number of Servings — 12

2 3-oz. pkg. cream cheese
1 c. mayonnaise
¼ c. sugar
1 c. nuts, chopped
1 c. pineapple, cubed
½ c. Maraschino cherries, drained
1 carton whipped cream or 1 pkg. dessert topping mix

Cream the cheese; add mayonnaise and sugar. Beat until smooth. Stir in nuts, pineapple and cherries. Fold in whipped cream or prepared dessert topping mix. Freeze.

Mrs. James Beebe, Scales Mound Community H.S.
Scales Mound, Illinois

FROZEN FRUIT-CHEESE SALAD

Number of Servings — 6

1 c. pineapple, drained and shredded
4 T. confectioners' sugar
¼ lb. cream cheese
8 marshmallows, chopped
1 c. mayonnaise
1 c. whipped cream
12 Maraschino cherries, chopped

Combine pineapple, sugar, cherries and marshmallows. Let stand until marshmallows melt. Mash cream cheese; add mayonnaise. Blend until smooth; add to fruit mixture. Add whipped cream; freeze.

Mrs. Frances E. Smith, Alpena H. S.
Alpena, South Dakota

FROZEN STRAWBERRY SALAD

Number of Servings — 8-10

16 lg. marshmallows
2 T. strawberry juice
1 c. strawberries, drained and sliced
½-1 c. crushed pineapple, drained
1 3-oz. pkg. cream cheese
½ c. mayonnaise
1 c. whipped cream
½ t. vanilla (Opt.)

Melt marshmallows in strawberry juice, in double boiler. Cool. Add strawberries and pineapple. Cream the cheese until smooth; add mayonnaise. Combine whipped cream and vanilla if desired; add to strawberry mixture. Freeze until firm.

This recipe submitted by the following teachers:

Mrs. Donna Blaue, Hiawatha High School
Hiawatha, Kansas

Mrs. Gladys Wirth, Community Unit #2
Liberty, Illinois

Mrs. Lois Lovas, Mayville High School
Mayville, North Dakota

FROZEN STRAWBERRY-PINEAPPLE SALAD

Number of Servings — 12

Crust:

1½ c. Graham cracker crumbs
¼ c. sugar
⅓ c. butter or margarine, melted

Combine sugar, melted butter and crumbs; mix well. Firmly press mixture into a greased 9 x 9-inch pan. Chill.

Salad:

1 c. sweetened strawberries, drained and sliced
1 9-oz. can pineapple tidbits, drained
8 marshmallows, chopped
¼ c. mayonnaise or salad dressing
1 c. whipped cream
¼ c. pecans, broken
1 envelope unflavored gelatin
2 T. cold pineapple syrup
¼ c. hot pineapple syrup
½ c. coconut

Soften gelatin in cold pineapple syrup; dissolve in hot pineapple syrup. Combine fruit, marshmallows and pecans. Add gelatin. Fold mayonnaise into whipped cream; add to fruit mixture. Fold in coconut or sprinkle over the top of fruit mixture. Spread in chilled crust or if desired, omit the crust and pour mixture into paper cups set in a muffin pan. Freeze.

This recipe submitted by the following teachers:

Mrs. Merlin R. Miller, Hettinger H. S.
Hettinger, North Dakota

Mrs. Miriam Bobo Templeton
Hickory Tavern H. S.
Gray Court, South Carolina

Ruth Fingerhut, Pasco H. S.
Dade City, Florida

Hallie Mattson, St. Louis County No. 70
Embarrass, Minnesota

Mrs. Lilla Schmeltekopf, Burleson H. S.
Burleson, Texas

FROZEN STRAWBERRY SALAD

Number of Servings — 12

1 pt. frozen sweetened strawberries
1 c. crushed pineapple, drained
½ c. pecans, chopped
½ lb. miniature marshmallows
1 c. whipped cream
1 c. salad dressing
1 3-oz. pkg. cream cheese

Combine strawberries, pineapple, pecans and marshmallows. Combine remaining ingredients; beat until smooth. Add to fruit mixture; mix well. Freeze.

Irma Haley, Castleford High School
Castleford, Idaho

STRAWBERRY SALAD SUPERB

Number of Servings — 6

1 6-oz. pkg. cream cheese
2 T. honey
1 c. sweetened strawberries, crushed
½ c. canned pineapple, diced
¼ c. lemon juice

Blend cheese with honey; add strawberries, pineapple and lemon juice. Freeze.

Sister Del Rey, St. Mary H. S.
Dell Rapids, South Dakota

STRAWBERRY-CHEESE SALAD

Number of Servings — 6-8

1 pt. strawberries
2 T. sugar
2 t. lemon juice
2 3-oz. pkg. cream cheese
½ c. whipped cream

Crush strawberries with sugar. Mix with cream cheese and lemon juice. Fold in whipped cream. Freeze.

Miss Rony E. Bolton, Seaman Local School
Seaman, Ohio

STRAWBERRY SALAD

Number of Servings — 8

2 pkg. strawberry gelatin
1 c. hot water
1 c. cold water
2 10-oz. pkg. frozen strawberries, thawed
1 envelope dessert topping mix, whipped
2 T. sugar
1 3-oz. pkg. cream cheese, softened

Dissolve gelatin in hot water; stir in cold water. Add 2 ice cubes; chill. Add strawberries. Pour half of mixture in oblong glass baking dish. Freeze. Chill remaining half of mixture until nearly set. Combine dessert topping mix, sugar and cream cheese. Beat until smooth. Spread dessert topping mixture on top of frozen layer; top with chilled gelatin. Chill for several hours.

Mrs. Fayma Drummond, Petersburg H. S.
Petersburg, Texas

Fruit Salads

APPLE SALAD WITH BLEU CHEESE DRESSING

Number of Servings — 4-5

2 c. unpared apples, diced
1 c. celery slices
1½ c. cantaloupe or honeydew melon balls
½ c. sour cream
⅓ c. mayonnaise
⅓-½ c. Bleu cheese, crumbled

Mix apples, celery and melon balls. Blend sour cream and mayonnaise; stir in Bleu cheese. Add to apple mixture and toss lightly. Chill.

Mrs. Louise E. Frame, Coraopolis Jr. H. S.
Coraopolis, Pennsylvania

BLEU-CHEESE WALDROF SALAD

Number of Servings — 6

2 c. unpared tart apples, diced
1 c. celery, diced
½ c. California walnuts, broken
¼ c. Bleu cheese, crumbled
¼ c. sour cream
¼ c. mayonnaise or salad dressing
Dash of salt

Combine apples, celery and walnuts. Mix remaining ingredients; add to first mixture; toss. Chill.

Elizabeth Davis Gibson, St. Peter Claver
Community House
Detroit, Michigan

EVELYN'S APPLE SALAD

Number of Servings — 6

4 juicy apples, chopped
¼ c. celery, diced
¼ c. dates, chopped
¼ c. nuts, chopped
3 T. sugar
Maraschino cherries

Combine apples, celery, dates and nuts. Sprinkle with sugar; Toss. Chill. Garnish with cherries. Salad keeps 4 to 5 hours.

Mrs. Mary Lou Demoise,
Conestoga Valley Sr. H. S.
Lancaster, Pennsylvania

HOOSIER APPLE SALAD

Number of Servings — 6

3 c. apples, diced
1 c. dates, chopped
1 c. celery, chopped
3 oranges, sectioned
French dressing
Cheese balls
Lettuce cups

Arrange mixed fruits in lettuce cups, decorate with cheese balls. Serve with French dressing.

Sue Hornung, Granville H. S.
Milwaukee, Wisconsin

WALDORF SALAD

Number of Servings — 6

2 c. Jonathan apples, cubed
1 c. celery, chopped
1 c. Queen Anne cherries, pitted
2 T. lemon juice
Nuts, chopped
½ c. mayonnaise
½ c. sour cream
2 T. sugar
¼ t. salt

Sprinkle apples with lemon juice. Add celery and cherries. Combine mayonnaise, sour cream, sugar and salt. Fold into apples. Chill 1 hour. Top with nuts.

Edna Stankovich, Washington H. S.
East Chicago, Indiana

FRESH FRUIT SALAD

Number of Servings — 8

4 medium Bananas, sliced
8 oranges, chopped
1 lb. Green or Red Grapes, seeded and halved
1½ c. miniature marshmallows
¼ c. nuts, chopped
Maraschino cherries
½ pt. whipping cream
¼ c. sugar

Mix all the fruit together. Add nuts and marshmallows. Chill. Just before serving, whip the cream; add sugar; mix into fruit. Top with Maraschino cherries.

Laurel R. Brice, Remus H. S.
Remus, Michigan

BANANA APPLE SALAD

Number of Servings — 10

1 c. sugar
2 T. flour
1 egg
1 No. 2½ can pineapple tidbits, drained
4 tart apples, sliced
8 bananas, sliced
18 marshmallows quartered
1 c. nuts, chopped
1 c. whipped cream

Combine juice drained from pineapple with sugar, flour and egg. Cook until thick. Chill. Add whipped cream. Fold mixture into remaining ingredients.

Mildred Young, Marlington H. S.
Alliance, Ohio

BANANA FRUIT SALAD

Number of Servings — 8

5 bananas, diced
3 apples, diced
1 small can pineapple, diced
1 c. pecans, chopped
12 marshmallows, diced
2 egg yolks, well beaten
½ c. lemon juice
½ can sweetened condensed milk

Combine fruits, marshmallows and nuts. Thoroughly mix remaining ingredients for a dressing; add to the fruit mixture.

Lanora Jane Etheredge, McLean H. S.
McLean, Texas

MILLIONAIRES SALAD

Number of Servings — 8

2 eggs, beaten
5 T. lemon or orange juice
5 T. sugar
2 T. butter
32 marshmallows
1 c. whipped cream
1 can pineapple, diced
1 can fruit cocktail
3 bananas, sliced

Combine eggs, juice, sugar, butter and marshmallows. Simmer until marshmallows are melted. Cool. Add remaining ingredients. Chill.

Mrs. Evelyn Attendorf, Warren H. S.
Warren, Minnesota

ANGEL SALAD

Number of Servings — 6-8

1 c. marshmallows, chopped
3 bananas or 1 lb. white grapes chopped
1 c. pineapple chunks drained and chopped
½ c. peanuts, crushed
½ c. whipped cream
⅔ c. pineapple juice
1 egg
2 T. sugar
1 T. cornstarch

Mix marshmallows and fruit; add nuts. Make a cooked dressing of the egg, cornstarch, sugar and juice. Cool; add whipped cream. Combine with salad mixture and serve on lettuce.

Mrs. Helen H. Wise, Manheim Township Sr. H. S.
Neffsville, Pennsylvania

FRUIT SALAD WITH DRESSING

Number of Servings — 8

2 oranges, diced
2 apples, diced
3 bananas, diced
8 marshmallows, diced
1 lge. can crushed pineapple, drained
1 lge. bottle cherries, drained
Coconut or nuts (opt.)
1 egg
1 c. sugar
2 T. flour
Juice from pineapple and cherries

Mix all fruits and marshmallows together. Combine egg, sugar, flour and fruit juices; cook in double boiler, stirring constantly until thick. Let cool. Add to fruit mixture. Chill. Will not lose color for several days.

Shirley McCain, Angie H. S.
Angie, Louisiana

FAVORITE FRUIT SALAD

Number of Servings — 10-12

1 c. sugar
1 T. flour
Juice of 1 lemon
1 egg, beaten
¼ c. pineapple juice
¼ c. boiling water
1 c. whipped cream,
5 apples, diced
3 bananas, sliced
1 small can crushed pineapple
12 Maraschino cherries, quartered

Sift sugar and flour together. Add egg, lemon juice, pineapple juice and water. Cook in double boiler until thickened. Cool. Add whipped cream; mix in fruits.

Marilyn Rennich, Wessington Springs Public School
Wessington Springs, South Dakota

WHITE FRUIT SALAD

Number of Servings — 15

3 oranges, cubed
1 No. 2 can pineapple chunks, drained
1 No. 2 can Royal Anne cherries, drained
1 lb. miniature marshmallows
1 c. whipped cream
3 egg yolks, well beaten
Juice of 2 small lemons
2 T. sugar
1½ T. flour
1 c. pineapple juice

Combine egg yolks, lemon juice, sugar, flour and pineapple juice until thickened. Remove from heat; stir in ½ of the marshmallows. Let cool. Fold in whipped cream. Gently fold in remaining ingredients.

Florence Tustison, Sentinel H. S.
Sentinel, Oklahoma

VELVET SALAD

Number of Servings — 12-15

3 eggs
Juice of 1 lemon
½ pkg. miniature marshmallows
1 can sliced pineapple, drained
1 can Royal Anne cherries, drained
½ pt. whipped cream

Beat eggs with a rotary egg beater until thick; add lemon juice. Cook, stirring constantly until mixture resembles scrambled eggs. Cool. Add fruit; mix lightly. Fold in whipped cream. Chill overnight for improved flavor.

Ann Stevens Hardy, Estill County H. S.
Irvine, Kentucky

CHERRY-PINEAPPLE SALAD

Number of Servings — 5-6

2 c. frozen cherries
1 9-oz. can crushed pineapple
2 c. marshmallows
2 T. sugar
½ c. nuts, chopped
½ c. mayonnaise
1 c. whipped cream

Combine cherries, pineapple, marshmallows, nuts and mayonnaise. Refrigerate until serving time. Fold in whipped cream sweetened with sugar just before serving.

Jo Ann Wolters, Fairbury H. S.
Fairbury, Nebraska

CITRUS SALAD WITH CRANBERRY DRESSING

Number of Servings — 6

Citrus Salad.
1 head lettuce
1 c. orange sections
1 c. grapefruit sections
2 c. melon balls
Maraschino cherries (garnish)

Arrange fruit attractively on individual lettuce cups. Garnish with cherries.

Cranberry Dressing:
1 c. jellied cranberry sauce
1 c. mayonnaise
2 T. lime or lemon juice
1 c. whipped cream (opt.)

Blend cranberry sauce and mayonnaise with electric mixer. Add juice. For a richer dressing, fold in whipped cream if desired.

Mrs. Thelma Hause, Stevens H. S.
Claremont, New Hampshire

CITRUS SALAD WITH LEMON MAYONNAISE DRESSING

Number of Servings — 6

2 grapefruit or 1 No. 303 can grapefruit sections
3 oranges
1 avocado
1 persimmon

Peel, section and remove membranes from citrus fruits. Peel avocado and slice lengthwise. Cut peeled persimmon into bite-size pieces. Arrange fruits attractively on lettuce. Serve with lemon mayonnaise.

Lemon Mayonnaise:
1 egg
¼ c. lemon juice
1 t. mustard
1 t. salt
1 t. sugar
¼ t. paprika
1 pt. salad oil

Combine all ingredients except salad oil. Slowly beat in salad oil. Continue beating until thick. Yield: 2½ cups mayonnaise.

Margarette C. Weeks, Highland Junior H. S.
Highland, California

GOLD COAST SALAD

Number of Servings — 6

1 head lettuce, torn in bite-size pieces
1 grapefruit, sectioned
2 oranges, sectioned

Pare grapefruit and oranges, cutting through white skin. Cut sections close to membrane and lift out. Arrange sections of grapefruit and orange on lettuce. Garnish with pomegranate seeds or avocado slices. Pass fruit dressing.

DRESSING:
½ c. sugar
1 t. salt
1 t. dry mustard
1 t. celery salt
1 t. paprika
1 t. grated onion
1 c. salad oil
¼ c. vinegar

Mix dry ingredients; add onion. Add oil, a small amount at a time, alternately with vinegar, the last addition being vinegar. Beat with a fork; then, if mixture seems to separate use rotary or electric beater.

Frances Shipley, Coon Rapids Community School
Coon Rapids, Iowa

CRANBERRY DELIGHT

Number of Servings — 6-8

1 lb. cranberries, coarsely ground
2 oranges, peeled. Reserve rind
3 or 4 pineapple slices, chopped
2 c. sugar
3 or 4 apples, chopped
Orange rind

Grind orange rind into cranberries; add sugar and mix well. Mix in orange and pineapple pieces. Add apples just before serving. Serve in a hollowed orange half if desired.

Fay C. Patterson, Mohall H. S.
Mohall, North Dakota

CRANBERRY FLUFF

Number of Servings — 8-10

2 c. raw cranberries, ground
3-4 c. miniature marshmallows
¾ c. sugar
1-2 c. unpared tart apples, diced
½ c. seedless green grapes (opt.)
½ c. walnuts, broken (opt.)
¼ t. salt (opt.)
1 c. whipped cream
Pineapple slices (opt.)

Combine cranberries, marshmallows and sugar. Cover and chill overnight. Add apples, grapes, walnuts and salt. Fold in whipped cream. Chill. Turn into a serving bowl or spoon onto pineapple slices in lettuce cups. Trim with a cluster of green grapes if desired.

This recipe submitted by the following teachers:

Mrs. Bessie Hutchins, Grady Municipal School
Grady, New Mexico

Mrs. Mary Edge, Augusta H. S.
Augusta, Wisconsin

Dorothy Watson, Nucla H. S.
Nucla, Colorado

Mrs. Jack Turner, Bourne H. S.
Bourne, Massachusetts

Eunice S. Marshall, Spaulding H. S.
Barre, Vermont

Mrs. Merle Brotherton, Lockney H. S.
Lockney, Texas

Ann Held, Horicon H. S.
Horicon, Wisconsin

Mrs. Charlene Kersten, Marion H. S.
Marion, Wisconsin

Anita Mielke, Wild Rose H. S.
Wild Rose, Wisconsin

Betty Bielenberg, Jefferson Community H. S.
Jefferson, Iowa

Mrs. Alfrieda Jacobson, Granite Falls H. S.
Granite Falls, Minnesota

CRANBERRY-FRUIT SALAD

Number of Servings — 8

1 lb. cranberries, ground
1¼ c. sugar
1 No. 303 can crushed pineapple
1 pkg. miniature marshmallows
4 bananas, sliced
1 c. whipped cream, sweetened

Combine cranberries, sugar, pineapple and marshmallows. Refrigerate overnight. Just before serving add bananas and whipped cream.

Shirley Keenlance, Manawa H. S.
Manawa, Wisconsin

CRANBERRY SALAD

Number of Servings — 4

1 c. cranberries, chopped
1 apple, diced
1 banana, diced
1 small can crushed pineapple, drained
⅔ c. sugar

Mix cranberries, apple, banana and pineapple. Stir in sugar until well blended. Refrigerate 2 or 3 hours before serving.

Mrs. Marilyn J. Fleener, Lakeview H. S.
Decatur, Illinois

CRANBERRY SALAD

Number of Servings — 8

3 c. miniature marshmallows
1 c. whipped cream
1 c. cranberries, ground
½ c. sugar
1 9-oz. can crushed pineapple, drained

Fold marshmallows into whipped cream. Chill for 2 hours. Combine cranberries and sugar, stirring to dissolve sugar. Let stand at room temperature for 2 hours. Add crushed pineapple to cranberry-sugar mixture. Fold cranberry mixture into whipped cream. Chill at least 6 hours or overnight.

Catherine Luker, H. S.
Martinsville, Indiana

CRANBERRY SALAD

Number of Servings — 6

¾ c. raw cranberries, ground
¾ c. sugar
1 10-oz. pkg. miniature marshmallows
1¼ c. crushed pineapple
1 c. whipped cream

Mix cranberries and sugar; let stand for 3 hours. Mix marshmallows and pineapple. Let stand 3 hours, stirring occasionally. Combine mixtures; fold in whipped cream. Chill.

This recipe submitted by the following teachers:

Arva Knight, Samnorwood H. S.
Samnorwood, Texas

Clinette L. Wolf, West Concord H. S.
West Concord, Minnesota

CRANBERRY SALAD

Number of Servings — 8

1 lb. raw cranberries, ground
1 c. crushed pineapple, drained
1 c. sugar
1 c. miniature marshmallows
1 c. whipped cream

Combine cranberries, pineapple and sugar. Let stand overnight. Add marshmallows and whipped cream just before serving.

Mrs. Dorothy Soderlund, Milaca H. S.
Milaca, Minnesota

FRESH CRANBERRY SALAD

Number of Servings — 8-12

1 lb. whole fresh cranberries, ground
1½-2 c. sugar
1½ c. applesauce
1½-2 c. crushed or tidbit pineapple, well drained
½ pkg. miniature marshmallows
1 c. nuts, coarsely chopped (opt.)
½ c. whipping cream
4 T. sugar

Combine cranberries, 1½-2 cups sugar and applesauce. Let stand several hours or overnight. Add pineapple, marshmallows and nuts; mix well. Whip cream; sweeten with sugar. Mix with cranberry mixture until just blended. Chill. Serve with poultry or pork.

Mrs. Mary Lou Michalewicz, T. F. Riggs Sr. H. S.
Pierre, South Dakota

CRANBERRY SALAD SUPREME

Number of Servings — 10-12

1 c. raw cranberries, chopped
1 c. sugar
2 c. seedless or Tokay grapes, chilled
½ c. canned pineapple, diced and chilled (opt.)
1 c. whipped cream
½-2 c. walnuts or pecans, chopped
½ c. marshmallows, quartered (opt.)

Combine cranberries and sugar. Blend. Refrigerate overnight. Drain off liquid. Combine grapes, pineapple, nuts and whipped cream. Fold into cranberry mixture. Add marshmallows and stir until evenly distributed.

This recipe submitted by the following teachers:

Nancy Lee, Cleburne H. S.
Cleburne, Texas

Margaret Miller, Henry County H. S.
New Castle, Kentucky

Miriam E. Moorman, Mt. Clemens H. S.
Mt. Clemens, Michigan

Mrs. Rowena Ballew, Richland Senior H. S.
Fort Worth, Texas

Mrs. June Nesbitt, Springfield H. S.
Springfield, Illinois

Mrs. Hallie Christensen, Truman Public School
Truman, Minnesota

Mrs. Alverna M. Thomas, Lewiston Senior H. S.
Lewiston, Idaho

CRANBERRY SALAD

Number of Servings — 14

2 cans whole cranberries
2 c. miniature marshmallows
2 c. apples, diced
3 bananas, sliced
3 c. orange sections, cut
½ c. pecans, broken

Mix ingredients. Refrigerate for several hours or overnight.

Mrs. Sharlene Swann, Columbus H. S.
Columbus, Wisconsin

STUFFED CRANBERRY-PEAR SALAD

4 c. fresh cranberries
1 whole orange, quartered and seeded
½ small grapefruit, sectioned and seeded
2 c. sugar or 1 c. sugar and 1 c. syrup
Pear halves

Put cranberries, oranges and grapefruit through food chopper. Add sugar and syrup. Mix well. Chill a few hours before serving. This relish will keep several days in refrigerator. Fill pear half with this mixture at serving time.

Mrs. Zella H. Mills, Hancock County H. S.
Sneedville, Tennessee

CREAM CHEESE SALAD

Number of Servings — 8

1 c. whipped cream
1 3-oz. pkg. cream cheese
¼ c. salad dressing
2½ c. mixed fruit
¼ c. cherries
¼ c. nuts, chopped
¼ c. marshmallows, cut
1 banana, diced

Combine whipped cream, cream cheese and salad dressing. Add remaining ingredients and chill 2 or 3 hours.

Mrs. Sharon K. Emery, Houghton Lake H. S.
Houghton Lake, Michigan

ICE COLD FRUIT SALAD

Number of Servings — 6

1 c. lge. pineapple chunks
1½ c. oranges, sliced
4 bananas
½ c. Maraschino cherries
⅓ c. sugar
1½ c. cracked ice
6 mint leaves or 6 pieces of Green mint leaf candy
Maraschino cherries

Mix pineapple, oranges, cherries and sugar. Refrigerate for 2 hours. Score bananas and make slanting slices ½-inch thick. Mix salad and serve at once in individual serving dishes packed in cracked ice. Garnish with mint leaf or candy and Maraschino cherry.

Mildred McNutt, Randolph H. S.
Randolph, Wisconsin

FRUIT SALAD WITH DELIGHTFUL DRESSING

Number of Servings — 6

¼ c. sugar
4 oranges
4 bananas, chopped
1 bunch purple grapes, seeded and halved
1 small can pineapple chunks, drained
Marshmallows (opt.)

Peel and section orange; remove all white membrane. Add remaining ingredients. Toss lightly. Add dressing just before serving.

Delightful Dressing:
¼ c. sugar
2 T. flour
1 egg yolk
2½ T. lemon juice
½ c. pineapple juice
1 c. whipped cream

Combine sugar, flour and egg yolk; slowly add lemon and pineapple juice. Cook until thick. Cool. Fold in whipped cream.

Mrs. James L. Patton, Bryan Station Senior H. S.
Lexington, Kentucky

OLD FASHIONED FRUIT SALAD

Number of Servings — 6

1 lge. orange, shredded
1 lge. banana, peeled and sliced
1 lge. apple, peeled and diced
1 c. crushed pineapple drained
1 c. green grapes, cut in half
6 lge. marshmallows, quartered
¼ c. fruit salad dressing (opt.)

Combine all ingredients. Mix well. Chill. Mold in custard cups.

Fruit Salad Dressing:
Grated rind and juice of 1 lemon
Grated rind and juice of 1 lime
Grated rind and juice of 1 orange
1 egg
1 c. sugar
1 c. whipped cream

Cook all ingredients except whipped cream in a double boiler, stirring constantly, until thickened. Cool. Chill. Fold in whipped cream.

Eleanor M. King, West Monroe H. S.
West Monroe, Louisiana

WARD-BELMONT FRUIT SALAD

Number of Servings — 10

1 pkg. marshmallows, cut in pieces
1 lge. can pineapple, drained and cut in small pieces
1 lge. can Royal Anne cherries, drained and halved
1 medium bottle red cherries, drained and halved
1 lge. can peaches, drained and cut in small pieces
8 small apples, cut in pieces
1 c. pecan or walnut pieces

Soak marshmallows in juice drained from pineapple. Mix well drained fruit with marshmallows and nuts.

Dressing:
4 eggs, beaten
6 T. boiling vinegar plus 2 T. water
2 T. butter, melted
1 pt. whipped cream
Salt, sugar and dry mustard to taste

Gradually add boiling vinegar and water to eggs. Add butter and cook in double boiler until thick. Cool completely. Season with salt, sugar and dry mustard. Fold in whipped cream. Alternate layers of fruit and dressing in a deep dish, ending with a layer of dressing. Refrigerate overnight.

Mrs. Mary Menking, Hallettsville H. S.
Hallettsville, Texas

FRUIT SALAD

Number of Servings — 8

2 eggs
4 T. sugar
3 T. vinegar
1 t. water
½ t. butter
12 marshmallows, quartered
1 c. grapes, halved
1 lge. can sliced pineapple, chopped
½ pt. whipped cream

Mix eggs, sugar, vinegar, water and butter together. Cook over low heat until thickened. Let stand until cool. Combine fruit with egg mixture. Add whipped cream. Refrigerate for 4 hours or overnight.

Patricia Dable, Thorp H. S.
Thorp, Wisconsin

PERFECTION FRUIT SALAD

Number of Servings — 16

2 lb. white grapes or white cherries
2 lb. canned pineapple
1 lb. blanched almonds
1 lb. marshmallows
Juice of 2 lemons
4 egg yolks
2 c. milk
1 lb. sugar
1 pt. whipped cream

Combine fruits; place half of the mixture in a bowl. Pour juice of 1 lemon over it. Add remaining fruit and lemon juice. Let stand. Heat egg yolks, milk and sugar to a boil; let cool. Add whipped cream. Pour cream mixture over fruit mixture. Let stand overnight.

Manona Brewer, Arestimba Union H. S.
Newman, California

GRAPE-CANTALOUPE SALAD

Number of Servings — 6-8

1 can chunk pineapple, drained
½ cantaloupe
1 c. miniature marshmallows
1½ c. Thompson seedless grapes
1 banana, sliced
1 T. cornstarch

Cut fruit into bite-size pieces. Heat pineapple juice; add cornstarch. Cool. Pour dressing over combined fruits and marshmallows.

Mrs. Eva Huston, Williamsburg H. S.
Williamsburg, Iowa

FRUIT SALAD SUPREME

Number of Servings — 10

1 lb. green grapes
1 small can pineapple, drained
1 lb. miniature marshmallows
1 can pears, drained
3 T. sugar
4 egg yolks
¼ c. pineapple juice
1 pt. whipped cream

Cook sugar, egg yolks and pineapple juice until it reaches the thickness of custard. Fold in whipped cream. Combine remaining ingredients. Pour cream mixture over fruit mixture.

Mrs. N. Bruce Thom, Granite Falls Sr. H. S.
Granite Falls, Minnesota

BANANA-PEANUT SALAD

Number of Servings — 1

1 banana
Commercial mayonnaise
Salted peanuts, chopped
Lettuce leaves

Slice banana lengthwise; place on lettuce leaf, sliced sides up. Spread generously with mayonnaise; sprinkle with peanuts.

Mrs. Sally McConnell, Punxsutawney Area H. S.
Punxsutawney, Pennsylvania

COTTAGE CHEESE SALAD

Number of Servings — 6

1 12-oz. pkg. Cottage Cheese
½ c. carrots, grated
½ c. celery, finely chopped
2 t. onion, minced
¼ c. salad dressing
Salt and pepper to taste

Combine cottage cheese, carrots, celery and onion. Add salad dressing, salt and pepper; mix well. Chill before serving.

Mrs. Lois Brichacek, Roosevelt Jr. H. S.
Great Bend, Kansas

CHEESE-AVOCADO SALAD

Number of Servings — 6

1 lge. pkg. cream cheese
1 c. sour cream
2 T. onion, finely chopped
2 lge. avocados, peeled and pitted
Salt to taste

Mix sour cream, cheese, onion and salt with electric mixer. Add avocados; blend. Serve on lettuce.

Mrs. Lillian S. Ealy, Gadsden H. S.
Anthony, New Mexico

COLORFUL QUICK FRUIT & MELON SALAD

Number of Servings — 6-8

1 can fruit cocktail or jar of fruits for salad, drained
½ c. whipped cream
1 cantaloupe or honeydew melon pared and sliced ½" thick
¼ t. vanilla
2 T. sugar
Various fresh fruits: apples, bananas, grapes
Maraschino cherries

Add vanilla and sugar to cream. Fold into fruit mixture. Place slice of melon on lettuce leaf. Fill hole with fruit mixture; top with a cherry.

Mrs. Geneva Gill Cooper, Wayne County H. S.
Monticello, Kentucky

CRANBERRY-PINEAPPLE SALAD

Number of Servings — 8

1 can cranberry sauce
1 can pineapple rings, well drained
1 box cottage cheese
8 Maraschino cherries

Place the sliced cranberry sauce on lettuce cups, put a ring of pineapple over the sauce, place a tablespoon of cottage cheese in the center of the pineapple. Place a cherry on top of cheese.

Mrs. Janice P. Cabler, East Senior H. S.
Nashville, Tennessee

FRUIT SALAD

Number of Servings — 4-6

1 small can fruit cocktail, drained
1 small can crushed pineapple, drained
1 small pkg. miniature marshmallows
½ c. sour cream
½ c. nuts or coconut (opt.)

Combine all ingredients. Toss.

Louise Greene, Anson H. S.
Wadesboro, North Carolina

GARDEN ISLAND SALAD

Number of Servings — 6

¼ section of medium-sized watermelon
1 c. pineapple chunks, drained
1 c. green grapes
2 bananas, diced
¼ c. lemon juice
¼ c. powdered sugar

Cut up fruits to chunk size. Combine all fruits. Pour over fruit. Chill. Serve on lettuce leaf. Combine fruits. Combine lemon juice and sugar. Gently toss together.

Jean Sanae Izumi, Ramona Jr. H. S.
Chino, California

GARLIC ORANGE-GRAPEFRUIT SALAD BOWL

Number of Servings — 8

1 No. 303 can grapefruit, drained
1 11-oz. can Mandarin oranges, drained
1 medium-size head of lettuce, torn in small pieces
1 pkg. garlic dressing

Prepare dressing according to package directions. Combine fruits and lettuce; serve with desired amount of garlic dressing. Remaining dressing will keep indefinitely in refrigerator.

Mrs. Gary Keech, Trimont Area School
Trimont, Minnesota

JIFFY CHERRY SALAD

Number of Servings — 9

16 Graham crackers, crushed
½ c. butter or margarine, melted
1 8-oz. pkg. cream cheese
1 c. whipped cream
1 c. powdered sugar
1 can cherry pie filling

Combine cracker crumbs and melted butter. Press mixture into bottom of a 9" square pan, reserving some for topping. Cream sugar and cream cheese. Combine sugar, cheese and whipped cream; spread over cracker crust. Pour cherries over top of mixture; sprinkle with reserved crumb mixture. Chill. Cut in squares and serve.

This recipe submitted by the following teachers:

Norma Strube, Hopkins Township H. S.
Granville, Illinois

Ruth Ann Stickelmaier, McLean-Waynesville H. S.
McLean, Illinois

ORANGE-LETTUCE SALAD BOWL

Number of Servings — 6

½ head lettuce, torn in small pieces
Juice of 1 orange or ½ can frozen orange juice, undiluted
1 T. sugar

Pour orange juice over lettuce. Sprinkle with sugar.

Mrs. Patricia Moore, Ionia H. S.
Ionia, Michigan

MOUNTAINEER SALAD

Number of Servings — 6-8

2 c. cabbage, shredded
1 c. small marshmallows
1 c. fresh green grapes
½ c. dried raisins
½ c. coconut, shredded
½ c. nuts, chopped
¼ c. fresh cream

Toss all ingredients until well moistened. Chill.

Mrs. J. M. Allen, Wall H. S.
San Angelo, Texas

ORANGE WALDORF SALAD

Number of Servings — 6

1 c. red apple, diced
1 c. orange, diced
½ c. dates, chopped
½ c. celery, chopped
⅓ c. walnuts, chopped
4 t. honey
1 t. poppy seed
¼ t. salt
Watercress
1½ c. sour cream

Carefully mix together fruits with celery and walnuts. Combine sour cream with honey, poppy seed and salt. Fold into fruit mixture. Place on bed of watercress and garnish with mint and walnuts if desired.

Cynthia Nanninga, Lamphere H. S.
Madison Heights, Michigan

PEAR-AVOCADO SALAD

Number of Servings — 4

1 No. 2½ can Bartlett pear halves, chilled
2 avocados, peeled and halved
Candied ginger, diced
Lettuce

For each serving arrange 2 pear halves and 1 avocado half on a lettuce leaf. Place 2 or 3 pieces of ginger in each piece of pear and avocado. Serve with Poppy Seed Dressing.

Mildred Williams, Austin H. S.
El Paso, Texas

QUICK 'N' EASY FRUIT SALAD

Number of Servings — 6

Salad greens
6 slices cantaloupe ¾" thick, peeled
Seasonal fruits: pears, cherries, melon balls, grapes, berries, etc.

For each serving place a cantaloupe slice on a bed of greens. Fill slice with seasonal fruit or top salads with a sweet fruit dressing.

Mrs. Margaret Tarsa, Weidman Community School
Weidman, Michigan

PINEAPPLE SANDWICH SALAD

Number of Servings — 4

4 t. Maraschino cherry juice
1 6-oz. pkg. cream cheese
4 t. Maraschino cherries, chopped
8 pineapple slices
Bibb lettuce
Maraschino cherry wedges

Combine cherry juice and cream cheese; blend until smooth. Add chopped cherries and mix well. For each serving place a slice of pineapple on lettuce; spread with cream cheese mixture and cover with a second slice of pineapple. Place a spoonful of the cream cheese mixture in the center of the pineapple and garnish with cherry wedges.

Mrs. Myrtle Deranger, Sunset H. S.
Sunset, Louisiana

PRONTO PINEAPPLE SALAD

Number of Servings — 8

1 c. crushed pineapple, heated
1 pkg. lime gelatin
1 c. cream, whipped or 2-oz. pkg. dessert topping mix
1 c. miniature marshmallows
1 c. cottage cheese
½ c. chopped pecans

Dissolve gelatin in heated pineapple. Cool to room temperature. Add marshmallows, cottage cheese and pecans to whipped cream. Fold cream and gelatin mixtures together. Salad may be served at once or molded for later use.

Mrs. Betty Vickers, Wapello Community School
Wapello, Iowa

QUICK PARTY SALAD

1 lge. can fruit cocktail, drained
1 small bottle Maraschino cherries, halved
2 c. miniature marshmallows
1 c. whipped cream, sweetened and flavored with Vanilla

Lightly toss all ingredients together just before serving.

Mrs. L. Iola Pennington, Wallace H. S.
Wallace, Nebraska

SPECIAL SALAD

Number of Servings — 8

1 head crisp, chilled lettuce
1 can cranberry sauce, chilled and cut in ¾" round slices
1 pkg. black walnuts, chopped
Mayonnaise to taste

Make a bed of lettuce in salad bowls. Add cranberry slices and top with mayonnaise. Sprinkle with walnuts.

Ina Hammons, Clayton H. S.
Clayton, Oklahoma

RADISH WING SALAD

Number of Servings — 6

6 pineapple slices
6 lettuce leaves
1 3-oz. pkg. cream cheese
Milk
6 radish roses
6 T. French dressing

For each serving, place a slice of pineapple in a lettuce cup. Soften cream cheese slightly with a small amount of milk; place a rounded tablespoonful of cheese in the center of each pineapple slice. Press thin sliced radish roses into the cheese to resemble wings. Place a tablespoon of dressing on each serving.

Lois Slise, Woodlin Public School
Woodrow, Colorado

STUFFED PEACH SALAD

Number of Servings — 6

6 peach halves
1 3-oz. pkg. cream cheese
¼ c. Maraschino cherries
½ c. pecans, chopped
½ c. mayonnaise
1 c. whipped cream
Red food coloring
Whole cloves

Cream the cheese with nuts and cherries. Fill the centers of each peach half with cheese mixture. Place a half peach on top of the cheese center, making a whole peach. Dilute a small bit of red coloring with water and brush over one corner of the peach to produce a blush. Stick a clove in one end for the stem.

Mrs. Willie Fay Spurlock, M. C. Napier H. S.
Hazard, Kentucky

WALDORF SALAD

Number of Servings — 6

4 medium apples, diced
¾ c. celery, chopped
⅜ to ½ c. nuts, coarsely chopped
2 to 5 T. mayonnaise or salad dressing
⅛ t. salt
½ head lettuce, chopped
Shake of nutmeg, (opt.)
Lemon juice

Sprinkle apples with lemon juice. Add celery, nuts, mayonnaise, and salt. Toss lightly. Serve on chopped lettuce.

This recipe submitted by the following teachers:

Mrs. Brenda Silva, Alvirne H. S.
Hudson, New Hampshire

Mrs. Storer De Merchant, Easton H. S.
Easton, Maine

WALDORF SALAD

Number of Servings — 10

1 c. mayonnaise
1 c. sour cream
2 T. honey
3 c. apples, diced
2 c. celery, diced
1 c. walnuts
2 c. red grapes, seeded and halved

Combine mayonnaise, sour cream and honey. Combine apples, celery, walnuts and grapes. Fold in dressing. Garnish with unpeeled apple slices. For variation ½ cup sliced dates may be used.

Mrs. Ethel Moons, Artesia H. S.
Artesia, California

FAVORITE FRUIT SALAD & DRESSING

Number of Servings — 16

1 c. watermelon balls
1 c. canteloupe balls
2 c. Mandarin oranges
2 c. pineapple tidbits
2 c. marshmallows
Almonds, chopped (opt.)

The oranges, pineapple, and marshmallows may be combined in advance, but melon balls should be added just before serving. Mix with dressing.

DRESSING:

2 eggs
2 T. sugar
¼ c. light cream
Juice of 1 lemon
1 c. whipping cream

Beat eggs until light, gradually add sugar, cream, and lemon juice. Cook in double boiler until smooth, stirring constantly. Cool, Fold in 1 cup of whipped cream.

Mrs. Ila Johnson, District #494
Elkton, Minnesota

LOW-CALORIE FRUIT SALAD

Number of Servings — 6

1 c. cantaloupe balls or cubes
½ c. orange sections, diced
2 bananas, diced
1 c. lettuce, chopped
2 T. low-calorie dressing

Chill all ingredients. Lightly toss together just before serving.

Ruth L. Auge, Belen Junior H. S.
Belen, New Mexico

FRESH FRUIT SALAD

Number of Servings — 6

½ lge. cantaloupe, cubed
1 c. fresh peaches, diced
2 or 3 plums, diced

Combine fruit and add salad dressing.

Salad Dressing:

¼ c. salad dressing
⅛ c. evaporated milk
1 T. sugar
1 t. prepared mustard

Mix sugar, mustard and salad dressing. Add enough evaporated milk to form salad dressing.

Mrs. Frances Hicks, Utopia H. S.
Utopia, Texas

PARTY RAINBOW FRUIT SALAD

Number of Servings — 10-12

2 c. fresh peaches, sliced
2 c. seedless grapes, halved
2 c. watermelon, diced
2 c. cantaloupe, diced
2 bananas
1 c. red raspberries or blueberries
Lettuce

Arrange peaches in bottom of bowl. Make a layer of grapes, a layer of watermelon and top with a cantaloupe layer. Chill. Just before serving peel and slice bananas and place on top of fruit. Pile fruit on lettuce leaf & garnish with raspberries. Serve with Lemon-Sweet Dressing.

Lemon-Sweet dressing

1 egg
2 T. sugar
¼ c. salad oil
2 T. lemon juice
¼ t. salt
¼ c. whipped cream

Beat egg slightly in top of double boiler. Stir in sugar and cook until sugar is dissolved. Remove from heat and beat until fluffy thick—slowly beat in salad oil, lemon juice, and salt. Chill. Fold in whipped cream just before serving.

Mrs. Martha Zimmerman, Taylorsville H. S.
Taylorsville, Illinois

FRESH FRUIT SALAD

Number of Servings — 6-8

3 Oranges, peeled and diced
3 Apples, diced
3 Bananas, sliced
1 small bunch seedless grapes
1 sl. watermelon, diced
3 Pears, diced
3 Peaches, peeled and diced
DRESSING:
¾ c. of salad dressing
⅛ c. of milk
1 t. of sugar

(Continued on next page)

Combine fruits. Mix dressing and fold into fruits. If the salad dressing is not desired, you may sprinkle powdered sugar over the fruit and mix. Repeat the powdered sugar about 3 times. Serve chilled.

Sylvia Schultz, Oconto Falls H. S.
Oconto Falls, Wisconsin

FRUIT SALAD

Number of Servings — 6-8

1 can concentrated orange juice
½ c. sugar
2 T. flour
¼ t. salt
1 c. whipped cream
2 medium cans pineapple tid-bits, drained
2 cans Mandarin oranges
1 c. miniature marshmallows
½ c. nuts, chopped

Combine orange juice, sugar, flour and salt. Cook in double boiler until thick. Let cool. Add whipped cream. Add remaining ingredients.

Lucie Fischer, Culver H. S.
Culver, Oregon

FRUIT SALAD SUPREME

Number of Servings — 8

2 eggs, beaten
5 T. lemon juice
5 T. sugar
2 T. butter
½ lb. marshmallows
2 c. Mandarin oranges, drained
1 c. pineapple tidbits, drained
1 c. bananas, sliced
1 c. whipped cream

Combine eggs, lemon juice, sugar and butter in top of double boiler. Beat well; stir and cook until mixture thickens. Melt marshmallows in hot mixture. Cool. Add oranges, pineapple and bananas to the custard. Fold in cream and chill.

Clara E. Dalton, Piute H. S.
Junction, Utah

MANDARIN ORANGE SALAD

Number of Servings — 8

1 8-oz. can Mandarin oranges, drained
1 13½-oz. can crushed pineapple, drained
1 8¾-oz. can seedless grapes, drained
1 8-oz. carton sour cream
10 Maraschino cherries, halved

Combine all ingredients; mix gently. Refrigerate overnight.

Janice Larson, Iron River H. S.
Iron River, Michigan

CALIFORNIA ROYALE

Number of Servings — 8

1 can Mandarin oranges, drained
1 can pineapple tidbits, drained
1 c. white seedless grapes
½ c. walnuts, chopped
2 c. miniature marshmallows
¼ c. Maraschino cherries, chopped
½ c. coconut, shredded
4 fresh peaches, sliced
3 bananas, sliced
1 pt. dairy sour cream

Combine first 7 ingredients; cover with sour cream. Refrigerate for at least 4-6 hours. Just before serving add bananas and peaches. Chopped cantaloupe may be substituted for peaches if desired.

Betty Ann Augustad, Orland
Madison, South Dakota

EASY FRUIT SALAD

Number of Servings — 6-8

1 can instant peach pie filling
1 can fruit cocktail, drained
1 can pineapple tidbits, drained
1 can Mandarin oranges, drained
1 c. apples, chopped (opt.)
1 can grapes, drained
1 c. miniature marshmallows
1 banana, sliced
1 c. nuts, chopped

Combine pie filling, fruit cocktail. pineapple, oranges, apples and grapes. Add marshmallows, banana and nuts. Refrigerate several hours before serving.

This recipe submitted by the following teachers:

Mrs. Steve Nickisch, Napoleon Public School
Napoleon, North Dakota

Mrs. Jane Pilcher Wirth, South Lyon H. S.
South Lyon, Michigan

"MAKE-AHEAD" FRUIT SALAD

Number of Servings — 6

1 1-lb. 13-oz. can peach slices, drained
1 c. miniature marshmallows
½ c. Maraschino cherries
1 lge. banana, sliced
¼ c. nuts, chopped
½ c. whipped cream
⅓ c. salad dressing
1 T. lemon juice

Combine peach slices, marshmallows, cherries, banana and nuts. Mix whipped cream, salad dressing and lemon juice together; add to fruit mixture. Chill for a few hours before serving.

Mrs. Louise McKamey, Belfast H. S.
Hillsboro, Ohio

FRESH PEAR SALAD AND DRESSING

Number of Servings — 4

Dressing:
2 T. flour
½ c. sugar
2 T. lemon juice

Mix all ingredients; cook over low heat until flour is cooked and clear. Cool.

2 c. fresh pears, diced or sliced
1 c. celery, diced
⅓ c. pecans
Salad greens
Maraschino cherries

Mix the celery and pears in the dressing; add nuts. Serve on salad greens. Garnish with cherries.

Mrs. Margaret Thornton, Thorndale H. S.
Thorndale, Texas

PINEAPPLE-BANANA SALAD

Number of Servings — 10

1 egg, beaten
⅓ c. sugar
1 T. flour
Pineapple juice
1 8-oz. pkg. marshmallows, quartered
3 bananas, sliced
1 can pineapple tidbits drained
1 c. whipped cream or 1 c. canned milk, whipped

Mix egg, sugar, flour and pineapple juice together, cook until it boils; stirring constantly—let cool. Add marshmallows, pineapple, bananas and whipped cream or milk. Serve immediately or chill for 24 hours.

Mrs. Edna Coleman, Holton H. S.
Holton, Kansas

PINEAPPLE-BANANA SALAD

1 lge. can pineapple, drained
1 c. pineapple juice
1 c. sugar
2 T. vinegar or lemon juice
4 bananas
12 marshmallows
2 eggs, beaten

Cook pineapple juice, sugar, flour and vinegar or lemon juice until thick. Remove from heat. Pour small amount of hot mixture slowly into eggs; stir constantly. Pour egg mixture into remaining hot mixture; cook for 2 minutes. Cool. Add pineapple, marshmallows and bananas.

Mrs. Judy Herbig, Timber Township H. S.
Glasford, Illinois

CREAM CHEESE-FRUIT SALAD

Number of Servings — 10

1 8-oz. jar Maraschino cherries
1 4-oz. Box Dream Whip
1 No. 2 can crushed pineapple
1 c. miniature marshmallows
1 8-oz. pkg. cream cheese
½ c. nut meats (opt.)

Let cream cheese reach room temperature. Add all remaining ingredients except dessert topping mix to the cream cheese; blend on low speed. When well blended fold in dessert topping mix prepared according to directions on the package.

Mrs. Helen Mason, Stilesville H. S.
Stilesville, Indiana

FRUIT COCKTAIL SALAD

Number of Servings — 12-15

2 c. fruit cocktail, drained
1½ c. chunk pineapple, drained
4 to 5 oz. cream cheese, softened
3 c. miniature marshmallows
Cream
Coconut, nuts or cherries (opt.)

Thin cheese with a small amount of cream. Add remaining ingredients. Chill until firm.

Mrs. Marlene Priebe, Valier H. S.
Valier, Montana

FRUIT SALAD

Number of Servings — 10

2 No. 2 cans pineapple, drained
½ lb. American cheese, cubed
1¼ c. pecans, chopped
1½ c. miniature marshmallows
2 T. flour
2 T. sugar
1 egg, beaten
1¼ pineapple juice

Combine pineapple, cheese, pecans and marshmallows. Combine remaining ingredients; cook in a saucepan, stirring constantly until thick. Cool. Pour over fruit-cheese mixture. Toss lightly.

Mrs. Naomi F. Stock, Lakota H. S.
West Chester, Ohio

PINEAPPLE & TOMATO CUBE SALAD

Lettuce
Pineapple rings
Tomato, cubed
Parsley

For each serving, make a bed of lettuce. Add a small amount of shredded lettuce and a pineapple ring. Arrange tomato cubes over pineapple. Garnish with parsley. Serve with Honey French Dressing.

Melba Dansie Stoffers, Hermiston Senior H. S.
Hermiston, Oregon

FRENCH PINEAPPLE SALAD

Number of Servings — 6-8

1 lge. pineapple
1 lge. orange, sectioned and peeled
2 peaches, sliced
1 banana, slant sliced
1 apple, sliced
1 pt. strawberries, hulled and sweetened
1 c. pecan halves

Cut pineapple in half lengthwise, remove fruit and cut into cubes. Dust cubes lightly with sugar. Combine all ingredients. Chill for 30 minutes. Lightly pile fruit mixture into pineapple shells.

Mrs. Marvel E. Wax, Bel Air H. S.
El Paso, Texas

FRUIT PLATE AND DRESSING

Number of Servings — 10

Pear halves
Peach halves
Cantaloupe slices
Pineapple rings
Bananas

Arrange fruits on platter. Pour dressing over all fruit.

Dressing:
2 eggs
3 T. sugar
1 T. cream
3 t. dry mustard
½ t. salt
3 T. lemon juice
1 pt. whipped cream;
1 c. marshmallows, diced
1 c. pecans, chopped

Combine eggs, sugar, cream, mustard, salt and lemon juice. Cook in double boiler until thick. Cool. Fold in remaining ingredients.

Mrs. Frances Morton, Tallulah H. S.
Tallulah, Louisiana

FRUIT SALAD

1 c. Maraschino cherries, drained
2 c. crushed pineapple, drained
2 c. Mandarin oranges, drained
1 c. miniature marshmallows
3 egg yolks
2 T. sugar
2 T. vinegar
2 T. pineapple juice
1 T. Butter
⅛ t. salt
1 c. whipped cream

Mix cherries, pineapple, oranges and marshmallows together. Combine all remaining ingredients except whipped cream. Cook until thickened. Let cool. Fold in whipped cream. Add fruit mixture. Let stand for 24 hours.

Mrs. Evelyn Piper, Minnenaukan, H. S.
Minnenaukan, North Dakota

CRACKER SALAD

Number of Servings — 12

¾ c. water
4 t. apple cider vinegar
7 saltine crackers
18 marshmallows
1 c. crushed pineapple
½ c. pecans, chopped
3 bananas, diced
1 c. whipped cream

Bring water, vinegar and crackers to a boil. Add marshmallows and stir until melted. Cool. Add pineapple, pecans and bananas. Chill. Fold in whipped cream and refrigerate several hours or overnight.

Mrs. Frances Alsup, Kopperl H. S.
Kopperl, Texas

HEAVENLY HASH SALAD

Number of Servings — 6-8

1 c. crushed pineapple, drained
1 small bottle cherries, drained and chopped
½ pkg. miniature marshmallows
1 c. hoop cheese, grated
1 c. whipped cream
½ c. mayonnaise
1 T. sugar

Combine cherries, pineapple, marshmallows and cheese. Combine cream and sugar; add mayonnaise. Fold into fruit-cheese mixture. Chill 2 or 3 hours.

Mrs. Mary C. Harbour, Philadelphia H. S.
Philadelphia, Mississippi

MILLIONAIRE SALAD

Number of Servings — 12

1 lge. can pineapple, drained and cut
1 lge. can Queen Anne cherries, drained
1 lb. marshmallows, cut
1 lb. blanched almonds, slivered
1 pt. whipped cream
5 T. lemon juice
2 T. sugar
3 egg yolks
1 heaping T. cornstarch
1½ t. salt
Juice from pineapple

Combine lemon juice, sugar, egg yolks, cornstarch, salt and pineapple juice. Cook in double boiler until very thick. Add remaining ingredients, folding in whipped cream last. Chill overnight. Stir once or twice.

Ola Mae Hawkins, Santa Fe H. S.
Alta Loma, Texas

MILLION DOLLAR FRUIT SALAD

Number of Servings — 12

1 No. 2 can white cherries, diced
½ lb. marshmallows, diced
1 No. 2 can pineapple chunks, diced
6 bananas, diced
4 egg yolks, slightly beaten
½ c. sugar
Juice of 1 lemon
1 t. cornstarch
½ c. milk
½ pt. whipped cream

Combine egg yolks, sugar, lemon juice, cornstarch and milk. Blend. Cook slowly in double boiler until thick, cool. Add whipped cream. Mix in fruit. Chill.

Norma Womble, Broadway School
Broadway, North Carolina

MANHATTAN SALAD

Number of Servings — 14

1 c. pineapple chunks, drained
¼ lb. blanched almonds
1 pt. sweet cream, whipped
½ lb. marshmallows, cut
3 eggs
1 T. sugar
2 T. milk
3½ T. vinegar
1 t. salt

Cook eggs, sugar, milk, vinegar and salt in double boiler. Stir constantly until thick. Put pineapple over marshmallows. Add egg mixture and almonds. Mix. Fold in whipped cream.

Willie M. Trotter, Batesburg Leesville H. S.
Batesburg, South Carolina

PINEAPPLE SALAD

Number of Servings — 14

6 T. sugar
2½ T. cornstarch
¼ t. salt
2 eggs, beaten
2 No. 2 cans pineapple tid-bits, drained and diced
Juice from 1 can pineapple
1 10½-oz. pkg. miniature marshmallows
¼ c. nuts, chopped

Mix sugar, cornstarch and salt; add eggs. Beat. Add pineapple juice. Cook until thick, stirring constantly. Remove from heat. Cool. Pour dressing over pineapple. Add marshmallows; stir. Just before serving add nuts.

Mrs. Berneta B. Hackney, McGuffey McDonald
McGuffey, Ohio

PINEAPPLE SALAD

Number of Servings — 6

1 No. 2½ can chunked pineapple, drained
1 c. nuts
½ c. marshmallows
1 c. whipped cream
Juice from pineapple
½ c. milk
1 egg, beaten
1 T. cornstarch

Mix fruit, nuts and marshmallows. Mix all remaining ingredients except cream. Cook until thick. Cool. Add whipped cream. Pour dressing over fruit; toss lightly.

Mrs. Janice Howell, New Riegel
New Riegel, Ohio

PINEAPPLE SALAD

Number of Servings — 8

1 can pineapple chunks, drained
1 pkg. miniature marshmallows
½ c. sugar
1 T. flour
1 c. pineapple juice
1 egg, well beaten

Mix pineapple juice, sugar, flour and egg together. Cook until mixture thickens, stirring constantly. Cool. Add pineapple and marshmallows.

Mary Lumsden, New Holland-Middletown H. S.
New Holland, Illinois

PINEAPPLE SALAD

Number of Servings — 10-12

2 No. 211 cans pineapple tidbits, drained
10 medium sized apples, peeled and cubed
1 10½-oz. bag miniature marshmallows
1 c. whipped cream
2 egg yolks
¼ t. salt
2 T. flour
¼ c. sugar
1 c. cold water
1 T. vinegar
Juice of 1 lemon
2 T. butter

Combine egg yolks, salt, flour, sugar, water, vinegar, lemon juice and butter. Cook until thickened, stirring constantly. Cool. Add pineapple, apples and marshmallows. Fold in whipped cream.

Mrs. Margery Might, Columbia City Joint H. S.
Columbia City, Indiana

PINEAPPLE SALAD

Number of Servings — 8-10

3 c. pineapple, drained, cut in wedges
1 c. nuts
½ lb. miniature marshmallows
2 T. cornstarch
2 eggs, well beaten
1 c. pineapple juice
1 c. sugar
Juice of 2 lemons

Mix cornstarch, eggs, pineapple juice and sugar together. Cook until thick. Add lemon juice. Cool. Add remaining ingredients.

Elizabeth L. Fox, Gustine ISD
Gustine, Texas

HEAVENLY PINEAPPLE SALAD

Number of Servings — 8

22 lge. marshmallows
1 small crushed pineapple
1 small can evaporated milk, chilled and whipped

Heat marshmallows and pineapple in double boiler. Let cool. Fold in whipped milk. Chill.

Addie Huckabay, Bolton H. S.
Alexandria, Louisiana

REFRIGERATOR FRUIT SALAD

Number of Servings — 10-12

3 egg yolks
3 T. sugar
2 T. vinegar
3 T. pineapple juice or syrup
2 T. butter
Dash of salt
2 c. canned white cherries, drained
2 c. canned pineapple bits drained
2 oranges, peeled and diced
1 c. strawberries
1½ c. whipped cream,
30 marshmallows, quartered
½ c. blanched almonds

Cook egg yolk, sugar, vinegar, pineapple juice, butter and salt on low heat until thick; stir constantly. Cool. Combine fruits; fold in marshmallows and egg yolk mixture. Fold in whipped cream. Sprinkle the top with almonds. Chill for 12 hours.

Veau Dell F. Prochazka, Atwood Community H.S.
Atwood, Kansas

PINEAPPLE SALAD

Number of Servings — 6

2 c. chunk pineapple, drained
1 c. white grapes
1½ c. marshmallows
½ c. sugar
2 T. cornstarch
2 egg yolks, beaten
2 egg whites, beaten
1 T. vinegar
1 T. butter
Pineapple juice

Mix together sugar, cornstarch, egg yolks, vinegar and butter. Add pineapple juice; cook until thick. Pour juice mixture over fruits. Chill. Add marshmallows and egg whites. Mix gently.

Mrs. Charles Mary Reece,
Warsaw Community H.S.
Warsaw, Indiana

PINEAPPLE SALAD

Number of Servings — 10

1 lge. can pineapple chunks, drained
½ pkg. marshmallows
2 eggs, beaten
2 T. cornstarch
5 T. sugar
1 T. butter
1 pt. whipped cream
Nuts (opt.)
Pineapple juice

Moisten cornstarch with pineapple juice, add sugar, eggs, and butter; cook until thick and cornstarch is thoroughly cooked. Cool. Add pineapple, marshmallows, whipped cream and nuts. Chill.

Mrs. Fern Todd, Bloomington Community School
Bloomington, Wisconsin

PINEAPPLE-CHEESE SALAD

Number of Servings — 8

1 No. 2 can pineapple tid-bits, drained
4 lge. bananas, diced
¾ lge. pkg. cream cheese, softened
1 T. sugar
2 T. pineapple juice
1 c. pecans, chopped
1 c. miniature marshmallows

Combine cream cheese and pineapple juice. Whip until mixture reaches the consistency of whipped cream. Add sugar. Add remaining ingredients. Chill for 2 or 3 hours.

Kathryn Hill, Comanche H. S.
Comanche, Texas

Party & Desserts Salads

MOLDED AMBROSIA SALAD

Number of Servings — 8

1 c. crushed pineapple
1 c. sugar
Juice of 1 lemon
1 pkg. lemon gelatin
1¾ c. boiling water
½ c. American cheese, shredded
1 c. whipped cream

Boil pineapple, sugar and lemon juice for 3 minutes. Dissolve gelatin in boiling water. Combine gelatin and boiled mixture. Cool until partially set. Fold whipped cream and cheese into gelatin mixture. Refrigerate until firm.

Mrs. Caroline E. Duffy, Turlock H. S.
Turlock, California

CONGEALED FRUIT AMBROSIA SALAD

Number of Servings — 6-8

1 pkg. lemon gelatin
2 c. hot water
3 c. orange sections, diced
1 c. coconut, flaked

Dissolve gelatin in hot water, add orange sections and coconut. Pour into individual molds. Chill. Serve with cooked dressing.

COOKED DRESSING:

2 eggs
Juice of 1 lemon
2 T. honey
1 c. whipped cream
2 T. candied ginger, chopped

Beat eggs until creamy. Add lemon juice and honey. Cook until thick. Cool. Fold in whipped cream and ginger.

Mrs. D. L. Hamilton, Michie H. S.
Selmer, Tennessee

JELLIED AMBROSIA SALAD

Number of Servings — 4-6

1 envelope plain gelatin
¼ c. cold water
¼ c. boiling water
2 T. sugar
1¼ c. orange juice
2 T. lemon juice
3 medium oranges, peeled and sectioned
1 lge. banana, peeled and sliced
¼ c. coconut, grated or shredded

Soften gelatin in cold water. Dissolve in boiling water. Add sugar; stir over low heat until completely dissolved. Add orange and lemon juice. Cool until thickened. Add fruit and coconut to orange juice mixture. Pour into molds; chill until firm. Garnish with orange sections, a sprinkle of coconut and sprigs of fresh mint.

Mrs. Avalene Swanson, St. Croix Central H. S.
Hammond, Wisconsin

MOLDED AMBROSIA

Number of Servings — 8

1 8-oz. can crushed pineapple, drained
1 pkg. orange gelatin
1 c. hot water
1 c. dairy sour cream
1 c. diced orange or Mandarin orange sections
½ c. coconut, flaked

Dissolve gelatin in hot water and stir in syrup. Chill until partially set. Add sour cream; whip until fluffy. Fold in pineapple, oranges and coconut. Pour into molds; chill.

Margaret Ann Ramsdale, Hutchinson Senior H. S.
Hutchinson, Kansas

HAWAIIAN DELIGHT

Number of Servings — 8

1 pkg. orange gelatin
¾ c. hot water
1 small can frozen orange juice concentrate
1 box Dream Whip
1 can Mandarin oranges, halved
1 small can crushed pineapple, undrained
½ c. miniature marshmallows
1 box coconut

Dissolve gelatin in hot water. Add frozen concentrate. Let stand until partially set. Prepare Dream Whip according to package directions. Fold into partially set gelatin. Add oranges, marshmallows and half of the coconut. Chill. Sprinkle remaining coconut on top of firm mixture.

Mrs. Doris Slack, White Pigeon H. S.
White Pigeon, Michigan

POLLY'S PARTY SALAD

Number of Servings — 12

2½ c. miniature marshmallows
1 c. milk or starlac if desired
1 pkg. lime gelatin
1 6-oz. pkg. cream cheese
1 No. 2 can crushed pineapple
1 can coconut, flaked
2 c. Dream Whip or 1 c. whipped cream

Combine marshmallows and milk in top of double boiler or in heavy pan over low heat and melt. Add jello and blend with rotary egg beater or mixer. Add cheese and blend same way. Fold in pineapple and coconut. Cool. Fold in dream whip or whipped cream—pour into pan and chill until firm. (I use pan 11 x 7). Can be used as dessert also. Keeps indefinitely so can be made in advance for parties or school affairs or large functions.

Mrs. Pauline G. Adkins, Sandy Hook, FWA Adviser
Sandy Hook, Kentucky

ORANGE GELATIN PARTY DESSERT

Number of Servings — 8-10

1 c. chunk pineapple, well drained
2 cans Mandarin orange slices, well drained
1 c. flaked coconut
1 c. sour cream
1 pkg. miniature marshmallows
½ c. nuts, chopped
1 pkg. of orange gelatin

Mix all ingredients except gelatin; chill overnight. Prepare gelatin according to package directions. Chill until firm. Top firm gelatin with chilled fruit mixture.

Cassandra Coker, Union Park Jr. H. S.
Orlando, Florida

FRUIT AMBROSIA SALAD

Number of Servings — 8-10

1 c. coconut, flaked
1 c. miniature marshmallows
1 c. Mandarin oranges, drained
1 8-oz. can pineapple tid bits, drained
1 c. seedless green grapes
1 c. sour cream

Combine all ingredients. Chill several hours, Serve on bibb lettuce.

Margaret Stampfly, Okemos H. S.
Okemos, Michigan

AMBROSIA SALAD IN ORANGE CUPS

Number of Servings — 6

6 oranges
1 lb. seedless grapes
1 small can grated coconut
½ c. whipping cream
3 T. sugar
2 T. lemon juice
2 T. grated orange rind
Nutmeg
6 Maraschino cherries

Remove a ½-inch slice from top of each orange. Remove pulp from oranges. Refrigerate orange cups. Remove seed and membranes from orange pulp. Add grated orange rind to whipping cream; chill. Whip cream until it forms soft mounds; add lemon juice and sugar. Fold in orange pulp, grapes and coconut. Spoon into orange cups. Garnish each with nutmeg and a cherry.

Mrs. Ernestine A. McLeod, Wickes H. S.
Wickes, Arkansas

CHEESE-MANDARIN SALAD

Number of Servings — 6-8

1 8-oz. carton small curd cottage cheese
1 8-oz. carton sour cream
1 11-oz. can Mandarin oranges, drained and coarsely chopped
1 7-oz. pkg. flaked coconut

Combine cottage cheese and sour cream. Fold in coconut and orange segments.

Mrs. Madge Addington, Altoona Rural H. S.
Altoona, Kansas

COCONUT-FRUIT BOWL

Number of Servings — 8

1 No. 2 can pineapple tidbits, drained
1 11-oz. can Mandarin oranges, drained
1 c. Thompson seedless grapes
1 c. miniature marshmallows
1 3½-oz. can flaked coconut
2 c. sour cream
¼ t. salt

Combine fruits, marshmallows and coconut. Stir in sour cream and salt. Chill overnight.

Mrs. Glenodine E. Holman, Lamesa H. S.
Lamesa, Texas

COTTAGE CHEESE AMBROSIA SALAD

Number of Servings — 10

1 No. 303 Can fruit cocktail, drained
1 No. 303 can pineapple tidbits, drained
1 c. miniature marshmallows
1 c. coconut
1 8-oz. carton small curd cottage cheese
1 c. sour cream
2 T. sugar

Mix cottage cheese, cream and sugar. Add pineapple, fruit cocktail, marshmallows, and coconut. Mix well and refrigerate for several hours or overnight.

Sandra Stinebring, Cissna Park H. S.
Cissna Park, Illinois

FRUIT SALAD

Number of Servings — 8-10

1 c. Mandarin orange sections, drained
1-2 c. pineapple chunks, drained
½ c. Maraschino cherries, drained (opt.)
1 c. Nuts (opt.)
1 c. miniature marshmallows
1 c. coconut, shredded
1 c. sour cream

Mix all ingredients together. Chill for several hours.

This recipe submitted by the following teachers:

Virginia Bert, Havana H. S.
Havana, Florida

Mary Ella Porter, Como H. S.
Como, Texas

Joyce Thorson, Shiocton H. S.
Shiocton, Wisconsin

Betty MacSpadden, Salinas H. S.
Salinas, California

Mrs. Jane Morris, Hardin Jefferson
Sour Lake, Texas

Mrs. Patsy Evans, Bridge City H. S.
Bridge City, Texas

Mrs. Nell Albrecht, Blum H. S.
Blum, Texas

Mrs. Kathryn J. Lumpkin, Randolph County H. S.
Wedowee, Alabama

Mary Carlyn Mitchell, Pelican Rapids, Public H. S.
Pelican Rapids, Minnesota

FIVE CUP SALAD

Number of Servings — 6-8

1 c. pineapple tidbits, well drained
1 c. flaked coconut
1 c. Mandarin orange slices, well drained
1 c. miniature marshmallows
1 c. commercial sour cream
½-1 c. pecans, chopped (opt.)
Maraschino cherries garnish

Mix all ingredients. Chill several hours or overnight. Garnish with cherries.

The teachers who submitted this recipe can be found on page 378.

FIVE CUP SALAD

Number of Servings — 8

1 c. pineapple chunks, drained
1 c. orange segments, drained
1 c. miniature marshmallows
1 c. coconut
1 c. whipped cream

Mix ingredients. Chill several hours.

This recipe submitted by the following teachers:

Mrs. Donald Struebing, David City Public Schools
David City, Nebraska

Mrs. Marshall S. Neff, Cairo H. S.
Cairo, Georgia

HAWAIIAN SALAD

Number of Servings — 6

1 c. pineapple tidbits, drained and chilled
1 c. miniature marshmallows
1 c. sour cream
1 c. Mandarin oranges, drained and chilled
1 c. angel flake coconut

Combine fruits. Add marshmallows and coconut. Fold in sour cream. Serve on crisp lettuce leaf. Top with Maraschino cherry.

Augusta M. Appenfelder, Scottsdale H. S.
Scottsdale, Arizona

HAWAIIAN FRUIT SALAD

Number of Servings — 8-10

1 c. fresh pineapple, cubed or canned pineapple chunks
1 c. white seedless grapes
1 c. cantaloupe or papaya, cubed
1 c. fresh shredded coconut or angel flake coconut
½ c. whipped cream or Dream Whip

Combine pineapple, grapes, cantaloupe and coconut. Toss lightly with cream or Dream Whip.

Mrs. Daisy Massey, Fredericksburg H. S.
Fredericksburg, Texas

HOMEWOOD FARM SOUR CREAM SALAD

Number of Servings — 6-8

1 c. pineapple chunks, drained
1 c. Mandarin orange slices, drained
1 c. small marshmallows
1 c. flaked coconut
1 c. sour cream
1 c. bananas, cubed (opt.)

Combine all ingredients. Chill for 24 hours.

This recipe submitted by the following teachers:

Dixie Giannini, Caldwell Co. High
Washington & Plumb
Princeton, Kentucky

Leona V. Jenson, Amphitheater H. S.
Tucson, Arizona

Edna Belling, Edgeley H. S.
Edgeley, North Dakota

Nona L. Dutson, Marsh Valley H. S.
Arimo, Idaho

Edith Stanley, Plateau School
District RE-5
Peetz, Colorado

MANDARIN ORANGE SALAD

Number of Servings — 6

1½-2 c. crushed or chunk pineapple
1 can Mandarin orange sections
2 c. miniature marshmallows
1 c. flaked coconut
1 small carton sour cream
⅓ c. nuts (opt.)

Mix ingredients well. Chill for several hours or overnight.

This recipe submitted by the following teachers:

Mrs. Doris Sutton, Delavan-Darien H. S.
Delavan, Wisconsin

Elizabeth Shirley, Chilton H. S.
Chilton, Texas

Mrs. Alma Points, Altoona H. S.
Altoona, Pennsylvania

MARSHMALLOW SURPRISE

Number of Servings — 8

1 pkg. miniature marshmallows, drained
1 can Mandarin oranges, drained
1 No. 303 can chunk pineapple
1 c. sour cream
1 c. coconut (opt.)

Combine all ingredients; chill for 24 hours before serving.

This recipe submitted by the following teachers:

Mrs. Shirlee J. Hora, Germantown H. S.
Germantown, Ohio

Violett Cheek, Henderson Settlement
Frakes, Kentucky

MARSHMALLOW DREAM

Number of Servings — 6

1 pkg. salad style marshmallows
1 c. Mandarin oranges
½ pt. sour cream
1 c. shredded coconut (opt.)

Combine marshmallows, oranges and sour cream. Refrigerate for at least 3 hours before serving. Can be molded.

Joan Brown, Farwell Area School
Farwell, Michigan

SOUR CREAM AMBROSIA

Number of Servings — 6-8

1 11-oz. can Mandarin oranges, drained
1 No. 2 can pineapple tidbits, drained
1½ c. miniature marshmallows
1 c. flaked coconut
1 c. dairy sour cream
3 bananas (opt.)

Blend oranges, pineapple, coconut and marshmallows with sour cream. Chill several hours. Add bananas if desired just before serving.

This recipe submitted by the following teachers:

Mrs. Anna Lee Morris, Paul G. Blazer H. S.
Ashland, Kentucky

Barbara Coddington, Dinuba H. S.
Dinuba, California

Mrs. Marguerite Cleveland, Coral Gables H. S.
Coral Gables, Florida

ONE-CUP FRUIT SALAD

Number of Servings — 10

1 c. crushed pineapple, drained
1 c. miniature marshmallows
1 c. flaked coconut
1 c. Mandarin oranges sections, drained
1 c. seedless or seeded grapes, chopped
1 c. sour cream
Few Maraschino cherries

Mix all ingredients together. Mold and refrigerate for 24 hours. Keeps well. Other fresh or well drained canned fruits may be added or substituted.

This recipe submitted by the following teachers:

Lucile Haney, Geddes H. S.
Geddes, South Dakota

Jean Mullen, Camp Lejeune H. S.
Camp Lejeune, North Carolina

SIX-CUP SALAD

Number of Servings — 10

1 c. cottage cheese
1 c. miniature marshmallows
1 c. coconut
1 c. fruit cocktail, drained
1 c. sour cream
1 c. chunk pineapple, drained

Combine all ingredients. Chill thoroughly.

Goldie Farmer, Mt. Carmel H. S.
Mt. Carmel, Illinois

SEVEN-CUP FRUIT SALAD

Number of Servings — 8

1 c. pineapple tidbits or chunks
1 c. Mandarin oranges
1 c. cantaloupe balls
1 c. watermelon balls
1 c. seedless grapes
1 c. coconut
1 c. miniature marshmallows
1 c. commercial sour cream

Drain fruit thoroughly; add cream, mix well. Let stand 24 hours. More cream may be added if desired.

Doreen Nielsen, Murray H. S.
Murray, Utah

QUICK FRUIT SALAD

Number of Servings — 8

1 c. Mandarin oranges, drained
1 c. pineapple tidbits, drained
1 c. seedless grapes
1 c. miniature marshmallows
1 c. coconut, flaked
½ c. mayonnaise
½ c. sour cream
Few drops food coloring (opt.)

Blend sour cream and mayonnaise until smooth; add food coloring if desired. Stir in coconut. Put aside. Combine fruits and marshmallows. Fold into sour cream mixture. Pour into mold. This is best if allowed to set overnight, however it may be used immediately.

Mrs. Richard Hurd, Lake Benton H. S.
Lake Benton, Minnesota

MILLIONAIRE FRUIT DELIGHT

Number of Servings — 10

1 c. Mandarin oranges, drained
1 c. coconut
1 c. miniature marshmallows
1 c. pineapple tidbits, drained
1 c. white grapes
1 T. sugar
½ c. sour cream
½ c. nuts (opt.)

Mix sugar and sour cream together. Add remaining ingredients. Chill before serving weight watchers: substitute ½ cup cottage cheese and 1 tablespoon skimmed milk for the sour cream and sugar.

This recipe submitted by the following teachers:

Aleen Hartman, Manderson-Hyattville H. S.
Manderson, Wyoming

Mrs. Zara Lee M. Baker, Plain Dealing H. S.
Plain Dealing, Louisiana

ORIENTAL DELIGHT

Number of Servings — 8

1-2 cans Mandarin oranges, drained
1 c. coconut, flaked
1 c. sour cream
1-2 c. crushed pineapple, drained
1 c. miniature marshmallows

Mix sour cream, fruits and coconut. Add marshmallows last. Toss salad until thoroughly mixed. Chill in covered glass bowl before serving.

This recipe submitted by the following teachers:

Mrs. Sue Warren, Terrell Wells Jr. H. S.
San Antonio, Texas

Mrs. Tom Hamilton, North Jr. H. S.
Waco, Texas

TROPICAL SALAD

Number of Servnigs — 8-10

2 c. pineapple tidbits, drained
2 c. diced orange sections, diced
2 c. coconut, freshly grated or flaked
2 c. miniature marshmallows
½ c. sugar
1 pt. sour cream
20 grapes, seeded and halved (opt.)

Toss together first four ingredients. Sprinkle sugar over top and lightly mix. Add sour cream and stir just enough to mix well, serve.

Niva J. Reddick, Dept. Chairman Largo, Sr. H. S.
Largo, Florida

FROSTED APRICOT SALAD

Number of Servings — 12

2 T. unflavored gelatin
1 c. cold water
1 c. sugar
Juice of 2 lemons (opt.)
1 No. 2½ can apricots, drained
1 c. whipped cream
1 small pkg. cream cheese
Pinch of salt

Soften gelatin in ½ c. water. Combine remaining water, sugar and syrup drained from apricots; bring to a boil. Add to softened gelatin. Set aside cup of the mixture to congeal slightly. Strain apricots into the remaining gelatin mixture; pour into 8x10 pan. Refrigerate until firm. Combine whipped cream, cheese and salt. Fold in the cup of slightly congealed gelatin and pour over the firm apricot layer. Serve with argyle dressing.

This recipe submitted by the following teachers:

Mrs. Darryl Emert, Sabetha Rural H. S.
Sabetha, Kansas

Hazel S. Wilkinson, Carroll H. S.
Ozark, Alabama

APRICOT-CHEESE DELIGHT

Number of Servings — 20-24

2 pkgs. orange gelatin
2 c. boiling water
½ c. pineapple juice
½ c. apricot juice
1 No. 2½ can apricots, diced or mashed
1 No. 2 can crushed pineapple
½ pkg. miniature marshmallows

Dissolve gelatin in boiling water. Add juices and fruit. Pour into 9 x 13 dish. Top with marshmallows. Congeal.

TOPPING:

½ c. sugar
2-3 T. flour
½ c. apricot juice
½ c. pineapple juice
1 egg, well beaten
2 T. butter
1 c. whipped cream or Dream Whip
Grated cheese (opt.)

Cook sugar, flour, egg and juice in double boiler until thick. Add butter. Cool. Add whipped cream. Spread over top of gelatin. Top with grated cheese and chill. Whipped cream may be seasoned and kept separate for a garnish.

This recipe submitted by the following teachers:

Estelle J. Garrison, Fayette County H. S.
Fayette, Alabama

Nellie McClure, Damascus Twp.
McClure, Ohio

Marjorie Scott, Bethany H. S.
Bethany, Illinois

Ruth G. Schmotter, Crooksville H. S.
Crooksville, Ohio

Ghlee Kershner, Montpelier Community
Montpelier, Indiana

Mrs. Dale Taylor, Warren H. S.
Warren, Arkansas

Delores Neiwert, Tekoa H. S.
Tekoa, Washington

Mrs. J. C. Embry, Forestburg H. S.
Forestburg, Texas

BING CHERRY FLING

Number of Servings — 6

1 can Bing cherries, drained
1 pkg. cherry gelatin
1 3-oz. pkg. cream cheese
½ c. pecans, coarsely broken
½ t. lemon juice
2 T. sugar

Prepare gelatin according to directions on package, using all but 3 tablespoons of juice drained from cherries as part of the liquid. Add cherries. Pour into salad mold. Chill until set. Add reserved cherry juice, lemon juice and sugar to the cream cheese; beat until smooth. Add nuts and blend. Spread over firm gelatin. Chill. Cover mold while in refrigerator to prevent drying. When ready to serve, invert mold.

Alice Hawley, Tuslaw H. S.
Massillon, Ohio

BING CHERRY SALAD

Number of Servings — 12

1 No. 2 can crushed pineapple, drained
1 No. 2 can Bing cherries, drained
2 pkg. cherry gelatin

Dissolve gelatin according to package directions; cool. Add fruit. Chill until firm.

Dressing:

2 egg yolks, beaten
1 T. water
3 T. sugar
3 T. vinegar
½ t. salt
½ pkg. miniature marshmallows
1 c. whipped cream

Cook egg yolks, water, sugar, vinegar and salt until thick. Add marshmallows. Stir until dissolved. Cool; add cream. Spread on firm gelatin. Chill.

Mary E. Myers, Barry Community Unit
Barry, Illinois

CHERRY-COKE SALAD

Number of Servings — 8-10

1 No. 2 can crushed pineapple, drained
1 can sweet black cherries, drained
2 pkg. cherry gelatin
2 c. cherry-pineapple juice and water
1 c. nuts, chopped
2 6-oz. bottles Coca-Cola
2 3-oz. pkg. cream cheese, softened

Bring juice to a boil; add to gelatin. Stir until dissolved. Cool. Add Coca-Cola to cooled gelatin. Chill until slightly thickened. Add drained pineapple, cherries and ¾ cup of nuts. Pour into a ring mold or an 8 x 8 x 2 pan. Chill until firm. Spread cream cheese on top of firm gelatin. Sprinkle with remaining nuts.

Mrs. Hazel Hasty, Urbana Senior H. S.
Urbana, Illinois

CRANBERRY-GELATIN SALAD

Number of Servings — 6-8

½ pt. sour cream
3 c. water
1 can whole cranberry sauce
2 pkg. cherry or raspberry gelatin

Dissolve gelatin in water. Let set until partially congealed. Spread cranberries evenly over the bottom of pan or molds. Pour gelatin slowly over cranberries, without moving berries. Chill until firm. Spread sour cream as evenly as possible over top. Chill.

Louise Hall, Amador County H. S.
Sutter Creek, California

FROSTED CONGEALED SALAD

Number of Servings — 12

2 pkgs. lemon gelatin
2 c. boiling water
2 c. Upper-10 or 7-Up
1 No. 2 can crushed or chunk pineapple, drained
2-4 medium bananas, sliced
½ c. miniature marshmallows

Dissolve gelatin in boiling water; dilute with Upper-10. Chill. Combine bananas, pineapple and marshmallows. Stir mixture into gelatin. Chill until firm.

TOPPING:

½ c. sugar
2 T. flour
1-2 T. butter (opt.)
1 c. whipped cream
¼ c. American cheese, shredded (opt.)
2-3 T. Parmesan cheese (opt.)
1 c. pineapple juice
1 egg, slightly beaten

Cook pineapple juice, egg, flour, butter and sugar until sauce is thick. Cool. Fold sauce into whipped cream. Frost salad. Sprinkle with cheeses. Salad will seep 3 to 4 days.

This recipe submitted by the following teachers:

Mrs. Louise Howard, Bradford H. S.
Bradford, Ohio
Marlys Wilmer, Henning H. S.
Henning, Minnesota
Florence Warren Evans, Deaver H. S.
Deaver, Wyoming
Mrs. Jane H. Brown, Enfield Comm.
Unit H. S.
Enfield, Illinois
Mrs. Linda Lewis, Joint School District No. 283
Kendrick, Idaho
Mrs. Charlotte Clarke, Central H. S.
Aberdeen, South Dakota
Mrs. J. A. Myron, Chester H. S.
Chester, Montana
Patricia Dwerlkotte, Concordia H. S.
Concordia, Kansas
Eileen S. Brenden, Independent School District 263
Elbow Lake, Minnesota
Nellie Merrill, St. David H. S.
St. David, Arizona
Mrs. Martha Swingle, Northwestern H. S.
West Salem, Ohio
Gaynelle C. James, Gardner, H. S.
Gardner, Illinois

FROSTED FRUIT SALAD

1 6-oz. pkg. lime gelatin
1 lge. can pear halves, drained
1 lge. can crushed pineapple, drained

Dissolve gelatin according to package directions using juice drained from pears and pineapple as part of liquid. Chill until slightly thickened. Place pear halves with rounded side up in bottom of dish. Add gelatin mixture. Chill until firm.

(Continued on next page)

Topping:
1 egg, slightly beaten
1 T. flour
1 T. lemon juice
2 T. pineapple juice
8 marshmallows
½ pt. whipped cream
1 pkg. sharp cheese, grated

Combine egg, flour, lemon and pineapple juice. Cook in double boiler until thickened. Add marshmallows; stir until melted. Cool. Fold in whipped cream. Spread on top of gelatin layer; sprinkle with grated cheese.

Mrs. Marie G. Reid, Rochester Area Jr.-Sr. H. S.
Rochester, Pennsylvania

DELUXE MANDARIN ORANGE SALAD

Number of Servings — 12

1 can Mandarin oranges, drained
2 pkg. orange gelatin
2 c. hot water
2 c. cold water
1 c. miniature marshmallows
2-3 bananas, sliced
1 c. mixed orange juice and water
½ c. sugar
2 T. flour
2 T. butter
1 egg, beaten
1 c. whipped cream
2 T. salad dressing

Dissolve gelatin in hot water; add cold water. When gelatin thickens add oranges, marshmallows and bananas. Chill until firm. Heat juice-water mixture with butter. Combine sugar, flour and egg. Add to hot liquid, stirring constantly until mixture thickens. Cool. Add salad dressing. Fold in whipped cream. Spread over firm gelatin. Refrigerate until ready to serve.

Mrs. Fleta L. Bruce, Hamburg Community School
Hamburg, Iowa

APRICOT NECTAR SALAD

2 pkg. orange gelatin
1½ c. hot water
2½ c. apricot nectar, heated
2 c. miniature marshmallows

Dissolve gelatin in hot water and nectar. Chill until partially set. Add marshmallows. Let set for several hours or overnight.

Topping:
½ c. sugar
Few grains salt
2 T. flour
1 egg, beaten
1 c. apricot nectar
1 pkg. Dream Whip, whipped
½ c. Cheddar cheese

Combine sugar, salt, flour, egg and nectar. Cook over medium heat, stirring constantly until thick. Cool. Fold in Dream Whip. Spread over the firm gelatin. Sprinkle with cheese.

Mrs. Margaret A. Campbell, Sierra Junior H. S.
Roswell, New Mexico

APRICOT DELITE

Number of Servings — 10

2 pkg. apricot gelatin
1 No. 2 can crushed pineapple, drained
1 c. miniature marshmallows

Prepare gelatin according to package directions. Add pineapple and marshmallows. Chill until firm.

Topping:
1 egg
½ c. sugar
2 T. butter
2 T. flour
½ c. pineapple juice
1 3-oz. pkg. cream cheese, softened
1 pkg. dessert topping mix
Chopped nuts

Cook egg, sugar, butter, flour and pineapple juice until thick. Cool. Whip dessert topping mix according to package directions. Fold cream cheese and dessert topping into cooled cooked mixture. Spread over firm gelatin. Sprinkle with nuts.

Violet Shaffner, Marshall H. S.
Marshall, Illinois

MOLDED APRICOT SALAD

Number of Servings — 10-12

2 3-oz. pkg. orange gelatin
1 No. 2 can sliced apricots, drained
1 9-oz. can crushed pineapple, drained
1 c. seedless green grapes, halved (opt.)

Prepare gelatin according to package directions; chill until partially set. Stir in apricots, pineapple and grapes. Turn into a mold; chill until firm.

Topping:
½ c. sugar
2 T. flour
1 c. mixed apricot-pineapple juice
1 egg, slightly beaten
2 T. butter
1 c. whipped cream (opt.)

Cook the sugar, flour, juice and egg until thick. Stir in butter. Chill. Fold in whipped cream. Spread over firm gelatin. Sprinkle with nuts if desired. Chill.

This recipe submitted by the following teachers:

Violet Nyhart, Danville H. S.
Danville, Ohio

Mrs. Marilyn Sampson, Dahlgren H. S.
Dahlgren, Illinois

FROSTED 7-UP FRUIT SALAD

Number of Servings — 12-15

2 pkg. lemon gelatin
2 c. boiling water
2 c. 7-Up
1 No. 2 can pineapple, drained
2 lge. bananas, sliced
1 c. miniature marshmallows

Dissolve gelatin in boiling water; add 7-Up. Chill until partially set. Add remaining ingredients. Chill until firm.

(Continued on next page)

Topping:
½ c. sugar
2 T. flour
1 c. pineapple juice
1 egg, beaten
2 T. butter
1 c. whipped cream
¼ c. American cheese, shredded

Combine sugar and flour in a saucepan; stir in pineapple juice and egg. Cook, stirring constantly until thickened. Add butter; cool. Fold in whipped cream. Spread over gelatin mixture. Sprinkle with cheese. Will keep for several days.

Delores Vondrak, Elk Point H. S.
Elk Point, South Dakota

LEMON GELATIN DELIGHT

Number of Servings — 10

2 pkg. lemon gelatin
4 c. boiling water
16 lge. marshmallows
1 No. 2 can crushed pineapple, drained
4 bananas, diced

Combine gelatin, water and marshmallows. Stir until dissolved. Cool until thickened. Fold in pineapple and bananas. Chill until firm.

Topping:
1 c. pineapple juice
½ c. sugar
Nuts, chopped or cheese, shredded
2 T. flour
2 T. butter
1 c. whipped cream

Combine sugar, flour, butter and juice. Cook in a double boiler until smooth and thick. Cool. Add whipped cream. Spread over gelatin mixture. Sprinkle with nuts or cheese. Chill.

Mrs. R. E. Hieronymus, Clinton H. S.
Clinton, Illinois

LIME PARTY SALAD

Number of Servings — 9

1 pkg. lime gelatin
1 c. boiling water
1 c. pineapple juice
1 c. pineapple chunks
2 bananas, cubed
½ c. pecan halves
½ pt. whipped cream
15 marshmallows, quartered
Maraschino cherries

Mix gelatin with hot water and juice; chill until partially set. Add pineapple, bananas and pecans. Chill until firm. Combine whipped cream and marshmallows; spread over firm gelatin. Garnish with Maraschino cherries.

Evelyn Mangold, Warrensburg-Latham H. S.
Warrensburg, Illinois

GOLDEN DELIGHT

Number of Servings — 15

2 pkg. lemon gelatin
1 No. 2 can diced or crushed pineapple, drained
4 bananas, sliced
1 pkg. marshmallows, cut in fourths
½ c. nuts, chopped (opt.)

Dissolve lemon gelatin according to package directions; cool until partially thickened. Add pineapple and bananas; also nuts and marshmallows if desired. Chill until firm.

TOPPING:
½ c. sugar
2 T. flour
1-2 eggs, well beaten
¼ t. salt (opt.)
1-2 T. butter (opt.)
1 c. pineapple juice and water
1 T. gelatin (opt.)
¼ c. cold water (opt.)
1 c. whipped cream
1 c. sharp cheese, grated

Mix sugar salt, flour and juice; stir in eggs. Cook over low heat until thick, stirring constantly. Soften unflavored gelatin in cold water and dissolve in hot mixture. Chill until partially thickened. Fold in cream; pile on firm lemon gelatin layer. Sprinkle with cheese if desired. Chill until firm.

This recipe submitted by the following teachers:

Mrs. Evelyn Van Vleet, Garden City H. S.
Garden City, Kansas

Mrs. Lorraine Nugent, Cimarron Consolidated School
Cimarron, Kansas

Norlene Ramhorst, Philip Independent School
Philip, South Dakota

Ermadee Meyer, Sac Community H. S.
Sac City, Iowa

Janice Wanklyn, Magnolia H. S.
Anaheim, California

Helen McGuire, Burlington H. S.
Burlington, Kansas

Mrs. Marjorie Bradley, Cameron H. S.
Cameron, Wisconsin

Mrs. Eunice Wood, Glendo H. S.
Glendo, Wyoming

Mary Beth Stine, Flora Township H. S.
Flora, Illinois

Mrs. Madra Fischer, Mendota H. S.
Mendota, Illinois

Margaret N. Phillips, Grant Community H. S.
Fox Lake, Illinois

MANDARIN SALAD

Number of Servings — 8

2 pkg. orange gelatin
1 c. crushed pineapple, drained
2 small cans Mandarin orange sections, drained
Orange and pineapple juice plus enough water to make 4 c. liquid

(Continued on next page)

½ pt. whipping cream
½ c. salad dressing
1 pkg. miniature marshmallows
¾ c. longhorn cheese, grated

Prepare gelatin according to package directions using juice-water mixture as liquid. When silghtly thickened, add fruit. Chill until firm. Whip cream and blend with salad dressing and marshmallows. Spread on firm gelatin. Top with cheese. Keep refrigerated.

Judith C. Hughes, Jefferson Local School
Dayton, Ohio

MANDARIN ORANGE SALAD

Number of Servings — 12

2 boxes lemon gelatin
4 c. hot water
3 bananas, sliced
1 c. miniature marshmallows
1 No. 2 can crushed pineapple
2 small cans Mandarin oranges, drained and cut

Dissolve gelatin in hot water; chill until slightly set. Whip thoroughly. Fold in bananas, marshmallows, pineapple and oranges. Pour in large pan and let set several hours until firm.

Topping:

1 c. whipped cream
1 c. pineapple juice
2 T. flour (heaping)
1 egg
½ c. sugar
¼ t. salt

Mix flour, sugar and salt. Add enough juice to blend and make mixture smooth. Beat in egg. Gradually add remaining juice. Cook until thick, stirring well. Chill until completely cold. Fold in whipped cream. Spread over salad 1-2 hours before serving.

Kathleen Dyer, Charlestown H. S.
Charlestown, Indiana

MANDARIN ORANGE SALAD

Number of Servings — 16

2 pkg. orange gelatin
2⅔ c. hot water
1 small can frozen orange juice
1 can crushed pineapple, drained
2 cans Mandarin oranges, drained

Dissolve gelatin in hot water. Add frozen orange juice and allow mixture to cool. Add pineapple and oranges. Pour in large pan. Chill until firm. Spread topping over gelatin. Chill in refrigerator overnight.

Topping:

1 pkg. lemon pie filling
½ pt. whipped cream
1 egg

Prepare according to directions on box of pie filling. Substitute 1 whole egg for the 2 egg yolks. Allow mixture to cool. Add whipped cream.

Mrs. Elsie Rosselit, Vassar H. S.
Vassar, Michigan

FROSTED LIME-NUT SALAD

Number of Servings — 8

1 pkg. lime gelatin
1 c. boiling water
1 No. 2 can crushed pineapple, undrained
1 c. cottage cheese
½ c. celery, chopped
½ c. walnuts or pecans, chopped
1 T. pimento (opt.)

Dissolve gelatin in boiling water. Cool until syrupy. Add remaining ingredients. Turn into a mold or loaf pan which has been rinsed with cold water. Chill until firm.

FROSTING:

3-6 oz. cream cheese
1 T. mayonnaise
1 t. lemon juice

Combine all ingredients. Spread on top of firm gelatin. Decorate as desired. Slice and serve.

This recipe submitted by the following teachers:

Mildred Timm Paxon, Brawley Union H. S.
Brawley, California

Helen S. Redmon, Southeast Guilford
Greensboro, North Carolina

Mrs. Eunie V. Stacy, Marthaville H. S.
Marthaville, Louisiana

Mrs. Coleen Dorris, Clarksville H. S.
Clarksville, Tennessee

Mrs. Robinette M. Husketh, South Granville H. S.
Creedmoor, North Carolina

Doris Stephens, Rabun County H. S.
Clayton, Georgia

Mrs. Dorothy Bent, Whitcomb H. S.
Bethel, Vermont

ORANGE CREAM SALAD

Number of Servings — 12-15

2 pkg. orange gelatin
2 c. boiling water
1 c. cold water
½ c. pineapple juice
1 c. marshmallows, cut
1 No. 2 can crushed pineapple

Combine first 5 ingredients. When mixture begins to set, add pineapple. Refrigerate until firm.

Topping:

1 egg, well beaten
½ c. sugar
½ c. pineapple juice
2 T. flour
2 T. butter
¼ c. cream cheese, softened
½ c. whipped cream

Combine egg, sugar, pineapple juice, flour and butter. Cook until mixture begins to thicken. Cool. Add cream cheese. Fold into whipped cream. Spread over firm gelatin.

Mrs. Rosa File, Mt. Auburn H. S.
Mt. Auburn, Illinois

ORANGE GLOW SALAD

Number of Servings — 8

1 pkg. orange gelatin
1 c. hot water
1 c. cold water
1 small can crushed pineapple
Marshmallows

Dissolve gelatin in hot water; add cold water and pineapple. Congeal. Cover with marshmallows.

Dressing:

2 egg yolks
Juice and grated rind of 1 orange
1 c. whipped cream
1 T. sugar
American cheese, grated

Cook yolks and orange juice until thick. Cool. Add whipped cream, sugar and orange rind. Spread over firm gelatin; top with cheese.

Mrs. Carol Bonynge, East Junior H. S.
Alton, Illinois

ORANGE-PINEAPPLE SALAD

Number of Servings — 6-8

1 3-oz. box orange or orange-pineapple gelatin
1 c. hot water
1 8½-oz. can pineapple, undrained
1 c. orange sections, diced
1 11-oz. can Mandarin oranges, drained
1 c. miniature marshmallows
1 c. dairy sour cream
2 T. mayonnaise
2 T. cheddar cheese, grated
Salad greens

Dissolve gelatin in hot water. Add pineapple and chill until slightly thickened. Fold in oranges and marshmallow. Pour into 8 x 8 x 2 pan; chill until firm. Mix sour cream and mayonnaise; spread on salad. Sprinkle with cheese. Serve on greens.

Mrs. Ida Sneath, Sterling H. S.
Sterling, Colorado

NECTARINE FLUFF DELIGHT

Number of Servings — 4-6

1 c. fresh nectarines, diced
1 envelope unflavored gelatin
¼ c. cold water
¾ c. boiling water
1 t. vanilla
¼ t. salt
½ c. sugar
3 egg whites

Soften gelatin in cold water; dissolve in boiling water. Stir in vanilla, salt and sugar. Chill until slightly thickened. Add egg whites and beat until thick. Fold in nectarines. Pour into 8½x4½ pan and chill until firm.

CREAMY FRUIT SAUCE:

½ c. butter
3 egg yolks, slightly beaten
½ c. sugar
¼ t. salt
⅓ c. light cream
1 T. grated lemon rind
2 T. lemon juice
2 c. nectarines, diced

Melt butter in top of double boiler. Add egg yolks, sugar, salt and cream. Cook, stirring constantly until thick. Remove from heat and add lemon juice and rind. Stir in nectarines. Chill. Serve with gelatin salad. Garnish with nectarines if desired. Dressing will keep for several days in refrigerator.

Lucille Johnston, Dunlap Township H. S.
Dunlap, Illinois

RED AND WHITE RASPBERRY SALAD

Number of Servings — 8

2 boxes red raspberry gelatin
2 c. boiling water
2 10-oz. boxes frozen red raspberries

Dissolve gelatin in hot water. Add raspberries, stir until berries are thawed. Chill until set.

Topping:

1 small pkg. cream cheese
¼ lb. miniature marshmallows
1 c. coffee cream
½ c. nuts

Blend together cream cheese, marshmallows and coffee cream. Let stand to thicken, preferably overnight. Spread on firm gelatin layer. Sprinkle with nuts.

Josephine Sherman, Clarinda Community School
Clarinda, Iowa

FROSTED RHUBARB SALAD

Number of Servings — 10-12

½ c. water
½ c. sugar
4 c. rhubarb, diced
2 pkg. strawberry gelatin
2 c. rhubarb syrup plus water
1½ c. cold water
2 T. lemon juice
¼ t. salt
⅛ t. cinnamon
1 3-oz. pkg. cream cheese

Bring ½ cup water and the sugar to boil. Add diced rhubarb; simmer until tender. Drain rhubarb; add enough hot water to the syrup to make 2 cups. Dissolve gelatin in this hot liquid. Stir in the cold water, lemon juice, salt and cinnamon. Reserve 1 cup cooked rhubarb. Combine remaining rhubarb with gelatin mixture and chill until firm in mold or pan. Soften the cream cheese; blend in reserved rhubarb. Frost firm salad with this mixture and return to refrigerator. Red coloring may be added to the cooked rhubarb.

Mrs. Larry Stomm, Auburn H. S.
Auburn, Indiana

SALAD SUPREME

Number of Servings — 8

2 c. applesauce
1 3-oz. pkg. lime gelatin
1 small bottle 7-Up
4 oz. miniature marshmallows
1 3-oz. pkg. cream cheese, crumbled
1 c. whipped cream

Heat applesauce; add gelatin and stir until dissolved. Stir in 7-Up. Chill until set. Mix cream cheese with marshmallows. Pour whipped cream over cheese-marshmallow mixture. Refrigerate overnight. Beat until smooth with rotary beater. Spread over lime gelatin before cutting into squares and serving.

Genevieve Olson, Osseo Senior H. S.
Osseo, Minnesota

SUNSHINE AND SNOW SURPRISE

Number of Servings — 9

1 3-oz. pkg. orange gelatin
1 c. hot water
1 c. apricot juice, chilled
1 No. 303 can apricot halves, drained
½ 2¼-oz. box dessert topping mix
¼ c. cold milk
½ t. vanilla
½ c. miniature marshmallows

Dissolve gelatin in hot water. Add chilled apricot juice. Pour into 8x8 pan and chill until partially set. Add apricot halves and return to refrigerator until firmly set. Mix dessert topping mix with cold milk. Whip until topping forms soft peaks. Fold in vanilla and marshmallows. Spread mixture over gelatin and return to refrigerator until time for serving.

Mrs. Lynda Rought, Orion H. S.
Orion, Illinois

 *RECIPE*

APRICOT-CHEESE SALAD WITH FRUIT-CHEESE TOPPING

Number of Servings — 12

1 No. 2½ can apricots, drained and finely cut
1 No. 2 can crushed pineapple, drained
2 pkgs. orange, cherry or lime gelatin
2 c. boiling water
1 c. combined apricot and pineapple juice
1 c. miniature marshmallows

Chill drained fruits. Dissolve gelatin in boiling water; add fruit juice. Chill until slightly congealed. Fold in fruit and marshmallows. Pour into 11x7x2 baking dish which has been rinsed with cold water. Chill until firm.

TOPPING:
½ c. sugar
3 T. flour
1 egg, slightly beaten
2 T. butter
1 c. whipped cream
¾ c. cheddar cheese, grated
1 c. combined apricot and pineapple juice

Combine sugar and flour; blend in egg. Gradually stir in juice. Cook over low heat until thickened, stirring constantly. Remove from heat and stir in butter; cool. Fold in whipped cream and spread over chilled gelatin layer. Sprinkle top with cheese. Chill. Gelatin salad may be made a day ahead of time but topping must be made the day it is served.

The teachers who submitted this recipe can be found on page 378.

ICE CREAM SALAD

Number of Servings — 10-12

1 pkg. strawberry gelatin
1 c. hot water
1 c. bananas, mashed
1 c. crushed pineapple
1 c. vanilla ice cream

Dissolve gelatin in hot water. Cool. Add remaining ingredients in order. Mix until ice cream is completely dissolved. Turn into a mold and refrigerate overnight. Serve with grapes that have been dipped in white sugar.

Alice Eckerle, Hart H. S.
Hart, Michigan

ICE CREAM SALAD

Number of Servings — 12

2 pkg. lime gelatin
1 qt. vanilla ice cream
1 No. 2 can crushed pineapple, undrained
1 medium can red or green Maraschino cherries, drained
2 c. boiling water
1 c. pecans, chopped

Dissolve gelatin in boiling water. Add ice cream and stir until melted. Refrigerate until mixture is syrupy. Fold in pineapple, nuts and cherries. Place in 9 x 13 cake pan or a 2-quart mold. Chill until firm.

Mrs. Lillian McKinney, Ashley Community School
Ashley, Michigan

CONGEALED SALAD

Number of Servings — 8-10

2 boxes apple gelatin
2 c. boiling water
1 pt. vanilla ice cream
2 c. fruit cocktail, drained

Dissolve gelatin in boiling water. Add ice cream and stir until melted. Refrigerate until mixture begins to thicken. Add fruit. Chill until firm.

Mrs. Ruth Deese, Cliff H. S.
Cliff, New Mexico

PARFAIT SALAD

Number of Servings — 8-10

1 pkg. lime gelatin
1 c. water
2 T. vinegar
1/8 t. salt
1 c. cucumbers, chopped
1 can crushed pineapple, drained
1 pt. vanilla ice cream

Dissolve gelatin in water; add vinegar and salt. Dissolve ice cream in gelatin; mix. Add cucumbers and pineapple. Pour into mold; congeal. Serve on endive.

Mrs. Louise Sturgeon, Cody H. S.
Detroit, Michigan

ORANGE DELIGHT

Number of Servings — 6

1 3-oz. pkg. orange gelatin
3/4 c. boiling water
1 c. vanilla ice cream
3 T. orange juice
1 9-oz. can crushed pineapple, undrained
1/2 c. pecans, chopped
Mandarin orange sections, drained

Dissolve gelatin in boiling water; stir in ice cream and orange juice. Chill until partially thickened. Stir in pineapple and nuts. Pour into 1-quart mold; chill until firm. Garnish with Mandarin orange sections.

Doris C. Sporleder, Hall H. S.
Spring Valley, Illinois

RASPBERRY ICE CREAM SALAD

Number of Servings — 6

1 pkg. raspberry gelatin
1 c. hot water
1-2 c. vanilla ice cream
3 T. orange juice (opt.)
1 9-oz. can crushed pineapple
1 medium banana, sliced
1/2 c. pecans, chopped

Dissolve gelatin in hot water. Mix in ice cream and orange juice. Chill until partially set. Add fruit and nuts. Pour into 1-quart mold; chill until firm.

This recipe submitted by the following teachers:

Mrs. Ruth F. Gamble, Northern Potter Joint
Ulysses, Pennsylvania

Elaine Carlson, Horton H. S.
Horton, Kansas

RED RASPBERRY RING

Number of Servings — 8-10

1 10-oz. pkg. frozen raspberries, thawed
2 3-oz. pkgs. red raspberry gelatin
2 c. boiling water
1 pt. vanilla ice cream
1 6-oz. can frozen pink lemonade concentrate, thawed
1/4 c. pecans, chopped

Drain raspberries; reserve syrup. Dissolve gelatin in boiling water. Add ice cream by spoonfuls, stirring until melted. Stir in lemonade concentrate and reserved raspberry syrup. Chill until partially set. Add raspberries and pecans. Turn into a 6-cup ring mold; chill until firm.

This recipe submitted by the following teachers:

Mrs. W. R. Temple, Fairfield Community H. S.
Fairfield, Illinois

Mrs. Eugene Romsos, Barron Sr. H. S.
Barron, Wisconsin

PINEAPPLE-ICE CREAM SALAD

Number of Servings — 8

1 pkg. lime or other flavored gelatin
1 c. boiling water
1 pt. vanilla ice cream
1 c. crushed pineapple
1/2-1 c. nuts, finely cut (opt.)

Dissolve gelatin in boiling water; add ice cream and stir until melted. Mix in pineapple and nuts if desired. Chill until firm. Do not freeze.

This recipe submitted by the following teachers:

Pearl Oliver, Cadillac Jr. H. S.
Cadillac, Michigan

Sally K. Kemp, Grand Ledge H. S.
Grand Ledge, Michigan

Mrs. Karen Christensen, Seymour H. S.
Seymour, Wisconsin

MOLDED CINNAMON-APPLE SALAD

Number of Servings — 6

1/2 c. red cinnamon candies
2 c. hot water
1 pkg. lemon gelatin
2 T. lemon juice
1 1/4 c. unpeeled apple, diced
1/4 c. toasted walnuts or filbert, broken
1 3-oz. pkg. cream cheese
1/4 c. cream
1/8 t. salt

Dissolve the candies and gelatin in boiling water. Cool. Add lemon juice. Chill until syrupy. Fold in apple and nuts. Pour half the gelatin mixture into an 8 x 8 inch square cake pan; chill until firm. Blend together cream cheese, cream and salt. Spread on firm gelatin layer. Carefully pour remaining half of gelatin over cheese layer. Chill until firm.

Mrs. Eleanor Hatch, Joseph H. S.
Joseph, Oregon

APPLE-CHEESE SALAD

Number of Servings — 8-10

1 c. boiling water
⅔ c. red cinnamon candies
1 3-oz. pkg. lemon gelatin
1½ c. sweetened or unsweetened applesauce
1 8-oz. pkg. cream cheese
½ c. nuts, chopped
½ c. celery, finely cut (opt.)
½ c. mayonniase or ¼ c. cream
¼ t. salt (opt.)

Dissolve candies in hot water. Add gelatin; stir until dissolved. Add applesauce. Pour half of mixture in 8x8x2 pan. Chill until firm. Blend cream cheese, nuts and celery; add mayonnaise or cream. Spread in layer over firm gelatin. Pour on remaining applesauce mixture. Chill until firm. Unmold. Garnish with sugared grapes, if desired.

This recipe submitted by the following teachers:

Mrs. Margaret Lott, New Oxford Area H. S.
New Oxford, Pennsylvania

Nola Kay Scott, Allensville H. S.
Allensville, Ohio

Joyce Wuehle, Galesburg Sr. H. S.
Galesburg, Illinois

Elva Williams Schrantz, Flandreau Indian School
Flandreau, South Dakota

Gladys Parry, Jr. Sr. H. S.
Two Harbors, Minnesota

Mrs. Eunice O. Stott, Altavista H. S.
Altavista, Virginia

Mrs. Ann Hunt, Nampa Sr. H. S.
Nampa, Idaho

Alda J. Ramsey, Cash H. S.
Cash, Arkansas

Marilyn Lynch, Valley Falls H. S.
Valley Falls, Kansas

Gladys C. Clemens, Connellsville Joint Sr. H. S.
Connellsville, Pennsylvania

Mrs. Vesta Glessner
Shanksville-Stonycreek Jr. H. S.
Shanksville, Pennsylvania

ORANGE-LIME APPLE SALAD

1 3-oz. pkg. lime gelatin
1 c. apples, chopped
1 c. nuts, chopped
⅓ c. pineapple
1 stalk celery, chopped
1 3-oz. pkg. orange gelatin
1 T. mayonnaise
1 3-oz. pkg. cream cheese

Prepare lime gelatin according to package directions. Mix apples, nuts, pineapple and celery; add to lime gelatin. Chill until firm. Prepare orange gelatin according to package directions. Mix mayonnaise and cream cheese into orange gelatin with electric mixer. Pour on top of firm lime layer. Chill.

Carolyn Gardner, Westfield
Westfield, Illinois

APPLE-LIME MOLDED SALAD

Number of Servings — 12

1 pkg. lime gelatin
1 c. boiling water
¾ c. cold water or fruit juice
3-4 apples, quartered, diced
1 stalk celery, diced
½ c. pecans, chopped
1 pkg. lime gelatin
1 c. boiling water
½ c. cold water or juice
1 3-oz. pkg. cream cheese, softened
½ c. crushed pineapple, drained
½ c. whipped cream

Dissolve one package of gelatin in boiling water; add cold liquid. Chill until partially set. Fold apples, celery, and nuts into gelatin; pour into 6 cup ring mold; chill until firm. Dissolve remaining gelatin in boiling water and add cold liquid. Chill until firm. Whip until foamy. Combine cream cheese and pineapple; fold into whipped gelatin. Fold in cream. Pour over first layer and chill until firm.

Mrs. Rosalynn Mickelson, Oakwood H. S.
Fithian, Illinois

PINK RIBBON SALAD

Number of Servings — 6-8

¼ c. red cinnamon candies
1 c. boiling water
1 pkg. lemon gelatin
1 c. applesauce
1 3-oz. pkg. cream cheese
2 T. cream
2 T. mayonnaise

Dissolve candies in boiling water. Pour liquid over lemon gelatin. Stir to dissolve. Add applesauce. Spoon half of mixture into loaf pan. Chill until set. Blend cream cheese, cream and mayonnaise; spoon over firm gelatin. Chill until set. Pour remaining gelatin over cheese layer. Chill until firm.

Beverly Schultz, Creston H. S.
Creston, Washington

APRICOT RIBBON RING

Number of Servings — 8-10

2 envelopes unflavored gelatin
¼ c. cold water
Syrup from crushed pineapple
1½ c. apricot nectar
¼ t. salt
¼ c. lemon juice
1 c. crushed pineapple, drained
1 7-oz. bottle 7-Up

Soften gelatin in cold water and pineapple syrup. Heat apricot nectar to boiling; stir in softened gelatin until completely dissolved. Add salt, lemon juice and crushed pineapple. Cool to room temperature. Carefully add the 7-Up, stirring as little as possible. Fill a 5½-cup ring mold ⅓ full; chill until firm.

(Continued on next page)

Filling:
1 3-oz. pkg. cream cheese, softened
Dash of salt
3 T. mayonnaise or salad dressing
1/3 c. celery, chopped
1/4 c. pecans, chopped

Blend together. Spread evenly over chilled gelatin layer. Add remaining gelatin. Chill until firm. Serve on crisp lettuce.

This recipe submitted by the following teachers:

Verna Buerge, Turlock H. S.
Turlock, California

Barbara Borgen, Senior H. S.
Chippewa Falls, Wisconsin

APRICOT-NECTAR SALAD

Number of Servings — 8

4 c. apricot nectar
2 pkg. lemon gelatin
1 small can crushed pineapple
1 8-oz. pkg. cream cheese
1/2 c. nuts, chopped
1/2 c. celery, chopped

First layer: Dissolve 1 package gelatin in 1 cup hot apricot nectar; add 1 cup cold water. Chill until thick. Add 1/2 can of pineapple. Pour into 9 x 9 inch pan and allow to set. Soften cream cheese with a little nectar; blend in nuts and celery. Frost the firm gelatin layer. Make second layer same as the first and allow to thicken slightly before pouring onto frosted layer. Chill thoroughly before serving.

Luella V. Henderson, Old Washington H. S.
Old Washington, Ohio

GOLD'N MOLD

Number of Servings — 8-10

3 c. heavy apricot puree
2 envelopes unflavored gelatin
1 small can pineapple, drained
5 T. sugar
2 T. lemon juice
1 4-oz. pkg. cream cheese, softened
3 drops almond extract
2 T. green pepper, minced

Soften gelatin in pineapple juice. Heat slowly until gelatin is dissolved and clear. Add sugar, lemon juice and apricot puree; blend well. Divide into three portions, making one portion larger than the other two. To the larger portion, add almond extract. Pour into a pyramid mold that has been rinsed in cold water. Chill in freezer until set, but not frozen. Whip cheese; fold cheese and green pepper into one of the remaining gelatin portions. Spoon on top of the chilled layer. Chill until set. Fold pineapple into the remaining gelatin portion; spoon over chilled layers. Chill overnight.

Mrs. Pearl Wheaton, Moscow Senior H. S.
Moscow, Idaho

BLUEBERRY SALAD

Number of Servings — 16

3 3-oz. pkg. raspberry gelatin
1 No. 2 can crushed pineapple, drained
1 No. 303 can blueberries, drained
2 pkg. Dream Whip
1 c. nuts, chopped
2 c. hot water
Pineapple and blueberry juice plus enough water to make 4 c. liquid

Dissolve gelatin in hot water; add juice-water mixture. Set aside 2 cups of the gelatin mixture. Add pineapple and blueberries to remaining gelatin. Chill until firm. Prepare Dream Whip according to package directions; add nuts. When reserved gelatin mixture reaches egg white consistency, combine with Dream Whip. Spread over firm gelatin layer. Chill until firm.

This recipe submitted by the following teachers:

Mrs. Beuford Rook, Clay Co. Community H. S.
Clay Center, Kansas

Clara Deiter, Dodge City Junior H. S.
Dodge City, Kansas

BLUEBERRY-CREAM CHEESE SALAD

Number of Servings — 8-12

1 lg. pkg. cream cheese
1 3-oz. pkg. lemon gelatin
2 3-oz. pkgs. lemon or a red gelatin
1/2 pt. cream or chilled evaporated milk, whipped
2 No. 2 cans blueberries, drained
1-3 T. sugar
1 t. vanilla
1 1/4 c. hot water
Blueberry juice plus enough water to make 3 c. liquid

Dissolve 1 pkg. of gelatin in hot water; cool. Cream the cheese and slowly mix in cooled gelatin. Add sugar and vanilla to whipped cream; fold into cheese mixture. Chill until firm. Heat juice-water mixture; pour over remaining gelatin to dissolve. Chill until slightly thickened. Add blueberries. Pour on top of firm gelatin-cheese mixture. Chill until firm.

This recipe submitted by the following teachers:

Mrs. Mayme W. Day, Refrigio H. S.
Refrigio, Texas

Esther F. Intermill, Chassell H. S.
Chassell, Michigan

BLUEBERRY-HONEYDEW MOLD

Number of Servings — 8

2 envelopes unflavored gelatin
1/2 c. cold water
3/4 c. hot water
1/2 c. sugar
1/4 t. salt
1 c. fresh lime juice
2 drops green food coloring
3 c. fresh honeydew melon balls
3/4 c. fresh blueberries
Mint leaves (garnish)

(Continued on next page)

Strain juice from melon rind and pulp. Add enough cold water, if necessary, to make ¾ cup liquid. Soften gelatin in cold water; add hot water, sugar and salt. Add lime juice and melon juice-water mixture. Arrange some of the melon balls and blueberries in bottom of an oiled 5-cup mold. Pour one-third of the gelatin mixture over the fruit; chill until firm. Add green food coloring to remaining gelatin mixture. Chill until mixture is the consistency of egg whites. Fold in remaining melon balls and berries. Pour on top of firm gelatin layer. Chill until firm. Garnish with mint leaves and melon balls if desired.

Mrs. Marguerite Kiss, Teaneck H. S.
Teaneck, New Jersey

BLUEBERRY FRUIT SALAD

Number of Servings — 8

2 pkg. raspberry gelatin
2½ c. hot water
1½ c. blueberry juice
1 c. whipped cream
1 No. 2 can blueberries, drained

Mix 1 package of gelatin with 1½ cups hot water. Add ½ cup blueberry juice. Cool until slightly set. Pour into 1-quart mold. Chill. Mix remaining gelatin with ¾ cup hot water and ½ cup blueberry juice. Cool. Add whipped cream and blueberries. Pour on top of chilled mixture. Chill several hours or overnight.

Mrs. Sara L. Stump, New Paris H. S.
New Paris, Indiana

TRIPLE DELIGHT

Number of Servings — 12

1 pkg. raspberry gelatin
1 c. hot water
1 pkg. frozen raspberries
1 pt. coffee cream
1 c. sugar
2 pkg. unflavored gelatin
¼ c. cold water
1 pt. sour cream
2 t. vanilla
1 pkg. raspberry gelatin
1 c. hot water
1 can blueberries, undrained

Dissolve 1 package gelatin in hot water. Stir in frozen raspberries until dissolved. Chill in square cake pan. Heat cream and sugar. Soak gelatin in the cold water. Add to hot mixture. Add sour cream and vanilla. Pour over firm layer. Dissolve the second package of raspberry gelatin in the hot water. Add blueberry juice. Chill until partly congealed. Add blueberries. Pour over sour cream layer. Chill until firm.

Barbara Gaylor, Gerrish Higgins H. S.
Roscommon, Michigan

CHERRY SALAD

Number of Servings — 15

2 pkg. cherry gelatin
1 c. boiling water
1 can dark pitted cherries, undrained
1 can crushed pineapple, undrained
1 bottle 7-Up or 1 c. ginger ale
1 lge. pkg. cream cheese
Milk
Juice of 1 lemon
1-2 c. nuts, finely chopped

Dissolve gelatin in boiling water; stir well. Add cherries and crushed pineapple. Add 7-Up or ginger ale and mix thoroughly. Chill half of the mixture until firm. Soften cream cheese with milk. Add lemon juice and nuts. Spread over firm gelatin. Pour remaining gelatin over cheese mixture. Chill until firm.

Mrs. Edith Donaldson, Gadsden H. S.
Anthony, New Mexico

CHERRY SALAD MOLD

Number of Servings — 8-10

1 1-lb. can dark, sweet cherries or 1 pt. frozen sweet cherries, drained and pitted
1 11-oz. can Mandarin orange sections, drained
2 pkg. orange gelatin
1 c. hot water
1 7-oz. bottle ginger ale
Cherry syrup plus enough water to make 1 c. liquid, heated
Orange syrup plus enough water to make 1 c. liquid
⅓ c. nuts, broken

Dissolve gelatin in hot water and cherry liquid. Add ginger ale and orange liquid; chill until mixture is syrupy. Pour ¾ cup of the thick mixture into a ring mold. When mixture starts to congeal, alternately place cherries and orange sections on top. Cover with remaining gelatin, nuts, cherries and orange sections combined. Chill until firm.

Grace Ormston, High School
St. Johns, Michigan

PARTY FRUIT SALAD

Number of Servings — 6-8

1 No. 2 can chunk pineapple, drained
1 1-lb. can Bing cherries, drained
½ c. lemon juice
2 pkg. cherry gelatin
2 T. light cream or milk
1 3-oz. pkg. cream cheese
½ c. pecans, chopped

Combine juice from fruit and lemon juice; add enough water to make 3½ cups liquid. Heat to boiling. Dissolve gelatin in boiling juice. Divide into two equal parts. To one part add pineapple. Chill until firm. Spread with cheese softened with cream or milk. Add pecans and cherries to remaining gelatin. Chill; pour over cheese layer. Chill until firm.

Jo Ann Thompkins, Three Rivers H. S.
Coshocton, Ohio

BING CHERRY SALAD MOLD

Number of Servings — 12

1 No. 2 can sliced pineapple, drained and cut in ⅛-in. pieces
1¾ c. pineapple juice and water
1 pkg. cherry gelatin
1 3-oz. pkg. cream cheese
2½ T. light cream
1 No. 2 can Bing cherries, drained
⅓ c. lemon juice
1 pkg. orange gelatin

Heat pineapple juice and water to boiling. Add cherry gelatin; stir until dissolved. Chill until partially set. Add pineapple. Pour into an 8-inch square pan. Chill until firm. Soften cream cheese with cream; spread over cherry gelatin. Chill until firm. Combine cherry juice, lemon juice and enough water to make 1¾ cup liquid; heat to boiling. Add orange gelatin; stir until dissolved. Chill until partially set. Add cherries. Pour over cheese-cherry layer. Chill.

Charlotte H. Thompson, Claremont Junior H. S.
Claremont, New Hampshire

CHERRY-PINEAPPLE LAYER SALAD

Number of Servings — 12-15

1 pkg. lemon gelatin
1 No. 2 can crushed pineapple, undrained
1 8-oz. pkg. cream cheese
2 pkg. cherry gelatin
2½ c. boiling water
2 No. 2 cans dark sweet cherries, drained
Milk
1½ c. cherry juice

Dissolve lemon gelatin in 1 cup boiling water. Cool until slightly thickened. Add pineapple. Pour into 8 x 11 pan and chill until firm. Whip cream cheese with a little milk until it reaches consistency of frosting. Spread over firm gelatin layer. Chill until set. Dissolve cherry gelatin in remaining boiling water; add cherry juice. Chill until slightly thickened. Add cherries and pour carefully over the cheese layer. Chill until firm.

Mrs. Louise S. Ventura, Arnold H. S.
Arnold, Pennsylvania

CHERRY-MINCEMEAT MOLD

Number of Servings — 8-10

2 pkgs. cherry gelatin
4 c. water
1 pt. brandied mincemeat
½ c. pecans, chopped

Dissolve gelatin in water. When mixture begins to thicken pour a small amount in the bottom of a greased 6-cup mold. Chill until firm. Mix remaining gelatin with mincemeat and pecans; pour over firm gelatin. Chill until firm.

Mrs. Carolyn Rose, Gettysburg School
Gettysburg, Ohio

BING CHERRY SALAD

Number of Servings — 15

3 pkg. black cherry or cherry gelatin
2⅓ c. boiling water
1 30-oz. can crushed pineapple, drained
1 30-oz. can Bing cherries, pitted and drained
⅓ c. lemon juice
⅓ c. whipping cream
⅓ c. mayonnaise
2 3-oz. pkg. cream cheese (room temp.)
Dash of salt
½ c. nuts, coarsely broken
About 3 c. reserved cherry and pineapple juice

Dissolve gelatin in boiling water. Mix pineapple, cherry and lemon juices with gelatin. Chill half of the gelatin mixture until partially set. Fold in pineapple. Spread evenly in a 9 x 13 x 2 pan; chill until firm. Whip cream, mayonnaise, cream cheese and salt together until light and fluffy; spread evenly over firm gelatin. Chill until firm. Chill remaining gelatin until partially set. Fold in cherries and nuts; spread over cheese layer. Chill until firm.

This recipe submitted by the following teachers:

Mrs. Shelba W. Barnes, Wayne Township School
Waynetown, Indiana

Alma Hicks, Elverado H. S.
Elkville, Illinois

Mrs. Betty Jo Hill, Gorham H. S.
Gorham, Illinois

DOUBLE-DECKER CHERRY SALAD

Number of Servings — 9

1 No. 2 can sliced pineapple, drained
1 3-oz. pkg. cherry gelatin
1 3-oz. pkg. cream cheese
2-3 T. light cream or top milk
Pineapple juice plus water to make 1¾ c. liquid
1 No. 2 can Bing cherries, pitted and drained
⅓ c. lemon juice
1 pkg. orange gelatin
½ c. stuffed olives, sliced

Heat mixed pineapple juice and water to boiling. Add cherry gelatin; stir to dissolve. Chill until partially set. Cut pineapple slices in ⅛-inch pieces; add to cherry gelatin mixture. Pour into an oiled 8-inch square pan. Chill until firm. Soften cheese with cream; spread over firm gelatin. Combine cherry juice and lemon juice; add water to make 1¾ cups liquid. Heat liquid to boiling; add orange gelatin and dissolve. Chill until partially set. Add cherries and olives. Spread over cheese. Chill until firm.

This recipe submitted by the following teachers:

Virginia B. Dotson, Buffalo H. S.
Buffalo, West Virginia

Helen McSparrin, Quakertown Community Sr. H.S.
Quakertown, Pennsylvania

RIBBON RING SALAD

Number of Servings — 10-12

1 3-oz. pkg. strawberry gelatin
2 c. whole cranberry sauce
3½ c. boiling water
1 3-oz. pkg. lemon gelatin
1 8-oz. pkg. cream cheese, softened
1 9-oz. can crushed pineapple, undrained
¼ c. salted pecans, chopped
1 3-oz. pkg. lime gelatin
2 T. sugar
2 c. grapefruit sections, undrained

Dissolve strawberry gelatin in 1¼ cups boiling water. Add cranberry sauce; mix well. Chill until partially set. Pour into an 8-cup ring mold. Chill until almost firm. Dissolve lemon gelatin in 1¼ cups boiling water. Add cheese and beat until smooth. Add pineapple; chill until partially set. Stir in pecans. Pour over cranberry layer. Chill until almost firm. Dissolve lime gelatin and sugar in 1 cup boiling water. Add grapefruit; chill until partially set. Pour over cheese layer. Chill overnight.

This recipe submitted by the following teachers:

Linda Cross, Overton H. S.
Memphis, Tennessee

Shirley Hueftle, Owyhee H. S.
Owyhee, Nevada

TWO LAYERED ORANGE-CRANBERRY MOLD

Number of Servings — 10-12

1 box strawberry gelatin
1 c. boiling water
1 box frozen orange-cranberry relish
1 13½-oz. can crushed pineapple, drained
1 box lemon gelatin
1¼ c. boiling water
½ c. whipped cream
2 c. miniature marshmallows
3 oz. cream cheese
½ c. mayonnaise

Dissolve strawberry gelatin in 1 cup boiling water. Add frozen cranberry-orange relish. Pour into a 6-cup mold. Chill until firm. Dissolve lemon gelatin in 1¼ cups boiling water plus enough pineapple syrup to make 2 cups. Add marshmallows and stir until melted. Chill until partially set. Blend cheese, mayonnaise together; fold in the cream; add to gelatin mixture. Stir in pineapple. Pour over cranberry mixture. Chill until firm.

Dorothy Davey, Junior H. S.
Iron Mountain, Michigan

TWO LAYER FRUIT MOLD

1 pkg. strawberry gelatin
1 c. hot water
1 10-oz. pkg. frozen strawberries

Dissolve strawberry gelatin in hot water, add frozen strawberries including juice. Pour into a 2-quart mold. Chill until firm.

1 envelope unflavored gelatin
¼ c. cold water
½ c. fruit cocktail syrup
¼ c. sugar
1 c. small curd cottage cheese
1 c. fruit cocktail, well drained
1 T. lemon juice
¼ t. salt
1 c. sour cream

Dissolve unflavored gelatin in cold water. Combine the fruit cocktail syrup and sugar; bring to a boil. Add to the soft gelatin; stir until dissolved. Chill slightly. Fold in the remaining ingredients and pour over the firm strawberry layer. Chill until firm.

Carolyn Mae Horky, Fremont Junior H. S.
Fremont, Nebraska

LIME-CHEESE GELATIN SALAD

Number of Servings — 12

1 lg. pkg. lime or lemon gelatin
1½ c. boiling water
1 8-oz. pkg. cream cheese
2 c. evaporated milk
1 c. salad dressing
½ c. nuts, chopped
1 small pkg. lime gelatin

Dissolve large package of gelatin in boiling water; add cheese and mash with a fork. Add milk. When mixture begins to set, add salad dressing and nuts. Place in a 7x11 dish. Congeal. Dissolve remaining gelatin according to package directions. Pour over first mixture; chill.

Mrs. Vera Moe, Pierceton H. S.
Pierceton, Indiana

LIME-GREENGAGE PLUM SALAD

Number of Servings — 16-20

2 pkgs. lime gelatin
1 No. 3 can greengage plums, drained and peeled
1 pkg. lemon gelatin
1 8-oz. pkg. cream cheese
½ c. miniature marshmallows
½ pt. whipped cream
2 c. hot water
Plum juice plus enough water to make 4 cups liquid

Dissolve 1 package lime gelatin in 2 cups juice-water mixture. Pour into 12x8 dish; chill until firm. Whip plums with electric beater. Dissolve lemon gelatin in hot water. Add cream cheese and marshmallows; stir until dissolved. Cool. Add plums. Partially congeal. Add whipped cream. Spoon over firm lime gelatin. Chill. Dissolve remaining lime gelatin in plum-water mixture. Chill until partially set. Spoon on top of plum layer. Chill.

Betty Lou Hawks, San Jacinto Jr. H. S.
Pasadena, Texas

LIME-DREAM WHIP SALAD

Number of Servings — 12

2 pkg. lime gelatin
1 envelope unflavored gelatin
1 c. boiling water
1 c. grapefruit-pineapple juice
2 c. lemon-lime soft drink
1 can crushed pineapple, well drained
1 can grapefruit sections, drained

Dissolve lime gelatin in boiling water. Soften unflavored gelatin in fruit juice; add to hot gelatin mixture and dissolve. Add soft drink; let jell. Add fruits. Pour half of mixture into a large flat pan; refrigerate until firm.

Filling:
1 pkg. Dream Whip
1 3-oz. pkg. cream cheese
½ t. vanilla
½ c. powdered sugar

Let cream cheese come to room temperature. Prepare Dream Whip according to directions on the package. Beat cream cheese, vanilla and powdered sugar together. Add Dream Whip. Pour mixture over firm gelatin layer. Add remaining gelatin and let set. Filling will be between the two layers of gelatin.

Minnette Luebber, Cashmere H. S.
Cashmere, Washington

RED TOP SALAD

Number of Servings — 9-12

1 pkg. lemon gelatin
2 c. hot water
10 marshmallows
1 c. crushed pineapple
½ c. celery, chopped
½ c. cheese, grated
1 c. whipped cream
¼ c. salad dressing
½ c. nuts, chopped
1 pkg. strawberry gelatin
2 c. hot water

Dissolve strawberry gelatin in 2 cups hot water. Pour into large mold. Chill until firm. Dissolve lemon gelatin and marshmallows in hot water. Cool. Whip until frothy. Add pineapple, celery and cheese. Whip mayonniase into whipped cream; stir in nuts. Add to marshmallow mixture. Pour over firm strawberry layer. Chill until firm.

Marilyn Peterson, Alexander Ramsey H. S.
St. Paul, Minnesota

UNDER THE SEA SALAD

Number of Servings — 8

1 pkg. lime gelatin
1½ c. boiling water
½ c. pear juice
¼-½ t. salt
1½ t. vinegar or 1 T. lemon juice
2 c. canned pears, diced
2 pkgs. cream cheese, softened
¼ t. ginger

Dissolve gelatin in boiling water; add pear juice, salt and 1 t. vinegar. Pour about ½ inch deep in molds. Chill until firm. Allow remainder of gelatin to cool until slightly thickened; whip with beater. Add cheese creamed with ½ t. vinegar and ginger, fold in diced pears. Pour over firm gelatin. Chill until firm.

This recipe submitted by the following teachers:

Mrs. Frances R. Greenleaf, Hoquiam H. S.
Hoquiam, Washington

Mrs. Pat Woodyard, Crystal River H. S.
Crystal River, Florida

Mrs. Alice Driver, Bath H. S.
Lima, Ohio

ORANGE GELATIN SALAD

Number of Servings — 8

2 small pkg. orange gelatin
2 c. hot orange juice
1 pkg. Dream Whip
1 6-oz. pkg. cream cheese
1 c. Mandarin oranges
1 small pkg. orange gelatin
1 c. hot orange juice
1 c. water

Mix 1 package gelatin with 1 cup hot orange juice. Let set until slightly congealed. Beat Dream Whip; add cream cheese. Mix cheese mixture with gelatin mixture. Add oranges. Chill until firm. Mix remaining gelatin with 1 cup hot orange juice and 1 cup water. Pour over congealed layer. Chill until firm.

Mrs. Carolyn Weaver, Lancaster School
Huntington, Indiana

SUNNY SALAD SUPREME

Number of Servings — 8

2 boxes orange gelatin
1 No. 2 can crushed pineapple, drained
1 small can Mandarin oranges, drained
½ pt. sour cream
¼-½ c. coconut

Dissolve 1 package of gelatin according to package directions. Chill until partially set. Add pineapple. Spread this mixture in the bottom of a 1½-quart dish. Chill until firm. Dissolve the remaining gelatin according to package directions. Chill until partially set. Add oranges. Spread sour cream over the firm gelatin and sprinkle with coconut. Spread the orange mixture over all. Chill until firm.

Judith Ann Kostura, Windber Area H. S.
Windber, Pennsylvania

PEACH MELBA-CHEESE MOLD

Number of Servings — 12

1 pt. frozen peaches, drained and finely chopped
2 T. lemon juice
1 envelope unflavored gelatin
1 12-oz. carton creamed cottage cheese
1 c. light cream
½ t. almond extract
1 pkg. raspberry gelatin
1 c. hot water
⅓ c. cold water
1 pkg. frozen raspberries

Combine peach juice, lemon juice and enough water to make ½ cup liquid. Combine unflavored gelatin and juice-mixture; heat in double boiler until gelatin is dissolved. Add cheese, cream, peaches and almond extract; chill. Dissolve raspberry gelatin in hot water; cool. Add raspberries and cold water; stir until raspberries separate. Chill until thickened, but not set. When cheese mixture is thickened, whip and pour into a loaf pan. Chill until partially set. Spoon raspberry mixture over top; chill. Cover with remaining cheese mixture; chill overnight.

Dressing:
1 c. sour cream
2 t. brown sugar
Dash of salt
2 t. crystallized ginger, finely chopped

Combine all ingredients. Pass. Do not pour over gelatin, but pass separately.

Mrs. Shirley Johnson, Langford H. S.
Langford, South Dakota

SPICY PEACH-CRANBERRY RING

Number of Servings — 8

1 No. 2½ can cling-peach halves, drained
1 t. whole cloves
1 3-inch stick cinnamon
¼ c. vinegar
1 pkg. lemon gelatin
⅓ c. granulated sugar
1¾ c. peach juice and water
1¾ c. hot water
1 pkg. cherry gelatin
1 c. fresh cranberries
½ medium orange, unpeeled

Combine peach juice-water, cloves, cinnamon and vinegar; simmer for 10 minutes. Add peaches; heat slowly for 5 minutes. Remove peaches from syrup; place peaches, with cut sides up, in a 2-quart mold. Strain syrup; combine syrup with enough hot water to make 1⅔ cups liquid. Add syrup to lemon gelatin; stir until dissolved. Pour over peaches. Chill until almost firm. Put cranberries and orange through the medium blade of food chopper. Stir in sugar. Add hot water to cherry gelatin; stir until dissolved, cool. Stir in cranberry-orange mixture. Pour over peach layer. Chill until firm.

Rosetta Skinner, Inman Rural H. S.
Inman, Kansas

PEACH SURPRISE SALAD

Number of Servings — 6

1 6-oz. pkg. peach gelatin
6 canned cling peach halves
1 8-oz. pkg. cream cheese, softened
¼ c. nuts, chopped

Prepare the gelatin according to the directions on package. Chill until slightly thickened. Pour half into 6-cup ring mold. Roll softened cream cheese into balls the size of walnuts. Roll the cheese balls in the nuts until they are coated. Stuff peach halves with cream cheese balls. Arrange cut side down in mold. Add gelatin. Chill until firm.

Grace Guenther, Cambria Union H. S.
Cambria, Wisconsin

SPICED PEACH SALAD

Number of Servings — 8-10

1 can spiced peaches
2 pkg. orange gelatin
2 c. hot water
1 c. peach juice
1 3-oz. pkg. cream cheese
1 c. cold water
⅔ c. crushed pineapple
⅓ c. nuts, chopped
½ c. celery, chopped
¼ c. pimento (opt.)

Place peaches in a mold with round side down. Dissolve 1 package orange gelatin in 1 cup hot water. Add 1 cup peach juice. Pour over peaches. Let set. Dissolve remaining gelatin in 1 cup hot water. While it is hot, beat in cream cheese. Add 1 cup cold water or peach juice. Pour over molded layer. Chill until firm. Add pineapple, nuts, celery and pimento. Pour over molded layer. Chill until firm.

Mrs. June L. Powell, Atkinson H. S.
Atkinson, Illinois

GREEN TOP SALAD

Number of Servings — 12

1 pkg. orange gelatin
1 pkg. lime gelatin
2 3-oz. pkgs. cream cheese
2 small or 1 lge. can crushed pineapple
½ lb. white miniature marshmallows
¼-½ c. salad dressing or mayonnaise
4 c. hot water
1 c. whipped cream

Mix orange gelatin with 2 cups hot water; pour over marshmallows. Stir cheese, pineapple and salad dressing into hot mixture; cool. Add whipped cream. Chill until very firm. Mix lime gelatin with remaining hot water. When cool but not set, pour on top of orange gelatin mixture. Chill until firm.

This recipe submitted by the following teachers:

Mrs. Rosamond Fuller, Danube H. S.
Danube, Minnesota

Mrs. Constance Hill, McPherson H. S.
McPherson, Kansas

GELATIN RIBBON SALAD

Number of Servings — 8-10

2 pkg. cherry gelatin
1 pkg. lemon gelatin
1½ c. pineapple juice
1 c. small curd cottage cheese
1 c. whipped cream

Dissolve 1 package cherry gelatin according to package directions; let set. Dissolve lemon gelatin in pineapple juice; let set until syrupy. Add cottage cheese and whipped cream. Pour lemon-mixture over cherry gelatin. Let set until firm. Dissolve remaining cherry gelatin according to package directions; pour over lemon-cherry layer. Chill.

Carolyn S. Howard, Box Elder H. S.
Brigham City, Utah

GREEN AND WHITE SALAD

Number of Servings — 8

1 pkg. lime gelatin
2½ c. boiling water
1 No. 303 can crushed pineapple
1 pkg. lemon gelatin
1 c. whipped cream
½ c. cottage cheese or 1 3-oz. pkg. cream cheese combined with almonds.

Dissolve lime gelatin in 1½ cups boiling water, cool. Add pineapple. Pour into mold or 8 x 13 pan; chill until firm. Dissolve lemon gelatin in 1 cup boiling water; cool until partially set. Add whipped cream and cottage cheese; beat. Combine with partially set lemon gelatin. Pour lemon mixture over the firm lime gelatin. Chill until firm.

Isabelle T. Staley, Huron H. S.
Huron, South Dakota

MOLDED COTTAGE CHEESE-PINEAPPLE SALAD

Number of Servings — 12

1 pkg. lemon gelatin
1 pkg. lime gelatin
2 c. boiling water
1 c. whipped cream
1½ c. cottage cheese
1 c. pineapple juice
1 c. pineapple, chopped
⅓ c. stuffed olives, sliced
⅓ c. walnut meats, broken

Dissolve lemon gelatin in 1 cup boiling water; cool slightly. Beat with egg beater until light; add cream. Beat and add cottage cheese. Pour into round mold. Chill until firm. Dissolve lime gelatin in remaining water and pineapple juice; cool. Add pineapple, olives and walnut meats. Pour over firm layer. Chill until firm.

Mrs. Charlotte Brainerd
Fennimore Community School
Fennimore, Wisconsin

LAYERED GELATIN SALAD

Number of Servings — 12

2 pkg. cherry gelatin
1 pkg. lemon gelatin
¼ lb. marshmallows
1 small can crushed pineapple
1 8-oz. pkg. cream cheese, softened
1 c. whipped cream
2 c. hot water (scant)

Prepare 1 package cherry gelatin according to package directions. Chill until firm. Dissolve lemon gelatin in hot water. Add marshmallows; stir until melted. Mix in pineapple. Whip cream cheese. Mix cheese and whipped cream; fold in lemon gelatin. Pour over firm cherry gelatin. Chill until firm. Dissolve remaining cherry gelatin according to package directions; pour over firm layer. Chill until firm.

Mrs. Jean Eliason, Mora H. S.
Mora, Minnesota

ORANGE PINEAPPLE MOLDED SALAD

2 pkg. orange gelatin
2½ c. hot water
1 3-oz. pkg. cream cheese, softened
¼ c. orange juice
2 T. lemon juice
1 8-oz. can crushed pineapple, undrained

Dissolve 1 package orange gelatin in 1½ cups hot water. Gradually blend into cream cheese. Add orange and lemon juice. Pour into mold. Chill until firm. Dissolve second package gelatin in 1 cup hot water. Add pineapple. Chill until syrupy. Pour over firm layer. Chill until firm.

Mrs. Lena Brown, Tecumseh H. S.
Tecumseh, Michigan

RUBY SALAD

Number of Servings — 15-18

1½ c. Milnot
16 marshmallows
1 pkg. lemon gelatin
3 T. cold water
1 8-oz. pkg. cream cheese
1 c. crushed pineapple
½ c. blanched almonds, chopped
2 pkg. strawberry or cherry gelatin
2 c. hot water
2 c. cold water

Melt marshmallows and 1 cup Milnot over low heat. Mix lemon gelatin and cold water; add to marshmallow mixture. Stir in cream cheese, ½ cup Milnot, pineapple and almonds, let set. Dissolve strawberry or cherry gelatin in 2 cups hot water; add cold water. Pour over lemon mixture. Chill until firm.

Dorothy Kimbley, Jeffersonville H. S.
Jeffersonville, Indiana

PINEAPPLE-GELATIN SALAD

Number of Servings — 8

1 pkg. lime gelatin
1 c. boiling water
1 c. cottage cheese
1 c. crushed pineapple
¾ c. whipped cream
1 pkg. red gelatin

Pour boiling water over lime gelatin. Chill until partially set; beat well. Blend in cottage cheese. Add pineapple and whipped cream. Refrigerate. Mix red gelatin according to package directions. Let cool. Pour over lime layer.

Mrs. Betty Herbel, Bowbells Public School
Bowbell, North Dakota

RIBBON SALAD

Number of Servings — 12

5 c. hot water
4 c. cold water
1 pkg. lemon gelatin
2 pkg. lime gelatin
2 pkg. apricot gelatin
¾ c. miniature marshmallows
1 c. pineapple juice
1 8-oz. pkg. cream cheese
1 No. 2 can crushed pineapple
1 c. whipped cream
½ c. mayonnaise

Dissolve lime gelatin in 2 cups hot water and 2 cups cold water. Chill until firm. Dissolve lemon gelatin in 1 cup of hot water and 1 can pineapple. Melt marshmallows and cream cheese in a double boiler. Whip; add mayonnaise, pineapple juice and whipped cream. Mix with lemon gelatin and pour onto set lime gelatin. Let stand overnight. Dissolve 2 packages apricot gelatin in 2 cups hot water and 2 cups cold water. Chill until syrupy and add as a third layer. Cut into squares.

Sonja Crummy, Wyoming Community H. S.
Wyoming, Illinois

PINEAPPLE-LIME MOLD

Number of Servings — 8

2 boxes lime gelatin
2 c. boiling water
2 small pkg. cream cheese
1 No. 2 can crushed pineapple, drained
2 c. pineapple juice plus water

Dissolve gelatin in hot water; add pineapple juice-water mixture. Reserve ½ the gelatin mixture. Add cream cheese to remaining gelatin. Whip with rotary beater. Spread in bottom of ring mold. Chill until firm. Add pineapple to reserved gelatin and pour over firm layer.

Mrs. Catharine Dahlquist, Plymouth H. S.
Plymouth, Illinois

RIBBON SALAD

Number of Servings — 24

1-2 3-oz. pkgs. lime gelatin
5 c. hot water
4 c. cold water
1 3-oz. pkg. lemon gelatin
½ c. or more miniature marshmallows
1 c. pineapple juice
1 8-oz. pkg. cream cheese
1 1-lb. 4-oz. can crushed pineapple, drained
1 c. whipped cream
1 c. mayonnaise (opt.)
1-2 3-oz. pkgs. cherry, raspberry or strawberry gelatin
½ c. pecans, chopped (opt.)

Dissolve lime gelatin in 2 cups hot water; add 2 cups cold water. Chill until partially set. Dissolve lemon gelatin in 1 cup hot water in top of double boiler. Add marshmallows; stir to melt. Remove from heat. Add pineapple juice and cream cheese; beat until well blended. Stir in pineapple. Cool slightly. Fold in whipped cream, mayonnaise and nuts if desired. Chill until thickened but not completely set. Pour over lime gelatin. Chill until almost set. Dissolve cherry gelatin in 2 cups hot water; add 2 cups cold water. Chill until syrupy. Pour over pineapple layer. Chill until firm.

This recipe submitted by the following teachers:

Mrs. Winifred Robinson, Homedale H. S.
Homedale, Idaho

Mrs. Vernon Sturlaugson, Benson County School
Maddock, North Dakota

Verla Mae Huston, Rolfe Community
Rolfe, Iowa

Lois Sandell, Nevada Community H. S.
Nevada, Iowa

Judith Maggert, Grant Community H. S.
Fox Lake, Illinois

Mrs. Bernice Anderson, Central Jr. H. S.
Reno, Nevada

Mrs. Olith Hamilton, Maple Valley H. S.
Nashville, Michigan

RIBBON SALAD

Number of Servings — 20

2 pkg. orange gelatin
1 pkg. lemon gelatin
1 c. mayonnaise
1 c. whipped cream
1 8-oz. pkg. cream cheese
1 c. miniature marshmallows
1 c. crushed pineapple, drained
2 pkg. lime gelatin

Prepare orange gelatin according to package directions; let congeal. Prepare lemon gelatin according to package directions. Add marshmallows; stir until dissolved. Add mayonnaise, whipped cream, cream cheese and pineapple. Pour on top of congealed orange layer. Let congeal. Prepare lime gelatin according to package directions. Let set until it begins to thicken; pour over orange and lemon layers.

Mary Elizabeth Walker, Deputy H. S.
Deputy, Indiana

SURPRISE SALAD

Number of Servings — 12

1 pkg. lemon or lime gelatin
½ lb. marshmallows, cut up
2 3-oz. pkg. cream cheese
½ c. mayonnaise (opt.)
1 lge. can crushed pineapple, drained
½ pt. whipped cream or Dream Whip
1 c. pecan pieces (opt.)
1 or 2 pkg. cherry or strawberry gelatin
1 c. pineapple juice
1 c. hot water
1 pt. boiling water

Dissolve lemon gelatin in boiling water; add marshmallows. Add cream cheese and mayonnaise if desired. Beat until mixture is smooth. Chill until partially congealed. Add pineapple and nuts if desired; fold in whipped cream. Refrigerate overnight. Prepare cherry gelatin using hot water and pineapple juice. Cool. Pour over firm gelatin. Chill until set.

This recipe submitted by the following teachers:

Mrs. Elizabeth Richard
Lakewood Public School System
Sunfield, Michigan

Mrs. Dorothye Hansen, Marshall H. S.
Marshall, Michigan

Mrs. Blanche Weaver, Herrin Township H. S.
Herrin, Illinois

Mrs. Sarah Perry, North Webster H. S.
North Webster, Indiana

TRIPLE-TREAT MOLDED SALAD

Number of Servings — 12

1 3-oz. pkg. lime gelatin
1 c. hot water
1 3-oz. pkg. lemon gelatin
1 c. hot water
1 3-oz. pkg. raspberry gelatin
2 c. hot water
1 9-oz. can sliced pineapple, drained
2 T. lemon juice
2 3-oz. pkgs. cream cheese
⅓ c. mayonnaise
2 c. bananas, sliced

Dissolve the lime raspberry and lemon gelatins separately in specified amounts of hot water. Add lemon juice to the pineapple syrup and enough water to make 1 cup of liquid. Add this to the lime gelatin. Chill until partially set. Cut pineapple slices in thirds, arranging in S design in bottom of a 10x5x3 loaf pan. Pour small amount of lime mixture over the pineapple and chill until set. Add the remaining lime mixture; chill until firm. Chill dissolved lemon gelatin until thick. Whip until light and fluffy. Blend cream cheese and mayonnaise. Fold into the lemon gelatin. Pour on top of firm lime layer. Slice bananas over lemon layer and top with raspberry gelatin. Chill.

Carol Machovec, Trempealeau H. S.
Trempealeau, Wisconsin

TWO-TONED GELATIN SALAD

Number of Servings — 6-8

1 pkg. orange gelatin
1 c. hot water
10 lge. marshmallows, quartered
1 can crushed pineapple, drained
1 small pkg. cream cheese
½ c. mayonnaise
½ pt. whipped cream
1 pkg. cherry gelatin
2 c. hot water

Dissolve orange gelatin in 1 cup hot water. Add marshmallows. Let set until mixture begins to set. Combine pineapple, cream cheese and mayonnaise; add to gelatin mixture. Let set for a few minutes longer. Add whipped cream. Pour into an oiled mold; chill until firm. Dissolve cherry gelatin in 2 cups hot water. Chill until partially set. Carefully spoon cherry gelatin over orange layer. Chill until firm.

Susann Farrell, Wasco H. S.
Wasco, California

VELVET SALAD

Number of Servings — 12-15

1 pkg. lemon gelatin
3 c. hot water
1 8-oz. pkg. marshmallows (opt.)
1 small can crushed pineapple
1 c. whipped cream or Dream Whip
1 3-oz. pkg. cream cheese
¾-1 c. salad dressing
1 pkg. raspberry gelatin
1 c. cold water
Nuts

(Continued on next page)

Dissolve lemon gelatin in 1 cup hot water. Place 1 cup hot water over heat; add marshmallows and stir until dissolved. Add marshmallow mixture to lemon gelatin; add pineapple. Combine cream, cheese and salad dressing; fold into gelatin mixture. Pour into mold; chill until firm. Dissolve raspberry gelatin in remaining cup of hot water. Add cold water; cool. Pour raspberry gelatin over lemon gelatin. Chill until firm. Sprinkle with nuts.

This recipe submitted by the following teachers:

Carolyn Cheney, Culbertson Public School
Culbertson, Nebraska

Patricia Dolven, Willson Junior H. S.
Bozeman, Montana

WISCONSIN SUNSET SALAD

Number of Servings — 12

1 pkg. strawberry gelatin
1 pkg. orange gelatin
2 c. hot water
1 c. cold water
½ c. pineapple juice
2 T. lemon juice
1 c. whipped cream
1 T. sugar
1 c. cream cheese, softened
1 c. pineapple, drained
1 c. carrots, grated

Dissolve gelatins together in hot water. Add cold water, pineapple juice and lemon juice. Pour about one quarter of this mixture into the bottom of a salad mold and chill. Cool remainder until jelly-like; beat until light and fluffy. Work cream cheese until smooth and creamy. Blend into the whipped gelatin. Fold carrots, pineapple and cream, sweetened with the sugar, into gelatin cheese mixture. Pour over the firm gelatin. Chill several hours. Garnish with greens and fresh fruit.

Mrs. Arlene Block, Sauk-Prairie H. S.
Prairie du Sac, Wisconsin

RASPBERRY RIBBON SALAD

Number of Servings — 9

1 pkg. raspberry gelatin
1 pkg. frozen raspberries
2 c. hot water
1 c. cold water
Cultured sour cream
1 pkg. cherry gelatin
1 small can crushed pineapple, undrained

Dissolve raspberry gelatin in 1 cup hot water. Add frozen raspberries and ½ cup cold water. Chill until set. Spread top of firm gelatin with a layer of sour cream about ½ inch thick. Dissolve cherry gelatin in remaining hot water. Add pineapple and ½ cup cold water. Cool until thick. Spoon cherry mixture on top of sour cream layer. Chill until firm.

Deeanne Enders, Hebron H. S.
Hebron, Nebraska

RASPBERRY-FILLED GELATIN SALAD

Number of Servings — 10-12

1 3-oz. box raspberry gelatin
1 small pkg. frozen raspberries, undrained
1 lge. stalk celery, finely diced
1 medium apple, pared and finely diced
1 c. boiling water

Dissolve gelatin in boiling water. Add frozen raspberries; stir until raspberries are completely thawed. Add celery and apples; stir well. Pour half of mixture into a mold. Congeal.

FILLING:

1 small pkg. cream cheese
⅔ c. sour cream
⅔ c. large marshmallows, cut-up
1 lg. stalk celery, finely diced
½ c. pecans, chopped (opt.)

Whip cheese with electric mixer. Blend in sour cream; fold in marshmallows, celery and nuts. Spread over firm gelatin mixture. Refrigerate. Add remaining gelatin mixture; refrigerate until firm.

Berniece M. Cobb, Westminster H. S.
Westminster, Colorado

RASPBERRY-PEACH MOLD

Number of Servings — 8

1 1-lb. can sliced peaches, drained
4 T. lemon juice
1 3-oz. pkg. lemon gelatin
2 t. milk
2 T. mayonnaise or salad dressing
1 3-oz. pkg. cream cheese, softened
2 T. pecans, finely chopped
1 10-oz. pkg. frozen red raspberries, thawed
1 3-oz. pkg. raspberry gelatin
2 c. hot water

Combine syrup drained from peaches and 2 tablespoons lemon juice; add enough cold water to make 1 cup liquid. Dissolve lemon gelatin in 1 cup hot water; add syrup mixture. Chill until partially set. Add peaches; pour into 6½-cup ring mold. Chill until almost set. Mix milk, mayonnaise and cream cheese; stir in pecans. Spread over peach layer. Chill. Combine syrup drained from raspberries and remaining lemon juice. Add enough cold water to make 1 cup liquid. Dissolve raspberry gelatin in 1 cup hot water; add syrup mixture. Chill until partially set; stir in raspberries. Pour over cheese layer; chill until firm. Unmold.

Mrs. Shirley Gulbranson, Flandreau Indian H. S.
Flandreau, South Dakota

RASPBERRY RIBBON SALAD

Number of Servings — 9

1 3-oz. pkg. red raspberry gelatin
¼ c. sugar
1¼ c. boiling water
1 10-oz. box frozen red raspberries
1 T. lemon juice
1 Graham cracker crumb crust (opt.)

(Continued on next page)

1 3-oz. pkg. cream cheese, softened
⅓ c. Confectioner's sugar
1 t. vanilla
¼ t. salt
1 c. whipped cream

Dissolve gelatin in boiling water; add sugar, frozen berries and lemon juice. Mix well and chill until mixture starts to congeal. Blend whipped cream into Confectioner's sugar, vanilla, salt and cream cheese. Line a 9-inch square pan with a Graham cracker crust if desired. Place half of the cream cheese mixture on the crust then half of the raspberry mixture. Repeat. Top with a layer of graham cracker crumbs if desired. Chill several hours or overnight.

This recipe submitted by the following teachers:

Mrs. Carrie Rowe, Bazine Rural H. S.
Bazine, Kansas

Betty M. Ross, Sandwich H. S.
Sandwich, Illinois

STRAWBERRY SALAD

Number of Servings — 12

2 boxes strawberry gelatin
1 c. boiling water
2 pkg. frozen strawberries, drained
1 med. can crushed pineapple, drained
2½ c. juice drained from pineapple and strawberries
1 pkg. dessert topping mix
3 oz. cream cheese
½ c. nuts, crushed

Dissolve gelatin in boiling water. Add pineapple-strawberry juice. Add strawberries and pineapple. Congeal. Prepare dessert topping mix according to directions on the package. Blend in cream cheese. Spread over firm gelatin. Top with nuts. Let stand at least 3 hours before serving.

Mrs. Clara W. Folmar, McGuffey Jr.-Sr. H. S.
Claysville, Pennsylvania

STRAWBERRY GLACE SALAD

Number of Servings — 6-8

2 pkgs. strawberry gelatin
1 8-oz. pkg. cream cheese, softened
½ c. nuts, finely chopped
1 pt. whole strawberries, lightly sugared or 1 lge. pkg. frozen strawberries
2 c. boiling water
2 c. cold water

Dissolve gelatin in hot water; add cold water. Chill until slightly thickened. Shape cream-cheese balls; roll in nuts. Alternate cheese balls and strawberries in 9" ring mold. Cover with a layer of gelatin. Continue making layers. Chill until firm. Fill center with pineapple sherbet.

This recipe submitted by the following teachers:

Frances Hallett, Southington H. S.
Southington, Connecticut

Mildred A. Graham, LaRue Co. H. S.
Hodgenville, Kentucky

STRAWBERRY CREAM SQUARES

Number of Servings — 9

2 pkgs. strawberry gelatin
2 c. boiling water
2 10-oz. pkgs. frozen strawberries
1 c. dairy sour cream or ½ c. sour cream and ½ c. cream cheese
1½-2 c. crushed pineapple
2-3 lge. firm ripe bananas, finely diced (opt.)
1 c. nuts, coarsely chopped (opt.)

Dissolve gelatin in boiling water. Add berries, stirring occasionally until thawed. Add pineapple, bananas and nuts if desired. Pour half of mixture into 8x8x2 pan; chill until firm. Spoon an even layer of sour cream over firm gelatin. Stir and gently pour remaining gelatin over sour cream; chill until firm. If desired nuts may be combined with sour cream instead of with the fruit and gelatin.

This recipe submitted by the following teachers:

Elaine L. Smith, Union City Community H. S.
Union City, Indiana

Claris Crotton, Browns Valley H. S.
Browns Valley, Minnesota

Mrs. Beverly Wruck, Clintonville Senior H. S.
Clintonville, Wisconsin

Lois Ann Knutson, Sibley H. S.
West St. Paul, Minnesota

Mrs. Ruth E. Brown, West Washington, H. S.
Campbellsburg, Indiana

Dorothy Chalfant, Pennridge Senior H. S.
Perkasie, Pennsylvania

Donna J. Hunt, St. Ansgar Senior H. S.
St. Ansgar, Iowa

Mrs. Phyllis Greene McAfee
Old Rochester Regional H. S.
Mattapoisett, Massachusetts

Mrs. Delores Dexter, Lead Public H. S.
Lead, South Dakota

Kay D. Gass, King City H. S.
King City, California

Mrs. Jane Hutchins, Bangor H. S.
Bangor, Michigan

Joann Sealock, Pittsfield H. S.
Pittsfield, Illinois

Mrs. Angelene Phillips, Fredericktown H. S.
Fredericktown, Ohio

Mrs. Eloise Hearin, Thomas Edison H. S.
Springfield, Illinois

Mrs. Audra Taylor, Jacksonville H. S.
Jacksonville, Illinois

Thelma Birt, Troy H. S.
Troy, Ohio

Dorothy Hiser, Anthony Wayne H. S.
Whitehouse, Ohio

LAYERED BERRY SALAD

Number of Servings — 8-10

2 pkg. strawberry or raspberry gelatin
1 carton sour cream
1 lge. box frozen strawberries or raspberries, thawed
3½ c. hot water

Dissolve gelatin in hot water. Add fruit. Pour half of mixture into an 8 x 8 pan. Chill until firm. Spread sour cream evenly over firm layer. Chill. Pour remaining gelatin over sour cream. Chill until firm.

Mrs. Doris Balbach, Warren Community H. S.
Warren, Illinois

RUBY RING MOLDED SALAD

Number of Servings — 8-10

2 3-oz. pkg. strawberry gelatin
1 10-oz. pkg. frozen strawberries, strained
¼ c. sour cream
¼ c. cream cheese
½ c. pineapple juice
⅓ c. crushed pineapple
⅓ c. walnuts, finely chopped
½ c. ripe bananas, mashed
1 c. hot water

Prepare 1 package of gelatin according to directions. Chill until syrupy. Reserve ⅓ cup berries. Add remaining berries to gelatin. Turn into a 5½-cup ring mold; chill until set. Beat sour cream and cream cheese together until smooth and a spreading consistency. Spread mixture evenly over firm gelatin. Chill until set. Dissolve remaining package of gelatin in hot water. Add pineapple juice and chill until mixture is consistency of egg whites. Fold in nuts, pineapple, banana and reserved strawberries. Pour over chilled cheese-cream layer. Chill until firm.

Mrs. Alice Bostic, Springfield H. S.
Petersburg, Ohio

STRAWBERRY SURPRISE SALAD

Number of Servings — 10-12

1 pt. frozen strawberries, partially thawed
1 pkg. strav berry gelatin
1 6-oz. pkg. sream cheese
1 c. crushed pineapple, drained
½ c. walnuts, chopped

Combine pineapple juice with enough hot water to make 4 cups liquid. Add gelatin; stir until dissolved. Slightly cool. Add strawberries and pineapple; mix. Chill until almost set. Roll nuts in small balls of cream cheese; place in rows in gelatin mixture. Chill.

Topping:
1 pt. whipped cream
1 jar pimento spread
20 small marshmallows, diced

Mix all ingredients. Spread over salad. Sprinkle with additional nuts, if desired.

Mildred Snell, Austintown-Fitch H. S.
Youngstown, Ohio

LAYERED STRAWBERRY AND CHEESE

Number of Servings — 6-8

1 pkg. strawberry or cherry gelatin
1 pkg. lemon gelatin
1 3-oz. pkg. cream cheese
¼ c. black walnuts, chopped

Prepare strawberry or cherry gelatin according to package directions. Chill until firm. Prepare lemon gelatin in same manner. Let stand until it reaches the consistency of jelly. Beat until foamy. Beat in softened cream cheese and nuts. Spread over firm gelatin. Chill until firm. Cut into cubes.

Ruth I. Schwarz, Galesburg Senior H. S.
Galesburg, Illinois

MOLDED STRAWBERRY SALAD

Number of Servings — 6-8

2 pkg. strawberry gelatin
1 c. boiling water
2 10-oz. pkg. partially thawed sliced strawberries
1 pt. sour cream
1 c. walnuts or pecans, chopped
2 red apples, coarsely chopped

Dissolve gelatin in boiling water. Add partially thawed strawberries. Pour half mixture in mold. Refrigerate until firm. Spread sour cream on firm gelatin. Sprinkle nuts and apples on cream. Add remaining gelatin. Refrigerate until firm.

Mrs. Helen Toelle, Excelsior H. S.
Norwalk, California

SHERBET-FRUIT SALAD

Number of Servings — 8-10

1 pkg. orange gelatin
1 c. hot water
1 can Mandarin orange sections, drained
1 can crushed or chunk pineapple, drained (opt.)
½-1 pt. orange or orange-pineapple sherbet

Dissolve gelatin in hot water; cool. Stir in sherbet until melted Chill until partially set. Add oranges; also pineapple if desired. Chill until firm.

This recipe submitted by the following teachers:

Betty Henderson, Jordan H. S.
Sandy, Utah

Eleanore Pehlke, Elmwood H. S.
Elmwood, Wisconsin

Audrey Bailey, Northfield H. S.
Northfield, Minnesota

Mrs. Louanna Kirkpatrick, Frankfort Sr. H. S.
Frankfort, Indiana

Mrs. Nancy Williston, Elkton-Pigeon-Bay Port Schools
Pigeon, Michigan

Mrs. Ferrol Maddox, H. S.
Palestine, Illinois

Mrs. Donna Henrikson, Lena-Winslow H. S.
Lena, Illinois

Frances Holben, Stonington H. S.
Stonington, Illinois

MANDARIN DUET SALAD

Number of Servings — 10-12

Ambrosia Fruit Salad:
1 11-oz. can Mandarin orange sections, drained
1 13-oz. can pineapple chunks
1 c. flaked coconut
1 c. miniature marshmallows
1 c. sour cream

Mix ingredients. Chill for several hours or overnight.

2 3-oz. pkg. orange gelatin
2 c. mixed orange juice and water
1 pt. orange sherbet
1 11-oz. can Mandarin orange sections, drained

Dissolve gelatin in boiling juice-water mixture. Add sherbet; stir until melted. Add oranges. Pour into 1½-quart ring mold. Chill until set. Unmold and fill the center with Ambrosia Fruit Salad.

This recipe submitted by the following teachers:

Anne Weisbrot, Wabeno H. S.
Wabeno, Wisconsin

Marilyn Rova, Alvarado H. S.
Alvarado, Minnesota

FROTHY ORANGE SHERBET SALAD

Number of Servings — 8

2 3-oz. pkg. orange gelatin
2 c. mixed orange and pineapple juice plus water
1 pt. orange sherbet
1 can Mandarin oranges, drained
1 small can crushed pineapple, drained
⅓ c. walnuts, chopped (opt.)

Heat juice-water mixture to boiling. Dissolve gelatin in hot liquid. Spoon in sherbet. When slightly congealed add Mandarin oranges, pineapple and nuts if desired. Chill until firm. If desired 1 cup boiling water and 1 cup cold orange soft drink may be substituted for juice-water mixture.

Patricia M. Bieber, Del Norte H. S.
Crescent City, California

ORANGE DELIGHT

Number of Servings — 6-8

1 3-oz. pkg. orange gelatin
1 c. boiling water
1 c. orange sherbet
½ c. crushed pineapple, drained
1 11-oz. can Mandarin oranges, drained
2 bananas, sliced (opt.)
⅓ c. nuts, chopped (opt.)

Dissolve gelatin in boiling water; stir in sherbet. Chill until partially set. Add remaining ingredients. Chill until firm.

This recipe submitted by the following teachers:

Mary Kay Labbe, Eastern Jr. H. S.
Silver Spring, Maryland

Nancy Stewart, Melvindale H. S.
Melvindale, Michigan

ORANGE-CHEESE SALAD

Number of Servings — 8-10

2 pkg. orange gelatin
2 c. hot water
1 No. 202 can crushed pineapple
1 pt. orange sherbet, softened
¼ c. cream
½ c. pecans, chopped
1 c. longhorn cheese, grated

Dissolve gelatin in hot water; cool. Add remaining ingredients. Chill until firm.

Mrs. Kathryn Fox, Willcox H. S.
Willcox, Arizona

ORANGE COOLER-GELATIN SALAD

Number of Servings — 8

1 3-oz. pkg. orange gelatin
1 small can Mandarin orange sections, drained
1 No. 2 can crushed pineapple, drained
1 pt. orange sherbet
1 c. boiling water
1 c. mixed orange and pineapple juice or water

Dissolve gelatin in boiling water. Add fruits. Add juice or water. Beat sherbet until soft and creamy. Fold into gelatin mixture. Chill.

Lois F. McComber, Senior H. S.
Mountain Home, Idaho

ORANGE SATIN SALAD

Number of Servings — 6-8

2 3-oz. pkg. orange gelatin
2 c. hot water
1 pt. orange sherbet
1 T. cooking sherry
2 c. Mandarin oranges, well drained

Dissolve gelatin in hot water. Mix thoroughly and let stand at room temperature for 5 minutes. Dissolve sherbet in gelatin mixture; add cooking sherry. Mix in oranges. Chill. Lime gelatin, lime sherbet and pineapple or raspberry gelatin, raspberries or cherries and raspberry sherbet may be used for variety.

Mrs. Lynne Wise, Clear Fork H. S.
Bellville, Ohio

ORANGE SHERBET SALAD

Number of Servings — 15

1 pkg. lemon gelatin
1 pkg. orange gelatin
2 c. boiling water
1 small can Mandarin oranges, drained
¾ c. mixed Mandarin orange juice and water
1 pt. orange sherbet

Dissolve gelatins in hot water; add juice-water mixture. Chill. Beat in sherbet; stir in oranges. Chill until firm.

Vera Murphy, Atchison County Community H. S.
Effingham, Kansas

ORANGE SALAD

Number of Servings — 8-10

2 cans Mandarin oranges, drained
2 pkg. orange gelatin
1 c. hot water
1 c. Mandarin orange juice
1 pt. orange sherbet

Dissolve gelatin in hot water. Add juice. Cool until mixture begins to thicken. Add sherbet, stirring until it softens. Add oranges. Chill until firm.

This recipe submitted by the following teachers:

Dorothy Withers, Senior H. S.
Hastings, Nebraska

Rosalie Vollmer, Campbellsport H. S.
Campbellsport, Wisconsin

Mary H. Olmanson, Cannon Falls H. S.
Cannon Falls, Minnesota

Mrs. Mary Lou Wright, Siren H. S.
Siren, Wisconsin

SALAD WITH ORANGE SHERBET

Number of Servings — 8-10

2 pkg. orange gelatin
2 c. boiling water
1 pt. orange sherbet
1 lge. can crushed pineapple undrained (opt.)
1 can Mandarin oranges, drained
Maraschino cherries, drained and chopped (opt.)

Dissolve gelatin in boiling water. Add orange sherbet; stir until melted. Add pineapple, oranges and cherries. Chill until set.

This recipe submitted by the following teachers:

Bessie L. Alford, Newman H. S.
Newman, Illinois

Mrs. Virginia H. Gustafson, Cloquet H. S.
Cloquet, Minnesota

Mrs. Betty Phillips, Fromberg H. S.
Fromberg, Montana

TRIPLE-ORANGE DESSERT SALAD

Number of Servings — 6

1 pkg. orange gelatin
1 c. boiling water
Juice of ½ lemon
½ pt. orange sherbet
½ c. whipped cream
½ c. Mandarin oranges, drained

Dissolve gelatin in water. Add lemon juice and sherbet, stirring until melted. Refrigerate until partially set. Fold in whipped cream and orange sections. Pour into a 1-quart ring mold and chill until set.

Mrs. Beverly Sampson, Redfield H. S.
Redfield, South Dakota

ORANGE SOUFFLE SALAD

Number of Servings — 6

1 3-oz. pkg. orange gelatin
1 pt. orange sherbet, softened
2 T. lemon juice
1 11-oz. can Mandarin orange slices, drained
Juice drained from oranges plus enough water to make 1 c. liquid

Heat juice-water mixture to boiling; add gelatin, stirring to dissolve. Immediately add sherbet and stir until melted. Add lemon juice. Cool until partially thickened. Add orange sections.

Mrs. Martha Engelberg, Mason County Eastern
Custer, Michigan

TWENTY-FOUR HOUR SALAD

Number of Servings — 8

1 No. 2 can crushed or chunk pineapple, drained
1 lb. Tokay grapes or 1 can white cherries
30 marshmallows, cut up
¼ lb. pecans, chopped
1 c. whipped cream

Dressing:

2 T. sugar
4 egg yolks
Juice of 1 lemon
½ t. salt
¼ t. mustard

Mix the sugar, egg yolks, lemon juice, salt and mustard. Bring to a boil. Cool. Add dressing to the combined fruits, marshmallows and nuts. Fold in the cream. Refrigerate 24 hours.

Deanna Brosten, McFarland H. S.
McFarland, California

TWENTY-FOUR HOUR SALAD

Number of Servings — 8-10

2 eggs, beaten
4-6 t. vinegar or lemon juice
4-6 t. sugar
2 t. butter (opt.)
1 c. whipped cream
2 c. Royal Anne cherries, diced
2 c. pineapple, diced
2 oranges, diced
2 c. peaches, diced (opt.)
2 c. miniature marshmallows

Cook eggs, vinegar and sugar in double boiler until thick and smooth. Cool. Fold in cream and fruit. Turn into ring mold or glass serving dish. Chill 24 hours.

This recipe submitted by the following teachers:

Mrs. Lora Hedegaard, Cheyenne-Eagle Butte
Eagle Butte, South Dakota

Mrs. Mildred E. Miller, Chico Senior H. S.
Chico, California

TWENTY-FOUR-HOUR SALAD

Number of Servings — 8-12

½ c. milk
4 egg yolks, beaten
Juice of 1 lemon
1 pt. whipped cream
1 lb. miniature marshmallows
1 lge. can white cherries, drained
1 lge. can Bartlett pears, drained and cut
1 lge. can pineapple chunks, drained

Heat ½ cup milk to boiling point; stir in egg yolks; cook in double boiler until thickened. Add lemon juice. Cool. Fold in cream. Add marshmallows; fold in fruit; chill for approximately 24 hours.

Mrs. Dorothy E. Cobb, Sebring McKinley H. S.
Sebring, Ohio

TWENTY-FOUR HOUR SALAD

Number of Servings — 12

¼ c. Maraschino cherries
1 c. pears, diced
1 c. pineapple, diced
1 c. grapes, diced
1 c. peaches, diced
2 eggs, beaten
¼ c. water
3 T. sugar
Juice of 1 lemon
½ pt. whipped cream
½ t. salt
½ lb. marshmallows

Combine fruits. Cook eggs, water, sugar and lemon juice until thickened. Cool. Add whipped cream, salt and marshmallows. Pour over fruits. Refrigerate for 24 hours.

Mrs. Arvella Curtis, Fulton School
Middleton, Michigan

TWENTY-FOUR HOUR SALAD

Number of Servings — 8

2 T. cornstarch
1 c. pineapple juice
½ c. butter or margarine
2 T. sugar
1/16 t. salt
2 T. lemon juice
1 egg, slightly beaten
4 slices pineapple, chopped
3 oranges, chopped
¼ c. nuts, chopped (opt.)
10 marshmallows, chopped
1 c. whipped cream
1 c. Bing cherries (opt.)

Make a paste of cornstarch and pineapple juice. Add remaining juice, butter, sugar and salt. Cook 10 minutes. Add egg; cook a few minutes longer, stirring constantly, until thick. Cool. Combine cooked mixture, fruit and nuts, fold in whipped cream. Refrigerate for 24 hours.

This recipe submitted by the following teachers:

Betty Sudduth, Westminster H. S.
Westminster, South Carolina

G. Kathleen Booth, Grove City H. S.
Grove City, Ohio

TWENTY-FOUR HOUR FRUIT SALAD

Number of Servings — 10-12

2 c. fresh or canned green grapes, or white cherries, drained
2 c. pineapple tidbits, drained
2 c. Mandarin oranges, drained (opt.)
2-3 c. miniature marshmallows
½-1 c. almond slivers
2 eggs
2 T. sugar
¼ c. light cream
Juice of 1 lemon or small orange
1 c. whipped cream

Combine fruits with marshmallows and almonds. Beat eggs until light and fluffy; gradually add sugar, light cream and lemon juice. Mix well. Cook in a double boiler until smooth and thick, stirring constantly. Cool. Fold in whipped cream. Pour over fruit mixture and mix lightly. Chill for 24 hours. Do not freeze.

This recipe submitted by the following teachers:

Kathy Daniels, Moose Lake Public H. S.
Moose Lake, Minnesota

Edith Minix Atcheson, Colonial H. S.
Orlando, Florida

Constance Ackerson, Grand Ledge H. S.
Grand Ledge, Michigan

Mrs. Layne Storment, Kahlotus H. S.
Kahlotus, Washington

Mrs. Magdaline Dhuey, Casco H. S.
Casco, Wisconsin

OVERNIGHT FRUIT SALAD (24 HOUR)

Number of Servings — 8-10

1 No. 2½ can chunk pineapple
1 can Mandarin oranges
1 c. seedless grapes (opt.)
1 c. angel flake coconut
1 c. miniature marshmallows
1 c. cultured sour cream

Mix ingredients together. Place in refrigerator for 24 hours. Serve. Excellent with chicken.

Mrs. Lucile Calhoun, Kelso H. S.
Kelso, Washington

OVERNIGHT FRUIT SALAD

Number of Servings — 12

1 lb. grapes, halved
1 lb. marshmallows, cut
1 small can crushed pineapple, drained
1 c. whipped cream
2 eggs
Juice of 1 lemon
1 c. sugar

Mix fruits and marshmallows; chill. Combine eggs, lemon and sugar; cook over low heat until thickened. Cool; fold in whipped cream. Fold cooked dressing into fruit mixture. Chill overnight.

Mrs. Bernice Dukerschein, Flambeau H. S.
Tony, Wisconsin

TWENTY-FOUR HOUR SALAD

Number of Servings — 6-8

Dressing:
2 eggs or 3 egg yolks
2 T. sugar
2 T. lemon juice
2 T. pineapple juice
1 T. butter
Salt
1 c. whipped cream

Cook in saucepan over low heat, stirring constantly until boiling. Remove from heat. Cool. Fold into whipped cream.

2 c. Queen Anne cherries, drained
2 c. pineapple tidbits, drained
2 oranges, pared or Mandarin oranges
2 grapefruit, pared
2 c. miniature marshmallows
½ c. pecans, chopped
½ c. Maraschino cherries
1 c. green grapes

Combine fruit and fold in dressing. Chill. Garnish with green grapes and mint leaves.

Beth Trotter, Morris H. S.
Morris, Illinois

TWENTY-FOUR HOUR SALAD

Number of Servings — 10

2 egg yolks
2 T.-½ c. plain cream
Pinch of salt (opt.)
Juice of ½ lemon (opt.)
1 T. sugar

Mix yolks, cream, salt and sugar. Cook in double boiler until mixture thickens. Cool.

2 c. Tokay grapes seeded (opt.)
1 No. 2½ can pineapples, drained and cubed
1 lb. marshmallows, cubed
¼ lb. pecans, or almonds, broken (opt.)
1 lge. bottle Maraschino cherries, cubed, (opt.)
1 pt. whipped cream

Mix fruits, nuts and marshmallows with cool dressing. Fold in whipped cream. Refrigerate for 24 hours.

This recipe submitted by the following teachers:

Mrs. Juanita M. Rogers, Paul G. Blazer H. S.
Ashland, Kentucky

Christine Applin, Stephen F. Austin H. S.
Austin, Texas

Mrs. Helen I. Becker, LaGrande Sr. H. S.
LaGrande, Oregon

Edith Nusser, Smith Center H. S.
Smith Center, Kansas

TWENTY-FOUR HOUR SALAD

Number of Servings — 6-8

2 eggs
4 T. vinegar
4 T. sugar
16 marshmallows
¼ c. Maraschino cherries
2 c. pears, drained and chopped
2 c. peaches, drained and chopped
2 c. crushed pineapple, drained
2 c. apricots, drained and chopped
1 c. evaporated milk, stiffly beaten
½ c. nuts, chopped (opt.)

Mix eggs, vinegar and sugar in double boiler. Cook 3-5 minutes until thick. Add marshmallows and stir until soft. Stir in cherries, pears, peaches, pineapple, apricots and nuts. Fold in evaporated milk. Pour into a loaf pan. Refrigerate for 24 hours.

Anne Whitmore, North Judson H. S.
North Judson, Indiana

TWENTY-FOUR HOUR SALAD

Number of Servings — 10

4 egg yolks
½ c. pineapple juice
Juice of 1 lemon
Pinch of salt
1 pt. whipped cream
1 9-oz. can crushed pineapple, drained
1 lb. marshmallows, cut
1 c. nuts, chopped
1 8-oz. jar Maraschino cherries (opt.)
1 No. 2 can Royal Anne cherries, or 1 lb. seedless grapes, drained

Mix egg yolks with pineapple juice in top of double boiler. Cook until thick. Cool. Add lemon juice and salt. Fold in whipped cream, fruits, marshmallows and nuts. Chill 24 hours before serving.

This recipe submitted by the following teachers:

Mrs. Charles Yount, Bandy's H. S.
Catawba, North Carolina

Mrs. Ralph Leach, Bird City Rural H. S.
Bird City, Kansas

TWENTY-FOUR HOUR SALAD

Number of Servings — 12-15

2 c. pineapple chunks, drained
2 c. Mandarin oranges or orange sections, diced
2 c. flaked coconut
8 lge. marshmallows, diced
2 c. commercial sour cream
2 c. seedless grapes, diced (opt.)

Combine all ingredients. If salad seems too dry, add some of the reserved pineapple and orange juice. Refrigerate for 24 hours. Serve on lettuce leaf if used as a salad. Good as a dessert.

This recipe submitted by the following teachers:

Betty Conant, Dundee Sr., H. S.
Carpentersville, Illinois

Mrs. Betty S. Turner, Chicod School
Greenville, North Carolina

Mrs. Clara Ann Maples, Sweeny H. S.
Sweeny, Texas

Mrs. Roy A. Gill, Barnesville, Sr. H. S.
Barnesville, Minnesota

Mrs. Iris Payne, Iola H. S.
Iola, Texas

TWENTY-FOUR HOUR SALAD

Number of Servings — 12

¼ c. water
3 T. orange juice
3 T. lemon juice
6 T. pineapple juice
½ c. sugar
2 T. flour
1 egg, beaten
1 lb. marshmallows, quartered
1 lb. white grapes
1 No. 2½ can pineapple cubes, drained
1 bottle Maraschino cherries, drained
1 c. whipped cream

Mix flour and sugar; add to liquid. Cook until thickened, stirring constantly. Add egg gradually and continue cooking 1 minute. Cool. Add marshmallows, grapes, pineapple and cherries. Refrigerate overnight. Several hours before serving fold in whipped cream.

Delores Weir, Comfrey H. S.
Comfrey, Minnesota

TWENTY-FOUR HOUR SALAD

Number of Servings — 8

4 egg yolks
2 T.-½ c. sugar
Juice of 1 or 2 lemons
1 pt. whipped cream
1 lb. white grapes or 1 can Queen Anne cherries
1 lb. marshmallows
1 No. 2 can pineapple, drained and cut in pieces
1 can fruit cocktail, drained (opt.)

Combine yolks, sugar and lemon juice; beat for 3 minutes. Cook over low heat until thick. Cool. Stir in remaining ingredients. Chill 24 hours before serving.

This recipe submitted by the following teachers:

Mary Jean Weeden, Adams City H. S.
Adams City, Colorado

Ethlyn Peters, Cassville H. S.
Cassville, Wisconsin

TWENTY-FOUR HOUR SALAD

Number of Servings — 10

1 No. 2 can pineapple chunks, drained
1 can Mandarin oranges, drained
1 can white grapes, drained
1 c. miniature marshmallows
½ c. coconut
½ pt. whipped cream
½ pt. commercial sour cream
2 T. powdered sugar

Fold sour cream and powdered sugar into whipped cream. Mix with fruits, coconut and marshmallows. Chill in refrigerator 24 hours. Serve on lettuce; garnish with Maraschino cherry.

Beverly Wilcoxon, Butte H. S.
Arco, Idaho

TWENTY-FOUR HOUR SALAD

Number of Servings — 8-10

2-3 egg yolks, beaten
2 T. sugar
2 T. lemon juice or vinegar
2 T. pineapple juice
⅛ t. salt
1 T. butter
1 c. whipped cream
2 c. white seedless grapes or white cherries, pitted
2 c. pineapple tidbits, drained
2 c. miniature marshmallows
2 oranges, sectioned or 1 c. Mandarin orange slices
½-1 c. Maraschino or candied cherries, diced (opt.)
½-1 c. blanched toasted almonds, slivered or whole (opt.)

Combine egg yolks, sugar, vinegar, pineapple juice, salt and butter in double boiler. Cook over hot water until thick. Cool. Fold in cream. Gently stir in fruits, marshmallows and nuts. Chill 24 hours. Serve on lettuce or in dessert bowls.

This recipe submitted by the following teachers:

Vivian Eggers, Chester H. S.
Chester, Illinois

Rosemary Freeborn, Santiam H. S.
Mill City, Oregon

Jane Bonander, Melvin-Sibley H. S.
Melvin, Illinois

Mrs. Dorothy T. Rabb, Lowe Jr. H. S.
Minden, Louisiana

Mable Gray, Savanna Community H. S.
Savanna, Illinois

Nora K. Gardner, Floyd County H. S.
Floyd, Virginia

Mrs. Virginia Henson, Central H. S.
Kirtland, New Mexico

Mrs. Jennette F. Buhler, Byron H. S.
Byron, Wyoming

Mrs. Frances Grein, Van Vleck, H. S.
Van Vleck, Texas

Mrs. Eleanor J. Lewis, Union Point School
Union Point, Georgia

Homoiselle House, Hempstead H. S.
Hempstead, Texas

Mrs. Ada Blankenship, Riley County H. S.
Riley, Kansas

Mrs. Judith R. Camden, Freeman H. S.
Freeman, Washington

Janice Hancock, Ipswich H. S.
Ipswich, South Dakota

Mrs. Jimmie W. Tew, Blue Springs H. S.
Clio, Alabama

Mrs. Joyce Cheatham, Monterey H. S.
Slaton, Texas

ANGEL SALAD (24 HOUR)

Number of Servings — 8-10

2 egg yolks, beaten
3 T. canned pineapple syrup
1 T. vinegar
2 T. sugar
Dash of salt
2 c. seedless green grapes, halved
½ lb. marshmallows
1 c. whipped cream

Combine egg yolks, pineapple syrup, vinegar, sugar and salt. Cook over hot water until thick, stirring constantly. Cool and pour over combined grapes and marshmallows. Mix well and let stand several hours or overnight. Just before serving fold in whipped cream.

Mrs. Miriam Erickson, Gibraltar Union H. S.
Fish Creek, Wisconsin

ANGEL HASH SALAD (24 HOUR)

Number of Servings — 10-12

2 T. cornstarch
¼ c. sugar
1 c. mixed pineapple syrup and water
2 egg yolks
1 c. whipped cream
1 No. 2 can pineapple tidbits, drained
¼ c. walnuts, chopped
15 marshmallows, quartered
6 bananas, sliced

Combine cornstarch and sugar. Gradually add pineapple syrup, stirring to blend. Cook, stirring constantly, until thickened. Add part of mixture to egg yolks; blend well and return to hot mixture. Cook, stirring constantly, for 2 minutes. Cool. Fold in whipped cream. Fold in pineapple, walnuts and marshmallows. Chill overnight. Add bananas just before serving. Garnish with maraschino cherries and serve in lettuce lined salad bowl.

Mrs. Marjorie Neilson, Arlington Public Schools
Arlington, South Dakota

CHERRY-FRUIT SALAD (24 HOUR)

Number of Servings — 8

Dressing:
4 eggs
1 c. sugar (scant)
4 T. vinegar
1 c. whipped cream

Mix eggs, sugar and vinegar. Cook over low heat until thick. Cool. Add whipped cream.

4 c. white cherries, drained and pitted
4 c. dark cherries, drained and pitted
4 c. pineapple cubes, drained
4 c. marshmallows, diced

Mix 1 cup of dressing with fruit. Refrigerate for 24 hours.

Janet Kohls, Waupun Senior H. S.
Waupun, Wisconsin

GUMDROP SALAD (24 HOUR)

Number of Servings — 10-12

1 No. 2 can pineapple chunks, drained
1 No. 303 can white grapes, drained
1 11-oz. can Mandarin orange sections, drained
1 8-oz. pkg. miniature marshmallows
1 c. assorted gumdrops, quartered (no licorice)
½ c. nuts, chopped
½ c. sugar
¼ c. sifted flour
Dash of salt
¼ c. lemon juice
1 c. pineapple juice
1½ c. whipped cream

Combine pineapple, grapes and orange sections with marshmallows, gumdrops and nuts; set aside. Combine sugar, flour and salt in saucepan. Stir in lemon and pineapple juices. Cook over low heat until thickened, stirring constantly. Cool. Fold in whipped cream and fruit mixture. Cover and chill for 12 to 24 hours.

Regina Johnson, Ely Memorial H. S.
Ely, Minnesota

GUMDROP-FRUIT SALAD (24 HOUR)

Number of Servings — 8

1 No. 2 can pineapple chunks, drained
¼ c. sugar
2 T. flour
¼ t. salt
3 T. lemon juice
1½ t. vinegar
⅓ c. pineapple juice
2 c. seedless grapes, halved
⅔ c. orange slice or assorted gumdrops, quartered
1 4-oz. bottle Maraschino cherries, drained and halved
¼ c. pecans, chopped
2 c. miniature marshmallows
1 c. whipped cream

Combine sugar, flour and salt. Add pineapple juice, lemon juice and vinegar. Cook, stirring constantly until mixture thickens and boils. Cool. Combine pineapple and all remaining ingredients except whipped cream. Fold in cooked dressing then whipped cream. Cover and refrigerate for 12 to 24 hours.

This recipe submitted by the following teachers:

Doris Meyer, Columbus Senior H. S.
Columbus, Indiana

Judith Adams, Stillwater Senior H. S.
Stillwater, Minnesota

Helen G. Long, Rushville H. S.
Rushville, Illinois

MOLDED TWENTY-FOUR HOUR SALAD

Number of Servings — 6-8

1 No. 2½ can pineapple, drained
1 8-oz. pkg. cream cheese, broken
¾ c. walnuts, chopped
1 c. celery, chopped
1 c. whipped cream

Dissolve gelatin according to package directions. Chill until thickened. Mix pineapple, cheese, celery and nuts. Fold into gelatin. Fold in cream. Chill for 24 hours. Top with pineapple dressing.

Pineapple Dressing:
1 c. pineapple juice
1 c. sugar
2 eggs, beaten
2 T. cornstarch or flour

Stir and cook ingredients until thick and smooth. Cool and add to salad.

June Houchins, Tuslaw H. S.
Massillon, Ohio

OVERNIGHT SALAD

Number of Servings — 25

1 lb. marshmallows
1 No. 2½ can pineapple slices, drained
1 can Royal Anne cherries, drained and pitted (opt.)
½-1 lb. grapes, seeded
½ lb. nuts

Cut all fruits into small pieces. Mix.

Dressing:
4 eggs, beaten
½ c. hot milk
Juice of 1 lemon
1 pt. whipped cream
¼ t. dry mustard (opt.)

Cook eggs, milk and lemon juice in double boiler until mixture coats a spoon. Remove from heat. When cold, add whipped cream. Mix with fruit; chill overnight.

This recipe submitted by the following teachers:

Mrs. Mary Ada Parks, Anna-Jonesboro H. S.
Anna, Illinois

Ruth I. Lamb, Central Kitsap Junior H. S.
Silverdale, Washington

OVERNIGHT FRUIT SALAD

1 No. 2½ can fruit cocktail, drained
1 No. 2 can crushed pineapple, drained
20 marshmallows, quartered
½ pt. whipped cream
½ c. salad dressing
¼ c. powdered sugar
1 3-oz. pkg. cream cheese, broken

Combine fruits. Whip salad dressing, cream cheese and powdered sugar into whipped cream. Beat until well blended. Add to fruit mixture. Stir in marshmallows. Chill several hours.

Mrs. Jenevieve Klug, Barnesville H. S.
Barnesville, Minnesota

OVERNIGHT FRUIT SALAD

Number of Servings — 12

1 can chunk pineapple, drained
½ lb. marshmallows, flavored
4 bananas, sliced
1 c. Maraschino cherries, halved
½ c. pineapple juice
2 egg yolks, beaten
3 T. sugar
1 T. cornstarch
1 c. whipped cream

Combine pineapple, marshmallows, bananas and cherries. Mix sugar and cornstarch; add to egg yolks. Gradually stir in pineapple juice. Cook until thick, stirring constantly. Cool. Add whipped cream. Combine dressing mixture with fruit. Chill overnight.

Ruth Peterson, Parkers Prairie H. S.
Parkers Prairie, Minnesota

PINEAPPLE OVERNIGHT SALAD

Number of Servings — 6

1-2 eggs, beaten
1 c. pineapple juice
2 T. flour
3-4 T. sugar
½ t. salt (opt.)
4-8-oz. miniature marshmallows
1 No. 2 can crushed pineapple, drained
1 c. whipped cream
2 T. lemon juice
1 t. lemon peel (opt.)
¼ c. maraschino cherries (opt.)

Combine eggs, pineapple juice, flour and sugar in a double boiler; cook until thickened add lemon juice & peel. Cool. Fold in marshmallows, pineapple and whipped cream. Chill overnight.

This recipe submitted by the following teachers:

Evangeline LaBarre, Belt Valley H. S.
Belt, Montana

Mary Frances Dungen, Yoakum H. S.
Yoakum, Texas

WHITE GRAPE SALAD (24 HOUR)

Number of Servings — 8-10

20 lge. marshmallows, cut very fine
1 small can crushed pineapple, drained
1 3-oz. pkg. cream cheese
½ pt. whipped cream
½-1 lb. white seedless grapes or 1 jar Maraschino cherries, quartered
¼ c. salad dressing

Thoroughly mix salad dressing with the cream cheese; add to marshmallows, grapes, and pineapple. Fold in whipped cream and mix lightly. Pour into a 6x10 pan. Chill for 24 hours.

This recipe submitted by the following teachers:

Ruth Haberlen, Greensburg Salem Sr. H. S.
Greensburg, Pennsylvania

Wanda M. Stacke
Home Economics Teacher, Sr. H. S.
Marshfield, Wisconsin

TOMORROW'S SALAD (24 HOUR)

Number of Servings — 8-10

DRESSING:
2 eggs, beaten
¼ c. sugar
¼ c. vinegar
2 T. butter

Combine eggs, sugar and vinegar. Cook in a double boiler until thick and smooth. Remove from heat; stir in butter. Cool.

2 c. marshmallows, quartered
2 c. white cherries, pitted or white grapes
2 c. pineapple chunks
2 c. Mandarin or small oranges, cut up
¼ c. candied cherries, cut in small pieces (opt.)
1 c. whipped cream

Mix ½ cup nuts, chopped (opt.) white cherries, pineapple, marshmallows, oranges and candied cherries. Combine whipped cream, dressing and fruits. Let stand 24 hours in coldest part of refrigerator. Do not freeze.

This recipe submitted by the following teachers:

Mrs. Kathryn Jeska, Swanton H. S.
Swanton, Ohio

Mrs. Grace L. Schindler, Wheelersburg H. S.
Wheelersburg, Ohio

Mrs. J. A. Gipson, Benton H. S.
Benton, Arkansas

Mrs. Alberta Collier, Paw Paw H. S.
Paw Paw, Illinois

Viola Gracey, Travis Jr. H. S.
Snyder, Texas

Maude Marshall Henderson, Gunston Jr. H. S.
Arlington, Virginia

Jane G. Roberts, Quincy Community H. S.
Quincy, Michigan

CINNAMON-APPLE SALAD

Number of Servings — 4

¾ c. sugar
¾ c. water
1 T. red cinnamon candies
¼ t. red food coloring
4 cooking apples
Cottage cheese or cream cheese

Cook sugar, water and candies until dissolved. Add food coloring to make syrup bright red. Meanwhile, core and pare apples, leaving 1 inch of the skin at the blossom end. Place apples in syrup; cover and slowly cook until barely tender. Turn apples after 7-10 minutes. Remove apples from syrup; place on rack. Continue cooking syrup until thick. Slowly dip syrup over apples. Chill. Place on lettuce. Cut each apple part of the way down, spreading sections open. Fill centers with cottage cheese or cream cheese.

Mrs. Nannie C. Edwards, Oxford Area H. S.
Oxford, Pennsylvania

STUFFED APPLE-CINNAMON SALAD

Number of Servings — 6

6 apples, pared and cored
½ c. red cinnamon candies
¼ c. sugar
2 c. water
2 T. pecans, broken
10 dates, pitted and chopped
½ c. crushed pineapple, drained
¼ c. mayonnaise
Grated cheese (opt.)

Dissolve candies and sugar in water over low heat. Add whole apples and cook slowly until transparent but not soft. Chill. Combine remaining ingredients; stuff apples. Serve on lettuce. Garnish with a small amount of grated cheese if desired.

This recipe submitted by the following teachers:

Mrs. Freddie E. Taylor, Dierks, H. S.
Dierks, Arkansas

Mrs. Wanda Newlin, Highland Community H. S.
Highland, Illinois

Kathleen Burchett, Flatwood
Jonesville, Virginia

Fern Peterson, North Jr. H. S.
Rapid City, South Dakota

STUFFED APPLE RING SALAD

Number of Servings — 8

5 red apples
Lemon or pineapple juice
1 8-oz. pkg. cream cheese
½ c. dates, chopped
¼ c. nuts, chopped

Wash apples but do not pare. Cut in ½-inch slices. Remove core with a small cutter, leaving a ring about ½-1-inch across. Brush with lemon or pineapple juice. Cream the cheese until smooth; add dates, nuts and a dash of lemon juice. Blend well. Place apple rings on a tray and fill with the cheese mixture, either spreading evenly over the surface or topping each ring with a ball of the cheese. Chill.

Sharon L. Bickel, Liberty Center School
Liberty Center, Indiana

CANTALOUPE CARNIVAL

Number of Servings — 8-10

1 medium cantaloupe, diced
2-3 medium bananas, sliced
1 c. miniature marshmallows
½ c. almonds, sliced
½ c. strawberries, sliced
⅓ c. salad dressing
½ c. strawberry ice cream, softened

Sprinkle lemon juice on bananas. Combine cantaloupe, bananas, marshmallows, almonds and strawberries. Chill. Just before serving whip salad dressing and ice cream. Pour over salad.

Mrs. Jeanne Damhof, Manton H. S.
Manton, Michigan

CANTALOUPE SALAD

Number of Servings — 6

1 medium cantaloupe
2 c. seedless green grapes
Lettuce leaves

Cut cantaloupe lengthwise into 6 sections; remove seeds and shell. Place each section on crisp lettuce leaf. Pile grapes on each section.

Dressing:
½ c. mayonnaise
2 T. frozen orange juice, concentrate

Mix well. Top each salad with desired amount of dressing.

Helen Hoermann, Jamestown Senior H. S.
Jamestown, North Dakota

FRUIT COCKTAIL SALAD

Number of Servings — 8

1 No. 2½ can fruit cocktail, drained
½ lge. bag miniature marshmallows
1 c. sour cream

Mix ingredients together. Cover and chill overnight.

Mrs. Betty Kandt, Herington H. S.
Herington, Kansas

MARSHMALLOW SURPRISE

Number of Servings — 10

1 No. 2 can crushed pineapple, drained
½ c. sugar
2 T. flour
2 eggs, beaten
1 pkg. miniature marshmallows
2 oranges, sectioned
1 c. pecans, chopped
1 c. evaporated milk, whipped

Combine juice drained from pineapple with sugar, flour and eggs. Cook until thick. Add marshmallows to hot mixture. Cool. Fold in pineapple, oranges, pecans and whipped milk. Refrigerate until firm.

Kathryn Williams, Ruidoso H. S.
Ruidoso, New Mexico

MELON SALAD WITH DRESSING

Watermelon balls or cubes
Cantaloupe balls or cubes
Honeydew melon balls or cubes
Banana slices (opt.)
Pineapple slices (opt.)
½ watermelon shell, cut lengthwise

Combine fruits. Place in scooped out watermelon shell.

DRESSING:
½ c. oil
2 T. vinegar
2 T. lemon juice
½ t. salt
¼ t. dry mustard
¼ t. paprika
4 T. confectioner's sugar

Put all dressing ingredients in a jar; shake well. Pour over fruits just before serving.

Darleen Pulkrabek, Mt. Iron H. S.
Mt. Iron, Minnesota

STUFFED PEAR SALAD

Number of Servings — 6

1¾ c. pear or raspberry and pear juice
1 pkg. raspberry gelatin
6 pear halves
1 c. fresh or frozen red raspberries, partially thawed
Lettuce
⅓ c. mayonnaise
Cream

Heat juice; add gelatin. Stir until gelatin is completely dissolved. Pour ⅛" layer into a glass baking dish that has been rinsed with cold water. Chill until gelatin layer is firm. Place pears, with hollow side up on gelatin; fill hollows with raspberries. Carefully pour remaining gelatin over berries. Chill until firm. Cut in squares with stuffed pears in the center. Serve on lettuce with mayonnaise and whipped cream.

Mrs. Helen L. Ware, Salem H. S.
Salem, New Jersey

PINEAPPLE CUP

Number of Servings — 6

1 lge. pineapple
1 c. whole strawberries
1 c. honeydew balls
1 c. cantaloupe balls
1 c. cherry liqueur

Cut pineapple in half lengthwise. Scoop out center, leaving a 1-inch shell. Remove core and cut fruit in cubes. Chill the pineapple shells. Combine pineapple cubes with strawberries, melon balls, and liqueur. Let stand at room temperature for 1 hour. Chill for at least 4 hours. To serve, spoon fruit and marinade into pineapple shells.

Mrs. Barbara Spears, Shafter H. S.
Shafter, California

STRAWBERRY DELIGHT

Number of Servings — 6

1 c. whipped cream
1¼ c. confectioner's sugar
¼ lb. butter
1 c. nuts, chopped
2 lge. eggs, slightly beaten
1 10-oz. pkg. frozen strawberries

Cream sugar and butter together; blend in eggs. Add nuts and strawberries. Fold in whipped cream. Chill. May be frozen for later use.

Fornadia Cook, Osborne Jr. H. S.
Marietta, Georgia

TARRAGON SALAD

Number of Servings — 8

4 egg yolks
¼ c. sugar
2-4 T. Tarragon vinegar
½ lb. pecans
½ lb. miniature marshmallows
1 c. pineapple chunks, drained
1 c. whipped cream

Cook egg yolks, sugar and vinegar in top of double boiler until slightly thick. Cool. Add nuts, marshmallows and pineapple; mix. Fold in whipped cream. Refrigerate in coldest part of the refrigerator for 4 hours. Salad will keep for a week if covered and refrigerated.

This recipe submitted by the following teachers:

Lavonda McCurdy, Yulee H. S.
Yulee, Florida

Vada Nolen, Smoot H. S.
Smoot, West Virginia

TROPICAL FRUIT SALAD

Number of Servings — 8-12

DRESSING:
1 T. butter
1 T. sugar
2 T. vinegar
2 eggs
Whipped cream

Mix ingredients. Cook over low heat until thick. Cool and mix with equal amount of whipped cream.

24 marshmallows, cut in pieces
1 lge. can diced pineapple
6 lge. oranges, cut in pieces
½-1 c. nuts (opt.)

Mix oranges, pineapple and marshmallows; let stand about an hour. Drain. Mix with dressing and whipped cream just before serving. Nuts may be added if desired.

Eliza Ninmann, Gresham H. S.
Gresham, Wisconsin

TUNA-FRUIT PARTY SALAD

Number of Servings — 6

2 c. white water packed chunk tuna
1 c. celery, chopped
1 c. pineapple chunks
½ t. salt
½ c. mayonnaise
½ c. salted almonds

Mix tuna, celery and pineapple. Add salt. Blend in mayonnaise; add almonds. Chill thoroughly. Serve on lettuce leaves and top with almonds.

Maybelle Nichols, Ridgeville H. S.
North Ridgeville, Ohio

WAFFLES A LA FRUIT SALAD

Number of Servings — 4-6

1-2 apples
1-2 oranges
1-2 bananas
1 medium can pineapple chunks
6-8 Maraschino cherries
4-5 marshmallows, cut up
Waffles
½ pt. whipped cream
3 T. powdered sugar
1 t. vanilla

Combine fruits and marshmallows. Mix whipped cream, sugar and vanilla; add to fruit mixture. Top waffles with salad.

Mrs. Carol Arnold, Cascade H. S.
Cascade, Idaho

WALDORF SPIRAL SALAD

Number of Servings — 6

6 red apples
4 c. cold water
⅓ c. lemon juice
1 c. celery, diced
⅓ c. seedless raisins
1 c. miniature marshmallows
¼ c. mayonnaise
¼ c. whipped cream
½ c. walnuts, coarsely
6 lettuce cups

Pare apples very thick, being sure each paring is long and unbroken. Add 3 tablespoons of lemon juice; to the water drop parings in to keep color bright. Core pared apples and dice fine; sprinkle with remaining lemon juice. Combine apple cubes, celery, raisins, marshmallows, and mayonnaise. Fold in whipped cream. Before serving, add nuts. Curl each paring into cup shape on lettuce. Fill with salad.

This recipe submitted by the following teachers:

Mrs. Shirley Boddie, Calvin H. S.
Calvin, Louisiana

Katherine Brooks, Pleasanton Rural H. S.
Pleasanton, Kansas

SUMMER FRUIT BOUNTY

Number of Servings — 2

1 honeydew melon
2 t. fresh fruit juice or pineapple juice
2 T. sugar
2 c. ripe peaches, sliced
1 medium pear, diced
1 banana, sliced
½ c. strawberries, sliced
½ pt. orange sherbet
Sprig of fresh mint

Early in day; cut honeydew in half. Remove seeds and scoop out meat. Cut into cubes and reserve. Scallop edges of melon. Turn melon halves up side down to drain, store in refrigerator. Combine fresh fruit or pineapple juice and sugar. Peel and slice pears, peaches and banana directly into sugar mixture. Add melon cubes, strawberries and toss well, cover and store in refrigerator until ready to serve. Fill melon halves with fruit and at last minute top with tiny balls of orange sherbet and a sprig of mint.

Laoma D. Clevenger, Ohio City-Liberty School
Ohio City, Ohio

WATERMELON BASKET

Number of Servings — 10-15

1 short, plump watermelon, chilled
1½ c. fresh or frozen cantaloupe and honeydew melon balls
1 small can pineapple juice
1 c. whole fresh strawberries, (opt.)
Few grape leaves or mint if desired

After watermelon is thoroughly chilled, cut lengthwise, slicing off top third. Use larger piece for fruit holder. Scoop out melon balls with melon-ball cutter or measuring teaspoon. Scallop top edge of shell. Fill with watermelon, cantaloupe, and honeydew melon balls. Add strawberries last. Pour pineapple juice over top. Tuck in grape leaves or mint.

Sharon Klickna, Tularosa H. S.
Tularosa, New Mexico

WATERMELON DELIGHT

Number of Servings — 12-15

½ watermelon, chilled
3 cantaloupes, chilled
3 lbs. white grapes, washed
4 lbs. fresh peaches, sliced

Use mellon "Baller" and scoop out watermelon and cantaloupes. Use the ½ watermelon rind as the bowl and cut jagged edges. Combine all the fruit and some of the juice. Variations: Any colorful fruits together. Canned fruit cocktail; wine for juice. Use a whole watermelon and have a lid.

Millie Sanderson, LaCrosse Rural H. S.
LaCrosse, Kansas

AVOCADO RING SALAD

Number of Servings — 6

1 c. boiling water
1 pkg. lemon gelatin
2 ripe avocados, mashed
¼ c. sour cream
2 T. white wine
⅛ t. salt
1 c. heavy cream, whipped

Dissolve gelatin in boiling water. Add avocado pulp, sour cream, wine and salt. Beat until smooth and fluffy. Chill until mixture begins to set. Fold in whipped cream. Pour into a ring mold. Chill until firm. Unmold onto crisp dry salad greens.

Dorothy E. Brevoort,
State Supervisor Home Economics Education,
State Department of Education
Trenton 25, New Jersey

AVOCADO-GRAPE FRUIT SALAD

Number of Servings — 10

2 3-oz. pkgs. lime gelatin
2 avocados, sieved
½ c. mayonnaise
2 fresh grapefruit, peeled and sectioned

Dissolve gelatin according to directions on package. Cool until partially set. Remove membranes from grapefruit sections. Arrange sections in bottom of an 8x12 pan. Pour half of the gelatin mixture over grapefruit. Chill. Pour remaining gelatin mixture into a bowl; add avocado and mayonnaise. Beat with electric or rotary beater until light and foamy. Pour over the grapefruit layer. Chill until firm. Cut in squares and serve foamy side up on a lettuce leaf. Garnish with whipped cream and a Maraschino cherry.

Mrs. Helen D. Andrus, Beaverhead County H. S.
Dillon, Montana

FRUIT DELIGHT SALAD

Number of Servings — 6

1¼ c. pineapple chunks, drained
1 pkg. frozen peaches, thawed and cut in 1-inch pieces
1 pkg. frozen strawberries, thawed
1 pkg. strawberry gelatin
1 c. whipped cream
¼ c. confectioner's sugar
⅛ t. salt
½ lb. seedless green grapes, or halved, seeded grapes
½ t. ground ginger
2 c. fruit juice plus water

Heat juice to boiling. Add gelatin and stir until dissolved. Chill until partially set. Combine sugar, cream, salt and ginger in large mixing bowl; whip until cream forms peaks. Fold fruits into whipped cream. Fold congealed gelatin into cream mixture. Turn into lightly oiled mold. Chill until firm.

Pauline E. Smith, Redbank Valley H. S.
New Bethlehem, Pennsylvania

FRUIT SALAD

Number of Servings — 6

1 pkg. cherry gelatin
1 pkg. cream cheese
½ pt. whipped cream
2 T. mayonnaise
¼ c. sugar
¼ t. salt
1 c. pineapple tidbits
1 can Mandarin oranges
½ c. pecans, chopped

Prepare gelatin according to package directions. Beat in cream cheese, whipped cream, mayonnaise, sugar and salt. Stir in fruits and nuts. Chill until firm.

Mrs. Deanna Egge, Forest Lake H. S.
Forest Lake, Minnesota

CREAM CHEESE RING

Number of Servings — 8-12

1 pkg. lime gelatin
1 8-oz. pkg. cream cheese
1 c. pecans, chopped

Prepare gelatin according to package directions. Fill ring mold ½-inch deep with the mixture. Chill until firm. Divide cheese into desired number of portions. Roll cheese in pecans, pressing the pecans firmly into the cheese. Place balls gently around on the firm gelatin. Add enough of the remaining gelatin to come up half way on the cheese-pecan balls. Chill until firm. Pour remaining gelatin over cheese-pecan balls. Chill until firm. Serve with unsweetened whipped cream or salad dressing. Recipe may be varied by using strawberry gelatin and fresh strawberries with cheese-pecan balls.

Mrs. L. C. Alley, Pecos H. S.
Pecos, Texas

TANGY FRUIT AND CHEESE MOLD

Number of Servings — 8

1 c. cranberry juice cocktail
1 pkg. lemon gelatin
Dash of salt
1 small bottle ginger ale, chilled
½ c. pineapple tidbits, drained
½ c. celery, finely chopped
1 3-oz. pkg. cream cheese
8 walnut halves

Dissolve gelatin in cranberry juice heated just to boiling; add salt. Cool. Add ginger ale. Chill until partially set. Stir in pineapple and celery. Set aside. Cut cream cheese into 8 squares. Form each square into ball around a walnut half. Place cheese balls in bottom of individual molds. Pour gelatin mixture over cheese balls. Chill until firm. Unmold on lettuce leaves.

Kathryn N. Lynch, West H. S.
Bremerton, Washington

BING CHERRY SALAD

Number of Servings — 12-16

2 pkgs. orange or black cherry gelatin
2 c. boiling water
1¾ c. cherry juice plus water
2 cans bing cherries, drained
1 6-oz. pkg. cream cheese, softened and whipped
1 3-oz. jar stuffed olives
1 c. pecans or blanched almonds broken into small pieces

Dissolve gelatin in boiling water. Add cherry juice. Chill until slightly thickened. Stuff cherries with cream cheese. Add cherries, sliced olives and pecans to gelatin mixture. Pour into molds. Chill until firm.

This recipe submitted by the following teachers:

Cetha G. Kuske, Britton H. S.
Britton, South Dakota

Ann Crews Daniels, Escambia H. S.
Pensacola, Florida

CHERRY-ALMOND SALAD

Number of Servings — 8

1 3-oz. pkg. cherry gelatin
1 c. dark sweet cherries, pitted and halved
1-2 T. milk
1 3-oz. pkg. cream cheese
¼ c. blanched, toasted almonds, chopped

Prepare gelatin according to package directions; set aside until mixture begins to thicken. Combine cheese and milk. Form mixture into tiny balls about the size of small marbles. Roll the balls in chopped almonds and place between 2 cherry halves. Drop into the slightly thickened gelatin. Chill until firm.

Norma Swenson Sandison, Port Angeles Sr. H. S.
Port Angeles, Washington

CHERRY-NUT SALAD

Number of Servings — 5-6

1 3-oz. pkg. cherry gelatin
1 c. boiling water
1 No. 303 can black cherries, chilled and drained
1 3-oz. pkg. cream cheese
½ c. walnuts, chopped
Cold cherry juice plus water to make 1 c. liquid

Dissolve gelatin in boiling water. Add juice-water mixture; mix well. Chill until mixture is consistency of egg whites. Form cream cheese into 1-incn balls; roll in nuts. Mix cherries and cheese balls with gelatin. Chill until firm. Serve with whipped cream or mayonnaise.

Mrs. Carol Stephenson, North Adams H. S.
North Adams, Michigan

DARK SWEET CHERRY SALAD

2 pkg. black cherry gelatin
1 can lge. sweet dark cherries, pitted and halved
Pecan halves
Cream cheese

Prepare gelatin according to package directions; chill until partially set. Fill half of the cherries with pecans and half with cream cheese. Add filled cherries to partially set gelatin. Chill until firm.

Mrs. Evelyn Kochenour, Hempfield Junior H. S.
Landisville, Pennsylvania

GRAPE-CHEESE BALL SALAD

Number of Servings — 6

SPICED GRAPES:
4 inches stick cinnamon
2 T. whole cloves
¾ c. sugar
¾ c. cider vinegar
1½ c. syrup drained from grapes
3 c. white seedless grapes, drained

Boil cinnamon, cloves, sugar, vinegar and grape syrup together for 15 minutes. Strain over grapes. Refrigerate overnight. Yield: 2½ c. drained spiced grapes.

1 pkg. lemon gelatin
⅛ t. salt
1 3-oz. pkg. cream cheese, cut in 6 sq.
½ c. pecans or walnuts, chopped
1 c. spiced grapes, drained

Prepare gelatin according to package directions. Chill in a ring mold until mixture is consistency of unbeaten egg whites. Form cream cheese squares and salt into balls; roll in some of the nuts. Stir remaining nuts and spiced grapes into slightly congealed gelatin. Arrange cheese balls in mold; press into gelatin mixture. Chill until firm.

Marie Weir, Hardin H. S.
Hardin, Montana

GRAPEFRUIT SALAD MOLD

Number of Servings — 8

1 3-oz. pkg. cream cheese
2 1-lb. cans grapefruit sections, drained
3½ c. grapefruit juice
2 pkgs. lime gelatin
¼ t. salt
¼ c. pimento, diced

Roll cream cheese into 8 small balls; chill. Heat 2 cups of the juice; pour over gelatin and salt. Stir until gelatin is dissolved. Add remaining juice; chill. Arrange some of the grapefruit sections and pimento and all of the cheese balls in the bottom of a 5-cup ring mold. Spoon in a little of the chilled gelatin and chill until almost firm. Cool remaining gelatin until slightly thickened. Fold in remaining grapefruit sections and pimento. Spoon into mold. Chill until firm.

Mrs. Esther P. Leeds, Piscataquis Community H.S.
Guilford, Maine

GRAPEFRUIT SALAD

Number of Servings — 12

3 lge. grapefruit, fruit and rind
2 pkgs. lemon gelatin
1 c. hot water

Cut grapefruit in half; long way. Remove the pulp break fruit into small pieces. Add water, if necessary to make 1 quart fruit and juice. Dissolve gelatin in boiling water and add to the 1 qt. grape fruit pulp. Pour into half rinds, scraped clean with a spoon. Chill until firm; cut each half in two. Serve on lettuce with fruit dressing.

DRESSING:

3 egg yolks
½ c. sugar
1 T. flour
1 c. pineapple juice
Juice of 2 lemons
12 marshmallows, chopped
½ pt. whipped cream.

Combine all ingredients. Cook in double boiler until thick. Remove from heat, stir in marshmallows. Chill. Fold in cream.

Mrs. Audrey S. Bowers, Byrnes H. S.
Duncan, South Carolina

LIME SALAD SURPRISE

Number of Servings — 8

1 pkg. lime gelatin
1 c. boiling water
½ c. cold water
1 3-oz. pkg. cream cheese
½ c. nuts, finely chopped
1 c. fruit cocktail, drained

Dissolve gelatin in boiling water; add cold water. Chill until slightly thickened. Mix cream cheese and chopped nuts; form in balls the size of small marbles. Add fruit cocktail and cream cheese balls to gelatin. Chill. Serve on lettuce.

Jacqueline Hardee, University H. S.
Los Angeles, California

PARADISE SALAD

Number of Servings — 8

1 pkg. lemon-lime gelatin
18 marshmallows
1 pkg. cream cheese, whipped
1 c. whipped cream
1 c. crushed pineapple
2 c. hot water

Stir gelatin and marshmallows in hot water until dissolved. Chill. Combine whipped cheese and whipped cream; add pineapple and beat. Stir creamy mixture into cooled gelatin mixture. Refrigerate until firm.

Mrs. Marion Ray, Dunlap Community
Dunlap, Iowa

GRAPEFRUIT SALAD WITH BUTTERCUP DRESSING

2 lge. fresh grapefruit, halved
1 No. 2 can crushed pineapple, undrained
1 pkg. lemon or orange gelatin
1 c. boiling water

Pour boiling water over gelatin. Cool until mixture begins to thicken slightly. Remove all sections from the grapefruit rind. Combine grapefruit sections with crushed pineapple. Add to the gelatin mixture. Pour into hollowed grapefruit halves. Chill until firm. If rind extends too far above the firm gelatin, trim with a knife. When ready to serve, cut grapefruit in half again. Serve plain or with Buttercup Dressing.

BUTTERCUP DRESSING:

3 T. flour
½ c. sugar
⅝ t. salt
½ c. fruit juice
2 eggs. separated
3 marshmallows
½ c. whipped cream
⅛ c. lemon juice
¼ c. pecans, chopped (opt.)

Heat fruit juice. Combine flour, salt and sugar; blend with just enough fruit juice to make a smooth paste. Add to remaining fruit juice and cook for 15-20 minutes or until thickened. Stir in slightly beaten egg yolks and cook for 5 minutes longer. Remove from heat; add marshmallows. Cool. Add nuts and lemon juice. Fold in stiffly beaten egg whites and whipped cream.

Mrs. Mary C. Dyches, Fort Mill H. S.
Fort Mill, South Carolina

PARTY SALAD

Number of Servings — 10-12

1 pkg. lime gelatin
1 pkg. lemon gelatin
2 c. hot water
1 c. sour cream
1 No. 2 can crushed pineapple, undrained
1 c. country style cottage cheese
1 c. stuffed olives, sliced
½ c. walnuts or blanched almonds, chopped

Disolve gelatins in boiling water. Add pineapple; cool. Add remaining ingredients. Pour into a 2-quart mold. Chill until firm.

Mrs. Mary E. Schwartz, Artesia H. S.
Artesia, California

PARTY SALAD

Number of Servings — 16

1 3-oz. pkg. lemon gelatin
2 3-oz. pkg. lime gelatin
4 c. boiling water or pineapple-water mixture
1 8-oz. pkg. cream cheese
2 c. American cheese, grated
2 c. cottage cheese
1 No. 2½ can crushed pineapple, well drained
½ pt. whipped cream

Dissolve gelatin in water or a mixture of heated water and pineapple juice. While still warm, add cream cheese and mash with fork until dissolved. Refrigerate. When partially congealed add remaining cheeses and pineapple. Fold in whipped cream; pour into oiled salad mold. Refrigerate until firm.

Mrs. Lois Sadogierski, Waupaca H. S.
Waupaca, Wisconsin

PINK PARTY SALAD

Number of Servings — 6-8

1 pkg. lemon gelatin
1 c. boiling water
1 c. pineapple juice
1 c. crushed pineapple
1 lge. pkg. cream cheese
¾ c. Maraschino cherries, cut up
2 T. cherry juice

Moisten cheese with cherry juice. Dissolve gelatin in boiling water; add pineapple juice. Let stand until it begins to congeal. Add cream cheese-cherry juice mixture, pineapple and cherries. Mix well. Pour into mold and chill.

Mrs. Georgia Adams, Hillsboro H. S.
Hillsboro, Illinois

RAINBOW PARTY SALAD

Number of Servings — 12

1 pkg. lime gelatin
1 pkg. strawberry gelatin
1 c. pineapple juice
½ c. water
1 pkg. orange gelatin
¼ c. sugar
Dash salt
½ pt. whipped cream

Dissolve lime and strawberry gelatins according to package directions. Congeal in separate square cake pans. Cut into cubes. Combine pineapple juice, water, sugar and salt in sauce-pan; bring to a boil. Add orange gelatin; chill until nearly firm. Add cream and gelatin cubes. Chill until firm.

Mrs. Nancy Zebrun, Forbes H. S.
Stoystown, Pennsylvania

REGAL PARTY SALAD

Number of Servings — 8

1 No. 2 can crushed pineapple
Juice of 1 lemon
1 c. sugar
1 envelope unflavored gelatin
¼ c. cold water
1 c. American cheese, grated
1 c. whipping cream

Soak gelatin in cold water. Heat pineapple, lemon juice and sugar until sugar dissolves. Add gelatin. Cool until mixture begins to thicken. Fold in whipped cream and cheese. Chill until firm.

Topping:
½ c. whipped cream
½ c. mayonnaise
½ c. celery, finely chopped
½ c. stuffed olives, finely chopped
1 t. onion, grated

Combine all ingredients 2 hours before serving. Serve on Party Salad.

Marjorie L. Benesh, State Industrial School
Mandan, North Dakota

PEACH BUFFET SALAD

Number of Servings — 8-10

2 c. peach slices, drained
1 c. hot peach juice
1 pkg. lemon gelatin
1 c. cottage cheese
½ c. pecans, chopped
½ c. celery, chopped
8-10 Maraschino cherries
1 c. evaporated milk, undiluted
2 T. lemon juice

Arrange some peach slices and cherries in petal form around a 1½-quart ring mold. Dissolve gelatin in hot peach juice; let set until thick. Fold in celery, pecans, remaining peaches and cheese. Chill milk in freezer until ice crystals form. Beat until stiff. Add lemon juice; beat until very stiff. Fold milk into gelatin mixture. Pour into mold. Chill until firm.

Mrs. George Raboin, Carney H. S.
Carney, Michigan

STUFFED SPICED PEACH SALAD

Number of Servings — 6-8

1 pkg. lemon gelatin
1 pkg. lime gelatin
2 c. boiling water
2 c. juice from spiced peaches plus water
1 small pkg. cream cheese
¼ c. pecans, chopped
1 jar spiced peaches, drained
Lemon and orange juice to soften cream cheese

Dissolve gelatins in boiling water; add the juice. Chill until thickened. Soften cream cheese with orange and lemon juice. Add pecans. Take seed out of each peach and stuff with cream cheese mixture. When jello becomes thick, pour into individual molds. Add a stuffed peach to each mold. Serve on lettuce and garnish with sprig of mint and more cream cheese dressing.

Mrs. Ann Spencer, East Lake Jr. H. S.
Chattanooga, Tennessee

TOMORROW'S SALAD

Number of Servings — 10

1 pkg. lemon gelatin
1 pkg. lime gelatin
1 No. 2 can crushed pineapple
1 c. mayonnaise or salad dressing
1 c. evaporated milk
1 lb. cottage cheese

Prepare gelatins according to package directions; let stand until partially set. Add remaining ingredients; mix well. Let set 2 hours or overnight.

Mrs. Gertrude J. Bennett, Chester H. S.
Chester, Vermont

BRIDE'S SALAD

1 c. cubed pineapple, drained
½ lb. marshmallows, finely cut
1 T. cornstarch
1 t. lemon juice
1 small head cabbage, shredded and chilled
½ pt. whipped cream

Bring juice drained from pineapple, cornstarch and lemon juice to a boil. Cool. Just before serving toss all ingredients together.

Mrs. Nancy Willard, East Haven H. S.
East Haven, Connecticut

CANDLESTICK SALAD

Number of Servings — 8

8 pineapple rings, drained
4 bananas, cut in halves crosswise
8 strawberries, Maraschino cherries or candied cherries
8 lettuce leaves
Shredded coconut
½ c. whipped cream or fruit salad dressing

Arrange a slice of pineapple on lettuce for the candle base or holder. Dip bananas in pineapple juice to prevent discoloration. Place half of banana in pineapple ring to make candle. Add cherry on strawberry for flame. Put coconut in cherry for wick. Dribble whipped cream down banana to make it look as if candle is melting. For a colorful Christmas salad, red or green candied apple rings may be used instead of pineapple, and lemon juice used on banana.

This recipe submitted by the following teachers:

Mrs. Lawrence A. Boyd, Vernon H. S.
Vernon, Texas

Fern E. Ruck, Rangely H. S.
Rangely, Colorado

CHRISTMAS SALAD

Number of Servings — 8-10

2 No. 2½ cans chunk pineapple
½ pkg. miniature marshmallows
½ c. red cinnamon candies
¾ c. whipped cream

Cut pineapple chunks in half; add marshmallows and candy. Mix well. Refrigerate overnight. Drain; fold into whipped cream.

Mrs. Helen Wright, Stevenson H. S.
Stevenson, Washington

HOLIDAY SALAD

Number of Servings — 6-8

2 eggs, beaten
4 T. white vinegar
4 T. sugar
2 T. butter
2 c. white cherries, halved
1 c. heavy cream, whipped
2 oranges, cut in pieces
2 c. marshmallows, quartered
1 c. pineapple tidbits, drained
Red or green Maraschino cherries (opt.)

Put eggs in saucepan; add vinegar and sugar. Heat, beating constantly until thick and smooth. Remove from the heat; add butter. Cool. Fold in whipped cream, fruits and marshmallows. Chill for 24 hours.

Mrs. Betty J. Hempel, Lyman Memorial H. S.
Lebanon, Connecticut

HOLIDAY FRUIT SALAD

Number of Servings — 10-12

1 c. red grapes, halved and seeded
1 c. pineapple chunks, drained
1 c. bananas, sliced
1 c. dates, chopped
2 oranges, cut in small pieces
½ c. walnuts, chopped
1 c. whipped cream
¼ c. sugar

Combine fruit in a large bowl. Add whipped cream and sugar just before serving.

Mrs. Elsie Vredenburg, Chesaning H. S.
Chesaning, Michigan

KRIS KRINGLE SALAD

Number of Servings — 4

1¼ c. water
½ c. sugar
¼ c. red cinnamon candies
2 apples, pared and cut in wedges
1 avocado, cut in wedges

Make syrup of water, sugar and cinnamon candies. Add apples; cook till just tender. Chill. Alternate apples and avacado on lettuce. Pass French dressing.

Mrs. Pecola L. Scott, Goodridge H. S.
Goodridge, Minnesota

HOLIDAY CRANBERRY SALAD OR DESSERT

Number of Servings — 20

1 lb. fresh cranberries, ground
3-4 medium apples, ground
1 10-oz. pkg. miniature marshmallows
1½ c. sugar
1 c. nuts, chopped
1 pt. whipped cream or 2 pkgs. dessert topping mix

Combine cranberries, apples and nuts. Add marshmallows and sugar; mix well. Gently fold in whipped cream or dessert topping mix prepared according to package directions. Chill before serving.

Bette Brown, Steamboat Springs H. S.
Steamboat Springs, Colorado

CHRISTMAS SALAD

Number of Servings — 12-15

1 pkg. lime gelatin
1 pkg. lemon gelatin
1 pkg. strawberry gelatin
1 1-lb. box cottage cheese
1 c. whipped cream
1 No. 2 can crushed pineapple, drained
1 3-oz. pkg. cream cheese
1 T. milk
2 c. hot water
1 c. pineapple juice

Mix lime gelatin according to directions on package. Let set until partially congealed. Fold in cottage cheese and pineapple. Let set until firm. Mix lemon gelatin with 1¼ cups hot water and ¾ cup pineapple juice; let set until partially congealed. Blend the cream cheese with the milk. Beat lemon gelatin, whipped cream and cheese together with an electric mixer. Spread lemon mixture over the lime mixture. Let set until firm. Mix strawberry gelatin with 1¾ cups hot water and ¼ cup pineapple juice. Cool. Pour over the lime-lemon layers.

Mrs. Helen Rapp, Eastern Local H. S.
Beaver, Ohio

CHRISTMAS SALAD

Number of Servings — 12

1 3-oz. pkg. strawberry gelatin
4½ c. hot water
¾ c. raw cranberries, ground
½ orange, ground
1 3-oz. pkg. lemon gelatin
2 3-oz. pkg. cream cheese
1 3-oz. pkg. lime gelatin
1 c. pineapple juice
1 9-oz. can crushed pineapple, drained

Dissolve strawberry gelatin in 1½ cups hot water. Add cranberries and orange. Pour into an 8 x 12 glass dish. Let congeal. Dissolve leman gelatin in 2 cups hot water. Beat in cream cheese. Let cool. Pour over strawberry layer. Congeal. Dissolve lime gelatin in 1 cup hot water and pineapple juice. Add the pineapple. Let cool. Pour over lemon layers. May be served with a cooked fruit dressing.

Mrs. Hilda Burt, Las Cruces H. S.
Las Cruces, New Mexico

CHRISTMAS SALAD

Number of Servings — 8

1 pkg. cherry gelatin
1 pkg. lime gelatin
1 pkg. miniature marshmallows
1 8-oz. pkg. cream cheese
½ c. mayonnaise
½ t. salt
1 9-oz. can crushed pineapple
1 c. celery, diced
½ c. nuts, chopped
1 c. whipped cream
1¾ c. hot water
1 c. boiling water

Dissolve cherry gelatin in hot water; let cool. Dissolve lime gelatin in boiling water. Melt marshmallows in lime gelatin. Combine cheese, Mayonnaise and salt together; add to lime mixture. Chill until partially set. Add pineapple, celery and nuts. Fold in whipped cream. Chill until set. Pour cherry gelatin over lime gelatin. Chill.

Vola May Miller, Sparta H. S.
Sparta, Illinois

AUNT TENA'S CHRISTMAS SALAD

Number of Servings — 12

1 pkg. lime gelatin
1 pkg. lemon gelatin
2 c. boiling water
1 qt. vanilla ice cream, softened
1 c. red and green Maraschino cherries, sliced
1 c. pineapple tidbits

Dissolve gelatins in boiling water. Immediately add ice ceram; stir until melted. Add fruit. Pour into an oiled 1-quart mold. Chill until firm.

Mrs. Janet Jacobson, Buena Vista H. S.
Saginaw, Michigan

CHRISTMAS APRICOT SALAD

Number of Servings — 8

1 pkg. lime gelatin
¾ c. boiling apricot juice
¼ c. apricot cordial
Juice of 1 lemon
Juice of 1 orange
16 canned apricot halves
1 pkg. cream cheese
¼ c. pecans, finely chopped
¼ c. Maraschino cherries, finely chopped
¼ c. dates, finely chopped
2 T. mayonnaise

Dissolve gelatin in boiling apricot juice; cool. Combine orange and lemon juice, cordial and enough water to make 1 c. liquid. Add to gelatin mixture. Mix cheese, cherries, nuts and dates with mayonnaise; form into balls. Stuff half of the apricots with cheese-mayonnaise mixture; cover with remaining apricot halves. Place 2 stuffed apricots in each individual mold. Pour gelatin over apricots. Chill until firm. Serve on lettuce cups topped with mayonnaise. Garnish with cherries cut to resemble poinsettias.

Mrs. Mabel Kitchrigs Owen, Monticello H. S.
Monticello, Arkansas

CHRISTMAS LAYER SALAD

Number of Servings — 9-10

LIME LAYER:
1 pkg. lime gelatin
1 c. pineapple tidbits, drained
1 c. hot water
⅓ c. pineapple juice

Dissolve gelatin in hot water. Add pineapple and juice. Chill until firm.

CHEESE LAYER:
1½ t. unflavored gelatin
2 T. cold water
1 8-oz. pkg. cream cheese
¼ c. milk

Sprinkle gelatin over cold water to soften. Add cream cheese softened with milk. Spread over firm lime layer.

CRANBERRY LAYER:
2 pkgs. strawberry gelatin
2 c. hot water
1 can whole cranberries

Dissolve gelatin in hot water. Add cranberries. Cool. Pour over cheese layer. Chill until firm.

This recipe submitted by the following teachers:

Mrs. Linda G. Wallace, York Suburban Sr. H. S.
York, Pennsylvania

Mrs. Nancy Sedarat, Edgerton H. S.
Edgerton, Wisconsin

Joyce Niedenthal, Parkway Jr. H. S.
Fort Lauderdale, Florida

CHRISTMAS SALAD

Number of Servings — 8

1 pkg. lemon gelatin
2 pkg. cream cheese
Juice drained from 1 lge. can pineapple, heated
½ c. celery, chopped
⅔ c. walnuts, chopped
½ pt. whipped cream
Pinch of salt.
1 lge. can crushed pineapple (opt.)
Pimentos (opt.)

Disolve gelatin in heated pineapple juice. Let partially set. Add remaining ingredients. Congeal.

Lois A. Auger, Lincoln H. S.
Park Falls, Wisconsin

EASY CHRISTMAS SALAD

Number of Servings — 8

1 pkg. lime gelatin
1 c. hot water
1 c. crushed pineapple, drained
Juice from pineapple plus water to make 1 c.
1 T. lemon juice
2 c. miniature marshmallows
1 small bottle Maraschino cherries, cut in pieces
½ c. walnuts, chopped

Dissolve gelatin in hot water. Add juices. Chill until nearly firm. Fold in pineapple, marshmallows, cherries and nuts. Chill until firm. For a festive touch: barely cover bottom of mold with diluted gelatin. Arrange cherries and marshmallows; chill until firm. Add mixture to this.

Mrs. Carolyn R. Stone, Whitingham H. S.
Jacksonville, Vermont

CHRISTMAS TREES

Number of Servings — 10

1 pkg. lime gelatin
1 c. hot water
½ c. cottage cheese drained
1 c. whipped cream
1 c. crushed pineapple, well drained
½ c. pecans, broken
½ c. Maraschino cherries, chopped
Juice drained from pineapple plus enough water to make 1 c. liquid
Mayonnaise
Whipped cream for garnish

Dissolve gelatin in boiling water; add juice-water mixture. Chill until partially set. Fold in whipped cream. Fold in cottage cheese which has been put through a fine sieve, pineapple, nuts and cherries; blend well. Pour into pointed waxed paper cups to chill. Unmold on a bed of lettuce; garnish with mayonnaise and fluff whipped cream. Let a small amount run down the sides of each tree. Top with a cherry wedge.

Mrs. Vera Troyer, Bennett County H. S.
Martin, South Dakota

OLIVE WREATH MOLD

Number of Servings — 8-10

1 No. 2 can crushed pineapple, drained
1 3-oz. pkg. lime gelatin
½ c. American cheese, grated
½ c. pimento, chopped
½ c. small stuffed olives, sliced
Curly endive
½ c. celery, finely chopped
⅔ c. walnuts or pecans, chopped
¼ t. salt
1 c. whipped cream or 1 small pkg. whipped dessert topping mix

Heat pineapple syrup to boiling; pour over gelatin and stir until dissolved. Cool. When gelatin begins to thicken, add pineapple, cheese, pimento, celery, nuts and salt. Fold in whipped cream. Place a row of sliced stuffed olives in bottom of 9-inch ring mold. Pour gelatin mixture into mold and chill until firm. Arrange endive on platter; unmold salad on top.

This recipe submitted by the following teachers:

Mrs. Joyce C. Rapes, Sebewaing Public School
Sebewaing, Michigan

Mrs. Mildred Bowles
Labette County Community H. S.
Altamont, Kansas

ST. NICK SALAD RING

Number of Servings — 8-10

2 pkgs. strawberry gelatin
3½ c. boiling water
2 T. lemon juice
1 T. vinegar
1 T. grated onion
1 t. salt
2 3-oz. pkg. cream cheese
⅓ c. parsley, chopped
2 grapefruit, sectioned
1 c. celery, diced
1 medium unpared apple, diced
1 avocado, diced

Dissolve gelatin in boiling water; stir in lemon juice, vinegar, onion and salt. Chill until syrupy. Form cream cheese into small balls about the size of marbles; roll in parsley. Lightly oil 1½-quart ring mold. Alternate cheese balls and grapefruit sections around bottom of mold, rounded side of fruit down. Spoon syrupy gelatin around design to depth of about ¼ inch. Chill until firm. Fold celery, avocado and apple into remaining syrupy gelatin. Pour into the mold. Chill several hours.

SNOW CREAM DRESSING:

1 c. sour cream
2 T. mayonnaise
2 t. sugar
2 t. lemon juice
½ t. salt

Chill to blend flavors. Serve with St. Nick Salad Ring.

Mrs. Mildred R. Turner, McKinleyville H. S.
Arcata, California

CHRISTMAS SNOWBALL SALAD

Number of Servings — 8

1 bottle of red Maraschino cherries, drained
1 pkg. white coconut
1 can green grapes, drained
1 pkg. small white marshmallows
1 pkg. sour cream
1 lge. pkg. cream cheese

Soak green grapes in food coloring for 1 hour or until they are a lively green color. Combine carefully all ingredients except cream cheese. Place in an attractive green or white bowl. Form small balls of cream cheese and place on top for garnish. A few red cherries may be saved for center. This makes a colorful christmas salad.

Mrs. Lucille Tready, Bishop Baraga Central H. S.
Marquette, Michigan

HOLIDAY FRUIT SALAD

Number of Servings — 12

1 pkg. lemon gelatin
1 c. hot water
1 c. pineapple juice plus water
1 pkg. raspberry gelatin
1 c. hot water
1 c. cold water
1 No. 211 can crushed pineapple, drained
1 heaping c. cranberries, ground
½ c. sugar
2 unpared apples, chopped fine
1 orange and rind, chopped
½ c. walnuts, chopped

Dissolve lemon gelatin in hot water and the pineapple juice-water mixture. Chill until syrupy. Add pineapple. Pour into a large mold; chill until firm. Dissolve raspberry gelatin in hot water; add cold water. Chill until partially set. Mix sugar with cranberries; combine apples, orange, and nuts. Combine with gelatin. Pour on firm layer. Chill until firm.

Mrs. Mabel Hammer, Wolsey H. S.
Wolsey, South Dakota

HOLIDAY SALAD

Number of Servings — 6

1 pkg. strawberry gelatin
1 c. hot water
½ c. cold water
1 orange and rind, ground
1 lb. can whole or jellied cranberry sauce
½ c. apples, chopped
¼ c. celery, chopped
¼ c. nuts, chopped

Dissolve gelatin in hot water. Add cold water. Chill until mixture begins to thicken. If whole cranberry sauce is used, drain. If jellied sauce is used, beat slightly with beater. Fold cranberry sauce, orange, apple, nuts and celery into gelatin. Pour into mold; chill until firm.

Mrs. Eleanor Tedford, Wiggins H. S.
Wiggins, Colorado

HOLIDAY SALAD

Number of Servings — 20

2 pkg. lime gelatin
3 pkg. lemon gelatin
8 marshmallows, cut in pieces
1 8-oz. pkg. cream cheese
1 c. crushed pineapple
1 pkg. Dream Whip
5 c. hot water
4 c. cold water

Dissolve lime gelatin in 2 cups hot water; add 2 cups cold water. Put in a 4-quart loaf pan and chill until set. Over low heat, combine 1 package lemon gelatin and 1 cup hot water. Add marshmallows and cream cheese. Crush with a fork until dissolved. Add pineapple and cool until mixture begins to set. Prepare Dream Whip according to package directions. Add to lemon gelatin mixture. Put on top of lime gelatin. Prepare remaining 2 packages of lemon gelatin with 2 cups of hot water and 2 cups of cold water. Let cool. Put on top of Dream Whip-gelatin layer.

Mary Jane Elliott, Constantine H. S.
Constantine, Michigan

RECEPTION SALAD

Number of Servings — 6-8

1 pkg. lemon gelatin
1 c. hot water
1 medium can crushed pineapple, drained
2 3-oz. pkg. cream cheese
1 small can pimento
½-1 c. celery, finely chopped
⅔ c. nuts, chopped
½ pt. whipped cream
⅛ t. salt

Heat pineapple juice and water to boiling. Dissolve gelatin in juice. Cool. Mash pimentos and cream cheese together. Mix celery, nuts and pineapple with thickened gelatin. Add cream. Allow to chill before serving.

This recipe submitted by the following teachers:
Sammie Saulsbury, Crockett Jr. H. S.
Odessa, Texas

Mrs. W. E. Cooper, Monticello Attendance Center
Monticello, Mississippi

Mrs. Aleta B. Nelson, Tidehaven H. S.
Blessing, Texas

Mildred H. Dodge, Wyalusing Valley H. S.
Wyalusing, Pennsylvania

Mrs. Mary Ann Hammontree, West Side High,
Rocky Face, Georgia

Dorothy Waugh, Strasburg H. S.
Strasburg, Virginia

Mrs. Mary Jo Gresham, Hickory Flat
Attendance Center
Hickory Flat, Mississippi

Mrs. Karl Joebrendt, Paoli H. S.
Paoli, Indiana

Mrs. Dorothy G. Pruitt, J. F. Webb H. S.
Oxford, North Carolina

SPECIAL HOLIDAY SALAD

Number of Servings — 6-8

6 lge. apples, chopped
6 bananas, chopped
4 stalks celery, chopped
1 No. 1 can pineapple tidbits
½ lb. marshmallows, cut
1 c. seedless grapes
1 small carton lge. curd cottage cheese
1 c. nuts, chopped
1 c. whipped cream, sweetened and flavored with vanilla
1 pkg. orange and 1 pkg. lime gelatin or 1 pkg. red gelatin and 1 pkg. lime gelatin
1¾ c. water

Use orange and lime gelatin for Thanksgiving and red and lime gelatin for Christmas. Prepare gelatin with water; chill. Cut into cubes. Toss fruits, marshmallows, celery, cottage cheese, nuts and whipped cream together. Combine with gelatin cubes.

Mrs. Kenny Handel, Freeman H. S.
Freeman, South Dakota

SAINT PATRICK'S SALAD

Number of Servings — 10

1 box lime gelatin
1 box lemon gelatin
2 c. boiling water
Few drops green food coloring
1 c. pineapple juice
1 c. crushed pineapple, drained
1 c. evaporated milk
1 c. mayonnaise
1 lb. cottage cheese
½ c. walnut meats

Dissolve gelatin in boiling water; add food coloring and pineapple juice. Chill until thickened. Fold in remaining ingredients. Chill until firm.

Betty Ann Boyle, Council Rock H. S.
Newtown, Pennsylvania

SWEETHEART SALAD

Number of Servings — 10-12

2 c. crushed pineapple
½ T. sugar
1½ T. unflavored gelatin
¼ c. cold water
2 T. lemon juice
2 T. Maraschino cherry juice
2 3-oz. pkg. cream cheese
12 Maraschino cherries, finely cut
½ pt. whipped cream

Heat pineapple with sugar. Soften gelatin in cold water; stir into pineapple mixture. Add lemon and cherry juices. Cool. Mash cream cheese and stir in cherries. Add a small amount of pineapple mixture to cheese at a time until all is mixed. Chill until slightly thickened. Fold in whipped cream. Mold in a 9 x 12 glass dish. Chill until firm.

Mrs. Jessie Rae Schweizer, Sumner H. S.
Sumner, Illinois

HONEYMOON SALAD

Number of Servings — 6

2 pkgs. lime jello
1 6-oz. pkg. cream cheese
1 c. hot water
1 medium can crushed pineapple
½ pt. whipped cream
½ c. chopped walnuts

Cream 2 packages of lime jello into 1 package of cheese. Add hot water. Blend well. Add pineapple. Fold in whipped cream. Add nuts. Mold and chill until firm.

Mrs. Diane S. Babcock, Port Allegany Union H. S.
Port Allegany, Pennsylvania

VALENTINE SALAD

Number of Servings — 6

¼ c. red-hot cinnamon candies
1 c. boiling water
1 pkg. lemon gelatin
1 c. unsweetened applesauce
1 3-oz. pkg. cream cheese
2 T. cream
2 T. mayonnaise

Dissolve red-hot candies in boiling water. Pour over lemon gelatin. Dissolve; allow to cool. Add applesauce. Put half of mixture in heart-shaped mold. Chill until set. Combine cheese, cream and mayonnaise. Spread on set gelatin mixture. Pour remaining gelatin on top of cheese. Chill until firm.

Mrs. Helen M. Godwin, Northwest H. S.
Greensboro, North Carolina

WEDDING SALAD

Number of Servings — 8

1 pkg. lime gelatin
1¼ c. boiling water
½ c. mayonnaise
2 t. onion, minced
1 c. creamed cottage cheese
½ pt. whipped cream
Black olives
Endive

Dissolve gelatin in hot water. Cool. Add mayonnaise, onion and cottage cheese. Fold in whipped cream. Put into mold. Chill until firm. Garnish with black olives and endive.

Mrs. Mary Kolischah, Chatham Sr., H. S.
Chatham, New Jersey

Molded Salads

APPLE CIDER DELITE

Number of Servings — 10-12

2 pkgs. lemon gelatin
4 c. (scant) apple juice or cider
3 c. applesauce, drained
Green food coloring

Heat cider. Add gelatin and stir until dissolved. Add applesauce and a few drops of green food coloring. Pour into a ring mold; chill until firm.

DRESSING:

1 c. cottage cheese
1½ c. whipped cream
24 marshmallows, chopped
½ t. almond extract
2 t. lemon juice

Combine ingredients; refrigerate for 2 hours. Heap in center of molded salad.

Mrs. Eleanore M. Dahl, Belgrade H. S.
Belgrade, Minnesota

APPLE-CIDER SALAD

Number of Servings — 6

2½ c. cold cider
2 T. unflavored gelatin
1 c. apples, chopped
½ c. celery, chopped
¼ t. salt
1 T. parsley, chopped
¼ c. nuts, chopped

Soak gelatin in ½ cup cold cider for 5 minutes. Bring remaining cider to boil. Pour into gelatin mixture, stirring until dissolved. Cool until mixture begins to thicken. Stir in remaining ingredients. Pour into individual molds. Chill until firm. Unmold on beds of watercress. Serve with French dressing, cooked salad dressing or mayonnaise.

Dianne J. MacPherson, Garden Spot H. S.
New Holland, Pennsylvania

APPLE-CRANBERRY SALAD

Number of Servings — 15

2 c. cranberries, ground
1 orange, ground
1 c. sugar
2 pkg. strawberry gelatin
3 c. hot water
2 c. apples, ground
1 c. pecans, chopped
1 small can pineapple
1 c. marshmallows

Combine cranberries, orange and sugar; let stand until juicy. Mix gelatin in hot water; cool. Add all remaining ingredients. Mold if desired. Refrigerate until firm.

Ethel Spradling, Bixby H. S.
Bixby, Oklahoma

APPLESAUCE-PINEAPPLE SALAD

Number of Servings — 6

1 pkg. raspberry gelatin
1 c. hot applesauce
Grated rind and juice of 1 orange
1 small c. crushed pineapple
1 small bottle 7-Up

Combine gelatin and hot applesauce. Mix in remaining ingredients. Stir occasionally until slightly cool. Refrigerate until firm.

Mrs. Opal Brovillard, Barnard H. S.
Barnard, South Dakota

APPLESAUCE RING

Number of Servings — 12

½ c. red cinnamon candies
2 c. hot water
2 pkgs. raspberry gelatin
4 c. applesauce

Simmer cinnamon candies in hot water until dissolved. Add gelatin; stir well. Add applesauce. Pour into a ring mold. Chill until firm.

Mrs. Bertha Leidahl, Willow River H. S.
Willow River, Minnesota

CELERY-APPLE SALAD

Number of Servings — 6

1 pkg. cherry gelatin
1 c. hot water
¼ c. red cinnamon candies
½ c. boiling water
1 c. pared apples, chopped
1 c. celery, chopped
½ c. nuts, chopped

Dissolve gelatin in hot water. Add cinnamon candies to boiling water; stir to dissolve. Add enough water to make 1 cup liquid. Add to dissolved gelatin. Cool until partially set. Add remaining ingredients. Pour into individual molds; chill until firm. Serve on crisp lettuce.

This recipe submitted by the following teachers:

Ruth C. Holder, Thorpe Junior H. S.
Hampton, Virginia

Mrs. Ruby H. Parrish, State School for the Blind
Aberdeen, South Dakota

APPLE SURPRISE SALAD

Number of Servings — 8

TOPPING:

½ c. whipped cream
2 T. mayonnaise
1 pkg. raspberry gelatin
½ c. apples, diced
½ c. celery, chopped
½ c. crushed pineapple
½ c. dates, chopped
¼ c. nuts, chopped
2 T. mayonnaise
½ c. whipped cream

(Continued on next page)

Prepare gelatin according to package directions. Chill until slightly thickened. Add fruit, celery and nuts. Combine whipped cream and mayonnaise; fold into gelatin mixture. Pour into individual molds. Chill until firm. Serve on lettuce leaf. Serve plain or with topping.

Mrs. Pete (Helen) Alberda, Manhattan H. S.
Manhatian, Montana

CINNAMON-APPLE CUPS

Number of Servings — 15

2 pkgs. lemon gelatin
½ c. red cinnamon candies
2 c. boiling water
2 c. unsweetened applesauce
1 T. lemon juice
Dash of salt
1 3-oz. pkg. cream cheese
½ c. walnuts, broken

Dissolve gelatin and candy in boiling water. Stir in applesauce, lemon juice and salt. Chill until partially set. Form cream cheese into tiny balls. Stir cheese balls and nuts into gelatin mixture. Chill until firm.

Mrs. David Reigel, Highland H. S.
Sparta, Ohio

CINNAMON-APPLESAUCE SALAD

Number of Servings — 9

½ c. red cinnamon candies
2 c. boiling water
2 3-oz. pkg. lemon gelatin
2 c. unsweetened applesauce
2 3-oz. pkg. cream cheese
¼ c. light cream
2 T. salad dressing

Dissolve candy in boiling water. Add gelatin and stir to dissolve. Stir in applesauce. Chill until mixture begins to thicken. Pour into 8"x8"x2" pan. Combine cream cheese, cream and salad dressing. Spoon on top of gelatin and swirl to make marbled effect. Chill until firm.

Deanna Smith, Creighton H. S.
Creighton, Nebraska

CINNAMON-APPLESAUCE SALAD

Number of Servings — 8

1 T. red cinnamon candies
1 c. hot water
1 pkg. cherry gelatin
2 c. applesauce, sweetened
½ c. celery, chopped
½ c. nuts, chopped

Dissolve candy in hot water; pour over gelatin. Add applesauce and chill until partially set. Fold in celery and nuts. Chill until firm.

Mrs. Verna Zeeb, Tripp H. S.
Tripp, South Dakota

LIMEAPPLE-CHEESE SALAD

Number of Servings — 6-8

1 pkg. lime gelatin
¾ c. boiling water
2 c. thick applesauce
1 c. cottage cheese
Crisp lettuce leaves
Mayonnaise
Paprika

Dissolve gelatin thoroughly in water. Fold in the applesauce and cottage cheese. Pour into individual molds; chill until firm. Unmold on lettuce leaves, and top with mayonnaise. Garnish with paprika.

Fern A. Soderholm, Willmar Jr. H. S.
Willmar, Minnesota

LIME-APPLE SALAD

Number of Servings — 8

1 No. 2 can applesauce
1 pkg. lime gelatin
1 7-oz. bottle 7-Up
½ c. miniature marshmallows
2 T. milk
1 c. whipped cream

Heat applesauce in saucepan; add gelatin. Stir until dissolved. Remove from heat; stir in 7-Up. Chill until firm. Dissolve marshmallows in milk in a double boiler. Cool. Fold in whipped cream. Serve on or with gelatin mixture.

Marilyn Berkseth Olson, Antioch Community H. S.
Antioch, Illinois

LIME APPLESAUCE DELIGHT

Number of Servings — 8

1 pkg. lime gelatin
½-1 c. sugar
1¼ c. applesauce
1 c. evaporated milk
1 T. lime or lemon juice

Heat applesauce. Add gelatin and sugar. Stir until dissolved. Chill milk until very cold; whip until stiff. Add lime or lemon juice. Fold whipped milk into gelatin mixture. Chill.

Mrs. Doris E. Gregory, Falls-Overfield School
Mill City, Pennsylvania

SPICED WALDORF SALAD

Number of Servings — 6

½ c. red cinnamon candies
½ t. salt
1 c. hot water
1 pkg. lemon or apple gelatin
1 c. cold water
1 c. red apple, unpeeled and diced
⅓ c. celery, finely sliced
⅓ c. nuts, chopped

(Continued on next page)

Mix candies salt and hot water together; heat until candies are dissolved. Add gelatin; stir until dissolved. Add cold water. Chill until slightly thickened. Fold in apples, celery and nuts. Chill until firm. Serve with cream cheese dressing.

Cream Cheese Dressing:

1 3-oz. pkg. cream cheese, softened
¼ c. mayonnaise
¼ c. celery, chopped
¼ c. nuts, chopped

Blend cheese and mayonnaise together. Add celery and nuts.

Avanelle Lavender, Buckeye Valley H. S.
Delaware, Ohio

SPICY APPLE SALAD

Number of Servings — 9

1 c. hot water
¼ c. red cinnamon candies
2 t. sugar
1 pkg. cherry gelatin
1 c. cold water
1 c. apple, diced
¼ c. walnuts, chopped

Dissolve sugar and candies in hot water. Heat to boiling and pour over gelatin. Add cold water. Chill until partially set. Add apples and nuts. Chill until firm.

Anna Mae Strickler, Chino H. S.
Chino, California

MOLDED WALDORF SALAD

Number of Servings — 6

1 envelope unflavored gelatin
⅓ c. sugar
½ t. salt
1½ c. water
¼ c. vinegar or lemon juice
2 c. tart apples, diced
½ c. celery, diced
¼ c. pecans, chopped

Mix gelatin, sugar and salt thoroughly in a small saucepan. Add ½ cup of the water. Stir over low heat, until gelatin is dissolved. Remove from heat; stir in remaining water, vinegar or lemon juice. Chill mixture until thickened. Fold in apples. celery and nuts. Chill until firm.

This recipe submitted by the following teachers:

Mrs. Johnnie Mae Proctor, Dilley H. S.
Dilley, Texas

Mrs. Constance White, West Allegheny Junior H. S.
Oakdale, Pennsylvania

Mrs. Jane Ann Courtney, East Central H. S.
Pascagoula, Mississippi

Lucille Whitney, Thetford Academy
Thetford, Vermont

WALDORF WHIP

Number of Servings — 6-8

1 - oz. pkg. lemon gelatin
1 c. hot water
3 T. lemon juice
½ c. mayonnaise
1 c. celery, chopped
½ c. walnuts, chopped
1½ c. apples, chopped
⅔ c. undiluted evaporated milk, whipped

Dissolve gelatin in hot water; cool. Add 1 tablespoon lemon juice. mayonniase, celery, nuts and apples. Mix well. Chill until mixture is the consistency of unbeaten egg whites. Chill evaporated milk in refrigerator tray until soft ice crystals form around edges; 10-15 minutes. Whip milk until stiff. Add the remaining lemon juice; whip 1 to 2 minutes or until very stiff. Fold whipped milk into gelatin mixture. Chill for 2 hours.

Mrs. Virginia J. Darling
Olivet Community Schools
Olivet, Michigan

WHITE GELATIN SALAD

Number of Servings — 8-10

1 pkg. lemon gelatin
1¼ c. hot water
1 T. lemon juice
½ c. pineapple juice
1 c. apples, diced
½ c. shredded pineapple
½ c. celery, diced
½ c. mayonnaise

Dissolve gelatin in hot water; add lemon and pineapple juice. Chill until slightly thickened. Fold in remaining ingredients. Chill until firm.

Mrs. Bernice Schenk, Oakland City H. S.
Oakland City, Indiana

APRICOT-CREAM CHEESE DELITE

Number of Servings — 15

1 6-oz. pkg. apricot gelatin
1 No. 2 can crushed pineapple
¾ c. sugar
1 c. apricot puree or 2 small jars strained baby food apricots
1 8-oz. pkg. cream cheese
1 lg. can evaporated milk, chilled
⅔ c. nuts, finely chopped

Combine gelatin and pineapple; heat until mixture simmers. Add sugar apricot puree and softened cream cheese. Continue heating; stirring occasionally until cheese melts. Remove from heat. Chill until mixture mounds when dropped from a spoon. Whip chilled evaporated milk until stiff peaks form. Fold into apricot mixture. Pour into 9x13x2⅝ pan. Chill until firm. Top with chopped nuts.

Patricia C. Harker, Waynesburg H. S.
Waynesburg, Pennsylvania

APRICOT CONGEALED SALAD

Number of Servings — 6-8

1 pkg. lemon gelatin
1 pkg. cream cheese
1 c. apricot nectar
4 t. mayonnaise
1 can fruit cocktail or other chopped fruit, drained
2 c. fruit juice plus water

Break cheese into gelatin. Heat juice; add to gelatin-cheese mixture. Stir thoroughly. Cool until syrupy. Add fruit and chill until firm.

Beulah Holt, Chester Independent
Chester, Texas

APRICOT GELATIN

Number of Servings — 4

1 pkg. apricot gelatin
3 ripe bananas, thinly sliced
1 small can crushed pineapple, drained
Dream Whip
2 T. sugar

Dissolve gelatin according to package directions, cool. Fold in bananas combined with pineapple. Chill until firm. Top with sweetened Dream Whip.

Mrs. Nancy York, St. Andrews H. S.
Charleston, South Carolina

APRICOT FRUIT SALAD

Number of Servings — 8-10

2 c. canned apricot halves, drained and quartered
8-10 cooked prunes, drained and quartered
¾ c. boiling water
1 3-oz. pkg. orange gelatin
1 c. evaporated milk, undiluted
2 T. lemon juice
½ c. celery, chopped
¼ c. nuts, chopped

Pour boiling water over gelatin; stir until dissolved. Chill until mixture is syrupy. Chill evaporated milk in refrigerator tray until soft crystals form around edges of tray. Whip milk until stiff; add lemon juice; whip until very stiff. Stir apricots, prunes, celery and nuts into gelatin. Fold in whipped milk. Chill until firm.

Evelyn Michelle, Coleridge H. S.
Coleridge, North Carolina

APRICOT SALAD

Number of Servings — 8-10

2 envelopes unflavored gelatin
½ c. cold water
2 cans apricots, drained
18 marshmallows
Juice of 1 lemon
½ t. salt

Dissolve gelatin in water. Bring apricot juice to boil; add marshmallows. Remove from heat and stir until marshmallows are melted. Add lemon juice, salt and gelatin to hot juice; cool. Add apricots. Chill until firm.

Janette Knox, Falkville H. S.
Falkville, Alabama

APRICOT-GINGER SALAD

Number of Servings — 6

1 pkg. Orange-Pineapple gelatin
1 c. boiling water
Orange Juice
1 medium can peeled apricots, drained
2 T. candied ginger, chopped or ginger marmalade
½ pkg. cream cheese
2 T. milk or cream

Dissolve gelatin in boiling water. Add enough cold orange juice to apricot juice to make cup liquid; add to gelatin. Chill until syrupy; Pour ½ inch layer of gelatin in bottom of mold. Place an apricot half-pit side up in gelatin. Fill cavity with cream cheese to which milk and ginger have been added. Cover with ½ apricot-pit side down. Fill mold with remaining gelatin and chill.

Susan B. Randlett, Molly Stark Jr. H. S.
Bennington, Vermont

APRICOT RING

Number of Servings — 10-12

1 No. 2½ can apricot halves, drained and sieved
1½ c. apricot juice
½ c. water
2 pkg. lemon or 1 lemon pkg. and 1 orange pkg. gelatin
Juice of 2 lemons
Juice of 1 orange
1 c. pecans, broken
2 3-oz. pkg. cream cheese, diced

Heat apricot juice and water. Add gelatin; stir until dissolved. Add enough water to lemon and orange juice to make 1 cup liquid. Add to the gelatin mixture. Add apricots. Chill until mixture begins to thicken. Add cream cheese and nuts. Chill until firm.

Mrs. Imogene Spring, Seymour H. S.
Seymour, Texas

APRICOT JUICE SALAD

1 pkg. lemon gelatin
1½ c. apricot juice
1 3-oz. pkg. cream cheese
1 can Mandarin oranges
1 c. whipped cream
½ c. water

Combine juice and water to make 2 cups liquid. Boil; pour over gelatin. Cream the cheese and beat into gelatin. Add whipped cream. Arrange oranges in a mold; pour remaining ingredients over top.

Gale Wolff, Byron H. S.
Byron, Minnesota

APRICOT SALAD

Number of Servings — 8

1 pkg. apple gelatin
1 can apricots, sliced
½ c. pecans, chopped
3 T. wine
2 c. hot apricot juice and water

Stir gelatin in hot juice-water mixture until dissolved. Chill until mixture begins to thicken. Add remaining ingredients. Chill until firm.

Mildred Mason, Cherokee Vocational H. S.
Cherokee, Alabama

APRICOT SALAD

Number of Servings — 6-8

1 No. 2 can apricots
1 lge. can diced pineapple
1 lb. small marshmallows
Juice of 1 lemon
2 T. sugar
1 egg well beaten

Combine lemon juice, butter, sugar and egg. Cook until thickened. Mix with fruits and marshmallows and refrigerate.

Helen E. Pyle, Christian County H. S.
Hopkinsville, Kentucky

APRICOT SALAD

Number of Servings — 8

2 Envelopes unflavored gelatin
½ c. cold water
Juice of 1 lemon
½ c. sugar
2 lg. cans peeled apricots, drained and sieved
Apricot juice

Soak gelatin in cold water for 5 minutes. Heat apricot juice with sugar until sugar is dissolved. Add gelatin. Remove from heat; add lemon juice. Let cool. Add apricots. Chill until firm.

Mrs. Virginia S. Sharbutt, Vincent School
Vincent, Alabama

APRICOT SALAD

Number of Servings — 8

1 lge. can apricots, drained
¾ c. sugar
½ lb. cheese, grated
2 T. flour
Nuts
Juice of lemon
2 eggs, beaten
Juice of apricots

Mix flour and sugar; add to eggs. Add lemon and apricot juice. Cook until thick. Cool. Make a layer of apricots, cheese and nuts in bottom of mold. Pour cool dressing over all. Chill. Cut in squares to serve.

Mrs. Berniece Wiginton, Big Sandy H. S.
Big Sandy, Texas

APRICOT SALAD SOUFFLE

Number of Servings — 9

2 c. apricot halves, drained and sliced
1 pkg. orange gelatin
½ c. orange juice
2 T. lemon juice
1 3-oz. pkg. cream cheese
1 9-oz. can pineapple tidbits, drained
1 c. red grapes, halved and seeded
½ c. mayonnaise
⅓ c. almonds, toasted and slivered
Dash of salt

Drain juice from apricots and add water to make 1 cup liquid. Heat to boiling; add gelatin and stir until dissolved. Add orange and lemon juice; salt. Blend in cream cheese until smooth. Chill until partially congealed. Beat gelatin mixture until fluffy. Fold in fruits, mayonnaise and almonds. Chill until firm. Garnish with sugared grapes.

Louise Green, Cedar Bluff H. S.
Cedar Bluff, Alabama

GOLDEN APRICOT MOLDS

Number of Servings — 8

1 No. 2½ can peeled apricot halves, drained
¼ c. vinegar
½ t. cloves
½ t. cinnamon
1 pkg. orange gelatin

Add vinegar and spices to apricot juice. Boil 10 minutes. Strain and measure. Add enough boiling water to make 2 cups liquid. Dissolve gelatin in the hot liquid. Place apricots in individual or a large mold. Slowly pour gelatin over apricot halves. Chill until firm.

This recipe submitted by the following teachers:
Mrs. Jamie Harris White, Signal Mountain Jr. H. S.
Signal Mountain, Tennessee
Ellen Anderson, Tolt H. S.
Carnation, Washington

JELLIED APRICOT NECTAR SALAD

Number of Servings — 6

1 T. unflavored gelatin
2 T. cold water
¾ c. boiling Apricot Nectar
Speck of salt
2 T. sugar
2 T. lemon juice
¾ c. ginger ale
¼ c. ripe olives, sliced
¼ c. celery, diced
½ c. pineapple

Soak gelatin in cold water for 5 minutes; dissolve in boiling apricot nectar. Add salt, sugar and lemon juice. Cool slightly; add ginger ale. Let partially set. Add olives, celery and pineapple. Pour mixture into mold; Set in cool place until mixture is firm.

Marjorie Corbin, Holly H. S.
Holly, Colorado

AVOCADO MOUSSE

Number of Servings — 8

1 T. unflavored gelatin
½ c. cold water
½ c. boiling water
1 t. salt
1 t. onion juice
2 t. Worcestershire sauce
2 T. lemon juice
2 c. avocado, mashed
½ c. heavy cream, whipped
½ c. mayonnaise

Soak gelatin in cold water; dissolve in boiling water. Add salt, onion juice, Worcestershire sauce, lemon juice and avocado pulp. Chill until mixture begins to set. Fold in whipped cream and mayonnaise. Turn into an oiled mold or individual molds. Chill until firm.

Mrs. Mary Belle Nutt, Cotulla H. S.
Cotulla, Texas

AVOCADO-PECAN SALAD

Number of Servings — 12

2 pkg. lime gelatin
2 c. boiling water
1 c. sour cream
1 c. mayonnaise
2 c. pecans, broken
1⅓ c. avocado, mashed
2 t. onion, minced
2 t. celery, minced
1 c. green pepper, chopped
1 t. salt

Dissolve gelatin in boiling water. Refrigerate until gelatin reaches the consistency of egg white. Whip until foamy. Beat in sour cream and mayonnaise. Blend thoroughly. Fold in remaining ingredients. Refrigerate until firm.

Myrtle Little, Hattiesburg H. S.
Hattiesburg, Mississippi

AVOCADO PERFECTION SALAD

Number of Servings — 8

1 pkg. Lime gelatin
1¼ c. hot water
⅛ t. salt
1 9-oz. can crushed pineapple
1 T. lemon juice
2 T. sweet pickle juice
2 T. sweet pickle, chopped
2 T. pimento, chopped
1 green onion, diced
1 avocado, chopped
1 c. cabbage, finely shredded

Combine hot water and salt. Add gelatin; dissolve. Add pineapple, lemon juice and pickle juice. Cool; add remaining ingredients. Pour into individual molds. Chill until firm.

Freda H. Montgomery, Central Union H. S.
Fresno, California

AVOCADO MOUSSE

Number of Servings — 8

1 T. unflavored gelatin
2 T. cold water
1 pkg. lime gelatin
2 c. hot water
1 c. ripe avocado, mashed
½ c. mayonnaise
½ c. whipped cream

Soften unflavored gelatin in cold water. Dissolve both gelatins in hot water. Chill until partially set. Stir in remaining ingredients. Pour into a mold greased with mayonnaise. Chill until firm. Unmold on crisp salad greens. Garnish with fruit and mint sprigs if desired.

Mrs. Blazita G. Flores, Ben Bolt-Palito Blanco H. S.
Ben Bolt, Texas

AVOCADO RING

Number of Servings — 8

1 T. unflavored gelatin
¼ c. cold water
½ c. boiling water
¼ c. lemon juice
1 c. sieved avocado
½ c. mayonnaise
½ c. whipped cream
½ c. celery, chopped
1 T. grated onion, or onion juice (opt.)

Soak gelatin in cold water; dissolve in boiling water. Cool until mixture begins to thicken. Add remaining ingredients. Turn into a ring mold; chill until firm. Fill center with ham, chicken or fruit salad if desired.

Augusta Jannett, Yoakum H. S.
Yoakum, Texas

AVOCADO SALAD

Number of Servings — 12

1 pkg. lime gelatin
1 c. boiling water
1 c. cold water
1 ripe avocado
1 small pkg. cream cheese
½ c. mayonnaise
¼ c. celery, finely cut
½ c. bell pepper, finely cut
Few drops onion juice
⅛ t. salt

Dissolve gelatin in hot water; add cold water. Let set until almost firm. Mash avocado and cream cheese; add to thickened gelatin. Add remaining ingredients; chill until firm.

Mrs. C. B. Carter, Kirbyville H. S.
Kirbyville, Texas

AVOCADO SALAD

Number of Servings — 8

2 3-oz. pkg. lime gelatin
2 c. boiling water
1 8-oz. pkg. cream cheese
1½ t. grated onion
1 t. salt
½ t. garlic powder
¼ t. pepper
2 Large avocados, mashed
1 c. celery, finely chopped
Stuffed olives, sliced (garnish)

Dissolve gelatin in boiling water. Chill over ice water, stirring frequently until syrupy. Beat cheese with electric mixer until creamy. Slowly add gelatin, beating constantly until mixture is blended. Chill until partially thickened. Fold in remaining ingredients. Turn into molds. Chill until firm. Garnish with olives.

Mrs. Pauline Quillin, Pymatuning Joint School
Jamestown, Pennsylvania

AVOCADO SALAD

1 pkg. lime gelatin
1 c. hot water
2 c. avocado, mashed, 3 average size
½ small onion, grated
½ c. mayonnaise
Juice of 1 lemon
½ t. salt
¾ c. whipped cream

Dissolve gelatin in hot water; cool until syrupy. Add avocado, onion, mayonnaise, lemon and salt. Fold in whipped cream. Mold.

Mrs. Susan R. Salter, Robert E. Lee H. S.
Montgomery, Alabama

AVOCADO SEAFOAM SALAD

Number of Servings — 10

1 avocado, peeled and cubed
1 3-oz. pkg. cream cheese
2 small stalks celery, chopped
1 small onion, grated
½ c. mayonnaise
1 or 2 pimentos, chopped
1 pkg. lime gelatin
1½ c. hot water

Dissolve gelatin in hot water. Chill until partially set. Mix mayonnaise and cream cheese until smooth and well blended. Add avocado. Add celery, onion and pimentos. Blend well. Add to gelatin. Spoon into individual molds. Chill until firm.

Mrs. Jean Aldredge, Moore Junior H. S.
Tyler, Texas

MOLDED AVOCADO-LIME SALAD

Number of Servings — 8

1 pkg. lime gelatin
½ c. warm water
1 No. 1 can crushed pineapple, drained
¾ c. whipped cream
½ c. mayonnaise
½ c. avocado, diced
½ t. salt
2 T. lemon juice
½ c. pineapple juice

Dissolve gelatin in warm water. Stir in pineapple juice. Cool until mixture begins to thicken. Add pineapple, salt and lemon juice. Fold in mayonnaise, whipped cream and avocado. Chill until firm.

Sarah Beth Galloway, Bonneville H. S.
Idaho Falls, Idaho

MOLDED AVOCADO SALAD

Number of Servings — 8

1½ T. unflavored gelatin
¼ c. cold water
2½ c. tomato juice
2 bay leaves
5 whole cloves
¼ c. onion, chopped
½ t. salt
⅛ t. pepper
3 drops Tabasco Sauce
2 avocados, peeled and diced
½ c. celery, chopped

Soak gelatin in cold water for 5 minutes. Combine tomato juice, bay leaves, cloves, onions, salt, pepper and Tabasco sauce. Boil for 5 minutes; strain. Add gelatin; stir until dissolved. Cool until syrupy. Add avocados and celery. Pour into individual molds; chill until firm.

Mrs. LeArta Hammond, West Side High
Dayton, Idaho

BLACKBERRY DELIGHT

Number of Servings — 8

1 blackberry gelatin
1 c. boiling water
1 c. sugar
1 3-oz. pkg. cream cheese
1 carton frozen blackberries
¼ c. nuts, chopped

Dissolve gelatin and sugar in boiling water. Soften cheese in 4 tablespoons of the hot mixture. Cool remaining gelatin mixture. Add frozen blackberries, nuts and cheese mixture to cooled gelatin. Refrigerate until firm.

Mrs. Clarice I. Snider, Unicoi County H. S.
Erwin, Tennessee

BLUEBERRY SALAD

Number of Servings — 8

1 pkg. lemon gelatin
1 c. boiling blueberry juice
1 c. pineapple juice
1 c. whipped cream
1 banana, mashed
1 c. blueberries, drained

Dissolve gelatin in hot blueberry juice. Stir in pineapple juice. Refrigerate until mixture thickens. Fold in whipped cream, blueberries and banana. Spoon into large mold or individual molds.

Bettye Robinson, LaPuente H. S.
LaPuente, California

BLUEBERRY SALAD

1 can blueberries, drained
1 pkg. black raspberry gelatin
1 can crushed pineapple, drained
1 c. pecans, chopped

Bring combined juices to a boil. Add gelatin; stir until dissolved. Add blueberries, pineapple and nuts. Chill until set.

Mrs. Matha L. Taylor, Algoma H. S.
Algoma, Mississippi

BLUEBERRY-GELATIN SALAD

Number of Servings — 8

2 3-oz. pkgs. red gelatin
1 pt. sour cream
15-02 can blueberries, undrained
2 c. hot water

Dissolve gelatin in hot water. Chill until partially set. Blend in sour cream and blueberries. Chill until firm. Garnish with sour cream, dressing or pineapple chunks if desired.

Grace Lamusga, Hosterman Jr. H. S.
Robbinsdale, Minnesota

BLUEBERRY MOLD

Number of Servings — 12

1 can blueberries, drained
2 pkg. lemon gelatin
1 c. heavy cream, whipped
1 lge. banana, mashed
2 T. sugar
Pineapple juice

Combine juice from blueberries and enough pineapple juice to make 3 cups liquid. Add gelatin and stir until dissolved. Chill until partially thickened. Fold in banana, sugar, cream and blueberries. Turn into mold and chill until firm.

Mary Jane Henderson, Bay H. S.
Bay, Arkansas

FRESH BLUEBERRY SALAD

Number of Servings — 12

2 3-oz. pkg. black cherry gelatin
3 c. boiling water
1 8-oz. can crushed pineapple
¼ c. Maraschino cherries, halved
2 c. fresh blueberries

Dissolve gelatin in boiling water. Cool. Add pineapple and chill until thickened. Fold in cherries and blueberries. Chill until firm.

DRESSING:

1 c. miniature marshmallows
2 c. sour cream
1 t. mayonnaise
½ t. vanilla

Mix ingredients and let stand several hours or overnight. Mix well and serve on blueberry salad.

Nora Peterson, Junior College
Virginia, Minnesota

LIME-BLUEBERRY MOLD

Number of Servings — 6-8

2 envelopes unflavored gelatin
1 c. cold water
1½ c. boiling water
½ c. sugar
¼ t. salt
¼ c. fresh lime juice
3 c. fresh blueberries

Soften gelatin in cold water. Add boiling water, sugar and salt; stir until gelatin dissolves. Add lime juice. Chill until mixture reaches the consistency of unbeaten egg white. Fold in blueberries.

Mrs. Carolyn Martin, Girard H. S.
Girard, Illinois

PURPLE LADY

Number of Servings — 12

2 pkg. raspberry gelatin
1 c. boiling water
1 No. 300 can blueberries
1 small can crushed pineapple, drained
½ pt. whipped cream

Dissolve gelatin in boiling water; add fruit. Mix well. Chill until partially set. Fold in whipped cream. Chill until firm.

Mrs. Ruth Marshall, Borger Senior H. S.
Borger, Texas

APPLE-CRANBERRY-MALLO SALAD

Number of Servings — 8-10

1 pkg. raw cranberries, ground
2 med. oranges, quartered and seeded
1 apple, cored and ground
2 c. sugar
1 pkg. strawberry or raspberry gelatin
1 c. hot water
½ c. cold water
1 c. toasted pecans
1 c. miniature marshmallows

Combine sugar with ground cranberry-orange-apple mixture. Set aside. Dissolve gelatin in hot water. Add cold water, chill until syrupy. Fold in fruit mixture pecans and marshmallows. Chill until firm.

Mrs. Frances C. Reynolds
Calhoun Attendance Center
Laurel, Mississippi

CONGEALED CRANBERRY AND CHEESE SALAD

Number of Servings — 8

1 pkg. raspberry gelatin
1 c. boiling water
1 small pkg. cream cheese
1 small can crushed pineapple, drained
1 c. whole cranberry sauce
½ c. nuts, chopped
1 small pkg. marshmallows (opt.)
2 oranges, peeled and sectioned (opt.)
½ c. pineapple juice and water

Dissolve gelatin in 1 cup boiling water. Add pineapple juice-water mixture. Cool. Mix cream cheese with a little pineapple juice. Add pineapple, cranberry sauce and nuts. Add to gelatin mixture. Chill until firm. Marshmallows and oranges may be added with other fruits for variety.

This recipe submitted by the following teachers:

Mrs. Christine C. Risher, Noxubee County H. S.
Macon, Mississippi

Mrs. Kathleen H. Land
Camp Hill, Alabama

Mrs. Kathleen Garrett, Albertville H. S.
Albertville, Alabama

CRANBERRY CUPS

Number of Servings — 8-9

1 9-oz. can crushed pineapple, drained
1 No. 2½ can sliced pineapple, drained
1 pkg. cherry gelatin
¼-1 c. sugar
1 T. lemon juice
1 whole unpeeled apple, cored (opt.)
1 c. fresh cranberries, ground
1-2 small orange, unpared, seeded and ground
1 c. celery, chopped (opt.)
½ c. walnuts or pecans, broken
Pineapple juice plus enough water to make 2 c. liquid

Combine gelatin, sugar and juice-water mixture. Heat until sugar and gelatin dissolve, stirring constantly. Add lemon juice. Chill until partially set. Add crushed pineapple, cranberries, orange, celery and walnuts. Pour into individual molds. Chill until firm. Unmold on pineapple slices. Top with mayonnaise and garnish with tiny lettuce leaves standing upright. If less orange flavor is desired, the orange may be peeled. If a firmer salad is desired 1 package softened unflavored gelatin may be added to the hot juice mixture.

This recipe submitted by the following teachers:

Irene Struble, Fairview H. S.
Farmer, Ohio

Mrs. Glenna Lober, Forrest-Strawn-Wing Unit
Forrest, Illinois

Mrs. Wilford W. Taylor, Hoxie Consolidated School
Hoxie, Arkansas

Mrs. Elizabeth McGee, East Lamar H. S.
Pattonville, Texas

Mrs. Effie L. Jones, Mineral Springs H. S.
Mineral Springs, Arkansas

Mrs. Robert L. Abney, Jr., Bay Springs H. S.
Bay Springs, Mississippi

Barbara A. Potter, Raceland H. S.
Raceland, Kentucky

Mrs. Suzanne Olds, Hosterman Junior H. S.
Minneapolis, Minnesota

Mrs. Helen Fetter, United Joint H. S.
New Florence, Pennsylvania

Hilda Harmon, Crowley H. S.
Crowley, Louisiana

CRANBERRY HOLIDAY SALAD

Number of Servings — 10

1 c. sugar
1 c. raw cranberries, ground
1 pkg. lemon or raspberry gelatin
½ c. boiling water
1 c. orange or pineapple juice
1-2 t. grated orange rind (opt.)
1 9-oz. can crushed pineapple
½-1 c. pecans, broken (opt.)
½-1 c. celery, chopped or unpeeled apple (opt.)

(Continued on next page)

Mix sugar and berries together; let stand 2 or more hours. Add gelatin to boiling water; stir until dissolved. Stir in orange juice and rind. Chill until syrupy. Fold in remaining ingredients. Pour into mold, refrigerate. Serve on crisp lettuce.

This recipe submitted by the following teachers:

Julia B. Simpson, Troutman H. S.
Troutman, North Carolina

Mrs. J. E. Clowdis, Gordon H. S.
Decatur, Georgia

Mrs. K. P. Jackson, Ponce de Leon
Ponce de Leon, Florida

Mrs. Frances S. Bruce, James A. Gray H. S.
Winston-Salem, North Carolina

Pauline Waggener, DuQuoin Township H. S.
DuQuoin, Illinois

Mrs. Verna I. Boyd, Pisgah School
Sand Hill, Mississippi

Nan Lindsey, Wade Hampton H. S.
Greenville, South Carolina

CRANBERRY DELIGHT

Number of Servings — 6

2 c. cranberries, ground
1 orange, finely chopped
1 c. sugar
1 c. nuts, finely chopped
1 c. crushed pineapple, drained
2 T. salad dressing
1 3-oz. pkg. cream cheese
1 pkg. cherry gelatin
Pineapple juice plus enough water to make 2 c. liquid

Dissolve gelatin in juice-water mixture. Set aside until mixture starts to congeal. Add remaining ingredients. Chill. Slice and serve on lettuce.

Mrs. Rosie Hurd, Thompson Junior H. S.
Lubbock, Texas

CRANBERRY DELIGHT

Number of Servings — 10-12

1 pkg. raw cranberries, ground
1½ c. sugar
1 pkg. strawberry gelatin
1¼ c. hot water
1 small can crushed pineapple
1 c. marshmallows, diced
1 c. nuts, chopped
½ c. flaked coconut

Combine ground cranberries and sugar. Chill overnight. Next morning, dissolve strawberry gelatin in hot water. Add to cranberries. Fold in pineapple, marshmallows and nuts. Mix well. Pour into molds; sprinkle with angel flake coconut. Chill until set.

Mrs. Margaret Kemp, Mountain View H. S.
Mountain View, Arkansas

CRANBERRY GELATIN SALAD

Number of Servings — 12

2 pkg. strawberry gelatin
2 c. whole cranberry sauce, heated
⅔ c. sugar
2 c. crushed pineapple, well drained
2 c. ginger ale
2 c. celery, diced
1 c. nuts, chopped
Grated rind of 2 oranges

Dissolve sugar and gelatin in the hot cranberry sauce. Cool; add pineapple and ginger ale. Chill until slightly congealed; stir in remaining ingredients. Pour into a ring mold and chill until firm.

Mrs. Margaret H. Davidson, East Henderson H. S.
Flat Rock, North Carolina

CRANBERRY GELATIN SALAD

Number of Servings — 16

2½ c. sugar
1 c. water
2½ T. unflavored gelatin
½ c. cold water
4 c. raw cranberries, ground
1 orange with rind, ground
1 c. celery, chopped
1 c. nuts, chopped

Soak gelatin in cold water. Cook sugar and 1 cup water to make a thin syrup. Add softened gelatin and stir until dissolved. Cool. Add remaining ingredients. Pour into a mold. Chill.

Mildred H. Morris, Reeltown H. S.
Notasulga, Alabama

CRANBERRY GELATIN SALAD

Number of Servings — 12-15

1 pkg. cranberries, washed
2 pkg. orange gelatin
1½ c. granulated sugar
1 lg. can crushed pineapple, undrained
1 c. celery, diced
½ c. walnuts

Cook cranberries in water until soft. Drain and press through sieve. Bring sieved mixture to boil. Add gelatin and sugar; stir until dissolved. Add pineapple. Cool until thickened. Stir in celery and walnuts. Chill.

Jeanette Weiss, Ovid H. S.
Ovid, Colorado

CRANBERRY-GELATIN SALAD

Number of Servings — 6

1 3-oz. pkg. lemon gelatin
½ c. hot water
½ c. crushed pineapple and juice
½ c. apple, grated
1 16-oz. can whole cranberries
½ c. orange juice
1 T. lemon juice
¼ c. nuts, chopped

Dissolve gelatin in the hot water; cool. Stir in remaining ingredients. Pour into a 1-qt. mold and chill several hours.

Neala R. Yde, John Muir Jr. H. S.
Burbank, California

CRANBERRY HOLIDAY SALAD

Number of Servings — 8

2 c. uncooked cranberries, chopped
1-3 thin-skinned oranges, chopped
1-3 red apples, chopped
1 c. celery, chopped (opt.)
1 pkg. lemon or raspberry gelatin
1 c. hot water
½ c. cold water
1½ c. sugar
½-1 c. nuts (opt.)

Dissolve gelatin in hot water; add cold water. Chill until partially set. Combine fruits, sugar, nuts, and celery. Fold into gelatin. Chill until firm.

This recipe submitted by the following teachers:

Mrs. Emma Catherine Lawson, Carrizozo H. S.
Carrizozo, New Mexico

Mrs. Betty Peters, Onsted Community Schools
Onsted, Michigan

Mrs. Beulah K. Sanders, Goldonna H. S.
Goldonna, Louisiana

Lucinda Beverage, Highland H. S.
Monterey, Virginia

LaVergne Wilken, Burlington H. S.
Burlington, Colorado

Mrs. Rama G. Steen, Caldwell H. S.
Caldwell, Ohio

CRANBERRY JEWEL SALAD

Number of Servings — 6

1 pkg. raspberry gelatin
1 unpeeled orange, ground
1 16-oz. can cranberries
1 c. hot water
½ c. cold water

Dissolve gelatin in hot water; add cold water. Chill until mixture begins to jell. Fold orange and cranberries into gelatin mixture. Chill until firm.

Mrs. Grace Montgomery, Kiona Benton
Benton, Washington

CRANBERRY JEWEL SALAD

Number of Servings — 4-6

1 pkg. raspberry or lemon gelatin
1 c. hot water
½ c. cold water
2 c. fresh cranberries
1 orange, quartered and seeded
1 c. sugar
½ c. walnuts, chopped (opt.)

Dissolve gelatin in hot water. Add cold water. Cool. Put raw cranberries and orange through food chopper. Add sugar and mix well. When gelatin begins to thicken, fold in cranberry mixture; pour into molds and chill until firm.

This recipe submitted by the following teachers:

Mrs. Mozelle B. Batchelor, Coopers H. S.
Nashville, North Carolina

Emma E. Bunyard, Jenks H. S.
Jenks, Oklahoma

Mrs. John Knecht, Langdon Public School
Langdon, North Dakota

Mrs. Juanita Willis, Carlsbad Senior H. S.
Carlsbad, New Mexico

Mrs. Elizabeth Hayton, Huntington Junior H. S.
Kelso, Washington

CRANBERRY-MARSHMALLOW MOLD

Number of Servings — 8

1 pkg. raspberry gelatin
1 c. boiling water
2 t. lemon juice
1 1-lb. can whole cranberry sauce
2 medium oranges, sectioned and chopped or
1 small can pineapple tidbits
⅓ c. walnuts, chopped
¾ c. miniature marshmallows

Dissolve gelatin in boiling water; add lemon juice. Stir in Cranberry sauce. Cool until syrupy. Fold in oranges or pineapple, nuts and marshmallows. Pour into star shaped mold and refrigerate until firm.

Arlene Trautman, Arickaree School
Anton, Colorado

CRANBERRY MOLD SALAD

Number of Servings — 6

1 c. raw cranberries, ground or chopped
1 c. unpared apple, diced
1 c. sugar
1 pkg. lemon gelatin
1 c. hot water
⅔ c. cold water
¼ c. walnuts, finely chopped

Combine cranberries, apple and sugar; let stand. Dissolve gelatin in hot water; add cold water. Chill until partially set. Add cranberry-apple mixture and nuts. Pour into individual molds; chill until firm.

Margaret Nowatzki, Hazen H. S.
Hazen, North Dakota

CRANBERRY MOLD

Number of Servings — 5-6

1 pkg. raspberry gelatin
½ t. salt
1 c. hot water
½ c. cold water
2 t. lemon juice
1 c. whole cranberry sauce
½ c. canned crushed pineapple, drained
½ c. celery, diced
½ c. apple, diced
¼ c. nuts

Dissolve gelatin and salt in hot water. Add cold water and lemon juice. Chill until slightly thickened. Fold in cranberry sauce, pineapple, celery, apple and nuts. Pour into molds. Chill until firm.

Mary Russell Cole, North Marshall H. S.
Calvert City, Kentucky

CRANBERRY MOLD

Number of Servings — 12-15

1 lb. fresh cranberries, ground
1½ c. sugar
1 small can pineapple, drained
1-1½ c. fresh orange juice
1 c. apples, peeled and chopped (opt.)
1 pkg. cherry or strawberry gelatin
1 pkg. lemon or orange gelatin
1 c. celery, chopped
1 c. nuts, chopped
Dash of salt (opt.)

Grind cranberries, add sugar, apple if desired and pineapple. Let stand 15 minutes. Dissolve gelatin in hot orange, pineapple and lemon juices. Add cranberry mixture, celery and nuts. Pour into greased mold and chill.

This recipe submitted by the following teachers:

Mrs. E. B. McWhorter, Milner H. S.
Milner, Georgia

Nina Diefenbach, Silver Creek H. S.
Sellersburg, Indiana

CRANBERRY-ORANGE MOLDS

Number of Servings — 6

2 c. uncooked cranberries
2 small oranges, peeled
1 c. sugar
Rind of 1 orange
1 pkg. lemon gelatin
1 c. boiling water

Put cranberries and orange rind through food chopper. Dice orange. Add orange and sugar to cranberry mixture. Dissolve gelatin in boiling water; cool. Add gelatin to cranberry-orange mixture. Pour into oiled molds; chill until firm.

Gladys H. Frye, Chilhowie H. S.
Chilhowie, Virginia

CRANBERRY MOLD

Number of Servings — 6-8

1 pkg. strawberry or cherry gelatin
1 c. whole cranberries, cooked or 1 can whole cranberry sauce
½-1 c. crushed pineapple, drained
Juice of 1 lemon (opt.)
1 c. hot water
½ c. pecans or English walnuts, chopped
½-1 c. celery, chopped
¼-1 c. sugar (opt.)
Pineapple syrup drained from pineapple
½ t. lemon peel, grated (opt.)

Dissolve gelatin in hot water. Add sugar, lemon juice and pineapple syrup. Stir until dissolved. Chill until thickened. Fold in remaining ingredients. Chill until firm. Serve on crisp lettuce with salad dressing.

This recipe submitted by the following teachers:

Rebecca C. Turner, State Supervisor
Home Economics Education
Little Rock, Arkansas

Mrs. Minta Skaggs, M. C. Napier H. S.
Hazard, Kentucky

Mary Jane L. Niboli, Tranquillity Union H. S.
Tranquillity, California

Ruth Bailey, Jonesboro H. S.
Jonesboro, Tennessee

Ruby Lucking, Augusta Community H. S.
Augusta Illinois

CRANBERRY SALAD

Number of Servings — 4-6

1 T. unflavored gelatin
1¼ c. cold water
2 c. cranberries
1 c. sugar
½ c. nuts, chopped
½-1 c. celery, chopped
½ t. salt
½ c. peeled orange sections, chopped (opt.)
1 small can crushed pineapple (opt.)

Cook cranberries in 1 cup water for 20 minutes or until soft; stir in sugar and cook for 5 minutes. Soften gelatin in cold water; add gelatin and salt to hot cranberries; stir until dissolved. Strain. Cool until thickened. Add celery and nuts. Orange sections and pineapple may also be added at this time if desired. Chill until firm.

This recipe submitted by the following teachers:

Nancy E. Anderson, Hennepin Township School
Hennepin, Illinois

Mrs. Lois Christian, Cottage Grove H. S.
Cottage Grove, Oregon

Mrs. Colleen T. Marshall, Lebanon H. S.
Lebanon, Tennessee

CRANBERRY-ORANGE RING

Number of Servings — 8

1 3-oz. pkg. cherry gelatin
1 c. boiling water
1 10-oz. pkg. frozen cranberry-orange relish, partially thawed
1 9-oz. can crushed pineapple
1 T. leman juice
½ c. celery, chopped
½ c. walnuts, chopped

Dissolve gelatin in boiling water. Add relish and stir until completely thawed. Stir in pineapple and juice; add lemon juice. Chill until partially set. Fold in celery and nuts. Spoon into 5-cup ring mold. Chill until firm.

Ann Scott Giles, Dixie Heights
South Fort Mitchell, Kentucky

CRANBERRY SALAD

Number of Servings — 8-10

2 c. raw cranberries
1½ c. water
1 c. sugar
1 pkg. cherry gelatin
½ c. crushed pineapple, drained
1 tart apple, peeled and finely chopped
½ c. nuts, chopped

Add water to cranberries; simmer 10 minutes. Add sugar, stir and add gelatin. Remove from heat; cool. Add pineapple, a little pineapple juice, apple and nuts. Pour into molds; chill.

Mrs. Edna Earle Beck, Anson H. S.
Anson, Texas

CRANBERRY SALAD

Number of Servings — 12

1 c. water
1 c. sugar
2 c. cranberries
1 pkg. raspberry gelatin
15 marshmallows
1 c. nuts, chopped
1 c. celery, chopped
1 c. apples, chopped (opt.)

Bring water and sugar to a boil; add cranberries. Boil until cranberries pop open. Remove from heat; add gelatin and marshmallows. Cool; add remaining ingredients. Chill until firm.

This recipe submitted by the following teachers:

Mrs. Doris Hutchison, Burkburnett H. S.
Burkburnett, Texas

Mrs. Inez Parkey, Amarillo H. S.
Amarillo, Texas

Mrs. Elouise Scheirman, Tonkawa H. S.
Tonkawa, Oklahoma

Mrs. Hazel Huckaby, Fowler H. S.
Fowler, Colorado

CRANBERRY SALAD

Number of Servings — 10-12

2 envelopes unflavored gelatin
1 c. unsweetened orange juice (fresh or frozen)
2 c. sugar
1 c. miniature marshmallows
1 small can crushed pineapple
1 c. pecans, chopped
1 c. celery, finely chopped
1 lb. cranberries, finely ground

Dissolve gelatin in heated orange juice. Add sugar, marshmallows, pineapple, pecans, celery and cranberries. Pour into a mold; chill overnight.

Mrs. Martha Cervenka, Granger H. S.
Granger, Texas

CRANBERRY SALAD

Number of Servings — 10-12

2 3-oz. boxes cherry or black cherry gelatin
2-3 c. boiling water
1 1-lb. can cranberry sauce
1 T. lemon juice (opt.)
1 pt. cultured sour cream

Dissolve gelatin in boiling water. Cool until syrupy. Blend in Cranberry sauce with a fork. Add lemon juice and sour cream. Pour into mold; let set.

Alma Frerichs, Grants Pass Sr. H. S.
Grants Pass, Oregon

CRANBERRY SALAD

Number of Servings — 8

1 lb. cranberries
1 small can crushed pineapple, drained
2 c. sugar
2 envelopes unflavored gelatin
1 c. nuts
½ c. cold water

Boil cranberries in juice drained from pineapple, until they pop. Add sugar. Dissolve gelatin in ½ cup cold water. Add to hot mixture. Add pineapple and nuts. Pour into mold. Chill until firm.

Thelma S. Land, Hickory School
Hickory, Mississippi

CRANBERRY SALAD

Number of Servings — 10-12

1 3-oz. pkg. raspberry gelatin
1 3-oz. pkg. lemon gelatin
4 c. hot water
2 c. fresh cranberries, ground
1 c. crushed pineapple, drained
1½ c. sugar
2 c. celery, finely chopped

Dissolve gelatin in hot water, chill until slightly thickened. Combine cranberries, pineapple, sugar and celery. Fold mixture into jello. Chill until firm.

Nellie F. Lower, Butler H. S.
Vandalia, Ohio

CRANBERRY SALAD

Number of Servings — 10

1 pkg. cherry gelatin
1 c. hot water
1 c. sugar
1 T. lemon juice
1 c. mixed pineapple and orange juice
2 c. raw cranberries, ground
1 c. crushed pineapple, drained
1 c. celery, finely chopped
2 c. apples, ground or diced
½ c. nuts, chopped

Dissolve gelatin in hot water; add sugar. Cool slightly. Add juices. Chill until partially set. Add remaining ingredients. Chill until firm.

Mrs. Marie L. Fuller, Liberty-Eylau
Texarkana, Texas

CRANBERRY SALAD

Number of Servings — 6

½ c. pineapple juice
4 T. water
1 pkg. orange gelatin
6 T. mayonnaise
¼ t. salt
½ c. canned milk, chilled
1 No. 303 can cranberry sauce
⅔ c. crushed pineapple
½ c. celery, diced

Boil pineapple juice and water, add gelatin; cool but do not chill. Add mayonnaise, salt, and chilled milk; let set until thick. Whip until fluffy. Fold in cranberry sauce, pineapple and celery. Refrigerate until ready to serve.

Mrs. Estelle Lair Greene, Yreka Union H. S.
Yreka, California

CRANBERRY SALAD

Number of Servings — 10

1 pkg. unflavored gelatin
¼ c. cold water
1 pkg. red fruit-flavored gelatin
1 c. hot water
1⅓ c. jellied cranberry sauce
Juice of 2 lemons
Juice of 2 oranges
1 t. grated rind from oranges and lemons
1 No. 2 can crushed pineapple, drained
2 or 3 apples, grated

Soften gelatin in cold water. Dissolve red gelatin in the hot water. Add cranberry sauce and softened gelatin. Mix well. Add fruit juices and grated rind. Chill until partly congealed; add pineapple and grated apples. Mold as desired.

Mrs. Reva B. Guinn, Young H. S.
Knoxville, Tennessee

CRANBERRY SALAD

Number of Servings — 20

1 qt. cranberries, ground
2 Delicious apples, ground
2 lge. oranges, diced
2 c. sugar
2 c. pecans
3 envelopes unflavored gelatin
¾ c. cold water
1 c. boiling orange juice

Soften gelatin in cold water. Dissolve in hot orange juice. Stir in sugar. Cool. Combine fruits and nuts. Fold into syrupy gelatin mixture. Chill until firm. May be frozen.

Mrs. Helen D. Jones, Buckatunna H. S.
Buckatunna, Mississippi

CRANBERRY SALAD

Number of Servings — 8

1½ c. boiling water
1 pkg. cherry gelatin
1 c. raw cranberries, ground
¾ c. sugar
1 c. crushed pineapple
½ c. celery, diced
½ c. apple, diced
½ c. walnuts, chopped (opt.)

Dissolve gelatin in water. Cool. Refrigerate until thickened. Add sugar to cranberries. Add all ingredients to gelatin. Refrigerate until set. Serve with salad dressing or whipped cream.

Nancy McCormack, North Gem H. S.
Bancroft, Idaho

CRANBERRY SALAD

Number of Servings — 8

1 pkg. raspberry, lemon or cherry gelatin
1 c. boiling water
1 c. cold water
1 unpeeled apple, ground
1 orange, peeled or unpeeled, seeded and ground
1-1½ c. cranberries, ground
1 t. orange rind, grated (opt.)
½ c. pecans, chopped
½ c. celery, chopped (opt.)
¼-½ c. sugar, to taste
¼ t. salt (opt.)

Dissolve gelatin in boiling water. Add cold water. Chill until thickened. Mix fruit with salt and sugar; add to the gelatin and mold.

This recipe submitted by the following teachers:

Monna Smith Miller, Lake City H. S.
Lake City, Tennessee

Mrs. Carline Cuttrell, Fannindel H. S.
Ladonia, Texas

Mrs. Beverly P. Boyer, North Plainfield H. S.
North Plainfield, New Jersey

CRANBERRY SALAD

Number of Servings — 8-10

1 pkg. orange gelatin
1 pkg. cherry gelatin
2 c. hot water
2 c. cold water
1 pkg. cranberries, ground
3 red apples, ground
Juice of 1 orange
Peel of ½ orange, ground
1½ c. sugar

Dissolve gelatins in hot water; add cold water. Let set until mixture begins to thicken. Add remaining ingredients. Chill until firm.

Deette Mefford, Altamont H. S.
Altamont, Illinois

CRANBERRY SALAD

Number of Servings — 12

1 lb. cranberries, ground
2 oranges, one unpeeled
2 T. gelatin
1 c. cold water
2 c. sugar
1 c. water
1 c. nuts, chopped
1 c. celery, finely diced
2 Delicious apples, ground
2 bananas, ground

Grind cranberries and oranges. Soak gelatin in cold water. Combine sugar and one cup water; cook 3 minutes. Add softened gelatin and cranberry mixture to sugar and water. Chill until partially congealed; add remaining ingredients.

Patricia Morgan, Laurel H. S.
Laurel, Montana

CRANBERRY SALAD

Number of Servings — 12

1 qt. cranberries, ground and drained
2 c. sugar
1 c. grated pineapple, drained
Juice from pineapple and cranberries
1 c. cold water
1 c. celery, diced
1 c. nuts
2 envelopes unflavored gelatin

Soak gelatin in cold water. Combine pineapple and cranberry juice with enough water to make 2 cups. Add sugar and boil 2 minutes. Dissolve gelatin in hot liquid. Chill. When mixture begins to thicken, stir in cranberries, pineapple, celery and nuts. Chill.

Fay Murray, Crockett H. S.
Crockett, Texas

CRANBERRY SALAD

Number of Servings — 8

1 c. canned whole cranberries
1½ c. boiling water
½ c. sugar
1 pt. pecans, chopped
1 pkg. cherry gelatin
1 small can crushed pineapple
Juice of 1 orange

Combine gelatin and boiling water, stirring until gelatin dissolves. Stir in sugar until dissolved. Mix in remaining ingredients. Chill until congealed.

Mrs. Laquita B. Neill, J. Z. George H. S.
North Carrollton, Mississippi

CRANBERRY SALAD

Number of Servings — 6-8

1 can cranberry sauce
1 c. miniature marshmallows
1 c. nuts
1 small can crushed pineapple, drained
1 pkg. raspberry gelatin
1 c. celery, chopped
1 T. gelatin
1½ c. pineapple juice and water

Heat liquid to boiling. Dissolve raspberry gelatin in hot liquid. Soak gelatin in ¼ cup cold water; add to hot liquid. Chill until mixture begins to thicken. Add cranberry sauce and beat well. Fold in remaining ingredients. Put into greased mold and chill.

Leacy Newell, Wilcox County H. S.
Camden, Alabama

CRANBERRY SALAD

Number of Servings — 10

2 eating apples, cored and diced
1 medium orange, peeled and chopped
1 pt. raw cranberries, ground
2 pkg. red gelatin
1 c. celery, finely diced
⅔ c. walnuts, chopped, black walnuts preferred
2 c. miniature marshmallows (opt.)
1 c. sugar
2 c. combined juice and water

Combine chopped fruits, drain and keep juice, measure juice; add enough water to make 2 cups. Heat 1 cup juice with the sugar. Pour over gelatin; stir until dissolved. Add remaining juice and cool. Add fruits, nuts, celery and marshmallows. Pour into individual molds or a square pan. Chill until firm.

Katy Jo Powers, Haysi H. S.
Haysi, Virginia

CRANBERRY SALAD

Number of Servings — 8

1 pkg. cherry gelatin
2 c. cranberries, ground
1 apple, diced
½ c. walnuts, chopped
1 c. sugar
1 c. boiling water
½ c. cold water

Dissolve gelatin in boiling water; add cold water. Chill until thickened. Combine fruits with sugar. Add nuts and fold into gelatin. Chill until firm.

Genevieve Overvaag, Mountain Lake H. S.
Mountain Lake, Minnesota

CRANBERRY SALAD

Number of Servings — 6

1 c. fresh cranberries, ground
1 c. red apples, unpeeled and ground
1 c. sugar
1 3-oz. pkg. lemon gelatin
1 c. hot water
1 c. pineapple juice
½ c. grape halves, seeded
¼ c. nuts, chopped
6 pineapple slices, drained

Combine cranberries, apple and sugar. Dissolve gelatin in hot water, add pineapple juice and chill until partially set. Add cranberry-apple mixture, grapes and nuts. Pour into individual molds; chill until firm. Unmold salads and place each salad on a slice of pineapple on lettuce.

Mrs. Joe H. Rainey Chester County H. S.
Henderson, Tennessee

CRANBERRY SALAD

Number of Servings — 6

1 qt. cranberries
3½ c. boiling water
1½-2 c. sugar
2 T. unflavored gelatin
½ c. cold water
½-1 c. nuts, chopped
1 c. diced pineapple, drained
1 c. white seedless or Tokay grapes

Cook cranberries in hot water, put through strainer and add sugar. Dissolve gelatin in cold water and add to hot fruit mixture. Let stand until cool. Add nuts, pineapple, and grapes. Chill and serve.

This recipe submitted by the following teachers:

Mary Ellen Rudd, Eaton Rapids H. S.
Eaton Rapids, Michigan

Wilma Davis, Sandy Hook H. S.
Sandy Hook, Kentucky

Mrs. Hazel Fuller, Orofino H. S.
Orofino, Idaho

CRANBERRY SALAD

Number of Servings — 20-25

2 pkg. raspberry or cherry gelatin
1 c. celery, diced
1 No. 2 can crushed pineapple, well drained
2 c. hot water
1 c. black walnuts, chopped
1 lb. pkg. fresh cranberries, ground

Dissolve gelatin in hot water. Cool. Add all ingredients to gelatin mixture; pour into mold. Chill for at least 2 hours. Salad will keep for several weeks in refrigerator. Serve with meats.

Mrs. Juanita Patton, Inola H. S.
Inola, Oklahoma

CRANBERRY SALAD

Number of Servings — 12

3 pkg. cherry gelatin
2 c. boiling water
1 can cranberry jelly
1 carton sour cream
3 c. cold water
1 small can crushed pineapple, drained
½ c. pecans, chopped

Dissolve gelatin in boiling water. Add cranberry jelly and sour cream; use rotary beater to completely mix. Add cold water; chill until thickened. Add pineapple and pecans. Pour into a 10 x 12 inch rectangular pan and allow to chill. Good with baked turkey and ham.

Nancy Russ, Falfurrias H. S.
Falfurrias, Texas

CRANBERRY SALAD

Number of Servings — 8

1 orange, peeled and seeded
1 apple, peeled and cored
1 lb. fresh cranberries, chopped
1½ c. water
1 pkg. raspberry gelatin
1 T. unflavored gelatin
1 c. sugar
¾ c. pecans, chopped

Put orange and apple through food grinder. Add cranberries and water. Bring to boil. Dissolve raspberry gelatin, 1 tablespoon gelatin and sugar in hot mixture. Chill until partially set. Add fruit and pecans. Pour into molds and chill until set.

Ellaine B. Scott, DeKalb H. S.
DeKalb, Mississippi

CRANBERRY SALAD

Number of Servings — 12

2 boxes cherry gelatin
2 c. hot water
1 medium can crushed pineapple and juice
1 can whole cranberry sauce
1 c. sour cream
1 c. pecans, chopped
¼ c. mayonnaise

Dissolve gelatin in hot water. Set aside until mixture thickens slightly. Thoroughly mix pineapple, cranberry sauce and pecans. Mix mayonnaise and sour cream adding a small amount of juice from the fruit mixture; blend well. Mix fruit and cream; blend well. Stir into gelatin. Chill overnight. Salad will keep for a week in refrigerator.

Mary Y. Thompson, Clay County H. S.
Ashland, Alabama

CRANBERRY SALAD

Number of Servings — 8

1 box cranberries, ground and drained
1 lemon and rind, ground and drained
2 oranges and rind, ground and drained
1 6-oz. can crushed pineapple, drained
1½ c. sugar
2 pkg. strawberry gelatin
2 c. boiling water
1½ c. juice from ground fruit

Add sugar to water and bring to boiling point to dissolve gelatin. Add drained fruit juices. Chill until slightly thickened. Fold in remaining ingredients. Chill. This salad is better after setting for several days. May be frozen or kept in the refrigerator several weeks.

Mrs. Helen S. Underwood,Shepherdsville H. S.
Shepherdsville, Kentucky

CRANBERRY SALAD

Number of Servings — 16

2 T. unflavored gelatin
6 T. cold water
4 c. cranberries, washed
2 oranges, unpeeled
2 c. sugar
½ c. boiling water
1 c. nuts, broken
1 c. celery, diced

Soak gelatin in 6 tablespoons cold water for 5 minutes. Put cranberries and oranges through food chopper into saucepan. Add sugar and boiling water to cranberry mixture; boil for 2 minutes. Stir in softened gelatin. Cool. Add nuts and celery. Pour into molds. Chill.

Mrs. Mary L. Whitley, Caledonia H. S.
Caledonia, Mississippi

CRANBERRY SALAD

Number of Servings — 6-8

1 3-oz. pkg. lemon gelatin
1½ c. hot water
1 c. jellied cranberry sauce
½ c. crushed pineapple, drained
½ c. pecans, chopped

Dissolve gelatin in hot water. Add cranberry jelly and cool. Beat with rotary beater until completely blended. Mix in crushed pineapple and nuts. Pour into 1-quart mold or ring mold. Chill.

Emily B. Person, John Graham H. S.
Warrenton, North Carolina

CRANBERRY SALAD

Number of Servings — 10

2 c. fresh cranberries, ground
½ c. sugar
1 small can crushed pineapple, drained
1 c. nuts, chopped
1 pkg. marshmallows, chopped
1 pkg. raspberry gelatin
1 orange, chopped

Dissolve gelatin according to package directions using drained pineapple juice as part of liquid. Cool until syrupy. Combine ground fruits, sugar, nuts and marshmallows. Fold into gelatin. Chill.

Marvolin Stephens, Thompson H. S.
Siluria, Alabama

CRANBERRY SALAD

Number of Servings — 6-8

1 envelope unflavored gelatin
¼ c. cold water
2 c. cranberries, ground
2 c. sugar
½ c. hot water
1 c. pecan meats
2 c. crushed pineapple, drained
1 pkg. miniature marshmallows

Soften gelatin by sprinkling over cold water; let stand for 5 minutes. Add hot water and stir to dissolve. Chill. Add sugar to ground cranberries. Mix well. Add pineapple, marshmallows and pecans. Add thickened gelatin to cranberry mixture; mix well. Pour into mold and chill until set.

Rosa Wirz, Barstow H. S.
Barstow, Texas

CRANBERRY SALAD

Number of Servings — 8-10

2 pkg. strawberry gelatin
1 c. hot water
2½ c. cold water
2 c. fresh cranberries, ground
1 c. orange sections, diced
1 c. crushed pineapple
½ c. sugar
1 c. nuts, chopped

Mix gelatin, sugar and hot water until well dissolved. Stir while adding cold water and cranberries. Add all ingredients to the gelatin. Chill or freeze in a mold.

Leila Mae Vickery, Elizabeth Cobb
Tallahassee, Florida

CRANBERRY SALAD

Number of Servings — 20

1 lb. cranberries, ground
2 c. sugar
4 pkg. raspberry gelatin
4 c. hot water
1 c. apple, chopped
1 c. crushed pineapple, drained
1 c. celery, chopped
1 c. nuts, chopped

Add the sugar to the cranberries. Chill overnight. In the morning, dissolve the gelatin in the hot water, cool. Combine remaining ingredients and add to cooled gelatin. Add cranberry—sugar mixture. Pour into a mold or into a large flat pan. Chill until set. Serve on lettuce with mayonnaise.

Mrs. Adeline B. Wiser, Calaveras H. S.
San Andreas, California

CRANBERRY STARS

Number of Servings — 6

1 c. ground raw cranberries
1 c. sugar
1 pkg. lemon or a red gelatin
1 c. hot water
1 c. pineapple syrup
1 c. crushed pineapple, well drained
½-1 c. walnuts, broken
1 c. celery, chopped

Combine cranberries and sugar. Allow to stand several hours. Dissolve gelatin in hot water; add syrup. Chill until partially set. Add cranberry mixture, pineapple, walnuts and celery. Pour into individual molds; chill until firm.

This recipe submitted by the following teachers:

Mrs. Beatrice Nuppenau, Winnebago H. S.
Winnebago, Illinois

Mrs. Merle Pierce, Central Junior H. S.
Bastrop, Louisiana

Rachel Bruner, Westminster H. S.
Westminster, South Carolina

Mrs. Wilma Tucker, Marion H. S.
Marion, Louisiana

CRANBERRY SALAD

Number of Servings — 12

1 lb. raw cranberries, medium ground
½ c. sugar
2 pkg. red gelatin
1 c. celery, diced
1 c. apples, diced with peeling if desired
1 c. crushed pineapple, drained
1 c. nuts, chopped

Mix cranberries and sugar, let stand for 1 hour. Add gelatin which has been dissolved, let chill until firm enough to hold fruit in suspension. Add remaining ingredients. Chill until firm.

Mary Wood, Atlanta H. S.
Atlanta, Texas

CRANBERRY-STRAWBERRY SALAD

Number of Servings — 12

2 3-oz. pkg. strawberry gelatin
2 c. boiling water
1 lb. pkg. frozen strawberries
1 10-oz. pkg. frozen cranberry relish
2 8-oz. cans crushed pineapple

Dissolve the gelatin in the boiling water. Add the frozen strawberries and cranberry relish. Stir until they are melted and mixed. Add the crushed pineapple. Chill until firm.

Betty Huey, Marysville H. S.
Marysville, Kansas

CRUNCHY CRANBERRY SALAD

Number of Servings — 6-8

1 pkg. strawberry, cherry or lemon gelatin
1½ c. boiling water
1 c. cranberries, ground
¾-1 c. sugar
½-1 c. celery, diced (opt.)
½-1 c. walnuts or pecans, chopped
1-2 oranges, ground (opt.)
Lemon juice (opt.)
Dash of salt (opt.)

Add sugar to cranberries and let stand 2 hours. Dissolve gelatin in boiling water. Chill until thickened. Fold in sweetened cranberries, celery, nuts, lemon juice and salt. Chill until firm.

This recipe submitted by the following teachers:

Marion T. Biscup, Grants Pass North Junior H. S.
Grants Pass, Oregon

Mrs. A. D. Wilder, Contentnea School
Kinston, North Carolina

Norma Jean Bewley, Edmonson County H. S.
Brownsville, Kentucky

Mrs. Frank Griffin, Detroit H. S.
Detroit, Texas

Billye Tingle, Edinburg H. S.
Carthage, Mississippi

CRANBERRY SOUFFLE SALAD

Number of Servings — 6

1 envelope unflavored gelatin
2 T. sugar
¼ t. salt
1 c. water
½ c. mayonnaise
2 T. lemon juice
1 t. grated lemon rind (opt.)
1 1-lb. can whole cranberry sauce
1 orange or apple, peeled and diced or 1 8½-oz. can pineapple tidbits
¼ c. walnuts, chopped

Mix gelatin, sugar and salt in a small saucepan. Add water. Stir over low heat, until gelatin is dissolved. Remove from heat; stir in mayonnaise, lemon juice and lemon rind. Blend with a rotary beater. Pour into a refrigerator tray. Quick chill in freezing unit 10 to 15 minutes, or until firm about 1-inch from edge but soft in center. Beat until fluffy. Fold in remaining ingredients. Chill until firm. Serve with mayonnaise.

This recipe submitted by the following teachers:

Mrs. Annie Laura Sayers, George Washington H. S.
Danville, Virginia

Nell P. Stevens, Indianola H. S.
Indianola, Mississippi

Lenora Ann Hill, Great Falls H. S.
Great Falls, Montana

Sara Thompson, Pineville H. S.
Pineville, Kentucky

Dora C. Fleming, Centerville H. S.
Sand Coulee, Montana

GLENADINE'S CRANBERRY SALAD

1 pkg. cranberries
¾ c. water
2 pkg. cherry gelatin
1 c. sugar
2 c. red grapes, halved
2 c. celery, chopped
1 c. nuts, chopped
1 No. 2 can crushed pineapple

Cook cranberries and water until berries pop; boil 5 minutes. Add gelatin and sugar; stir until dissolved. Chill until thickened. Fold in grapes, celery, nuts and pineapple. Chill until firm.

DRESSING:

1 3-oz. pkg. cream cheese
16 marshmallows, quartered
1 c. whipping cream

Combine ingredients; chill overnight. Whip before serving.

Margaret Crosby and Joyce Douglas,
Robinson H. S.
Robinson, Illinois

CRANBERRY SOUFFLE SALAD

Number of Servings — 6

1 pkg. lemon gelatin
1 c. hot water
½ c. mayonnaise
1-2 T. lemon juice
¼ t. salt
1 16-oz. can whole cranberry sauce
½ c. celery
1 9-oz. can crushed pineapple, drained

Dissolve gelatin in hot water. Add mayonnaise, lemon juice, salt and ½ cup of cranberry sauce. Blend thoroughly with rotary beater. Turn into freezing tray in automatic refrigerator and chill until firm about 1-inch from side of tray, but soft in center. Turn into bowl and whip with rotary beater until fluffy. Fold in remaining cranberry sauce, celery and pineapple. Lour into 1-quart mold. Chill until firm.

Martha Jane Rackley, Messick H. S.
Memphis, Tennessee

CRANBERRY STAR MOLD

Number of Servings — 8-10

1 c. crushed pineapple, drained
Pineapple juice plus enough boiling water to make 1¼ c. liquid
1 pkg. raspberry gelatin
2 c. whole cranberry sauce
1 t. grated orange rind
1 c. Mandarin orange sections, drained
1 c. heavy cream, whipped

Dissolve gelatin in hot juice-water mixture. Chill until partially set. Fold in cranberry sauce, orange rind, orange sections and pineapple. Fold in whipped cream. Pour into a 1½-quart star mold. Chill until firm. Garnish with additional whipped cream.

Mrs. Lillian Moran, Filer H. S.
Filer, Idaho

MOLDED CRANBERRY-ORANGE SALAD

Number of Servings — 12

1 T. unflavored gelatin
½ c. water
4 c. cranberries, ground
2 small oranges, seeded and ground or 2 medium apples, ground
1 c. sugar
1 pkg. lemon gelatin

Soak the unflavored gelatin in ¼ c. water. Over low heat dissolve the sugar, remaining ¼ c. water, lemon gelatin and unflavored gelatin by stirring. Remove from heat; add ground fruit. Place mixture in a mold which has been rubbed with salad dressing or mayonnaise. Chill overnight.

Mrs. Edwin F. Cook, Union County H. S.
Blairsville, Georgia

FAVORITE CRANBERRY SALAD MOLD

Number of Servings — 8-10

1 pkg. raspberry or strawberry gelatin
1 c. hot water
½ c. cold water or pineapple juice
1 small orange, peeled
½-1 c. crushed pineapple, drained
1 16-oz. can whole or jellied cranberry sauce
¼ c. nuts, chopped (opt.)
½ c. celery, chopped (opt.)

Dissolve gelatin in hot water. Add cold water and chill until partially thickened. Cut orange segments in half. Fold orange, pineapple, cranberry and nuts into gelatin. Pour into 1-quart mold or individual molds; chill until firm. Turn out on chilled plate and serve with sour cream or mayonnaise; garnish with crisp greens.

This recipe submitted by the following teachers:

Mrs. Clara Grace Spence, Pitkin H. S.
Pitkin, Louisiana

Mrs. Adry Fifer, Wynne H. S.
Wynne, Arkansas

Mrs. Mildred G. Grundy
South Middleton Township H. S.
Boiling Springs, Pennsylvania

Sally Worth, Rancocas Valley Regional H. S.
Mt. Holly, New Jersey

Mrs. Margaret Lee, Tylertown H. S.
Tylertown, Mississippi

JOYCE'S CRANBERRY SALAD

Number of Servings — 8

2 c. cranberries
1¼ c. water
1 pkg. cherry gelatin
¾ c. nuts
¾ c. celery, diced

Cook berries in water until they pop. Pour hot berries over gelatin. Stir until gelatin dissolves. Chill until thickened. Fold in nuts and celery. Mold as desired.

Margaret McIntire, Mitchell H. S.
Mitchell, Indiana

MOLDED CRANBERRY SALAD

Number of Servings — 10

1 qt. cranberries, ground
1 c. sugar
2 pkg. lemon gelatin
2 c. nuts, chopped
2 small cans crushed pineapple

Pour sugar over cranberries and soak. Mix gelatin according to directions on package and allow to partly congeal. Add pineapple and nuts. Chill until firm.

Mrs. Josephine P. Clark, Fairview H. S.
Fairview, Tennessee

MOLDED CRANBERRY SALAD

Number of Servings — 12

1 lb. cranberries, ground
1 orange, peeled and ground
½ c. pecans, chopped
1 c. crushed pineapple, drained
4 T. lemon juice
1 c. sugar
2 c. water
2 pkg. cherry gelatin

Combine ground cranberries and orange with nuts, pineapple, lemon juice and sugar. Mix thoroughly and let stand overnight. Next morning, mix 2 packages gelatin with only 2 cups water. Combine fruit mixture with gelatin mixture; pour into individual molds and refrigerate until firm.

Mrs. Betty Parrett, Ramona H. S.
Ramona, Oklahoma

MOLDED CRANBERRY SALAD

Number of Servings — 12

2 T. unflavored gelatin
½ c. cold water
1 qt. cranberries, chopped
1½ c. boiling water
2 c. sugar
1 t. salt or to taste
1½ c. apples, pineapple or seeded grapes, diced
1 c. celery, diced
½-1 c. nuts, diced

Dissolve gelatin in cold water. Cook cranberries in boiling water for 3 minutes, stirring constantly. Add sugar and salt; cook 5 minutes longer. Remove from heat. Add gelatin mixture. Chill until mixture begins to thicken. Add apples, celery and nuts. Mix together and pour into mold. Let set overnight if possible. Serve on lettuce.

This recipe submitted by the following teachers:

Marie Perdue, Chapmanville H. S.
Chapmanville, West Virginia

Mrs. Cornelia C. Peterson, North Stanley H. S.
New London, North Carolina

Mrs. Mary Elizabeth Watkins, Lily High School
Lily, Kentucky

PINEAPPLE-CRANBERRY MOLD

Number of Servings — 8-10

1 No. 2 can crushed pineapple and water
2 pkg. lemon gelatin
½ c. lemon juice
⅓ c. walnuts, chopped
3 T. orange peel, shredded or chopped
3 c. whole cranberry sauce

Drain syrup from pineapple and add enough water to make 1½ c. liquid. Heat to boiling and pour over gelatin. Stir until completely dissolved. Stir in pineapple and remaining ingredients. Turn into mold. Chill until firm. To unmold, dip into hot water about 15 seconds; invert.

Maggie Beth Watts, Era H. S.
Era, Texas

RAW CRANBERRY SALAD

Number of Servings — 50

2 boxes cranberries, ground
4 c. sugar
3 c. apples, chopped
3 c. celery, chopped
2 c. pecans, chopped
1 small can frozen orange juice, undiluted
1 orange, chopped
3 pkg. raspberry gelatin
1 c. hot water

Mix sugar and cranberries; set aside. Dissolve gelatin in hot water; cool. Mix all ingredients with gelatin. Refrigerate until firm. Salad will keep indefinitely in refrigerator.

Nell Criswell, Northwest H. S.
Justin, Texas

RAW CRANBERRY SALAD

Number of Servings — 12

2 pkg. lemon gelatin
2 c. sugar
1 orange rind, grated
2 c. hot water
1 lb. cranberries, ground
2 oranges, finely chopped
1 c. nuts

Dissolve gelatin and sugar in hot water; Chill until thickened. Combine the fruit, rind and nuts; add to gelatin. May be congealed in molds or in large pan and cut into squares for serving.

Mrs. Bob Farris, Altus-Denning H. S.
Altus, Arkansas

THREE HOUR JELLIED CRANBERRY RING

Number of Servings — 12

2 pkg. raspberry or cherry gelatin
2 c. hot water
2 c. raw cranberries, ground
1 orange, ground, seeds removed
1 apple, ground
1/4 c. nuts, chopped
3/4-1 c. sugar

Dissolve gelatin in hot water. Chill until partially set. Mix cranberries, orange, apple, nuts and sugar. Fold into gelatin. Place in a quart mold. Refrigerate until firm. About 3 hours.

Mrs. Phoebe Stout, Logan Senior H. S.
Logan, West Virginia

SPICED CRANBERRY SALAD

Number of Servings — 8

1 1/2 c. cranberry juice
1/4 t. oil of cinnamon
9 whole cloves
1 pkg. lemon gelatin
1 7-oz. can whole cranberries

DRESSING:

Mix 1/4 t. dry horseradish to
1 pt. sour cream

Combine juice, oil of cinnaman and cloves. Bring to boil; strain out cloves. Dissolve gelatin in hot mixture. Cool; chill until partially set. Fold in whole cranberries. Serve with horseradish dressing.

Elizabeth A. M. Mitchell, Bridgeville H. S.
Bridgeville, Delaware

THANKSGIVING SALAD

Number of Servings — 8-10

2 pkg. lemon gelatin
1 lb. cranberries, ground
1 whole orange, ground
1 c. nuts, cut fine
1 c. orange juice
3 c. water
1 c. celery, cut fine
1 1/2 c. sugar

Dissolve gelatin in 2 cups hot water. Add 1 cup cold water and the orange juice. Chill until thickened. Combine sugar with ground cranberry-orange mixture. Fold into gelatin and chill until firm.

Frances L. Lynch, Buckhannon-Upshur Senior H. S.
Buckhannon, West Virginia

GOOSEBERRY SALAD

Number of Servings — 6-8

2 c. boiling water minus 1 T.
1 pkg. lemon gelatin
1 c. gooseberries, drained
1 T. lemon juice
1 c. celery, cut fine
1 orange, diced
½ c. nuts, chopped

Dissolve gelatin and marshmallows in hot water. Cool. Add the gooseberries, lemon juice, celery, orange and nuts. Chill until firm.

TOPPING:
1 3-oz. pkg. cream cheese
1 c. sour cream
2 c. miniature marshmallows, cut fine

Beat with mixer and use as dressing for Gooseberry salad.

Elvira Benne, Columbus Sr. H. S.
Columbus, Nebraska

GOOSEBERRY SALAD

Number of Servings — 8

1 can gooseberries, drained
1 pkg. any flavor gelatin
Juice of gooseberries and water to make 2 c.
1 c. miniature marshmallows
⅔ c. sugar
1 c. celery, finely chopped
1 orange, grated

Dissolve gelatin and marshmallows in heated juice-water mixture. Chill until thickened. Combine gooseberries and sugar. Grate rind of the orange and chop the pulp. Add fruits and rind to gelatin. Chill until firm.

Ethel R. McKinley, South San Antonio H. S.
San Antonio, Texas

GOOSEBERRY SALAD

1 pt. gooseberries, drained
1 pkg. lemon gelatin
1 c. sugar
3 bananas
1 pt. boiling water
½ c. nuts
1 c. marshmallows, finely cut
Salt

Add sugar to gooseberries; heat slowly and stir until sugar dissolves. Cool. Dissolve gelatin in boiling water. Chill until it starts to jell. Combine all ingredients. Chill until firm.

Mrs. Austin Noblitt, Rockville H. S.
Rockville, Indiana

CONGEALED FRUIT SALAD

Number of Servings — 6

1 pkg. raspberry gelatin
1 c. hot water
1 pkg. cream cheese
1 can fruit cocktail, undrained
½ c. nuts, chopped

Dissolve gelatin in hot water. Stir in cream cheese; mix until thoroughly dissolved. Add fruit cocktail and nuts. Chill until firm.

Mrs. La'Nelle Howard, Martin Junior H. S.
Natchez, Mississippi

CONGEALED SALAD WITH POPPY SEED DRESSING

1 pkg. raspberry gelatin
1 c. hot water
1 t. unflavored gelatin
¼ c. water
1 c. applesauce
½ c. nuts, chopped
1 small can crushed pineapple

Dissolve unflavored gelatin in ¼ cup water; add raspberry gelatin and hot water. Stir until dissolved. Chill until partially set. Add remaining ingredients. Chill until firm. Serve with poppy seed dressing.

Poppy Seed Dressing:
1 t. powdered mustard
1 t. salt
½ c. sugar
1 T. onion, grated
5 T. vinegar
1 c. salad oil
1 t. poppy seed

Combine mustard, salt, sugar, onion and 2 tablespoons vinegar. Mix well. Slowly add remaining vinegar, oil and poppy seed.

Mrs. Ouida Hicks, Sidney Lanier H. S.
Montgomery, Alabama

RASPBERRY BAVARIAN SALAD

Number of Servings — 8

1 pkg. raspberry gelatin
1 c. boiling water
1 pkg. frozen raspberries
1 c. miniature marshmallows
½ c. whipped cream

Dissolve gelatin in boiling water. Add raspberries and marshmallows. Refrigerate until mixture starts to jell. Whip. Combine whipped cream and whipped gelatin mixture. Put into individual molds and chill.

Sylvia Benson, Grant Union H. S.
John Day, Oregon

QUICK RASPBERRY GELATIN

Number of Servings — 4

1 c. boiling water
1 regular size pkg. black raspberry gelatin
1 10-oz. pkg. frozen raspberries
1 banana, sliced

Dissolve gelatin in boiling water. Add frozen raspberries. Chill until thick. Add banana. Chill until firm.

Mrs. Mary Westfall, Colusa H. S.
Colusa, California

RED RASPBERRY SALAD

Number of Servings — 6

1 pkg. raspberry gelatin
1 pkg. frozen raspberries
½ pt. sour cream
1 c. boiling water

Dissolve gelatin in boiling water; add raspberries. When raspberries are thawed, add sour cream. Mix well. Chill until firm.

Mrs. Doris Waller, Chino H. S.
Chino, California

RASPBERRY-APPLESAUCE SALAD

Number of Servings — 6

1 pkg. red raspberry gelatin
1 c. boiling water
1 pkg. frozen red raspberries
1 c. applesauce

Dissolve gelatin in boiling water. Add frozen raspberries; stir until berries are melted. Add applesauce. Chill until firm.

Martha Sterrett, Franklin Area Jr. H. S.
Murrysville, Pennsylvania

RASPBERRY DELIGHT SALAD

Number of Servings — 10

1 c. boiling water
1 c. sugar
2 pkg. raspberry gelatin
Juice of 1 lemon
1 can crushed pineapple
1 c. whipped cream
½ c. Velveeta cheese, grated

Combine boiling water, gelatin, sugar and lemon juice. Stir until gelatin and sugar is dissolved. Add pineapple; stir. Chill until mixture begins to thicken. Fold in whipped cream and cheese. Chill until firm.

Alice Dyer, Bixby Junior H. S.
Bixby, Oklahoma

RASPBERRY FIZZ SALAD

Number of Servings — 6

1 box raspberry gelatin
1½ c. applesauce, strained
1 7-oz. bottle 7-Up
Juice of 1 orange
½ c. celery, diced
¼ c. nuts, chopped

Dissolve gelatin in applesauce. Bring to a boil. Remove from heat; add 7-Up and orange juice. Chill until partially set, stirring occasionally so foam from 7-Up mixes thoroughly. Add celery and nuts. Chill until firm.

Barbara Jane Anderson, Rochelle Township H. S.
Rochelle, Illinois

RASPBERRY GELATIN SALAD

Number of Servings — 9

2 10-oz. pkg. frozen raspberries
2 pkg. raspberry gelatin
½ c. lemon juice
2 c. boiling water
1 c. watermelon balls

Thaw raspberries and drain. Add enough water to raspberry syrup to make 1½ cups liquid. Dissolve gelatin in boiling water. Stir in raspberry syrup, lemon juice and raspberries. Chill until partially set. Add melon balls. Pour into individual molds or a 9-inch square pan. Chill until firm.

Mrs. Stephanie T. Mulford, Salem, H. S.
Salem, New Jersey

RASPBERRY SALAD

Number of Servings — 6

2 c. sour cream
12 marshmallows, diced
2 pkg. raspberry gelatin
3 c. hot water
½ c. applesauce
2 pkg. frozen raspberries

Mix marshmallows and sour cream together. Let stand overnight. Dissolve gelatin in hot water. Add applesauce and raspberries. Chill until firm. Serve with sour cream mixture.

Sarah E. Cooper, Del Mar H. S.
San Jose, California

RASPBERRY SALAD

1 small pkg. frozen raspberries, thawed
1 pkg. raspberry gelatin
1½ c. hot water
1 3-oz. pkg. cream cheese, grated
½ c. pecans, broken

Dissolve gelatin in hot water; add raspberries. Let cool. Add cheese and pecans. Chill until firm.

Suzie L. Kelly, Union H. S.
Broken Arrow, Oklahoma

RASPBERRY SALAD

Number of Servings — 6

1 pkg. raspberry gelatin
1¼ c. boiling water
1 pkg. frozen raspberries, unthawed
1 c. crushed pineapple, undrained
½ c. pecan halves

Dissolve gelatin in boiling water; add raspberries. Let raspberries thaw gently. Add pineapple and nuts. Chill until firm.

Elsa Graham, Moorestown Jr. H. S.
Moorestown, New Jersey

RASPBERRY SNOW

Number of Servings — 8

1 pkg. raspberry gelatin
1 c. boiling water
1 c. cold water
1 t. lemon juice
2 egg whites, beaten

Dissolve gelatin in boiling water; stir in cold water and lemon juice. Chill until slightly thickened. Place bowl of gelatin in a bowl of ice; whip until light and fluffy. Add egg whites; continue beating until well blended. Let stand over ice until thickened.

Miss DeWayne Law, Valley H. S.
Hot Springs, Virginia

RASPBERRY SURPRISE GELATIN

Number of Servings — 4-6

1 pkg. raspberry gelatin
1 c. applesauce
1 7-oz. bottle 7-Up
1 No. 9 can crushed pineapple, drained
⅓ c. pecans, chopped

Heat applesauce; add gelatin. Stir until gelatin is dissolved. Cool mixture to lukewarm. Stir in the 7-Up. Add pineapple and pecans. Mix thoroughly. Chill until firm.

Mrs. Stenson Terry, San Perlita H. S.
San Perlita, Texas

CONGEALED STRAWBERRY SALAD

Number of Servings — 6

1 pkg. strawberry gelatin
1 pkg. unflavored gelatin
1 10-oz. pkg. frozen strawberries, thawed
1 can grapefruit sections, drained

Dissolve strawberry gelatin according to package directions. Add dissolved unflavored gelatin; cool. Stir in strawberries; add grapefruit sections. Mold as desired. Chill until firm.

Mrs. Evelyn R. Sheets, Yatesville H. S.
Yatesville, Georgia

RASPBERRY TANG GELATIN

Number of Servings — 8

1 pkg. raspberry gelatin
2 c. hot water
2 pkgs. cream cheese
¼ c. mayonnaise
1 banana, mashed
1 small can crushed pineapple
¼ c. shredded coconut
½ c. walnuts, chopped

Dissolve gelatin in hot water; chill until thickened. Whip until light. Mix cream cheese with mayonnaise; add to gelatin. Add banana, pineapple, coconut and walnuts. Mix well. Chill until firm.

Mrs. Ethelyn Richman, Wawaka H. S.
Wawaka, Indiana

CONGEALED STRAWBERRY-PINEAPPLE SALAD

Number of Servings — 10-12

2 pkg. strawberry gelatin
1¼ c. hot water
1 pkg. frozen strawberries, thawed
1 No. 2 can crushed pineapple, drained
3 ripe bananas, mashed
1 c. sour cream (opt.)

Dissolve gelatin in hot water. Let set until mixture is consistency of jelly. Add strawberries, pineapple and bananas. Refrigerate until firm. Spread sour cream on top 2 hours before serving.

Maurine Taylor, East Mountain School
Gilmer, Texas

GELATIN-FRUIT SALAD

Number of Servings — 8

2 pkg. strawberry gelatin
1 pkg. Dream Whip
1 can fruit cocktail, drained
½ c. nuts

Prepare gelatin according to package directions. Congeal. Beat firm gelatin for 1 minute with mixer. Prepare Dream Whip according to package directions. Fold fruit cocktail, Dream Whip and nuts into beaten gelatin. Refrigerate for several hours before serving. Garnish with nut halves.

Mrs. Katie M. Smith, Evadale H. S.
Evadale, Texas

STRAWBERRY-COTTAGE CHEESE SALAD

Number of Servings — 6

1 small can crushed pineapple, undrained
1 box strawberry gelatin
1 small carton cottage cheese
1 c. nuts, chopped
1 c. whipped cream

Boil pineapple and gelatin together for 3 minutes. Add cottage cheese and nuts. Fold in sweetened whipped cream. Chill until firm.

Shelby H. Morris, Antioch H. S.
Antioch, Tennessee

STRAWBERRY BAVARIAN

Number of Servings — 8-10

1 pkg. strawberry gelatin
1 c. hot water
1 c. cold water
1 pkg. Dream Whip
1 10-oz. pkg. frozen strawberries, thawed

Dissolve gelatin in hot water; add cold water. Chill until partially set. Prepare Dream Whip according to package directions; beat into gelatin. Fold in strawberries. Chill until firm.

Mrs. Nancy Luttrell, Beaver Dam H. S.
Beaver Dam, Kentucky

STRAWBERRY-CHEESE MOLD

Number of Servings — 8

2 pkg. strawberry gelatin
2 small pkg. cream cheese
1 c. apple, finely chopped
1 c. celery, finely chopped
1 lge. pkg. marshmallows
1 T. water
1 small can pineapple and a few chopped nuts may be added, if desired

Mix gelatin according to directions on package. Chill until slightly congealed. Whip. Melt marshmallows with the water. Blend cheese; add marshmallows and fruit; Add to the gelatin. Chill until firm.

Mrs. Frydis M. Hanbrough
Magee Attendance Center
Magee, Mississippi

STRAWBERRY DELIGHT

Number of Servings — 8-10

1 pkg. lemon gelatin
1 pkg. strawberry gelatin
2 c. boiling water
2 pkg. frozen strawberries
1 c. crushed pineapple
2 bananas, cubed

Thoroughly dissolve gelatins in boiling water. Add strawberries; stir until berries separate and thaw. Mixture will begin to congeal. Add pineapple and bananas. Pour mixture into a mold. Chill until firm. Top with desired dressing.

DRESSINGS:
Cream cheese softened with milk to desired consistency. Prepare just before serving.

1 c. dairy sour cream
72 miniature marshmallows

Combine sour cream and marshmallows. Refrigerate for several hours before using.

Mrs. Mary E. Jackson, Bad Axe H. S.
Bad Axe, Michigan

STRAWBERRY-CREAM DELIGHT

Number of Servings — 6

1 c. crushed pineapple
½ c. sugar
1 pkg. strawberry gelatin
1 c. cold water
1 c. American cheese grated
1 c. nuts
1 c. whipped cream

Dissolve gelatin in cold water. Bring ¼ cup sugar and pineapple to a boil; pour over gelatin. Cool until slightly thick. Add cheese; let set until slightly thickened. Add nuts and whipped cream sweetened with ¼ cup sugar. Refrigerate overnight.

Frances Nesmith, Monterey H. S.
Lubbock, Texas

STRAWBERRY DELIGHT

Number of Servings — 6-8

1 regular size box strawberry gelatin
1 3-oz. pkg. cream cheese
1 c. crushed pineapple, drained
½ c. nuts, chopped
10 ice cubes
1 c. boiling water

Dissolve gelatin in boiling water; Add ice cubes; stir constantly for 2 or 3 minutes or until gelatin begins to thicken. Remove unmelted ice. Chill until thick, but not set. Soften cream cheese with crushed pineapple. Beat until smooth with a mixer. Add nuts. Fold cheese mixture into the gelatin mixture.

Mrs. Glenn A. Britt, Greenwood H. S.
Greenwood, Mississippi

STRAWBERRY DELIGHT

1 pkg. strawberry gelatin
1 pkg. frozen whole strawberries, thawed and drained
1 8-oz. can crushed pineapple

Prepare gelatin according to package directions substituting juice for part of the liquid. Add strawberries and pineapple. Chill until firm.

Judith Ann Shannon, New River Junior H. S.
Fort Lauderdale, Florida

STRAWBERRY DELIGHT

Number of Servings — 15

1 pkg. unflavored gelatin
1 pkg. strawberry gelatin
1 c. water
2 T. lemon juice
2 T. sugar
1 pkg. frozen strawberries, thawed and drained
3 oranges, diced and drained
Juice from strawberries and oranges

Prepare unflavored gelatin according to package directions substituting strawberry and orange juice for part of the liquid needed. Dissolve strawberry gelatin in 1 cup water; mix with unflavored gelatin. Chill until partially set. Add remaining ingredients. Chill until firm.

Mrs. Ruth M. Smith, D. W. Daniel H. S.
Central, South Carolina

STRAWBERRY GLAZE

Number of Servings — 4-6

1 pkg. strawberry gelatin
1 c. hot water
1 c. cold water
1 pkg. cream cheese
1 t. cream
¾ c. pecans, chopped
½ box frozen strawberries, thawed

Dissolve gelatin in hot water; add cold water and set aside to cool. Blend the cheese with the cream; add pecans. Roll mixture into small balls. Place balls on bottom of dish. Pour the strawberries over balls. Pour gelatin over all. Chill until firm.

Mrs. Jeannette Thompson, Winnsboro H. S.
Winnsboro, Louisiana

STRAWBERRY SALAD

Number of Servings — 6-8

1 pkg. strawberry gelatin
1 c. hot water
1 pkg. frozen strawberries, unthawed
1 small pkg. cream cheese
1 c. whipped cream

Dissolve gelatin in hot water. Separate frozen strawberries with a fork. Soften cream cheese with a small amount of strawberry juice. Add separated, frozen strawberries to gelatin. When mixture begins to thicken, quickly add softened cream cheese and fold in whipped cream.

Frances Flint, Dimmitt Jr. H. S.
Seattle, Washington

STRAWBERRY DESSERT OR PARTY SALAD

Number of Servings — 8

1 pkg. strawberry gelatin
1½ c. hot water
1 No. 2½ can fruit cocktail
1 c. pecans, chopped
1 c. whipped cream

Dissolve gelatin in hot water. Chill until thick. Whip gelatin until fluffy. Add fruit cocktail and pecans. Fold in whipped cream. Pour in shallow pan; chill until firm.

Mrs. Mary Ruth Dorris, Bassfield H. S.
Bassfield, Mississippi

STRAWBERRY SALAD

Number of Servings — 6

1 pkg. strawberry gelatin
1 3-oz. pkg. cream cheese
1 c. boiling water
1 small can crushed pineapple, undrained
¾ c. pecans
½ pt. whipped cream

Thoroughly cream gelatin and cheese. Gradually add boiling water, stirring until cheese and gelatin dissolves. Add pineapple and pecans. Chill until firm. Fold in sweetened whipped cream. Refrigerate until serving time.

Mrs. Mary Evelyn Cook, Glynn Academy
Brunswick, Georgia

STRAWBERRY SALAD

Number of Servings — 6

1 pkg. strawberry gelatin
1 c. boiling water
1 small pkg. frozen strawberries, partially thawed
1 c. applesauce
1 small can crushed pineapple

Dissolve gelatin in boiling water; let cool. Add strawberries, applesauce and pineapple. Chill until firm.

Bertha K. MaHarry, Morrisonville Community, Unit 1
Morrisonville, Illinois

STRAWBERRY SALAD

Number of Servings — 18

2 6-oz. pkgs. strawberry or cherry gelatin
3 c. hot water
1 No. 2½ can applesauce
3 10-oz. pkg. frozen strawberries, thawed
Sour cream or whipped cream

Dissolve gelatin in hot water; cool until mixture is consistency of egg whites. Add applesauce and strawberries; chill until firm. Top with sour cream or whipped cream.

Mrs. Louella Pence, Macon H. S.
Macon, Illinois

STRAWBERRY SALAD

Number of Servings — 6

1 pkg. strawberry gelatin
1 c. hot water
1 c. 7-Up, chilled
1 pt. frozen strawberries, drained
1 c. celery, diced
1 c. crushed pineapple, drained
1 c. nuts, chopped (opt.)

Dissolve gelatin in hot water; cool. Add 7-Up strawberries, celery, pineapple and nuts. Chill until firm.

Mrs. Maxine Stelovich, Littleton H. S.
Littleton, Colorado

STRAWBERRY SALAD

Number of Servings — 6

1 c. crushed strawberries, sweetened to taste
1 pkg. lemon gelatin
1 c. boiling water
2 T. mayonnaise
1 c. whipped cream

Dissolve gelatin in boiling water; cool slightly. Mix whipped cream and mayonnaise together. Add strawberries and whipped cream to gelatin.

Mrs. Robert T. Thompson, Branchville H. S.
Branchville, South Carolina

STRAWBERRY SHASTA

Number of Servings — 8

1 box strawberry gelatin
1 10-oz. box frozen strawberries
1 8-oz. pkg. cream cheese
½ c. walnuts, chopped
1 c. whipped cream

Mix strawberry gelatin as directed on package. Chill until partially set. Add frozen strawberries; refrigerate until softly congealed. Soften cream cheese with a small amount of cream; add walnuts. Form into balls about the size of a marble. Drop balls into gelatin. Chill until firm. Top with whipped cream just before serving.

Virginia W. Eoff, Hiram Johnson H. S.
Sacramento, California

SUNRISE PINK DESSERT SALAD

Number of Servings — 12

2 3-oz. pkg. strawberry gelatin
2 c. boiling water
2 10-oz. pkg. frozen strawberries
1 medium banana, mashed
2 T. lemon juice
1 pt. sour cream or 1½ c. sour cream and ½ c. mayonnaise

Dissolve gelatin in boiling water; add frozen berries and stir until thawed. Add banana and lemon juice. Stir mixture into sour cream. Chill until set.

Mrs. Bobbie Jean Pope, Holly Pond H. S.
Holly Pond, Alabama

SUNSET SALAD

Number of Servings — 6

2 pkg. strawberry gelatin
2 c. hot water
1 c. cold water
1 can cranberry sauce, mashed
4 bananas, diced
½ c. pecans, chopped

Dissolve gelatin in hot water, add cold water. Chill until partially thickened. Fold cranberry sauce, bananas and nuts into gelatin. Pour into molds that has been rinsed in cold water. Chill until firm.

Mrs. Bettye T. Brumley, Weston H. S.
Jonesboro, Louisiana

TROPICAL SALAD

Number of Servings — 8

1 3-oz. pkg. strawberry gelatin
1 3-oz. pkg. orange gelatin
2 c. hot water
3 oranges, sectioned
1 8½-oz. can sliced pineapple, undrained and cut in wedges
1 10-oz. pkg frozen strawberries

Dissolve gelatins in hot water. Add oranges, pineapple wedges and frozen strawberries. Stir until strawberries are thawed. Chill until firm.

Doris Kolb, Allegany H. S.
Cumberland, Maryland

YUM-YUM SALAD

Number of Servings — 12-16

1 6-oz. box strawberry gelatin
2 c. boiling water
2 c. pineapple juice
1 No. 2 can crushed pineapple
1 8-oz. pkg. cream cheese
½ pt. whipped cream or 1 2-oz. envelope Dream Whip and ½ c. milk, whipped

Mix gelatin and water. Add pineapple juice, pineapple and cream cheese. Combine with a fork. Refrigerate. When mixture begins to set add whipped cream or Dream Whip. If salad is to be molded, reduce liquid ½ cup. Pour into mold brushed with salad oil.

Mrs. Betty Mackey, Ridgemont H. S.
Ridgeway, Ohio

ANGEL SALAD

Number of Servings — 15

2 pkg. lime or cherry gelatin
2 c. boiling water
1 pt. cottage cheese
¼ c. mayonnaise
½ pt. whipped cream
1 can crushed pineapple, drained
2 c. miniature marshmallows

Dissolve gelatin in boiling water; cool. Mix cheese, mayonnaise, whipped cream, pineapple and marshmallows. Add to gelatin. Pour into mold; chill until firm.

Mrs. Sue B. Mays, Dungannon H. S.
Dungannon, Virginia

COTTAGE CHEESE SALAD

Number of Servings — 8

1 box lime gelatin
1¼ c. hot water
1 c. crushed pineapple
12 lg. marshmallows, quartered
1 small carton cottage cheese
⅓ c. mayonnaise
¼ c. walnuts, chopped

Dissolve gelatin in hot water; cool. Whip. Fold in mayonniase. Gently fold in remaining ingredients; pour into a mold. Refrigerate until thoroughly congealed.

Mrs. Violet Dirstine, Natoma Rural H. S.
Natoma, Kansas

COTTAGE CHEESE SALAD MOLD

Number of Servings — 6-8

1 pkg. lemon gelatin
1 pkg. lime gelatin
1 c. boiling water
½-1 c. milk, chilled
1-1½ c. creamed cottage cheese
1 No. 2 can crushed pineapple
Salad greens
½ c. nuts (opt.)

Drain pineapple. Combine juice and enough water to make ⅔ cup liquid. Dissolve gelatin in boiling water; add pineapple juice-water mixture. Cool until mixture is consistency of jelly. Fold in milk, cottage cheese and pineapple. Pour into lightly oiled mold and chill until firm. Unmold on salad greens and serve with mayonnaise or sour cream dressing.

This recipe submitted by the following teachers:

Blanche Maxwell, Spring Valley Public Schools
Spring Valley, Wisconsin

Mrs. Fred Blohm, Central Senior H. S.
Helena, Arkansas

Mrs. Rebecca Burns Drone, College Grove H. S.
College Grove, Tennessee

COTTAGE CHEESE SALAD

Number of Servings — 6

1 pkg. lemon gelatin
½ c. boiling water
½ c. pineapple juice
1 c. whipped cream
1 c. crushed pineapple
1 c. celery, minced
1 c. cottage cheese
½ c. walnuts, chopped

Dissolve gelatin in boiling water. Add pineapple juice; mix. Chill until the mixture starts to congeal. Beat with a rotary beater until light and fluffy. Fold in whipped cream. Add pineapple, celery, cottage cheese and walnuts; blend thoroughly. Chill.

Eleanor Sturman, Blue Ridge Joint School
New Milford, Pennsylvania

COTTAGE CHEESE SALAD

Number of Servings — 8

2 pkg. lemon or lime gelatin
¾ c. boiling water
1 lb. cottage cheese, put through a sieve
1 c. mayonnaise
2 pimentos or green peppers, chopped
1 c. nuts, chopped
1 T. vinegar
1 t. salt

Dissolve gelatin in boiling water; add cottage cheese. Add remaining ingredients in order given. Let set for 4 hours.

Mrs. Merle Twesme, H. S.
Arcadia, Wisconsin

GELATIN-LEMON-LIME SALAD

Number of Servings — 12

1 pkg. lemon gelatin
1 pkg. lime gelatin
¾ c. hot water
¾ c. cold water
½ c. celery, chopped (opt.)
1 small can crushed pineapple
1-2 c. cottage cheese
¼-1 c. nuts, chopped
¼-1 c. Maraschino cherries, chopped
¼ c. lemon juice (opt.)

Mix water and gelatin; chill to jelly stage. Add all ingredients; mix well. Pour into mold. Chill until firm. Most delicious.

This recipe submitted by the following teachers:

Mrs. Gladys McDaniel, Broaddus H. S.
Broaddus, Texas

Mrs. Charles Eager, Brown City Community School
Brown City, Michigan

CREAM FLUFF COTTAGE CHEESE SALAD

Number of Servings — 4-6

1 c. whipping cream
1 pkg. lime gelatin
1½ c. cottage cheese
1 small can crushed pineapple, drained
¼ lb. marshmallows, cut up
½ c. nuts, chopped

Heat juice drained from Pineapple. Add gelatin and boil for 2 minutes. Cool. Whip cream and cooled gelatin. Add remaining ingredients. Chill until firm.

Mrs. Agnes Husenko, Mark Morris Sr., H. S.
Longview, Washington

GREEN GODDESS

Number of Servings — 10

1 c. boiling water
2 pkg. lemon gelatin
1 No. 2½ can crushed pineapple, drained
1 pt. cottage cheese
1 4-oz. pkg. cream cheese
1 c. cucumbers, diced
Few drops green food coloring
½ c. salad dressing
1 c. pineapple juice and water

Dissolve gelatin in boiling water; cool. Blend pineapple juice and cottage cheese together. Blend in cream cheese and salad dressing. Stir cheese mixture into gelatin. Add food coloring. Fold in pineapple and cucumber. Chill for 4 hours.

Estelle Delgado, Banning H. S.
Banning, California

HEALTH SALAD

Number of Servings — 8

1 pkg. lemon gelatin
1 c. boiling water
Dash of salt
1 1 -lb. carton cottage cheese
1 No. 2½ can fruit cocktail, undrained

Dissolve gelatin in boiling water; add salt. Let cool. Add fruit cocktail and cottage cheese. Chill until firm.

Augusta Richardson, Caddo H. S.
Caddo, Oklahoma

LIME-CHEESE SALAD

Number of Servings — 5-6

1 pkg. lime gelatin
1 4-oz. pkg. cream cheese, creamed cottage cheese or sour cream
Fruit

Mix gelatin according to package directions; chill until partially set. Cream the cheese until smooth; blend with gelatin. Blender or mixer does it very fast. Add a fruit if desired.

Betty Welty, Gervais Union H. S.
Gervais, Oregon

LIME DELIGHT

Number of Servings — 16

2 pkg. lime gelatin
2 c. boiling water
2 T. sugar
Pinch of salt
1 carton cottage cheese
1 small can crushed pineapple
1 c. miniature marshmallows
1 pt. whipped cream
1 c. nuts, chopped

Combine gelatin, water, sugar and salt. Let mixture stand until cool and begins to congeal. Add gelatin mixture to whipped cream. Add remaining ingredients. Chill until firm.

Mrs. Margaret Helton, Harrodsburg H. S.
Harrodsburg, Kentucky

LIME GELATIN DELIGHT

Number of Servings — 12-15

1 family size pkg. lime gelatin
Dash of salt
1 c. boiling pineapple juice and water
8-12 ice cubes
1⅔ c. canned milk
1 No. 303 can crushed pineapple, drained
1 lb. cottage cheese

Dissolve gelatin and salt in hot juice and water. Add ice cubes; stir until the mixture begins to thicken; remove remaining ice. Fold in milk, cottage cheese and pineapple. Chill until firm.

Pat Davina, Mesa Jr. H. S.
Roswell, New Mexico

LIME-PINEAPPLE DELIGHT

Number of Servings — 5-7

1 box lime gelatin
1 c. boiling water
1 c. cold water
1 small box cottage cheese
1 small can crushed pineapple
1 c. pecans, chopped

Dissolve gelatin in boiling water; add cold water. Chill until thick. Stir in remaining ingredients. Chill until firm.

Mrs. Kenneth W. Hammons, Elaine H. S.
Elaine, Arkansas

MARY MINNICK'S SALAD

Number of Servings — 9

1 pkg. lime gelatin
1 c. hot water
1 c. ginger ale
1 16-oz. carton creamed cottage cheese
1 small can crushed pineapple, drained
½ c. celery, finely diced
½ c. nuts, chopped

Dissolve gelatin in hot water. Let cool. Add ginger ale, cottage cheese, pineapple, celery and nuts. Chill until firm.

Nancy Kimbrell, Florida H. S.
Tallahassee, Florida

LIME MOLDED SALAD

Number of Servings — 12

2 pkg. lime gelatin
½ c. sugar
1 No. 2 can crushed pineapple, drained
1 pt. cottage cheese
1 c. whipped cream
¼ lb. marshmallows
1 c. walnuts, finely cut (opt.)
Juice drained from pineapple plus enough water to make 2 c. liquid

Combine juice—water mixture, sugar, marshmallows and gelatin. Heat in top of double boiler until marshmallows melt and sugar dissolves. Cool until partially set. Add whipped cream, cottage cheese, pineapple and nuts; stir. Pour into mold. Refrigerate until set.

Mrs. Donna Standley, Redmond Union H. S.
Redmond, Oregon

PINEAPPLE-CHEESE SALAD

Number of Servings — 12

1 pkg. lime gelatin
1 pt. creamed cottage cheese
1 small can crushed pineapple
20 pitted ripe olives, sliced (opt.)

Prepare gelatin as directed on package omitting ¼ cup water. Chill until mixture starts to thicken; add cheese and pineapple. Pour into flat 9" x 13½" pan. Garnish with olives if desired. Small strips of pimento may be added also. Cut in squares and serve on lettuce leaf. This salad may be extended by adding a package of lemon gelatin dissolved according to package direction.

This recipe submitted by the following teachers:

Florence R. Coslet, Glasgow H. S.
Glasgow, Montana

Mrs. Mary Davis Faison, Weldon H. S.
Weldon, North Carolina

SPEARS' SALAD

Number of Servings — 8

1 pkg. lime gelatin
1 c. hot water
½ c. celery, finely chopped
½ c. pecans, chopped
½ c. mayonnaise
1 carton cottage cheese
¼ c. evaporated milk
1 small can crushed pineapple

Dissolve gelatin in hot water. Combine remaining ingredients; add to gelatin mixture. Mix well. Chill until firm.

Mrs. Ruth Spears, Deep Run School
Deep Run, North Carolina

HAWAIIAN PINEAPPLE-CHEESE MOLD

Number of Servings — 8

1 pkg. lime gelatin
1 c. boiling water
1 c. evaporated milk
1 c. cottage cheese
2½ c. crushed pineapple, well drained
½ c. mayonnaise
¼-½ c. celery, chopped
¼-½ c. walnuts, chopped

Dissolve gelatin in boiling water. Stir in remaining ingredients. Chill until firm.

Mrs. Manuel Cox, Scappoose H. S.
Scappoose, Oregon

PINEAPPLE-PIMENTO SALAD

Number of Servings — 12

½ c. mayonnaise
1 lge. can crushed pineapple, drained
1 small jar pimentos, mashed
1 pt. cottage cheese
1 c. nuts, chopped
1 pkg. lemon gelatin
1 pkg. lime gelatin
½ pt. whipped cream
2 T. sugar

Combine mayonnaise, pineapple, pimentos, cottage cheese and nuts. Add juice from pineapple and ¼ cup water. Prepare gelatin according to package directions. Cool until partially congealed. Combine gelatin with first mixture; fold in cream sweetened with sugar. Chill until firm.

Mrs. Mary B. Mills, Vina H. S.
Vina, Alabama

SUNSHINE SALAD

Number of Servings — 15

1 pkg. lemon gelatin
1 c. hot water
12 lge. marshmallows, diced
2 stalks celery, diced
2 carrots, diced
1 c. crushed pineapple
1 c. mayonnaise or salad dressing
½ pt. whipped cream
1 c. cottage cheese
½ c. pecans, chopped

Dissolve gelatin in hot water. Add marshmallows, celery, carrots and pineapple. Fold in salad dressing, whipped cream, cottage cheese and nuts. Chill overnight.

Mrs. Ione Thompson, Phillips H. S.
Phillips, Texas

LEMON-LIME CHEESE SALAD

Number of Servings — 8

2 pkg. lime gelatin
1 pkg. lemon gelatin
3 c. hot water
3 c. cold water
1 lb. cottage cheese

Add 3 cups hot water to gelatin; stir until dissolved. Add 3 cups cold water. Refrigerate until mixture is syrupy. Blend in cottage cheese with beater, pour into 2 quart mold. Chill.

Mrs. Vivian McDonald, Chardon H. S.
Chardon, Ohio

CHEESE SALAD

Number of Servings — 10-12

2½-4 c. crushed pineapple
1 pkg. lemon gelatin
2 3-oz. pkg. cream cheese
1 small can pimentos
½ c. celery, chopped
⅔ c. walnuts or pecans, chopped
1 c. whipped cream
⅛ t. salt

Heat juice drained from pineapple. Add gelatin and dissolve. Cream pimento and cheese; add to juice-gelatin mixture. Combine all ingredients and pour in molds. Chill several hours.

This recipe submitted by the following teachers:

Mrs. Janice K. Flynt
New Hebron Attendance Center
New Hebron, Mississippi

Mrs. Johnie Dismuke, Lytle H. S.
Lytle, Texas

CONGEALED MARSHMALLOW-CHEESE SALAD

Number of Servings — 8

1 pkg. lime gelatin
1 c. boiling water
1 c. miniature marshmallows
¼ c. sugar
1 8-oz. pkg. cream cheese
Pinch of salt
2 T. lemon juice
1 small can crushed pineapple
½ pt. whipped cream
½ c. pecans, chopped (opt.)

Pour gelatin into boiling water; add marshmallows and stir well. Put in large mold and refrigerate until almost firm. Thoroughly cream the cheese with the sugar; add to gelatin. Add lemon juice, salt, pineapple and nuts if desired. Fold in whipped cream. Chill until firm.

Mrs. Mabel Harrison, Heath H. S.
West Paducah, Kentucky

CHEESE SALAD

Number of Servings — 6-8

1 pkg. lemon gelatin
1 c. hot water
1 small pkg. cream cheese
1 c. sharp yellow cheese, grated
1 T. sugar
1 c. water
1 small can pineapple
1 T. mayonnaise or ½ c. whipped cream

Dissolve gelatin in hot water. Add cheeses and sugar; stir until melted. Add remaining water; let set. Add pineapple, mayonnaise or whipped cream.

Mrs. Ruth C. Huffine, Chardon H. S.
Chardon, Ohio

CHERRY-CHEESE-PINEAPPLE SALAD

Number of Servings — 8-10

1 pkg. apple gelatin
1 small can crushed pineapple
1 small can cherries, chopped
2 3-oz. pkg. cream cheese
½ c. nuts, chopped

Dissolve gelatin as indicated on package. Dissolve cream cheese in the hot mixture. Stir until cheese is almost dissolved. Chill until thickened. Fold in pineapple, cherries and nuts. Chill until set.

Miss Marlowe Davis, South Hall H. S.
Gainesville, Georgia

CINNAMON-CHEESE SALAD

Number of Servings — 6

1 box strawberry gelatin
½ c. cinnamon candies
1 c. cold water
½ c. boiling water
½ c. apples, diced
½ c. celery, diced
½ c. nuts, chopped
1 4-oz. pkg. cream cheese

Melt cinnamon candy in boiling water. Add to gelatin; stir to dissolve. Add cold water and cream cheese. Beat until smooth. Chill until thickened; add apples, celery and nuts. Chill until firm.

Twyla M. Regula, Northeastern H. S.
Springfield, Ohio

CREAM CHEESE SALAD

Number of Servings — 4-6

1 pkg. lime gelatin
½ c. pecans, broken
1 pkg. cream cheese, crumbled
½ c. crushed pineapple, drained

Prepare gelatin according to directions on package, substituting pineapple juice for part of the cold water if desired. Mix cream cheese, pineapple and pecans; add to gelatin. Chill until firm. Garnish with Maraschino cherries and parsley if desired.

Mrs. Jo Nell Baker, Kemp H. S.
Kemp, Texas

CONGEALED CHEESE SURPRISE

Number of Servings — 8

1 pkg. lemon gelatin
1 c. hot water
1 4-oz. pkg. cream cheese
1 small can crushed pineapple, drained
1 c. celery, diced
1 c. nuts, chopped
1 carrot, grated (opt.)
1 c. pineapple juice and water

Dissolve gelatin in hot water. Melt cheese in hot mixture. Add pineapple-juice water mixture. Add remaining ingredients. Chill until firm.

Mrs. Mary Jo Lyle, Putnam County H. S.
Eatonton, Georgia

CONGEALED CREAM CHEESE SALAD

Number of Servings — 8-10

2 3-oz. pkg. cream cheese
2 pkg. lime or lemon gelatin
3 c. boiling water
1½ T. lemon juice
½ c. pecans, chopped
1 c. celery, chopped
1 c. whipped cream

Cream the cheese and gelatin. Add water and lemon juice. Cool until mixture is consistency of egg whites. Fold in pecans and celery. Chill until thick. Fold in whipped cream.

Juanita Spinks, Ferris H. S.
Ferris, Texas

CREAM CHEESE SALAD

Number of Servings — 10

1 pkg. lemon gelatin
1 c. Royal Anne cherries, drained
1 c. crushed pineapple, drained
1 c. marshmallows, chopped
1 c. nuts, chopped
1 c. whipped cream
¼ c. salad dressing
1 8-oz. pkg. cream cheese
1 c. mixed juice from cherries and pineapple

Prepare gelatin according to package directions substituting 1 cup cherry-pineapple juice mixture for liquid. Chill until syrupy. Add remaining ingredients in order given. Chill until firm.

Mrs. Nadine Kaiser, Hydro H. S.
Hydro, Oklahoma

CREAM CHEESE SALAD

Number of Servings — 10

2 pkg. lime gelatin
1 pkg. cream cheese
1 medium can crushed pineapple
1¾ c. pineapple juice, heated
1¾ c. thin cream
1 c. nuts
Dash of powdered ginger
Dash of salt

Dissolve gelatin in heated juice; cool. Blend cream cheese and cream until smooth. Add all ingredients to gelatin-juice mixture. Turn into a greased mold. Chill until firm.

Lida Connatser, Sevier County H. S.
Sevierville, Tennessee

CREAM CHEESE SALAD

Number of Servings — 8

1 pt. whipped cream
1 lge. green pepper, diced
1 lge. can pineapple bits, drained
3 T. unflavored gelatin
1 c. cold water
½ c. hot pineapple juice
1 c. nuts, chopped
3 small pkg. or 1 lge. pkg. cream cheese, softened
1 c. salad dressing

Dissolve gelatin in cold water; mix with pineapple juice. Mix cream cheese with salad dressing; add green pepper, pineapple and nuts. Mix with gelatin. Fold in whipped cream. Pour into mold and refrigerate until firm.

Mrs. Flora Taylor, Augusta H. S.
Augusta, Arkansas

CREAM CHEESE SALAD

Number of Servings — 12

1 12-oz. pkg. cream cheese
1 small can pineapple
1 pkg. lemon gelatin
1 pkg. raspberry gelatin
1 c. boiling water
½ c. mayonnaise
1 lge. can evaporated milk
Chopped pecans to taste

Pour boiling water over mixed gelatins; mix well. Cool. Add pineapple. Combine cream cheese and mayonnaise. Gradually add milk to cheese mixture. Add nuts. Add cheese mixture to gelatin. Chill until firm.

Mrs. Margaret T. Rayfield, Weogufka H. S.
Weogufka, Alabama

CREAM CHEESE SALAD

Number of Servings — 12

1 pkg. lemon gelatin
1 c. warm pineapple juice
15 marshmallows, quartered
1 c. crushed pineapple
1 3-oz. pkg. cream cheese
⅓ c. salad dressing
1 c. whipped cream

Dissolve gelatin in warm pineapple juice. Add marshmallows and pineapple. Mix cream cheese with salad dressing; add whipped cream. Add to gelatin mixture. Put in mold and chill until firm.

Mrs. Loretta Baumbach, Sheyenne H. S.
Sheyenne, North Dakota

CREAM CHEESE-GELATIN SALAD

Number of Servings — 8-10

1 pkg. orange or orange-pineapple gelatin
1 c. boiling water
1 4-oz. pkg. cream cheese
1 small can crushed pineapple
2 bananas, diced
1 small bottle Maraschino cherries, undrained
½ c. nuts, chopped
1 c. cream, whipped

Combine gelatin, water and cream cheese. Stir until thoroughly mixed and dissolved. Let set until thick. Add pineapple, bananas, cherries and nuts. Mix gently. Fold in whipped cream. Chill until firm.

Mrs. Esther J. Anderson, Bear River H. S.
Tremonton, Utah

GAINESVILLE CREAM CHEESE SALAD

Number of Servings — 8

2 pkg. cream cheese, broken in pieces
2 c. crushed pineapple
1 pkg. lemon gelatin
1 T. unflavored gelatin
1 T. cold water
Juice of 1 lemon
¼ c. pimento, chopped
½ c. nuts, chopped
1 stalk celery, chopped
6 marshmallows
¼ t. salt
½ pt. whipped cream

Drain pineapple. Combine juice and enough water to make 2 cups liquid. Heat to boiling point; pour over lemon gelatin. Mix cold water and unflavored gelatin; combine with lemon gelatin mixture. Add lemon juice and salt; chill until partially set. Mix pineapple, cream cheese, pimento, nuts, celery and marshmallows. Add to gelatin mixture. Fold in whipped cream. Pour into a mold. Chill.

Mrs. Marie M. Mingledorff, Coffee County H. S.
Douglas, Georgia

CREAM CHEESE SALAD

1 pkg. lime gelatin
1 6-oz. pkg. cream cheese
1 medium can fruit cocktail, drained
⅔ c. nuts
½ c. mayonnaise
1 c. boiling water

Thoroughly cream the cheese and gelatin powder. Add boiling water; cool slightly. Add mayonnaise, nuts and fruit cocktail. Stir and refrigerate.

Emma Lou Garst, Las Cruces H. S.
Las Cruces, New Mexico

CREAM CHEESE 7-UP SALAD

Number of Servings — 6-8

1 8-oz. pkg. cream cheese
1 pkg. lemon gelatin
1 c. boiling water
1 t. sugar
1 small can crushed pineapple, drained
4 drops green food coloring
½ c. pecans, chopped
1 7-Up

Dissolve gelatin in boiling water; add cheese, pineapple, sugar, food coloring and 7-Up. Stir in pecans. When mixture is partially congealed, pour into individual molds. Chill until firm.

Mrs. Elden Brunet, Oakdale H. S.
Oakdale, Louisiana

MOLDED FRUIT SALAD

Number of Servings — 18

2 T. unflavored gelatin
1 c. cold water-pineapple juice
2 c. boiling water
¾ t. salt
½ c. sugar
¼ c. vinegar
Juice of 1 lemon
2 3-oz. pkg. cream cheese, softened
1 c. mayonnaise
1½ c. crushed pineapple, drained
2 c. miniature marshmallows
1½ c. pecans, chopped
1 medium bottle Maraschino cherries

Soak gelatin in cold water-pineapple juice. Add boiling water, salt, sugar, vinegar and lemon juice. Stir until gelatin is dissolved. Chill until partially thickened. Mix cream cheese, mayonnaise, pineapple, pecans and cherries together. Fold into gelatin mixture. Chill until firm.

Mrs. Nonie Lee Hardage, Carthage H. S.
Carthage, Mississippi

FRUIT-NUT CHEESE MOLD

Number of Servings — 6-8

1 No. 2 can crushed pineapple
1 pkg. lime gelatin
2 3-oz. pkg. cream cheese, softened
⅓ c. pimento, chopped
1 c. whipped cream
½ c. celery, diced
1 c. California walnuts, chopped

Heat pineapple to boiling point; add gelatin and stir until dissolved. Chill until partially set. Combine cream cheese and pimento; add to gelatin mixture. Blend. Fold in whipped cream, celery and nuts. Chill

Robbye Keel, Stewart County H. S.
Dover, Tennessee

HAWAIIAN CRUNCH SALAD

Number of Servings — 8

1 pkg. lime or lemon gelatin
2 c. boiling pineapple juice and water
1 c. crushed pineapple, drained
1 c. walnuts, chopped
1 c. celery, chopped
2 3-oz. pkg. cream cheese
2 T. mayonnaise

Dissolve gelatin in the boiling water and juice; chill until partially set. Heat mayonnaise and cream cheese until melted. Add pineapple, nuts and celery. Gently stir cheese mixture into the gelatin mixture. Pour into individual molds. Chill until set.

Eileen R. Quinn, Wattsburg Area H. S.
Wattsburg, Pennsylvania

HEAVENLY CHEESE SALAD

Number of Servings — 12

1 box lemon or lime gelatin
1 c. pineapple juice or water
1 8-oz. pkg. cream cheese
4 slices pineapple, diced
½ c. English walnuts
¾ pt. whipped cream

Bring pineapple juice or water to a boil; pour over gelatin. Cool. Add cheese, pineapple and nuts. Fold in whipped cream. Chill.

This recipe submitted by the following teachers:

Mrs. Frank G. Haltom, Prescott H. S.
Prescott, Arkansas

Virginia Hearne, Marsh Junior H. S.
Fort Worth, Texas

LUCY'S SALAD

Number of Servings — 8-10

1 pkg. lime or cherry gelatin
1 envelope unflavored gelatin
1½ c. hot water
1 6-oz. pkg. cream cheese, mashed
1 c. mayonnaise
1 c. crushed pineapple
½ c. chopped pecans

Combine gelatins and hot water. Chill until thickened. Blend cream cheese, mayonnaise and pineapple together. Add to gelatin mixture; add nuts. Pour into a mold that has been greased with mayonnniase. Chill until firm.

Mrs. Eleanor Roberts, Thompsonville Comm. H. S.
Thompsonville, Illinois

PARADISE SALAD

Number of Servings — 16

2 pkg. cream cheese
1 small can pimentos, chopped and drained
1 small can crushed pineapple, drained
½ c. pecans, chopped
1 c. celery, chopped
½ pt. whipped cream
1 pkg. lemon gelatin

Dissolve gelatin in juice drained from pineapple and pimentos. Combine all ingredients, folding in whipped cream last. Refrigerate until firm.

Mrs. Dorothy Martin, Frost H. S.
Frost, Texas

PINEAPPLE-CHEESE SALAD

Number of Servings — 6

1 No. 1 can pineapple chunks
1 c. cream cheese, cubed
1 c. miniature marshmallows
2 T. butter
1 T. flour
2 T. sugar
1 egg yolk
1 egg white, beaten

Drain pineapple; reserve juice. Combine marshmallows, pineapple and cheese. Set aside. Combine butter, flour, sugar and egg yolk with pineapple juice. Boil; pour over first mixture. Fold in beaten egg white. Chill.

Dolores Jean Armstrong, Salem Community H. S.
Salem, Illinois

PINEAPPLE-CREAM CHEESE SALAD

Number of Servings — 8-10

1¾ c. boiling pineapple juice and water
2 boxes lime gelatin
1 medium can crushed pineapple, drained
2 small pkg. cream cheese, mashed
1 c. pecans, finely chopped
½ pt. whipped cream

Combine hot juice—water mixture and cheese; blend well. Add gelatin, pineapple and nuts. Let stand at room temperature for 1 hour. Fold in whipped cream. Refrigerate 6-8 hours. Do not freeze.

Mrs. William V. Creekmur, R. O. V. A. H. S.
Oneida, Illinois

PINEAPPLE-CREAM CHEESE SALAD

Number of Servings — 15

1 c. crushed pineapple
1 c. sugar
Juice of 1 lemon
2½ T. unflavored gelatin
2 3-oz. pkg. cream cheese
1 pt. whipped cream, or 1 can whipped evaporated milk

Heat pineapple, sugar and lemon juice. Add gelatn; stir to dissolve. Cool. Mix cream cheese and whipped cream together. Add pineapple mixture to cheese and cream. Chill until firm.

Lois S. Gass, Mahanoy Joint H. S.
Herndon, Pennsylvania

PINEAPPLE-ORANGE-CHEESE SALAD

Number of Servings — 10

1 11-oz. can Mandarin orange slices, drained
1 No. 2 can crushed pineapple, drained
1 can concentrated tangerine juice
1 box orange gelatin
2 3-oz. pkg. cream cheese, chopped

Combine orange, pineapple and tangerine juices. Heat but do not boil. Add gelatin; stir until dissolved. Add cream cheese. Some will melt and some will not. Cool until thickened. Add pineapple and oranges.

Marjorie J. Reynard, Rogers Township H. S.
Rogers City, Michigan

PINEAPPLE-LIME GELATIN SALAD

Number of Servings — 6-8

1 lge. pkg. lime gelatin
2 small pkg. cream cheese
4 oz. marshmallows
1 small can crushed pineapple
⅓ c. nuts, chopped (opt.)

Mix gelatin according to package directions. Chill until firm. Dissolve marshmallows and cheese over low flame. Combine mixtures and nuts. Cool until firm. Stir once as mixture thickens.

Mrs. Jo Nita Schwarz, Central H. S.
San Angelo, Texas

PECAN SALAD

Number of Servings — 10-12

1 pkg. lemon gelatin
2 small pkg. cream cheese
½ pt. whipped cream
2 c. pecans, chopped
1 small bottle Maraschino cherries, sliced
1 No. 2½ can crushed pineapple, drained

Heat pineapple juice; add gelatin. Stir until dissolved. Chill until thickened. Mash cream cheese; add whipped cream. Fold into thickened gelatin. Add pineapple, cherries and pecans. Pour into mold and chill until firm.

Rachel Brewster, Petrolia H. S.
Petrolia, Texas

SPRING SALAD

Number of Servings — 8-10

2 small pkg. cream cheese
1 pkg. lemon gelatin
1 pkg. lime gelatin
1 c. pecans, finely chopped
3 c. boiling water
24 lge. marshmallows
Pineapple juice
1 small can pineapple, drained
2 T. vinegar

Pour boiling water over gelatin and marshmallow; stir until dissolved. Chill until mixture begins to thicken. Mix cream cheese with vinegar; blend until smooth; add pineapple juice; blend thoroughly. Add pecans and pineapple. Chill. Combine cheese and gelatin mixtures. Chill until firm.

This recipe submitted by the following teachers:

Hilda Harman, Smithville H. S.
Smithville, Mississippi

Nancy G. Jones, Pink Hill
Pink Hill, North Carolina

Mary E. Roddam, Curry H. S.
Jasper, Alabama

SUPERB CREAM CHEESE SALAD

Number of Servings — 9

1 pkg. lime gelatin
1 pkg. lemon gelatin
2 c. hot water
1 8-oz. pkg. cream cheese
1 c. mayonnaise
2 T. horseradish
1 c. milk
1 c. crushed pineapple, drained

Dissolve gelatins in water. Gradually add cream cheese; blending until smooth. Chill until slightly thick. Add remaining ingredients. Chill until firm.

Madge Arlene Humphrey, Weston Union H. S.
Cazenovia, Wisconsin

CHEESE-PINEAPPLE SALAD

Number of Servings — 4

¾ c. pineapple juice
1 t. vinegar
1 c. whipped cream
¾ lb. miniature marshmallows
1 T. cornstarch
1 egg, beaten
½ lb. cheese, grated
1 No. 2½ can crushed pineapple

Combine pineapple juice, vinegar, cornstarch and egg in double boiler; cook until thick. Cool. Add cream, cheese, marshmallows and pineapple; mix. Chill overnight.

Sarah Henry, Redwater H. S.
Redwater, Texas

CHEESE AND PINEAPPLE SALAD

Number of Servings — 6-8

1 T. (1 envelope) unflavored gelatin
¼ c. cold water
¾ c. sugar
½ c. pineapple syrup
1 c. crushed pineapple, drained
1 c. grated American cheese
1 c. heavy cream, whipped

Soften gelatin in cold water. Dissolve sugar in pineapple syrup over low heat; add gelatin, stir until dissolved. Chill until partially set; add pineapple and cheese; fold in whipped cream. Turn into 1-quart mold. Chill until firm.

This recipe submitted by the following teachers:

Mrs. Joy Barkowsky, Flower Grove
Ackerly, Texas

Mrs. Barbara E. Wenner, Warrington Junior H. S.
Pensacola, Florida

Mrs. Maxie Lee Dixon, Walker H. S.
Walker, Louisiana

Lillah L. Ball, Arvin H. S.
Arvin, California

Mary Lee Egbert, Teton H. S.
Driggs, Idaho

Mrs. J. E. Carson, Decatur H. S.
Decatur, Texas

Rita Fielder, Biggers-Reyno H. S.
Biggers, Arkansas

CHEESE-PINEAPPLE SALAD

Number of Servings — 12-15

1 pkg. lemon gelatin
2 c. boiling water
1 c. crushed pineapple, drained
1 c. American cheese, grated
1 c. whipped cream
1 c. marshmallows, diced

Dissolve gelatin in boiling water; chill until partially set. Mix pineapple, and marshmallows; add to gelatin mixture. Add cheese; fold in whipped cream. Chill until firm.

Mrs. Joyce Meek, Yamhill-Carlton Union H. S.
Yamhill, Oregon

CHEESE SALAD

Number of Servings — 6-12

1 pkg. lemon, lime or cherry gelatin
½ envelope unflavored gelatin (opt.)
1 pt. hot water
1 small can crushed pineapple
½-¾ c. nuts, chopped
½ lb. cheese, grated
1 c. whipped cream
1 T. sugar (opt.)

Dissolve gelatins in hot water; refrigerate until mixture begins to thicken. Add pineapple; cool completely. Add nuts and cheese. Fold in whipped cream. Turn into mold. Chill until firm.

This recipe submitted by the following teachers:

Mrs. Anne T. Page, Cool Spring H. S.
Cleveland, North Carolina

Mrs. Mary Eula Cowles, Newkirk H. S.
Newkirk, Oklahoma

Mrs. Jane Davidson, South Park H. S.
Beaumont, Texas

GOLDEN SALAD

Number of Servings — 6-8

2 pkg. lemon gelatin
1 can pimento, ground
1 lge. can sliced pineapple, drained and ground
1 c. whipped cream
½ lb. American cheese, ground
2 c. hot pineapple juice-water

Dissolve gelatin in pineapple juice-water mixture. Add pimento, pineapple, cheese and whipped cream. Pour into a large mold or individual molds; congeal.

Mrs. Mabel Williamson, Lafayette Senior H. S.
Lexington, Kentucky

PIMENTO CHEESE MOLD

Number of Servings — 8

1 pkg. lime gelatin
1 small can crushed pineapple
2 c. marshmallows
2 c. nuts
Juice of 1 lemon
1 t. vinegar
1 c. hot water
Pinch of salt
½ pt. whipped cream
1 jar pimento cheese spread

Dissolve gelatin in hot water; cool. Add pineapple, marshmallows, nuts, lemon juice, vinegar and salt. Combine cream and cheese spread; blend with gelatin mixture. Refrigerate for 8 hours.

Mrs. Gwyndola Jackson, Longville H. S.
Longville, Louisiana

FRUIT-N-CHEESE RINGS

Number of Servings — 6

2½ c. crushed pineapple, drained
1 3-oz. pkg. lemon gelatin
1 c. hot water
½ c. mayonnaise or salad dressing
1 5-oz. jar pimento cheese spread
1 c. carrots, grated
¾ c. pineapple juice

Dissolve gelatin in hot water. Add mayonnaise and pimento cheese; beat until smooth with electric or rotary beater. Stir in pineapple juice. Chill until partially set. Fold in carrots and pineapple. Turn into a 5½-cup ring mold. Chill until firm. Unmold. Fill center with grapes or other fruit.

Norma Kay Jenni, Moore H. S.
Moore, Montana

MARSHMALLOW-CHEESE SALAD

Number of Servings — 6

1 glass pimento cheese
½ c. salad dressing
1 c. whipped cream or whipped evaporated milk
12 lg. marshmallows
1 9-oz. can crushed pineapple, drained
½ c. nuts, chopped

Combine marshmallows and pineapple; let stand for a few minutes. Combine cheese and salad dressing. Combine the mixtures; fold in whipped milk or cream and nuts. Refrigerate for 12 hours.

Janet C. Clark, Rigby H. S.
Rigby, Idaho

PINEAPPLE DELIGHT

Number of Servings — 6

1 c. crushed pineapple
1 c. sugar
Juice of 1 lemon
1 pkg. lemon gelatin
1 c. hot water
1 c. whipped cream
½ c. pimento cheese, grated

Combine pineapple, sugar and lemon juice. Boil 3 minutes. Dissolve gelatin in the hot water. Add to the hot mixture. Let set until partially congealed. Add cream and cheese. Chill.

Reva Wilson, Drummond H. S.
Drummond, Montana

PIMENTO-OLIVE-CHEESE SALAD

Number of Servings — 8

1 5-oz. glass neufchatel pimento-olive cheese spread
⅓ c. mayonnaise
1 8¾-oz. can crushed pineapple, well drained
½ pt. whipped cream
1½ c. salad marshmallows

Combine cheese and mayonnaise; mix well. Add pineapple. Fold in whipped cream; add the marshmallows. Place mixture in a rectangular dish for easy cutting or in individual molds. Chill at least 2 hours.

Mrs. Armalea Hopperstad
Independence Community College
Independence, Kansas

PINEAPPLE-CHEESE SALAD

Number of Servings — 12

1 No. 2 can crushed pineapple, undrained
½ c. sugar
Juice of 1 lemon
2 T. unflavored gelatin
¾ c. pimento cheese grated in long curls
1 c. whipped cream.
½ c. cold water

Dissolve gealtin in cold water. Heat pineapple and sugar to boiling point; add lemon juice. Remove from heat and add gelatin; stir until dissolved. Cool until partially set; whip until light and fluffy. Fold in cheese and whipped cream. Let set until firm.

Mrs. C. H. Simpson, McEwen H. S.
Athena, Oregon

THREE-FLAVOR MOLD

Number of Servings — 12

1 pkg. lemon gelatin
2 glasses pimento cheese
⅔ c. walnuts, finely chopped
1 c. whipped cream
⅓ t. salt
1 lge. can crushed pineapple, undrained

Drain pineapple; add enough water to make 2 cups liquid. Bring juice-water mixture to a boil. Add gelatin; chill until syrupy. Add pineapple and cheese; blend. Add walnuts and salt. Fold in whipped cream. Chill.

Mrs. Mary Van Fleet, Indio H. S.
Indio, California

BING-A-LING SALAD

Number of Servings — 10

1 lge. can Bing cherries
2 pkg. cherry gelatin
2 c. grape juice
Juice of 1 lemon
1 carton cottage cheese
1 c. nuts

Heat juice from cherries and add to gelatin. Cool. Add grape and lemon juice. When slightly thickened, add cherries, cottage cheese and nuts. Chill until firm.

Ola Lee W. Robinson, North H. S.
North, South Carolina

BING CHERRY SALAD

Number of Servings — 8

1 pkg. raspberry gelatin
1 c. hot cherry juice
1 T. gelatin
¼ c. pineapple juice
1 c. pecans, chopped
1 small can crushed pineapple, drained
1 c. orange sections, drained
1 can Bing cherries
1 small Coca-Cola or 1 c. Mogen David wine
1 c. whipped cream
1 T. mayonnaise

Dissolve raspberry gelatin in hot cherry juice. Add gelatin softened in the pineapple juice. Stir until dissolved. Chill until thickened; add fruits, nuts and wine or Coca-Cola. Combine cream and mayonnaise. Fold into gelatin mixture. Chill.

Ethel D. Johnson, Jackson H. S.
Jackson, Alabama

BING CHERRY CONGEALED SALAD

Number of Servings — 6

1 pkg. cherry gelatin
1 8-oz. pkg. cream cheese
1 No. 2 can Bing cherries
1 small pkg. pecans, almonds or walnuts
1 c. hot cherry juice
1 c. cold water

Dissolve gelatin in boiling cherry juice. Add cold water. Cool. Cream the cheese until soft. Add nuts. Stir into thickened gelatin. Add cherries. Chill until firm.

This recipe submitted by the following teachers:

Mary Nan Marek, William Adams H. S.
Alice, Texas

Mrs. Helen Pinkham, DeKalb H. S.
DeKalb, Texas

Mrs. Grace Hunt, Sturgis H. S.
Starkville, Mississippi

Mrs. Bernadette Schoen, East Troy H. S.
East Troy, Wisconsin

BING CHERRY CONGEALED SALAD

Number of Servings — 8

1 can sweetened, pitted Bing cherries, drained
1 small can crushed pineapple, drained
1 pkg. cherry or black cherry gelatin
1 3-oz. pkg. cream cheese
1 6½-oz. cold Coca-Cola, Seven-Up or 1 c. pineapple juice
1 c. pecans or other nuts

Heat 1 cup cherry juice. (Add pineapple juice if necessary to make 1 cup liquid.) Dissolve gelatin in hot juice. Pour a little of the hot mixture over cream cheese. Blend until very smooth. Add remaining hot gelatin mixture; blend well. Add Coca-Cola or pineapple juice; cream and beat thoroughly. Chill until fairly firm. Beat again with chilled beaters, until mixture begins to fluff. Fold in cherries, pineapple and nuts. Pour into mold that has been rinsed in cold water. Chill 6 to 8 hours or until firm. One package of strawberry gelatin prepared according to package directions may be added to extend this recipe.

This recipe submitted by the following teachers:

Mrs. Pauline B. Commer
Crowder White Attendance Center
Crowder, Mississippi

Marolyn W. Howell, Bainbridge H. S.
Bainbridge, Georgia

Hattie Hunt, Science Hill H. S.
Johnson City, Tennessee

Rose Ann Miller, Vaiden H. S.
Vaiden, Mississippi

Mrs. Ralph Johnson, Scottsville H. S.
Scottsville, Kentucky

Mrs. Patsy Ruth Agee, Evans H. S.
Orlando, Florida

BING CHERRY SALAD

Number of Servings — 6

1 pkg. cherry gelatin
1 can Bing cherries, drained
Juice of 1 orange
Juice of 1 lemon
Cooking sherry (opt.)
½-¾ c. nuts, chopped
1 c. cherry juice, heated
1 3-oz. bottle stuffed olives, sliced (opt.)

Dissolve gelatin in hot cherry juice. Combine orange and lemon juice; and enough cooking sherry to make 1 cup liquid. Add to gelatin mixture. Chill until thickened. Add nuts, cherries and olives if desired; chill until firm.

This recipe submitted by the following teachers:

Mrs. Eloise W. Gilreath, Wilkes Central H. S.
North Wilkesboro, North Carolina

Mrs. J. B. Morris, Gooding H. S.
Gooding, Idaho

BING CHERRY SALAD

Number of Servings — 6

1 pkg. cherry gelatin
½ c. sherry or grape wine
½ c. pineapple juice
1 c. cherry juice
1 #300 can black cherries, pitted and drained
½ c. pecans, chopped
1 small can crushed pineapple (opt.)

Dissolve gelatin in heated liquids. Chill until thickened. Add cherries and nuts. For extra firmness, soften ½ envelope plain gelatin in ¼ cup water and add to hot mixture. Chill for several hours before serving.

Catherine D. Magel, Shawnee H. S.
Camden, Ohio

BING CHERRY SALAD

Number of Servings — 15

1 No. 303 can pineapple chunks, drained and sliced in ⅓'s
2 pkgs. raspberry or cherry gelatin
2 c. hot water
Syrup drained from pineapple plus enough cold water to make 2 c.
1 No. 303 can bing or dark sweet cherries, pitted
1 c. celery, chopped
1 small bottle stuffed olives, sliced
1 6 oz. pkg. cream cheese, cut in small pieces
½ c. pecan halves

Dissolve gelatin in hot water. Add pineapple syrup and cold water. Chill until mixture thickens slightly. Add pineapple, cherries, celery and olives. Fold in the bits of cream cheese. Top salad with pecan halves. Chill until firm.

Joan McCready, Missouri Valley H. S.
Missouri Valley, Iowa

BING CHERRY SALAD

Number of Servings — 8-10

1 No. 2 can Bing cherries, pitted
1 box lemon gelatin
1¼ c. grape juice
½ c. pecans, broken (opt.)
1 pkg. cream cheese
½ c. mayonnaise

Heat juice from cherries; add gelatin and stir until dissolved. Add enough grape juice to make 2 cups liquid. Chill. When slightly congealed, add cherries and nuts. Chill until firm. Serve with a dressing made by blending the cream cheese and mayonnaise.

Mrs. E. T. Parker, Connally H. S.
Waco, Texas

BING CHERRY SALAD

Number of Servings — 10-12

1 No. 2 can Bing cherries or 1 10½-oz. bottle Maraschino cherries, diced
1-2½ c. crushed pineapple, drained (opt.)
2 pkg. cherry, lime or blackberry gelatin
2 Coca-Colas
2 c. fruit juice
1 c. nuts, chopped (opt.)
Whipped cream (opt.)

Heat juices drained from pineapple and cherries. Pour over gelatin; stir well. Cool. Add Coca-Cola. Chill until partly congealed. Add remaining ingredients. Chill until firm. Garnish with whipped cream if desired.

The teachers who submitted this recipe can be found on page 378.

CHERRY-COLA SALAD

Number of Servings — 8

1 No. 2 can black Bing cherries, drained
2 pkg. cherry gelatin
2 6-oz. bottles Coca-Cola
1 c. nuts
Whipped cream (opt.)

Dissolve gelatin in heated cherry juice. Add cherries, nuts and Coca-Colas. Chill and serve. Garnish with whipped cream if desired.

This recipe submitted by the following teachers:

Mrs. Annie Varnell, Dora Municipal School
Dora, New Mexico

Etta Mae Westbrook, Leetonia H. S.
Leetonia, Ohio

COCA COLA SALAD

Number of Servings — 12

1 lge. can Bing cherries
1 No. 2 can crushed pineapple
1 c. celery, cut medium fine
2 pkg. cherry gelatin
2 pkg. (3 oz.) cream cheese, broken in small chunks
2 regular sized bottles Coca Cola
Chopped nut meats, if desired

Heat juice of cherries and pour over gelatin. Let cool. Add Coca Cola and stir in other ingredients. Put mixture into mold, individual molds, or square pans for easy cutting into serving pieces. Chill until firm. Serves 12 generously.

Jean B. Gilleece, Lamar H. S.
Lamar, Colorado

BING CHERRY SALAD

Number of Servings — 18-20

1 No. 2 can Bing cherries, seeded and drained
1 No. 2 can crushed pineapple, drained
2 c. juice and water
1 pkg. black cherry gelatin
1 pkg. raspberry, cherry or strawberry gelatin
2 bottles Coca-Cola, Pepsi Cola or Seven-Up
2 small pkg. cream cheese
1 c. celery, finely diced (opt.)
1 c. nuts, coarsely chopped
½ c. flaked coconut (opt.)

Heat fruit juice to boiling; pour over the gelatin. Stir until dissolved. Add Coca-Colas; chill until slightly thickened. Break up or beat cream cheese and add to fruits and nuts. Fold into gelatin. Chill until firm. Amounts of pineapple, cherries, cream cheese and nuts may be varied to taste.

The teachers who submitted this recipe can be found on page 378.

BING CHERRY SALAD MOLD

Number of Servings — 8-10

1 pkg. cherry gelatin
1 c. boiling water or cherry juice
1 3-oz. pkg. cream cheese
1 c. pineapple juice
1 c. pecans, chopped
1 c. crushed pineapple, drained
1 c. canned Bing cherries, pitted

Dissolve gelatin in hot liquid. Add cream cheese, softened with a little of the gelatin mixture and pineapple juice. Stir until smooth. Chill until syrupy. Beat until fluffy. Fold in nuts, pineapple and cherries. Chill until firm.

This recipe submitted by the following teachers:

Charlotte Willard, Elsie H. S.
Elsie, Michigan

Mrs. Virginia Ryan McLain, Daingerfield H. S.
Daingerfield, Texas

Mrs. Ethelyne P. Wooten, Ruleville Public School
Ruleville, Mississippi

BLACK CHERRY SALAD

Number of Servings — 8-10

1 No. 2 can black cherries, drained
1 small can crushed pineapple, drained
1 c. nuts
1½ pkg. cherry gelatin
1 c. grape juice

Dissolve gelatin in hot cherry and pineapple juice. Add grape juice. When almost set, stir in pineapple, cherries, and nuts.

Mrs. George G. Walker, Flora H. S.
Flora, Mississippi

BLACK CHERRY SALAD

Number of Servings — 6

1 box black cherry gelatin
1 c. boiling water
1 can black cherries
1 can white grapes
½ c. pecan pieces
1 c. juice, drained from cherries

Dissolve gelatin in boiling water. Add cherry juice. Chill until slightly thickened. Stir in fruit and nuts. Pour into mold. Chill until set.

Lilliam B. Cockram, Floyd County H. S.
Floyd, Virginia

BLACK CHERRY SALAD

Number of Servings — 8

1 No. 2½ can pitted Bing cherries, drained
⅓ c. lemon juice
1 pkg. orange-gelatin
¾ c. pecans, chopped
⅓-oz. bottle stuffed olives, sliced

Add water to cherry syrup and lemon juice to make 1¾ cups liquid. Heat; pour over gelatin and stir until dissolved. Chill until partially set. Add cherries, nuts, and olives. Chill until firm.

Cozette Wilson, West Union H. S.
West Union, Ohio

BLACK CHERRY SALAD

Number of Servings — 6

2 c. canned black cherries, drained and pitted
1 pkg. black cherry gelatin
1 c. juice from cherries or water
1 c. port wine or ½ c. water and ½ c. wine
1 c. pecans or walnuts, broken (opt.)
1 3-oz. pkg. cream cheese
½ c. whipped cream
¼ c. mayonnaise
1 T. sugar (opt.)

Dissolve gelatin in the cup of boiling juice. Add port wine. Chill until syrupy. Stir in black cheries and nuts if desired. Congeal. Cream the cheese. Fold in the whipped cream and mayonnaise. Add sugar if desired. Use as dressing.

This recipe submitted by the following teachers:

Mrs. Velma Shaffer, State Department of Education
Little Rock, Arkansas

Joyce Wolfgang, State FHA Executive Secretary
State Department of Education
Tallahassee, Florida

Mrs. R. M. Sill, Camden Junior H. S.
Camden, South Carolina

BLACK CHERRY SALAD WITH FLUFFY RUFFLE DRESSING

Number of Servings — 6

1 can black cherries, pitted
1 pkg. cherry or raspberry gelatin
1 small can crushed pineapple
2 c. cherry juice
½ c. toasted pecans, chopped (opt.)

Measure cherry juice; add enough water to make 2 cups. Heat and pour over gelatin to dissolve. Cool. Add cherries, nuts and drained pineapple; chill. Serve with Fluffy Ruffle Dressing if desired.

Fluffy Ruffle Dressing
2 eggs, well beaten
½ c. lemon juice
1 T. flour
1 t. salt
2 T. sugar
10 marshmallows, diced
1 c. whipped cream
1 c. pecans, chopped

Mix eggs, lemon juice, salt, sugar and flour. Cook in double boiler until thick. Add marshmallows. Cool. Just before serving, add cream and pecans.

This recipe submitted by the following teachers:

Mrs. Anne Dodenhoff Nelson, J. E. B. Stuart H. S.
Falls Church, Virginia

Bobbie Rhae Keeter, Central H. S.
Muskogee, Oklahoma

Mrs. Kathryn D. Brown
Quakertown Com. Junior H. S.
Quakertown, Pennsylvania

Alliene Allen, Fairfield H. S.
Fairfield, Texas

Mrs. John Tsui, Brookfield H. S.
Brookfield, Ohio

CHERRY-CATSUP SALAD

Number of Servings — 6

1 pkg. cherry gelatin
½ c. catsup
1 c. boiling water
½ c. celery, chopped
1 c. nuts, chopped
12 small ripe olives, sliced

Dissolve gelatin in boiling water; cool. Add remaining ingredients. Chill until firm.

Mrs. Louisa M. Krebs, Rapid City Sr. H. S.
Rapid City, South Dakota

CHERRY-COKE SALAD

Number of Servings — 8

1 can sour pitted cherries
1 c. sugar
1 pkg. cherry gelatin
1 small Coca-Cola
1 small can crushed pineapple, drained well
1 c. hot cherry juice
½ c. nuts, chopped

Combine cherries with sugar and heat until cherries absorb sugar. Dissolve gelatin in hot cherry juice. Add cold coke, pineapple and nuts. Pour in a ring mold and congeal.

Mrs. Carolyn Garland, Seneca H. S.
Seneca, South Carolina

CHERRY-COKE SALAD

Number of Servings — 8

2 small Coca-Colas
2 pkg. black cherry gelatin
1 No. 303 can tart pie cherries, mashed and drained
1 No. 303 can crushed pineapple, drained
1 8-oz. pkg. cream cheese
2 T. milk or cream
½-1 c. walnuts or pecans, chopped
½-1 c. celery, chopped (opt.)

Heat the cokes to almost boiling, dissolve gelatin in coke. Add juice drained from fruits. Chill until it begins to thicken. Soften cream cheese with milk. Fold cherries, pineapple, cheese, nuts and celery into thickened gelatin. Pour into 2-quart mold and chill until set.

Mrs. Sarah Beth Golson Axtell H. S.
Axtell, Texas

CHERRY-COKE SALAD

Number of Servings — 6

1 pkg. cherry gelatin
1 small can crushed pineapple
1 small bottle Maraschino cherries
1 6-oz. bottle Coca-Cola
1 3-oz. pkg. cream cheese
½ c. celery, finely chopped (opt.)
⅛ t. salt (opt.)
½-1 c. pecans, chopped

Dissolve gelatin in heated pineapple and cherry juice. Stir in cream cheese until smooth. Chill until very thick. Add remaining ingredients and pour into a 1-quart mold. Chill until firm. Lime gelatin and 7-Up may be substituted for cherry gelatin and Coca-Cola if a green salad is desired. Cheese may be folded in last instead of melted in the hot juice.

This recipe submitted by the following teachers:

Mrs. Mabel Heath, Jacksonville Senior H. S.
Jacksonville, Texas

Mrs. Mary Louise Dworaczyk, Falls City H. S.
Falls City, Texas

Mrs. Emma Frances McCluskey
Cotton Center School
Cotton Center, Texas

Mrs. Alice M. Pouncey, Beatrice H. S.
Beatrice, Alabama

Barbara Jean Hemeter, New Augusta H. S.
New Augusta, Mississippi

CHERRY GELATIN SALAD

Number of Servings — 15

1 pkg. cherry gelatin
1 pkg. raspberry gelatin
2 cans sour pie cherries, drained
1 No. 2 can crushed pineapple, drained
1½ c. sugar
Juice of 2 oranges
Juice of 1 lemon
1 c. black walnuts or hickory nuts or ½ c. each
2 c. hot water

Combine juices drained from cherries and pineapple with orange and lemon juice to make 2 cups of liquid. Add sugar and boil 5 minutes. Dissolve gelatin in hot water; add to juice-sugar mixture. Add cherries and pineapple to the hot mixture. Add nuts. Pour into individual molds or 12 x 8 glass dish. Refrigreate for several hours. Soften cream cheese with pineapple or orange juice for dressing to serve on salad if desired.

Virginia Riddel, Spencer H. S.
Spencer, West Virginia

CHERRY-GELATIN SALAD

Number of Servings — 10

2 c. crushed pineapple
1½ c. sugar
1½ pkg. unflavored gelatin
¼ c. cold water
1 3-oz. pkg. cream cheese
12 Maraschino cherries
2 T. cherry juice
2 T. lemon juice
½ pt. whipped cream
½ c. pecans (opt.)

Heat the pineapple and sugar until melted. Mix water and gelatin, add to pineapple mixture. Stir in cream cheese until smooth. Cool. Add cherries, juices and pecans. Fold in whipped cream. Pour into mold if desired. Refrigerate.

Mrs. Marie Slover, Springlake H. S.
Earth, Texas

CHERRY-NUT SALAD

Number of Servings — 10-12

1 pkg. cherry gelatin
1 pkg. raspberry gelatin
8-oz. pkg. cream cheese
3 c. water
2 c. dark sweet cherries, halved
1 c. crushed pineapple
½ c. walnuts, broken

Dissolve gelatins in water; Stir in bite-size pieces of cream cheese. Chill until slightly thickened. Add cherries, pineapple and nuts. Chill until firm.

Judith Kuehn, Mid-County Jr. H. S.
Lacon, Illinois

CHERRY-NUT SALAD

Number of Servings — 8-12

1 16-oz. can red sour cherries, pitted and drained
Cherry juice plus enough Dr. Pepper or Pepsi-Cola to make 2 c. liquid
1 c. sugar
4 drops red food coloring
1¾ c. cold Dr. Pepper or Pepsi-Cola
1 c. celery, chopped
1 c. pecans, chopped
1 c. stuffed olives, sliced (opt.)
1 3-oz. pkg. cold cream cheese, diced
2 3-oz. pkg. cherry gelatin

Combine cherries, sugar, food coloring and cherry juice mixture. Bring to a boil. Dissolve gelatin in the hot mixture. Cool. Add cold Dr. Pepper. Chill until slightly thickened. Fold in celery, pecans, olives and cream cheese. Chill until firm. Serve with mayonnaise, sour or whipped cream if desired.

This recipe submitted by the following teachers:

Mrs. Estelle Caffey, Friona H. S.
Friona, Texas

Patricia Severin, Hopewell Junior H. S.
Aliquippa, Pennsylvania

CHERRY-PECAN SALAD

Number of Servings — 6

1 pkg. cherry gelatin
1 pkg. lemon gelatin
1 c. sugar
2 c. boiling water
1 can crushed pineapple, undrained
1 can pie cherries, undrained
2 c. pecan halves

Dissolve gelatin and sugar in boiling water. Cool slightly. Add pineapple and cherries. Place pecan halves on top. Chill until firm.

Hilda S. Wright, Hanceville H. S.
Hanceville, Alabama

CHERRY-PINEAPPLE MOLDED SALAD

Number of Servings — 12

1 1-lb. can pitted sour cherries, drained
1 No. 2 can crushed pineapple, drained
½ c. orange juice
3 T. lemon juice
½ c. sugar
2 pkg. cherry gelatin
½ c. pecans, chopped

Bring juice drained from pineapple and cherries to a boil. Add sugar; stir until dissolved. Bring liquid to a boil the second time. Add gelatin; Stir until dissolved. Add orange and lemon juice, cherries, pineapple and pecans. Pour into individual molds or one large mold. Chill until firm. This salad is very good with meats.

Frances Conway, Walla Walla H. S.
Walla Walla, Washington

CHERRY-PINEAPPLE CONGEALED SALAD

Number of Servings — 8

1 No. 2 can sour pitted cherries, drained
1 c. sugar
2 pkg. black cherry gelatin
1 No. 2 can crushed pineapple

Combine sugar and cherry juice; bring to a boil. Dissolve gelatin in hot juice. Add enough water to the gelatin mixture to make 4 cups liquid. Add cherries and pineapple. Pour into molds; chill until firm.

Mrs. Floyd Craig, Divide H. S.
Nolan, Texas

CHERRY-PINEAPPLE SALAD

1 pkg. lemon gelatin
1 pkg. unflavored gelatin
1 No. 2 can crushed pineapple, drained
1 No. 2 can Bing cherries, drained
1 c. pecans, chopped
Pineapple and cherry juice plus enough water to make 2 c. liquid

Soak unflavored gelatin in a small amount of cold water. Heat juice-water mixture to boiling; stir into lemon gelatin. Add unflavored gelatin; let set until almost firm. Add fruit and nuts, chill until firm.

Mrs. Nancy Myers, Jessamine County H. S.
Nicholasville, Kentucky

CHERRY-SOUR CREAM SALAD

Number of Servings — 6

1 pkg. cherry gelatin
1 small can crushed pineapple, drained (opt.)
1 No. 2 can dark sweet cherries, drained and pitted
½ c. nuts, chopped
½ pt. sour cream

Add enough water to juice drained from cherries and pineapple to make 1½ cups liquid; heat. Dissolve gelatin in the hot liquid. Chill until mixture thickens. Add pineapple, cherries and nuts; fold in cream. Pour into molds and chill.

This recipe submitted by the following teachers:

Broxie C. Stuckey, Gordo Home Economics Dept.
Gordo, Alabama

Mrs. Hazel P. Lowe, Chatham H. S.
Chatham, Virginia

CHERRY SALAD

Number of Servings — 8-12

2 t. vinegar
2 pkg. cherry gelatin
1 c. boiling water
1 No. 2 can sliced pineapple, drained
1 No. 2 can pitted cherries
1½ c. pecans, chopped
1 t. red food coloring
1 c. sugar
Juice of 1 lemon
Pineapple juice plus enough water to make 1 c. liquid

Dissolve gelatin in boiling water. Boil cherries, lemon juice and sugar for 10 minutes. Add pineapple-juice water mixture. Combine all ingredients. Pour into molds. Chill until firm.

Ivah Lou Ashley, Irvin H. S.
El Paso, Texas

CHERRY SALAD

Number of Servings — 12

2 pkg. raspberry gelatin
2 c. hot water
1 c. cottage cheese
2 c. whipped cream
2 c. nuts, chopped
1 c. red cherries, chopped
2 c. crushed pineapple, drained
Red food coloring

Dissolve gelatin in hot water. Chill until thick but not firm. Fold in remaining ingredients. Chill until firm.

Melba Wilson, Norcross H. S.
Norcross, Georgia

COLA-BUFFET SALAD

Number of Servings — 8-10

1 pkg. cherry gelatin
1 pkg. strawberry gelatin
1 8-oz. pkg. cream cheese
1 lge. can Bing cherries, drained and seeded
1 lge. can crushed pineapple, drained
1 c. pecans, chopped
2 c. cola beverage
Juice from cherries and pineapple, heated

Dissolve gelatin in juice from cherries and pineapple. Let cool. Mix pineapple, cheese, nuts and cherries together; add to gelatin mixture; blend well. Add cola beverage; blend again. Chill until firm.

This recipe submitted by the following teachers:

Mrs. Carolyn W. Baxlay, Paul Knox Junior H. S.
North Augusta, South Carolina

Mrs. Bonnie Bess C. Alexander, Warrington Jr. H. S.
Pensacola, Florida

COCA-COLA SALAD

Number of Servings — 8

2 bottles of Coca-Cola
1 pkg. raspberry gelatin
Juice of 1 lemon
½ c. nuts, chopped
½ c. seedless dates, diced

Heat 1 Coca-Cola in double boiler to dissolve the package of raspberry gelatin. To this mixture add 1 cold Coca-Cola and the lemon juice. Chill until slightly thickened. Beat with a rotary egg beater. Add nuts and dates. Pour into molds; chill until firm.

Grace Womack Buford, Plainview-Rover School
Plainview, Arkansas

COCA-COLA SALAD

Number of Servings — 12

1 can water-packed cherries, drained
2 pkg. cherry gelatin
1 c. sugar
2 6-oz. bottles Coca-Cola
1 can crushed pineapple
1 c. pecans, broken

Mix cherry juice, gelatin and sugar in saucepan. Heat, but do not boil. Remove from heat; cool until mixture begins to thicken. Add Coca-Colas, cherries, pineapple and pecans. Chill until firm.

Mrs. Erlene Dunn, Harper H. S.
Harper, Texas

COKE SALAD

Number of Servings — 8-10

2 small or 1 king-size Coca-Cola
1-2 pkg. cherry gelatin
1 No. 2½ can crushed pineapple, drained
1 No. 2½ can Bing cherries, pitted, drained
Juice from canned cherries
1 lge. pkg. cream cheese, grated in slivers
1 c. pecans, chopped
1 small jar olives, chopped (opt.)
4 T. mayonnaise (opt.)

Bring to boil 1 cup Coca-Cola. Add gelatin; stir until dissolved. Add remainder of Coca-Cola and juice from cherries. Chill until thickened. Add pineapple and cherries to mixture. Add cheese, pecans and mayonnaise. Chill in separate molds. Garnish with mayonnaise or whole nuts.

This recipe submitted by the following teachers:

Mrs. Barbara B. Henson, Santa Rosa H. S.
Santa Rosa, Texas

Janice Ayres, Navasota H. S.
Navasota, Texas

Mrs. Iva Stringer, Shady Grove H. S.
Laurel, Mississippi

COKE-GELATIN SALAD

Number of Servings — 6

1 pkg. cherry gelatin
1 c. hot water
1 c. cold Coca-Cola
1 c. celery, finely chopped
½ c. nuts, chopped
1 c. canned pears, grapes, canned apples, or other light-colored fruit, diced

Dissolve gelatin in hot water; slowly add Coca-Cola. When slightly thickened add celery, nuts and fruit. Chill until firm. Cut in squares and serve with slivers of cheddar cheese.

Lenore Whitmore, Cotopaxi H. S.
Cotopaxi, Colorado

COCA-COLA SALAD

Number of Servings — 8

2 pkg. cherry gelatin
1 can pineapple chunk or crushed, drained
1 can tart pie cherries, drained
2 6-oz. Coca-Colas
1 8-oz. pkg. cream cheese bits (opt.)
1 c. nuts, chopped

Heat drained juices and use to dissolve gelatin. Cool; add Coca-Colas. Chill until thick. Stir in cheese, fruit and nuts. Very good served with meats.

This recipe submitted by the following teachers:

Mrs. Glenna Boland, Hector H. S.
Hector, Arkansas

Martha Kay Johnson, B. B. Comer
Sylacauga, Alabama

Mary W. Wilhoit, Ooltewah H. S.
Ooltewah, Tennessee

COKE SALAD

Number of Servings — 6-8

2 Coca-Colas
2 pkg. cherry gelatin
1 can Bing cherries
1 small can pineapple
¼ c. pecans, chopped

Heat Coca-Colas until hot; mix with gelatin stirring until completely dissolved. Slowly add the cherries, pineapples and pecans. Chill until firm.

This recipe submitted by the following teachers:

Mrs. Sam Crow, Hollis H. S.
Hollis, Oklahoma

Janice Spaeth, Big Spring H. S.
Big Spring, Texas

COCA-COLA SALAD

Number of Servings — 10-12

2 small pkg. red cherry gelatin
2 c. juice from cherries and pineapple
1-2 c. Bing cherries
1-2 c. chunk or crushed pineapple
1 6-oz. cream cheese or less, diced
1 c. nuts, chopped
2 small Coca-Colas
2 c. miniature marshmallows (opt.)

Heat fruit juices and stir in gelatin. Chill until thickened. Mix in cream cheese, cherries, pineapple, nuts and Coca-Colas. Stir until completely mixed. Chill until firm.

This recipe submitted by the following teachers:

Carolyn Mullins, Puryear H. S.
Puryear, Tennessee

Zona Beth Cates, Tempe Union H. S.
Tempe, Arizona

Mrs. W. C. Caldwell, Bienville H. S.
Bienville, Louisiana

Mrs. Ted Kirby, Kermit H. S.
Kermit, Texas

Caroll Treece, Cutter Morning Star
Hot Springs, Arkansas

Mrs. Barbara C. Tyner, Runnelstown
Hattiesburg, Mississippi

Mrs. Joyce Mauldin Redstone, Weir H. S.
Weir, Mississippi

Mrs. Ben Bolton Jr., Terrell H. S.
Dawson, Georgia

MARION CLUB SALAD

Number of Servings — 28

4 T. unflavored gelatin
1 pt. cherry juice
1 pt. pineapple juice
½ c. sugar
1 pt. mayonnaise
1 pt. whipped cream
1 No. 2 can pineapple, diced
1 No. 2½ can Royal Anne cherries, pitted
½ lb. almonds, slivered (opt.)
1 t. salt
½ pkg. miniature marshmallows

Soak gelatin in 1 cup fruit juice; dissolve over hot water. Add remaining fruit juice, sugar and salt. Chill. When slightly congealed, add cream, mayonnaise, cherries, pineapple, nuts and marshmallows if desired. Do not use fresh or frozen pineapple. Chill until firm.

This recipe submitted by the following teachers:

Mrs. Doris G. Kruger, Peotone H. S.
Peotone, Illinois

Evelyn Henry, Salina H. S.
Salina, Oklahoma

MOLDED CHERRY SALAD

Number of Servings — 8

1 No. 2 can dark sweet cherries, pitted and drained
1 pkg. raspberry gelatin
1 No. 1 can crushed pineapple
1 c. pecans, chopped
Cherry juice plus water to make 1 c. liquid

Heat cherry juice-water to boiling. Dissolve gelatin in hot mixture. Chill until partially set. Add remaining ingredients; stir well. Pour into ring mold. Chill until firm.

Mrs. Billye D. Freeland, Eastwood H. S.
El Paso, Texas

RED CHERRY SALAD

Number of Servings — 10

1 pkg. orange gelatin
1 c. boiling water
1 c. cherry juice
1 can red pie cherries, drained
¾ c. sugar
1 c. pecans
1 c. celery, finely cut

Dissolve gelatin in boiling water. Add cherry juice and sugar; cool. Add remaining ingredients. Chill until firm.

Mrs. Juanita Goss, Avoca H. S.
Avoca, Texas

SOUR CHERRY SALAD

Number of Servings — 6

1 can sour pie cherries
1 c. sugar (scant)
¼ t. salt
2 pkg. cherry gelatin
2 c. hot water
½ envelope unflavored gelatin
⅛ c. pineapple juice
1 c. American cheese, grated
1 small can crushed pineapple, drained
1 t. almond flavoring

Bring cherries, sugar and salt to a boil. Cool. Dissolve unflavored gelatin in pineapple juice. Dissolve cherry gelatin in hot water; add unflavored gelatin. When gelatin mixture begins to thicken, add cherry mixture, cheese, pineapple and almond flavoring. Mix well. Turn into a mold. Chill until firm.

Mrs. Juanita G. LaConte, Elbert County H. S.
Elberton, Georgia

GELATIN-GINGER ALE SALAD

Number of Servings — 8

2 c. ginger ale
1 No. 2 can crushed pineapple, drained
¾ c. sugar
½ c. orange juice
2 T. lemon juice
¾ c. pineapple juice
1 pkg. lemon gelatin
1 pkg. lime gelatin

Mix all ingredients except gelatins and pineapple; heat until sugar melts. Remove from heat and add gelatins stirring until dissolved. Add pineapple; mix well. Chill until firm. Serve with mayonnaise as a salad or with whipped cream as a dessert.

Mrs. Mary R. Gibbs, Richardson Junior H. S.
Richardson, Texas

GINGER ALE SALAD

Number of Servings — 8

2 pkgs. lemon gelatin
1 c. boiling water
¼ t. salt
1 pt. ginger ale
Juice of 1 lemon
1 c. celery, chopped
½ c. apples, chopped
½ c. pecans, chopped
2 T. crystallized ginger

Dissolve gelatin in boiling water; add salt. Cool. Add ginger ale and lemon juice. When mixture begins to thicken, add remaining ingredients. Chill until firm.

Mrs. Barbara Hickey, Hobson School
Hobson, Montana

GINGER ALE SALAD

Number of Servings — 6

3 T. unflavored gelatin
3 T. cold water
⅓ c. boiling water
2 t. sugar
½ t. salt (opt.)
¼ c. lemon juice
2 c. ginger ale
Few drops of food coloring
1 c. apples, chopped
1 c. celery, chopped
¾ c. crushed pineapple, drained
½ box crystallized ginger

Soak gelatin in cold water for 5 minutes; dissolve it in boiling water. Add sugar, salt, lemon juice and ginger ale; cool. Color mixture with food coloring. Add apples, pineapple, celery and ginger. Mold and chill.

Minta McAninch, Raton H. S.
Raton, New Mexico

GINGER ALE SALAD

Number of Servings — 8

1 9-oz. pkg. cream cheese
2 pkg. lime gelatin
1 qt. ginger ale
½ t. Worcestershire sauce
½ pt. whipped cream

Soften cheese over hot water; add gelatin and mix thoroughly. Heat ginger ale to boiling and slowly pour over cheese gelatin mixture. Beat until smooth. Chill until syrupy. Add Worcestershire sauce. Fold in whipped cream. Turn into a 2-quart mold or individual molds. Chill until firm.

Mrs. Marvel Hughes, Nooksack Valley H. S.
Nooksack, Washington

GINGER ALE SALAD

Number of Servings — 6

1 T. unflavored gelatin
2 T. cold water
½ c. boiling water
½-1 c. ginger ale
2 T. lemon juice
4 T. sugar
1 c. canned peaches or pears, sliced
1 c. orange sections
¼ c. fresh strawberries, sliced
¼ c. grapes, seeded and halved
½ c. crushed pineapple (opt.)

Soften gelatin in cold water; add boiling water and stir until dissolved. Add ginger ale, lemon juice and sugar. Cool. When mixture begins to thicken, fold in fruit. Pour into molds and chill until firm. Serve on salad greens with Sour Cream Dressing.

This recipe submitted by the following teachers:

Mrs. Adeline Scarborough, Sumter Senior H. S.
Sumter, South Carolina

Lynette Calcote Tuggle, North Forrest
Hattiesburg, Mississippi

GINGER ALE SALAD

1 pkg. lemon gelatin
1 c. boiling pineapple juice or water
¼ t. paprika
1 c. ginger ale
½ c. purple grapes
¾ c. crushed pineapple, drained
⅓ c. nuts, chopped

Dissolve gelatin in hot juice or water. Cool to lukewarm. Add remaining ingredients. Turn into a mold; chill until firm.

Carol Wilhorn, Nekoosa Public
Nekoosa, Wisconsin

GINGER ALE SALAD

Number of Servings — 6

1 pkg. lime gelatin
1 c. hot water
1 c. ginger ale
¼ c. nuts, chopped
¼ c. celery, chopped
1 c. sweetened peaches, drained or apples, finely chopped

Dissolve gelatin in hot water; add ginger ale. Chill until slightly thickened. Fold in remaining ingredients. Turn into molds and chill until firm.

Dressing:
½ c. sour cream
½ c. mayonnaise

Whip sour cream until thick; fold in mayonnaise.

This recipe submitted by the following teachers:

Vera C. Souter, Boerne H. S.
Boerne, Texas

Beatrice Campbell, Leland Consolidated School
Leland, Mississippi

Carolyn Nelson, Plains H. S.
Plains, Texas

GINGER-FRUIT SALAD

Number of Servings — 6

1 pkg. lemon gelatin
1 c. ginger ale
½ t. ground ginger
1½ c. mixed fruit, diced
1 c. hot water
1 3-oz. pkg. cream cheese
½ c. undiluted evaporated milk
½ c. nuts (opt.)

Dissolve gelatin in hot water. Stir in ginger ale. Mash cream cheese; add ginger and stir in milk. Add to gelatin mixture. Chill until mixture begins to thicken. Beat chilled mixture with egg beater for 1 minute or until fluffy. Fold in fruit and nuts. Pour into an oiled mold. Chill until firm.

Mrs. Rosemary K. Harwood, North Stanly H. S.
Albemarle, North Carolina

GRAPE SALAD

Number of Servings — 8

1 pkg. unflavored gelatin
¼ c. cold water
1 can crushed pineapple, drained
2 c. fruit juice and water
1 pkg. lemon gelatin
1½ c. seedless grapes, washed
1 pt. sour cream
1 c. almonds, shredded

Soak gelatin in cold water. Bring juice-water mixture to a boil and pour over lemon gelatin. Add soaked gelatin. Stir until dissolved. Cool. Add pineapple, grapes, sour cream and almonds. Place in refrigerator until set.

Irene H. Nelson, Alabama School for the Deaf
Talladega, Alabama

GRAPE-LIME MOLD

Number of Servings — 8

1 16-oz. can spiced, seedless grapes, drained and chilled
2 pkg. lime gelatin
2 c. hot water
1½ c. ice water
3 T. lime juice

Dissolve gelatin in hot water. Add ice water and lime juice. Chill until slightly congealed. Fold in grapes. Pour into a 5-cup ring mold. Chill until firm. Fill center of mold with red strawberries dusted with powdered sugar. Dress with whipped cream accented with mayonnaise.

Judith A. Balsam, Summerfield, Petersburg,
Petersburg, Michigan

GRAPE RING

Number of Servings — 12

2 pkg. grape gelatin
2 c. boiling water
1 6-oz. can concentrated frozen grape juice
1 No. 2 can crushed pineapple and juice
½ c. nuts, chopped

Dissolve gelatin in the boiling water. Stir in the frozen grape juice and the pineapple with its juice. Allow to jell slightly; add the nuts. Pour into ring mold and refrigerate until firm. Unmold and fill the center with cream filling.

CREAM FILLING:
1 c. whipped cream
½ c. pimento cheese spread
5 T. marshmallow creme

Add cheese and marshmallow creme to whipped cream and beat.

Eileen Miller, McCook Sr. H. S.
McCook, Nebraska

MOLDED GRAPE SUPREME

Number of Servings — 6

1 envelope unflavored gelatin
¼ c. cold water
1 c. boiling water
½ c. sugar
Dash of salt
1 6-oz. can frozen grape juice concentrate
3 T. lemon juice
¾ c. seedless grapes, halved
2 medium bananas, diced
¼ c. nuts, chopped

Sprinkle gelatin over cold water to soften. Add boiling water, sugar and salt; stir until dissolved. Stir in grape and lemon juice. Refrigerate until partially thickened. Fold in fruits and nuts. Pour into 1-quart mold. Refrigerate until firm.

Mrs. Beth Jones, Overton H. S.
Nashville, Tennessee

WHITE SALAD

Number of Servings — 10-12

1 T. unflavored gelatin
1 c. milk
4 egg yolks, well beaten
¾ lb. miniature marshmallows
Juice of 1 lemon
¾ lb. blanched almonds
1 lge. can diced pineapple, drained
1 lge. can pitted white cherries, drained and diced
1 pt. whipped cream

Dissolve gelatin in milk. Add egg yolks; scald mixture in top of double boiler. Cool. Fold in marshmallows, lemon juice, nuts, pineapple and cherries. Fold in whipped cream. Pour into well oiled mold or loaf pan. Refrigerate.

Mrs. Lucille Bradbury, Central H. S.
San Angelo, Texas

WHITE SALAD

Number of Servings — 10

3 eggs, well beaten
½ t. salt
3 T. vinegar
2 T. sugar
1 T. unflavored gelatin
2 T. cold water
1 small can crushed pineapple, drained
1 c. nuts, chopped
1 c. white grapes or cherries
12 marshmallows, quartered
½ pt. whipped cream
½ c. pineapple juice

Cook eggs, salt, sugar and vinegar in double boiler until thickened. Dissolve gelatin in cold water; add juice. Combine gelatin and cooked mixture. Cool. When mixture begins to set, add fruit, nuts and marshmallows. Fold in whipped cream. Refrigerate overnight.

DRESSING:

¼ c. sugar
1 T. flour
Juice of 1 orange
Juice of ½ lemon
¼ c. pineapple juice
½ c. whipped cream

Cook sugar, flour and orange juice until clear. Add lemon and pineapple juice. Cool. Just before serving fold in whipped cream.

Betty J. Cockrel, Livingston Community H. S.
Livingston, Illinois

SPICED GRAPE SALAD

Number of Servings — 6-8

1 No. 2 can spiced white grapes, drained
1 8-oz. can crushed pineapple, drained
1 T. unflavored gelatin
3 T. cold water
1 T. lemon juice
½ c. celery, chopped
¼ c. nuts

Heat syrup drained from fruit plus enough water to make 1¾ cups liquid. Soften gelatin in cold water and lemon juice. Combine gelatin with juice-water mixture. Chill until partially set. Add fruit, celery and nuts.

Lemon Dressing:

1 egg
1 T. lemon juice
1 c. sugar
1 T. butter
1 c. whipped cream

Cook egg, sugar, butter and lemon juice together until thick. Cool. Stir cooked mixture into whipped cream. Serve over spiced grape salad.

Marian Joe Wilson, Odessa H. S.
Odessa, Texas

CITRUS SALAD

Number of Servings — 12-15

1 pkg. lemon gelatin
1 pkg. orange gelatin
1 No. 303 can citrus salad fruit, undrained
1 No. 303 can grapefruit sections, undrained
1 c. crushed or chunk pineapple, undrained
2 c. boiling water

Dissolve gelatins in boiling water. Add citrus salad fruit and grapefruit sections. Add pineapple; stir well. Pour into large loaf pan. Chill until firm.

Nancy M. Riley, M & M H. S.
McConnelsville, Ohio

MOLDED GRAPEFRUIT SALAD

Number of Servings — 6

1 envelope unflavored gelatin
¼ c. cold water
½ c. hot water
½ c. sugar
Pinch of salt
1 c. unpared apples, diced
2½ c. grapefruit, undrained
½ c. walnuts, broken

Soften gelatin in cold water; Dissolve in hot water. Add sugar and salt. Cool. Add apples and grapefruit. Chill until partially set. Add nuts. Chill until firm.

Mrs. Sarah S. Steffey, Reynolds Area Joint Jr.-Sr. H. S.
Greenville, Pennsylvania

CITRUS MOLDED SALAD

Number of Servings — 6-8

1 3-oz. pkg. lemon gelatin
1 3-oz. pkg. lime gelatin
2 c. boiling water
1 No. 303 can grapefruit sections, undrained
1 8-oz. can mandarin orange sections, undrained
1 6½-oz. can crushed pineapple, undrained

Dissolve gelatin in boiling water. Add fruits. Chill until firm.

Mrs. Amy Day, Elizabeth-Forward Sr. H. S.
Elizabeth, Pennsylvania

GRAPEFRUIT SALAD

Number of Servings — 12

1 No. 2 can grapefruit, drained
1 No. 2 can Royal Anne cherries, pitted and drained
1 No. 2 can sliced pineapple, drained and cubed
2 envelopes unflavored gelatin
½ c. cold water
Juice of 1 lemon
Pinch of salt
1 c. almonds, slivered

Soften gelatin in cold water. Combine grapefruit, cherry and pineapple juices; bring to a boil. Remove from heat; add softened gelatin and lemon juice. Cool. Add remaining ingredients. Pour into molds and chill until firm.

Mrs. Ned R. Mitchell
The High School of Charleston
Charleston, South Carolina

MOLDED CITRUS SALAD WITH AVOCADO DRESSING

Number of Servings — 6-8

1 pkg. lime gelatin
½ c. boiling water
1½ c. ginger ale, chilled
1 1-lb. can grapefruit sections, well drained
1 11-oz. can Mandarin oranges, well drained

Dissolve gelatin in boiling water. Chill slightly. Add ginger ale; chill until partially set. Fold in grapefruit and oranges. Turn into a mold and chill until firm.

Avocado Dressing:
1 3-oz. pkg. cream cheese, softened
2 ripe avocados, peeled
1 T. lemon juice
1 t. onion, grated
¼ t. salt
3 T. cream

Mash avocados with lemon juice. Combine all ingredients and blend until smooth.

Gladys Crawford, McDaniel Junior H. S.
Denison, Texas

GRAPEFRUIT-CHERRY MOLD

Number of Servings — 6-8

1 No. 2 can Royal Anne cherries, drained
1 No. 2 can grapefruit sections, drained or equivalent amount of fresh grapefruit sections
¼ c. celery, sliced
1 avocado, sliced (opt.)
1 pkg. lemon gelatin
Cherry and grapefruit juice plus cold water to make 2 c. liquid
Cottage cheese

Heat 1 cup of juice to boiling. Add gelatin; stir to dissolve. Add remaining juice. Chill. Combine fruit and celery; place in slightly oiled ring mold. Use avocado slices for design if desired. Pour chilled gelatin mixture over fruit. Chill until firm. Fill center of ring with cottage cheese.

Mrs. Anne Ward Broman
Sidney Lanier Jr.-Sr. H. S.
Austin, Texas

GRAPEFRUIT-CHERRY SALAD

Number of Servings — 8

1 pkg. cherry gelatin
1 small can grapefruit sections, drained and cut into pieces
1 small can pitted cherries, drained and cut into pieces
Grapefruit and cherry juice plus water to make 2 c. liquid

Heat 1 cup of juice; dissolve gelatin in hot liquid. Add remaining juice-water mixture. Add fruit. Chill until firm.

Mrs. Eloise Bayer Hawkins, Walterboro Sr. H. S.
Walterboro, South Carolina

LEMON-CIDER SALAD

Number of Servings — 10

Juice of 1 lemon
1 8-oz. bottle Maraschino cherries, drained
1 small can crushed pineapple, drained
4 c. cider
6 cloves
2 sticks cinnamon
Juice from cherries and pineapple
2 pkg. lemon gelatin

Combine lemon juice, cherry and pineapple juice with cider. Add cloves and cinnamon; bring to a boil. Simmer gently for 10 minutes; pour over gelatin. Add pineapple and cherries. Chill overnight.

Mrs. Clova Bryson, Rochelle H. S.
Rochelle, Texas

LEMON-CREAM DELIGHT SALAD

Number of Servings — 12

1 pkg. lemon gelatin
1 c. hot water
1 3-oz. pkg. cream cheese
1 c. crushed pineapple, drained
½ c. celery, finely chopped
1 4-oz. bottle Maraschino Cherries, drained
Walnuts, chopped
¼ pt. whipped cream
Pineapple and cherry juice plus enough water to make 1 c. liquid

Combine gelatin and hot water; mix well. Add juice-water mixture; cool to lukewarm. Stir in cream cheese. Cool until partially congealed. Stir in all remaining ingredients except cream. Fold in whipped cream last. Congeal.

Florence Shaffer, Berwick Sr. H. S.
Berwick, Pennsylvania

LEMON-CRYSTAL SALAD

Number of Servings — 8-10

1 pkg. lemon gelatin
1 c. boiling water
⅔ c. pineapple juice
1 c. celery, diced
1 c. unpeeled apple, diced
1 c. miniature marshmallows
1 c. crushed pineapple
½ c. mayonnaise
1 c. whipped cream

Dissolve gelatin in boiling water; add pineapple juice. Chill until mixture starts to congeal. Add remaining ingredients. Pour into salad mold or bowl. Chill until firm.

This recipe submitted by the following teachers:

Mrs. Marianne Abramowski, Madison H. S.
Madison, Minnesota

Mrs. Mildred Williams, Cadott H. S.
Cadott, Wisconsin

LEMON DELIGHT

Number of Servings — 6

1 pkg. lemon gelatin
1 c. hot water
1 c. cold water
½ c. celery, diced
½ c. walnuts, broken
½ c. miniature marshmallows
1 c. crushed pineapple, drained

Dissolve lemon gelatin in hot water; add cold water. Chill for 1 hour. Stir in celery, pineapple, walnuts, marshmallows. Chill until firm.

Virginia Zaffke, Johnson, Central H. S.
Crookston, Minnesota

LEMON GELATIN SALAD

Number of Servings — 10-12

1 pkg. lemon gelatin
½ pt. whipped cream
1 small pkg. cream cheese
1 No. 1 can crushed pineapple
1 stalk celery, chopped
½ c. nuts, finely chopped

Prepare gelatin according to package directions. Chill until partially set. Combine remaining ingredients; add to gelatin. Chill until firm.

Judith L. Roush, M & M H. S.
McConnelsville, Ohio

LEMON CROWN SALAD

Number of Servings — 6

2 egg yolks
½ c. sugar
Juice of 1 lemon
1 c. boiling fruit cocktail juice
1 pkg. lemon gelatin
2 c. fruit cocktail, drained
1 c. whipped cream

Slowly cook egg yolks, sugar and lemon juice until thickened; stir occasionally. Cool. Dissolve gelatin in boiling fruit cocktail juice; let cool. Slowly blend gelatin into egg yolk mixture. Add fruit cocktail. Fold in whipped cream. Chill.

Mrs. Margaret Olson, Gaylord Public H. S.
Gaylord, Minnesota

LEMON-GINGER ALE SALAD

Number of Servings — 6

1 pkg. lemon gelatin
1 c. boiling water
1 c. ginger ale
12 lge. marshmallows, cut
2 pineapple slices, cut
1 c. whipped cream

Dissolve gelatin in hot water; cool. Add ginger ale. When mixture begins to thicken, add marshmallows and pineapple. Let set. Fold in whipped cream just before serving.

Rosalie Kilbourn, Neillsville H. S.
Neillsville, Wisconsin

LEMON-PUDDING SALAD

Number of Servings — 6

1 pkg. lemon pudding
1 small can pineapple, drained
3 bananas, sliced
½ pkg. miniature marshmallows
1 c. whipped cream

Cook pudding according to package directions; let cool. Add remaining ingredients. Chill for 2 hours.

Betty Johnson, Nashwauk-Keewatin Senior H. S.
Nashwauk, Minnesota

COLORADO DELIGHT SALAD

Number of Servings — 12

1 3-oz. pkg. cream cheese, broken
1 pkg. lime gelatin
1 c. boiling water
½ pt. whipped cream
1 c. pecans, chopped
2 c. fruit cocktail
15 marshmallows, diced

Combine cheese and gelatin. Gradually add hot water; stir until blended. Chill until nearly firm. Add fruit cocktail, nuts and marshmallows. Fold in cream and chill until firm.

This recipe submitted by the following teachers:

Marjorie De Sardi, Homer H. S.
Homer, Louisiana

Mrs. Rachel Dunsmore, Boyle County H. S.
Danville, Kentucky

CONGEALED FRUIT SALAD

Number of Servings — 8-10

1 pkg. lime gelatin
1 c. hot water
1 c. marshmallows
½-1 c. cottage cheese
⅓ c. nuts, chopped
2 t. lemon juice
1 small can crushed pineapple, drained
¼ c. sugar
½-1 c. whipped cream

Dissolve gelatin and marshmallows in hot water. refrigerate until mixture begins to thicken. Add remaining ingredients. Chill until firm.

Mrs. G. T. Lilly, Murray H. S.
Murray, Kentucky

CONGEALED LIME SALAD

Number of Servings — 8-10

1 pkg. lime gelatin
1 c. boiling water
1 envelope unflavored gelatin
½ c. cold water
1 small pkg. cream cheese, softened
½-1 c. pecans or walnuts, chopped
1 small can crushed pineapple
Pinch of salt

Dissolve lime gelatin in boiling water. Dissolve unflavored gelatin in cold water. Add to the lime gelatin. Chill until partially set. Cream the cream cheese; add nuts. Add cheese mixture and pineapple to the gelatin mixture. Chill.

This recipe submitted by the following teachers:

Jo Dunn, Arab H. S.
Arab, Alabama

Ruth Anne Girardat, Clarion-Limestone Jr. H. S.
Strattanville, Pennsylvania

CONGEALED LIME SALAD

Number of Servings — 12

2 pkg. lime gelatin
1 small can crushed pineapple, drained
2 pkg. cream cheese
1 c. pecans, broken
1½ pimentos, diced
2 c. whipped cream
Juice drained from pineapple plus enough water to make 2 pt. liquid

Heat pineapple juice-water mixture to boiling; add gelatin, stirring to dissolve. Gradually add hot gelatin mixture to cream cheese, mixing well. Refrigerate until mixture begins to congeal. Add pineapple, pimento and pecans. Fold in whipped cream. Chill until firm. Substitute ½ cup cherries for pimento if used as a dessert.

Mrs. Kathryn Patrick, Cummings Junior H. S.
Brownsville, Texas

EMERALD ISLE MOLDED SALAD

Number of Servings — 6

1 3-oz. pkg. lime gelatin
1 c. boiling water
1 9-oz. can crushed pineapple, drained
½-1 c. creamy cottage cheese
½ c. mayonnaise
½ c. whipped cream or whipped canned milk (opt.)
¼-1 c. nuts, chopped
Juice from pineapple
1-2 T. horseradish or less (opt.)

Dissolve gelatin in boiling water. Add pineapple juice. Chill until slightly thickened. Beat until frothy. Fold in remaining ingredients. Chill until firm.

This recipe submitted by the following teachers:

Jeanne Mackie, Milwaukie Senior H. S.
Milwaukie, Oregon

Mrs. Ione G. Stroud, El Paso H. S.
El Paso, Texas

Mrs. Margaret Swigart, Bainville H. S.
Bainville, Montana

Mrs. Margaret G. Wilson, Waynesboro Area H. S.
Waynesboro, Pennsylvania

EMERALD SALAD

Number of Servings — 6-8

1 pkg. lime gelatin
½ c. cottage cheese
½ c. Marashino cherries, sliced
½ c. walnuts, chopped
1 c. crushed pineapple
1 c. whipped cream
1 c. boiling water

Dissolve gelatin in boiling water; add cottage cheese. Chill until stightly thickened. Add remaining ingredients. Chill until firm.

Mrs. Betty Tasker, Rice Lake H. S.
Rice Lake, Wisconsin

GARNETT'S EMERALD GREEN SALAD

Number of Servings — 8-10

16 lge. marshmallows
1 c. sweet milk
1 pkg. lime gelatin
1 3½-oz. pkg. cream cheese
1 small can crushed pineapple
½ pt. whipped cream
1 c. pecans, finely chopped

Heat marshmallows and milk in double boiler until marshmallows are melted. Add gelatin. Set aside to cool. Beat cream cheese until light and fluffy. Add pineapple to the cream cheese. Combine cheese mixture with gelatin mixture. Fold in cream and pecans. Chill until firm.

Mrs. Rachel M. Pearce, Castleberry H. S.
Fort Worth, Texas

GREEN PARTY SALAD

Number of Servings — 12

¼ lb. marshmallows
1 c. milk
1 pkg. lime gelatin
2 3-oz. pkg. cream cheese
1 No. 2 can crushed pineapple, drained
1 c. whipped cream
⅔ c. mayonnaise
1 c. pecans, chopped (opt.)

Melt marshmallows in milk in top of a double boiler. Pour hot mixture over lime gelatin, stirring until dissolved. Stir in cream cheese. When cheese is dissolved add pineapple. Cool. Blend in whipped cream, mayonnaise and nuts if desired. Chill until firm.

This recipe submitted by the following teachers:

Merle S. Crocker, Union H. S.
Union, South Carolina

Mrs. George Sansom, Campbell H. S.
Smyrna, Georgia

Mrs. Ruth Womick Williams, Belmont H. S.
Belmont, North Carolina

Mrs. Dixie Dunn Ruby, Charles Town, Senior H. S.
Charles Town, West Virginia

Mrs. Jean F. Goodman, Robert E. Lee Jr. H. S.
Danville, Virginia

GREEN GAGE PLUM SALAD

Number of Servings — 8

1 No. 2½ can plums, drained
1 pkg. lime gelatin
1 c. hot water
1 c. plum juice
2 T. sugar
1 small pkg. cream cheese
¼ c. salad dressing
3 T. whipped cream
1 c. nuts

Dissolve gelatin in hot water; add sugar and plum juice. Cool until slightly congealed. Cream the cheese and salad dressing. Add cream and cheese mixture together. Pour over plums; add nuts. Pour into mold and chill for several hours.

Mrs. Ruth Kenner, Crowell H. S.
Crowell, Texas

GREEN MAGIC SALAD

Number of Servings — 4-6

1 pkg. lime gelatin
1 c. boiling water
½ lb. marshmallows
1 c. cold water
½ c. mayonnaise
1 4-oz. pkg. cream cheese
1 small can crushed pineapple
1 c. whipped cream

Dissolve gelatin in boiling water. Melt marshmallows in hot mixture over low heat. When marshmallows are dissolved add 1 cup cold water. Cream mayonnaise and cheese; add pineapple. Combine with gelatin mixture. Chill until nearly set. Fold in whipped cream. Chill until firm.

Annette Ducote, Raceland H. S.
Raceland, Louisiana

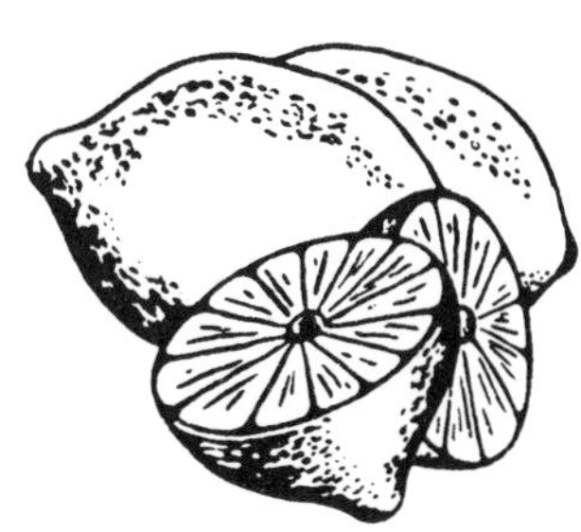

HEAVENLY SALAD

Number of Servings — 10-12

1 pkg. lime gelatin
2 c. boiling water
1 pkg. cream cheese, crumbled
18 lge. marshmallows, finely cut
1 T. vinegar (opt.)
1 No. 303 can pineapple tidbits
1 c. pecans, chopped
1 c. whipped cream

Dissolve gelatin in 1 cup boiling water; add cheese, marshmallows and remaining boiling water. Stir until gelatin is dissolved. Add vinegar. Chill until syrupy. Mix pineapple and pecans together. Fold in the whipped cream. Fold the whipped cream mixture into the gelatin mixture. Chill until firm.

This recipe submitted by the following teachers:

Addie Kellum, Chico H. S.
Chico, Texas

Georgia Robertson, Paradise School
Paradise, Texas

JOY SALAD

Number of Servings — 15-20

1 3-oz. pkg. lime gelatin
1 c. hot water
10 ice cubes
½ pt. whipped cream
1 8-oz. pkg. cream cheese
1 No. 2 can crushed pineapple
½ c. nuts, chopped

Dissolve gelatin in hot water. Add ice cubes; stir until mixture begins to thicken. Add cream cheese to whipped cream; whip. Fold fruit and nuts into the whipped cream mixture. Beat the gelatin for 3 minutes. Fold the whipped cream mixture into the gelatin. Refrigerate.

Mrs. Sharon Brittain, Britton Macon Area School
Britton, Michigan

LIME-CHEESE SALAD

Number of Servings — 8-10

1 pkg. lime gelatin
1 c. boiling water
2 c. miniature marshmallows
1 c. whipped cream or 1 pkg. dessert topping mix, whipped
Dash of salt
1 9-oz. can crushed pineapple
1 c. cottage cheese, drained

Dissolve gelatin in boiling water. Add marshmallows; stir until melted. Stir in salt and pineapple. Chill till slightly thickened. Fold in cottage cheese and cream. Let stand until firm.

Edna Mae Van Tuyl, Linn Rural H. S.
Linn, Kansas

LIME-COTTAGE CHEESE SALAD

Number of Servings — 8-10

1 pkg. lime gelatin
1 c. boiling water
1 T. lemon juice or dash of salt
1 c. crushed pineapple
½ c. cottage cheese
½ c. nuts, chopped
12 marshmallows, cut in eighths
1 c. whipped cream

Dissolve gelatin in boiling water; add marshmallows; stir until melted. Add lemon juice or salt and pineapple; cool until mixture begins to congeal. Add nuts and cottage cheese. Chill until almost set; fold in whipped cream. Chill until firm.

This recipe submitted by the following teachers:

Loretta Sawin, Dickinson County Community H. S.
Chapman, Kansas

Mrs. Sue T. Glovier, Old Fort H. S.
Old Fort, North Carolina

Lacquita Olson, Colman H. S.
Colman, South Dakota

LIME CHIFFON SALAD

Number of Servings — 6-8

1 box lime gelatin
1½ c. hot water
8 marshmallows
½ c. nuts, chopped
½ pt. whipped cream
1 small can crushed pineapple
1 small pkg. cream cheese
Mayonnaise

Dissolve lime gelatin and marshmallows in hot water. Stir until completely dissolved. Cool until almost set. Combine pineapple, nuts and whipped cream. Fold into gelatin mixture. Congeal until firm. Soften cream cheese with mayonnaise and use as dressing.

Mrs. Elizabeth C. Wilson, Greensboro H. S.
Greensboro, Alabama

LIME DELIGHT

Number of Servings — 8

1 small can crushed pineapple
4 T. water
1 pkg. lime gelatin
1 c. cottage cheese
½ c. pecans, chopped
½ pt. whipped cream

Heat pineapple and water. Add gelatin; stir until dissolved. Chill until mixture begins to thicken. Fold in remaining ingredients. Pour into an oiled mold. Chill until firm.

Betty L. Beaty, York Institute
Jamestown, Tennessee

LIME FRUIT SALAD

Number of Servings — 6-8

1 pkg. lime gelatin
¾ c. boiling water
1 3-oz. pkg. cream cheese
14 marshmallows
2 bananas (opt.)
½ c. crushed pineapple
½ c. evaporated milk
⅓ c. mayonnaise
1 t. lemon juice
½ c. pecans, chopped
½ c. pineapple juice

Combine gelatin, boiling water, cream cheese and marshmallows. Stir over low heat until gelatin is thoroughly dissolved. Cool. Add pineapple, evaporated milk, mayonnaise, lemon juice, pineapple juice, pecans and bananas. Refrigerate until firm.

Cecile Foxworth, Lealman Junior H. S.
St. Petersburg, Florida

LIME GELATIN DELIGHT

Number of Servings — 10-12

1 pkg. lime gelatin
12 marshmallows
1 c. cottage cheese
1 c. hot water
1 No. 2 can crushed pineapple
1 c. cream, whipped
1 c. nuts, chopped

Dissolve gelatin in hot water. Add marshmallows while mixture is hot. Cool until gelatin begins to congeal; whip. Fold in cottage cheese, pineapple, whipped cream and nuts. Chill until firm.

Mrs. Marilyn Breiding, Prospect H. S.
Mt. Prospect, Illinois

LIME GELATIN SALAD

Number of Servings — 9

1 box lime gelatin
1 c. boiling water
1 3-oz. pkg. cream cheese
Cream
½ c. crushed pineapple
¼ c. black walnuts, chopped
¼ c. Maraschino cherries, chopped

Dissolve gelatin in boiling water; cool until mixture is ready to set. Add cream cheese blended with enough cream to make 1 cup. Add pineapple, walnuts and cherries. Chill until firm.

Mary Ann DeVore, Fort Recovery H. S.
Fort Recovery, Ohio

LIME FRUIT SALAD

Number of Servings — 8

1 c. boiling water
1 pkg. lime gelatin
1 No. 2 can fruit cocktail, undrained
1 No. 2 can crushed pineapple, undrained
1 c. pecans, chopped
1 3-oz. pkg. cream cheese

Pour boiling water over gelatin; stir until dissolved. Blend the cream cheese, a small amount at a time, with the gelatin. Add fruit cocktail, pineapple and pecans. Pour into mold and chill until firm.

Joyce Duncan, Wm. Adams H. S.
Alice, Texas

LIME GELATIN SALAD

Number of Servings — 10

2 pkg. lime gelatin
2 c. hot water
1 can crushed pineapple
1 c. cottage cheese
1 c. pecans
1 can sweetened condensed milk

Dissolve gelatin in hot water. Combine remaining ingredients; add to gelatin. Chill until firm.

Dorothy B. Byrd, South Gwinnett H. S.
Snellville, Georgia

LIME DELIGHT

Number of Servings — 16

1 No. 2 can crushed pineapple, undrained
¼ oz. bottle red cherries, chopped
1 c. celery, chopped
1 c. nuts, chopped
1 envelope unflavored gelatin
1 lge. pkg. lime gelatin
1 lge. pkg. cream cheese
36 marshmallows, cut in small pieces
1 c. hot water
1 c. pineapple juice

Mix gelatins and hot water. Add to marshmallows and cream cheese. This will partially melt them. Add pineapple juice and remaining ingredients; stir. Pour into greased salad mold.

Mrs. Julia Quinn Powers, Gordon Military H. S.
Barnesville, Georgia

LIME GELATIN SALAD

Number of Servings — 12

1 pkg. lime gelatin
1 c. boiling water
1-2 c. miniature marshmallows
1 small can crushed pineapple, drain
½ c. pecans, chopped
1 c. cottage cheese
½ pt. whipped cream

Dissolve gelatin in boiling water; add marshmallows and stir until dissolved. Stir in pineapple, pecans and cottage cheese; cool. Fold in whipped cream. Chill until firm. Or, if desired, dissolve gelatin in boiling water; let set until firm. Cut firm gelatin into cubes; mix thoroughly with remaining ingredients. Chill.

This recipe submitted by the following teachers:

Ruth Conn, Cave-In-Rock, H. S.
Cave-In-Rock, Illinois

Judith Cary, Ramsey H. S.
Ramsey, Illinois

LIME GELATIN SALAD

Number of Servings — 8

1 pkg. lime gelatin
1 c. boiling water
1 small pkg. cream cheese
½ c. pineapple juice
½ c. cold water
⅓ c. pecans, chopped
6 Maraschino cherries, chopped
1 c. miniature marshmallows

Dissolve gelatin and cream cheese in hot water. Add pineapple juice and cold water. Chill until almost set. Whip gelatin; add remaining ingredient. Chill until firm.

Mrs. Janice Furnish, Henryville
Henryville, Indiana

LIME GELATIN SALAD

Number of Servings — 8

1 pkg. lime gelatin
1 c. boiling water
1 No. 306 can crushed pineapple
1 T. pimento, chopped
½ c. celery, finely cut
1 c. small curd cottage cheese
1 3-oz. pkg. cream cheese
1 T. mayonnaise
1 t. lemon juice
Dash of Paprika
⅓ c. nuts, chopped

Dissolve gelatin in boiling water; cool until partially set. Add pineapple, pimento, nuts, celery and cottage cheese. Chill until firm. Blend cream cheese, mayonnaise and lemon juice together; spread over gelatin mixture. Sprinkle with paprika.

Bettie Lou Graham, Jackson H. S.
Jackson, Ohio

LIME GELATIN MOLD

Number of Servings — 8-10

1 pkg. lime gelatin
1 3-oz. pkg. cream cheese
1 small can crushed pineapple
6 Maraschino cherries, quartered
½ c. pecans, finely chopped
1 c. hot water
½ c. cold water

Dissolve gelatin in hot water. Add cold water. Chill until the mixture begins to thicken. Cream the cheese thoroughly; beat into gelatin. Fold in pineapple, cherries and nuts. Let set until firm.

Maude Haynes, Lawhon School
Tupelo, Mississippi

LIME GELATIN SALAD

Number of Servings — 6-8

1 pkg. lime gelatin
1 c. boiling pineapple juice
2 T. powdered sugar
¼ c. mayonnaise
1 c. cottage cheese
1 c. crushed pineapple, drained
1 carrot, finely grated
½ c. ice water
1 T. lemon juice
½ c. dry milk

Dissolve gelatin in boiling juice. Chill until syrupy. Whip dry milk, lemon juice and ice water together. Add powdered sugar and mayonnaise; beat. Fold in gelatin; add remaining ingredients. Chill until firm.

Mrs. Martha J. O'Neil, Montgomery-Area
Joint School
Montgomery, Pennsylvania

LIME GELATIN SALAD

Number of Servings — 10

1 box of lime gelatin
1 c. of boiling water
⅛ c. sugar
1 small can crushed pineapple, drained
1 c. cottage cheese
Pinch of salt
Juice of ½ lemon
1 c. marshmallows
½ pt. whipped cream
½ c. pecans

Mix gelatin, sugar, salt, marshmallows and lemon juice in boiling water. Chill until thick. Add cottage cheese, whipped cream, pineapple and nuts.

Mrs. Sylvia B. Prater, Southeastern H. S.
Richmond Dale, Ohio

LIME GELATIN SALAD

Number of Servings — 8

1 pkg. lime gelatin
1 No. 2 can crushed pineapple, drained
1 c. cottage cheese
1 T. sugar
Pineapple juice
¼ t. salt
½ c. nuts, chopped
1 c. evaporated milk, whipped or whipped cream

Dissolve gelatin in hot pineapple juice. Let cool. Mix pineapple, cottage cheese, sugar, salt and nuts together; add gelatin. Fold in whipped cream. Refrigerate until firm.

Mrs. Stella C. Woody, Robertsville Junior H. S.
Oak Ridge, Tennessee

LIME-MARSHMALLOW SALAD

Number of Servings — 8

1 pkg. lime gelatin
1 c. boiling water
2 c. marshmallows
1 c. marshmallow cream
Pinch of salt
2 T. lemon juice
1 small can crushed pineapple
1 c. cottage cheese
1 c. whipped cream or whipped evaporated milk
⅛ c. pecans, chopped

Dissolve gelatin in boiling water. Add marshmallows and marshmallow cream; stir until dissolved. Add salt and lemon juice. Chill until syrupy. Add remaining ingredients. Refrigerate until serving time.

Mrs. Louise Forsythe, Butler County H. S.
Morgantown, Kentucky

LIME MIST MOLD

Number of Servings — 10

1 c. boiling water
1 pkg. lime gelatin
1 9-oz. can pineapple
1 c. cottage cheese
½ c. mayonnaise
Pineapple juice

Dissolve gelatin in boiling water; add pineapple juice. Chill until slightly thick. Beat until frothy. Fold in pineapple, cottage cheese and mayonnaise. Chill until firm.

Carolyn Corley, La Grange Senior H. S.
Lake Charles, Louisiana

LIME MIST SALAD

Number of Servings — 8

1 No. 2 can applesauce
1 pkg. lime gelatin
1 small bottle 7-Up
¼ lb. marshmallows, cut
1 3-oz. pkg. cream cheese, broken in small pieces
½ pt. whipped cream

Heat applesauce and dissolve gelatin in it. Add 7-Up; stir well. Refrigerate overnight. Combine marshmallows, cheese and cream. Chill overnight. The next day beat marshmallow mixture until thick. Spread over salad. Garnish with chopped nuts and cherries.

Sister M. Aloysius, PBVM O'Gorman H. S.
Sioux Falls, South Dakota

LIME SALAD

Number of Servings — 6-8

½ c. mayonnaise
½ c. cottage cheese
1 8-oz. pkg. cream cheese
1 pkg. lime gelatin
1 small can crushed pineapple, drained
1 c. pecans, chopped

Prepare gelatin according to package directions. Combine mayonnaise and both cheeses. Whip with a rotary beater or electric mixer. Add to gelatin mixture. Add pineapple and nuts. Chill until firm.

Mrs. Dorothy M. Andrews, Pine Forest H. S.
Fayetteville, North Carolina

LIME-APPLE SAUCE MOLDED SALAD

Number of Servings — 8

2 boxes lime gelatin
2 can applesauce
1 c. celery, finely cut
1 c. nuts, chopped
1 small jar red pimentos
2 small bottles 7-Up

Heat applesauce and dissolve gelatin in the applesauce. Let cool and add remaining ingredients. Pour in large mold or individual molds.

Hope Wood, Norman H. S.
Norman, Oklahoma

LIME-NUT SALAD

Number of Servings — 6

1 pkg. lime gelatin
1 c. boiling water
3 oz. pkg. cream cheese
1 small can crushed pineapple, drained
½ c. pecans
1 c. miniature marshmallows (opt.)
Pineapple juice

Dissolve gelatin and cream cheese in boiling water. Add pineapple, pecans and marshmallows if desired. Refrigerate until firm.

This recipe submitted by the following teachers:

Faye Owens, Jefferson County H. S.
Monticello, Florida

Mrs. Elsie H. Strole, Swansboro H. S.
Swansboro, North Carolina

Mae H. Smith, Rio Hondo H. S.
Rio Hondo, Texas

LIME PARTY SALAD

Number of Servings — 12-15

1 pkg. lime gelatin
1 pkg. lemon or lime gelatin
2 c. hot water
1 No. 2 can crushed pineapple, undrained
2 T. horseradish (opt.)
1 pt. cottage cheese
1 c. mayonnaise
1 small can condensed milk
¾-1 c. nuts, chopped

Dissolve gelatins in hot water. Cool until syrupy. Add remaining ingredients; chill until firm.

This recipe submitted by the following teachers:

Mrs. Louise A. Liddell, Whitehaven H. S.
Memphis, Tennessee

Vades Koonst, Sherman County H. S.
Moro, Oregon

Sandra Parrish, Miami Trace H. S.
Washington Courthouse, Ohio

LIME-PINEAPPLE SALAD

Number of Servings — 8

1 pkg. lime gelatin
2 c. hot water
20 lge. marshmallows
1 c. nuts, chopped
1 c. crushed pineapple
1 c. cottage cheese, drained or cheddar cheese, grated
1 c. whipped cream

Combine gelatin, water and marshmallows; stir until marshmallows are completely dissolved. Chill until thick. Add nuts, cheese, whipped cream and pineapple. Chill until firm.

Mrs. Blanche Hitson, Lordsburg H. S.
Lordsburg, New Mexico

LIME-PINEAPPLE SALAD

Number of Servings — 10-12

1 No. 2 can crushed pineapple
2 pkg. lime gelatin
1 3-oz. pkg. cream cheese
1 T. pineapple juice
½ c. pecans, chopped

Reserve 1 tablespoon pineapple juice from pineapple to use in topping. Bring pineapple and juice to boiling point. Stir in gelatin until dissolved. Chill until set. Soften cream cheese with pineapple juice. Add chopped pecans. Use to garnish salad.

Mrs. Phyllis Kennedy, Stedman H. S.
Stedman, North Carolina

LIME-PINEAPPLE SALAD

Number of Servings — 10-12

1 box lime gelatin
1 c. boiling water
1 4-oz. pkg. cream cheese
½ pt. half and half cream
½ c. pecans, chopped
1 small can crushed pineapple, drained
1 small can apricots

Dissolve gelatin in boiling water. Cool until thick. Mix cream cheese and cream. Add cream cheese mixture to gelatin; stir well. Add nuts and fruits. Chill until firm.

Nancy Roberson McClure, Ooltewah Junior H. S.
Ooltewah, Tennessee

LIME SALAD

Number of Servings — 8

1 pkg. lime gelatin
¾ c. boiling water
1 3-oz. pkg. cream cheese
15 lge. marshmallows
1 small can crushed pineapple
½ c. whipped cream or canned milk
⅓ c. mayonnaise
½ c. nuts, chopped
Dash of salt (opt.)

Stir gelatin in boiling water until dissolved. Add cream cheese and marshmallows; stir until dissolved. Cool slightly. Add pineapple, whipped cream, mayonnaise, salt and nuts. Fold together. Refrigerate until firm.

This recipe submitted by the following teachers:

Mrs. Nina B. Freas, Walnut Cove H. S.
Walnut Cove, North Carolina

Jean Suttle, Lathrop H. S.
Fairbanks, Alaska

Mrs. Arlene Willson, Fremont H. S.
Fremont, Michigan

LIME SALAD

Number of Servings — 6-8

1 pkg. lime gelatin
1 pkg. cream cheese, softened
1 can grated pineapple, drained
½ pt. whipped cream
12 marshmallows, diced
½ c. cut up pecans
¼ c. maraschino cherries

Prepare gelatin according to directions on package. Pineapple juice may be used as part of liquid. Chill until mixture reaches the consistency of jelly. Cream the cheese; add pineapple, whipped cream and marshmallows. Mix well. Pour gelatin over cheese mixture. Separate filling into islands; let set. Garnish with nuts and cherries.

Ada Campbell, Sterting Jr. H. S.
East Wenatchee, Washington

LIME SALAD

Number of Servings — 6-8

1 pkg. lime gelatin
1 c. boiling water
1 No. 2 can crushed pineapple, drained
½ c. celery, finely sliced
½ c. nuts, chopped
1 c. small curd cottage cheese, drained

Dissolve gelatin in boiling water. Cool until syrupy. Stir in remaining ingredients. Chill until firm.

Mrs. Olive Lambert, N. Potter Joint H. S.
Ulysses, Pennsylvania

LIME SALAD

Number of Servings — 10

1 pkg. lime gelatin
1 No. 2 can crushed pineapple, drained
1 c. boiling water
1 c. pineapple juice
1 4-oz. pkg. cream cheese
½ pt. whipped cream

Dissolve gelatin in hot water; add pineapple juice. Chill until quite firm. Whip until light and foamy. Mash cream cheese; fold into pineapple. Fold this mixture into whipped gelatin. Fold in the whipped cream. Chill until firm. Serve with a whipped cream-fruit dressing.

Mrs. Esther Nelson, Leuzinger, H. S.
Lawndale, California

LIME SALAD

Number of Servings — 8

1 pkg. lime gelatin
1 c. hot water
1 c. crushed pineapple
1 pkg. cream cheese, softened
1 c. whipped cream
½ c. nuts, chopped
1 pimento, chopped (opt.)

(Continued on next page)

Dissolve gelatin in hot water; cool. Add pineapple and let stand until mixture beings to thicken. Combine softened cream cheese and whipped cream; add to gelatin mixture. Add nuts and pimento. Pour into mold.

Mrs. Thora E. Stieler, Freeborn
Freeborn, Minnesota

LIME SUPREME SALAD

Number of Servings — 6-8

2 3-oz. pkg. lime gelatin
4 c. boiling water
¼ c. sliced Maraschino cherries
½ c. celery, chopped
½ c. nuts, chopped
1 small pkg. cream cheese, softened
2 T. mayonnaise

Dissolve gelatin in boiling water. Chill. Add all other ingredients; chill until partially set. Whip with fork until fluffy. Pour into molds and chill until firm.

Mildred Taylor Marsh, Colonial H. S.
Orlando, Florida

LIME SUPREME

Number of Servings — 8

2 pkg. lime gelatin
2 c. hot water
10-14 ice cubes
½ pt. whipped cream
1 6-oz. pkg. cream cheese, softened
1 small can crushed pineapple, drained
1 c. salad marshmallows
¼ to ⅓ c. nuts, broken

Dissolve gelatin in hot water; add ice cubes and stir until mixture is set. Slowly pour whipped cream into the cream cheese, beating until smooth. Carefully mix all ingredients into gelatin. Pour into mold and chill until firm.

Joyce M. Wingate, Marshall H. S.
Marshall, Michigan

LIME VELVET SALAD

Number of Servings — 10

1 pkg. lime gelatin
1 pkg. cream cheese
1 No. 1 can crushed pineapple, drained
1 c. celery, diced
1 c. whipped cream (opt.)
Juice from pineapple

Heat pineapple juice; add gelatin. Stir in cheese; stir until gelatin and cheese have dissolved. Mix pineapple and celery with whipped cream; add to gelatin. Chill until firm.

Mrs. Emily Watts Norriss, Maurice H. S.
Maurice, Louisiana

LIME WHIP SALAD

Number of Servings — 9

1 pkg. lime gelatin
1 c. boiling water
1 c. small curd cottage cheese, drained
1 c. whipped cream
1 c. crushed pineapple, drained
½ c. walnuts, chopped
¼ c. Maraschino cherries, chopped
½ c. celery, diced (opt.)
½ c. miniature marshmallows (opt.)

Dissolve gelatin in boiling water. When slightly cooled, add the cottage cheese. Cool until slightly congealed. Mix cream, pineapple, walnuts and cherries. Fold into the gelatin-cottage cheese mixture. Add celery and marshmallows if desired. Chill until firm.

Mrs. Marge Harouff, Pierce H. S.
Pierce, Nebraska

MOLDED LIME GELATIN SALAD

Number of Servings — 12

2 pkg. lime gelatin
2 c. boiling water
1 lge. can crushed pineapple
2 c. cottage cheese
1 c. celery, finely diced
2 T. pimento, chopped
1 c. black walnuts, chopped
1 pkg. cream cheese
1 t. lemon juice
1 T. mayonnaise

Dissolve gelatin in boiling water. Add pineapple, cottage cheese, celery, pimento and walnuts. Chill. Thoroughly mix cream cheese, lemon juice and mayonnaise together. Spread cream cheese mixture over gelatin mixture.

Mrs. David Farries, George Rogers Clark H. S.
Winchester, Kentucky

PARTY SALAD

Number of Servings — 10

1 pkg. lime gelatin
1 pkg. lemon gelatin
2 c. boiling water
1 can crushed pineapple
1 pkg. cream cheese
½ pt. whipped cream
16 marshmallows

Dissolve gelatins in boiling water. Add marshmallows and stir until dissolved. Let mixture stand until it starts to congeal. Soften cheese in a little of the gelatin mixture; stir until lumps are dissolved. Add to first mixture. Let gelatin stand until it starts to congeal. Add pineapple and whipped cream. Pour into mold; congeal.

Mabel Brill, Moorefield H. S.
Moorefield, West Virginia

MEN'S DELIGHT SALAD

Number of Servings — 6

1 pkg. lime gelatin
1 c. boiling water
1 c. miniature marshmallows
1 3-oz. pkg. cream cheese
½ c. cold water
½ c. pineapple juice
1 small can chopped, sliced pineapple, drained
1 c. celery, chopped
1 c. nuts, chopped

Dissolve gelatin in boiling water; add marshmallows and cream cheese. Mix well. Add cold water and pineapple juice. Add remaining ingredients. Mix well. Chill.

Louise O. Gurley, Sun Valley School
Monroe, North Carolina

MEN-LIKE-IT SALAD

Number of Servings — 6-8

1 pkg. lime gelatin
1¾ c. boiling water
1 small pkg. cream cheese
1 small can crushed pineapple
1 c. celery, diced
½ c. pecans, chopped
Salt to taste

Dissolve gelatin and salt in boiling water. Cool. Mash cream cheese; blend in pineapple, celery, and nuts. Add cheese mixture to gelatin. Pour into an oiled mold. Chill.

This recipe submitted by the following teachers:

Mrs. Evelyn Gose Owens, Valley H. S.
Albuquerque, New Mexico

Mrs. G. P. Grindstaff, Damascus H. S.
Damascus, Virginia

PARTY DELIGHT

Number of Servings — 6-8

1 envelope unflavored gelatin
¼ c. cold water
1 pkg. lime gelatin
1 No. 2 can fruit cocktail or crushed pineapple, drained
1 c. evaporated milk
Juice drained from fruit cocktail plus enough water to make 2 c. liquid
½-1 c. nuts, chopped
1 c. cottage cheese
½ c. mayonnaise (opt.)
1 T. sugar (opt.)

Dissolve unflavored gelatin in cold water. Dissolve lime gelatin in heated juice-water mixture. Add softened unflavored gelatin; mix well. When cold add remaining ingredients. Chill.

This recipe submitted by the following teachers:

Mrs. Emily Daniel, Talbot County School
Talbotton, Georgia

Mrs. Betty H. Foust, Bledsoe County H. S.
Pikeville, Tennessee

SEAFOAM SALAD

Number of Servings — 10

1 pkg. lime gelatin
1 medium can pineapple chunks, drained
1 lge. pkg. cream cheese
1 small jar Maraschino cherries, drained
1 c. nuts, chopped
½ pt. whipped cream

Heat fruit juice plus enough boiling water to make 1 cup liquid. Combine gelatin and hot juice-water mixture. Stir until gelatin is dissolved. Add softened cream cheese; pineapple, cherries and nuts. Cool, but do not let mixture set. Fold in whipped cream. Place in mold or 9x9 square pan. Congeal.

Mrs. Iris Hendershot, Southern Fulton Schools
Warfordsburg, Pennsylvania

FROSTED MELON SALAD

Number of Servings — 6-8

1 medium size cantaloupe, peeled
1 pkg. lime gelatin
1 ¾ c. water
1 6-oz. jar cream cheese, softened

Dissolve gelatin according to package directions. Using 1¾ cup water. Chill until slightly thickened. Cut open stem end so that just the edge of the seed pocket is exposed. Scoop out seeds and membrane. Fill pocket with the gelatin. Secure the lid with tooth picks. Place in refrigerator in up-right position until gelatin is firm. Before serving frost cream cheese. Slice crosswise.

Lois Moss, New Plymouth H. S.
New Plymouth, Idaho

CANTALOUPE PARTY SALAD

Number of Servings — 4

1 T. unflavored gelatin
¾ c. grapefruit juice
⅓ c. sugar
⅛ t. salt
½ c. cold water
⅓ c. lemon juice
2 c. cantaloupe balls
Cream cheese

Soften gelatin in ¼ cup grapefruit juice; melt over hot water. Add remaining grapefruit juice, salt, sugar, water and lemon juice. Chill until mixture begins to thicken. Fold in cantaloupe balls. Oil a 2½-cup mold and a 1½-cup mold; fill each with cantaloupe mixture. Refrigerate until firm. Just before serving unmold large salad onto serving plate. Center small salad on top of larger one. Garnish with cream cheese and serve with mayonnaise or fruit salad dressing.

Mrs. Gladys Evans, Central H. S.
Camp Point, Illinois

HONEYDEW SURPRISE

Number of Servings — 8

1 pkg. lime gelatin
1 c. boiling water
1 c. chunk pineapple, drained
1 c. Mandarin oranges
1 medium honeydew melon
Cottage cheese
Salad greens
French dressing

Dissolve gelatin in boiling water; cool until partially set. Add pineapple and oranges. Peel whole melon. Cut a slice from one end; remove seeds. Fill center with fruit gelatin. Wrap in cellophane; refrigerate until gelatin is firm. Slice; place on bed of greens. Spoon cottage cheese on top. Serve with French dressing.

Rhoda M. Grushkin, Union H. S.
Union, New Jersey

POLKA DOT MELON SALAD

Number of Servings — 4-6

1 pkg. lemon or lime gelatin
1 c. hot water
1 c. cold water
2 t. lemon juice
1 c. honeydew melon balls

Dissolve gelatin in hot water; add cold water and lemon juice. Let stand for 10 or 15 minutes. Chill until slightly thickened. Add melon balls. Pour into a 2½ cup melon mold. Chill until firm.

Mrs. Nelda Shows Turner, Jones Junior H. S.
Laurel, Mississippi

MINT-MELON SOUFFLE MOLD

Number of Servings — 4-6

1 c. hot water
1 3-oz. pkg. lemon gelatin
2 or 3 sprigs fresh mint
½ c. cold water
2 T. lemon juice
½ c. mayonnaise
½ t. salt
1 c. honeydew melon, diced
1 c. cantaloupe, diced
¼ c. toasted and blanched almonds, slivered

Pour hot water over gelatin and mint sprigs; stir until gelatin is dissolved. Let steep for 5 minutes. Remove mint; add cold water, lemon juice, mayonnaise and salt. Blend well with electric or rotary beater. Pour into refrigerator tray; quick-chill in freezer for 15 to 20 minutes or until firm about 1-inch from edge, but soft in center. Beat until fluffy. Fold in remaining ingredients. Chill until firm.

Mrs. Barbara Rawdon, Grants Sr. H. S.
Grants, New Mexico

RASPBERRY-MELON RING

Number of Servings — 5

3 10-oz. pkg. frozen raspberries, thawed and drained
2 envelopes unflavored gelatin
½ c. lemon juice
1¼ c. boiling water
¾ c. sugar
¼ t. salt
¾ c. melon balls
2 c. raspberry syrup

Soften gelatin in lemon juice; dissolve in boiling water. Stir in sugar, salt and raspberry syrup. Chill until partially set. Add melon balls and raspberries. Chill until firm.

Mrs. Ruth L. West, Butler County H. S.
Morgantown, Kentucky

WEDDING RING SALAD

Number of Servings — 8-10

1 6-oz. pkg. lemon gelatin
1 lb. Thompson green grapes
1 11-oz. can Mandarin orange sections, drained
1 c. pecans, chopped
2 medium cantaloupes, peeled
2 c. hot water
Juice drained from oranges plus enough water to make 1 c. liquid

Dissolve gelatin in hot water; cool. Add juice-water mixture. Cool until gelatin mixture thickens. Add grapes, oranges and nuts. Remove stem ends of cantaloupes; carefully scoop out seeds. Fill cavity with gelatin mixture. Let set 12 to 24 hours or until congealed. Slice cantaloupe into ½ to ¾-inch circles to serve.

Lorene Featherstone, Northside
Jackson, Tennessee

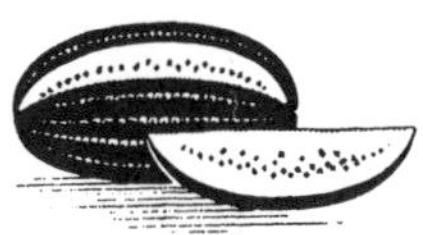

WATERMELON DELIGHT

Number of Servings — 5

1 pkg. cherry gelatin
2 c. watermelon balls

Prepare gelatin as directed on package, omitting ¼ cup of water. Refrigerate until mixture reaches the consistency of egg white. Add watermelon balls. Chill until firm.

Mrs. Marilee Steward, Ionia H. S.
Ionia, Michigan

ALASKAN FRUIT SALAD

Number of Servings — 6-8

1 6-oz. can frozen lemonade concentrate
1 envelope unflavored gelatin
1 pkg. regular vanilla pudding mix
1 c. whipped cream
¼ c. Maraschino cherries, halved
1 2-oz. can Mandarin orange segments, drained
1 8¾-oz. can crushed pineapple, drained
1 c. miniature marshmallows

Prepare lemonade according to directions. Soften gelatin in ¼ cup lemonade. Blend in pudding mix and an additional 1¾ cups lemonade. Cook and stir until mixture comes to full boil and thickens. Cool. Fold whipped cream into pudding mixture with remaining ingredients. Chill well.

Mrs. Sula Majure Sanford, Tchula H. S.
Tchula, Mississippi

ALASKAN FRUIT SALAD

Number of Servings — 8

1 6-oz. can frozen lemon or limeade concentrate
1 envelope unflavored gelatin
1 pkg. regular coconut pudding
1 c. whipped cream
½ c. blanched almonds, slivered
¼ c. Maraschino cherries, halved
1 11-oz. can Mandarin oranges, drained
1 8¾-oz. can crushed pineapple, drained
1 c. miniature marshmallows
Pineapple juice

Prepare lemonade according to directions, substituting pineapple juice as part of the liquid. Soften gelatin in ¼ cup lemonade. Blend pudding mix into remaining lemonade. Cook until mixture comes to a full rolling boil and thickens. Add gelatin; stir until it dissolves. Cool until mixture begins to set. Fold in whipped cream. Add remaining ingredients. Chill until firm.

Kathryn Schermerhorn, Butterfield-Odin H. S.
Butterfield, Minnesota

COLA-FRUIT SALAD

Number of Servings — 6

1 envelope unflavored gelatin
2 T. sugar
¼ c. water
Juice of 1 lemon
1½ c. cola or ginger ale
1½ c. mixed fruit, diced (fresh, frozen or canned)

Combine gelatin and sugar with water and lemon juice. Stir over low heat, until gelatin and sugar dissolves. Remove from heat. Add cola. Chill until slightly thickened. Fold in fruit. Chill until firm.

Mildred Few, Blue Ridge H. S.
Greer, South Carolina

CONGEALED FRUIT SALAD

Number of Servings — 6-8

1 envelope unflavored gelatin
¼ c. cold water
¼ c. cherry juice
1 c. mayonnaise or salad dressing
1 pkg. cream cheese
1 c. crushed pineapple
1 c. peaches, chopped
¼ c. Maraschino cherries, cut
1 c. whipped cream

Put gelatin into a measuring cup. Add cold water. Place measuring cup in a pan of hot water to dissolve gelatin. Blend mayonnaise, cream cheese, cherry juice and dissolved gelatin. Refrigerate 15 to 20 minutes or until mixture is partially congealed. Add pineapple, peaches and cherries. Fold in whipped cream. Pour into molds and congeal.

Mrs. Lorene H. English, Norcross H. S.
Norcross, Georgia

CONGEALED SALAD

Number of Servings — 8

1 pkg. lemon gelatin
1 No. 2 can fruit cocktail, drained
3 T. lemon juice
1 c. ginger ale
1 c. fresh or 1 10-oz. pkg. frozen strawberries, sliced
¾ c. fruit cocktail juice, heat
3 medium bananas, chopped
½ c. pecans, chopped

Mix heated fruit cocktail juice with lemon gelatin. Add lemon juice; cool. Add ginger ale and let set until mixture begins to congeal. Add remaining ingredients. Chill.

Mrs. Janie J. Gleason, Fairy Rural H. S.
Hico, Texas

CONGEALED LOW-CALORIE COMBINATION SALAD

Number of Servings — 12

1 pkg. orange gelatin
1 pkg. lemon gelatin
2 c. boiling water
8 ice cubes
2 t. lemon juice
1 medium red apple, chopped and peeled
1 medium red apple, chopped and unpeeled
1 No. 2 can crushed pineapple
1 c. celery, finely chopped
1 lge. carrot, grated
½ t. salt
Dash of red pepper
½ c. low calorie salad dressing or ¼ c. mayonnaise

Dissolve gelatins in boiling water; add ice cubes. Add remaining ingredients in order given. If mayonnaise is used, use ½ mayonnaise and ½ cottage cheese if desired.

Juliet W. Jenkins, Mayewood School
Sumter, South Carolina

EMERALD FRUIT SALAD WITH HONEY DRESSING

Number of Servings — 6-8

1 3-oz. pkg. lime gelatin
1½ c. boiling water
1½-2 c. pineapple chunks
1 orange, sectioned and cut
½ c. green grapes, cut and seeded
½ c. red grapes, cut and seeded
1 medium banana

Pour boiling water over gelatin; stir until dissolved. Cool. Add fruits. Chill until firm. Serve with honey dressing.

Honey Dressing:
½ c. mayonnaise
2-3 t. honey
2-3 t. lemon juice
Mace to taste

Mix all ingredients; blend well.

Mildred Williams, Lee H. S.
Columbus, Mississippi

FROSTY FRUIT SALAD

Number of Servings — 40

2 boxes lemon gelatin
1½ c. hot water
1 c. fruit juice
2 3-oz. pkg. cream cheese
2 lge. cans fruit cocktail, drained
1 lge. bottle Maraschino cherries, drained
1 c. mayonnaise
1 lge. pkg. marshmallows
1 lge. can evaporated milk, whipped

Dissolve gelatin in hot water; add fruit juice. Let stand until syrupy. Beat until light and foamy. Mash cream cheese with a fork; add mayonnaise, fruit and marshmallows. Fold cheese mixture into gelatin. Fold in whipped milk. Refrigerate until firm. Garnish with additional cherry slices.

Mrs. Helen Larabee, Central H. S.
Elizabeth City, North Carolina

FRUIT NECTAR SALAD

Number of Servings — 6

1 envelope unflavored gelatin
2 T. sugar
¼ t. salt
1 12-oz. can apricot nectar
½ c. water
8 whole cloves
1 T. lemon juice
1½ c. drained, diced mixed fruit fresh, canned or frozen (thawed)
1½ c. mixed fruits, drained

Thoroughly mix gelatin, sugar and salt together. Place in a small saucepan. Add apricot nectar, water and cloves. Place over low heat and stir until gelatin is dissolved. Simmer for 5 minutes. Remove from heat; strain to remove cloves. Add lemon juice. Chill until mixture reaches the consistency of unbeaten egg white. Fold in mixed fruit. Chill until firm.

This recipe submitted by the following teachers:

Agnes Sublette, Fulton County H. S.
Hickman, Kentucky

Mrs. Saralu C. Jenkins, Clarkston H. S.
Clarkston, Georgia

Melba M. Hackett, Henrico H. S.
Richmond, Virginia

FRUIT SALAD SQUARES

Number of Servings — 8

2 c. fruit cocktail, drained
¾ c. fruit cocktail juice
1 pkg. lemon gelatin
¼ c. lemon juice
1⅔ c. pineapple, drained
1 c. nuts, chopped
¼ c. Maraschino cherries
1 c. evaporated milk
2 T. lemon juice

Heat fruit cocktail juice to boiling. Add gelatin; stir until dissolved. Add lemon juice. Chill until mixture reaches the consistency of unbeaten egg whites. Add fruits and nuts. Chill milk until soft crystals form; whip until stiff. Fold milk into gelatin mixture. Chill until firm.

Mrs. Paul Cocke, Altavista H. S.
Altavista, Virginia

FRUIT SALAD

Number of Servings — 12-16

1 lge. can fruit cocktail, drained
1 can Royal Anne cherries, drained
1 med. can crushed pineapple, drained
1 med. can sliced peaches, drained
2 envelopes unflavored gelatin
1 lge. pkg. cream cheese
½ pt. whipped cream
½ c. mayonnaise
Juice from all fruit

Soak gelatin in ½ cup of the fruit juice. Heat in double boiler until gelatin melts. Add remaining juice. Blend cheese with mayonnaise. Add whipped cream. Fold cheese and remaining ingredients into gelatin. Chill until firm.

Ovelle Bennefield, Sylvania H. S.
Sylvania, Alabama

FRUITY SNOW SALAD

Number of Servings — 8-10

1 T. unflavored gelatin
2 T. lemon juice
1 3-oz. pkg. cream cheese, softened
½ c. pecans, chopped
½ c. sugar
1 c. whipped cream
¼ c. mayonnaise or salad dressing
1 No. 2½ can fruit cocktail, drained

Soften gelatin in lemon juice; dissolve over hot water. Blend cream cheese and mayonnaise together. Stir in gelatin, fruit cocktail and pecans. Gradually add sugar to whipped cream; fold into fruit mixture. Chill until firm.

Mrs. Katherine H. Ross, Dudley Hughes H. S.
Macon, Georgia

GRANDMA BOLEY'S FRUIT SALAD

Number of Servings — 6-8

2 Delicious apples, cored and diced
2 bananas, sliced
1 No. 2 can sliced pineapple, drained and cut up
Juice of 1 orange
Juice of 1 lemon
¾ c. sugar
2 T. minute tapioca
Pinch of salt
Whipped cream (opt.)
Chopped walnuts (opt.)

Combine juice drained from pineapple, lemon and orange juice, sugar and salt; blend well. Cook over medium heat. When mixture begins to boil, slowly sprinkle in tapioca, stirring until mixture thickens and tapioca is transparent. Cool. Combine apples and pineapple; add cooled dressing. Add bananas just before serving. Serve on lettuce as a salad. For a dessert, top with whipped cream and walnuts.

Mrs. Barbara Rosell Walker, Anaheim, H. S.
Anaheim, California

GEL-FRUIT SALAD

Number of Servings — 6

1 envelope unflavored gelatin
2 T. sugar
¼ c. water
Juice of 1 lemon
1½ c. ginger ale
1 apple, diced
½ c. fresh strawberries, diced
1 banana, diced
1 11-oz. can Mandarin orange segments, diced

Mix gelatin and sugar in a saucepan. Add water and lemon juice. Stir constantly over low heat until gelatin and sugar dissolves. Remove from heat. Add ginger ale. Chill until mixture reaches the consistency of unbeaten egg white. Fold in fruits. Chill until firm.

Mrs. Anona Moore, Alvin Junior H. S.
Alvin, Texas

GOLDEN FRUIT MOLD

Number of Servings — 6

1 pkg. lemon gelatin
1 c. cold water
1 c. hot water
2 oranges, diced
1 banana, sliced
1 red apple, diced
½ c. celery, thinly sliced
¼ c. pecans

Dissolve gelatin in hot water; add cold water. Chill until slightly thickened. Add fruit, celery and nuts. Chill until firm.

Jane Frudy, Tahlequah Junior H. S.
Tahlequah, Oklahoma

MARTHA'S SALAD

Number of Servings — 12

1 pkg. cream cheese
1 box lime gelatin
1 c. boiling water
¾ c. mayonnaise
1 envelope unflavored gelatin
¼ c. cold water
1 c. fruit juice
1 No. 2 can fruit cocktail, drained
1 No. 2 can pineapple chunks, drained
1 small jar Maraschino cherries, drained
1 c. pecan halves

Soak gelatin in cold water. Blend lime gelatin and cream cheese; add boiling water and stir until dissolved. Add softened unflavored gelatin, mayonnaise and fruit juice. Add fruit and nuts. Chill until firm.

Alma Barnes, North Junior H. S.
Johnson City, Tennessee

LIME-FRUIT MOLD

Number of Servings — 6

1 pkg. lime gelatin
1½ c. fruit juice or water
⅔ c. evaporated milk
1 c. fruit, drained and cut up
½ c. nuts, chopped

Dissolve gelatin in fruit juice. Pour into a 1½-quart bowl. Chill until firm. Beat with an electric mixer on low speed until gelatin is broken into small pieces. Beat in evaporated milk. Continue beating at high speed until mixture fills the bowl. Fold in fruits and nuts.

Mrs. Glenn Hodges, Cobb Memorial
Ruffin, North Carolina

MADALINE'S SALAD

Number of Servings — 8

1 envelope unflavored gelatin
1 pkg. cream cheese
⅔ c. whipped cream
¼ c. mayonnaise
1 can fruit cocktail, drained
½ c. nuts, chopped
½ c. sugar
2 T. lemon juice

Dissolve gelatin in a small amount of cold water. Bring sugar and juice of fruit cocktail to a boil. Add gelatin to hot syrup. Add lemon juice. Let cool. Mix cream cheese, mayonnaise and whipped cream; add to gelatin mixture. Add fruit and nuts.

Mrs. James W. Irwin, Tatum H. S.
Tatum, Texas

MOLDED FRUIT SALAD

Number of Servings — 4-6

1 c. grapefruit, cut in pieces
1 c. oranges, cut in pieces, undrained
1 c. apples, unpeeled and cubed
1½ T. unflavored gelatin
¼ c. cold water
½ c. sugar
½ c. boiling water
2 T. lemon juice
⅓ c. pecans, broken in small pieces

Soak gelatin in cold water for 5 minutes; dissolve sugar and gelatin in boiling water. Combine remaining ingredients; add to gelatin mixture. Cool. Pour into a mold that has been rinsed with cold water. Chill until firm.

This recipe submitted by the following teachers:

Jean Garceau, Harvey H. S.
Harvey, North Dakota

Mrs. Jean Foreman, Eureka Springs H. S.
Eureka Springs, Arkansas

HARVEST FRUIT SALAD

Number of Servings — 8-10

1 pkg. lime gelatin
¾ c. hot water
1 c. cottage cheese
1½ c. canned fruit cocktail, drained
½ c. nuts, chopped
½ c. apples, unpeeled and chopped
¼ c. lemon juice
1 c. evaporated milk, undiluted

Dissolve gelatin in hot water. Cool slightly. Add remaining ingredients. Mix well. Chill until firm.

Emma Lois Stephens, Elm City School
Elm City, North Carolina

PARTY SALAD

Number of Servings — 12

1 T. gelatin
¼ c. lemon juice
½ c. boiling water
¼ c. sugar
⅛ t. salt
½ c. mayonnaise
¾ c. evaporated milk
1 c. yellow cheese, grated
1 c. pineapple cubes
1 c. almonds, slivered
1 c. fruit cocktail, drained
1 can Queen Anne cherries

Soften gelatin in lemon juice; add sugar, salt and boiling water. Stir until gelatin is dissolved. Let cool. Whip milk until very stiff. Fold or beat in mayonnaise; add gelatin mixture. Stir in remaining ingredients.

Minnie Brier, McMinnville City H. S.
McMinnville, Tennessee

PERFECTION FRUIT SALAD

Number of Servings — 10

1 pkg. strawberry gelatin
1 c. boiling water
1 3-oz. pkg. cream cheese
1½ c. pineapple, drained
½ c. cherries, diced
2 T. mayonnaise
1 c. whipped cream
½ c. nuts
2 T. sugar

Dissolve gelatin in water; let cool. Soften cream cheese with a small amount of whipped cream; add remaining cream. Mix all remaining ingredients together; add to cream cheese mixture. Add cheese mixture to gelatin. Chill until firm.

Mrs. Mamie Goettee, Wade Hampton H. S.
Hampton, South Carolina

MOLDED FRUIT SALAD

Number of Servings — 8

1 pkg. lime gelatin
1 c. hot water
1 6-oz. can evaporated milk
1 17-oz. can fruit cocktail
1 c. miniature marshmallows
½ c. pecans, chopped

Dissolve gelatin in hot water. Let cool. Whip milk until stiff. Fold fruit, marshmallows, nuts and gelatin into the whipped milk. Pour into a greased mold. Chill until firm.

Helene Arnold, Franklin County H. S.
Frankfort, Kentucky

TROPICAL TRIUMPH

Number of Servings — 15

2 T. unflavored gelatin
½ c. cold water
1 No. 2½ can fruitcocktail, drained and cut up
½ c. lemon juice
1 8-oz. bottle ginger ale
1 No. 2 can sliced pineapple
1 11-oz. can Mandarin oranges, drained
1 8½-oz. can white grapes
Few grains of salt
2 c. juice from fruits

Sprinkle gelatin on water; let stand for 5 minutes. Bring fruit juice to boil; add gelatin; stir until gelatin is dissolved. Cool. Add lemon juice, salt and ginger ale. Chill until syrupy. Add fruit-cocktail, pineapple, oranges and grapes. Chill until firm.

Mrs. Evelyn E. Tompkins, Shelby Public
Shelby, Michigan

A CONGEALED FRUIT SALAD

Number of Servings — 8

1 8½-oz. small can crushed pineapple, undrained
1 11-oz. can Mandarin orange sections, undrained
1 pkg. orange gelatin
1 c. boiling water

Dissolve gelatin in boiling water; cool. Add pineapple and orange sections. Chill until firm.

Mrs. Margaret A. Scruggs
Alabama Institute for Deaf and Blind
Talladega, Alabama

CHERRY-ORANGE SALAD

Number of Servings — 16

2 boxes lemon gelatin
1 c. crushed pineapple, drained
1 c. cherries
1 c. frozen orange juice
2 pkg. cream cheese or ⅔ c. cottage cheese
½ c. nuts
2 t. salad dressing
20 miniature marshmallows
½ c. whipped cream

Mix gelatin with half of the water called for on package. Cool. Add all remaining ingredients except whipped cream. Fold in cream. Chill until firm.

Mrs. Cleota Ballery, Franklin County H. S.
Frankfort, Kentucky

CREAMY ORANGE SALAD

Number of Servings — 6

1 pkg. orange gelatin
1 c. hot water
1 pkg. cream cheese
¼ c. orange juice
2 T. lemon juice
1 T. grated orange rind
2 oranges, sectioned or ½ c. Mandarin oranges

Dissolve gelatin in hot water. Gradually add cream cheese, blending until smooth. Add juices. Chill until slightly thickened. Add orange sections and rind. Pour into molds and chill until firm.

This recipe submitted by the following teachers:

Dorothy S. McGoogan, St. Pauls H. S.
St. Pauls, North Carolina

Geneva Franklin, Powderly H. S.
Powderly, Texas

FRUIT SALAD

Number of Servings — 15-20

2 pkg. orange gelatin
2 c. boiling water
2 c. fruit juice
1 lge. can apricots, drained
1 lge. can chunk pineapple, drained
¾ c. miniature marshmallows
½ c. sugar
2 T. butter
3 T. flour
1 egg
1 c. whipped cream

Dissolve gelatin in boiling water—add 1 cup fruit juice. Let set until partially thickened. Add apricots, pineapple and marshmallows. Chill until firm. Combine sugar, butter, flour, remaining fruit juice, and egg; cook until thick. Cool. Fold in whipped cream. Spread cream mixture over gelatin.

Irma D. Bonebreak, Central H. S.
Martinsburg, Pennsylvania

FLUFFY ORANGE-PINEAPPLE SALAD

Number of Servings — 6-8

1 pkg. orange gelatin
1 c. whipped cream
1 9-oz. can crushed pineapple, drained
½ c. pecans
1 c. hot water
½ c. cold water

Dissolve gelatin in hot water; Add cold water. Chill until partially set. Beat with rotary or electric mixer until light and fluffy. Fold in cream, pineapple and nuts. Chill until firm.

Shirley Hensley, Cub Run
Cub Run, Kentucky

GELATIN MOLD

Number of Servings — 12

16 lge. marshmallows
1 c. milk
1 pkg. orange gelatin
2 3-oz. pkg. cream cheese
1 No. 2 can crushed pineapple, undrained
2 cans Mandarin oranges, drained
½ pt. whipped cream
½ c. mayonniase
½ c. nuts

Melt marshmallows in milk. Add gelatin; stir until dissolved. Blend in cream cheese. Add pineapple and oranges. Cool for 1 hour. Blend in remaining ingredients. Chill until firm.

Margaret Konesky, Starbuck H. S.
Starbuck, Minnesota

GELATIN SALAD

Number of Servings — 15

2 pkg. orange gelatin
2 c. boiling water
1 c. miniature marshmallows
½ c. sugar
2 T. flour
1 lge. can apricot halves, drained
1 lge. can pineapple tid-bits, drained and finely cut
1 c. juice from apricots and pineapple
½ pt. whipped cream
1 egg

Dissolve gelatin in boiling .water; add fruit juices. Chill until partially set. Add apricots, pineapple and marshmallows; chill until firm. Combine sugar, flour and egg. Cook until thick; cool. Add whipped cream. Spread over gelatin mixture.

Martha Smith, Washington College Academy
Washington College, Tennessee

FRUIT SALAD

Number of Servings — 10-12

2 pkg. orange tapioca pudding
3 c. milk
1 c. whipped cream
2 cans Mandarin oranges, drained
1 can crushed pineapple, drained
1 can fruit cocktail, drained
1 pkg. small marshmallows
2 or 3 bananas (opt.)

Cook tapioca pudding and milk as directed on package. Cool. Add fruits. Fold in whipped cream and marshmallows. Chill.

Hazel R. Freeman, West Valley H. S.
Yakima, Washington

HAWAIIAN DELIGHT

Number of Servings — 8

1 pkg. orange gelatin
¾ c. hot water
1 can orange concentrate
1 box dessert topping mix
1 can Mandarin oranges, halved
1 small can crushed pineapple, undrained
½ c. miniature marshmallows
½ box coconut

Dissolve gelatin in hot water; add orange concentrate. Chill until almost set. Prepare dessert topping mix according to package directions; fold into gelatin mixture. Fold in remaining ingredients.

Mrs. Doris Slack, White Pegen H. S.
White Pegen, Michigan

MANDARIN ORANGE SALAD

Number of Servings — 15

1 pkg. orange gelatin
1½ c. boiling water
1 can frozen orange juice
1 small can crushed pineapple, drained
1 small can Mandarin oranges, drained
2 bananas
2 c. miniature marshmallows
½ c. sugar
1 egg, beaten
1 T. flour
1 c. whipped cream
¼ c. cheese, grated
Juice from pineapple and oranges

Dissolve gelatin in boiling water; add orange juice, pineapple, oranges, bananas and marshmallows. Combine sugar, egg, flour and juice from pineapple and oranges. Cook juice-flour mixture over low heat until thick; add to gelatin mixture. Stir until marshmallows are melted. Let cool. Fold in whipped cream; top with cheese. Chill until firm.

Julia G. Williams, Washington College Academy
Washington College, Tennessee

MANDARIN FRUIT MOLD

Number of Servings — 9

1 lge. box lemon gelatin
1½ c. boiling water
8 ice cubes
1 small can frozen orange juice
1 can Mandarin oranges, drained
1 c. celery, diced
1 c. pineapple tid-bits, drained
½ pt. whipped cream
2 T. sugar

Dissolve gelatin in boiling water. Add ice cubes and orange juice; stir till thickened. Stir in oranges, pineapple and celery. Sweeten whipped cream with sugar; fold into gelatin mixture. Chill until firm.

Joy L. Ward, Oakdale Joint Union H. S.
Oakdale, California

MANDARIN ORANGE-AVOCADO SALAD

Number of Servings — 8

1 pkg. lemon gelatin
1 c. hot water
2 T. sugar
⅔ c. cold water
1 t. vinegar
1 can Mandarin oranges, drained
1 avocado, diced
1 T. pimento, diced
1 t. lemon rind, grated
1 t. orange rind, grated

Dissolve gelatin in boiling water; add cold water, sugar and vinegar. Chill until syrupy. Add remaining ingredients. Chill until firm.

Mrs. Alma Martin, St. Maries H. S.
St. Maries, Idaho

MANDARIN ORANGE SALAD

Number of Servings — 8

2 pkg. lemon gelatin
1 c. boiling water
1 c. cold water
1 12-oz. can frozen orange juice, undiluted
1 T. lemon juice
2 8-oz. cans Mandarin oranges, drained
1 c. sour cream
½ c. mayonnaise
1 T. sugar
½ c. crushed pineapple, drained
1 banana, mashed

Dissolve gelatin in boiling water; add cold water and orange juice. Let set until mixture begins to congeal. Add oranges and lemon juice. Pour into an oiled mold. Chill. Combine remaining ingredients in order given. Chill. Spread over gelatin mixture.

Mrs. Adele Charlson, Deimar H. S.
San Jose, California

MANDARIN ORANGE MOLD

Number of Servings — 12-14

2 pkg. orange gelatin
3½ c. boiling water
1 No. 2 can crushed pineapple
2 cans Mandarin oranges, drained
1 small can concentrated frozen orange juice, undiluted

Combine gelatin, boiling water and orange juice; stir until gelatin dissolves. Add pineapple and oranges. Pour into a ring mold. Chill until firm.

Mrs. Fran Pratt, Wm. Adams H. S.
Alice, Texas

MANDARIN ORANGE SALAD

Number of Servings — 8

1 box orange gelatin
1 pkg. dessert topping
1 can Mandarin oranges, drained

Prepare gelatin according to package directions. Let set until thick. Add half of the oranges. Beat at high speed on mixer until well mixed. Prepare dessert topping mix according to package directions; add remaining oranges. Chill.

Louise Adon Hall, Mulvane H. S.
Mulvane, Kansas

MOLDED ORANGE SALAD

Number of Servings — 14-16

2 pkg. orange gelatin
1 small can frozen orange juice
2 cans Mandarin oranges, drained
1 No. 2 can crushed pineapple, drained
1 c. boiling water
3 orange juice cans cold water

Dissolve gelatin in boiling water. Cool until partially congealed. Mix frozen orange juice with cold water. Add juice, oranges and pineapple to gelatin; Mix well. Pour into molds and chill until firm.

Arlene H. Oettmeier, Big Rapids H. S.
Big Rapids, Michigan

MANDARIN ORANGE SALAD

Number of Servings — 10

1 pkg. peach gelatin
1 can Mandarin orange sections, drained
1 can water chestnuts, thinly sliced
1 heaping c. miniature marshmallows
2 c. juice from Mandarin oranges and frozen orange juice

Heat orange juice; add gelatin and stir until dissolved. Let cool until thickened. Add remaining ingredients. Chill until firm.

Mrs. Eugene S. Turner, Lexington H. S.
Lexington, Tennessee

MANDARIN ORANGE SALAD

Number of Servings — 6

2 pkg. orange or lemon gelatin
2 c. orange juice
1 c. hot water
1 small can crushed pineapple
Juice of 1 lemon
1 lemon rind, grated
2 cans Mandarin oranges

Dissolve gelatin in hot water; let cool. Add orange juice; cool until mixture reaches the consistency of unbeaten egg white. Add remaining ingredients. Chill.

Carolyn J. Dennis, Kate Duncan Smith School
Grant, Alabama

MANDARIN ORANGE SALAD

Number of Servings — 8

1 pkg. orange gelatin
1 c. boiling water
1 can frozen orange juice
½ c. cold water
1 can Mandarin oranges, drained
2 bananas, sliced

Dissolve gelatin in hot water; add frozen orange juice and cold water. Chill. Add Mandarin oranges and bananas. Chill until firm.

This recipe submitted by the following teachers:

Mrs. Zella Weidenbach, Parkston H. S.
Parkston, South Dakota

Hazel E. Schaad, Fulton H. S.
Fulton, Illinois

MANDARIN SALAD

Number of Servings — 6

1 pkg. orange gelatin
1 c. boiling water
1 6-oz. can orange juice concentrate
¾ orange juice can cold water
2 T. lemon juice
1 9-oz. can crushed pineapple, undrained
1 11-oz. can Mandarin oranges, drained

Dissolve gelatin in boiling water. Add orange concentrate, water, lemon juice and pineapple. Let stand until mixture begins to thicken. Add oranges. Chill until firm.

Beverly Anne Edwards, Newnan H. S.
Newnan, Georgia

MANDARIN SALAD

Number of Servings — 6

1 c. juice from oranges and pineapple
1½ t. vinegar
¼ t. salt
½ pkg. orange gelatin
1 c. pineapple tid-bits, drained
1 c. Mandarin orange slices, drained
1½ c. miniature marshmallows
½ pt. sour cream
½ c. coconut

Heat fruit juice, vinegar and salt together. Add gelatin; stir until dissolved. Chill until partially set. Fold in remaining ingredients. Chill until firm.

Marjanna Norton, Piner Junior H. S.
Sherman, Texas

MOLDED FRUIT SALAD

Number of Servings — 8

2 pkg. orange gelatin
1 c. cold water
2 c. fruit cocktail
1 c. crushed pineapple
1 c. sugar
1 c. whipped cream
½ c. cheese, grated

Mix fruit cocktail, pineapple and sugar together; heat to boiling point. Mix gelatin and water together; pour over hot mixture. Let set until partially congealed. Fold in whipped cream and cheese. Chill.

Voncile Owens, Sonora Union H. S.
Sonora, California

MOLDED MANDARIN ORANGE SALAD

Number of Servings — 10-12

2 pkg. lemon gelatin
1 c. boiling water
1 c. cold water
1 12-oz. can frozen orange juice
2 11-oz. cans Mandarin oranges, drained

Dissolve gelatin in boiling water; add cold water and frozen orange juice. Mix thoroughly. Add oranges. Pour in ring mold; refrigerate until set.

DRESSING:
1 pt. whipped cream
2 bananas, diced
½ pt. mayonnaise
1 small can crushed pineapple, drained

Prepare dressing just before serving. Mix all ingredients together and put in center of salad. Decorate with Maraschino cherries and mint if desired.

Mrs. Jean Otterson, S. L. O. Jr. H. S.
San Luis Obispo, California

MOLDED MANDARIN ORANGE SALAD

Number of Servings — 8-10

2 pkg. orange gelatin
2 c. hot water
1 12-oz. can frozen orange juice
2 small cans Mandarin oranges, undrained

Dissolve gelatin in hot water. Add orange juice. Let set until partially congealed. Add oranges. Mix well. Chill until firm.

La Donna Snyder, South Central H. S.
Greenwich, Ohio

ORANGE BUFFET SALAD

Number of Servings — 6

2 T. unflavored gelatin
¼ c. lemon juice
¾ c. boiling water
1½ t. liquid sugar substitute
¼ t. salt
1½ c. orange juice
⅓ c. sour cream
1 c. orange sections

Soften gelatin in lemon juice; dissolve it in boiling water. Add sugar substitute, salt, orange juice and sour cream; stir until well blended. Chill until mixture begins to thicken; fold in orange sections. Pour into mold; chill until set.

Sally Rhoads Parks, Audubon H. S.
Audubon, New Jersey

ORANGE COCA-COLA SALAD

Number of Servings — 8-10

2 3-oz. pkg. cream cheese
2 pkg. orange gelatin
4 small Coca-Colas
1 c. nuts, chopped

Cream together the cheese, gelatin and ½ bottle Coca-Cola. Using a blender or beater. Heat the remaining 3½ Coca-Colas to boiling. Combine with cheese and gelatin mixture. Add nuts. Pour into a greased mold. Chill until firm.

Marjorie W. Browning, Pensacola H. S.
Pensacola, Florida

ORANGE-COCONUT SALAD

Number of Servings — 12

2 c. boiling water
1 6-oz. pkg. orange gelatin
1½ c. cheese, grated
1 c. pecans or walnuts
⅓ c. sugar
2 c. crushed pineapple
1 c. whipped cream
1 pkg. coconut

Dissolve sugar and gelatin in boiling water; stir in cheese and pineapple. Let stand until almost stiff. Add whipped cream, ½ cup coconut and nuts. Sprinkle remaining coconut over top.

Kay Ragan, Covina H. S.
Covina, California

ORANGE-DATE SALAD

Number of Servings — 6-8

1 pkg. orange gelatin
1 c. hot water
1 c. orange juice
4-6 fresh oranges, peeled, trimmed and cut up
½-1 c. dates, pitted and sliced
½-1 c. pecan halves
1 fresh avocado
Mayonnaise

Dissolve gelatin in hot water; add orange juice. Pour into a flat glass container; add oranges, dates and nuts. Mix well. Chill until firm. Mash avocado with enough mayonnaise to make a creamy mixture; season to taste. Spoon into mound over salad.

Helen Harbour Nix, Pomona H. S.
Pomona, California

ORANGE-DATE SALAD

Number of Servings — 4-6

1 pkg. orange gelatin
1 c. hot water
1 8-oz. pkg. cream cheese
½ c. orange juice
2 T. lemon juice
1 c. orange sections
1 c. dates, chopped

Dissolve gelatin in hot water; gradually add cream cheese. Blend until smooth. Add orange and lemon juice. Chill until slightly thickened. Add orange sections and dates. Chill until firm.

Mrs. Roy E. Skinner, Wingo H. S.
Wingo, Kentucky

ORANGE DELIGHT

Number of Servings — 12

1 6-oz. pkg. orange gelatin
2 c. fruit juice and water
1 can Mandarin oranges, drained
1 small can crushed pineapple, drained
1 c. seedless green grapes
1 c. flaked coconut
1 c. miniature marshmallows
1 c. sour cream

Heat fruit juice to boiling point; add gelatin. Stir until dissolved. Chill until mixture begins to thicken. Mix remaining ingredients; blend well. Fold into the gelatin mixture. Chill for several hours.

Mrs. Byrle Daugherty, Bessemer H. S.
Bessemer, Alabama

ORANGE DELIGHT

Number of Servings — 6

1 box orange gelatin
1 c. hot water
1 small pkg. cream cheese
½ c. cold water
1 can Mandarin orange sections, undrained
½ c. pecans, chopped

Dissolve gelatin in hot water. Add cream cheese; mix thoroughly. Add cold water. Add orange sections and pecans. Chill.

Mrs. R. Watson Durham, Patrick Henry H. S.
Ashland, Virginia

ORANGE DELIGHT

Number of Servings — 12

1 pkg. orange gelatin
24 lge. marshmallows
1 c. hoop cheese, grated
1 c. crushed pineapple, drained
1 c. pineapple juice
1 c. boiling water
½ pt. whipped cream

Pour hot water over gelatin and marshmallows. Let marshmallows melt. Cool. Add remaining ingredients, folding in whipped cream last.

Evelyn H. Ford, South Cobb H. S.
Austell, Georgia

ORANGE GELATIN SALAD

Number of Servings — 8-10

2 envelopes unflavored gelatin
1 c. cold water
1 c. boiling water
⅔ c. sugar
⅛ t. salt
½ c. lemon juice
1 c. orange juice
1 c. orange sections

Sprinkle gelatin on cold water to soften. Add sugar, salt and boiling water. Stir until dissolved. If necessary, place container over boiling water to dissolve the gelatin. Add orange and lemon juice; stir. Chill until partially set; add orange sections. Chill until firm.

Evelyn M. Crippen, John L. Foust Junior H. S.
Owensboro, Kentucky

ORANGE-GINGER ALE RING

Number of Servings — 6-8

2 envelopes unflavored gelatin
½ c. lemon juice
½ c. granulated sugar
½ t. salt
1¼ c. orange juice
2 c. ginger ale
2 c. orange sections
⅔ c. walnuts or pecans, chopped
Orange slices
Cottage cheese

Sprinkle gelatin over lemon juice to soften; stir over hot water until dissolved. Combine sugar, salt, orange juice and ginger ale; add to gelatin. Refrigerate; stir often until mixture reaches the consistency of unbeaten egg white. Fold in nuts and orange sections. Pour into a 1½-quart ring mold. Chill until firm. Unmold. Fill center with cottage cheese. Garnish with orange slices.

Mrs. Elaine S. Washburn, Mayville, H. S.
Mayville, Wisconsin

ORANGE GLOW SALAD

1 c. orange juice, heated
1 pkg. orange gelatin
1 c. buttermilk, room temperature
1 c. Mandarin orange sections

Dissolve gelatin in hot orange juice; cool to room temperature. Add buttermilk and oranges. Chill.

DRESSING:
1 8-oz. pkg. cream cheese, softened
¼ c. orange juice
1 T. orange peel, shredded
Dash of salt
½ c. whipped cream
Yellow food coloring (opt.)

Beat the cheese. Add orange juice, peel and salt. Beat until mixture is light and fluffy. Add a few drops of food coloring if desired. Fold in whipped cream. Serve with salad.

Mildred F. Frederickson, Blooming Prairie H. S.
Blooming Prairie, Minnesota

ORANGE MOLDED SALAD

Number of Servings — 8

1 pkg. orange gelatin
1 c. boiling water
16 marshmallows, quartered
1 c. fresh orange juice, heated
1 c. crushed pineapple
1 c. bananas, sliced
¼ c. Maraschino cherries, quartered
1 c. sugar
¼ c. lemon juice
⅓ c. orange juice
¼ c. pineapple juice
2 eggs, beaten
1 c. whipped cream

Dissolve gelatin in boiling water. Melt marshmallow in heated orange juice; add to the gelatin mixture. Chill until mixture begins to set; add pineapple, bananas and cherries. Mix lightly. Chill until firm. Combine sugar, lemon juice, orange juice and eggs. Cook until thickened; cool. Fold in whipped cream; serve with gelatin mixture.

Mrs. Dorothy Nelson, Bonneville H. S.
Idaho Falls, Idaho

ORANGE-PEACH SALAD

Number of Servings — 4-6

1 pkg. orange gelatin
1 c. boiling water
⅔ c. pineapple juice
4 fresh peaches, peeled and diced
1 c. pineapple, drained and diced
½ c. seedless green grapes

Dissolve gelatin in boiling water; add pineapple juice. Refrigerate until mixture begins to thicken. Fold in remaining ingredients. Cover with Saran wrap; chill.

Dorothy G. Scothorn, Kennedy Community School
Kennedy, Minnesota

ORANGE-PINEAPPLE SALAD

Number of Servings — 12

2 pkg. orange gelatin
1 c. boiling water
1 6-oz. can frozen orange juice
1 c. pineapple tid-bits, drained
1 c. orange sections, diced
Pineapple juice plus enough water to make 2 c. liquid.

Dissolve gelatin in boiling water. Add orange juice. Mix well. Add pineapple juice-water mixture. Let set until partially thickened. Add pineapple and orange. Chill until firm.

Mrs. Paul Blake, Walnut Township Schools
New Ross, Indiana

ORANGE-PINEAPPLE SALAD

Number of Servings — 10-12

1 pkg. orange or pineapple-orange gelatin
1 c. hot pineapple juice or water
1 c. cheese, grated
1 c. carrots, grated
1 small can crushed pineapple
1 lge can evaporated milk
½ c. nuts, chopped

Dissolve gelatin in hot juice or water. Add cheese, carrots, pineapple, milk and nuts. Mix well. Chill several hours or overnight.

Ruby Jo Chancey, Hale County H. S.
Moundville, Alabama

ORANGE-PINEAPPLE SALAD

Number of Servings — 8

1 c. crushed pineapple, drained
3 oranges, sectioned and drained
1 3-oz. pkg. cream cheese
1 pkg. lemon gelatin
½ c. boiling water
½ c. evaporated milk
½ c. pecans, chopped
Juice drained from oranges and pineapple plus enough water to make ¾ c. liquid

Dissolve gelatin in boiling water. Set aside to cool. Gradually add milk to cream cheese; whip with a fork until smooth. Add to gelatin. Add juice-water mixture; mix thoroughly. Add fruits and nuts. Pour into mold and chill until firm.

Mrs. Adele K. Lytle, Fort Mill H. S.
Fort Mill, South Carolina

ORANGE-PINEAPPLE SALAD

Number of Servings — 10

2 boxes orange gelatin
3½ c. boiling water
1 No. 303 can crushed pineapple undrained
1 can Mandarin oranges, drained
Miniature marshmallows
1 pkg. dessert topping mix
1 c. Longhorn cheese, grated

Dissolve gelatin in boiling water; let cool. Add pineapple and oranges. Cover with marshmallows. Chill 2 or 3 hours. Whip dessert topping mix; spread over gelatin mixture. Sprinkle with cheese. Chill for 12 hours.

Marie B. King, Ligonier Valley School District
Ligonier, Pennsylvania

ORANGE-PINEAPPLE SALAD

Number of Servings — 8

1 2-lb. can crushed pineapple, drained
1 pkg. orange gelatin
2 T. lemon juice
¼ t. salt
1 13-oz. can cold evaporated milk
½ c. celery, chopped
½ c. nuts, chopped
1 t. orange food coloring
1½ c. pineapple juice and water

Heat pineapple juice and water; add gelatin. Stir until gelatin is dissolved. Add lemon juice and salt. Chill until mixture begins to thicken. Stir in milk, celery, pineapple, nuts, and food coloring; mix thoroughly. Chill until firm.

Mrs. Elizabeth K. Stewart, New Boston H. S.
New Boston, New Hampshire

ORANGE POSIES

Number of Servings — 5

1¾ c. orange juice
1 envelope unflavored gelatin
¼ c. sugar
⅛ t. salt
5 orange slices
5 Maraschino cherries

Place ¾ cup orange juice in saucepan. Add gelatin, sugar and salt. Set aside for 2 minutes or until gelatin has taken up part of liquid. Stir over low heat until gelatin and sugar are dissolved. Combine with remaining orange juice. Place orange slices in round individual molds. Pour gelatin mixture over orange slices. Chill until set. unmold onto lettuce leaves and place a cherry in center of salad.

Mrs. Nadine Elder, Union H. S.
Warsaw, Ohio

ORANGE SALAD

2 boxes orange gelatin
¾ c. hot water
1 small can crushed pineapple
1 lge. can condensed milk
1 c. medium sharp American grated cheese

Pour hot water over gelatin. Stir well; cool until slightly thick. Add pineapple, milk and cheese. Chill until firm.

Mrs. Theresa H. Smith, Northside H. S.
Warner Robins, Georgia

PINEAPPLE-MANDARIN ORANGE SALAD

Number of Servings — 8-10

1 pkg. lemon gelatin
2/3 c. hot water
1 pkg. unflavored gelatin
1/4 c. cold water
1 1/2 cans frozen orange juice, diluted with 1 can water
1/4 c. sugar
1 can Mandarin oranges, undrained
1 can crushed pineapple

Dissolve lemon gelatin in hot water. Soften unflavored gelatin in cold water; add to lemon gelatin. Add orange juice and sugar; stir until dissolved. Add oranges and pineapple. Chill until firm.

Alice M. Ford, Central H. S.
Cheyenne, Wyoming

ORANGE SPICE

Number of Servings — 4

1 pkg. orange gelatin
1 c. boiling water
1 stick cinnamon bark
8 whole cloves
8 ice cubes
1 can Mandarin orange sections
1/2 c. nuts, chopped

Combine gelatin and boiling water; stir until gelatin is dissolved. Add cinnamon and cloves; simmer for 10 minutes. Remove spices; add ice cubes. Stir until mixture is chilled. Remove any remaining bits of ice. Add oranges and nuts. Chill until firm.

Donna M. Dickenson, Penns Valley Area Joint School
Spring Mills, Pennsylvania

SPICED MANDARIN ORANGE MOLDS

Number of Servings — 12

Juice drained from oranges plus enough water to make 3 c. liquid
1/3 t. salt
2 3-inch pieces stick cinnamon
1/2 t. whole cloves
1 c. + 2 T. orange gelatin
3 c. cold water
1/4 c. lemon juice
2 c. Mandarin oranges, drained
Whipped cream
Chopped walnuts

Combine juice-water mixture, salt, cinnamon and cloves. Cover and simmer for 10 minutes. Remove from heat and let stand, covered, for 10 minutes to steep. Strain. Dissolve gelatin in hot spice mixture. Stir in cold water and lemon juice. Chill until partially set. Fold in oranges. Pour into individual molds. Chill until firm. Garnish with whipped cream and walnuts.

Betty Berk, Othello H. S.
Othello, Washington

ORANGE SALAD

Number of Servings — 6

1 pkg. orange gelatin
1 1/2 c. orange juice
1 pkg. cream cheese
Chopped nuts
1 1/2 c. hot water

Dissolve gelatin in boiling water. Add orange juice. Chill until mixture begins to thicken. Form cream cheese into 2 or 3 small balls; roll in chopped nuts. Add to gelatin. Chill until firm. Serve with pineapple, grapefruit and Mandarin oranges if desired.

Mrs. Evelyn Pence, Jr. H. S.
Bend, Oregon

SPICED ORANGE GELATIN MOLD

Number of Servings — 12

1 3/4 c. juice from oranges and water
1 11-oz. can Mandarin orange sections, drained
1/4 t. salt
1 6" stick cinnamon
1/2 t. whole cloves
2 3-oz. pkg. orange gelatin
2 c. cold water
3 T. lemon juice
1/2 c. walnuts

Combine juice-water mixture, salt, cinnamon and cloves. Cover and simmer for 10 minutes. Remove from heat; steep for 10 minutes. Strain. Dissolve gelatin in juice—water mixture. Add cold water and lemon juice. Chill until partially set. Add oranges and nuts. Chill until firm.

Frances Schneider, Menomonie, H. S.
Menomonie, Wisconsin

SPRINGTIME SALAD

Number of Servings — 6-8

1 pkg. lime or orange gelatin
1 c. hot water
1 No. 2 can grapefruit-orange sections, undrained

Dissolve gelatin in hot water. Add grapefruit—orange sections. Chill until firm. Serve with fruit salad dressing.

FRUIT SALAD DRESSING:

1/2 c. pineapple juice
1 T. flour
3 T. sugar
1 egg, beaten
1 1/2 T. lemon juice
1/4 pt. whipped cream

Mix flour and sugar in double boiler; add egg. Combine pineapple and lemon juice; add to egg mixture. Cook over hot water until thick. Cool. Fold in whipped cream just before serving.

Mrs. Rita Simones, Lakeville H. S.
Lakeville, Minnesota

ORANGE-PRUNE SALAD

Number of Servings — 8

2 pkg. lemon gelatin
20 cooked prunes, drained and chopped
1 c. prune juice
3 c. water
Grated rind of 1 orange
2 T. orange juice
½ c. whipped cream
⅓ c. celery, diced
1 banana, mashed

Dissolve gelatin in prune juice and water. Let set until partially congealed. Add prunes, orange juice and rind. Pour into a ring mold. Chill until firm. Combine whipped cream, celery and banana. Fill center of gelatin ring with cream mixture.

Jean Passino, Keewatin-Nashwauk Junior H. S.
Keewatin, Minnesota

QUEEN ANNE SALAD

Number of Servings — 12

2 eggs, beaten or 4 egg yolks
4 T. vinegar
4 T. sugar
2 T. butter
2 boxes orange gelatin
2 c. boiling fruit juice
2 c. marshmallows, chopped
1 c. whipped cream
1 No. 2 can Queen Anne cherries, drained
1 No. 2 can crushed pineapple, drained
3 oranges, sectioned and diced

Combine eggs, vinegar, sugar and butter; cook until thick. Dissolve gelatin in boiling fruit juice. Add marshmallows; stir until dissolved. Combine cherries, pineapple and oranges. Combine all mixtures. Fold in whipped cream. Chill until firm.

Mrs. Frances Jones, Littlefield H. S.
Littlefield, Texas

TEN-MINUTE ORANGE-FRUIT SALAD

Number of Servings — 12

2 pkg. orange gelatin
1 pkg. lemon gelatin
1½ c. boiling water
2 6-oz. cans frozen orange juice concentrate
1 8-oz. can crushed pineapple, undrained
3 bananas, mashed
2 c. whipped cream

Dissolve gelatin in boiling water. Add frozen orange juice, stirring constantly. Add pineapple. Cool mixture until it molds from spoon. Fold in bananas and whipped cream. Chill until firm.

Ruth E. Kuhn, La Conner H. S.
La Conner, Washington

CHIFFON FRUIT SALAD

Number of Servings — 6

1½ c. peach slices, well drained
1 c. hot peach syrup and water
1 pkg. lemon gelatin
½ c. celery, diced
½ c. nuts chopped
⅓ c. mayonnaise
2½ c. whipped instant dry milk

Line bottom of mold with 8 peach slices for garnish. Chop remaining peach slices. Mix peach syrup—water mixture with gelatin; stir until dissolved. Chill until thickened. Add celery, peaches, nuts, and mayonnaise to gelatin. Mix in whipped instant milk. Spoon into salad mold. Chill until firm.

Mrs. Margaret Fagot, Fairbury-Cropsey H. S.
Fairbury, Illinois

MOLDED PEACH SALAD

Number of Servings — 9

1 pkg. raspberry gelatin
2 t. vinegar
9 canned peach halves
Softened cream cheese
Chopped nuts
Crisp lettuce leaves

Prepare gelatin according to package directions. Add vinegar; chill until slightly thickened. Arrange the peach halves, cut side up, in an 8-inch square pan. Pour the thickened gelatin over the peaches. Chill until firm. Cut in 9 squares. Serve on crisp lettuce. Place softened cream cheese in the center of each peach half; sprinkle with chopped nuts.

Mrs. Nola Y. Coates, Union City Area H. S.
Union City, Pennsylvania

PEACH-ALMOND GLOW

Number of Servings — 6

1 pkg. orange gelatin
1 c. hot water
1 No. 2 can peaches, diced and drained
½ t. almond extract
1 c. peach juice and water

Dissolve gelatin in hot water; add peach juice—water mixture and almond extract. Chill until slightly thickened. Fold in peaches. Chill until firm.

Claudia Bringle, University H. S.
Iowa City, Iowa

CONGEAL SPICED PEACH SALAD

Number of Servings — 6

1 pkg. orange gelatin
1 c. boiling water
1 c. peach juice
6-8 spiced peaches, seeded
1 4-oz. pkg. cream cheese, softened
3-4 T. celery, diced

Dissolve gelatin in boiling water. Add peach juice. Let cool until slightly thicken. Mix cream cheese and celery together. Form into balls; place cheese balls in peach where seed was. Arrange in ring mold. Pour gelatin over peaches. Chill until firm.

Lilliam Y. Wynn, Sicily Island H. S.
Sicily Island, Louisiana

PEACH ASPIC

Number of Servings — 8

1 pkg. peach gelatin
1 No. 2½ can peaches, drained
2 c. peach juice and water
1 3-oz. pkg. cream cheese, softened
1 T. mayonnaise

Reserve 1 peach half; dice remaining peaches. Heat peach juice to boiling; pour over gelatin. Stir until gelatin is dissolved. Chill until thick. Add peaches. Chill until firm. Blend cream cheese and mayonnaise together. Mash the reserved peach half; stir it into the cheese mixture. Serve the cheese mixture with gelatin mixture.

Frances Rast, Byars-Hall H. S.
Covington, Tennessee

PEACH-CHEESE BALL SALAD

Number of Servings — 6

1 pkg. raspberry gelatin
1 c. hot water
1 c. peach juice and water
2 t. tarragon vinegar
6 peach halves
1 3-oz. pkg. cream cheese
Nuts, chopped
Salad greens
French dressing or mayonnaise

Dissolve gelatin in hot water; add peach juice-water mixture and vinegar. Pour a thin layer into a loaf pan; chill until firm. Chill remaining gelatin until partially thickened. Arrange peach halves, with rounded side up, on firm gelatin. Pour partially thickened gelatin over peaches; chill until firm. Roll cheese in 6 balls; roll in nuts. Unmold gelatin, cut in squares an place on salad greens. Place a cheese ball on the center of each peach half. Serve with French dressing or mayonnaise.

Mrs. Marion Montgomery, McKinney H. S.
McKinney, Kentucky

PEACH-COCONUT MOLD

Number of Servings — 12

1 3-oz. pkg. mixed-fruit gelatin
1 c. boiling water
1 c. milk
1 c. sugar
6 fresh peaches, peeled, sliced and sweetened
Dash of salt
2 c. whipped cream
1½ c. flaked coconut
1 t. vanilla

Dissolve gelatin in boiling water; cool to lukewarm. Scald milk; add sugar and salt; stir until dissolved. Cool until lukewarm. Gradually add milk mixture to gelatin, stirring constantly. Chill until syrupy. Beat until thick and fluffy. Fold whipped cream, coconut and vanilla into gelatin. Spoon into a 2-quart ring mold; chill until firm. Unmold on a large plate; spoon peaches in center.

Mrs. Pat Vaughan, Fairfield H. S.
Fairfield, Illinois

PEACH-CRANBERRY SALAD

Number of Servings — 8

1 pkg. peach gelatin
1 c. hot water
¾ c. cold water
2 c. Cranberry Relish
½ c. pecans, chopped

Dissolve gelatin in hot water; add cold water. Stir in Cranberry Relish and pecans. Pour into mold; chill.

Cranberry Relish:
2 med. oranges
1 lb. cranberries
1 med. apple, unpeeled
2 c. sugar

Peel oranges; discard white part of rind. Put orange pulp and rind, cranberries and apples through a food chopper. Add sugar; mix well. Relish can be frozen or it will keep in refrigerator for about 2 weeks. Makes 2 pints.

Mrs. Jean G. Sands, Rocky Gap H. S.
Rocky Gap, Virginia

PEACH PICKLE SALAD MOLD

Number of Servings — 10-12

2½ c. boiling peach juice
2 pkg. orange or lemon gelatin
2 lge. jars or cans spiced peaches, drained and diced
2 cans white seedless grapes, drained
1 No. 2 can pineapple tidbits, well-drained
1 c. almonds or pecans, chopped

Dissolve gelatin in boiling peach juice. Let cool. Combine peaches, grapes and pineapple. Add to gelatin. Add nuts. Chill until firm.

Myrtis L. McAlhany, St. George H. S.
St. George, South Carolina

PEACH PICKLE ASPIC

Number of Servings — 6

1 T. unflavored gelatin
3 T. cold water
2½ c. hot juice drained from pickled peaches
1 T. lemon juice

Soften gelatin in cold water; dissolve in hot pickle juice. Add lemon juice. Chill until firm.

Mrs. Runette Davis, Savannah H. S.
Savannah, Georgia

PEACH SALAD

Number of Servings — 8-10

2 c. canned peaches, drained and cut up
1 c. crushed pineapple, drained
¼ c. Maraschino cherries, drained and cut up
¼ c. pecans, chopped
1 3-oz. pkg. cream cheese
1 pkg. orange gelatin
2 c. peach, pineapple and cherry juice

Heat fruit juice; add cream cheese. Stir until melted. Add gelatin and stir until dissolved. Add remaining ingredients. Chill until firm.

Ila S. Williams, New Kent H. S.
New Kent, Virginia

PICKLED PEACH SALAD

Number of Servings — 8

2 boxes lemon gelatin
1 c. boiling water
2 c. water and peach juice
3 oranges, sliced
1 jar peach pickles, drained and chopped
1 c. nuts, chopped
1 small bottle cherries, sliced

Dissolve gelatin in boiling water. Add peach juice-water. Stir in nuts and fruits. Chill until firm.

Mrs. Geraldine Jenkins, Emanuel County Institute
Twin City, Georgia

PICKLED PEACH SALAD

Number of Servings — 8

2 pkg. lemon gelatin
1 lge. jar pickled peaches
1 lge. pkg. cream cheese
3 c. water-peach juice
½ c. nuts, chopped
Cayenne pepper
Cream

Heat liquid and pour over gelatin. Soften cheese with cream; add nuts, salt and cayenne pepper. Remove seeds from peaches; stuff with cheese mixture; place in custard cups. Pour gelatin over peach and chill. Garnish with mayonnaise.

Myrtle Sands, Ware County H. S.
Waycross, Georgia

SPICED PEACH SALAD

1 1-lb. 14-oz. can spiced peaches, drained and chopped
1 c. peach syrup and water
1 3-oz. pkg. orange gelatin
¾ c. celery, chopped
½ c. pecans, chopped
¼ c. mayonnaise
1 c. evaporated milk, undiluted
2 T. lemon juice

Heat peach syrup to boiling point; add gelatin. Blend. Chill until syrupy. Add peaches, celery, nuts and mayonnaise. Chill milk in refrigerator tray until soft ice crystals form. Whip until stiff. Add lemon juice; whip until very stiff. Fold milk into gelatin mixture. Chill for about 2 hours.

This recipe submitted by the following teachers:

Neva T. Bailey, Hicks Memorial
Autaugaville, Alabama
Gladys Helm, Milford H. S.
Milford, Nebraska

SPICED PEACH SALAD

Number of Servings — 6-8

1 lge. jar whole spiced peaches, drained
1 pkg. lemon gelatin
1 c. hot water
1 c. cold peach juice and water
1 3-oz. pkg. cream cheese
1 t. lemon juice
½ c. nuts, finely chopped
Mayonnaise, cream or milk

Dissolve gelatin in hot water; add peach juice and water. Let cool. Mix cream cheese with enough mayonnaise, cream or milk to thin; add lemon juice and nuts. Stuff peaches with cream cheese mixture; place in individual molds. Fill molds with gelatin. Chill until firm.

Allene Elliott, Gulfport H. S.
Gulfport, Mississippi

SPICED PEACH SALAD

Number of Servings — 12-14

1 jar spiced peaches, drained and cut in half
1 envelope unflavored gelatin
1 8-oz. pkg. cream cheese
Juice from peaches
¼ c. cold water
Cream or mayonnaise
Ground pecans

Soak gelatin in cold water; dissolve it in warm peach juice. Mix cream cheese, mayonnaise and nuts together. Stuff center of peaches with cheese mixture. Pour gelatin mixture over peaches. Chill.

This recipe submitted by the following teachers:

Mrs. Leo Thames, Robert E. Lee H. S.
Baton Rouge, Louisiana
Marilyn Cooper, Delhi H. S.
Delhi, Louisiana

CONGEALED PEAR SALAD

Number of Servings — 10-12

1 pkg. lime gelatin
1 lge. can pears, drained
1 c. hot water
1 8-oz. pkg. cream cheese
Juice of ½ lemon
¼ t. salt
½ c. pear juice

Dissolve gelatin in hot water. Beat cream cheese until it reaches the consistency of thick cream; add pears. Continue beating until pears are beaten into pieces. Add salt and lemon juice. Add gelatin and pear juice. Chill.

Mrs. L. S. Coers, Buda Ind. Co. Line
Buda, Texas

LIME-PEAR SALAD

Number of Servings — 24

1 lge. can pears, drained and diced
2 pkg. lime gelatin
2 c. hot pear juice and water
2 c. whipped cream
2 pkg. cream cheese

Dissolve gelatin in hot pear juice; let cool. Soften cream cheese by blending in 3 or 4 tablespoons of gelatin; blend well after each addition. Add remaining gelatin. Fold in whipped cream and pears. Chill until firm.

Rose Chandler, Calhoun City H. S.
Calhoun City, Mississippi

LIME-PEAR SALAD

Number of Servings — 6-8

1 lge. or 2 small pkg. cream cheese
1 small pkg. lime gelatin
1-1½ c. pear juice
1 c. pears, drained
½ pt. whipped cream
2 T. cream (opt.)

Dissolve gelatin in boiling pear juice. Mash cream cheese or soften it with cream; add to gelatin. Let cool. Mash half of the pears; dice the remaining half. Add pears and whipped cream. Refrigerate for several hours.

This recipe submitted by the following teachers:

Jane Milligan, Lake County H. S.
Ridgely, Tennessee

Mrs. Ruth Mae Weber, Brandon Valley H. S.
Brandon, South Dakota

PEAR-CHEESE SALAD

Number of Servings — 10-12

3 pkg. lime gelatin
1 lge. pkg. cream cheese, crumbled
3 c. boiling water
1 lge. can pears, undrained
1 c. pecans, chopped

Mix gelatin and cream cheese together. Add boiling water. Blend with a rotary beater. Chill until thickened. Beat pears with a rotary beater. Add pears and nuts to gelatin mixture. Chill.

Mrs. Roceil Graves, Leakey H. S.
Leakey, Texas

PEAR-LIME GELATIN SALAD

Number of Servings — 8

1 3-oz. pkg. lime gelatin
1 c. pear juice, heated
1 8-oz. pkg. cream cheese
2 T. sweet cream
2 c. cooked or canned pears, drained
1 c. whipped cream

Dissolve gelatin in the hot pear juice. Add cream cheese which has been softened with the sweet cream. Chill until partially set; add pears and whipped cream. Chill until firm.

Mrs. Lois Watts, Bismarck Sr. H. S.
Bismarck, North Dakota

SEA FOAM SALAD

Number of Servings — 8-10

1 pkg. lime gelatin
1 c. pear or pineapple juice
1 qt. pears, mashed or crushed pineapple, drained
1 small pkg. cream cheese
3 T. cream
Speck of salt
1 c. whipped cream

Dissolve gelatin in juice. Soften cream cheese with cream. Add mashed pears or pineapple and salt. Combine cheese mixture with gelatin. Fold in whipped cream. Chill until firm.

Sally Adams, Fremont, H. S.
Fremont, Michigan

SEA FOAM SALAD

Number of Servings — 6-8

1 No. 2½ can pears, chopped
2 3-oz. pkg. cream cheese, softened
1 pkg. lime gelatin
1 envelope whipped Dream Whip
Pear juice

Heat juice from pears. Pour over gelatin. Chill. Ad softened cheese to Dream Whip; beat until smooth. When gelatin begins to thicken, add to the beaten mixture. Fold pears into mixture. Chill until firm.

Mrs. Virgil Olson, Clinton H. S.
Clinton, Wisconsin

SEA FOAM SALAD

Number of Servings — 6-8

1 pkg. lime gelatin
1 c. hot pear juice
2 small pkg. cream cheese
1 c. whipped cream
2 T. salad dressing
1 No. 2 can pears, drained and mashed

Dissolve gelatin in hot pear juice. Blend in cream cheese, whipped cream and salad dressing. Let stand until mixture begins to congeal. Add pears. Beat. Chill until firm.

This recipe submitted by the following teachers:

Mrs. Margaret Morgan, Austin H. S.
Austin, Minnesota

Mrs. Mary Nestande, Fairfax Public School
Fairfax, Minnesota

Margaret Jones, United Joint H. S.
New Florence, Pennsylvania

SEA FOAM SALAD

Number of Servings — 4-6

1 pkg. lime gelatin
2 c. hot pear juice
1 3-oz. pkg. cream cheese
¼ c. mayonnaise or salad dressing
2 c. canned pears, diced
⅛ t. ginger

Dissolve gelatin in hot pear juice. Gradually add cream cheese, blending until smooth. Chill until slightly thickened. Add mayonnaise or salad dressing; beat until light and fluffy. Fold in pears and ginger. Chill until firm.

Mrs. Gerre Thompson, Blackford H. S.
San Jose, California

CRUNCHY PINEAPPLE MOLD

Number of Servings — 6

1¼ c. hot water
1 pkg. lemon gelatin
½ c. pineapple juice
1 No. 2 can crushed pineapple, drained
¼ c. celery, diced
½ c. apple, diced
¼ c. walnuts
2 t. pickle relish

Pour hot water over gelatin; stir until dissolved. Chill until mixture reaches the consistency of unbeaten egg whites; stir occasionally. Fold in remaining ingredients. Chill until firm.

Mrs. Gladys Hendren, Central Junior H. S.
Holly Hill, Florida

CHILLED HAWAIIAN SALAD

Number of Servings — 4

1 pkg. lime gelatin
¾ c. pineapple juice
⅔ c. crushed pineapple, drained
½ t. onion, minced
4 T. green pepper, minced
1 c. cucumber, minced and drained
¾ c. salad dressing

Dissolve gelatin in boiling pineapple juice. Cool. Add vegetables and fruit. Let stand until syrupy. Fold in salad dressing. Chill until firm.

Becky Bahnsen, Reed City H. S.
Reed City, Michigan

CONGEALED SALAD

Number of Servings — 8-10

3 egg yolks
3 T. sugar
3 T. vinegar
1 envelope unflavored gelatin
¼ c. water
1 pkg. miniature marshmallows
1 small can crushed pineapple
1 c. nuts, chopped
½ pt. whipped cream

Cook yolks, vinegar and sugar until thick. Cool. Dissolve gelatin in water; add to cooked mixture. Add marshmallows, pineapple and nuts. Fold in whipped cream. Chill until firm.

Billie Crawford, Jacksboro H. S.
Jacksboro, Texas

FLUFFY FRUIT SALAD

Number of Servings — 6-8

¾ c. sugar
1 T. unflavored gelatin
¼ c. water
1 egg white, stiffly beaten
1 c. whipped cream
¼ c. mayonnaise or salad dressing
1 9-oz. can pineapple tidbits, drained
¼ c. seedless white grapes
½ c. California walnuts, broken

Combine sugar, gelatin and water. Bring to a boil, stirring constantly. Pour slowly over egg white; beat until thick. Cool. Fold in cream and mayonnaise; add grapes, nuts and pineapple. Chill until firm.

This recipe submitted by the following teachers:

Mrs. Jane Poteet, Fox H. S.
Fox, Oklahoma

Mrs. Sonia M. Cole, Huntington Local H. S.
Chillicothe, Ohio

CONGEALED SALAD

Number of Servings — 10-12

1 small can crushed pineapple
1 pkg. any flavor gelatin
1 medium sweet apple, diced
1 lge. banana, diced
½ c. pecans, chopped
1 c. whipped cream

Heat pineapple to boiling point. Remove from heat and stir in gelatin until dissolved. Add apple, banana and nuts. Cool quickly. Fold in whipped cream. Chill until firm.

Lola Hardaway, Strawberry H. S.
Strawberry, Arkansas

FLUFFY SALAD

Number of Servings — 10

1 pkg. lemon or lime gelatin
1 small can evaporated milk
1 small can crushed pineapple, undrained
½ c. nuts, chopped
¼ c. Maraschino cherries
1 c. boiling water

Dissolve gelatin in boiling water. Let cool. Whip. Chill evaporated milk in freezer tray until ice crystals form; whip milk. Fold milk into gelatin. Fold in pineapple, nuts and cherries. Chill until firm.

Mrs. Prudence Sheldon, Airport Community H. S.
Carleton, Michigan

FRUIT MOUSSE

Number of Servings — 10-12

¾ c. boiling water
1½ c. sugar
2 T. orange rind, grated
2 envelopes unflavored gelatin
1½ c. orange juice
⅓ c. pineapple juice
¾ c. cold water
¾ c. instant non-fat dry milk
⅓ c. lemon juice
½ c. Maraschino cherries, drained and chopped
½ c. crushed pineapple, drained
1½ c. blanched almonds, chopped

Combine sugar, orange rind, gelatin and boiling water in a saucepan. Stir and boil for 1 minute. Add orange and pineapple juices. Cool until mixture is partially set and of the consistency of jelly. Sprinkle dry milk on ¾ cup water; beat. When milk is partially whipped, add lemon juice. Beat until stiff. Fold milk mixture into gelatin mixture. Fold in cherries, pineapple and nuts. Chill until firm.

Mrs. Peggy S. Jackson, Fairforest H. S.
Fairforest, South Carolina

FRUIT GELATIN MOLD

Number of Servings — 8

1 pkg. lime gelatin
1 c. hot water
1 c. pineapple juice and water
1½ c. crushed pineapple, drained
¾ c. miniature marshmallows
1 lge. banana, sliced
½ c. pecans, broken
¼ c. Maraschino cherries, cut

Dissolve gelatin in hot water. Add pineapple juice; chill until partially set. Add fruits and nuts. Chill until firm.

Elizabeth Stump Rice, Colonial H. S.
Orlando, Florida

GINGER ALE FRUIT SALAD

Number of Servings — 8

2 T. gelatin
2 T. cold water
⅓ c. boiling water
¼-⅓ c. lemon juice
2-3 T. sugar
Few grains salt
1 c. ginger ale
⅓ c. white grapes or Malaga grapes, skinned and seeded
⅓ c. celery, chopped
⅓ c. apples pared and cut Julienne style
½-1 c. canned pineapple wedges
2 T. candied ginger, chopped (opt.)

Soak gelatin in cold water; dissolve it in hot water. Add lemon juice, sugar, salt and ginger ale; cool until mixture begins to thicken. Add remaining ingredients. Pour into an oiled ring mold; refrigerate.

This recipe submitted by the following teachers:

Avis Thompson, Tigerton H. S.
Tigerton, Wisconsin

Mrs. Emadele L. McCleary, West Junior H. S.
Waco, Texas

GREEN MOUNTAIN SALAD

Number of Servings — 6

2 pkg. lime gelatin
1 c. boiling water
1 c. pineapple juice
½ c. crushed pineapple, drained
1 pt. sour cream
1 c. miniature marshmallows
¼ c. Maraschino cherries, cut
½ c. nuts, chopped (opt.)

Dissolve gelatin in boiling water; add pineapple and sour cream. Fold in mayonnaise, cherries and nuts.

Mrs. Anita Lewis, Cumberland Valley Jr. H. S.
Mechanicsburg, Pennsylvania

GOLDEN SALAD

Number of Servings — 12

2 egg yolks
1 t. salt
1 T. butter
⅔ c. milk
½ c. sugar
⅓ c. mild vinegar
1 pkg. lemon gelatin
1 c. boiling water
4 c. crushed pineapple
1 c. whipped cream

Dissolve gelatin in boiling water. Chill until mixture starts to set. Combine yolks, salt, butter, milk, sugar and vinegar in order. Cook until mixture is custard consistency. Cool. Add pineapple and whipped cream. Add to gelatin. Turn into molds and chill until firm. Salad needs no dressing.

Mrs. Adrienne Carter, Alleghany District H. S.
Shawsville, Virginia

GREEN SALAD

Number of Servings — 8

1 T. unflavored gelatin
¼ c. cold water or pineapple juice
½ c. sugar
¼ t. salt
½ c. hot water
¼ c. mild vinegar
Few drops green food coloring
½ c. blanched almonds, chopped
½ c. stuffed olives, sliced
½ c. pineapple, drained, cut in small pieces
½ c. small sweet pickles, diced

Soak gelatin in cold water for 5 minutes. Add sugar, salt, hot water; stir until all are dissolved. Add vinegar and food coloring. Mix almonds, olives, pineapple and pickle together. Pour gelatin mixture over pineapple mixture. Chill until firm.

Josephine S. Loyd, Oneonta H. S.
Oneonta, Alabama

GREEN AND WHITE SALAD

Number of Servings — 6

2 T. gelatin
1 ¾ c. boiling water
¼ c. vinegar
½ c. sweet pickles, diced
¼ c. cold water
½ c. sugar
¾ c. pineapple, diced
½ c. blanched almonds, diced
¼ c. whipped cream
¼ c. salad dressing

Soak gelatin in cold water for 5 minutes. Add sugar and boiling water. Stir until dissolved. Let set until mixture begins to thicken. Add pineapple and vinegar. Add almonds and pickles. Chill until firm. Mix whipped cream and salad dressing together; serve with gelatin mixture.

Mrs. Vanora Fry, H. S.
Little River, Kansas

GREEN SALAD

Number of Servings — 12

2 boxes lime gelatin
2 c. boiling water
1½ c. pineapple juice-water
1 c. olives, chopped
1 c. sweet pickles, chopped
1 c. nuts
1 No. 303 can pineapple chunks
1 c. celery, diced

Dissolve gelatin in boiling water. Add pineapple juice; chill until mixture reaches the consistency of egg whites. Add remaining ingredients. Chill until firm.

Mrs. Elizabeth Nesbitt, Seeger H. S.
West Lebanon, Indiana

IMPERIAL SALAD

Number of Servings — 6-8

1 c. boiling water
1 pkg. lemon gelatin
1 small can crushed pineapple
½ c. nuts, chopped
½ c. celery, chopped
¼ c. pimento, chopped
2 T. lemon juice
½ t. salt

Dissolve gelatin in boiling water; add remaining ingredients. Chill until firm.

Mrs. Kay W. Nicholson, Lexington H. S.
Lexington, South Carolina

LIME FRUIT SALAD

Number of Servings — 8

2 pkg. lime gelatin
1 c. boiling water
1 No. 2 can crushed pineapple, drained
1 pt. sour cream
½ c. Maraschino cherries, drained
½ c. nuts, chopped

Dissolve gelatin in boiling water. Let set until mixture begins to set. Add pineapple. Let set a short time. Fold in sour cream, cherries and nuts. Chill until firm.

Mrs. Gloria Lorenz, Prospect H. S.
Mt. Prospect, Illinois

LIME GELATIN SALAD

Number of Servings — 6

1 pkg. lime gelatin
1 c. hot water
1 c. crushed pineapple, undrained
½ c. sour cream
⅛ t. salt

Dissolve gelatin in hot water. Cool until partially congealed and syrupy. Add pineapple, sour cream and salt; stir. Congeal.

Mrs. Phyllis B. Grose, Warwick Senior H. S.
Newport News, Virginia

LIME-MALLOW SALAD

Number of Servings — 8

1 pkg. lime gelatin
2 c. miniature marshmallows
1 No. 2 can crushed pineapple, undrained
1 c. whipped cream or 1 pkg Dream Whip plus ½ c. milk

Dissolve gelatin and marshmallows in boiling water. Chill until partially set. Whip gelatin mixture with beater on high speed until smooth and creamy. Mix in pineapple. Fold in whipped Dream Whip or whipped cream. Pour into a mold that has been rinsed with cold water. Chill until firm.

Mrs. Anne McCord, Kilgore H. S.
Kilgore, Texas

LIME-PINEAPPLE SALAD

Number of Servings — 6-8

1 pkg. lime gelatin
1 small can pineapple, sliced
½ c. stuffed olives, chopped

Mix gelatin according to directions on package. Chill until mixture reaches the consistency of egg whites. Add pineapple and olives. Pour into mold and refrigerate until firm.

Opal Wood, Navasota H. S.
Navasota, Texas

LIME-SOUR CREAM MOLD

Number of Servings — 12

2 pkg. lime gelatin
2 c. boiling water
1 No. 2 can crushed pineapple, drained
¾ c. nuts, chopped
1 pt. sour cream

Dissolve gelatin in boiling water. Cool. Add sour cream, pineapple and nuts. Chill until firm.

Jane C. Richardson, Toccoa H. S.
Toccoa, Georgia

MARSHMALLOW DELIGHT SALAD

Number of Servings — 8

1 pkg. orange gelatin
1 c. boiling water
1 c. pineapple juice
14 marshmallows, diced
½ c. cheese, grated
6 slices pineapple, chopped
½ c. whipped cream
½ c. pecans, chopped

Dissolve gelatin in boiling water. Add pineapple juice. Add cheese and marshmallows while mixture is still hot. Cool. Add pineapple and pecans. When mixture begins to congeal fold in whipped cream. Place in molds and chill until firm. Serve on lettuce with mayonnaise.

Mrs. Doris V. Griffith, Elmore County H. S.
Eclectic, Alabama

MARION CLUB SALAD

Number of Servings — 8

1 T. unflavored gelatin
½ c. pineapple juice
½ c. cherry juice
3 T. sugar
½ c. whipped cream
½ c. mayonnaise
1 c. Royal Anne cherries, pitted
1 c. pineapple tidbits
½ lb. almonds, blanched and chopped
¼ t. salt

Soak gelatin in 3 tablespoons of fruit juice. Dissolve over hot water. Add remaining fruit juice and sugar; chill. When mixture begins to congeal, add remaining ingredients in order. Pour mixture into 8 individual molds. Chill until firm.

Mary Lou Myers, Charlestown H. S.
Charlestown, Indiana

MARSHMALLOW SALAD

Number of Servings — 6-8

2 eggs
2 T. vinegar
2 T. water
Dash of salt
32 marshmallows, diced
1 can crushed pineapple, drained
1 c. pecans, chopped
1 pt. sweet cream or 1 lge can evaporated milk, whipped
1 T. unflavored gelatin
¼ c. pineapple juice

Dissolve gelatin in pineapple juice. Whip eggs with water until light; add salt and vinegar. Cook until thick, stirring constantly. Add gelatin-juice mixture. Cool. Add all ingredients to whipped cream. Pour into molds. Refrigerate for several hours or overnight.

Mrs. Frances Rawls Kolb, McLaurin Junior H. S.
Sumter, South Carolina

MINTED PINEAPPLE SALAD

Number of Servings — 10

1 pkg. lemon gelatin
1 pkg. lime gelatin
2½ c. boiling water
1 T. vinegar
1 4½-oz. can minted pineapple, drained and chopped
1 c. pineapple juice and water
1 c. celery, chopped
¼ c. green pepper, chopped
1 2-oz. jar pimento, chopped
½ c. walnuts, chopped

Dissolve gelatin in boiling water; add pineapple juice and vinegar. Chill until partially thickened. Add remaining ingredients. Chill until firm.

Nellie P. Millar, Beaver Dam Sr. H. S.
Beaver Dam, Wisconsin

MOLDED FRUIT SALAD

1 pkg. lime gelatin
1 pkg. lemon gelatin
2 c. boiling water
1 c. crushed pineapple, drained
1 c. whipped cream
1 c. mayonnaise
½ c. walnuts, chopped
1 c. miniature marshmallows
1 t. horseradish

Dissolve gelatins in boiling water. Chill until partially set. Combine remaining ingredients; fold into the gelatin mixture.

Mrs. Sereen N. Taylor, Waterville, H. S.
Waterville, Maine

MOLDED JEWEL SALAD

Number of Servings — 8

2 envelopes unflavored gelatin
⅓ c. sugar
¼ t. salt
1 1-lb. 4-oz. can pineapple chunks, drained
2 c. pineapple juice and water
⅓ c. lemon juice
1 c. raw carrots, coarsely grated
1½ c. orange scetions, diced

Mix gelatin, sugar and salt together. Add 1 cup juice-water mixture. Place over low heat, until gelatin is dissolved. Stir constantly. Remove from heat. Add remaining 1 cup juice-water mixture and lemon juice. Chill until mixture reaches the consistency of unbeaten egg whites. Stir in carrots, orange and pineapple chunks. Chill until firm.

Helen Craft, Clinton County H. S.
Albany, Kentucky

SPRING SALAD

Number of Servings — 12

3 c. boiling water
2 pkg. lemon gelatin
1 No. 2 can crushed pineapple, drained
12 marshmallows, finely chopped
3 bananas, cubed
1 c. pineapple juice
1 egg, beaten
1½ T. flour
½ c. sugar
½ whipped cream

Dissolve gelatin in boiling water. Chill until partially thick. Combine pineapple, marshmallows and bananas; fold into gelatin mixture. Chill until firm. Heat pineapple juice; add egg, flour and sugar. Let cool. Fold in whipped cream. Spread cream mixture over gelatin.

Mrs. James Poulton, Spencerville, H. S.
Spencerville, Ohio

MOLDED TANGY FRUIT SALAD

Number of Servings — 6

1 pkg. orange-pineapple gelatin
1 can Mandarin orange sections, drained
1 can pineapple tid-bits, drained
⅓ c. cooking sherry
1 c. seedless white grapes, halved
1⅔ c. juice from oranges and pineapple

Heat 1 cup of the juice and dissolve gelatin in it. Add remaining juice. Let cool. Add cooking sherry. Let set until partially congealed. Add orange sections, pineapple and grapes.

Mrs. Eleanor Weathermon, Wink H. S.
Wink, Texas

ORANGE-PINEAPPLE SALAD

Number of Servings — 9

1 pkg. lime gelatin
1 medium can crushed pineapple, drained
1 can Mandarin Oranges, drained
1 c. hot water
1 c. cold water

Dissolve gelatin in hot water; add cold water. Add remaining ingredients. Refrigerate until firm.

Mrs. Rena Nelson, Sheffield Area Joint School
Sheffield, Pennsylvania

PINEAPPLE-APRICOT SALAD

Number of Servings — 12-14

1 pkg. pineapple gelatin
1 pkg. orange gelatin
2 c. hot water
2 c. pineapple and apricot juice
1 c. pineapple chunks or tid-bits, drained
1 c. apricot halves, drained
1 c. sour cream

Dissolve gelatins in hot water; stir in fruit juices. Cool until partially set. Fold in pineapple and apricots. Gently fold in sour cream. Chill until firm.

Mrs. Maurietta Cusey, Wapella H. S.
Wapella, Illinois

PINEAPPLE AND CAPER SALAD

Number of Servings — 8-10

2 pkg. lemon gelatin
3 c. hot water
1 No. 2 can crushed pineapple
1 bottle capers, drained
1 small bottle sweet onions, drained and quartered or sweet pickles
¼ c. roasted almonds, finely cut

Dissolve gelatin in hot water. Chill until partially thickened. Add remaining ingredients. Chill until firm.

Eloise Peterson, University H. S.
Spokane, Washington

PINEAPPLE-SOUR CREAM SALAD

Number of Servings — 6-8

1 pkg. lemon gelatin
1⅓ c. boiling water
1 13½-oz. can crushed pineapple, undrained
1 c. sour cream
¼ c. celery, chopped
¼ c. water chestnuts, chopped

Dissolve gelatin in boiling water. Chill until syrupy. Blend in remaining ingredients. Chill for 2 or 3 hours.

Mrs. Frankie B. Skeels
Area Supervisor of Home Economics
Alexandria, Louisiana

PINEAPPLE DELIGHT

Number of Servings — 8

1 pkg. fruit gelatin
½ c. boiling water
½ c. cold water
8 marshmallows, finely cut
1 9-oz. can crushed pineapple
½ c. nuts, broken
⅔ c. evaporated milk, chilled

Dissolve gelatin in boiling water; stir in cold water. Add marshmallows, pineapple and nuts. Let stand. Whip the evaporated milk in a cold bowl until milk is stiff; fold into gelatin. Chill.

Mrs. Catherine Russell, McCollum H. S.
San Antonio, Texas

PINEAPPLE DELIGHT

Number of Servings — 8

¾ c. evaporated milk, chilled
½ c. cold water
10 marshmallows, finely cut
½ c. nuts, chopped
1 pkg. lime gelatin
½ c. boiling water
1 9-oz. can crushed pineapple, undrained

Chill milk in tray until almost frozen. Dissolve gelatin in boiling water; add cold water. Add nuts, pineapple and marshmallows. Let stand at room temperature. Whip milk until stiff; fold into gelatin mixture. Cover and chill.

Mrs. C. R. Ledbetter, Black Rock H. S.
Black Rock, Arkansas

PINEAPPLE SALAD

Number of Servings — 8

1 No. 2 can pineapple tid-bits, drained
2 T. flour
2 T. sugar
2 eggs, well beaten
1 envelope unflavored gelatin
¼ c. water
1 c. whipped cream
2 c. miniature marshmallows

Heat pineapple juice in sauce pan. Combine flour, sugar and eggs. Add to juice and cook until thick. Soak gelatin in water. Add to cooked mixture. Cool. Fold in whipped cream, pineapple tidbits and marshmallows. Put in 8x12 glass dish and chill.

Mrs. Janice Brunk, Wilton Community School
Wilton Junction, Iowa

PINEAPPLE-OLIVE SALAD

Number of Servings — 12

2 pkg. orange gelatin
1 envelope unflavored gelatin
1 No. 2 can crushed pineapple, drained
1 5-oz. jar Maraschino cherries drained and sliced
1 3-oz. jar stuffed olives, drained and sliced
½ c. pecans, chopped
Pineapple and cherry juice plus 1 T. olive juice and enough water to make 4 c. liquid

Soften unflavored gelatin in ¼ c. juice-water mixture. Prepare orange gelatin according to package directions substituting remaining 3¾ cups juice-water mixture as liquid. When partially congealed, add nuts, olives, cherries and pineapple. Pour into 12 individual molds and chill.

Dressing:
Grated rind and juice of 1 lemon
Grated rind and juice of 1 orange
1 egg, beaten
1 T. flour
½ c. sugar
1 c. whipped cream

Mix orange and lemon juice with egg, flour and sugar. Cook in double boiler until thick. Add orange and lemon rind; cool. Refrigerate. Add whipped cream just before serving.

Mrs. Adilaid P. Maddox, Riverside H. S.
Avon, Mississippi

PINEAPPLE SALAD

Number of Servings — 8

2 egg yolks
1½ T. vinegar
2 T. sugar
¾ c. boiling water
1 10-oz. pkg. marshmallows
1 envelope unflavored gelatin
1 No. 2 can crushed pineapple, undrained
½ pt. whipped cream
¼ c. cold water

Combine egg yolks, vinegar and sugar. Cook in double boiler until smooth. Slowly add boiling water and marshmallows. Soften gelatin in ¼ cup water; add to hot mixture. Cool. Add pineapple. Add whipped cream.

Louise Curry, Richfield H. S.
Waco, Texas

ROSY GELATIN SALAD

Number of Servings — 8

1 3-oz. pkg. cherry gelatin
1 c. boiling water
1 c. pineapple syrup and water
1 or 2 oranges, diced
1 c. pineapple cubes
½ medium banana, sliced
½ apple, diced
½ c. English walnuts or pecans, broken

Dissolve gelatin in boiling water; add pineapple syrup. Chill until partially set. Add fruit and nuts; chill until firm.

Joyce Thornton, Rosebud H. S.
Rosebud, Texas

SOUR CREAM MOLDS

Number of Servings — 16-20

3 c. pineapple juice and water
1 No. 2½ can crushed pineapple, drained
2 boxes lime gelatin
1-2 c. sour cream
½-1 c. nuts, chopped
1 c. white grapes (opt.)

Dissolve gelatin in hot liquid. Cool until slightly thickened. Add sour cream, pineapple, nuts and grapes; whip gently. Chill until set. Garnish with whipped topping or salad dressing.

This recipe submitted by the following teachers:

Sarah Leonard Morey, Brookville H. S.
Lynchburg, Virginia

Mrs. Ruth M. Dreyer, Circle H. S.
Circle, Montana

WHITE FRUIT SALAD

Number of Servings — 9-12

1 No. 2 can Royal Anne cherries, drained and pitted
1 9-oz. can crushed pineapple, drained
1 envelope unflavored gelatin
⅔ c. evaporated milk, undiluted
Juice drained from pineapple
¼ c. cherry juice
¾ c. mayonnaise
½ c. almonds, slivered

Soften gelatin in cherry juice. Heat pineapple juice to boiling. Add to gelatin. Let cool. Combine cherries, pineapple, almonds, mayonnaise and milk. Stir gelatin mixture into fruit mixture until liquid ingredients and mayonnaise are smooth. Chill until firm.

Mrs. Katherine V. Fisher, Colonial H. S.
Orlando, Florida

PINK CHAMPAGNE FRUIT SALAD

Number of Servings — 6-8

1 envelope unflavored gelatin
2 T. cold water
½ c. boiling water
Dash of salt
1 T. sugar
½ c. pink champagne
1 T. lemon juice
½ c. whipped cream
½ c. pineapple, diced
1 c. seedless grapes, sliced
½ c. celery, diced
½ c. pecans, chopped

Soften gelatin in cold water; add boiling water. Stir until gelatin is dissolved. Add sugar, salt, lemon juice and champagne. Chill until slightly thickened. Fold in fruits, celery, nuts and cream. Chill.

Maggie Johnson, Varnado School
Varnado, Louisiana

WHITE SALAD

Number of Servings — 6

2 pkg. unflavored gelatin
½ c. water
1 small can crushed pineapple, drained
1 jar Royal Anne cherries, drained
½ pkg. marshmallows, diced
½ c. mayonnaise
1 c. whipped cream
Juice from pineapple and cherries, heated

Soak gelatin in water. Add juice from pineapple and cherries. Chill until thick. Add pineapple, cherries and marshmallows. Add mayonnaise and whipped cream. Chill until firm.

Mrs. Linda S. Wright, Houston H. S.
Houston, Mississippi

YUM YUM SALAD

Number of Servings — 8

1 box cherry gelatin
1 c. boiling water
⅔ c. pecans, chopped
1 small can crushed pineapple
1 small pkg. miniature marshmallows
½ pt. whipped cream

Dissolve gelatin in boiling water; add pineapple juice. Cool. Add marshmallows, pecans and pineapple. Fold in cream. Chill until firm.

Mrs. John C. Clark, North Side H. S.
Jackson, Tennessee

CARROT-LIME SURPRISE SALAD

Number of Servings — 18

1 6-oz. pkg. lime gelatin
2 c. boiling water
2 c. carrots, grated
1 c. crushed pineapple
1½ c. cold water
1 c. miniature marshmallows
½ c. walnuts, chopped

Dissolve gelatin in boiling water. Add cold water. Chill until mixture reaches the consistency of egg whites. Whip with electric mixer or rotary beater until light and fluffy. Add carrots, pineapple, marshmallows and walnuts. Mix thoroughly. Chill until firm.

Mrs. Verda E. McConnell, Adams City Sr. H. S.
Adams City, Colorado

COMPLEXION SALAD

Number of Servings — 6-8

1 pkg. lemon or orange gelatin
1 c. hot water
1 c. pineapple juice drained from pineapple
1½ c. raw carrots, grated
1¼ c. crushed pineapple, drained
1 stalk celery, chopped (opt.)
½ c. pecans, chopped (opt.)

Dissolve gelatin in hot water; add pineapple juice. Chill until slightly thickened. Add grated carrots and pineapple. Pour into molds and chill. Unmold on crisp lettuce, serve with mayonnaise.

This recipe submitted by the following teachers:

Mrs. Ray Welborn, Glade H. S.
Laurel, Mississippi

Emma Steele, Ochelata H. S.
Ochelata, Oklahoma

Mrs. Tillie Gandy, Weatherford Junior H. S.
Weatherford, Texas

Mrs. R. D. Dyson, Cairo H. S.
Cairo, Georgia

Mrs. Elaine Matawich, No. 703 Mt. Iron School
Mountain Iron, Minnesota

Mrs. Rebecca B. Sisk, Brentwood Junior H. S.
Pensacola, Florida

Mrs. Willa Graves Didway, Post H. S.
Post, Texas

Mrs. Virginia H. Brown, Soddy-Daisy Junior H. S.
Daisy, Tennessee

CHEESE PARTY SALAD

Number of Servings — 8

1 c. hot water
1 pkg. cream cheese
1 pkg. lime gelatin
1 c. carrots, grated
1 c. celery, finely cut
1 8-oz. can pineapple, drained
1 c. whipped cream
½ c. nuts

Heat water, gelatin and cheese. Cool. Add carrots, celery, pineapple, whipped cream and nuts. Top with dressing.

DRESSING:

2 eggs, beaten
¾ c. pineapple juice
¼ c. sugar

Combine eggs, pineapple juice and sugar. Cook over low heat until mixture slightly thickens, stirring constantly.

Marel Bolger, Bentley Sr. H. S.
Flint, Michigan

CRUSHED PINEAPPLE-CARROT MOLD

Number of Servings — 10

1 No. 2 can crushed pineapple, drained
1½ c. juice plus water
1 pkg. lemon gelatin
½ c. sugar
¼ t. salt
2 T. lemon juice
1 c. carrots, finely grated
½ pt. whipped cream

Combine pineapple juice and water; heat to boiling. Add gelatin; stir until dissolved. Add sugar, salt and lemon juice. Chill until slightly thickened. Add pineapple and carrots. Fold in cream. Pour into 8″ ring mold. Chill until firm.

This recipe submitted by the following teachers:

Juanita Hamil, Forsyth County H. S.
Cumming, Georgia

Mrs. Joanne Snider, Dimmitt H. S.
Dimmitt, Texas

GOLDEN SALAD

Number of Servings — 6

1 envelope unflavored gelatin
¼ c. cold water
1¼ c. pineapple juice
¼ c. lemon juice
½ t. salt
1 c. crushed pineapple
1 c. carrots, grated

Soften gelatin in cold water; dissolve over hot water. Add pineapple juice, lemon juice and salt. Chill until partially set. Fold in pineapple and carrot. Turn into a 1-quart mold and refrigerate until firm.

Mrs. Jean Harris, Eastern Junior H. S.
Owensboro, Kentucky

DOUBLE GLOW SALAD

Number of Servings — 8-10

1 pkg. orange gelatin
1 pkg. lemon gelatin
2 c. boiling water
2 c. cold water
1 No. 2 can crushed pineapple
4-6 raw carrots, grated
¼ lb. or more grated cheese (opt.)
1 c. nuts, chopped (opt.)

Dissolve gelatin in boiling water; add cold water. Chill until mixture begins to thicken. Add carrots, cheese or nuts if desired and pineapple; chill until firm. To serve a smaller number, 1 package of gelatin and 2 cups liquid may be omitted.

This recipe submitted by the following teachers:

Mrs. Alice Wood, Greenwood Jr.-Sr. H. S.
Greenwood, Indiana

Helen W. Brink, South Williamsport Senior H. S.
South Williamsport, Pennsylvania

Norine R. Edwards, Kilbourne H. S.
Kilbourne, Louisiana

Bertrice Robertson, Collins H. S.
Collins, Mississippi

GOLDEN GLOW SALAD

Number of Servings — 8

1 pkg. orange or lemon gelatin
1 c. boiling water
Pineapple juice plus water to make 1 c. liquid
½-1 c. crushed pineapple, drained
½ c. sharp cheese, grated
½ c. carrots, grated
¼-½ c. nuts, chopped
1 pkg. marshmallows, cut up (opt.)

Dissolve gelatin in boiling water. Add juice-water mixture. Cool until mixture thickens. Add cheese, carrots, pineapple, nuts and marshmallows if desired. Chill until firm.

This recipe submitted by the following teachers:

Mrs. Annie H. Seaford, China Grove Junior H. S.
China Grove, North Carolina

Marilyne Burgess, DuPont H. S.
Old Hickory, Tennessee

GOLDEN GLOW OR SUNSHINE SALAD

Number of Servings — 6

1 3-oz. pkg. lemon or orange gelatin
1 c. hot water
1 c. mixed pineapple syrup and water
1-2 T. vinegar or lemon juice (opt.)
½ t. salt (opt.)
½-1 c. raw carrots, grated
1 No. 2 can crushed pineapple, drained
½ c. pecans, chopped or ½ c. celery, chopped

Dissolve gelatin in hot water. Add pineapple syrup-water, vinegar and ½ teaspoon salt. Chill until slightly thickened. Season carrots with ¼ teaspoon salt; add pineapple and nuts. Fold into gelatin mixture. Chill until firm. One cup pineapple juice and 2½ cups shredded red apples may be substituted for pineapple syrup-water and crushed pineapple.

This recipe submitted by the following teachers:

Mrs. Frank Grace, Dardanelle H. S.
Dardanelle, Arkansas

Mrs. Denean Dixon, Appling County H. S.
Baxley, Georgia

Mrs. Virginia N. Tardy, Lexington H. S.
Lexington, Virginia

Mrs. Kemper R. Russell, Logansport H. S.
Logansport, Louisiana

Mrs. Mildred West Pirgan, Boca Ciega Senior H. S.
St. Petersburg, Florida

GOLDEN GLOW SALAD WITH PINEAPPLE DRESSING

1 pkg. lemon gelatin
1½ c. hot water
½ t. salt
⅔-1 c. crushed pineapple, drained
½ c. pineapple juice
1 T. lemon juice or vinegar
1 c. raw carrot, coarsely grated
½ c. nuts, chopped (opt.)

Dissolve gelatin in hot water. Add lemon and pineapple juices and salt. Chill until slightly thickened. Fold in pineapple and carrot. Chill until firm. Serve with mayonnaise or Pineapple Dressing.

Pineapple Dressing:
1½ T. butter
½ c. sugar
1 T. flour
2 eggs, beaten
1 c. pineapple juice, heated
½ pt. whipped cream

Cream butter and sugar. Add eggs and flour. Add hot pineapple juice. Cook over low heat for 3 minutes or until mixture is thick. Cool. Add whipped cream just before serving.

This recipe submitted by the following teachers:

Mrs. Phyllis Price, Montello H. S.
Montello, Wisconsin

Mrs. Nanette Whichard, Erwin H. S.
Erwin, North Carolina

Mable Henderson, Tahlequah H. S.
Tahlequah, Oklahoma

Frances Yvonne Stepp, Oak Hill H. S.
Lenoir, North Carolina

HAWAIIAN GOLDEN SALAD

Number of Servings — 10

1 No. 2 can crushed pineapple, drained
1 c. golden Hawaiian punch
1½ pkg. orange-pineapple gelatin
1 c. American cheese, grated
½ c. pecans, broken
1 8-oz. jar Maraschino cherries

(Continued on next page)

1 c. miniature marshmallows
1 c. whipped cream

Bring juice drained from pineapple and Hawaiian punch to a boil. Stir in gelatin until thoroughly dissolved. Cool. Add pineapple, cheese, nuts, cherries and marshmallows. Refrigerate until mixture begins to thicken. Fold in whipped cream and chill until firm.

Anna Mae Ogle, Sevier County H. S.
Sevierville, Tennessee

ORANGE-CREAM CHEESE SALAD

Number of Servings — 9

1 pkg. orange gelatin
15 lge. marshmallows
1 3-oz. pkg. cream cheese
1 c. carrots, grated
1 c. crushed pineapple
½ c. nuts
1 c. whipped cream

Prepare gelatin according to package directions. While mixture is still hot whip in marshmallows and cheese. Chill until syrupy. Add remaining ingredients. Chill until firm.

Mrs. William Keiner, Madison Central H. S.
Madison, South Dakota

ORANGE-PINEAPPLE GOLDEN SALAD

Number of Servings — 6

1 envelope unflavored gelatin
¼ c. sugar
¼ t. salt
¾ c. canned pineapple juice, heated
¼ c. orange juice
¼ c. vinegar
1 c. crushed pineapple, drained
½ c. orange sections
½ c. raw carrots, coarsely grated

Mix gelatin, sugar and salt; dissolve in hot pineapple juice. Add orange juice and vinegar. Chill until mixture is consistency of unbeaten egg whites. Fold in pineapple, orange sections and carrots. Turn into a 3-cup mold. Chill until firm.

Mrs. A. J. Robertson, Quitman H. S.
Quitman, Arkansas

SUNGLOW RAISIN SALAD

Number of Servings — 6

⅔ c. light or dark raisins
1 pkg. lemon gelatin
1¼ c. hot water
2 T. lemon juice
1 c. crushed pineapple, undrained
¼ t. salt
1¼ c. carrots, grated

Rinse raisins; cover with water and boil for 5 minutes. Cool and drain. Dissolve gelatin in hot water. Blend in lemon juice, pineapple and salt. When slightly thickened, fold in raisins and carrots. Turn into individual molds. Chill until firm.

Joyce Pietila, Park Rapids Central H. S.
Park Rapids, Minnesota

ARIZONA DESSERT

Number of Servings — 12

1 pkg. cherry gelatin
1 c. hot water
12 lge. marshmallows
1 pkg. Dream Whip
1 pt. cottage cheese
1 No. 300 can crushed pineapple, undrained

Combine gelatin and water. Dissolve marshmallows in hot mixture. Cool until syrupy; beat with an egg beater if desired. Prepare Dream Whip according to package directions. Fold Dream Whip, cottage cheese and pineapple into gelatin mixture. Chill until firm.

Pat Oglesby, Fort Vancouver, H. S.
Vancouver, Washington

AUNT JENNY'S SALAD

Number of Servings — 8

1 pkg. lime gelatin
½ c. hot water
1 8-oz. can crushed pineapple and juice
1 c. cottage cheese
12-14 marshmallows, cut up
½ c. nuts, finely chopped
1 pkg. Dream Whip or ½ c. whipped cream

Mix gelatin in hot water, stir over low heat until gelatin is dissolved. Cool. Add all remaining ingredients except Dream Whip in order; cool. Prepare Dream Whip according to package directions, or use whipped cream. Fold into cooled mixture. Chill until firm.

This recipe submitted by the following teachers:

Wilma Heggaton, Birch Run Area H. S.
Birch Run, Michigan

Bertha Hundley, Red Bank H. S.
Chattanooga, Tennessee

FRUIT-CHEESE SALAD

Number of Servings — 5

2 t. unflavored gelatin
2 T. plus 2 t. cold water
½ c. boiling pineapple juice
⅔ c. crushed pineapple, drained
½ c. banana, diced
⅔ c. cottage cheese
88 miniature marshmallows
⅛ t. salt
⅓ c. mayonnaise
⅓ c. whipped cream
2 t. lemon juice

Soak gelatin in cold water for five minutes; add pineapple juice. Stir until gelatin is dissolved. Add pineapple, banana, cottage cheese, marshmallows and salt. Chill until mixture begins to thicken. Fold in whipped cream, mayonniase and lemon juice. Chill until firm.

Mrs. Barbara D. Straker, Chelsea H. S.
Chelsea, Michigan

BUFFET SALAD

Number of Servings — 12

2 pkg. lime gelatin
2 c. hot water
1 No. 2 can crushed pineapple, undrained
1 c. cottage cheese
½ c. nuts, chopped
2 T. pimento
2 T. horseradish

Dissolve gelatin in hot water; let stand until partially set. Fold in remaining ingredients. Pour into a 1½-quart mold. Chill.

Mrs. Evelyn Wester, Crossville
Crossville, Alabama

COTTAGE CHEESE SALAD

Number of Servings — 10

1 pkg. lemon gelatin
1 pkg. lime gelatin
2 c. hot water
1 No. 2 can crushed pineapple, undrained
2 T. lemon juice
⅓ c. orange juice
1 c. sweetened condensed milk, chilled
1 c. mayonnaise
½ lb. cottage cheese
1 c. nuts

Dissolve gelatins in hot water. Add pineapple, orange and lemon juice. Cool. Mix in remaining ingredients. Turn into a ring mold. Chill until firm.

Nancy Hinkemeyer, Big Piney H. S.
Big Piney, Wyoming

HEAVENLY SALAD

Number of Servings — 8-10

1 pkg. lime gelatin
1 pkg. lemon gelatin
2 c. boiling water
1 c. marshmallows
1 c. cottage cheese
2 t. sugar (opt.)
½ c. pecans, chopped
1 small can crushed pineapple
½ pt. whipped cream

Dissolve gelatin, sugar and marshmallows in boiling water or a ½ water and ½ juice mixture. Chill until mixture begins to congeal. Add cheese, pecans, pineapple and whipped cream. Chill until firm. For a richer salad, one box of the gelatin and 1 cup of water may be omitted.

This recipe submitted by the following teachers:

Mary A. Kirby, Greenville Senior H. S.
Greenville, Texas

Mrs. Winnie Sanders, Taylor County H. S.
Campbellsville, Kentucky

Beda Sue Hogue, Green Forest H. S.
Green Forest, Arkansas

GELATIN DELIGHT

Number of Servings — 8

2 boxes lemon gelatin
3 c. hot water
1 No. 2 can crushed pineapple
1 carton small curd cottage cheese
1 c. pecans, chopped
1 c. whipped cream

Dissolve gelatin in hot water. Cool until mixture reaches the consistency of jelly. Add pineapple, cheese and nuts; mix well. Fold in whipped cream. Chill until firm.

Sarah H. Bogard, Mooresville H. S.
Mooresville, Indiana

MOTHER CHURCH'S SALAD

Number of Servings — 8-10

2 pkg. lemon gelatin
2 c. hot water
1 No. 2 can crushed pineapple
½ c. Maraschino cherries, quartered
½ c. walnuts, chopped
1 8-oz. pkg. cream cheese
1 12-oz. pkg. small curd cottage cheese
1 c. whipped cream

Stir gelatin, hot water and pineapple together until gelatin is dissolved. Chill until firm. Blend the cheeses together with electric mixer. Add cherries, nuts and cheese mixture to gelatin mixture. Fold in whipped cream. Chill.

Mary E. Eastman, Adams H. S.
Adams, Minnesota

PINEAPPLE-COTTAGE CHEESE LOAF

Number of Servings — 12

1 No. 2 can crushed pineapple
2 envelopes unflavored gelatin
1 lb. cottage cheese
¾ c. mayonnaise
1 T. sugar
1 c. walnuts, broken
1 medium green pepper, chopped
1 4-oz. can pimento, drained and chopped
1 c. whipped cream

Reserve 2 tablespoons pineapple for garnish. Drain juice from remaining pineapple into glass measuring cup; soften gelatin in juice. Place measuring cup in pan of boiling water; stir until gelatin dissolves. Combine pineapple and cottage cheese with remaining ingredients; stir in gelatin. Pour into a loaf pan and refrigerate until firm. Garnish with green pepper ring filled with reserved pineapple.

This recipe submitted by the following teachers:

Mrs. Dianna M. Watson, New Braunfels H. S.
New Braunfels, Texas

Mrs. Bert Johnson, Bruce H. S.
Bruce, Mississippi

CONDENSED MILK-PINEAPPLE SALAD

Number of Servings — 12

1 pkg. lemon gelatin
1 pkg. lime gelatin
1 c. boiling water
1 No. 2 can crushed pineapple
1 small box cottage cheese
1 lge. can condensed milk

Dissolve gelatin in boiling water. Immediately add the milk, pineapple and cottage cheese. Stir until thoroughly mixed. Pour into mold. Chill until firm.

Virginia Searles, Westville Public Schools
Westville, Oklahoma

PINEAPPLE-CHEESE SALAD

Number of Servings — 6-8

1 pkg. lemon gelatin
1 pkg. lime gelatin
1 small can milk, chilled
½ lb. small curd cottage cheese
1 c. crushed pineapple, chilled
½ c. nuts (opt.)

Dissolve the gelatin in 2 cups of hot water. Chill until slightly congealed. Using electric mixer, beat in milk, cottage cheese, pineapple, nuts (if used) in this order. Pour into a 3½-cup mold. Let set until firm.

Mrs. Richard H. Garrett, Gragg School
Memphis, Tennessee

PINEAPPLE-NUT FRUIT SALAD

Number of Servings — 10

1 box lemon gelatin
1 box lime gelatin
2 c. boiling water
½-1 c. mayonnaise
1 can evaporated or sweetened condensed milk
2-2½ c. crushed pineapple, drained
1 pt. or less cottage cheese
½-1 c. pecans or walnuts, chopped
2 T. lemon juice (opt.)

Dissolve gelatins in hot water; cool. Chill until thickened. Combine mayonnaise and milk. Fold into gelatin. Add pineapple, cottage cheese, nuts and lemon juice if desired. Chill until firm. For a richer salad, 1 package of gelatin and 1 cup water may be left out.

This recipe submitted by the following teachers:

Mrs. Maxine King, Unity H. S.
Mendon, Illinois

Mrs. Marie W. Davis, John Rundle H. S.
Grenada, Mississippi

Jeannette Reynolds, Crowville H. S.
Crowville, Louisiana

Mrs. Virginia Bonds, Shady Spring H. S.
Beaver, West Virginia

Mrs. Wilma Sonne, Plankinton H. S.
Plankinton, South Dakota

Mrs. Dorothy Hutchison Hanks, Vancleave H. S.
Vancleave, Mississippi

PINEAPPLE-COTTAGE CHEESE SALAD

Number of Servings — 12

1 pkg. lime gelatin
1 pkg. lemon gelatin
2 c. hot water
1-2½ c. crushed pineapple, drained
1 pt. cottage cheese
1 c. mayonnaise
1 c. whipped cream or Dream Whip
½-1 c. nuts. chopped
1-2 T. horseradish
1 c. celery, chopped (opt.)

Dissolve gelatins in hot water; let stand until partially set. Add remaining ingredients in order given; mix well. Refrigerate until firm.

This recipe submitted by the following teachers:

Elda Kaufman, Central Junior H. S.
Clifton, Illinois

Harrietta H. White
Hyndman-Londonderry Merged H. S.
Hyndman, Pennsylvania

Mrs. Patricia Langston, Alamosa H. S.
Alamosa, Colorado

Mrs. Elaine B. Kiester
Slippery Rock, Pennsylvania

Mrs. Leon Potts, Kossuth H. S.
Kossuth, Mississippi

Mrs. Frances W. Smith, Johnson County H. S.
Mountain City, Tennessee

Peggy Allison, Thomas Downey H. S.
Modesto, California

Emma Andreae, Bellows Falls H. S.
Bellows Falls, Vermont

PINEAPPLE PARTY SALAD

Number of Servings — 10

1 No. 2 can crushed pineapple, drained
1 pkg. lime gelatin
1 pkg. lemon gelatin
½ c. nuts, chopped
¼ t. salt
1-2 c. cottage cheese
1 c. mayonnaise

Combine juice drained from pineapple with enough water to make 2 cups liquid. Heat to boiling. Pour over gelatins; stir until dissolved. Add salt. Cool until slightly thickened. Fold in remaining ingredients. Chill until firm.

This recipe submitted by the following teachers:

Mrs. Charlene Broome Strickland
Madison County H. S.
Danielsville, Georgia

Mrs. Ina Mae Perry, Lexington H. S.
Lexington, Texas

PINEAPPLE SALAD

Number of Servings — 9

2½ c. crushed pineapple
½ c. sugar
1 box lime gelatin
1 c. cottage cheese
1 small box Dream Whip or 1 c. whipped cream
½ c. pecans, chopped

Bring sugar and pineapple to a boil. Dissolve gelatin in mixture. Cool until thickened. Prepare Dream Whip according to package directions. Add Dream Whip or whipped cream and cottage cheese. Mix well. Add nuts and pour into square flat dish or mold. Refrigerate.

Beulah Riegel, Brookville H. S.
Brookville, Ohio

PINK SALAD

Number of Servings — 6

1 pkg. strawberry gelatin
1 6-oz. can crushed pineapple, undrained
1 c. whipped cream
1 c. small curd cottage cheese
½ c. pecans, coarsley chopped

Combine gelatin and pineapple in saucepan. Bring to a boil, stirring occasionally to prevent sticking. Cool. Fold in cream, cottage cheese and pecans. Place in 1 quart mold and refrigerate 2 to 3 hours or until firm.

Mrs. Lynn L. Keim, Alwood H. S.
Woodhull, Illinois

GREEN PINEAPPLE SALAD

Number of Servings — 16

1 or 2 pkg. lime gelatin
2 c. pineapple juice and water
½-1 c. celery, diced
½-1 c. walnuts or pecans, finely chopped
1 small jar pimento strips
1 No. 2 can crushed pineapple, drained
2 pkg. cream cheese
½ pt. whipped cream

Dissolve gelatin in pineapple juice and boiling water. Cool until thickened. Blend cheese and pineapple; add to gelatin. Fold in celery, nuts and pimento. Fold in whipped cream. Pour into 2 ring molds and chill.

This recipe submitted by the following teachers:

Mrs. Patricia Johansen, Rockford H. S.
Rockford, Minnesota

Katie Jackson, Cass City H. S.
Cass City, Michigan

Mrs. Eunice Gunter, Eagle Lake H. S.
Eagle Lake, Texas

FRUIT GELATIN

Number of Servings — 9-12

2 pkg. lemon gelatin
2 c. boiling water
8-12 ice cubes
1 lge. can crushed pineapple, drained
2 small pkg. cream cheese, diced
1 c. pecans, chopped

Dissolve gelatin in hot water or pineapple juice. Add ice cubes; stir until slightly congealed; remove unmelted cubes. Add remaining ingredients. Chill until firm.

Nancy A. Miller, Morganfield H. S.
Morganfield, Kentucky

MOLDED PINEAPPLE-CREAM CHEESE

Number of Servings — 6-8

1 pkg. lime gelatin
1 pkg. lemon gelatin
1 No. 2 can pineapple
2 small pkg. cream cheese
2 T. vinegar
½ c. pecans, chopped

Prepare gelatin according to directions on package. Cool. Combine cream cheese and vinegar; stir until smooth. Add crushed pineapple and nuts to cream cheese mixture. Combine mixture with chilled gelatin and pour into molds.

Angela Martin, Southside H. S.
Gadsden, Alabama

MOLDED PINEAPPLE-NUT SALAD

Number of Servings — 6

1 pkg. lemon or lime gelatin
1 pkg. cream cheese
1 small can crushed pineapple, drained
½ c. pecans, chopped
2 c. pineapple juice plus water

Heat pineapple juice and water to boiling, add gelatin. Stir until dissolved and let cool. Mix a small amount of the cooled gelatin with the cream cheese. Add to remaining gelatin when it is about ready to set. Add pineapple and pecans. Chill in desired mold.

Mrs. Ruth A. Holliday, Lamar County H. S.
Vernon, Alabama

PINEAPPLE CHIFFON SALAD

Number of Servings — 8

1 pkg. lime gelatin
1 c. crushed pineapple, drained
1 c. hot water
1 pkg. cream cheese
2 c. whipped cream

Dissolve gelatin in hot water or pineapple juice. Cool; add cream cheese. When mixture is thick, beat. Add whipped cream. Chill.

Mrs. Margaret Daugherty, Chestnut—Ridge H. S.
Fishertown, Pennsylvania

GELATIN-PINEAPPLE SALAD

Number of Servings — 15

1 pkg. lemon gelatin
1 c. boiling pineapple juice
1 pkg. cream cheese
1 c. crushed pineapple
12 Maraschino cherries
½ c. whipped cream

Dissolve gelatin in pineapple juice and cool to the consistency of egg whites. Mash cream cheese with a fork; add pineapple and crush together. Add cherries and whipped cream. Fold into gelatin mixture. Place in a round mold. Chill until firm. Unmold and fill the center with cottage cheese.

Barbara Schneitman, Live Oak Union H. S.
Live Oak, California

PINEAPPLE-CHEESE RING

Number of Servings — 8-10

1 No. 2½ can crushed pineapple
1 6-oz. pkg. leman gelatin
½ c. stuffed olives, sliced
¼ lb. cream cheese (cubed)
¼ c. nuts, chopped (opt.)
½ pt. heavy cream, unwhipped

Heat crushed pineapple to the boiling point. Add gelatin. Remove from heat and stir until gelatin is dissolved. Cool until lukewarm. Add olives, cubes of cheese and nuts, if desired and heavy cream. Do not whip the cream. Refrigerate until set. This is enough for a large size ring mold. This salad stays solid for hours. It is excellent for carrying to picnics even in warm weather.

Mrs. Helen L. Wilson, Washington Senior H. S.
Sioux Falls, South Dakota

PINEAPPLE-CITRUS MOLD

Number of Servings — 18-20

1 pkg. lemon gelatin
1 pkg. lime gelatin
1½ c. hot water
1 No. 2 can crushed pineapple
1 c. mayonnaise
1 c. pecans, chopped
1 lge. pkg. cream cheese
1 13-oz. can evaporated milk, whipped

Dissolve gelatin in water. Soften cream cheese with mayonnaise and small amounts of gelatin mixture. When mixture is thin enough, blend in remaining gelatin. Chill until partially thickened. Add pineapple and pecans. Fold in milk. Refrigerate until firm.

Mrs. Maudine R. Baldwin, Bruce H. S.
Pittsboro, Mississippi

PINEAPPLE-CHEESE SALAD

Number of Servings — 12

1 pkg. lemon gelatin
2 c. hot water
1 4-oz. pkg. cream cheese
1 small can crushed pineapple
½ c. nuts, chopped
2 T. mayonnaise

Mix gelatin, water and cream cheese. Stir until well blended. Chill until set. Add pineapple, nuts and mayonnaise. Chill until firm.

Mrs. John H. Graves, Central H. S.
Sumner, Texas

PINEAPPLE-CHEESE SALAD

Number of Servings — 8-10

1 No. 2 can crushed pineapple and juice
½ c. sugar
1 pkg. lemon gelatin
1 3-oz. package cream cheese, softened
½ c. nuts, chopped
1 c. evaporated milk, chilled or whipped cream

Bring sugar and pineapple to a boil. Stir in gelatin until it dissolves. Chill until thickened. Add nuts and cheese. Whip the chilled milk until stiff. Carefully fold the whipped milk or cream into the gelatin mixture. Chill until set.

Mrs. Ellen S. Racht, Northeast Bradford H. S.
Rome, Pennsylvania

PINEAPPLE-CREAM CHEESE SALAD

Number of Servings — 8

1 pkg. lime gelatin
1 c. marshmallows
1 T. sugar
1 c. boiling water
1 pkg. cream cheese
1 No. 2 can crushed pineapple
½ pt. whipped cream

Dissolve gelatin, marshmallows, cheese and sugar in boiling water. Cool. Fold in pineapple and whipped cream. Chill.

Mrs. Mary Kay Bacon, Thomas Walker H. S.
Ewing, Virginia

PINEAPPLE-CREAM CHEESE SALAD

Number of Servings — 8

1 pkg. lime or lemon gelatin
1 c. boiling water
1 3-oz. pkg. cream cheese
1 c. half and half cream
1 c. crushed pineapple, drained
½ c. nuts, chopped

Dissolve gelatin in boiling water; chill until partially set. Blend cheese and cream until smooth. Add pineapple and nuts to cheese mixture. Fold into gelatin and refrigerate until firm.

Helen Phillips, Metamora H. S.
Metamora, Ohio

PINEAPPLE-CREAM CHEESE SALAD

Number of Servings — 15

2 medium cans crushed pineapple
2 3-oz. pkg. cream cheese
2 1-oz. envelopes unflavored gelatin
1 small bottle Maraschino cherries
1 c. cold water

Soak gelatin in cold water for 5 minutes. Heat pineapple and cream cheese until cheese melts. Add softened gelatin. Add cherries; blend until gelatin is dissolved. Pour into 13 x 10 pan. Chill until firm.

Fruit Salad Dressing:
2 eggs, beaten until light
2 T. flour
⅔ c. sugar
Juice of 1 lemon
Juice of 1 orange
1 c. pineapple juice
½ c. whipped cream

Blend eggs, sugar and flour in double boiler. Gradually add juices. Cook until thickened. Cool; fold in whipped cream.

Mrs. Winifred S. Elliott, Rockville H. S.
Rockville, Connecticut

PINEAPPLE-CREAM CHEESE SALAD

Number of Servings — 14

1 pkg. lemon gelatin
1 pkg. lime gelatin
2 c. crushed pineapple, drained
2-3 drops green food coloring (opt.)
1 8-oz. pkg. cream cheese, softened
1 c. coffee cream

Combine pineapple juice and enough water to make 2¾ cups liquid. Dissolve gelatin in boiling water and juice. Add pineapple and food coloring; cool. Blend cream cheese and cream. Add to gelatin mixture. Refrigerate.

Mrs. Elizabeth W. Smith, Austin H. S.
El Paso, Texas

PINEAPPLE-CREAM CHEESE SALAD

Number of Servings — 6-8

1 pkg. orange gelatin
1 c. boiling water
1 c. pineapple juice
1 c. crushed pineapple, drained
1 4-oz. pkg. cream cheese
18 marshmallows

Pour boiling water over gelatin. Add pineapple juice and pineapple. Melt marshmallows and cream cheese in top of double boiler. Add this to the gelatin pineapple mixture. Chill until firm.

Mrs. Grace S. Wells, Huntington Local School
Chillicothe, Ohio

PINEAPPLE DELIGHT

Number of Servings — 6-8

1 small can crushed pineapple, drained
1 pkg. lemon gelatin
1 3-oz. pkg. cream cheese
Pineapple juice plus enough water to make 1 c. liquid
1 c. whipped cream
½ c. pecans, chopped

Bring pineapple juice-water mixture to a boil. Pour half of the hot liquid over gelatin and half over cream cheese. Stir the two mixtures together; cool. Fold in pineapple, pecans and whipped cream. Chill.

Mrs. Ellen Gressett, Hermleigh H. S.
Hermleigh, Texas

PINEAPPLE DELIGHT

Number of Servings — 12

1 3-oz. pkg. lemon gelatin
½-1 c. celery, finely cut
½ pt. whipped cream
1 No. 303 can crushed pineapple, drained
⅛ t. salt (opt.)
1 small can pimento, chopped
2 3-oz. pkg. cream cheese
⅔-1 c. nuts, chopped

Moisten cream cheese with chopped pimento. Add celery, nuts, pineapple and salt. Set aside. Heat juice drained from pineapple to boiling; stir in gelatin. Let thicken, then whip until bubbly. Add all ingredients except whipped cream. Let mixture stand until it starts to set. Fold in whipped cream. Refrigerate.

This recipe submitted by the following teachers:

Mrs. Caroline Daniels, Freedom Area H. S.
Freedom, Pennsylvania

Mrs. Esther Magill, Kimball H. S.
Kimball, South Dakota

Mrs. Mary Pinkston Whaley
Tuscaloosa County H. S.
Northport, Alabama

PINEAPPLE-LIME DELIGHT

Number of Servings — 6

1 3-oz. pkg. lime gelatin
1 No. 2 can crushed pineapple, drained
2 3-oz. pkg. cream cheese
1 c. evaporated milk
1 c. celery, finely chopped
1 c. nuts, chopped
Juice from canned pineapple

Heat pineapple juice and gelatin until gelatin is dissolved; cool. Mix cheese and milk together until smooth; add celery, pineapple and nuts. Fold into thickened gelatin. Pour into oiled mold or 10 x 6 x 1½ inch pan. Chill until firm.

Mary Ann Eltife, Windthorst H. S.
Windthorst, Texas

PINEAPPLE-LIME GELATIN SALAD

Number of Servings — 6

1 pkg. lemon or lime gelatin
1 c. boiling water
1 3-oz. pkg. cream cheese
½-2½ c. crushed pineapple, drained
½ c. nuts, chopped
1 c. pineapple juice plus water

Dissolve gelatin and cream cheese in hot water. Add juice and water mixture. Chill until partially set. Add pineapple and nuts. Chill until firm.

This recipe submitted by the following teachers:

Margaret M. Golden, Millport H. S.
Millport, Alabama

Mrs. Francys Putnam, Phillips Junior H. S.
Chapel Hill, North Carolina

Marguerite Steele, Green Springs H. S.
Green Springs, Ohio

YO-YO SALAD

Number of Servings — 8

1 pkg. lime gelatin
12 marshmallows
1½ c. boiling water
½ c. pineapple juice
1 3-oz. pkg. cream cheese
1 8-oz. can crushed pineapple
1 c. pecans, chopped
3 T. mayonnaise
1 c. whipped cream

Dissolve gelatin and marshmallows in boiling water. Add pineapple juice; chill until thickened. Cream together cheese, pineapple, nuts and mayonnaise. Combine with gelatin mixture. Fold in whipped cream. Congeal and serve on lettuce. Garnish with whipped cream and Maraschino cherries if desired.

Norma T. Yelverton, Lee Woodard School
Black Creek, North Carolina

YUM-YUM SALAD

Number of Servings — 12

2 c. crushed pineapple
¾ c. sugar
Juice of 1 lemon
1 pkg. lemon gelatin
1 pkg. unflavored gelatin
¼ c. cold water
2 small pkg. cream cheese
2 T. cream
½ c. olives, sliced
½ c. nuts, chopped
½ pt. whipped cream

Soak gelatin in cold water for 10 minutes. Heat pineapple, sugar and lemon juice. Add soaked gelatin and lemon gelatin to the hot mixture. Moisten cheese with cream and add to gelatin mixture. When beginning to set add olives, nuts and whipped cream. Chill until firm.

Bobbie Jones McGee, Ware Shoals School
Ware Shoals, South Carolina

CHEESE-PINEAPPLE SALAD

Number of Servings — 6-8

¼ lb. Velveeta cheese, cubed
1 No. 2 can pineapple chunks
12 marshmallows
Pinch of salt
1 egg, beaten
2 T. cornstarch

Drain pineapple. Combine juice and egg; mix well. Mix cornstarch with a small amount of the juice-egg mixture to form a paste. Combine paste with remaining juice-egg mixture. Heat slowly until thickened; stirring constantly. Pour over cheese, pineapple, and marshmallows. Mix lightly and chill.

Luella Davis, Cheboygan H. S.
Cheboygan, Michigan

PINEAPPLE CHEESE MOLD

Number of Servings — 4-5

1 c. crushed pineapple
1 c. pineapple juice
¼ c. lemon juice
½ c. sugar
1½ envelopes gelatin
½ c. American cheese, grated
½ c. whipped cream

Dissolve gelatin in ½ cup of water for 10 minutes. Bring pineapple and juice, lemon juice and sugar to a boil. Remove from heat and add gelatin. Chill until partially set. Add cheese and whipped cream. Chill until firm. Top with dressing.

Dressing:

1 c. salad dressing
⅛ c. onion juice
⅛ c. celery, finely chopped
⅛ c. green pepper, finely chopped

Combine ingredients and serve on salad.

Mrs. Cynthia R. Cutter, LaRue County H. S.
Hodgenville, Kentucky

PINEAPPLE-CHEESE SALAD

Number of Servings — 8-12

2 pkgs. orange gelatin
1 c. hot water
2½ c. cold water
2 c. crushed pineapple, drained
24 marshmallows, cut up
1 c. cheese, grated
1 c. whipped cream
1 T. salad dressing

Dissolve gelatin in hot water. Add cold water, pineapple, marshmallows and cheese. Mix. Let set. When mixture begins to congeal add whipped cream and salad dressing.

Carol Biere, Nebraska City H. S.
Nebraska City, Nebraska

LIME SURPRISE

Number of Servings — 8

1 pkg. lime gelatin
1 pkg. dessert topping mix
1 small can crushed pineapple, drained
1 small pkg. Velveeta cheese, cubed
¼ c. pecans, chopped

Mix gelatin according to package directions. Chill until syrupy; beat until frothy. Mix dessert topping mix as directed on package. Fold gelatin, pineapple, pecans and cheese in dessert topping mix. Chill.

Mrs. Nadine Tooley, Effingham, H. S.
Effingham, Illinois

MOLDED PINEAPPLE SALAD

Number of Servings — 8

1 pkg. lemon gelatin
1½ c. hot water
½ c. mayonnaise
½ c. canned condensed milk
1 No. 2 can crushed pineapple
1 c. cheese, grated
½ c. nuts, chopped

Dissolve gelatin in boiling water. Chill until partially set. Combine with remaining ingredients. Put into molds; chill until set.

Rozena N. Oaks, Bonneville H. S.
Ogden, Utah

PINEAPPLE-CHEESE SALAD

Number of Servings — 6-8

1 pkg. lemon gelatin
1½ c. boiling water
1 small can crushed pineapple
¼ c. mayonnaise
½ pt. whipped cream
1 c. cheese, grated

Dissolve gelatin in boiling water. Let set until syrupy. Mix pineapple and mayonnaise together; fold into gelatin mixture. Fold in whipped cream. Sprinkle top with cheese.

Mrs. James D. Jones, Mountainburg H. S.
Mountainburg, Arkansas

PINEAPPLE-CHEESE SALAD

Number of Servings — 8

1½ c. boiling water
1 pkg. orange, lemon or lime gelatin
½ c. sugar
Juice of 1 lemon
1 15-oz. can crushed pineapple, drained
1 c. whipped cream or whipped evaporated milk
1 c. cheddar cheese, grated

Dissolve gelatin and sugar in boiling water; add lemon juice. Chill until thickened. Fold in pineapple, whipped cream or milk and cheese. Refrigerate until firm.

Barbara Law, McCaulley H. S.
McCaulley, Texas

PINEAPPLE-CHEESE SALAD

Number of Servings — 12-15

1 No. 2½ can crushed pineapple, drained
1 lb. American cheese, grated
1 c. pecans, chopped
1 pkg. lime gelatin
1 tall can evaporated milk, chilled and whipped or 1 c. whipped cream

Heat pineapple juice. Dissolve gelatin in hot juice. Add grated cheese; mix well. Add pineapple and nuts. Chill until partially congealed. Whip milk. Fold the gelatin mixture into the milk or cream. Chill until firm.

Mrs. Louise Simpson, New Site H. S.
Alexander City, Alabama

PINEAPPLE-CHEESE SALAD

Number of Servings — 6

1 envelope gelatin
¼ c. cold water
½ c. hot water
1 c. crushed pineapple
1 T. sugar
¼ t. salt
⅔ c. American cheese or cream cheese, grated
½ c. whipped cream
2 T. lemon juice

Sprinkle gelatin on top of cold water. Let soak 5 minutes. Add sugar, salt and softened gelatin to hot water; stir until dissolved. Add lemon juice. Chill until thickened. Beat in cheese and whipped cream. Turn into molds that have been rinsed in cold water and chill.

Mrs. Dorothy Smith, Palacios Senior H. S.
Palacios, Texas

PINEAPPLE-CHEESE SURPRISE

Number of Servings — 8

1 pkg. lemon gelatin
1 No. 300 can pineapple tid-bits, or crushed pineapple
1 lge. can evaporated milk, whipped, or whipped cream
1-2 T. mayonnaise
¼ c. pecans, or walnuts chopped
¼ c. candied cherries or Maraschino cherries, chopped
½-¾ c. American cheese, finely diced

Place pineapple in a saucepan; bring to a boil. Add gelatin; stir until dissolved. Place saucepan in a bowl of ice water, stirring occasionally until it becomes thick and syrupy. Gently fold pineapple into whipped milk. Quickly fold in mayonnaise, pecans, cherries and cheese. Chill until firm.

This recipe submitted by the following teachers:

Mrs. Janet Latham, Buhl H. S.
Buhl, Idaho

Mrs. Anne Boersma, Ephrata Jr. H. S.
Ephrata, Washington

PINEAPPLE-CHEESE SQUARES

Number of Servings — 10-12

1 pkg. lemon gelatin
1 c. hot water
1 c. pineapple juice-water
¾ c. sugar (opt.)
1 c. crushed pineapple, drained
1 c. whipped cream
¾-1 c. American cheese, grated

Dissolve gelatin in hot water; add juice-water mixture and sugar. Chill until slightly thickened. Fold in remaining ingredients. Chill until firm. Cut in squares.

This recipe submitted by the following teachers:

Mrs. Normagene Manning, Livingston H. S.
Livingston, California

Mrs. Robert Klein, Brookland Junior H. S.
Richmond, Virginia

PINEAPPLE CREAM DELIGHT

Number of Servings — 6-8

1 No. 2 can crushed pineapple
½-1 c. sugar
1 pkg. lemon or lime gelatin
1 c. hot water
1 c. nuts
½ lb. cheese, grated
½ pt. whipped cream

Boil pineapple and sugar 3 minutes, pour over gelatin, which has been dissolved in the hot water. Cool. Add nuts and cheese. Refrigerate until it begins to jell. Fold in cream. Chill until firm.

This recipe submitted by the following teachers:

Mrs. Lynn Mathews, Centerville H. S.
Centerville, Texas

Peggy M. Ivey, Hudler School
Monahans, Texas

Elizabeth Conduff, St. James H. S.
Greenville, Tennessee

Mrs. William Cooper, Paxton H. S.
Paxton, Illinois

YELLOW WONDER

Number of Servings — 6

1 No. 2 can crushed pineapple
½ c. sugar
1 pkg. lemon gelatin
1 c. hot water
1 c. walnuts, chopped
½ lb. cheddar cheese, grated
1 c. whipped cream

Cook pineapple and sugar together for three minutes. Dissolve gelatin in the hot water. Add to pineapple mixture. Cool. Add nuts and cheese. Refrigerate until mixture begins to jell. Add whipped cream. Mold and Chill.

Mrs. Karmen Miles W. Setty, George L. Dilworth Jr. H. S.
Sparks, Nevada

REFRESHMENT SALAD

Number of Servings — 8

1 No. 2 can crushed pineapple, drained
1 pkg. lemon gelatin
1½ c. hot liquid
2 T. lemon juice (opt.)
½ lb. American cheese, grated
½ c. blanched almonds or other nuts, chopped coarsely
1 c. whipped cream

Dissolve gelatin in water and pineapple juice. Add lemon juice and cool. Add pineapple, cheese and nuts. When mixture is slightly thickened fold in cream. Chill until firm. Grated cheese may be sprinkled on salad as a garnish.

This recipe submitted by the following teachers:

Mrs. Sadie Belle Propst, Circleville H. S.
Circleville, West Virginia

Patricia Everett, Mayfield H. S.
Mayfield, Kentucky

SALAD WITH A MULTITUDE OF SINS

Number of Servings — 6-8

1 pkg. lime gelatin
2 c. boiling water
2 c. miniature marshmallows
1 c. sharp Cheddar cheese, grated
1½ c. celery, chopped
1 No. 2 can crushed pineapple, drained
½-¾ c. nuts, chopped
2 T. lemon juice
½ pt. whipped cream
⅓ c. mayonnaise

Stir gelatin and marshmallows in hot water until melted. Chill until mixture begins to thicken. Add cheese, celery, pineapple, nuts and lemon juice. Add combined whipped cream and mayonnaise. Pour into an 8 x 12 x 2 glass dish. Refrigerate for at least 12 hours before serving.

Yvonne M. Camagna, Ceres Union H. S.
Ceres, California

YUM-YUM SALAD

Number of Servings — 8

1 pkg. lime gelatin
1 flat can crushed pineapple, undrained
½ c. sugar
1 c. mild Cheddar cheese, finely grated
½ c. pecans, chopped
1 c. whipping cream
2 T. sugar

Prepare gelatin according to package instructions; set aside to thicken slightly. Cook pineapple with ½ cup sugar until no liquid remains and pineapple is slightly candied. Cool. Add cheese and pecans. Add pineapple mixture to gelatin; fold in whipped cream sweetened with 2 Tablespoons sugar. Refrigerate until firm.

Mrs. Jo Ann Gray, Waxahachie H. S.
Waxahachie, Texas

YUM-YUM PINEAPPLE SALAD

2 c. crushed pineapple
Juice of 1 lemon
¾-1 c. sugar
2 T. gelatin
½ c. cold water
1 c. cheese, grated
2 T. green pepper, chopped or 2 T. green Maraschino cherries (opt.)
2 T. red sweet pepper or pimento, chopped or 2 T. red Maraschino cherries, minced (opt.)
½ c. stuffed olives (opt.)
½ c. nuts, chopped (opt.)
1 c. whipped cream

Heat pineapple with lemon juice and sugar. Soak gelatin in cold water for 10 minutes. Add to hot mixture. Cool until thickened. Add cheese and any of the optional ingredients desired. Fold in whipped cream last. Chill until firm. NOTE: Chilled, whipped evaporated milk may be substituted for whipped cream if desired.

This recipe submitted by the following teachers:

Mrs. Ruth Bell, Trinity H. S.
Trinity, Texas

Mrs. Beulah Y. Collins, Elkin H. S.
Elkin, North Carolina

Frances J. Williams, Newton-Conover H. S.
Newton, North Carolina

Mrs. Jo Anna W. Boyens, Many H. S.
Many, Louisiana

Mildred E. Peterson, Senior H. S.
Pendleton, Oregon

Mrs. Mary K. Adams, Galien H. S.
Galien, Michigan

Loraine Fowles, Hailey H. S.
Hailey, Idaho

Mrs. Johnny Morrow, Waco H. S.
Waco, Texas

Mrs. Jesse Clausel, Thrasher H. S.
Booneville, Mississippi

Mrs. Reba Jean Fite Cook
Clarksdale-Coahoma H. S.
Clarksdale, Mississippi

Lois Ghent Ousley, Hartsville Junior H. S.
Hartsville, South Carolina

Elizabeth Thornburg, Montrose H. S.
Montrose, Colorado

RASPBERRY-RHUBARB SALAD

Number of Servings — 6

1 c. hot sweetened rhubarb sauce
1 box red raspberry gelatin
1 c. pineapple juice
1 c. crushed pineapple, drained
1 lge. raw apple, diced
½ c. nuts

Dissolve gelatin in hot rhubarb sauce; add pineapple juice. Chill until partially set. Add remaining ingredients. Chill until firm.

Mildred Christofeno, Baugo Township School
Elkhart, Indiana

PINEAPPLE-RHUBARB MOLD

Number of Servings — 6-8

2 c. fresh rhubarb, cut in 1" slices
⅓ c. sugar
½ c. water
1 No. 2 can pineapple tid-bits, drained
1 pkg. strawberry gelatin
2 t. lemon juice, fresh, frozen, or canned
1¾ c. syrup from pineapple and rhubarb

Combine rhubarb, sugar, and water; cover and cook just until tender, about five minutes. Drain thoroughly, reserving syrup. Heat the pineapple and rhubarb syrups to boiling; add to gelatin; stir until dissolved. Add lemon juice. Cool. Chill until partially set. Fold in rhubarb and pineapple; pour into 1-quart mold. Chill until set.

Mrs. Sharon Lampman, Ruthton H. S.
Ruthton, Minnesota

RHUBARB SALAD

Number of Servings — 8

1 pkg. strawberry or lemon gelatin
2 c. cooked and sweetened rhubarb
2 T. orange concentrate or juice of 1 orange
Juice of 1 lemon
1 pkg. cream cheese
½ c. chilled and whipped milnot

Dissolve gelatin in sweetened rhubarb. Add orange and lemon juice; chill until partially set. Blend in cream cheese. Fold in whipped milnot. Chill overnight. If lemon gelatin is used, a few drops of red food coloring may be added.

Mrs. Reta Neff, East Side School
Nappanee, Indiana

RHUBARB MOLDED SALAD

Number of Servings — 8

1 pkg. frozen or 2 c. fresh rhubarb
2 pkg. strawberry gelatin
2 c. pineapple juice
2 c. apples, chopped
1 c. nuts, chopped
Pinch of salt

Cook rhubarb as directed on package. Add 1 cup pineapple juice; bring to a boil. Add gelatin and stir until dissolved. Add salt and remaining pineapple juice. Let cool. Add apples and nuts. Chill until firm.

Jean Haynes, Whittle Springs Junior H. S.
Knoxville, Tennessee

RHUBARB SALAD

3 c. rhubarb, cut in ½-inch pieces
1 c. water
1 pkg. raspberry gelatin
1 c. sugar
1 c. celery, diced
1 c. nuts

Cook rhubarb in 1 cup water for 5 or 10 minutes. Add gelatin and sugar; stir until dissolved. Cool until syrupy. Add celery and nuts. Chill until firm. For a dessert substitute 1 cup miniature marshmallows for the celery.

Mrs. Barbara Sackett, Monona Grove H. S.
Madison, Wisconsin

RHUBARB-RASPBERRY SALAD

Number of Servings — 15

4 c. fresh rhubarb, diced
1 qt. water
2 c. sugar
2 pkgs. red raspberry gelatin
2 c. cold water
1 c. chunk pineapple, drained
1 c. nuts, chopped
¼ c. lemon juice
1 c. celery, diced

Combine rhubarb, water and sugar. Cover and cook until tender. Dissolve gelatin in hot rhubarb. Stir in lemon juice and cold water. Chill until syrupy. Fold in pineapple and nuts.

Mrs. Ethel Haun, Sr. H. S.
Junction City, Kansas

7-UP SALAD

Number of Servings — 6-8

1 box lemon gelatin
1 c. hot water
1 t. sugar
1 8-oz. pkg. cream cheese, softened
¼ c. pecans, chopped
1 t. vanilla
¼ c. cherries, chopped
1 small can crushed pineapple
1 bottle 7-Up

Dissolve gelatin in hot water; add sugar. Chill until slightly thickened. Beat cream cheese until very creamy; gradually add gelatin. Beat constantly. Add remaining ingredients. Chill until firm.

Mrs. Marybeth C. Pitman, North Clayton H. S.
College Park, Georgia

ORANGE-APPLESAUCE SALAD

Number of Servings — 6

1 can applesauce
1 pkg. orange gelatin
Juice of 1 orange
Rind of 1 orange, grated
1 7-oz. bottle 7-Up

Heat applesauce; add gelatin and stir until dissolved. Add remaining ingredients. Chill until firm.

Mrs. Martha R. LaCourse, Folsom H. S.
Folsom, California

ORANGE-CHEESE SALAD

Number of Servings — 12-16

3 pkgs. orange gelatin
3 c. reconstituted frozen orange juice
3 small bottles 7-Up or Squirt, chilled
3 3-oz. pkgs. cream cheese, softened
1 can Mandarin orange sections, drained and chilled
1 can pineapple tidbits, drained and chilled

Pour boiling orange juice over the gelatin; stir until dissolved. Add 7-Up or Squirt. Chill until mixture begins to thicken. Add cream cheese; beat with electric mixer until well blended. Pour into large ring mold and chill until set. Unmold on large serving plate. Fill center of mold with orange sections and pineapple tidbits.

Catherine Stall, Greenville Sr. H. S.
Greenville, Michigan

7-UP SALAD

Number of Servings — 8

1 pkg. lime gelatin
1 3-oz. pkg. cream cheese
1 c. crushed pineapple
1 6-oz. bottle 7-Up
½ c. nuts, chopped
2 T. hot water

Heat 7-Up; pour over gelatin. Mix cream cheese with hot water until smooth. Add cheese and remaining ingredients together. Chill.

Mrs. Ava Bush, Latexo Ind. School
Latexo, Texas

7-UP SALAD

Number of Servings — 6-9

1 3-oz. pkg. lemon or lime gelatin
1 c. boiling water
1 8-oz. pkg. cream cheese, broken in small pieces
1 No. 2 can crushed pineapple, drained
1 t. sugar
1 t. vanilla
½ c. nuts, chopped (opt.)
½ c. Maraschino cherries (opt.)
1 c. 7-Up
Few drops green food coloring (opt.)

Dissolve gelatin in boiling water; add cream cheese. Beat with electric mixer at low speed until smooth. Stir in pineapple, sugar, vanilla, food coloring, if desired, pecans. Add 7-Up. Chill until set. Stir when partially set to keep nuts from coming to top.

This recipe submitted by the following teachers:

Barbara E. Vines, Rupert H. S.
Rupert, West Virginia

Mrs. Geneva Christian, North Junior H. S.
Waco, Texas

Patricia Copeland, Pinckney Comm. School
Pinckney, Michigan

7-UP SALAD

Number of Servings — 6

1 pkg. lime gelatin
1 c. hot water
2 small pkg. cream cheese
1 small can crushed pineapple
1 T. sugar
1 t. vanilla
1 6-oz. bottle 7-Up

Dissolve gelatin in hot water. Cool. Add remaining ingredients. Chill.

Carrie E. Hinton, Stone School
Wiggins, Mississippi

7-UP SALAD

Number of Servings — 8

1 box cherry gelatin
1 No. 303 can applesauce
1 bottle 7-Up

Heat applesauce. Add gelatin and stir until dissolved. Let cool. Add 7-Up. Chill.

Mrs. Evelyn W. Hansen, Buffalo H. S.
Buffalo, Minnesota

ASPARAGUS SALAD

Number of Servings — 6-8

2 envelopes unflavored gelatin
½ c. hot water
¾ c. sugar (less if desired)
Pinch of salt
½ c. vinegar
1 c. water
1 c. celery, chopped
½ c. toasted pecans, chopped
1 can asparagus, cut in bite-size pieces
1 can pimento, cut in strips
Juice of ½ lemon
1 T. onion, scraped

Combine sugar, vinegar, water and salt; bring to a boil. Continue boiling for 5 minutes. Dissolve gelatin in hot water. Remove boiling mixture from heat and add gelatin. Cool. Combine remaining ingredients and add to liquid mixture. Chill until firm.

Mrs. Mary J. Higgins, Marietta H. S.
Marietta, Georgia

CONGEALED ASPARAGUS SALAD

Number of Servings — 6

1 No. 300 can green cut asparagus, drained
1 box lime gelatin
1 c. boiling water
¼ t. salt
1 c. mayonnaise
½ c. milk
½ c. cheese, grated
1 T. onion, grated
1 T. vinegar
Dash of red pepper or a few drops Tabasco sauce

Dissolve gelatin in boiling water. Cool until syrupy. Mix mayonnaise, milk, salt, cheese, onion, vinegar and pepper. Fold into thickened gelatin. Add asparagus. Turn into oiled molds. Congeal.

This recipe submitted by the following teachers:

Elizabeth Heard, Central H. S.
Jackson, Mississippi

Mrs. Anna Wheeler Phillips, Enterprise School
Brookhaven, Mississippi

ASPARAGUS OR BROCCOLI MOLD

Number of Servings — 8-10

1 can asparagus or 1 pkg. frozen broccoli, cooked
1 T. unflavored gelatin
¼ c. cold water
½ c. mayonnaise
½ c. whipped cream
1 t. salt
2-4 T. lemon juice
1 c. almonds

Dissolve gelatin in cold water; let stand until partially set. Drain hot liquid from vegetables and add enough water to make 1 cup liquid. Combine liquid and gelatin mixture. Fold in whipped cream, mayonnaise, salt and lemon juice. Add vegetables and almonds. Congeal. Serve with mayonnaise whipped with a small amount of lemon juice.

Mrs. J. W. Gant, White County H. S.
Sparta, Tennessee

BEET SALAD

Number of Servings — 6-8

1½ c. mixed water and beet juice
1 No. 2 can shoe-string beets, drained
1 pkg. lemon gelatin
1½ T. vinegar
1 t. salt
1½ T. onion, grated
¼ c. stuffed olives, sliced
2 T. horseradish
1¼ c. celery, chopped
½ c. nuts (opt.)

Heat water-beet juice mixture to boiling; add gelatin and stir until clear. Add vinegar and salt. Chill until partially set. Stir in remaining ingredients. Pour into mold. Chill until firm.

May Lohmann, Miami H. S.
Miami, Oklahoma

BEET SALAD

Number of Servings — 6

1 1-lb. can shoe-string beets, drained
2 T. vinegar
1 small onion, grated
1 t. prepared horseradish
½ t. celery salt
1 3-oz. pkg. lemon gelatin
1½ c. boiling water
1 c. celery, thinly sliced

Marinate beets in mixture of vinegar, onion, horseradish and celery salt. Dissolve gelatin in boiling water. Let thicken slightly. Add celery and beet mixture. Turn into individual molds and chill until firm. Serve with mayonnaise seasoned with curry.

Mrs. Florence Lenox, Runnels Jr. H. S.
Big Spring, Texas

BEET SALAD

Number of Servings — 8

1 pkg. lemon gelatin
1 c. boiling water
¾ c. canned beet juice
3 T. vinegar
½ t. salt

(Continued on next page)

2 t. onion, minced
1 t. horseradish
1 c. canned beets, drained and diced
1 c. celery, chopped
½ c. cucumbers, diced (opt.)

Dissolve gelatin in boiling water. Add beet juice, vinegar onion, horseradish and salt. Chill until partially thickened. Add remaining ingredients. Pour into mold. Chill until firm.

Volina Wilson, Greenville Jr. H. S.
Greenville, South Carolina

MOLDED BEET SALAD

Number of Servings — 9

1 T. unflavored gelatin
¼ c. lemon juice
1 c. hot beet juice
2 T. sugar
1 c. beets, chopped
1 c. celery, diced
¼ c. pecans, chopped
½ t. salt
Dash of pepper

Soak gelatin in lemon juice for 5 minutes. Dissolve in hot beet juice. Cool. Add remaining ingredients. Chill until firm.

Mrs. C. F. Hammer, West End H. S.
Nashville, Tennessee

BEET-CABBAGE SOUFFLE

Number of Servings — 4-6

1 pkg. lemon gelatin
1¼ c. hot water
¼ c. beet juice
1 T. vinegar
½ c. mayonnaise
¼ t. salt
Dash of pepper
1 c. cabbage, shredded
1 T. onion, finely chopped
1 c. beets, drained and diced

Dissolve gelatin in hot water. Add beet juice, vinegar, mayonnaise, salt and pepper. Blend well with rotary beater. Pour into refrigerator freezing tray. Quick-chill in freezing unit for 15 to 20 minutes or until firm about 1-inch from edge but soft in center. Whip with rotary beater until fluffy. Fold in beets, cabbage and onion. Chill for 30 to 60 minutes.

Jean Penrose, Loveland Senior H. S.
Loveland, Colorado

BEET-RASPBERRY SALAD

Number of Servings — 6

1 pkg. raspberry gelatin
2 c. cooked shoe-string beets
½ c. celery, finely chopped

Prepare gelatin according to package directions. Let partially thicken. Add remaining ingredients, stirring once. Chill.

Hilma R. Davis
Kansas State College, College High
Pittsburg, Kansas

BEET RINGS

Number of Servings — 6

1 pkg. lemon gelatin
1 c. hot water
1 c. mixed cold water and beet juice
1 lge. stalk celery, chopped
1 can beets, drained and cut in strips
½ c. prepared horseradish
1¼ t. salt
Pepper to taste

Dissolve gelatin in hot water; add cold water-beet juice mixture. Chill until mixture reaches the consistency of unbeaten egg whites. Combine beets, celery, horseradish, salt, and pepper. Add to gelatin mixture. Chill until firm.

Mrs. Alton D. Lewis, Lexington H. S.
Lexington, Tennessee

BROCCOLI SALAD

Number of Servings — 6

1 can hot beef consomme
1 envelope unflavored gelatin
¼ c. cold water
1 c. mayonnaise
1 pkg. frozen broccoli spears
6 hard-cooked eggs
½ t. salt
1 t. onion juice
1 t. Tabasco sauce
Juice of 1 lemon
1 t. Worcestershire sauce

Cook broccoli according to package directions. Cool and cut into small pieces. Soak gelatin in cold water; dissolve in hot consomme. Cool completely. Add remaining ingredients. Pour into individual molds. Chill until firm.

Mrs. Frances E. Poole, Mary Persons H. S.
Forsyth, Georgia

BROCCOLI SALAD

Number of Servings — 6-8

2 pkgs. broccoli, cooked and mashed
1 envelope unflavored gelatin
4 hard-cooked eggs, chopped
½ c. mayonnaise
Dash of Tabasco and Worcestershire sauce
2 c. hot beef consomme

Dissolve gelatin in hot consomme. Cool slightly. Add remaining ingredients. Pour into oiled molds; Chill.

Dionetta K. Talley, Demoplis H. S.
Demopolis, Alabama

MOLDED CARROT SALAD

Number of Servings — 8-10

1 pkg. lime gelatin
2 T. lemon juice
1½ c. carrot, grated
Salad greens
Salad dressing

Dissolve gelatin according to package directions. Add lemon juice; blend. Chill until partially set. Add carrot. Let stand until partially set. Pour into a ring mold; chill until firm. Garnish with salad greens. Serve with desired salad dressing.

Mrs. Joyce Miller, Hiland H. S.
Berlin, Ohio

CARROT DELIGHT SALAD

Number of Servings — 6

1 pkg. lime gelatin
2 c. boiling water
1 6-oz. pkg. cream cheese
1 c. carrots, grated
½ c. pecans, chopped
1 pkg. dessert topping mix, stiffly beaten

Dissolve gelatin in boiling water. Add cream cheese and stir until well mixed. Cool until partially congealed. Fold in carrots and nuts. Fold in whipped dessert topping mix. Chill until firm. Serve on lettuce.

Mrs. Stella Geiger, Columbus Grove H. S.
Columbus Grove, Ohio

CARROT-PINEAPPLE SALAD

Number of Servings — 6-8

1 pkg. orange gelatin
1 c. carrots, grated
1 c. crushed pineapple, drained
2 c. hot water

Dissolve gelatin in hot water; chill until partially set. Add carrots and pineapple. Chill until firm.

Elizabeth M. Vail, J. U. Blacksher
Uriah, Alabama

CARROT AND CELERY SALAD

Number of Servings — 6

1 envelope unflavored gelatin
¼ c. sugar
½ t. salt
1½ c. water
¼ c. lemon juice
1½ c. carrot, grated
¼ c. celery, finely diced
¼ c. green pepper, diced

Thoroughly mix gelatin, sugar and salt. Add ½ cup of water. Stir constantly over low heat until gelatin is dissolved. Remove from heat and stir in remaining 1 cup water and lemon juice. Chill mixture to unbeaten egg white consistency. Fold in mixed vegetables. Turn into a 3-cup mold or individual molds. Chill until firm. Unmold. Garnish with salad greens, scallions and radishes.

Mattie Mary Green, McLain H. S.
Neely, Mississippi

"14-CARROT GOLD" SALAD

Number of Servings — 6

1 pkg. orange gelatin
1½ c. hot water
1½ t. vinegar
½ t. salt
Grated onion
1½ c. carrots, coarsely grated
1 red apple, diced or a few radishes, chopped
¼ c. cabbage, shredded
½ small can crushed pineapple

Dissolve gelatin in hot water. Add vinegar, salt and small amount of onion. Chill until consistency of unbeaten egg whites. Add remaining ingredients. Pour into an oiled 1-quart mold or individual molds. Chill. Serve on greens.

Mrs. Doris Gustafson, Brethren H. S.
Brethren, Michigan

CABBAGE MOLD

Number of Servings — 8

1 pkg. lime gelatin
½ c. crushed pineapple, drained
½ c. cabbage finely shredded
Green pepper, chopped (opt.)
Celery, chopped (opt.)
1 T. salad dressing
½ c. Cheddar cheese, shredded
½ c. carrot, grated

Prepare gelatin as directed on the package. Stir in salad dressing. When partially set add remaining ingredients. Chill until firm.

Mrs. Bessie Hackett, Danvers H. S.
Danvers, Illinois

CABBAGE SALAD

Number of Servings — 10

1 T. unflavored gelatin
⅓ c. cold water
3 T. flour
1 t. salt
½ c. sugar
2 T. vinegar
Pineapple juice
Juice of 1 lemon
2 egg whites, beaten
1 pt. whipped cream
1 qt cabbage, shredded
1 pkg. marshmallows
1 No. 2½ can crushed pineapple, drained

Soak gelatin in cold water. Mix flour, salt, sugar, vinegar, pineapple juice and lemon juice together. Fold in egg whites. Cook and stir over low heat until thick. Remove from heat. Add gelatin. Combine remaining ingredients. Fold cooked mixture into cabbage mixture. Chill. This salad will keep for several days.

Dona Louise Woolery, Henry Senochwine, H. S.
Henry, Illinois

COLESLAW SOUFFLE

Number of Servings — 8-10

1 pkg. lemon gelatin
1 c. hot water
½ c. cold water
2 T. vinegar
¼ t. salt
Dash of pepper (opt.)
⅓-½ c. mayonnaise
1-2 c. cabbage, finely chopped
2-3 T. green pepper, chopped
1 T. onion, chopped
½-1 c. celery, chopped (opt.)
¼ t. celery seed (opt.)
¼-1 c. carrots, grated (opt.)

Dissolve gelatin in hot water; add cold water, vinegar, salt, mayonnaise and pepper. Beat until fluffy. Quick-chill in freezing unit until firm around the edges. Beat until fluffy. Chill until firm. Serve on lettuce.

This recipe submitted by the following teachers:

Mary B. McGlone, St. Francisville School
St. Francisville, Illinois

Mrs. Retha George, Bioloxi Sr., H. S.
Biloxi, Mississippi

Mae Clare Kemmer, Killdeer H. S.
Killdeer, North Dakota

Mrs. Marilyn Bushnell, Avonworth School
Pittsburgh, Pennsylvania

Virginia O. Savedge, Northampton H. S.
Eastville, Virginia

Mrs. Bess Snyder Mohl, Petersburg H. S.
Petersburg, West Virginia

MOLDED CABBAGE SALAD

Number of Servings — 10

1 pkg. lime gelatin
1 c. boiling water
1 c. marshmallows
½ c. whipped cream
1 c. mayonnaise
1 c. crushed pineapple
1 c. cabbage, finely shredded
½ c. almonds, slivered
½ c. whipped cream
3 T. mayonnaise
Sprigs of parsley, finely cut

Melt marshmallows in boiling water. Add gelatin; stir until dissolved. Add ½ cup whipped cream, 1 cup mayonnaise, pineapple, cabbage and almonds. Chill. Combine remaining ingredients; serve with gelatin mixture.

Mrs. Marie Anderson, St. Paul Park H. S.
St. Paul Park, Minnesota

CHEESE 'N' VEGETABLE SALAD

Number of Servings — 6

3½ c. hot water
2 pkg. lime gelatin
1 c. cabbage, shredded
½ c. celery, diced
1c. sharp cheese, coarsely grated
6 pear halves
6 apricot halves

Pour hot water over gelatin; stir until dissolved. Chill until mixture reaches the consistency of unbeaten egg whites; stir occasionally. Add cabbage, celery and cheese. Chill until firm. Garnish with pear and apricot halves.

Mrs. Eva Benson, Sweet Home Union H. S.
Sweet Home, Oregon

SEAFOAM COLESLAW

Number of Servings — 8

1 pkg. lime gelatin
1 c. hot water
¾ c. cold water
¾ t. salt
2 T. vinegar
⅔ c. salad dressing
Dash of pepper
¾ t. celery seed
1 T. onion, grated
2 c. cabbage, finely grated

Dissolve gelatin in hot water; add cold water, salt and vinegar. Let set until partially congealed; add salad dressing, pepper, celery seed, onion and cabbage. Mold and chill until firm.

Mrs. Ann H. Malone, South Middleton Twp. H. S.
Boiling Springs, Pennsylvania

COLESLAW PARFAIT SALAD

Number of Servings — 6-8

1 pkg. lemon gelatin
1 c. hot water
½ c. mayonnaise
½ c. cold water
2 T. vinegar
¼ t. salt
1½ c. cabbage, finely shredded
½ c. radishes, sliced
½ c. celery, diced
2-4 T. green pepper, diced
1 T. onion, diced
1 c. cottage cheese (opt.)

Dissolve gelatin in hot water. Blend in mayonnaise, cold water, vinegar and salt. Chill until partially set. Beat until fluffy. Add remaining ingredients. Pour into individual molds or 1-quart mold. Chill until set. Unmold on ruffles of lettuce and garnish with thin slices of radish and mint leaves.

This recipe submitted by the following teachers:

Mrs. Ethel H. Hale, Hackberry, H. S.
Hackberry, Louisiana

Mrs. Maralee H. Garland, Unicoi County H. S.
Erwin, Tennessee

Mrs. Catherine Taylor, Lamesa H. S.
Lamesa, Texas

OLD-FASHIONED COLESLAW

Number of Servings — 6

1 pkg. lemon gelatin
½ t. salt
1 c. hot water
½ c. cold water
½ c. mayonnaise
½ c. sour cream
1 t. onion, grated
1 T. prepared mustard
2 T. vinegar
1 t. sugar
2 c. cabbage, finely chopped

Dissolve gelatin and salt in hot water; add cold water. Chill until syrupy. Fold in all remaining ingredients except cabbage. Chill until slightly thickened. Fold in cabbage. Chill until firm.

Louisa Liddell, North Thurston H. S.
Lacey, Washington

PERFECTION SALAD

Number of Servings — 6

1 pkg. lemon gelatin
1 c. boiling water
1 t. lemon juice
1 c. mixed pineapple juice and water
1 c. cabbage, shredded
1 c. crushed pineapple, drained

Combine lemon juice and boiling water. Dissolve gelatin in boiling mixture; add pineapple juice. Let set until slightly cool. Add cabbage and pineapple. Refrigerate.

Mrs. Mary M. Radford, Centralia School
Chillicothe, Ohio

GELATIN DELIGHT

Number of Servings — 12

1 pkg. lime gelatin
1 c. crushed pineapple
1 c. pineapple juice
1 c. boiling water
1 c. cabbage, finely shredded
1 c. marshmallows, finely chopped
½ c. nuts, chopped
½ pt. whipped cream

Dissolve gelatin in boiling water. Add marshmallows and all remaining ingredients except whipped cream. Chill until partially set. Fold in whipped cream. Chill.

Mrs. Zelma Goben, Antelope Valley H. S.
Lancaster, California

GREEN SALAD

Number of Servings — 8

1 3-oz. pkg. lime gelatin
1 c. boiling water
½ c. pineapple juice
1 c. whipping cream
1 c. crushed pineapple, drained
1 c. cabbage, finely chopped
8 marshmallows, finely cut

Dissolve gelatin in boiling water; add pineapple juice. Chill until partially set. Whip until frothy. Add whipped cream, crushed pineapple, cabbage and marshmallows; mix well. Pour into a mold and chill until firm. Unmold onto shredded lettuce. Serve with mayonnaise.

Irene E. Krause, Shawano Senior H. S.
Shawano, Wisconsin

PINEAPPLE SOUFFLE SALAD

Number of Servings — 8

1 pkg. lime gelatin
1 c. boiling water
½ c. cold water
2 T. lemon juice or vinegar
½ c. salad dressing
2 c. cabbage, shredded
¾ c. crushed pineapple

Dissolve gelatin in boiling water. Add cold water and lemon juice or vinegar. Cook. When mixture is partially set beat with a rotary beater until fluffy. Beat in salad dressing. Fold in cabbage and pineapple. Chill until firm.

Mrs. Phebe G. Walker, Lebanon Sr. H. S.
Lebanon, New Hampshire

LIME GELATIN DELIGHT

Number of Servings — 6

1 pkg. lime gelatin
1 c. crushed pineapple, drained
1 c. cabbage, finely shredded
12 lge. marshmallows, quartered
2 T. salad dressing
½ c. pecans, chopped
2 c. boiling water

Dissolve gelatin in boiling water; add marshmallows. Stir occasionally while cooling to melt marshmallows. When cool add remaining ingredients. Chill until firm.

Mrs. Harry N. Young, Holgate Local H. S.
Holgate, Ohio

THIRTY-BELOW SLAW

Number of Servings — 10-12

1 pkg. pineapple gelatin
1 c. boiling water
2 t. lemon juice
19-oz. can crushed pineapple, undrained
½ c. mayonnaise
3 c. cabbage, finely chopped
¼ c. green pepper, finely chopped

Dissolve gelatin in boiling water; add lemon juice, pineapple and mayonnaise. Beat with rotary beater until thoroughly blended. Chill until slightly thickened. Fold in cabbage and pepper. Chill until firm.

Mrs. Grace Richmond, Chesaning Union H. S.
Chesaning, Michigan

ONE CUP CELERY-NUT SALAD

Number of Servings — 4-6

1 pkg. lime gelatin
1 c. hot water
1 c. cold water
1 c. celery, diced
1 c. pecan halves

Dissolve gelatin in hot water; add cold water, Refrigerate until thickened. Fold in celery and pecans. Let set for several hours or overnight.

Mrs. Janet Killian, Thebes H. S.
Thebes, Illinois

CUCUMBER SALAD

Number of Servings — 6

1 pkg. lime gelatin
1 t. salt
1 c. hot water
2 t. vinegar
1 t. onion juice
1 c. sour cream
¼ c. mayonnaise
1 cucumber, grated

Dissolve gelatin in hot water. Add salt; cool. Stir in remaining ingredients; blend well. Turn into ring mold. Chill until firm.

Dorothy B. Gifford, Sepulveda Junior H. S.
Sepulveda, California

CUCUMBER SALAD

1 pkg. lime gelatin
1 t. salt
1 c. boiling water
1 T. vinegar
1 t. onion, grated
Pepper
1 c. sour cream
¼ c. mayonnaise
1 c. cucumber, shredded and drained

Combine gelatin and salt; add boiling water. Add vinegar, onion and pepper. Chill until mixture is consistency of unbeaten egg whites. Fold in sour cream and mayonnaise. Fold in cucumber. Chill for 3 hours.

Mrs. Karen Frohrip, Sturgis H. S.
Sturgis, South Dakota

CUCUMBER SALAD

Number of Servings — 8

1 pkg. lime gelatin
1 c. boiling water
1 c. cold water
1 t. salt
2 T. vinegar
1 t. onion, diced
1 c. cucumber, grated

Dissolve gelatin in boiling water. Add cold water, salt and vinegar. Stir until salt is dissolved. Chill until partially thickened. Add cucumber and onion; mix well. Chill until firm.

Carolyn Gilmer, Morton H. S.
Kinnear, Wyoming

CUCUMBER ASPIC

Number of Servings — 4

2 T. unflavored gelatin
¾ c. cold water
½ c. boiling water
½ c. sugar
¼ c. vinegar
1 c. cucumber, grated
1 c. crushed pineapple
Pinch of salt
Green food coloring

Soften gelatin in cold water; dissolve in boiling water. Add sugar, vinegar, cucumber, pineapple and salt. Stir until combined. Add food coloring; blend. Chill until firm.

Mrs. Margaret M. Lee, Briarcliff H. S.
Atlanta, Georgia

CUCUMBER SALAD

Number of Servings — 10-12

1 pkg. lime gelatin
¾ c. boiling water
1 lge. cucumber, finely chopped
1 medium onion, finely chopped
1 c. cottage cheese
1 c. mayonnaise
1 T. lemon juice
Pecans or English walnuts, chopped (opt.)

Dissolve gelatin in boiling water; chill until syrupy. Whip. Gently add remaining ingredients. Chill until firm.

Mrs. Kathy Hoar, South Junior H.S.
Rapid City, South Dakota

COOL-AS-A-CUCUMBER SALAD

Number of Servings — 8-10

1 T. unflavored gelatin
½ c. cold water
½ t. salt
1 medium cucumber, pared, seeded and grated
½ small onion, finely grated
3 c. cream-style cottage cheese
1 8-oz. pkg. cream cheese
½ c. mayonnaise
⅔ c. celery, finely chopped
⅓ c. nuts, broken and toasted

Soften gelatin in water; add salt. Stir over low heat until gelatin dissolves. Combine cheeses; beat until blended. Stir in gelatin. Add remaining ingredients. Pour into a 6-cup ring mold. Chill until firm.

Mrs. Billy Marks, Bodenham, H. S.
Pulaski, Tennessee

COOL-AS-A-CUCUMBER SALAD

Number of Servings — 8

1 pkg. lime gelatin
1 c. boiling water
¾ c. cold water
¼ c. lemon juice
½ c. non-fat dry milk
½ c. dairy sour cream
¼ c. green pepper, chopped
2 c. unpeeled cucumber, thinly sliced
1 t. onion juice (opt.)
⅛ t. salt

Dissolve gelatin in boiling water. Add cold water and lemon juice. Chill until mixture begins to thicken. Add dry milk; beat until fluffy. Fold in remaining ingredients. Turn into molds; chill until firm.

This recipe submitted by the following teachers:

Marie Green, Newton Community H. S.
Newton, Illinois

Mrs. K. Marie Wright, Poolville H. S.
Poolville, Texas

CUCUMBER-CABBAGE SALAD

Number of Servings — 8

1 pkg. lime gelatin
1 c. hot water
½ c. mayonnaise
1 c. cabbage, finely chopped
½ c. cucumber, finely chopped
2 T. green pepper, chopped
½ t. celery seed
2-4 T. onion, finely chopped

Dissolve gelatin in hot water; cool. Whip in mayonnaise. Add remaining ingredients. Chill until firm.

Janice Brown, Flagler H. S.
Flagler, Colorado

COOL-AS-A-CUCUMBER SALAD

Number of Servings — 6

1 pkg. lime gelatin
¾ c. hot water
¼ c. lemon juice
1 t. onion juice
1 c. sour cream or tart mayonnaise
1 c. unpared cucumber, chopped

Dissolve gelatin in hot water. Add lemon and onion juice. Chill until partially set. Stir in sour cream or mayonnaise and cucumber. Pour into individual molds or ring mold. Chill until firm. If desired center of ring-molded salad may be filled with crab or shrimp salad.

This recipe submitted by the following teachers:

Janet E. Metz, McArthur H. S.
Hollywood, Florida

Marguerite L. Corkill, Forks H. S.
Forks, Washington

Ida Lou N. Holmes, Calvin Coolidge H. S.
Washington, D. C.

Cleo Codas, Northern H. S.
Durham, North Carolina

Theresa Zettel, Reedsville H. S.
Reedsville, Wisconsin

COOL-AS-A-CUCUMBER SALAD

Number of Servings — 6

1 pkg. lime gelatin
¾ c. hot water
¼ c. lemon juice
1 c. dairy sour cream, whipped
1 c. cucumber, chopped
Tomato wedges (garnish)

Dissolve gelatin in hot water; add lemon juice. Chill until partially set. Add cucumber; fold in whipped cream. Pour into oiled molds; chill until firm. Unmold on crisp lettuce. Garnish with tomato wedges.

Mrs. Jean Wollum, Eagle River H. S.
Eagle River, Wisconsin

CUCUMBER-COTTAGE CHEESE

Number of Servings — 8-10

1 pkg. lime gelatin
1 c. boiling water
1 t. lemon juice
1 medium cucumber, ground or finely chopped
½ lge. onion, ground or finely chopped
1 c. cottage cheese
½ c. mayonnaise

Dissolve gelatin in boiling water; add lemon juice. Cool. Mix cottage cheese and mayonnaise. Add to drained onion and cucumber. Combine with cooled gelatin mixture. Chill until firm.

Mrs. Mary Elenbaas, Tucker H. S.
Richmond 29, Virginia

CUCUMBER-CREAM CHEESE-RING

Number of Servings — 6-8

2 T. unflavored gelatin
¼ c. cold water
½-¾ c. boiling water
2-4 T. sugar
½ t. salt
2-3 T. lemon juice
1 t. onion, grated
1 c. cucumber, grated and drained
2 to 3 3-oz. pkgs. cream cheese
Canned pears, drained
Lettuce
¼ lb. red cinnamon candies

Soften gelatin in cold water; dissolve in boiling water. Add sugar; cool. Add salt, lemon juice, onion and cucumber. Soften cream cheese with ¼ cup gelatin mixture. Chill remaining gelatin until partially thickened. Beat chilled mixture with an egg beater until foamy. Combine with cheese gelatin mixture. Pour into a ring mold and chill until firm. Heat pear juice and candy until candy is dissolved. Add pears and let stand for 1 hour in the candy syrup. Unmold the cucumber ring on a chop plate; fill the center with lettuce and garnish with pears in crisp lettuce cups.

This recipe submitted by the following teachers:

Rosetta Haire, Wellington H. S.
Wellington, Illinois

Carol Cain, Hastings, H. S.
Hastings, Minnesota

CUCUMBER-LIME SALAD

Number of Servings — 6-8

1 pkg. lime gelatin
1 c. boiling water
1 c. cucumber, chopped
1 small onion, chopped
¼ c. mayonnaise
Salt and pepper

Dissolve gelatin in boiling water; cool. Add remaining ingredients; mix well. Chill until firm.

Mrs. Thelma Vogel, McAlester H. S.
McAlester, Oklahoma

CUCUMBER-LIME SALAD

Number of Servings — 6-8

1 pkg. lime gelatin
¾ c. boiling water
¾ c. cucumber, grated
1 T. onion, grated
1 c. cottage cheese
1 c. mayonnaise
⅓ c. pecans or almonds, chopped

Dissolve gelatin in boiling water. Cool until partially set. Fold in remaining ingredients. Chill until firm.

Mrs. Charles Corlew, Greenwood Jr. H. S.
Clarksville, Tennessee

CUCUMBER-LIME SALAD

Number of Servings — 6

1 c. boiling water
1 3-oz. pkg. lime gelatin
½ c. whipped cream
½ c. mayonnaise
2 T. onion, grated
1 small cucumber, grated
1 c. cottage cheese

Dissolve gelatin in boiling water. Chill until partially set. Beat until frothy. Fold in whipped cream and mayonnaise. Chill until almost set. Fold in remaining ingredients. Chill until firm.

Muriel Olson, Warroad H. S.
Warroad, Minnesota

CUCUMBER SOUFFLE SALAD

Number of Servings — 6-8

1 pkg. lime or lemon gelatin
3 T. vinegar or lemon juice
½ c. mayonnaise
¼ t. salt
Dash of pepper
1½-2½ c. cucumber, diced

Prepare gelatin according to package directions, using ½ cup less water than is called for. Blend in all ingredients except cucumbers with a rotary beater. Freeze in refrigerator tray for 15-20 minutes or until mixture is firm around edges but soft in center. Turn into bowl; whip until fluffy. Fold in cucumbers. Pour into mold. Chill until firm.

Mrs. Gayle Pfeil, Monona Grove H. S.
Madison, Wisconsin

JELLIED CUCUMBER SALAD

Number of Servings — 6

1 pkg. lime gelatin
1 c. hot water
1 c. canned grapefruit juice
1 t. onion, scraped
Dash of salt
1 c. cucumber, diced
½ c. radishes, thinly sliced

Dissolve gelatin in hot water. Add grapefruit juice, onion and salt. Chill until slightly thickened. Fold in cucumbers and radishes. Turn into molds. Chill until firm. Unmold on lettuce. Serve with mayonnaise.

Dorothy S. Giller, Narbonne H. S.
Harbor City, California

CUCUMBER MOLD

Number of Servings — 4-6

1 medium unpeeled cucumber, ground
1 small onion, ground
1½ pkg. lemon gelatin
½ c. boiling water
1 T. vinegar
1 pt. cottage cheese
½ c. mayonnaise
¼ c. whipping cream

Dissolve gelatin in boiling water; add vinegar. Chill until partially set. Add cottage cheese, mayonnaise, cucumber and onion. Add whipped cream. Pour into a mold and chill until firm.

Patricia Roppel, Ketchikan H. S.
Ketchikan, Alaska

CUCUMBER MOLDED SALAD

Number of Servings — 6

1 pkg. lime gelatin
1 c. boiling water
½ t. salt
1 c. cucumber, diced
¼ c. onion, chopped
¾ c. salad dressing
1 c. cottage cheese

Dissolve gelatin and salt in boiling water. When mixture begins to thicken add remaining ingredients. Pour into molds; chill until firm.

Opal Pierce, Montebello Senior H. S.
Montebello, California

ASHEVILLE SALAD

Number of Servings — 15

3 pkgs. cream cheese, softened
1 pt. mayonnaise
1 c. cold water
3 envelopes unflavored gelatin
2 cans tomato soup
½ c. celery, chopped
½ c. nuts, chopped
2 T. onion, minced

Soften gelatin in cold water. Blend mayonnaise and cheese. Heat soup; add gelatin. Add remaining ingredients. Chill until firm.

Mrs. Helen C. Borders, Waco
Waco, North Carolina

ASHEVILLE SALAD

Number of Servings — 16-20

2 cans of tomato soup
2 8-oz. pkg. cream cheese
4 T. unflavored gelatin
⅓ c. cold water
1 c. celery, finely chopped
1 c. onion, finely chopped
1 c. green pepper, finely chopped
1 c. mayonnaise
½ c. pecans, chopped (opt.)

Soak gelatin in cold water. Heat cheese and soup together. Add gelatin; mix until dissolved. Cool. Add nuts, mixed vegetables and mayonnaise. Pour into large ring mold or individual molds. Chill. Serve on lettuce with small portion of mayonnaise, if desired.

Mrs. Alice Harvard, Effingham County H. S.
Springfield, Georgia

ASHEVILLE SALAD

Number of Servings — 6

1 can tomato soup, heated
1 small pkg. cream cheese
1 c. celery, chopped
1 lge. green pepper, chopped
½ c. mayonnaise
1 T. unflavored gelatin
½ c. water

Dissolve gelatin in water; pour into hot soup. Mash cheese into soup; dissolve. Add celery, green pepper, and mayonnaise. Chill until firm.

Jean Palmer, Channelview H. S.
Channelview, Texas

TOMATO-ASPARAGUS SALAD

Number of Servings — 8

2 c. canned tomatoes or tomato juice
1 t. salt
Dash of pepper
1 small bay leaf
3 whole cloves
3 T. onion, minced
1 pkg. lemon gelatin
1 T. vinegar
2 T. cold water
1¼ c. cottage cheese
2 T. green pepper, minced
½ c. celery, diced
1 c. cooked asparagus, cooled
Salt to taste
⅓ c. mayonnaise or salad dressing

Combine tomatoes or juice, salt, pepper, bay leaf, cloves and onion. Cook gently for 20 minutes. Remove bay leaf after 10 minutes. Force mixture through a sieve; measure and add hot water to make 1½ cups. Dissolve gelatin in hot tomato mixture. Add vinegar. Measure ½ cup mixture; add cold water. Turn into ring mold or individual molds. Chill until firm. Chill remaining gelatin mixture until slightly thickened. Combine cottage cheese with remaining ingredients and fold into thickened gelatin mixture. Turn into mold over firm gelatin layer. Chill until firm. Unmold on crisp lettuce.

Mrs. Virginia Vance, Central Lake H. S.
Central Lake, Michigan

TOMATO ASPIC SALAD

Number of Servings — 6

1 pkg. lemon gelatin
2 c. boiling tomato juice
1 c. celery, chopped
¼ c. onion, chopped

Dissolve gelatin in hot tomato juice. Cool until syrupy. Add celery and onion. Chill until firm.

Mrs. Helen Campbell, Watertown Junior H. S.
Watertown, South Dakota

TOMATO ASPIC

Number of Servings — 6

1 c. hot water
2 pkg. lemon gelatin
3 c. tomato juice
1 c. whole shrimp
1 c. shrimp pieces
¾ c. celery, finely chopped
1 small green pepper, finely chopped

Dissolve gelatin in hot water; add tomato juice. Chill until mixture begins to thicken. Add remaining ingredients. Chill until firm.

Sharon Hill, Missoula County H. S.
Missoula, Montana

TOMATO ASPIC

Number of Servings — 6

2½ c. tomatoes
1 slice onion
1 stalk celery
½ bay leaf
2 cloves
½ t. salt
3 drops Tabasco sauce
1 T. unflavored gelatin
½ c. cold water

Cook tomatoes with all ingredients except gelatin and cold water. When tomatoes are quite soft, puree the mixture. Return to heat and bring to boiling point. Remove from heat. Soften gelatin in cold water; add to hot tomato liquid. Put in mold; chill. Serve on lettuce leaf with mayonnaise.

Frances Bailey, State FHA Advisor
State Department of Education
Little Rock, Arkansas

TOMATO ASPIC SALAD

Number of Servings — 8

1 pkg. lemon gelatin
2¼ c. tomato juice
3 T. onion, chopped
1 c. celery, chopped
1 c. pecans, chopped
½ t. whole cloves
½ t. whole allspice
1 2-inch strip of cinnamon bark
Dash of Cayenne pepper

Simmer spices and onion in tomato juice for 10 minutes. Strain over gelatin; stir until dissolved. Chill until mixture begins to set. Add celery and pecans. Pour into a large mold or individual molds. Chill until firm.

Mrs. Louise J. McDonald, Bernice H. S.
Bernice, Louisiana

BARBECUE TOMATO ASPIC

Number of Servings — 8

1 pkg. lemon gelatin
1¼ c. hot water
1 8-oz. can tomato sauce
1 t. onion juice or ½ t. Worcestershire sauce (opt.)
1½ T. white vinegar
½ t. salt
Dash of pepper
½ c. sharp Cheddar cheese, cut in ¼-inch cubes

Dissolve gelatin in hot water. Add all remaining ingredients except cheese. Chill until partially thickened. Place 6 or 8 cheese cubes in mold. Pour gelatin mixture over them. Add more cheese cubes and gelatin. Chill until firm.

Mrs. Eleanor L. Miller, Wahama H. S.
Mason, West Virginia

TOMATO ASPIC SALAD

Number of Servings — 8-10

1 3-oz. pkg. lemon gelatin
2 c. tomato juice, heated
1 small can tomato sauce, chilled
Diced carrots, celery, olives or desired vegetables

Dissolve gelatin in hot tomato juice. Add tomato sauce. Chill until mixture begins to thicken. Add desired vegetables; mix well. Chill until firm.

Mrs. Ethel A. Nale, Indianola H. S.
Indianola, Ohio

TOMATO ASPIC

Number of Servings — 8-10

1 T. unflavored gelatin
½ c. cold water
1 10½-oz. can condensed tomato soup
⅓ c. sugar
1 t. salt
1 T. tarragon vinegar
1 T. vinegar
2 T. lemon juice
¼ t. celery salt
1 c. sweet pickles, chopped
1 c. stuffed olives, sliced
1 small onion, grated
1 small green pepper, chopped
1 cucumber, finely chopped
½ c. pecans, chopped

Soften gelatin in cold water for 5 minutes. Add sugar and salt to soup; bring to boil. Add gelatin; stir until dissolved. Add vinegars, lemon juice and celery salt; stir until mixed. Chill until thickened. Add remaining ingredients. Pour into mold. Chill overnight.

Lela A. Tomlinson, Director Home Economics Education, Louisiana Dept. of Education
Baton Rouge, Louisiana

TOMATO-VEGETABLE ASPIC

Number of Servings — 5-6

1 envelope unflavored gelatin
¼ c. cold tomato juice
1¾ c. boiling tomato juice
1 T. onion, grated
1 t. salt
¾ c. cabbage, finely shredded
¼ c. celery, chopped

Soften gelatin in cold tomato juice. Add gelatin, onion and salt to boiling tomato juice; stir. Chill until slightly thickened. Fold in cabbage and celery. Chill until firm.

Mrs. Frances Chappell, Apel District School
Apel, North Carolina

EASY TOMATO ASPIC

Number of Servings — 8

2 pkgs. lemon gelatin
2 c. tomato juice
2 T. vinegar
½ t. salt
½ t. seasoned salt

Prepare gelatin according to package directions; add remaining ingredients. Chill until firm.

Mrs. Florence D. Sorrell, Benson H. S.
Benson, North Carolina

TOMATO ASPIC ON SLAW

Number of Servings — 6

1 pkg. lemon gelatin
1¼ c. hot water
1 8-oz. can tomato paste
2 T. vinegar
½ t. salt
Dash of pepper
Dash of celery seed

Dissolve gelatin in hot water. Add remaining ingredients. Pour into molds and chill until firm.

DRESSING:
1 egg
½ c. water
¼ t. mustard
1 t. sugar
1 T. vinegar
Dash of salt
Dash of pepper
Dash of celery seed
3 c. green cabbage, shredded

Mix all ingredients except cabbage and cook until thick. Cool. Mix cabbage with dressing. Make a nest of slaw on each salad plate and fill nest with aspic mold.

Mary Lynch Chesnutt, Fulton H. S.
Knoxville, Tennessee

GREEN SALAD WITH ASPIC CUBES

Number of Servings — 8

1 pkg. lemon gelatin
½ t. salt
¾ c. hot water
1 8-oz. tomato sauce
1½ T. vinegar
½ c. Bleu cheese, crumbled
Dash of pepper
6 c. mixed salad greens
½ c. small sprigs watercress
¼ c. scallions, sliced
¼ c. olives, sliced
1 c. grapefruit sections
Garlic salad dressing.

Dissolve gelatin and salt in hot water. Add pepper, tomato sauce and vinegar. Add Bleu cheese; mix well. Chill until firm. Cut into ½-inch cubes. Just before serving combine salad greens, scallions, olives and grapefruit sections. Sprinkle with salad dressing and toss lightly. Serve in individual salad bowls, topped with cheese-aspic cubes.

Lillian Whaley, New Monroe Community School
Monroe, Iowa

TOMATO ASPIC RING

Number of Servings — 6-8

½ c. cold water
2 T. unflavored gelatin
2 1-lb. cans stewed tomatoes, undrained
2 T. sugar
½ t. salt
2 T. cider vinegar
1 T. prepared horseradish
1 T. onion, grated
½ t. Worcestershire sauce
3 hard-cooked eggs, quartered

Lightly oil a 5½-cup ring mold with salad or cooking oil; set aside to drain. Soften gelatin in cold water; dissolve over hot water. Break tomatoes into large pieces with a spoon. Stir in sugar, salt, vinegar, horseradish, onion and Worcestershire sauce. Heat to boiling. Stir in dissolved gelatin. Chill until mixture begins to congeal. Stir occasionally. Arrange egg quarters, cut side down, around the bottom of mold. Spoon gelatin mixture into mold; chill until firm. Unmold onto a chilled serving plate; garnish with crisp salad greens, scored cucumber slices and carrot straws. Sprinkle vegetables with French dressing.

Mrs. Laura Webb, Imperial Junior H. S.
Ontario, California

TOMATO ASPIC SUPREME SALAD

Number of Servings — 10-12

1 can tomato soup, undiluted
1 lge. pkg. cream cheese
1½-2 T. unflavored gelatin
¼-½ c. cold water
1 c. mayonnaise
½-1 c. celery, chopped
½ c. green pepper, chopped
1 small onion, chopped
½ c. pecans, chopped (opt.)

Bring tomato soup to a boil. Add cream cheese and stir until smooth. Soften gelatin in cold water. Add to hot liquid and stir until dissolved. Cool. Add remaining ingredients. Pour into mold and chill until firm. Serve on salad greens. Meat, chicken, tuna, shrimp hard-cooked eggs, olives, etc. may be added for variety.

This recipe submitted by the following teachers:

Mrs. Erma L. Reynolds, Lincoln Jr. H. S.
Bridgeville, Pennsylvania

Mrs. Audra Rasco, Monahans Sr. H. S.
Monahans, Texas

Mrs. Marguerite Craig, Fulton Local
Swanton, Ohio

QUICK TOMATO ASPIC SALAD

Number of Servings — 6

1 pkg. lemon gelatin
2 c. tomato juice
1 T. vinegar
½ t. Worcestershire sauce
Salt to taste
1 c. celery, chopped
1 can cocktail shrimp
1 t. onion juice or onion, finely chopped

Heat 1 cup tomato juice to boiling. Add to gelatin and dissolve. Add remaining tomato juice. Chill until mixture starts to congeal. Add remaining ingredients. Chill overnight.

Joan Bull, Dallas Junior H. S.
Dallas, Oregon

TOMATO CREAM CHEESE SALAD

Number of Servings — 8

1 can tomato soup
3 pkg. cream cheese
2 T. unflavored gelatin
½ c. water
1 c. mayonnaise
½ c. celery, chopped
½ c. green pepper, chopped
½ c. onion, chopped

Heat soup to boiling point; add cheese and stir until smooth. Combine water and gelatin. Add to soup-cheese mixture. Add mayonnaise. Cool. Add remaining ingredients. Chill until firm.

Mary D. Thompson
Montgomery-Wabash Township School
Owensville, Indiana

JELLIED TOMATO-CHEESE SALAD

Number of Servings — 10

1 can condensed tomato soup
3 3-oz. pkg. cream cheese
2 T. unflavored gelatin
½ c. cold water
1 c. mayonnaise
1 c. celery, chopped
¼ c. green or red pepper, chopped
1 T. onion, minced
½ t. salt
Dash of cayenne pepper
Dash of black pepper

Heat soup to boiling; remove from heat. Add cheese; beat until blended. Soak gelatin in cold water for 5 minutes. Dissolve in hot soup mixture. Cool but do not let mixture thicken. Stir in mayonnaise, vegetables and seasonings. Pour into mold. Chill until firm.

Mrs. Walter Edwards, Tulia H. S.
Tulia, Texas

JELLIED TOMATO SURPRISE

Number of Servings — 8

1 pkg. lemon gelatin
1 can tomato soup or 1 c. tomato juice
1 c. boiling water
1 small bottle olives, chopped
1 3-oz. pkg. cream cheese, cubed
3-4 stalks celery, finely diced
Few drops onion juice

Dissolve gelatin in boiling water; add tomato soup or juice. Cool until mixture is consistency of egg whites. Add olives, cream cheese and celery. Add onion juice last. Spoon into individual molds or a ring mold. Chill until firm.

Dorothy F. Kingsbury-Area Supervisor
Home Economics Education
Keene State College
Keene, New Hampshire

PRIZE TOMATO CHEESE SALAD

Number of Servings — 10

1 can tomato soup
3 small pkgs. cream cheese
2 T. unflavored gelatin
½ c. cold water
1 c. mayonnaise
¼ c. onion, chopped
¼ c. pimento, chopped
¼ c. green pepper, chopped
¾ c. celery, chopped

Bring tomato soup to a boil; add cheese. Beat with rotary beater until smooth. Soften gelatin in cold water; add to hot tomato-cheese mixture. Cool. Add remaining ingredients. Chill until firm.

Marguerite Goldsworthy, Sarasota Jr. H. S.
Sarasota, Florida

TOMATO CHIFFON SALAD

Number of Servings — 6-8

2 T. unflavored gelatin
2¼ c. tomato juice
3 T. onion, chopped
3 T. green pepper, chopped
½ t. celery salt
1 bay leaf
½ c. instant non-fat dry milk powder
½ c. water
2 T. lemon juice
Salad greens
Cottage cheese (opt.)

Soften gelatin in ½ cup tomato juice. Combine remaining tomato juice, onion, green pepper, bay leaf and celery salt in a saucepan. Simmer about 10 minutes; remove bay leaf. Add gelatin; stir until dissolved. Cool until mixture reaches the consistency of jelly. Sprinkle non-fat milk powder over water; beat until stiff. Blend in lemon juice. Fold milk mixture into tomato mixture. Pour into a mold that has been rinsed with cold water. Chill until firm. Unmold on salad greens and serve with cottage cheese, if desired.

Janet R. Stark, Blooming Prairie H. S.
Blooming Prairie, Minnesota

ZIPPY TOMATO CHEESE MOLD

Number of Servings — 8

2 envelopes unflavored gelatin
½ c. cold water
1 pkg. cream cheese
1 can tomato soup
1 c. mayonnaise
1 t. horseradish
1½ c. celery, chopped
½ c. pepper, chopped
½ c. onion, diced

Soften gelatin in cold water. Combine with cheese and soup. Simmer over low heat until gelatin is dissolved. Remove from heat; cool. Stir in mayonnaise, horseradish, celery, green pepper and onion. Chill until firm.

Mrs. Virginia Watson
Albion, Nebraska

TOMATO SOUP SALAD

Number of Servings — 6

1 can tomato soup
2 T. unflavored gelatin
⅔ c. cold water
1 8-oz. pkg. cream cheese, crumbled
1 c. mayonnaise
½ c. celery, chopped
½ c. green pepper, chopped

Soak gelatin in water. Heat soup; add cheese and gelatin. Beat until smooth. Cool. Add remaining ingredients. Pour into mold; chill until firm.

Mrs. Raye L. Evers, McGregor H. S.
McGregor, Texas

PINK LADY SALAD

Number of Servings — 8-10

1½ T. unflavored gelatin
½ c. cold water
1 c. tomato soup
2 3-oz. pkgs. cream cheese
¾ c. mayonnaise
1 c. celery, chopped
2 T. green pepper, chopped
1 t. onion, minced
½ c. nuts, chopped

Dissolve gelatin in cold water. Heat tomato soup; blend in gelatin. Cool. Combine cheese and mayonnaise. Add with remaining ingredients to gelatin mixture. Chill.

Antoinette Kelemen, Shelbyville H. S.
Shelbyville, Kentucky

SURPRISE GELATIN SALAD

Number of Servings — 8-10

1 can tomato soup
1 pkg. cherry gelatin
½ c. celery, chopped
½ c. green pepper, chopped
½ c. onion, chopped
1 c. cottage cheese
½ c. salad dressing
½ c. nuts, chopped

Heat tomato soup; add gelatin. Remove from heat and stir until gelatin is dissolved. Cool. Add remaining ingredients in order. Mix well. Chill until firm.

Mrs. Mary L. Scott, H. S.
Lyman, Nebraska

TOMATO SOUP SALAD

Number of Servings — 6-8

2 pkg. lemon gelatin
1 pt. boiling water
1 can tomato soup
1 lge. pkg. cream cheese
1 c. mayonnaise
1½ T. onion, grated
1½ c. celery, chopped
1 c. nuts, chopped
1 medium green pepper, chopped

Dissolve gelatin in boiling water. Cool. Combine soup and cream cheese; heat and stir until cheese melts. Add mayonnaise to soup-cheese mixture; stir until blended. Add combined onion, celery, nuts and green pepper. Mix well and stir with gelatin. Pour into molds and refrigerate. Salad will keep indefinitely.

Mrs. Donald W. Emery, Patterson H. S.
Patterson, California

TOMATO SOUP SALAD

Number of Servings — 12

1 c. hot water
2 pkg. lemon gelatin
1 c. cold water
1 can tomato soup
3 small pkg. cream cheese
1¼ c. celery, diced
1 small green pepper, diced
1 small cucumber or apple, diced
1 onion, grated
1 c. salad dressing

Dissolve gelatin in hot water; add cold water. Heat tomato soup to boiling. Add cheese; beat until smooth. Combine gelatin and tomato soup mixture. Cool. Add celery, green pepper, cucumber and onion. Fold in salad dressing.

Sharon Busskohl, Lyons H. S.
Lyons, Nebraska

TOMATO SOUP SALAD

Number of Servings — 12-15

2 T. unflavored gelatin
1 pkg. lemon gelatin
1 c. boiling water
1 c. mayonnaise
1 3-oz. pkg. cream cheese, softened
1 can tomato soup
1 No. 2 can crushed pineapple, drained
1 c. celery, chopped
1 c. pecans, chopped
1 c. carrots, grated

Dissolve gelatins in boiling water. Mix cream cheese with mayonnaise; add to gelatin mixture. When mixture is partially congealed add remaining ingredients. Turn into molds. Chill until firm.

Mrs. Marshall J. King, Gatesville H. S.
Gatesville, Texas

TOMATO SOUP SALAD

1 medium can tomato soup
1 lge. pkg. cream cheese
1 c. mango, finely chopped
1 c. celery, finely chopped
1 c. onion, finely chopped
1 c. mayonnaise
1 T. unflavored gelatin
¼ c. water

Heat tomato soup to a boil; add cream cheese. Stir until cheese is dissolved. Cool completely. Dissolve gelatin in water. Add celery, onion, mango, mayonnaise and gelatin to cooled soup mixture. Stir until smooth. Chill.

Mrs. Ruth Riale
Central Columbia Joint School
Bloomsburg, Pennsylvania

TOMATO SOUP SALAD

Number of Servings — 6

1 can tomato soup
2 pkgs. cream cheese
2 T. unflavored gelatin
½ c. cold water
1 c. celery, chopped
1 c. nuts, chopped
1 c. mayonnaise
1 can shrimp
Stuffed olives, sliced (opt.)

Soak gelatin in cold water. Heat tomato soup. Add cream cheese; stir until smooth. Add softened gelatin. Remove from heat and stir in remaining ingredients. Chill until firm.

Mrs. Rush Valentine, Starkville H. S.
Starkville, Mississippi

TOMATO SOUP SALAD

Number of Servings — 8-10

1 can tomato soup, heated
1 3-oz. pkg. cream cheese
1 pkg. lemon gelatin
1 c. water
¾ c. celery, chopped
¼ c. onion, chopped
¼ c. green pepper, chopped
½ c. nuts, chopped
½ c. mayonnaise

Dissolve gelatin in hot soup. Add remaining ingredients. Chill.

Mrs. Glen Wuester, Beattie H. S.
Beattie, Kansas

CORNFLOWER SALAD

Number of Servings — 10

2 No. 2 cans cream corn
1 t. onion, grated
1 t. salt
2 T. sugar
3 envelopes unflavored gelatin
Pepper to taste
½ c. water
6 cooked carrots
6 medium green peppers, hollowed

Blend corn, onion, salt, pepper and sugar. Soften gelatin in water; dissolve over hot water. Add to corn mixture. Put a piece of carrot in each hollowed out pepper and fill with corn mixture. Set peppers in muffin pan to steady them while chilling. Slice and serve on salad greens with dressing.

Opal Pruitt, Western H. S.
Buda, Illinois

CARDINAL SALAD

Number of Servings — 6-8

1 pkg. lemon gelatin
1 c. boiling water
¾ c. beet juice
3 T. vinegar
½ t. salt
1 T. horseradish
2 t. onion, grated
¾ c. celery, diced
1 c. cooked beets, diced

Dissolve gelatin in boiling water. Add beet juice, vinegar, salt, horseradish, and onion. Chill until Partially set. Fold in celery and beets. Pour into molds and chill until firm.

Mrs. Roberta Britton, Socastee H. S.
Myrtle Beach, South Carolina

CELERY-PEPPER CONGEALED SALAD

Number of Servings — 6-8

1 pkg. lemon gelatin
1 c. hot water
1 c. mayonnaise
1 c. cottage cheese
Pinch of salt
1 c. celery, chopped
2 T. onion, finely chopped
¼ c. green pepper, chopped
Green food coloring (opt.)
Chopped pimento (opt.)

Dissolve gelatin in hot water. Let cool. Stir in mayonnaise, cottage cheese, and salt. Add remaining ingredients. Let set for several hours.

Virginia L. Langston
State Department of Education
Baton Rouge 4, Louisiana

COTTAGE CHEESE-VEGETABLE SALAD

Number of Servings — 6

1 pkg. lime gelatin
1½ c. boiling water
⅓ c. carrots, shredded
¼ c. pepper, chopped
1 T. onion, minced
½ c. celery, cut
½ c. crushed pineapple
1 c. dry cottage cheese
½ t. salt
¼ c. whipping cream
½ c. salad dressing

Dissolve gelatin in boiling water; chill until partially set. Add vegetables, cottage cheese, pineapple and salt. Blend cream and salad dressing together; add to gelatin mixture. Chill.

Shirley Nasset, Regent Public School
Regent, North Dakota

COTTAGE CHEESE RING

Cucumber Layer:
1 pkg. lime gelatin
1 c. boiling water
¼ c. lemon juice
¼ t. salt
¼ t. dry mustard
⅓ c. instant non-fat dry milk
¼ c. sour cream
¼ c. green pepper, chopped
¾ c. cucumber, chopped
1 t. onion, finely chopped

Dissolve gelatin in boiling water. Add lemon juice, salt, mustard and milk; stir well. Chill until firm then beat gelatin mixture for about 5 minutes or until light and fluffy. Fold in sour cream. Add pepper, cucumber and onion; mix well. Pour into an oiled mold. Chill until firm.

Pineapple Layer:
1 pkg. lime gelatin
1 c. boiling water
1 c. crushed pineapple
Cottage cheese (garnish)
Salad greens (garnish)

Dissolve gelatin in boiling water. Add pineapple; cool. Add to cucumber layer and chill until firm. Garnish with mounds of cottage cheese and salad greens if desired.

Mrs. Nina B. Moore, Sharpsville H. S.
Sharpsville, Indiana

COTTAGE CHEESE-VEGETABLE SALAD

2 pkg. lemon gelatin
1½ c. boiling water
½ c. green pepper, ground
1 medium onion, ground
6 carrots, ground
1 pkg. cottage cheese
1 c. coffee cream or milk
1 c. salad dressing
1 t. salt

Dissolve gelatin in boiling water; cool. Add remaining ingredients. Chill.

Mrs. Joan Mattson, Ishpeming Senior H. S.
Ishpeming, Michigan

COTTAGE CHEESE-VEGETABLE RING

Number of Servings — 8

2 envelopes unflavored gelatin
½ c. cold water
1½ c. creamed cottage cheese
1¼ c. salad dressing or mayonnaise
¾ c. whipped cream
2 T. parsley, chopped
2 T. pimento, chopped
2 T. onion, chopped
1 T. lemon juice
½ t. Worcestershire sauce
Dash of Tabasco sauce
½ t. Accent
Salt to taste

Sprinkle gelatin on cold water; dissolve over hot water. Cool slightly. Combine cottage cheese and salad dressing. Stir in dissolved gelatin. Fold in whipped cream. Add parsley, pimento, onion, lemon juice and remaining seasonings. Turn into an oiled 5-cup ring mold. Chill until firm. Unmold on a large platter.

VEGETABLE SALAD MEDLEY:
2 16-oz. cans mixed vegetables or
2 12-oz. pkgs. frozen mixed vegetables, cooked and cooled
½ c. salad oil
½ t. paprika
½ t. garlic salt
Dash of Tabasco sauce
2 T. vinegar

Combine salad oil, vinegar, garlic salt, Tabasco and paprika. Beat with rotary beater. Pour over mixed vegetables. Chill. Fill center of gelatin mold with vegetables.

Mrs. Buford N. Irwin, Central H. S.
Knoxville, Tennessee

DEE'S MAIN DISH SALAD

Number of Servings — 6

1 envelope unflavored gelatin
¼ c. cold water
1 c. hot chili sauce
2 c. small curd cottage cheese
1 c. mayonnaise
½ pt. whipped cream

Soak gelatin in cold water. Add chili sauce, cottage cheese and mayonnaise. Blend. Chill until mixture starts to congeal. Blend in whipped cream. Mold. Chill until firm.

1 envelope unflavored gelatin
¼ c. cold water
1 T. lemon juice
¼ t. salt
¼ c. sugar
¾ c. pineapple juice
1 c. crushed pineapple
1 small pimento, minced
½ c. carrot, finely grated
½ c. frozen peas, cooked
½ c. celery, diced

TOPPING:

Soak gelatin in cold water; stir. Add remaining ingredients. Pour over firm gelatin. Refrigerate until set.

½ pt. whipped cream
⅓ c. mayonnaise
2 c. flaked crab, flavored with lemon juice and salt

Combine ingredients. Serve over firm gelatin.

Mrs. Bernice Gorsuch, Bellingham H. S.
Bellingham, Washington

EMERALD SALAD

Number of Servings — 8

1 pkg. green gelatin
½ c. cold water
3 carrots, grated
½ c. crushed pineapple
1 c. boiling water
1 apple, unpeeled, and finely cut
½ c. celery pieces

Dissolve gelatin in boiling water; add cold water. Add remaining ingredients. Pour into an oiled mold. Chill until firm.

Mrs. Clifton E. Whitney, Northfield H. S.
Northfield, Vermont

FROSTY MOUNTAIN SALAD

Number of Servings — 8

2 pkg. unflavored gelatin
½ c. lemon juice
½ c. lime juice
3 c. hot water
2 c. cabbage, finely shredded
½ c. green pepper, finely chopped
½ c. sugar
1 c. crushed pineapple, drained
2 c. seedless green grapes

Soften gelatin in lime and lemon juice. Dissolve gelatin in hot water; add sugar. Cool until syrupy. Beat until frothy. Add remaining ingredients. Chill until firm. Serve with a fruit dressing.

Mrs. Gladys M. Dunkle
Ashton Community Unit School No. 275
Ashton, Illinois

FRUIT-VEGETABLE SALAD

Number of Servings — 8

1 pkg. lime or lemon gelatin
½ c. cold water
1 small can crushed pineapple, drained
Juice from pineapple
½ c. sugar
½ c. vinegar
1 small can pimento, diced
3 dill or sweet pickles
¼ t. ground red pepper
½ t. salt
½ c. celery, chopped
½ c. pecans, chopped

Dissolve gelatin in cold water. Bring pineapple juice, sugar and vinegar to a boil; pour over gelatin. Add remaining ingredients. Chill until firm.

Mrs. Jesse Safley, Bellevoe H. S.
Bellevoe, Tennessee

DILL PICKLE SALAD

Number of Servings — 8

1 pkg. lemon gelatin
1 small can crushed pineapple, drained
2 T. pimento, chopped
¼ c. dill pickle, chopped
¼ c. pecans, chopped

Prepare gelatin according to package directions. Let set until partially thickened. Add remaining ingredients. Let set until firm.

Mrs. Dorothy Faulk, Burkburnett H. S.
Burkburnett, Texas

GREEN GODDESS SALAD BOWL

Number of Servings — 10

1 pkg. lime gelatin
1½ t. garlic salt
¾ c. hot water
Dash of black pepper
¾ c. sour cream
¼ c. mayonnaise
1 T. vinegar
1 2-oz. can anchovies, minced
1 9-oz. pkg. frozen artichoke hearts
1 grapefruit, sectioned
1 c. tomatoes, diced
½ c. olives, sliced
¼ c. green onions, chopped
3 qts. salad greens, cut in bite-size pieces
1 c. French dressing

Dissolve gelatin and garlic salt in hot water. Add pepper, sour cream, mayonnaise, vinegar and anchovies. Beat with egg beater until well blended. Pour into a loaf pan; chill until firm. Cut into 1-inch squares. Cook artichoke hearts according to package directions; drain. Cut each artichoke in half; chill. Combine remaining ingredients except French dressing. Toss and chill. Mix artichokes and salad greens mixture. Toss lightly. Arrange anchovy squares on top.

Betty Pate, Clinton H. S.
Clinton, Arkansas

LIME-AVOCADO SALAD

Number of Servings — 12-15

2 pkg. lime gelatin
3 c. boiling water
2 3-oz. pkg. cream cheese
1 c. salad dressing
2 ripe avocados, mashed
1 green pepper, chopped
¾-1 c. celery, diced
2 T. onion, grated

Dissolve gelatin in boiling water. Combine cream cheese with salad dressing; add to hot gelatin mixture. Chill until partially set. Add green pepper, celery, onion and avocado. Chill until firm. Cut into squares and serve.

Mrs. Shirley F. Campbell, Alexis Com. H. S.
Alexis, Illinois

HUMPTY-DUMPTY SALAD

Number of Servings — 4-6

1 envelope unflavored gelatin
¾ c. cold water
½ t. salt
2 T. lemon juice
¼ t. Tabasco sauce
¾ c. mayonnaise or salad dressing
1 c. celery, finely diced
¼ c. green pepper, finely diced
¼ c. pimento, chopped
4 hard-cooked eggs, chopped

Sprinkle gelatin on cold water. Place over low heat, stirring constantly, until gelatin is dissolved. Remove from heat, stir in salt, lemon juice and Tabasco sauce. Cool. Gradually stir into mayonnaise; blend. Fold in remaining ingredients. Turn into a 3-cup mold. Chill until firm.

Mildred L. Phillips, Santa Cruz H. S.
Santa Cruz, New Mexico

LIME GELATIN SALAD

Number of Servings — 8

1 pkg. lime gelatin
½ c. boiling water
1 lb. cottage cheese
½ c. evaporated milk
½ c. mayonnaise
1 t. onion, grated
2 T. carrot, grated

Dissolve gelatin in boiling water; cool until mixture starts to set. Add remaining ingredients.

Mrs. Marjorie Carpp, Lawrence Public School
Lawrence, Michigan

LIME-VEGETABLE SALAD

Number of Servings — 8

1 pkg. of lime gelatin
1 c. hot water
½ c. cold water
4 t. vinegar
½ c. mayonnaise
1 c. carrots, grated
½ c. cabbage, shredded
2 t. onion, grated
1 c. crushed pineapple
½ c. fresh cucumbers, grated
Few grains salt

Dissolve gelatin in hot water; add cold water and vinegar. Let set until thick enough to whip. Add mayonnaise; whip. Add remaining ingredients. Let set.

Mrs. Ruth Hale, Cheyenne-Eagle Butte H. S.
Eagle Butte, South Dakota

LIME GELATIN-VEGETABLE SALAD

Number of Servings — 10

1 family size pkg. lime gelatin
½ c. onion, finely chopped
¼ c. green pepper, chopped
1 or 2 cucumbers, thinly sliced

Mix gelatin according to directions on package. Let set until slightly thickened. Fold in vegetables. Let set until firm.

Jane L. Burnham, Ashland Community H. S.
Ashland, Maine

MOLDED GARDEN SALAD

Number of Servings — 12

4 envelopes unflavored gelatin
½ c. cold water
1 c. boiling water
½ c. sugar
1¼ c. cold water
1¼ c. vinegar
2 t. salt
1½ c. radishes, sliced
1¾ c. cucumbers, peeled and sliced
1¼ c. green onions, chopped
1 t. dill seed
1½ c. sour cream
½ c. mayonnaise
½ t. salt
2 t. vinegar

Soften gelatin in ½ cup cold water; add boiling water and sugar. Blend remaining cold water, 1¼ cups vinegar, and 2 teaspoons salt; add to gelatin mixture. Add radishes, cucumbers, onion and dill seed. Let set until firm. Combine sour cream, mayonnaise, ½ teaspoon salt and 2 teaspoons vinegar. Serve sour cream mixture with gelatin mixture.

Mrs. Mary Irey, Red Bluff Union H. S.
Red Bluff, California

MOLDED LETTUCE SALAD

Number of Servings — 6

1 pkg. lime gelatin
2 c. luke warm water
2 c. lettuce, shredded
½ c. radishes, diced
1 t. salt
½ t. white pepper

Dissolve gelatin in water. Chill until partially set. Fold in remaining ingredients. Refrigerate until set.

Margaret L. Jones, Armstrong Township H. S.
Armstrong, Illinois

LUNCHEON SALAD

Number of Servings — 6

1 T. unflavored gelatin
½ c. cold water
⅓ c. sugar
½ t. salt
1 c. hot water
¼ c. mild vinegar or lemon juice
2 apples, unpeeled and diced
½ c. celery, chopped
¼ c. carrots, grated
¼ c. nuts

Soften gelatin in cold water. Add sugar, salt and hot water; stir until dissolved. Add lemon juice or vinegar; mix thoroughly. Pour into a refrigerator tray. Quick-chill in freezer until mixture begins to thicken. Add apples, celery, carrots and nuts. Pour into a mold that has been rinsed in cold water. Chill until firm.

Mrs. Elsie C. Dolin, Newberry H. S.
Newberry, Florida

MOLDED GARDEN SALAD

Number of Servings — 4-6

2 pkgs. lemon gelatin
2 T. lemon juice
½ c. green onions finely sliced
¾ c. cucumbers, diced
½ c. radishes, thinly sliced
½ c. celery, thinly sliced
½ c. raw cauliflowerets
1 t. salt

Prepare gelatin according to package directions. Chill until partially set. Add remaining ingredients. Chill until firm.

Anne Cole, Livingston H. S.
Livingston, Kentucky

MOLDED RELISH SALAD

Number of Servings — 8

1 pkg. lime gelatin
1 pkg. lemon gelatin
3 c. boiling water
1 c. celery, chopped
½-1 c. nuts, chopped
1 bell pepper, chopped
4 T. chili sauce
4 T. India relish
1 small bottle olives, chopped
1 small can pimento, chopped
Pinch of salt

Dissolve gelatin in boiling water. Chill until partially set. Combine remaining ingredients; fold into gelatin mixture. Chill until firm.

Virginia C. Lee, Memphis Technical H. S.
Memphis, Tennessee

NEOPOLITAN VEGETABLE SALAD

Number of Servings — 12

2 pkgs. lemon gelatin
4 c. hot water
3 T. vinegar
3 t. salt
1½ c. raw carrots, finely chopped
1¾ c. cabbage, finely chopped
1 t. onion, minced
1½ c. raw spinach, finely chopped

Dissolve gelatin in hot water; add vinegar and salt. Divide gelatin into 3 parts. Chill each part until partially thickened. Add carrots to one layer of gelatin. Chill until firm. Combine cabbage and another gelatin layer. Pour over first layer. Chill until firm. Add onion and spinach to remaining gelatin layer. Pour over firmly chilled mixture. Chill until firm.

This recipe submitted by the following teachers:

Pauline K. Fish, Mt. Lebanon Sr. H. S.
Pittsburg, Pennsylvania

Ann Guth, Palisade H. S.
Palisade, Colorado

PEPPER POT SALAD

Number of Servings — 8-10

1 T. unflavored gelatin
¼ c. cold water
1 can pepper pot soup
1 can water
1 small can English peas, drained
1 can tuna or other meat

Add ¼ cup cold water to gelatin. Add 1 can of water to soup; heat to boiling point. Pour hot soup over gelatin. When mixture begins to cool, add peas and tuna. Pour. Refrigerate until firm.

Lillian Talbot, Area Supervisor of Home Economics
Ruston, Louisiana

PERFECTION CHEESE LOAF

Number of Servings — 6

2 pkgs. lime gelatin
2 c. hot water
1¾ c. cold water
4 T. lemon juice
½ c. cabbage, shredded
½ c. celery, chopped
½ c. carrots, shredded
¼ c. radishes, thinly sliced
2 c. cottage cheese
1 t. onion, grated
1 t. salt

Dissolve gelatin in hot water; stir in cold water and lemon juice. Divide mixture in half; chill one-half until syrupy; keep remaining mixture at room temperature. Fold celery, cabbage, carrots and radishes into syrupy mixture; chill until firm. Chill remaining gelatin until syrupy. Fold in combined cheese, onion and salt. Spoon over firm layer. Chill until firm.

Mrs. Maxine M. Miller, Fairview H. S.
Fairview, West Virginia

"SOUP-ER" SALAD

Number of Servings — 24

1 can condensed tomato soup
1 lge. pkg. cream cheese
2 pkgs. lemon gelatin
2 c. boiling water
½ c. salad dressing
2 c. celery, chopped
½ c. green pepper, chopped
1 small cucumber, finely chopped
1 T. onion, minced

Heat soup until hot; pour over cream cheese. Beat until blended. Add salad dressing. Dissolve gelatin in boiling water; cool. Refrigerate until gelatin begins to thicken; add soup mixture, celery, green pepper, cucumber and onion. Pour in mold; refrigerate until firm.

Mrs. Frances M. Whited, Toledo H. S.
Toledo, Oregon

SUNSET DELIGHT SALAD

Number of Servings — 6

1 pkg. lemon-lime gelatin
½ c. hot water
1½ c. cold water
½ c. small cocktail onions
½ c. small stuffed olives
½ c. cucumbers, sliced or diced

Dissolve gelatin in hot water; add cold water. Chill until partially set. Add remaining ingredients. Chill until firm.

Maurine Sullivan Frederick, Copperas Cove H. S.
Copperas Cove, Texas

PINEAPLE-VEGETABLE SALAD

Number of Servings — 6

¾ c. pineapple juice
¾ c. water
⅓ c. lemon juice
2 sticks cinnamon
1 t. cloves
1 t. allspice
½ t. salt
2 envelopes unflavored gelatin
2 t. horseradish
1 12-oz. bottle ginger ale
½ c. celery sliced
¼ c. green pepper, chopped
¼ c. radishes, sliced
2 T. pimento
6 pineapple slices

Combine pineapple juice, ¼ cup water, lemon juice, cinnamon, cloves, allspice and salt; simmer for 5 minutes. Soften gelatin in ½ cup water. Strain hot liquid into gelatin; stir until dissolved. Let cool. Add horseradish, ginger ale and vegetables. Arrange pineapple slices in bottom of a ring mold. Pour gelatin mixture over pineapple slices. Chill for several hours.

Mrs. Marjorie West, Northeast Vocational H. S.
Lauderdale, Mississippi

RIVERSIDE SALAD

Number of Servings — 8

1 pkg. lemon gelatin
2 hardcooked eggs, sliced
1 small bottle olives, diced
1 c. celery, diced
Salt to taste

Prepare gelatin according to package directions. Chill until partially set. Fold in olives, celery and salt. Carefully drop in egg slices. Do not stir. Chill until firm.

Mrs. Helen M. Scott, Fairmont H. S.
Fairmont, North Carolina

SPRING SALAD

Number of Servings — 8

1 pkg. lemon gelatin
½ c. boiling water
1 t. vinegar
¼ t. salt
1 lb. cottage cheese
1 lge. cucumber, unpeeled and diced
1 small onion, diced
½ c. salad dressing
½ c. nuts

Dissolve gelatin in boiling water; add vinegar and salt. Add cottage cheese, cucumber, onion, salad dressing and nuts. Refrigerate until firm.

Mrs. Gladys Wolven, St. Louis H. S.
St. Louis, Michigan

SPRING GARDEN MOLD

Number of Servings — 6-8

2 T. unflavored gelatin
1 c. cold water
1 c. boiling water
3 T. lemon juice
½ c. catsup
¼ t. garlic salt
½ t. salt
1 c. cabbage, shredded
½ c. cucumber, chopped
½ c. celery, chopped
½ c. stuffed olives, sliced
¼ c. green pepper, chopped
2 T. green onion, sliced

Soften gelatin in cold water. Dissolve in boiling water. Stir in lemon juice, catsup, garlic salt and salt. Chill until mixture begins to congeal. Add vegetables. Chill until firm.

Mrs. Hazel Hughes Dalton, Kimball H. S.
Kimball, West Virginia

SUMMER VEGETABLE SALAD

Number of Servings — 6

1 3-oz. pkg. lemon gelatin
1 c. boiling water
¾ c. cold water
1 T. vinegar
½ t. salt
Small red and yellow tomatoes
Green pepper, cut in thin strips
¼ c. celery, sliced
¼ c. cucumber, thinly sliced

Dissolve gelatin in boiling water. Add salt, cold water and vinegar. Chill until slightly thickened. Add remaining ingredients. Chill until firm.

Mrs. Mary Stockslager, Farmersville H. S.
Farmersville, Ohio

SUNSHINE SALAD

Number of Servings — 6-8

1 pkg. orange gelatin
1 c. hot water
½ t. salt
1 c. cold water
1 c. raw carrot, shredded
1 c. green onion, diced
1 c. celery, diced

Dissolve gelatin in hot water; add salt and cold water. Chill until mixture begins to congeal. Fold in remaining ingredients. Pour into oiled 1½-quart mold. Chill until firm.

Mrs. Lon Stephens, Wheatland H. S.
Wheatland, Wyoming

SWEET PICKLE SALAD

Number of Servings — 8

¾ c. boiling water
¾ c. cold water
1 pkg. lime gelatin
½ c. cheese, grated
¼ c. celery, diced
¾ c. pecans, chopped
1 red pimento, chopped
⅓ c. pineapple
1 c. sweet pickles, chopped

Dissolve gelatin in boiling water; add cold water. Cool. Add remaining ingredients; mix thoroughly. Pour into lightly oiled molds and chill until firm. Serve on lettuce with mayonnaise.

Mrs. Fran Caldwell, Garland Sr. H. S.
Garland, Texas

SUNSET AND SOUR SALAD

Number of Servings — 10

1 pkg. lime gelatin
1 c. hot water
1 c. cottage cheese
½ c. mayonnaise
½ c. celery
½ c. bell peppers, chopped
½ c. onions, chopped

Dissolve gelatin in hot water. Let set until partially congealed. Add remaining ingredients. Pour into molds that have been rinsed with cold water. Let set until firm.

Earle H. Vallentine, Edisto School
Cordova, South Carolina

CONGEALED VEGETABLE SALAD

Number of Servings — 8-10

2 T. unflavored gelatin
½ c. cold water
1½ c. boiling water
1 c. mayonnaise
¼ c. vinegar
Juice of 1 lemon
¼ c. sugar
¾ t. salt
1 c. celery, diced
1 c. cabbage, shredded
¾ c. carrots, shredded
1 small green pepper, shredded
1 onion, grated
1 pimento, shredded

Soak gelatin in cold water. Add boiling water; stir. Add sugar, salt, vinegar and lemon juice. Chill. Add mayonnaise. Mix all vegetables; add ¾ c. gelatin mixture. Chill. Add remaining gelatin mixture; stir. Pour into mold. Refrigerate.

Mrs. Elizabeth G. Mosley
George Washington H. S.
Danville, Virginia

VEGETABLE ASPIC

Number of Servings — 8

1 box lemon gelatin
1¾ c. boiling water
¼ c. vinegar
½ t. salt
1 c. cabbage, shredded
½ c. celery, finely chopped
1 small can pimentos, finely cut
1 green bell pepper, finely chopped
½ c. pecans, chopped

Dissolve gelatin in boiling water. Add salt and vinegar; cool. Refrigerate until mixture begins to congeal. Add remaining ingredients in order given. Pour into an oiled mold. Chill until firm.

Constance Day, LaGrange H. S.
LaGrange, Georgia

CONGEALED VEGETABLE SALAD

Number of Servings — 6

1 T. unflavored gelatin
¼ c. cold water
1¼ c. hot pineapple juice
1 t. salt
½ c. sugar
¼ c. lemon juice
2 T. vinegar
2 T. green pepper, chopped
1 c. cabbage, shredded
½ c. carrots, cut
¼ c. olives, sliced
1 c. celery, chopped

Soften gelatin in cold water; dissolve in boiling pineapple juice. Add salt, sugar, lemon juice and vinegar. Chill until partially set. Add remaining ingredients. Chill in an oiled mold.

Mrs. Maria A. Hurt, Albemarle H. S.
Charlottesville, Virginia

CONGEALED VEGETABLE SALAD

Number of Servings — 6

1 pkg. lemon gelatin
1 c. boiling water
¾ c. cold water
1 T. onion, minced
½ t. salt
1 T. vinegar
½ c. cabbage, finely shredded
½ c. carrot, finely shredded
½ c. celery, chopped
1 T. pimento, chopped

Dissolve gelatin in boiling water; add cold water. Add onion, salt and vinegar; blend well. Chill until syrupy. Fold in remaining ingredients. Chill until firm.

Ruby L. Meis, Mt. Pleasant Senior H. S.
Mt. Pleasant, Michigan

CONGEALED VEGETABLE SALAD

Number of Servings — 8

1 c. tomato soup
1 3-oz. pkg. cream cheese
1 envelope unflavored gelatin
2⅔ T. cold water
½ c. celery, chopped
½ c. olives, chopped
½ c. green peppers, chopped
¼ c. onions, finely cut
¼ c. mayonnaise
½ c. pecans, chopped

Dissolve gelatin in cold water. Dissolve cream cheese in soup over low heat. Add gelatin; mix well. Cool. Add vegetables, nuts and mayonnaise. Pour in mold and chill. Serve on lettuce or other green of choice.

Mrs. Hal Puett, North Cobb H. S.
Acworth, Georgia

CRISP VEGETABLE SALAD

Number of Servings — 4-6

1 pkg. lemon gelatin
1 c. hot water
1 c. cold water
1 T. vinegar
1 t. salt
¾ c. cucumber, diced
½ c. red radishes, thinly sliced
½ c. young onions, thinly sliced

Dissolve gelatin in hot water. Add cold water, vinegar and salt. Chill until slightly thickened. Fold in cucumbers, radishes and onions. Pour into individual molds, or a 1-quart mold. Chill until firm. Unmold on crisp greens.

Bette Jo Switzer, Salem-Oak Harbor H. S.
Oak Harbor, Ohio

VEGETABLE GELATIN

Number of Servings — 10

1 pkg. lemon gelatin
1 pt. hot water
10 marshmallows, quartered
1 c. crushed pineapple
½ c. celery, finely cut
¼ lb. cheese, grated
½ c. walnuts, chopped
1 c. whipped cream
¼ c. salad dressing
1 pkg. red gelatin

Dissolve lemon gelatin with 1 pint hot water. Add marshmallows. Cool until mixture begins to thicken. Add pineaple, celery, cheese, nuts, whipped cream and salad dressing. Chill until firm. Prepare red gelatin according to package directions; pour over firm mixture. Chill until firm.

Delores Hickenbottom, Sargent H. S.
Sargent, Nebraska

MOLDED VEGETABLE SALAD

Number of Servings — 12

1 c. cold water
1 envelope unflavored gelatin
1 pkg. lemon gelatin
1 c. hot water
⅓ c. vinegar
Juice of 1 lemon
1 t. salt
1 t. sugar
2 carrots, chopped
1 pimento, chopped
2 stalks celery, chopped
½ green pepper, chopped
1 T. onion, chopped

Soak unflavored gelatin in ¼ cup cold water. Dissolve lemon gelatin in hot water; add remaining cold water. Combine lemon juice and vinegar; add enough water to make 1 cup liquid. Mix gelatin mixtures and lemon juice-vinegar mixture together. Add sugar and salt. Let set until partially thickened. Add remaining ingredients.

Mrs. Ethel D. Finley, Montgomery Blair H. S.
Silver Spring, Maryland

VIRGINIA SALAD

Number of Servings — 8-10

1 pkg. lime gelatin
½ c. hot water
½ c. green pepper, diced
¼ c. onion, diced
½ c. celery, diced
1 small carton cottage cheese
½ pt. whipped cream
½ c. salad dressing
½ c. nuts, chopped

Dissolve gelatin in hot water. Combine vegetables, cottage cheese, salad dressing and nuts. Fold whipped cream into this mixture. Stir in the cooled gelatin. Chill.

Mrs. Eleanor F. Shadley, Cumberland H. S.
Toledo, Illinois

VEGETABLE SOUFFLE

Number of Servings — 12

1 lge. or 2 small pkg. lemon gelatin
1 c. boiling water
1 c. milk
1 c. salad dressing
1 c. small curd cottage cheese
1 green pepper, finely chopped
3 medium size carrots, grated
1 medium size onion, finely chopped

Dissolve gelatin in boiling water. Add remaining ingredients in order given. Pour in a lightly greased mold. Chill until firm.

Mrs. Carol MacQueen, Fruitport H. S.
Fruitport, Michigan

PERFECTION VEGETABLE SALAD

Number of Servings — 8

4 c. boiling water
3 pkgs. lemon gelatin
½ c. vinegar
Pimento
2 c. cabbage, finely shredded
1 c. carrot, shredded
¼ c. green pepper, diced
Chicory
French Dressing

Dissolve gelatin in boiling water; stir until completely dissolved. Add vinegar; cool. Chill until mixture begins to thicken. Spoon a small amount of gelatin mixture into the bottom of a 6-cup mold; arrange cutouts of pimento. Chill until set. Fold cabbage, carrot and green pepper into remaining gelatin mixture; pour pimento-gelatin. Chill until set. To unmold loosen edges with small spatula; dip mold briefly in warm water. Invert mold over serving plate; shake gently to loosen. Garnish with chicory and serve with a tart French dressing.

Mrs. Ella Baker, Martin H. S.
Laredo, Texas

VEGETABLE SOUFFLE SALAD WITH TUNA

Number of Servings — 4-6

1 pkg. lime gelatin
1 c. hot water
½ c. cold water
4 t. vinegar
½ c. mayonnaise
¼ t. salt
Dash of pepper
1 c. raw carrots, shredded
1 c. cabbage, shredded
¼ c. cucumber, finely diced and drained
1 T. onion, finely chopped
1 7-oz. can tuna, drained

Dissolve gelatin in hot water. Add cold water, vinegar, mayonnaise, salt and pepper. Blend well with rotary beater. Pour into refrigerator tray. Chill in freezing unit for 15-20 minutes, or until mixture is firm around edges but soft in the center. Turn mixture into bowl and whip with rotary beater until fluffy. Fold in vegetables. Pour into a 1-quart mold or individual molds. Chill until firm in refrigerator (not freezing unit), about 30 minutes. Unmold and garnish with salad greens. Serve with tuna and additional mayonnaise.

Hazel Edberg, Denair H. S.
Denair, California

OLD FASHIONED PERFECTION VEGETABLE SALAD

Number of Servings — 8-10

2 envelopes unflavored gelatin
½ c. sugar
1 t. salt
1½ c. boiling water
½ c. vinegar
1½ c. cold water
2 T. lemon juice
2 c. cabbage, finely shredded
1 c. celery, chopped
¼ c. green pepper, chopped
¼ c. pimento, diced
⅓ c. stuffed green olive slices

Dissolve gelatin, sugar and salt in boiling water; add cold water, lemon juice and vinegar. Chill until partially set. Add remaining ingredients. Pour into a greased loaf pan. Chill until firm.

This recipe submitted by the following teachers:

Mrs. Mary Jo Stephens, Kite H. S.
Kite, Georgia

Mrs. Ann Hoit, Ousley Jr. H. S.
Arlington, Texas

PERFECTION VEGETABLE SALAD

Number of Servings — 4-8

1 envelope of unflavored gelatin
¼ c. sugar
½ t. salt
1¼ c. water
¼ c. vinegar
1 T. lemon juice
½ c. cabbage, finely shredded
1 c. celery, chopped
1 small jar pimento, cut into small pieces

Thoroughly mix gelatin, sugar and salt in a small saucepan. Add ¼ cup of the water. Place over low heat, stirring constantly until gelatin is dissolved. Remove from heat; stir in remaining water, vinegar and lemon juice. Chill until mixture reaches the consistency of unbeaten egg white. Fold in cabbage, celery and pimento. Chill until firm.

Angeline Novak, Flatonia H. S.
Flatonia, Texas

PERFECTION VEGETABLE SALAD

Number of Servings — 6

1 T. gelatin
⅓ c. cold water
⅔ c. boiling water
¼ c. sugar
⅓ c. lemon juice
2 t. vinegar
½ c. cabbage, minced
1 T. green pepper, chopped
1 T. pimento, chopped

Mix gelatin and cold water; let stand for 5 minutes. Dissolve gelatin and sugar in boiling water. Add lemon juice and vinegar. Chill until mixture reaches the consistency of unbeaten egg whites. Stir in vegetables. Chill until firm.

Betty Jo Ryan, West Point School
Cullman, Alabama

VEGETABLE SALAD

Number of Servings — 6-8

1 3-oz. box lemon gelatin
1 t. salt
1 c. boiling water
Dash of pepper
2 T. vinegar
2 stuffed green olives, sliced
1 1-lb. can solid-packed tomatoes, drained and chopped
1 1-lb. can sliced carrots, drained
1 1-lb. can green lima beans, drained
Salad greens
Mayonnaise

Dissolve gelatin and salt in boiling water. Add pepper and vinegar. Arrange olive slices and tomatoes in a pattern on bottom of loaf pan. Add a layer of carrot slices, then lima beans. Pour gelatin mixture over vegetables. Chill 3 hours or until firm. Unmold on greens and serve with mayonnaise.

Mrs. Moore, Sharpsville H. S.
Sharpsville, Indiana

VEGETABLE SOUFFLE

Number of Servings — 4-6

1 pkg. lime gelatin
1 c. hot water
½ c. cold water
4 t. vinegar
½ c. mayonnaise
Dash of pepper
Salt
1 c. raw carrots, shredded
1 c. cabbage, shredded
¼ c. cucumber, finely diced and drained
1 T. onion, finely chopped

Dissolve gelatin in hot water. Add cold water, vinegar, mayonnaise, salt and pepper. Blend well with rotary beater. Quick-chill in freezing unit until firm about 1 inch from edge but soft in center. Whip with rotary beater until fluffy. Fold in vegetables. Pour into a 1-quart mold. Chill until firm.

This recipe submitted by the following teachers:

Mrs. Ivy W. Cross, Patrick Henry H. S.
Ashland, Virginia

Mrs. Anita Himbury, Shidler H. S.
Shidler, Oklahoma

Vegetable Salads

ARTICHOKE-GRAPEFRUIT SALAD

Number of Servings — 6

1 head crisp green lettuce
1 bunch endive
1 can artichoke hearts
2 onions, sliced and separated into rings
2 grapefruit, sectioned
Garlic French dressing or Roquefort dressing

Make a nest of lettuce and endive. Place artichoke hearts, onion rings and grapefruit sections on nest. Season with dressing.

Monna S. Ray, George Washington H. S.
Alexandria, Virginia

STUFFED ARTICHOKE SALAD

Number of Servings — 4

2 c. cooked chicken, cubed
¼ c. celery, finely diced
1 6-oz. can water chestnuts, cut in strips
¾ c. tart mayonnaise
4 artichokes
1 T. salt
2 T. salad oil
½ lemon, cut up
1 clove garlic
12 stuffed olives
1 T. capers

Mix chicken, celery, water chestnuts and mayonnaise. Toss lightly with a fork. Refrigerate several hours. Cut stems from artichokes. Cook about 1 hour in boiling water with salt, oil, lemon and garlic. Drain; cool and refrigerate several hours. Carefully spread leafy spines of cooled artichokes from tip so the inner leaves can be removed. Use a spoon to remove the "choke." Fill cavity with chilled chicken salad. Garnish with olives and sprinkle with capers.

Margaret Lopp, Chandler H. S.
Chandler, Arizona

ASPARAGUS-RADISH SALAD

Number of Servings — 4

3 T. olive oil
1 T. vinegar
1 t. salt
Freshly ground black pepper
1 small clove garlic, crushed
Green asparagus, cooked and chilled
20-25 radishes, thinly sliced
Salad greens

Mix oil, vinegar, salt, pepper and garlic. Add radishes and marinate for 2 to 3 hours. Place asparagus on salad greens. Arrange the radishes on top. Pour remaining marinade over radishes.

Mrs. Aussie A. Miller, Newton H. S.
Newton, Texas

AVOCADO SALAD

Number of Servings — 4

1 lge. avocado
¼ lb. cheese, grated
1 small onion, finely chopped
1 canned green chili pepper
1 T. mayonnaise
1 T. vinegar
Dash of sugar
1 t. salt

Cream avocado. Add remaining ingredients; mix. Serve on lettuce.

Mrs. Leda Callahan, Ysleta H. S.
El Paso, Texas

AVOCADO SALAD

Number of Servings — 6

2 T. dill pickle, finely chopped
2 T. sour pickle, finely chopped
¼ c. onion, chopped
1 tomato, diced
2 ripe avocados, diced
1 hot green chili pepper, seeded and chopped
2 T. mayonnaise
Dash of salt
Lettuce, shredded
Stuffed olives, sliced

Combine pickles and onion. Blend in pepper. Add tomato, avocado and salt. Toss lightly with mayonnaise. Serve on lettuce. Garnish with olives.

Mrs. Homer D. Shurbet, Katy H. S.
Katy, Texas

BEAN RELISH SALAD

Number of Servings — 12

1 can cut green beans, drained
1 can whole green beans, drained
1 can lima beans, drained
1 can kidney beans, drained
1 c. green pepper, chopped
2 T. onion, chopped
¾ c. sugar
⅔ c. vinegar
⅓ c. salad oil
1 T. salt
Dash of pepper

Mix vegetables. Thoroughly mix remaining ingredients; pour over vegetables. Let stand overnight in refrigerator.

Elizabeth C. Harrington, Colonial H. S.
Orlando, Florida

THREE-BEAN SALAD

Number of Servings — 12

¼ c. chopped onion
1 can green beans
1 can yellow wax beans
1 can red kidney beans

Drain all vegetables. Toss lightly with dressing. Marinate several hours.

DRESSING:

½ c. salad oil
½ c. vinegar
¾ c. sugar
½ t. salt
½ t. pepper

Serve salad well chilled.

This recipe submitted by the following teachers:

Carolyn Shidaker, Lakeville H. S.
Lakeville, Indiana

Gladyce Davis, Poteau H. S.
Poteau, Oklahoma

Mrs. Jean Wilkinson, Ector H. S.
Odessa, Texas

Mrs. Lucille Horton, Del Rio H. S.
Del Rio, Texas

Mrs. Annie Fred Wright, Blacksburg H. S.
Blacksburg, Virginia

Sara Jane Threadgill, Atwood H. S.
Atwood, Tennessee

Mrs. Jeanne Wainwright Park, Ocoee H. S.
Ocoee, Florida

Mrs. Connie Appleton, Grand Saline H. S.
Grand Saline, Texas

Mrs. Bernice W. Trice, Southampton H. S.
Courtland, Virginia

Mrs. Myral Burns Thomas, Rogers Junior H. S.
Ft. Lauderdale, Florida

Mrs. Ollie Lee Arter, Kiowa H. S.
Kiowa, Oklahoma

BEAN SALAD

Number of Servings — 10

1 No. 2 can green beans, drained
1 No. 2 can English peas, drained
1 small green pepper, diced
1 small onion, thinly sliced
1 2-oz. jar pimentos, sliced
4 stalks celery, chopped
¾ c. sugar
1 c. vinegar
½ c. salad oil

Combine beans, peas, green pepper, onion, pimento and celery. Mix sugar, vinegar and oil. Cook until mixture comes to a rolling boil. Cool; add to salad. Refrigerate for 24 hours before serving.

Euna Anderson, Paris H. S.
Paris, Texas

BEAN SALAD

Number of Servings — 10-12

1 c. canned cut green beans, drained
1 c. canned yellow wax beans, drained
1 c. canned kidney beans, drained
1 c. garbanzo beans, (opt.)
½ c. salad oil
½ c. cider vinegar
¾ c. sugar
1 t. salt
½ t. pepper
½ c. onions, thinly sliced

Combine beans. Combine oil, vinegar, sugar, salt and pepper, heat, if desired. Pour over beans. Add onions. Let stand overnight in the refrigerator.

This recipe submitted by the following teachers:

Bonnie Barber, Wakpala H. S.
Wakpola, South Dakota

Dorothy F. Reese, Boiling Springs H. S.
Spartanburg, South Carolina

THREE-BEAN SALAD

Number of Servings — 8-10

2 c. canned green beans, drained
2 c. canned wax beans, drained
2 c. canned red kidney beans, drained
½ c. green pepper, chopped
⅓ c. onion, chopped
2 pimentos, chopped (opt.)
½ c. celery, chopped (opt.)
½-⅔ c. vinegar
⅓-½ c. salad oil
½ t. pepper
½ t. salt
½ c. sugar
½ t. Worcestershire sauce (opt.)
Garlic salt (opt.)
½ t. celery seed (opt.)

Mix beans. Add pepper, onion, celery and pimento if desired. Mix remaining ingredients. Pour over vegetable mixture. Cover and refrigerate for 12 to 48 hours. Drain and serve. Salad will keep for several days in the refrigerator. Dressing ingredients may be varied to suit taste.

This recipe submitted by the following teachers:

Mrs. Ralph Ayecock, Dumas H. S.
Dumas, Arkansas

Nellie S. Moore, Perrin H. S.
Perrin, Texas

Lucy White, Wethersfield H. S.
Kewanee, Illinois

Jolene Eggen, Nebraska City Public Schools
Nebraska City, Nebraska

Thelma Jean Malone, Crab Orchard H. S.
Marion, Illinois

Sue Baylor, Georgetown H. S.
Georgetown, Indiana

Mrs. Alice Blakeney, Runge H. S.
Runge, Texas

BEAN SALAD

Number of Servings — 20

1 c. white vinegar
½ c. water
2 c. sugar
1 T. salt
1 can green beans, drained
1 can yellow beans, drained
2 cans kidney beans, washed
1 pkg. frozen lima beans, cooked
1 green pepper, thinly sliced
2 or 3 stalks celery, diced
1 small can pimento, chopped
2 medium onions, thinly sliced in rings

Bring vinegar, water, sugar and salt to a boil. Cool to lukewarm. Pour over mixed vegetables. Refrigerate for 24 hours. Drain before serving. Salad will keep for several weeks in the refrigerator.

Mrs. Dalton Bednarik, Morris Community H. S.
Morris, Illinois

BEAN SALAD

Number of Servings — 6

1 No. 2 can kidney beans, drained
¼ c. celery, diced
½-1 small onion, minced
2-4 hard cooked eggs, chopped
½ t. salt
⅛ t. pepper
3 dill or sweet pickles, chopped (opt.)
¼ c. mayonnaise
Grated cheese

Lightly mix all ingredients with mayonnaise. Chill. Garnish with grated cheese.

This recipe submitted by the following teachers:

Margaret S. Campbell, Chumuckla H. S.
Milton, Florida

Virginia H. Bible, North Greene
Greeneville, Tennessee

BEAN SALAD

Number of Servings — 8-10

1 can string beans
1 can wax beans
1 can pinto beans
1 c. relish
1 onion, chopped
½ c. vinegar
½ c. salad oil
½ c. brown sugar

Drain beans. Combine beans, relish and onion. Mix vinegar, oil and brown sugar. Pour over vegetables and marinate overnight.

Mona Faye Fordham, Sikes H. S.
Sikes, Louisiana

BEAN SALAD

Number of Servings — 12

1 No. 303 can wax beans, drained
1 No. 303 can green beans, drained
1 No. 303 can kidney beans, drained
1 small onion, minced
¼ c. sugar
1 t. salt
¼ t. pepper
½ c. vinegar
¾ c. salad oil
2 hard cooked eggs, sliced

Combine beans and onion. Thoroughly mix sugar, salt, pepper, vinegar and oil. Add to mixed vegetables. Garnish with egg slices.

Wanda Raye Judson, Chaplin Special School
Cheyenne, Wyoming

BEAN SALAD

Number of Servings — 4-6

2 No. 303 cans yellow wax beans
4 hard cooked eggs
¼ c. green pepper, finely chopped
¼ c. onion, finely chopped
1 T. vinegar
1 T. cream
¾ c. mayonnaise

Dice 3 of the eggs. Mix vegetables and diced eggs. Mix cream, vinegar and mayonnaise. Pour over vegetables. Chill before serving. Garnish with slices of remaining egg.

Elaine Kirkpatrick, T. L. Handy H. S.
Bay City, Michigan

BEAN SALAD

Number of Servings — 10

¾ c. salad oil
¾ c. cider vinegar
1 c. sugar
½ medium green pepper, sliced into strips
1 medium onion, sliced into strips or cut into rings
2 c. canned cut green beans
2 c. canned cut yellow beans
1 c. red kidney beans
1 c. cici beans
Garlic powder to taste

Thoroughly mix salad oil, vinegar and sugar. Add green pepper, onion and beans. Mix thoroughly. Add garlic powder. Mix. Cover and refrigerate at least 3 hours or overnight. Serve chilled.

Patricia Laughna, Byron H. S.
Byron, Michigan

BEAN SALAD

Number of Servings — 12

1 can red kidney beans
1 can small green beans
1 can wax beans
1 pkg. frozen lima beans
1 puprle onion, sliced and separated into rings
1 small green pepper, shredded
1 can pimentos, sliced
¾ c. vinegar
⅓ c. salad oil
¾ c. sugar
½ t. salt
⅛ t. pepper
½ t. prepared mustard
1 t. salad lift

Combine vegetables. Make a marinade of remaining ingredients; pour over vegetables. Refrigerate for 24 hours before serving. Salad will keep for weeks in refrigerator.

Mrs. Roxanne Self, Sarasota H. S.
Sarasota, Florida

BEAN SALAD

Number of Servings — 12

1 can green beans
1 can yellow beans
1 can kidney beans
1 can garbanzo beans (opt.)
1 lge. purple onion, sliced in rings
1 green pepper, sliced in rings
⅓ c. vinegar
½ c. oil
⅔ c. sugar
Salt and pepper to taste

Mix beans together. Place onion and green pepper on top of beans. Mix vinegar, oil, sugar, salt and pepper; pour over beans. Let stand overnight.

Verona Wegley, Beach H. S.
Beach, North Dakota

CHILLED LIMA BEAN SALAD

Number of Servings — 8

2 pkgs. frozen baby lima beans
2 T. garlic vinegar
2 T. salad oil
2 t. sugar
2 T. chopped parsley or dried flakes
2 t. salt
1 c. sour cream

Cook lima beans as directed on package, but without salt. Drain. While still hot add vinegar, salad oil, sugar, parsley, salt and cream in order. Chill overnight. Serve from lettuce lined bowl.

Faye Quinley, Corsicana H. S.
Corsicana, Texas

CELERY-GREEN BEAN SALAD

Number of Servings — 4

FRENCH DRESSING:
½ t. salt
⅛ t. white pepper
1 speck cayenne
4 T. salad oil
2 T. vinegar
Paprika (opt.)

Pour ingredients into jar. Close tightly and shake vigorously.

2 c. cut green beans, drained
1 c. celery, diced
1 slice onion, slivered
4 pimento strips

Marinate beans for 1 hour in dressing. Drain. Combine beans, celery and onions. Serve in lettuce cups; garnish with pimento strips.

Barbara Record, White Cloud H. S.
White Cloud, Michigan

"ECONOMICAL" PORK AND BEAN SALAD

Number of Servings — 8-10

1 lge. can pork and beans, drained and chilled
2 medium size tomatoes, diced
½ green sweet pepper, diced
½ medium onion, diced
½ c. salad dressing

Combine beans, tomatoes, peppers, and onion, add salad dressing. Chill for 1 hour.

Mrs. Margaret Ann Durham, Hereford Sr. H. S.
Hereford, Texas

FOUR-BEAN SALAD

Number of Servings — 12

1 No. 303 can kidney beans, rinsed and drained
1 No. 303 can wax beans, drained
1 No. 303 can green beans, drained
1 No. 303 can lima beans, drained
2 hard cooked eggs, diced (opt.)
1-2 green peppers, chopped
1 onion, chopped
Pimento, chopped (opt.)
½-¾ c. vinegar
½-1 c. sugar
½ c. salad oil
Salt and pepper to taste

Combine vegetables and eggs. Mix remaining ingredients; pour over vegetables. Refrigerate overnight.

This recipe submitted by the following teachers:

Sadie Weedman, Dale H. S.
Dale, Indiana

Barbara Myers Shaw, Hemlock H. S.
Hemlock, Michigan

Mrs. Theora M. S. Whelchel, Hudson H. S.
Hudson, Iowa

FOUR-BEAN SALAD

Number of Servings — 25

1 No. 303 can red beans, drained
1 No. 303 can lima beans, drained
1 No. 303 can cut green beans, drained
1 No. 303 can cut yellow string beans, drained
½ c. green pepper, chopped
½ c. onions, chopped or finely sliced
½ c. salad oil
½ c. vinegar
¾ c. sugar
1 T. salt
2 t. celery seed

Combine beans, green pepper and onion. Mix salad oil, vinegar, sugar, salt and celery seed. Pour over bean mixture. Refrigerate until serving time.

Mrs. Myrna Walldorff
Lakeview Community Schools
Lakeview, Michigan

FOUR BEAN SALAD

Number of Servings — 12

1 1-lb. can green beans, drained
1 1-lb. can cut yellow wax beans, drained
1 1-lb. can red kidney beans, drained
1 1-lb. can black-eyed peas or lima beans, drained
1 medium green pepper, thinly sliced in rings
1 medium onion, thinly sliced in rings
½ c. sugar
½ c. wine vinegar
½ c. salad oil
1 t. salt
½ t. dry mustard
½ t. dry tarragon leaves, crumbled
½ t. basil leaves
2 T. parsley, snipped

Mix vegetables together. Combine remaining ingredients; mix well. Pour dressing over vegetables. Cover. Let stand for several hours or overnight. Stir several times. Stir and drain before serving.

Elizabeth G. Voland, Franklin Community H. S.
Franklin, Indiana

GREEN BEAN DELIGHT

Number of Servings — 10-12

1 No. 303 can whole green beans, drained
1 No. 303 can french-style green beans, drained
1 medium onion, sliced into thin rings
½-1 c. French dressing

Marinate beans and onions overnight in dressing.

Rosemary C. Patout, Jeanerette H. S.
Jeanerette, Louisiana

GREEN BEAN SALAD

Number of Servings — 8-10

1 No. 2 can cut or whole green beans, drained
1 No. 2 can English peas, drained
1 small-medium onion, chopped
4 stalks celery, sliced (opt.)
1 small can pimentos
1 green pepper, chopped
½-1 t. salt
1 c. vinegar
¾-1 c. sugar
½-1 c. salad oil
½-1 t. paprika
½ t. mustard seed (opt.)
½ t. celery seed (opt.)

Combine vegetables. Thoroughly mix remaining ingredients. Pour over vegetables. Refrigerate overnight. Serve cold.

This recipe submitted by the following teachers:

Mrs. Richard Caldwell, Sulphur Springs, H. S.
Sulphur Springs, Texas

Mrs. Dolly Taylor, Maplewood H. S.
Nashville, Tennessee

Dorene Nehr, Three Rivers H. S.
Three Rivers, Texas

Mrs. Margaret Blasing, Lake Crystal Public School
Lake Crystal, Minnesota

GREEN BEAN SALAD

Number of Servings — 8-10

3 c. whole green beans, drained
½ c. sugar
¼ c. water
2 T. salad oil
½ c. garlic wine vinegar
1 lge. onion, chopped
1 lge. tomato, chopped
½ c. ripe olives, chopped

Bring sugar, vinegar and water to a boil. Remove from heat; add oil. Pour over beans. Refrigerate overnight. Add remaining ingredients just before serving.

Mrs. Shirley Farmer, Denton H. S.
Denton, Texas

FRENCH STYLE BEAN SALAD

Number of Servings — 3-4

1 No. 303 can French style green beans, drained
2 t. lemon juice
⅛ t. salt
2⅓ T. mayonnaise
1⅓ T. onion, chopped

Mix lemon juice, salt, mayonnaise and onion. Pour over beans; toss well. May be served immediately or refrigerated for several hours and then served. Dressing keeps indefinitely in refrigerator.

Elisabeth Neumeyer, D. C. Everest H. S.
Schofield, Wisconsin

GOLDEN GATE BEAN BOWL

Number of Servings — 8

2 pkg. frozen Italian green beans
1 c. cauliflowerets
½ c. celery, sliced
2 T. pimento, chopped
French dressing
4 slices bacon, fried and crumbled
Lettuce leaves

Cook beans according to package directions; drain. Add cauliflowerets, celery and pimento. Toss lightly with French dressing. Chill. Serve on lettuce leaf with crumbled bacon on top.

Mrs. Sam S. Smith, Piketon H. S.
Piketon, Ohio

GREEN BEAN SALAD

Number of Servings — 8

2 No. 2 cans whole beans
1 lge. onion, sliced
Commercial Italian dressing
1 lge. avocado, sliced

Marinate beans and onion overnight in Italian dressing. Add avocado just before serving.

Mrs. Carolyn Ibert, Hammond H. S.
Hammond, Louisiana

GREEN BEAN SALAD

Number of Servings — 6

1 No. 2 can French-style beans
1 No. 2 can bean sprouts
⅔ c. sugar
⅔ c. cooking oil
⅔ c. vinegar

Mix vinegar, oil and sugar; bring to a boil. Add beans and sprouts; bring to a boil. Simmer about 5 minutes. Cool. Let stand in juice overnight. Drain before serving.

Mrs. W. B. Killebrew, Port Neches Jr. H. S.
Port Neches, Texas

GREEN BEAN SALAD

Number of Servings — 12

FRENCH DRESSING:

2 c. salad oil
¼-½ c. vinegar
1 t. Worcestershire sauce
¾ t. paprika
2 garlic buds
Juice of 1½ lemons
Juice of 1½ oranges
¾ c. powdered sugar
1 t. salt
½ t. mustard

Blend all ingredients well.

2 No. 2 cans whole green beans, drained
1 No. 2 can English peas, drained
½ c. stuffed olives, sliced
4 carrots, cut in small, thin strips
¼ lb. blanched almonds, sliced
4 c. celery, cut in small, thin strips
1 bunch green onions, finely cut
2 green peppers, finely cut

Combine all ingredients. Marinate overnight in French dressing. Drain well before serving. Salad will keep several days.

This recipe submitted by the following teachers:

Alma Keys, Director Home Economics
Education, State Department of Education
Little Rock, Arkansas

Evelyn Cotney, Northeast District Supervisor
Home Economics Education
Montevallo, Albama

GREEN BEAN SALAD

Number of Servings — 6-8

1 onion, sliced in thin rings
1 lge. green pepper, sliced in thin rings
1 c. celery, diced
1 can English peas, drained
1 can whole green beans, drained
¾ c. cider vinegar
¼ c. garlic wine vinegar
½ c. water
1 T. sugar
¼ c. salad oil
Salt and pepper to taste

Combine vegetables. Mix remaining ingredients; pour over vegetables. Refrigerate for 24 hours. Do not stir until serving time.

This recipe submitted by the following teachers:

Thelma Maxey, Larenzo H. S.
Larenzo, Texas

Velma Grizzle, Meeker H. S.
Meeker, Oklahoma

GREEN BEAN SALAD

Number of Servings — 4

Dressing:
1 T. salad oil
2-3 T. vinegar
¾ t. sugar
Salt and pepper to taste
1 No. 2 can green beans
1 c. celery, chopped
2 medium tomatoes, cut in bite size pieces
⅓ c. onion, diced

Mix dressing ingredients. Pour over vegetables. Chill for 30 minutes before serving.

Patricia McGee, Conrad H. S.
Conrad, Montana

GREEN BEAN SALAD

Number of Servings — 6

2 c. green beans, drained
½ c. celery, chopped
½ c. fresh tomatoes, diced
1 T. onion, chopped
1 medium bell pepper, chopped
1 T. pimento, chopped
¼ t. salt
⅛ t. white pepper
¼ c. salad oil
3 T. vinegar
¼ t. Accent

Mix vegetables. Combine salt, pepper, salad oil, vinegar and Accent in a jar; shake well. Pour over vegetables. Refrigerate 1 to 2 hours before serving.

Odessa Smith, Foreman H. S.
Foreman, Arkansas

GREEN BEAN PARMESAN

Number of Servings — 8-10

2 lbs. raw green beans
¼ c. onion minced
½ c. salad oil
¼ c. wine vinegar
1 t. salt
¼ t. pepper
½ c. Parmesan cheese, grated
Radish slices
Lettuce cups

Wash beans; cut off ends and cut in halves lengthwise. Cover and cook in 1-inch deep boiling salted water until tender, about 15 minutes. Drain; cool. Toss with onion, salt, oil, vinegar, pepper and cheese. Cover; chill thoroughly, stirring occasionally. Serve in lettuce cups; garnish with radish slices.

Swanie Smoot, Scott H. S.
Madison, West Virginia

GREEN BEAN SALAD

Number of Servings — 10-12

1 c. celery, diced
1 c. onion, diced
1 c. green pepper, diced
1 c. pimento, diced
1 c. sweet pickles, diced
1 No. 2 can green beans, slightly chopped
⅓ c. vinegar
1 c. sugar

Combine vegetables. Cover with sugar-vinegar mixture and let stand overnight.

Mrs. Rosemary Visser, Wakefield Rural H. S.
Wakefield, Kansas

GREEN BEAN SALAD

Number of Servings — 10-12

1 can green string beans, drained
1 can English peas, drained
1 can kidney beans, drained
1 small can pimento
1 c. celery, diced
2 small onions, diced
Salt and pepper to taste
Pinch of rosemary
¾ c. tarragon vinegar
¾ c. sugar
½ c. salad oil

Mix first 7 ingredients. Mix remaining ingredients and pour over vegetables. Refrigerate for 24 hours.

Mrs. Juanita Williams, Graceville H. S.
Graceville, Florida

GREEN VEGETABLE SALAD

Number of Servings — 12

1 can peas, drained
1 can baby lima beans, drained (opt.)
2 cans green beans, drained
1 bunch celery, cut in narrow strips
1 green pepper, cut in narrow strips
2 pimentos, thinly sliced
1 medium onion, thinly sliced
1-1½ c. sugar
½ c. salad oil
½-1 c. vinegar
2 T. water

Mix vegetables; sprinkle with salt. Let stand 2-3 hours. Drain. Mix sugar, oil, vinegar and water. Pour over vegetables; mix well. Refrigerate for 24 hours. Serve on crisp greens.

This recipe submitted by the following teachers:

Mrs. Nora Estrem, Battle Lake H. S.
Battle Lake, Minnesota

Betty Otteson, Pearl City H. S.
Pearl City, Illinois

GREEN BEAN SALAD

Number of Servings — 6

1 can whole green beans, drained
2 medium tomatoes, quartered
1 medium onion, thinly sliced and separated into rings.

Combine beans, tomatoes and onion, chill. Serve with oil and vinegar.

Mrs. Joye Weaver, Leonard H. S.
Leonard, Texas

HEARTY BEAN SALAD

Number of Servings — 15

1 No. 2 can garbanzo beans, drained
1 No. 2 can red kidney beans, rinsed and drained
1 No. 2 can French cut green beans, drained
1 c. celery, diced
½ c. green pepper, diced
¼ c. green onions, chopped
1 c. French dressing

Lightly toss ingredients. Refrigerate several hours before serving.

Ethel C. Glenn, Smiley Junior H. S.
Durango, Colorado

HOT GREEN BEAN SALAD

Number of Servings — 3-4

3 c. French-style green beans
¾ t. salt
1 small onion, thinly sliced
2 pieces canned pimento, thinly sliced
¼ c. French dressing
Dash of black pepper

Cook beans and salt in small amount of water so no extra liquid will be left. While beans are cooking, mix the remaining ingredients. Combine beans and dressing. Serve hot.

Mrs. D. W. Kneeshaw, New Hope H. S.
Goldsboro, North Carolina

KIDNEY BEAN SALAD

Number of Servings — 8

1 can kidney beans, drained
1 small head lettuce, cut in bite size pieces
1 small onion, chopped
1 small green pepper, chopped
½ c. mayonnaise
1 t. salt

Combine all ingredients.

Mrs. Charles A. Malin, Rector H. S.
Rector, Arkansas

KIDNEY BEAN SALAD

Number of Servings — 8

3 c. canned kidney beans, drained
1 c. sweet pickle, chopped
5 hard cooked eggs, sliced
¾ c. celery, diced
¾ c. mayonnaise
Lettuce

Combine beans, pickles, eggs and celery; toss lightly. Add mayonnaise and blend. Chill thoroughly. Serve on shredded lettuce or in lettuce cups; garnish with egg wedges if desired.

Mrs. Iva W. Ammon, Beth-Center Jr. H. S.
Brownsville, Pennsylvania

KIDNEY BEAN SALAD

Number of Servings — 3-5

1 No. 2 can red kidney beans, drained
1 c. celery, sliced
1 T. onion, chopped
¼ c. sweet pickle relish
1 t. salt
¼ t. chili powder
½ t. prepared mustard

Combine all ingredients, being careful not to mash beans. Chill and serve with mayonnaise on lettuce.

Sarah Judith Pitts, Century H. S.
Century, Florida

LIMA-DILL SALAD

Number of Servings — 4-5

1 pkg. frozen baby lima beans
2 T. parsley, chopped
½ c. celery, chopped
¼ c. mayonnaise
1 T. vinegar
1 T. onion, grated
½ t. whole dill seed
½ t. salt
¼ t. pepper

OPTIONAL GARNISHES:
Whole vienna sausages
Quartered tomatoes
Hard cooked egg slices
Crisp bacon, bits

Cook limas until just tender. Drain and chill. Add parsley and celery. Mix together mayonnaise, vinegar, onion, dill seed, salt and pepper. Pour over bean mixture. Toss until well mixed. Serve in lettuce-lined bowl.

Wilma Garrity, North Vernon H. S.
North Vernon, Indiana

LUCY'S PICNIC SALAD

Number of Servings — 12-15

2 No. 2 cans green beans
4 carrots, cooked
4 stalks celery, chopped
½ medium green pepper, cut in half rings
1 small can pimento, chopped
1 medium sweet onion, sliced and separated into rings
2 c. vinegar
1½ c. sugar
1 T. Ac'cent
Pinch of garlic salt
1 t. salt

Combine beans, carrots, celery, pepper, pimento and onion. Heat vinegar, sugar, Ac'cent, garlic salt and salt to boiling point. Pour hot mixture over vegetables. Chill. Will keep several weeks in refrigerator.

Mrs. Marjorie Dye, Homer Community School
Homer Michigan

MARINATED GREEN BEANS

Number of Servings — 10-12

1 16-oz. can French style or whole green beans
1 c. salad oil
1 c. vinegar
½ c. sugar
1 small onion, sliced in rings

Mix all ingredients together. Cover. Refrigerate for 24 hours.

Mrs. Euzelia M. Vollbracht, Burns At Fallston H. S
Fallston, North Carolina

OVER-NIGHT VEGETABLE SALAD

Number of Servings — 15

1 No. 2 can peas, drained
1 No. 2 can French style beans, drained
1 No. 2 can whole kernel corn, drained (opt.)
1 c. celery, diced
½ c. green pepper, diced
1 medium onion, diced
1 2-oz. jar pimentos, cut
Salt to taste
1½ c. white sugar
1 c. vinegar
½ c. salad oil
2 t. water
½ t. paprika

Mix peas, beans, corn, celery, onion pimentos and salt together. Combine sugar, vinegar, oil, water and paprika. Mix until sugar is dissolved. Pour liquid mixture over vegetables. Chill for 24 hours.

Mrs. Virginia Johnson, Madelia Ind. Dist. 837
Madelia, Minnesota

MARINATED VEGETABLES

Number of Servings — 10-12

1 can cut green beans, drained
1 can English peas, drained
1 can water chestnuts, drained
1 small can pimento, drained
1 c. celery, sliced
1 lge. onion, cut in rings
¾ c. sugar
1 c. vinegar
¾ c. water
1 bell pepper, cut in rings
Salt and pepper to taste

Combine all ingredients. Marinate for 24 hours before serving.

Georgia F. Sharbrough, Fielding Wright H. S.
Rolling Fork, Mississippi

MIXED VEGETABLE SALAD

Number of Servings — 12-16

1½ c. salad dressing
1 medium onion, chopped
1 t. mustard
1 t. Worcestershire sauce
4 T. salad oil
Dash of Tasbasco sauce
3 hard cooked eggs, chopped
1 pkg. frozen lima beans
1 pkg. frozen green beans
1 pkg. frozen green peas

Serve immediately or let stand overnight. Cook beans and peas; drain. Make a sauce with the remaining ingredients. Pour sauce over vegetables. Serve immediately or let stand overnight.

Mrs. Martha Carden, East Jr. H. S.
Tullahoma, Tennessee

PEA AND BEAN RELISH SALAD

Number of Servings — 6-8

1 pt. canned green beans, cubed
1 small green pepper, cubed
1 small can pimentos, diced
1 t. salt
1 T. water
½ c. vinegar
1 stalk celery, cubed
1 c. small green peas
1 small onion, diced
¼ c. salad oil
¾ c. sugar

Combine beans, pepper and pimento. Combine remaining ingredients; add to bean mixture. Toss. Refrigerate overnight. Drain. Reserve liquid drained from salad as it can be used again.

Mrs. Ruth Fishburn, Adair H. S.
Adair, Oklahoma

MIXED VEGETABLE SALAD

Number of Servings — 8

1 8-oz. can green beans, drained
1 8-oz. can yellow wax beans, drained
1 8-oz. can kidney beans, drained
1 c. frozen baby lima beans, cooked and drained
1 small green pepper, diced
1 small can pimento, cut
¾ c. white sugar
⅔ c. vinegar
⅓ c. fresh salad oil
1 t. salt
Italian purple onion rings

Combine beans, pepper and pimento. Combine sugar, salt, vinegar and oil; stir until dissolved. Pour liquid mixture over vegetables. Refrigerate for 4 to 6 hours. Drain. Garnish with Italian purple onion rings.

Mrs. Irma Ewing, Durand Area Schools
Durand, Michigan

MIXED VEGETABLE SALAD

Number of Servings — 20

1 can peas
1 can green or yellow beans, cut
1 medium bunch celery, diced
1 medium onion, diced
1 small can pimentos, diced
1 green pepper, diced
1½ c. sugar
1 c. salad oil
1 c. vinegar
2 T. water
¼ t. paprika
½-1 t. salt

Mix sugar, salad oil, vinegar, water, paprika and salt. Add to combined vegetables. Mix well. Let stand several hours. Stir well before serving. Salad will keep for 3 weeks in the refrigerator.

Lila L. Paisley, Mindoro H. S.
Mindoro, Wisconsin

PATIO SALAD

Number of Servings — 20

4 15-oz. cans kidney beans, drained
8 hard cooked eggs, diced
1 c. onion, chopped
2 c. celery, diced
1⅓ c. pickle relish
2 c. sharp Cheddar cheese, shredded
2 c. sour cream

Mix beans, eggs, onion, celery, pickle relish and cheese. Add sour cream; toss lightly. Serve on lettuce; garnish with additional hard cooked egg if desired.

Mrs. Mary Frances B. Wilson
Cherokee County H. S.
Centre, Alabama

TWENTY-FOUR HOUR BEAN SALAD

Number of Servings — 16-24

1 No. 303 can green beans
1 No. 303 can yellow wax beans
1 No. 303 can kidney beans
1 No. 303 can small lima beans
1 No. 303 can bean sprouts
½ c. vinegar
½-1 c. oil
½-¾ c. sugar
½ c. green pepper, chopped
Garlic salt to taste
½ c. celery, chopped (opt.)
½ c. onion, chopped (opt.)

Drain kidney beans and wash. Drain half of the liquid off remaining beans if desired. Combine all ingredients. Refrigerate overnight.

This recipe submitted by the following teachers:

Betty L. Carter, Ephrata H. S.
Ephrata, Washington

Verana R. Ballou, Hall H. S.
Spring Valley, Illinois

VEGETABLE SALAD

Number of Servings — 10

1 can green beans
1 can wax beans
1 can kidney beans
1 c. celery, diced
1 c. onions, diced
1 c. vinegar
1 c. honey
1 T. salad oil

Mix the liquids. Pour over combined vegetables and let stand for 2 hours.

Bergliot Larson, Cook H. S.
Cook, Minnesota

VEGETABLE SALAD

Number of Servings — 6

1 c. sugar
1 c. vinegar
½ c. salad oil
1 T. salt (scant)
½ t. paprika
1 can peas, drained
1 can French style green beans, drained
1 small can pimento, drained
4 pieces celery, finely chopped
1 green pepper, finely chopped
1 small onion, finely chopped

Mix sugar, vinegar, oil, salt and paprika together. Combine remaining ingredients. Pour liquid mixture over vegetable mixture. Let stand overnight. Drain before serving.

Mrs. Myrna Baer, Rockwood Area H. S.
Rockwood, Pennsylvania

VEGETABLE SALAD

Number of Servings — 8

1 can whole string beans
4 stalks celery, chopped
1 small can pimento
3 small onions, cut in rings
1 bell pepper, cut in rings
1 can tiny English peas
½ c. salad oil
1 c. vinegar
½ c. sugar
1 T. water
1 T. salt
1 T. pepper

Combine beans, celery, pimento, onion, bell pepper and peas. Mix remaining ingredients together; pour over vegetable mixture. Toss.

Mrs. Dorothy Chapman, Irwin H. S.
Oilla, Georgia

VEGETABLE SALAD

Number of Servings — 6-8

1 No. 2 can French cut green beans or wax beans, drained
1 No. 2 can kidney beans, drained
2 stalks celery, finely diced
1 green pepper, finely cut
1 c. sugar
1 T. salt
2 t. freshly ground pepper
1 c. vinegar
½ c. salad oil
¼ t. celery seed

Beat or shake sugar, salt, pepper, vinegar, salad oil and celery seed until well mixed. Pour over mixed vegetables. Refrigerate for 24 hours. Drain just before serving. Save the liquid to use as a salad dressing on other vegetable salads.

Dorothy Wynkoop, Greenville H. S.
Greenville, Ohio

VEGETABLE SALAD AND DRESSING

Number of Servings — 12

2 c. green beans
4 stalks celery, chopped
1 small green pepper, chopped
1 c. tiny green peas
1 medium onion, chopped
1 small can pimento, chopped

DRESSING:
1 T. salt
¼ c. salad oil
1 T. water
¾ c. sugar
½ c. vinegar
Dash of paprika

Combine dressing ingredients; pour over mixed vegetables. Refrigerate overnight, stirring occasionally. Drain 1 hour before serving.

Mrs. Irene Clements, Clinton H. S.
Clinton, Oklahoma

WORKING GAL'S VEGETABLE SALAD

Number of Servings — 6

1 small onion, diced
3 stalks celery, diced
1 green pepper, chopped
1 No. 3 can English peas
1 No. 3 can cut or French green beans
1 small jar pimentos, chopped
1 t. salt

DRESSING:
¾ c. sugar
1 c. vinegar
½ c. corn oil
½ t. paprika

Combine vegetables; spinkle with salt. Refrigerate overnight. Next morning, drain and mix with dressing. This salad will keep in the refrigerator for several days.

Dorotha Prowell, Hereford Sr. H. S.
Hereford, Texas

BROCCOLI VINAIGRETTE

Number of Servings — 6

2 10-oz. pkg. frozen chopped broccoli
1 bottle Italian salad dressing
2 hard-cooked eggs, chopped
1 2-oz. jar pimento, chopped
8 black olives, chopped

Cook broccoli according to package directions; drain and chill. Just before serving moisten broccoli with Italian dressing and garnish with combined eggs, pimento and olives.

Dorothy L. Anderson, Princeton H. S.
Princeton, Minnesota

CABBAGE SALAD

Number of Servings — 4

1 qt. cabbage, shredded
½ red pepper, chopped
½ green pepper, chopped
2 t. salt
1½ c. water
1 c. sugar
½ c. vinegar
1 t. mustard seed
2 stalks celery, chopped

Combine cabbage, peppers, salt and 1 cup water. Refrigerate for 1 hour. Drain. Boil sugar, vinegar, ½ cup water and mustard seed. Cool. Pour over cabbage and peppers. Add celery. Refrigerate overnight.

Mrs. Donald Berkland
Minnesota Lake Public School
Minnesota Lake, Minnesota

CABBAGE SALAD

Number of Servings — 6

1 small head cabbage, shredded
2 apples, chopped
1 onion, minced
2 pimentos, minced
3 hard cooked eggs
¼ t. salt
1 T. sugar
1 t. dry mustard
1 T. melted butter
⅓ c. lemon juice
½ c. whipped cream
Parsley

Mash egg yolks to a paste; add salt, sugar, mustard and butter. Mix thoroughly. Add lemon juice. Mix. Add whipped cream. Add cabbage, apple, onion and pimento. Mix well. Garnish with egg whites and parsley.

Mrs. Thomas E. Maxwell, Big Sandy Public School
Big Sandy, Montana

CABBAGE SALAD

Number of Servings — 8-10

1 head cabbage, chopped
1 green pepper, chopped
1 lge. onion, chopped
1 c. boiling water
1 T. salt
1 c. white vinegar
1 c. white sugar or sugar substitute
1 t. celery seed
1 t. mustard seed
1 pimento, chopped (opt.)

Combine cabbage, pepper, onion, water and salt. Let stand for 1 hour. Drain. Add remaining ingredients.

Lucile Cooper, Algoma H. S.
Algoma, Wisconsin

CABBAGE SALAD

Number of Servings — 25

1 gal. cabbage, shredded
1 green pepper, finely cut
2 onions, sliced
¾ c. vinegar
¾ c. oil
1½ c. sugar
1 T. salt
1 t. celery seed

Place cabbage and pepper in large jar. Place onions on top of cabbage mixture. Bring vinegar, oil, sugar, salt and celery seed to boil; pour over cabbage mixture. Let stand 1½ hours. Refrigerate overnight. Stir before serving.

Mrs. Pauline Kirby, Marcellus H. S.
Marcellus, Michigan

CALICO CABBAGE SALAD

Number of Servings — 6-8

1 medium onion
2 c. green cabbage, shredded
2 c. red cabbage, shredded
2 small unpared apples, sliced
½ c. salad oil
¼ c. vinegar
1 t. celery seed
1 t. salt

Slice half of onion into rings; chop remaining half. Combine chilled cabbage with chopped onion in a large bowl. Arrange row of chilled apple slices and onion rings on top. Combine salad oil, vinegar, celery seed and salt. Just before serving pour over salad and toss.

Norma Wallace, Marion Sr. H. S.
Marion, Virginia

CABBAGE SALAD WITH CREAM DRESSING

Number of Servings — 10

1 cabbage, thinly sliced
3 t. sugar
1 t. salt
Pepper to taste
¾ c. minus 4 t. heavy cream
¼ c. vinegar

Combine sugar, salt, pepper and cream. Stir until sugar and salt dissolve. Add vinegar. Pour dressing over cabbage.

Nancy L. Suydam, Hale-Ray H. S.
Moodus, Connecticut

CABBAGE-PARSLEY TOSS

Number of Servings — 5-6

2 c. cabbage, shredded
½ c. fresh parsley, chopped
½ c. green onions, chopped or chives
Green pepper, chopped (opt.)
3 T. sugar
3 T. red wine vinegar
1 t. salt
2 T. salad oil

Combine vegetables. Combine remaining ingredients; mix well. Just before serving, toss vegetables with the dressing.

This recipe submitted by the following teachers:

Doris Everson, Jim Hill Junior H. S.
Minot, North Dakota

Mrs. Adeline Henderson, Penn Manor Jr. H. S.
Millersville, Pennsylvania

CABBAGE PEANUT SALAD

Number of Servings — 8

4 c. cabbage, shredded
¾ c. mayonnaise
¼ c. sugar
2 T. cider vinegar
¼ t. monosodium glutamate
Few grains pepper
1 c. salted
Spanish peanuts

Chill cabbage. Blend together mayonnaise, sugar, vinegar, monsodium glutomate and pepper. Chill. Just before serving, toss cabbage and dressing together. Pour the chilled dressing over the cabbage. Toss lightly until cabbage is well coated. Mix in peanuts.

Marianne Estes, Artesia H. S.
Artesia, California

CABBAGE-PINEAPPLE SALAD

Number of Servings — 10

2½ c. cabbage, finely shredded
1 t. salt
1½ c. pineapple, drained
1 c. red apple, chopped
8 marshmallows, quartered
Mayonnaise
Cream

Combine cabbage, salt, pineapple, apple and marshmallows. Add enough mayonnaise and cream to moisten all ingredients. Serve immediately.

Betty Sue Gregory, Zama H. S.
Zama, Mississippi

DINNER SALAD WITH COTTAGE CHEESE DRESSING

Number of Servings — 4

4 tomatoes, peeled and cut in eighths
1 T. onion, minced
1½ t. salt
1½ T. vinegar
¼ t. dry mustard
½ c. evaporated milk
1 c. cottage cheese
4 hard cooked eggs, sliced
4 c. cabbage, shredded

Sprinkle tomatoes with onion and ½ teaspoon of the salt. Mix remaining salt, vinegar and mustard. Stir slowly into milk, then into cheese. Arrange cabbage, tomatoes, eggs and cottage cheese dressing in layers in salad bowl. Toss with fork. Serve immediately.

Mrs. Laura Anderson, Sutherlin H. S.
Sutherlin, Oregon

EDNA ALSUP'S CABBAGE SALAD

Number of Servings — 10-12

2-3 qt. cabbage, shredded
2 green peppers, shredded
1 red pepper or 1 small jar pimento, shredded
4 medium onions, shredded
1 pt. vinegar
2-2½ c. sugar
1½ t. salt
1 t. celery seed
¼ t. tumeric
1½ t. dry mustard (opt.)

Bring vinegar, sugar, salt, celery seed, tumeric and mustard to a boil. Pour hot liquid over vegetables. Let stand overnight. Will keep for several days.

This recipe submitted by the following teachers:

Ruth L. Smith, Hillman Community School
Hillman, Michigan

Mrs. Helene Van Dyke, West Geauga H. S.
Chesterland, Ohio

CABBAGE-RAISIN SALAD

Number of Servings — 6

Mayonnaise Dressing:
1 t. dry mustard
2 t. confectioner's sugar
1 t. salt
Dash of cayenne pepper
2 egg yolks
¼ c. vinegar
1½ c. salad oil, chilled

Blend mustard, sugar, salt and pepper together. Add egg yolks. Mix well. Add ½ teaspoon vinegar. Gradually add oil, a few drops at a time, until about 2 tablespoons have been used. Beat thoroughly after each addition. Add a little more vinegar and oil, beating until mixture becomes stiff. Add remaining vinegar and oil. Beat well.

3 c. cabbage shredded
1½ c. raisins
1 carrot, grated
1 c. mayonnaise dressing
½ t. salt

Combine cabbage, raisins, carrot and salt. Add enough mayonnaise dressing to moisten.

Janice M. Mountz, Brandywine Heights Joint H. S.
Topton, Pennsylvania

OLD FASHION PEANUT-CABBAGE SALAD

Number of Servings — 10

2 T. flour
¾ c. sugar
Salt and pepper to taste
2 beaten eggs
1½ c. water
½ c. vinegar
3 T. mustard
1 lge. head cabbage, shredded
½ c. peanuts, broken

Sift together flour, sugar, salt and pepper. Combine eggs, water, vinegar and mustard. Mix well. Add to dry mixture. Cook until mixture becomes a sauce. Cool. Pour sauce over cabbage and peanuts; mix well.

Katie B. Whorton, Cabot H. S.
Cabot, Arkansas

CABBAGE-PINEAPPLE-NUT SALAD

Number of Servings — 6-8

3 c. cabbage, shredded
1 c. crushed pineapple, drained
½ c. nuts, chopped
6 or 8 maraschino cherries, chopped (opt.)

Combine cabbage, pineapple and nuts.

DRESSING:

½ small pkg. cream cheese
3 T. mayonnaise
3 T. pineapple juice
⅛ t. salt

Combine all ingredients; blend well. Pour dressing over salad; toss. Chill. Garnish with Maraschino cherries.

Mrs. Gladys Jo Ridgeway, Moselle
Moselle, Mississippi

CABBAGE-TOMATO SALAD

Number of Servings — 12

1 head cabbage, finely grated
3 ripe tomatoes, coarsley chopped
18 garlic pods, finely minced
1 t. salt
2 t. red pepper
3 T. lemon juice
2 T. olive oil

Combine cabbage and tomatoes. Combine remaining ingredients; add to cabbage. Mix well. If desired, let stand overnight.

Elgie M. Dautriel, East Beauregard H. S.
De Ridder, Louisiana

CLOTHESLINE SALAD

Number of Servings — 16

4 lbs. cabbage, grated
3 carrots, grated
1 green pepper, grated
1 onion, grated
1 T. unflavored gelatin
¼ c. cold water
1 c. vinegar
1½ c. sugar
1 t. celery seed
1 c. salad oil
Salt to taste
Pepper to taste

Combine cabbage, carrots, green pepper and onion. Put in a cloth bag and hang on the clothesline for 4 to 6 hours. Mix vinegar, sugar, celery seed, salt and pepper; boil. Dissolve gelatin in cold water; add to boiling mixture. Cool. Stir in salad oil. Mix with cabbage. Serve.

Donna Anderson, Woodbine Community School
Woodbine, Iowa

CONFETTI SALAD

Number of Servings — 8-10

3 c. green cabbage, finely shredded
3 c. red cabbage, finely shredded
¾ c. green onions, thinly sliced
6 strips bacon, crisply fried and crushed
2-3 T. bacon drippings
2 t. flour
2 t. sugar
½ t. salt
1 t. dry mustard
Dash of cayenne pepper
1 egg
¼ c. vinegar
1 c. sour cream
¼ c. milk

Blend bacon drippings, flour, sugar, salt, dry mustard and pepper. Beat egg and vinegar together; add to mixture in skillet. Cook over low heat until smooth and thick; stir constantly. Combine milk and sour cream. Stir into thickened mixture. Chill thoroughly. Pour over cabbage, onions and bacon.

Mrs. Arva Nell Needham, La Grange H. S.
La Grange, Texas

FAVORITE ALASKAN VEGETABLE SALAD

Number of Servings — 6

2 c. raw cabbage, chopped
½ c. raw spinach, cut with scissors or torn
⅓ c. parsley, cut
Onion to taste
Salt and pepper to taste
Mayonnaise

Combine all ingredients. Toss lightly with a fork.

Mary Lou Tucker, Palmer H. S.
Palmer, Alaska

GREEN CABBAGE SALAD

Number of Servings — 10-12

2 c. sugar
½ c. water
1 c. vinegar
1 lge. head cabbage, shredded
1 T. salt
½ bunch celery, chopped
½ t. celery seed
½ t. mustard seed
1 green pepper, chopped
1 red pepper, chopped

Boil sugar, water and vinegar for 2 minutes. Let cool. Mix cabbage with salt; let stand for 1 hour. Squeeze out all juice. Add remaining ingredients. Mix cabbage mixture with boiled mixture.

Mrs. Ladonna Nelson, Marietta Public School
Marietta, Minnesota

MARINATED VEGETABLE SALAD

Number of Servings — 20

2 qt. cabbage, shredded
2 green peppers, shredded
1 red pepper, shredded or 1 pimento, chopped
1 pt. vinegar
2½ c. sugar
1 t. celery seed
1½ t. salt
1½ t. mustard seed
½ t. tumeric

Combine vegetables. Mix remaining ingredients together; bring to a boil. Pour over vegetables. Let stand for 12 hours. Will keep indefinitely.

Nancy W. Anderson, Hanover Horton H. S.
Horton, Michigan

RED CABBAGE TOSS

Number of Servings — 4-5

2 c. red cabbage, finely shredded
1 c. cauliflowerets, sliced
½ c. celery, sliced
2 T. onions, finely sliced
1 T. sugar
1 t. salt
⅓ c. tarragon vinegar
3 T. salad oil
8-10 green pepper rings

Toss cabbage, cauliflowerets, celery and onion together. Combine remaining ingredients except pepper rings; pour over vegetables. Toss lightly. Chill for 1 hour. Garnish with green pepper rings.

Mrs. Guy Mitchell, Chataignier H. S.
Chataignier, Louisiana

CABBAGE SKILLET SALAD

Number of Servings — 6-8

4 slices cooked, crisp bacon, crumbled
¼ c. vinegar
1 T. brown sugar
1 t. salt
1 T. onion, finely chopped
4 c. cabbage, shredded
½ c. parsley, chopped

Add vinegar, sugar, salt and onion to bacon drippings. Add crumbled bacon. Heat thoroughly. Remove from heat. Toss cabbage and parsley in hot dressing.

This recipe submitted by the following teachers:

Mrs. Glendine Crider, Molina Jr. H. S.
Corpus Christi, Texas

Mrs. Ruth H. Hughes, Abbeville H. S.
Abbeville, South Carolina

TWENTY-FOUR HOUR CABBAGE SALAD

Number of Servings — 10-12

1 T. unflavored gelatin
¼ c. cold water
1½ c. sugar
1 c. white vinegar
1 t. celery seed
1 t. salt
¼ t. pepper
1 c. salad oil
6-8 c. cabbage, shredded
2 green peppers, grated
2 carrots, shredded
1 onion, grated

Soften gelatin in cold water. Heat sugar and vinegar until sugar dissolves; cool. Add celery seed, salt and pepper. Combine gelatin and vinegar mixtures. Cool until mixture is a thickness of cream. Beat in salad oil. Combine cabbage, peppers, carrots and onion. Add enough of the dressing to moisten. Refrigerate for 24 hours.

Mrs. Jeannine M. Brady, Crosby Public School
Crosby, North Dakota

TWENTY-FOUR HOUR CABBAGE SALAD

Number of Servings — 16

4 c. cabbage, shredded
1 small onion, chopped
1 small green pepper, chopped
1 small red pepper or pimento, chopped

Combine all ingredients.

Dressing:
1 c. sugar
1 c. vinegar
½ c. salad oil
½ c. water
¼ t. salt

Mix ingredients thoroughly; pour over vegetables. Mix thoroughly. Put into tightly covered container; refrigerate for 24 hours.

Mrs. Harold Garnick, Ord H. S.
Ord, Nebraska

WHITE SALAD

Number of Servings — 8

1 No. 2½ can pineapple tidbits, drained
1 lb. marshmallows
1 pt. cabbage, shredded
1 c. almonds or pecans, chopped
¾ c. sugar
2 T. flour
Juice of 1 lemon
Juice from pineapple
1 pt. whipped cream

Mix sugar and flour together. Add lemon and pineapple juice; cook until mixture thickens. Cool. Add whipped cream. Combine marshmallows and nuts. Dry cabbage and pineapple; add to marshmallows and nuts. Mix dressing thoroughly with salad. Serve immediately.

Mrs. Patricia A. Mikulecky, Sunny Hills H. S.
Fullerton, California

WHITE SALAD

Number of Servings — 12

1 small head cabbage, grated
1 c. almonds, slivered
1 c. marshmallows, diced

Combine all ingredients.

WHITE DRESSING:
¼ c. sugar
½ t. flour
1 T. vinegar
Juice of 1 lemon
1 egg white
1 c. whipped cream
Salt to taste

Combine all ingredients except whipped cream and salt. Cook in a double boiler until mixture is thick. Cook. Add whipped cream. Pour over salad and add salt.

Mrs. Ann Manzer, Mt. View H. S.
Kingsley, Pennsylvania

CABBAGE COLESLAW

Number of Servings — 6-8

½ head cabbage, shredded
2 carrots, coarsely grated
1 bell pepper, chopped
6 radishes, sliced
¼ c. sweet dill strips, chopped
1 t. celery seed
½ t. dry mustard
1 t. salt
½ t. paprika
2 T. mayonnaise
2 T. sweet dill pickle juice

Toss lightly all ingredients; serve immediately.

Edna Bryan, Susan Moore H. S.
Blountsville, Alabama

CABBAGE SLAW

Number of Servings — 25

14 c. cabbage, shredded
1 medium onion, shredded
1 medium green pepper, shredded
3 medium carrots, shredded
¾ c. plus 2 T. white vinegar
¾ c. plus 2 T. salad oil
1½ c. sugar
1 T. salt

Combine vinegar, oil, sugar and salt. Bring to a boil. Pour hot mixture over cabbage, onion, pepper and carrots. Let stand for 1½ hours. Refrigerate. Will keep for several days.

Mrs. Mary Esther Rowe
Swartz Creek Community School
Swartz Creek, Michigan

CABBAGE COLESLAW

Number of Servings — 4

2 c. shredded cabbage
¼ c. vinegar
¼ c. sugar
1 t. salt

Mix sugar, vinegar and salt. Bring to a boil; let cool. Pour over cabbage. Toss.

Jo Ann Willis, Cotaco H. S.
Somerville, Alabama

BEST YET SLAW

Number of Servings — 10-15

2-3 heads of cabbage, shredded
4 bell peppers, chopped
3 onions, chopped
½ lb. bacon, fried and chopped
2 c. of mayonnaise
1 T. mustard
1 t. Worcestershire sauce
½ box of brown sugar

Combine mayonnaise, mustard, Worcestershire sauce and brown sugar. Heat over medium heat; cool. Combine cabbage, onion, pepper and bacon. Cool bacon drippings; add to mayonnaise mixture. Combine the two mixtures; chill.

Lillian S. Aplin, Harrisonburg H. S.
Harrisonburg, Louisiana

OLD-FASHIONED CABBAGE SLAW

Number of Servings — 4-6

1 t. salt
¼ t. pepper
½ t. dry mustard
½-1 t. celery seed
2 T. sugar
¼ c. green pepper, chopped
1 T. pimento, chopped (opt.)
½ t.-1 T. onion, grated
2-3 T. vegetable oil
⅓ c. white vinegar
3 c. cabbage, finely chopped

Place ingredients in a large bowl in order given. Mix well. Cover and chill thoroughly. Serve in lettuce cups and garnish with sliced or whole stuffed olives if desired.

This recipe submitted by the following teachers:

Shirley M. Bandy, Fort Benton Jr.-Sr. H. S.
Fort Benton, Montana

Judy Daniels,
Panama City, Florida

Naomi N. Risner, Feds Creek, H. S.
Feds Creek, Kentucky

CABBAGE SLAW WITH COOKED DRESSING

Number of Servings — 8-10

1 small head cabbage, shredded
½ c. celery, finely diced
½ c. pecans, chopped
3 medium bananas, sliced
1 T. flour
½ c. sugar
1 egg
½-1 c. water
½ c. vinegar

Combine flour, sugar, egg, water and vinegar. Cook over low heat until thick. Mix remaining ingredients. Add dressing.

Mrs. Doris Roberts, Ninnekah Sr. H. S.
Ninnekah, Oklahoma

CABBAGE SLAW DUO

Number of Servings — 4

VEGETABLE OR FRUIT SLAW DRESSING:

¾ c. salad dressing
¼ c. evaporated milk
Juice and grated rind or 1 lemon
1½ t. sugar
½ t. dry mustard
⅓ c. sour cream

Combine all ingredients; mix well. Chill. Serve with vegetable or fruit slaw.

VEGETABLE SLAW:

1½ c. cabbage, shredded
½ c. carrots, grated
2 T. onion and tops, finely chopped
¼ c. salted peanuts
½ t. celery seed
½ t. salt
½ t. Worcestershire sauce
½ t. prepared horseradish
½ t. pepper

Combine all ingredients. Chill. Serve with slaw dressing.

FRUIT SLAW:

1½ c. cabbage, shredded
⅓ c. raw cranberries, chopped
⅓ c. Mandarin orange sections
2 T. raisins
1 T. honey
½ t. salt
⅛ t. Tabasco

Combine all ingredients. Chill. Serve with slaw dressing.

Mrs. Evelyn Meeks, Glenn County Union H. S.
Willows, California

RED CABBAGE SLAW

Number of Servings — 6-8

3 c. red cabbage, shredded
¼ c. parsley, chopped
2 T. garlic vinegar
1 t. sugar
½ t. salt
2 T. capers
1 T. onion
½ c. sour cream

Combine all ingredients. Mix well.

Nelda L. Roark, LaSalle H. S.
Olla, Louisiana

RED CABBAGE SLAW

Number of Servings — 4

3 c. cabbage, finely shredded
¼ t. salt
⅛ t. white pepper
½ c. sugar
1 T. vinegar
¼ c. dessert topping mix
Lettuce
Paprika

Combine all ingredients except lettuce and paprika. Stir until sugar is dissolved. Serve on lettuce, sprinkled with paprika.

Mrs. Elbert "Red" Preston, Barnsdall H. S.
Barnsdall, Oklahoma

CABBAGE SLAW RELISH

Number of Servings — 12

1 lge. head cabbage, grated
1 lge. white onion, grated
1 lge bell pepper, grated
1 small can pimento pepper, finely chopped
1 pod hot green pepper (opt.)
1½ c. vinegar
1½ T. prepared mustard
1-2 T. salt
2 T. sugar
1 t. black pepper

Combine cabbage, onion, bell pepper, pimento and green pepper. Add vinegar. Add remaining ingredients; mix well. Will keep several weeks in refrigerator.

Mrs. Marie R. Duggan, Wrightsville H. S.
Wrightsville, Georgia

CABBAGE-TOMATO-PEPPER SLAW

Number of Servings — 6

½ medium head cabbage, shredded
2 medium tomatoes, pared and chopped
½ medium green pepper, chopped
1 t. celery seed
½ c. salad dressing
1 t. mustard
1 T. milk
Salt and pepper to taste

Combine cabbage, tomatoes and green pepper. Mix lightly with celery seed. Combine salad dressing, mustard, milk, salt and pepper. Add dressing to vegetables; mix lightly. Chill before serving.

Linda Lee Benson, Tampico Township H. S.
Tampico, Illinois

CALICO SLAW

Number of Servings — 8

1 head cabbage, shredded
1 red onion, chopped
1 red pepper or pimento, chopped
1 green pepper, chopped
1 c. vinegar
¾ c. oil
1 c. sugar
1 T. salt
1 T. celery salt
1 T. dry mustard

Combine cabbage, onion red pepper or pimento and green pepper. Mix remaining ingredients together; pour over cabbage mixture. Let set for 24 hours. Will keep for 1 week.

Ruth Riffe, Hobart H. S.
Hobart, Oklahoma

COLESLAW AMERICANE

Number of Servings — 4-5

⅓ c. Italian or onion dressing
¼ c. mayonnaise
4 c. cabbage, shredded
1 T. pimento, chopped
1 T. green pepper, chopped
1 t. onion, grated

Gradually blend dressing into mayonnaise. Combine remaining ingredients; add dressing mixture. Toss lightly.

Dorothy L. Jones, Wheatley H. S.
Wheatley, Arkansas

COLESLAW

Number of Servings — 4

¼ c. light cream
1 T. vinegar
½ t. salt
2 t. sugar
⅛ t. dry mustard
Pepper to taste
2 c. cabbage, shredded

Combine cream, vinegar, salt, sugar, mustard and pepper. Mix well. Add shredded cabbage and toss lightly. Serve immediately. If desired, make dressing in advance and refrigerate but do not mix with cabbage until ready to serve.

Mrs. Coma Funderburk, West Lamar H. S.
Petty, Texas

COLESLAW

Number of Servings — 4-6

½ head cabbage, shredded
1 medium onion, chopped
2 T. vinegar
¼ c. sour or heavy cream
¼ c. salad dressing
¼ t. salt
Dash of pepper
½ t. dry mustard
Paprika (opt.)

Combine cabbage with onion, and vinegar. Mix remaining ingredients together; add to cabbage. Toss. Sprinkle with paprika if desired.

This recipe submitted by the following teachers:

Mrs. George Hedges, Akron Community School
Akron, Iowa

Mrs. Willie V. Hill, Neshoba County H. S.
Philadelphia, Mississippi

COLESLAW

Number of Servings — 10-12

2 small heads cabbage, shredded
1 green pepper, chopped
1 small onion, thinly sliced
¾ c. vegetable oil
¾ c. vinegar
1½ c. sugar
1 t. salt

Combine vegetable oil, vinegar, sugar and salt. Bring to a rapid boil. Slowly pour hot mixture over cabbage, pepper and onion. Do not stir. Let set for 1 hour. Refrigerate. Will keep for several weeks if refrigerated.

Grace L. Hollen, Turner Ashby H. S.
Dayton, Virginia

COLESLAW

4 c. cabbage, finely shredded
3 small tomatoes, coarsely chopped
¾ c. sour cream
1 T. vinegar
2 t. sugar
1 t. celery seed
½ t. salt
Dash of paprika

Combine cream, vinegar, sugar, celery seed, salt and paprika. Blend thoroughly. Pour over cabbage and tomatoes.

Mrs. Erma Little, Caswell Public Schools
Caswell, Oregon

COLESLAW

Number of Servings — 6

4 c. cabbage, shredded
½ c. green pepper, chopped
2 T. sugar
1 t. salt
1 t. celery seed
2 T. tarragon vinegar
½ c. salad dressing
1 t. prepared mustard
Dash of pepper

Combine sugar, salt, celery seed, tarragon vinegar, mustard, pepper and salad dressing. Chill. Add to cabbage and green pepper.

Elsie Waller, Mt. Enterprise H. S.
Mt. Enterprise, Texas

CREAM COLESLAW

Number of Servings — 6

4 c. cabbage, shredded
½ c. celery, finely sliced
¼ c. green pepper, finely sliced
¼ c. sweet red pepper, finely sliced or carrot
2 T. green onions, finely sliced
¾ c. sour cream
3 T. vinegar
3 T. sugar
1 t. salt
⅛ t. white pepper
1 t. celery seed

Combine cabbage, celery, peppers and onions. Combine remaining ingredients; pour over cabbage mixture. Mix lightly.

Gladys M. Harris, Buchanan H. S.
Buchanan, Michigan

COLESLAW

Number of Servings — 6-8

1 small head of cabbage, finely chopped
2 lge. onions, finely chopped
1/4 t. sugar
3 T. mayonnaise
5 small sweet pickles, finely chopped (opt.)

Combine all ingredients.

Mrs. Zenoba Cumbie
Ralls, Texas

COLESLAW WITH BASIC BOILED SALAD DRESSING

Number of Servings — 6

1 1/2 qt. cabbage, finely shredded
1/4 c. celery and leaves, finely chopped
1/4 c. onion, finely chopped
1 T. parsley
1 T. green or red pepper
1/4 c. mayonnaise or salad dressing
1/2 to 3/4 c. Basic salad dressing

Combine all ingredients. Chill before serving.

BASIC SALAD DRESSING:

Makes 3 c.

1/4 c. flour
2 t. salt
1 t. mustard
1/2 t. pepper
1/4 t. paprika
Dash of garlic or celery salt (opt.)
4 beaten eggs
3/4 c. vinegar
1/4 c. water
1 c. milk

Combine flour, salt, mustard, pepper, paprika and garlic or celery salt. Add eggs. Mix well. Cook over low heat, stirring constantly until thick. Boil 1 minute. Cool. Refrigerate will keep indefinitely.

Mrs. John Wandell, Eastern Lebanon County H. S.
Myerstown, Pennsylvania

DELICIOUS EVERYDAY SLAW

Number of Servings — 8

4 c. cabbage, shredded
1/2 c. green onions, sliced
1 c. celery, sliced
1/3 c. sugar
1/3 c. vinegar
2/3 c. salad oil
1/2 t. salt

Combine cabbage, onions and celery. Mix sugar vinegar, salad oil, and salt. Blend well. Pour desired amount of dressing over cabbage mixture.

Mrs. Mary Sallee, Pocahontas H. S.
Pocahontas, Arkansas

FANCY COLESLAW

Number of Servings — 10

1 c. cabbage, grated
1 c. apple, grated
1 c. crushed pineapple
1 c. miniature marshmallows
1/2 c. shredded coconut
Maraschino cherries

Combine all ingredients. Toss with desired dressing.

Mrs. Deanna Thomas, Manassa H. S.
Manassa, Colorado

GOLDEN CABBAGE SLAW

Number of Servings — 4

4 hard-cooked eggs, finely chopped
3/4 t. sugar
3/4 t. salt
2 t. prepared mustard
2 t. vinegar
1/4 c. mayonnaise
2 c. cabbage, shredded
1/3 c. sweet pickle, chopped
Parsley, chopped

Combine all ingredients except parsley. Tossing lightly. Chill. Sprinkle generously with parsley.

Linda Oldenburg, Osseo H. S.
Osseo, Wisconsin

HOT CABBAGE SLAW

Number of Servings — 4

2 c. cabbage, shredded
2 slices bacon
1/4 c. onion, chopped
1/2 c. water
1/2 c. vinegar
5 T. sugar
1 t. salt
1/4 t. pepper
2 T. flour

Fry bacon until crisp and onions until transparent. Drain and reserve drippings. Combine water, vinegar, salt, sugar and pepper. Cook until mixture boils. Add bacon, onion and the flour which has been mixed with the reserved drippings. Cook, stirring constantly, until mixture thickens. Serve over cabbage. This dressing is also good over green beans.

Malta O. Ledford, Jupiter H. S.
Jupiter, Florida

HOT COLESLAW

Number of Servings — 8

2 eggs, beaten
¼ c. water
¼ c. vinegar
2 T. sugar
2 T. butter
¼ t. salt
¼ t. mustard
Pinch of celery seed
Shredded cabbage

Combine eggs, water, vinegar, sugar, salt, mustard and celery seed. Cook in double boiler until thickened, stirring constantly. Just before serving add butter. Pour hot over cabbage.

Mrs. Sharon McCormack, Madelia H. S.
Madelia, Minnesota

HOT SLAW

Number of Servings — 6

1 medium green cabbage, coarsely shredded
6 sl. bacon, coarsely chopped
½ t. celery seed
¼ c. brown sugar, packed
½ t. dry mustard
¼ c. vinegar
½ t. salt

Cook bacon over low heat until crisp. Remove bacon pieces. Add remaining ingredients except cabbage and bacon to the drippings. When mixture is hot, add cabbage. Toss until well coated with the hot dressing. Remove from heat and sprinkle with bacon pieces.

Lucille Cook, Wilmer-Hutchins H. S.
Hutchins, Texas

MARINATED CABBAGE SLAW

Number of Servings — 10-12

1 lge. head green cabbage, shredded
1 lge onion, chopped
1 small green pepper, chopped
Ice water

DRESSING:

½ c. salad oil
½ c. vinegar
¾ c. sugar
½ t. salt
1 t. celery seed
¼ t. black pepper

Combine cabbage onion and pepper. Mix. Cover with ice water. Cover tightly; refrigerate for 30 minutes. Mix all ingredients in jar or shaker. Shake vigorously until sugar dissolves. Drain vegetables; add dressing. Toss. Cover container tightly. Refrigerate 3-24 hours.

Mrs. Maurice Silk, Cooper H. S.
Abilene, Texas

NINE-DAY SLAW

Number of Servings — 20

3-lbs cabbage, shredded
1 green pepper, shredded
1 medium onion, shredded
2 c. sugar
1 c. salad oil
1 c. vinegar
2 T. celery seeds
2 T. sugar

Combine cabbage, pepper, onion and 2 cups sugar. Mix remaining ingredients together; bring to a boil. Pour hot mixture over cabbage mixture. Let cool. May be kept for several days if covered and refrigerated.

Mrs. Mary Nelle Hamilton, Gibson H. S.
Gibson,Tennessee

OVERNIGHT COLESLAW

Number of Servings — 8

1 head cabbage, shredded
½ green pepper, chopped
1 c. celery, chopped
1 t. mustard seed
1 t. celery seed
1½ c. sugar
1 c. vinegar
2 t. salt

Combine cabbage, pepper, celery, mustard seed and celery seed. Mix vinegar, sugar and salt together; pour over cabbage mixture. Let stand overnight. May be kept for several days if covered and refrigerated.

Mrs. Frances McLaughlin, Connersville H. S.
Connersville, Indiana

PEANUT-CRUNCH SLAW

Number of Servings — 6-8

4 c. cabbage, shredded
1 c. celery, finely cut
½ c. commercial sour cream
½ c. mayonnaise
1 t. salt
¼ c. green onions, chopped
¼ c. green pepper, chopped
½ c. cucumber, chopped
1 T. butter
½ c. salted peanuts, coarsely chopped
2 T. Parmesan cheese

Toss cabbage and celery together. Chill. Mix sour cream, mayonnaise, salt, onions, green pepper and cucumber. Chill. Lightly brown peanuts in butter; stir in cheese. Just before serving, toss chilled vegetables with dressing. Sprinkle peanuts on top.

Mrs. Kay Pitts, Humble H. S.
Humble, Texas

PINE-APPLE SLAW

Number of Servings — 4-6

3 c. cabbage, shredded
1 c. pineapple tidbits, drained
1 c. apples, unpared and diced
1 c. miniature marshmallows
½ c. celery, chopped
½ c. mayonnaise

Combine all ingredients. Toss until mixture is coated with mayonnaise.

This recipe submitted by the following teachers:

Mrs. Mary Kay S. Bisignani
Hempfield Area Sr. H. S.
Greensburg, Pennsylvania

Mrs. Arlene Simek, Wagner H. S.
Wagner, South Dakota

REFRIGERATOR COLESLAW

Number of Servings — 12-15

1 lge. head of cabbage, finely chopped
1 or 2 small onions, finely chopped
3 or 4 stalks celery, finely chopped
1 bell pepper, finely chopped
1 c. sugar
1 c. vinegar
1 t. white mustard seed
1 t. turmeric
Salt and pepper to taste

Combine cabbage, onion, celery, bell pepper, salt and pepper. Heat sugar, vinegar, mustard seed and turmeric to boiling point. Pour over cabbage mixture. Cover and refrigerate. Will keep for 1 week in refrigerator.

Gladys S. Esslinger, New Hope H. S.
New Hope, Alabama

REFRIGERATED SLAW

Number of Servings — 15-20

8 c. cabbage, shredded
1 lge onion, thinly sliced
1-1½ c. sugar
1 c. vinegar
¾ c. salad oil
1 t. mustard
1 t. celery seed
Salt to taste

Alternate layers of cabbage, onion and sugar. Combine remaining ingredients; bring to a boil. Simmer until well blended. Pour boiling liquid over cabbage mixture. Cover and let set for about 3 hours. Stir. Let set for 2 or 3 hours. Refrigerate. Will keep for 5 or 6 weeks if refrigerated.

This recipe submitted by the following teachers:

Fern S. Zimmerman, Clayton H. S.
Clayton, New Mexico

Mrs. Esther Moorhead, Berryhill School
Tulsa, Oklahoma

SLAW

Number of Servings — 8

1 medium head cabbage, grated
1 small onion, grated
3-4 t. white vinegar
Juice of ½ lemon
1 t. sugar
1 t. prepared mustard
¼ t. celery seed
1 c. salad dressing

Combine all ingredients except cabbage and onion. Cook over low heat until thoroughly blended. Stir occasionally. Pour dressing over cabbage and onion. Mix thoroughly. Chill 3-4 hours.

Natalie M. Summerour, Lucedale H. S.
Lucedale, Mississippi

STAY CRISP GARDEN SLAW

Number of Servings — 10

8 c. cabbage, shredded
2 carrots, shredded
1 green pepper, cut in thin strips
½ c. onion, chopped
¾ c. cold water
1 envelope unflavored gelatin
⅔ c. sugar
⅔ c. vinegar
2 t. celery seed
1½ t. salt
¼ t. black pepper
⅔ c. salad oil

Mix cabbage, carrots, green pepper and onion. Sprinkle with ½ cup cold water; Chill. Soften gelatin in remaining ¼ cup cold water. Combine sugar, vinegar, celery seed, salt and pepper in a saucepan; bring to boil. Stir in softened gelatin. Cool until slightly thickened; beat. Gradually beat in salad oil. Drain vegetables; add dressing. Mix until all vegetables are coated with dressing.

This recipe submitted by the following teachers:

Mrs. Inez P. Curvin, Benjamin Russell
Alexander City, Alabama

Mrs. Barbara D. Stanley, Matoaca H. S.
Petersburg, Virginia

Mary R. Ruble, Cocke County H. S.
Newport, Tennessee

Mrs. Diana Grosz, Bowman Public H. S.
Bowman, North Dakota

Rose Marie Whiteley, Deuel County H. S.
Chappell, Nebraska

Jenette Roake, Newport H. S.
Newport, Oregon

Mrs. Betty Hudson, Groom H. S.
Groom, Texas

SLAW

Number of Servings — 24

1 lge. head cabbage, shredded
1 lge. green pepper, chopped
1 small onion, chopped
2 stalks celery, chopped
2 c. sugar
2 t. salt
½ c. cider vinegar
1 t. celery seed
1 t. white mustard seed

Combine sugar, salt, vinegar, celery seed and mustard seed. Add remaining ingredients. Let stand overnight.

Mrs. Caroll Deem, Decker H. S.
Decker, Indiana

SOUR-CREAM SLAW IN CABBAGE BOWL

Number of Servings — 4-6

1 lge. head cabbage
1 t. salt
⅛ t. pepper
2 T. onion, minced
2 T. carrot, grated (opt.)
1 c. sour cream
2 T. granulated sugar
2 T. wine vinegar

Slice off ⅓ of the top of cabbage. Hollow out base to form a bowl. Refrigerate bowl. Chop enough remaining cabbage to make 3 cups. Add salt, pepper, onion and carrot. Refrigerate. About 10 minutes before serving, combine sour cream, sugar, vinegar and slaw mixture. Heap into cabbage bowl.

Mrs. Earl Reese, Lakefield Public Schools
Lakefield, Minnesota

TWENTY-FOUR HOUR COLESLAW

Number of Servings — 8

1 medium head cabbage, shredded
1 medium onion, diced
1 medium green pepper, chopped
6-10 stuffed olives, sliced
½-¾ c. granulated sugar

Combine all ingredients.

Dressing:
½ c. salad oil
1 c. vinegar
1 t. salt
1 t. celery seed
½-1 t. dry mustard

Combine all ingredients. Boil 3 minutes. Pour hot mixture over vegetable mixture. Cover tightly. Refrigerate 24 hours.

Mrs. Ida Moon, Las Cruces H. S.
Las Cruces, New Mexico

TWENTY-FOUR HOUR SLAW

Number of Servings — 10

1½ c. vinegar
¾ c. sugar
1 T. powdered mustard
1 t. salt
1 c. salad oil
1 lge. head cabbage, shredded
2 medium Bermuda onions, chopped

Bring vinegar, sugar, mustard and salt to a boil. Remove from heat. Combine salad oil, cabbage and onion. Pour hot sauce over cabbage mixture. Cover and refrigerate. Will keep about 3 weeks in refrigerator.

Maitland W. Newsome, Meek H. S.
Arley, Alabama

COLESLAW SURPRISE

Number of Servings — 6

2 c. crushed pineapple, drained
1 qt. cabbage, shredded
1½ c. miniature marshmallows
½ t. salt
Dash of pepper
1 t. sugar
⅓ c. mayonnaise

Combine all ingredients. Mix lightly but thoroughly. Chill.

Barbara McColgin, Union Area Jr.-Sr. H. S.
New Castle, Pennsylvania

KRAUT SALAD

Number of Servings — 6-8

1 15-oz. can kraut
1 green pepper, chopped
1 small can pimentos, chopped and/or 2 c. celery, chopped
1 c. onions, chopped (opt.)
¾ c. sugar

Combine all ingredients. Chill for several hours.

This recipe submitted by the following teachers:

Mrs. Jolene Corcoran, Lefers H. S.
Lefers, Texas

Kathleen Gee, Medicine Lodge H. S.
Medicine Lodge, Kansas

Mrs. Genevieve Dillon, Rio Grande H. S.
Albuquerque, New Mexico

KRAUT SALAD

Number of Servings — 6

1 No. 2½ can sauerkraut
1 c. celery, minced
1 medium onion, minced
1 green pepper, minced
1¼ c. oil
1⅓ c. vinegar
1¼ c. sugar

(Continued on next page)

Wash and rinse sauerkraut. Wash again. Add celery, onion and green pepper. Mix oil, vinegar and sugar together; pour over vegetable mixture. Let stand overnight. Keeps in refrigerator for several days.

Mrs. Martha Ervin, Hagerstown H. S.
Hagerstown, Indiana

CARROT SALAD

Number of Servings — 6

4 medium carrots, scraped and grated
2 tart apples, peeled and coarsely grated
½ c. white raisins
Pineapple (opt.)
4 T. mayonnaise
¼ t. salt

Combine carrots and apples. Add raisins, salt and pineapple if desired. Mix in mayonnaise. Chill.

Mrs. Nina T. Smith, Picayune Memorial H. S.
Picayune, Mississippi

CARROT-COCONUT SALAD

Number of Servings — 4-5

1 c. flaked coconut
1½ c. raw carrots, shredded
¼ c. seedless raisins
2 T. lemon juice
½ t. ground ginger
¼ c. mayonnaise
Mandarin orange sections, drained (garnish)

Combine all ingredients; mix well. Chill. Serve on crisp lettuce with additional mayonnaise. Garnish with orange sections if desired.

Sandra M. Cuchna, La Farge H. S.
La Farge, Wisconsin

CARROT-COCONUT SALAD

Number of Servings — 4

1½ c. raw carrot, shredded
½ c. flaked coconut
2 T. lemon or orange juice
¼ c. mayonnaise
2 T. sour cream
Mandarin orange sections, drained (garnish)

Blend mayonnaise and sour cream. Combine all ingredients; mix well. Serve on crisp lettuce. Garnish with additional coconut and/or orange sections.

Bertha C. Stefan, Prophetstown Community H. S.
Prophetstown, Illinois

CARROT CONCOCTION

Number of Servings — 6

1½ c. carrots, grated
½ c. crushed pineapple, drained
⅓ c. raisins
¼ c. salted peanuts
½ c. cooked dressing
½ t. prepared mustard
1 T. sugar
2 T. sweet cream

Soak raisins in water until they become plump. Mix raisins, carrots, pineapple and peanuts together. Refrigerate for 1 hour. Combine dressing, mustard, sugar and cream. Whip until smooth. About 15 minutes before serving combine salad and dressing. Toss.

Catherine Nelson, Jeffers Public School
Jeffers, Minnesota

CARROT AND LEMON SALAD

Number of Servings — 4

2 c. carrots, grated
¼ c. sugar
Juice of 1 lemon

Mix ingredients; let stand for 1 hour. Serve on lettuce.

Mrs. Nettie Waller, Deer River H. S.
Deer River, Minnesota

CARROT-ORANGE-RAISIN SALAD

Number of Servings — 4

½ c. raisins
1 lge. orange, cubed
1½ c. raw carrots, grated
¼ c. mayonnaise
1 T. lemon juice
1 t. sugar
¼ t. salt
Lettuce

Cover raisins with boiling water; let stand for 5 minutes. Drain and cool. Add carrots and orange. Combine mayonnaise, lemon juice, sugar and salt. Add to carrot mixture. Toss. Serve on lettuce.

Mrs. Adeline H. Kirk, Central H. S.
San Angelo, Texas

CARROT-RAISIN SALAD

Number of Servings — 6

1½ c. carrots, shredded
½ c. seedless raisins
1½ c. orange, diced
Mayonnaise

Toss carrots, raisins and orange pieces together; moisten with mayonnaise. Serve on lettuce.

Mrs. Jimmie Cain, Thrall H. S.
Thrall, Texas

LEMONED CARROTS

Number of Servings — 4

12 small carrots, peeled
1 6-oz. can frozen lemonade, undiluted
6 whole cloves
Lettuce

Boil carrots in small amount of water until tender. Drain. Add lemonade and cloves; simmer gently for 5 minutes. Cool. Chill thoroughly. Drain. Serve on lettuce.

Mrs. Doveta Hunt, Pecos H. S.
Pecos, Texas

VITAMIN-CARROT SALAD

Number of Servings — 6

2 c. raw carrots, grated
2 T. lemon juice
1 c. celery, diced
¼ c. nuts, finely chopped
Salad dressing

Lightly toss all ingredients with salad dressing. Chill. Serve on salad greens.

Mrs. Carolyn W. Yeatts. Prince Edward Academy
Farmville, Virginia

RAW CAULIFLOWER SALAD

Number of Servings — 6

1 small head cauliflower, thinly sliced
3 unpeeled red apples, diced
1 c. celery, sliced
3 small green onions, sliced
¾ c. parsley, chopped or 1 small bunch watercress, chopped
1 clove garlic, cut
½ t. salt
¼ c. red wine vinegar
¼ c. salad or olive oil
Pepper to taste

Thoroughly chill cauliflower, apples, celery, onions and parsley. Rub salad bowl with cut garlic clove and salt. Shake vinegar, oil and pepper vigorously in a tightly covered jar. Pour over mixed fruit and vegetables; toss lightly.

Mrs. Ruth S. Park, Bend Senior H. S.
Bend, Oregon

RAW CAULIFLOWER SALAD

Number of Servings — 4

1 small head cauliflower, chopped
3 T. onion, diced
1 lge. tomato, diced
¼ green pepper, chopped

SOUR CREAM DRESSING:

½ c. sour cream
4 t. white vinegar
1 T. sugar
Dash of salt

Mix cauliflower, onion, tomato and pepper. Stir sour cream and vinegar together; add sugar and salt. Add to cauliflower mixture.

Julie Gorman, Mound City H. S.
Mound City, Kansas

CAULI-SLAW

Number of Servings — 6

½ head fresh cauliflower, finely grated
¼ c. carrots, grated
¼ c. celery, finely chopped
¼ c. green pepper, finely chopped
¼ t. vinegar
¼ t. sugar
Salt and pepper to taste
Mayonnaise
Hard-cooked eggs, sliced (garnish)
Paprika (garnish)

Combine all ingredients; mix well. Chill. Sprinkle with paprika or garnish with hard-cooked egg slices arranged in petal fashion if desired.

Carol Jean McConnell, Home Economic Department, Beth-Center Sr. H. S.
Fredericktown, Pennsylvania

CELERY SLAW

Number of Servings — 6

1 t. salt
1½ t. sugar
⅛ t. pepper
Dash of paprika
⅓ c. salad oil
2 T. vinegar
¼ c. sweet or sour cream
2 c. celery, thinly sliced
2 T. pimento, slivered
Salad greens
Green pepper rings

Combine salt, sugar, pepper, paprika, oil and vinegar. Beat with a rotary beater. Add cream; continue beating until smooth. Marinate celery in dressing for a few minutes. Add pimento; toss. Place greens in salad bowl; pile celery mixture in center. Garnish with green pepper rings.

Mrs. Dorothy Maxwell, Westville Township H. S.
Westville, Illinois

CELERY-KRAUT SALAD

Number of Servings — 8

¼ c. wine vinegar
1 c. sugar
1 medium can sauerkraut
1 medium onion, chopped
1 green pepper, chopped
1 c. celery, chopped

Combine vinegar and sugar; heat until sugar dissolves. Cool and pour over combined vegetables. Refrigerate for at least 2 hours or overnight.

Edith Kral, Pampa Sr. H. S.
Pampa, Texas

CELERY RINGS

Number of Servings — 8

3 T. butter
1 3-oz. pkg. cream cheese
3 T. tomato paste
Salt and red pepper to taste
1 bunch celery

Cream butter; add cheese and tomato paste. Mix well. Add salt and red pepper. Stuff celery stalks with mixture. Put celery hearts together; place remaining pieces of celery around to make the stalk into its original shape. Wrap in waxed paper; chill. Slice into rings.

Evelyn Ford, Clarke County H. S.
Berryville, Virginia

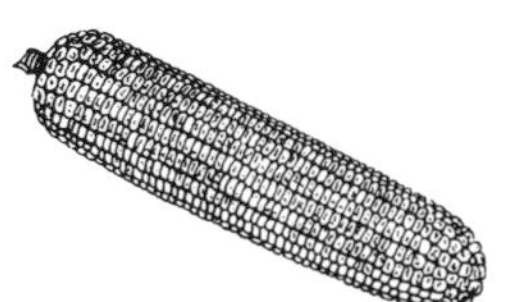

CORN RELISH SALAD

Number of Servings — 8-10

Dressing:
⅔ c. salad oil
2½ T. vinegar
2½ t. salt
½ t. pepper
1¼ t. dry mustard

Combine all ingredients.

1 No. 2 can whole kernel corn
½ green pepper, chopped
2½ t. pimento, diced
5 small stalks celery, diced
1 medium onion, chopped

Mix vegetables; add dressing. Refrigerate for 24 hours.

Jessie Chambers, East H. S.
Cheyenne, Wyoming

CORN SALAD

Number of Servings — 4

1 No. 2 can whole kernel corn, drained
1 pimento, chopped
1 small onion, chopped
1 small green pepper, chopped
1 small cucumber, chopped
½ c. French dressing

Combine all ingredients. Serve on lettuce cups. If desired, mayonnaise may be substituted for French dressing and the salad used for stuffing tomatoes.

Mrs. Judy Brumley, Kyle H. S.
Kyle, Texas

CUCUMBER SALAD

Number of Servings — 8

3-4 lge. cucumbers, sliced
2 lge. tomatoes, cubed
1 pkg. Swiss cheese, diced
2 No. 303 cans mixed carrots and peas, drained
1 lge. onion, chopped
1 pt. mayonnaise
⅔ c. sugar
¾ bottle Italian dressing
⅔ c. milk
Garlic salt to taste
1-2 c. cooked shrimp or ham, diced (opt.)

Combine cucumbers, tomatoes, cheese, onion, carrots and peas. Combine Italian dressing and milk; add sugar. Cook and stir over low heat until sugar is dissolved. Cool. Add mayonnaise and garlic salt; blend thoroughly. Add to vegetable mixture. Add shrimp or ham if desired.

Mrs. Ella Jo Adams, Allen Sr. H. S.
Allen, Texas

CUCUMBER COOLER

Number of Servings — 4-6

¼ c. vinegar
1 T. lemon juice
1 t. celery seed
2 T. sugar
1 t. salt
⅛ t. pepper
¼ t. Accent
¼ c. onion, chopped
2 T. parsley, chopped
3 medium cucumbers, thinly sliced

Mix all ingredients except cucumbers in jar or plastic container. Add cucumbers; toss to coat with dressing. Chill thoroughly. Turn or shake container several times while chilling.

Mrs. Emely Sundbeck, Manor H. S.
Manor, Texas

GRANDMA'S CUCUMBER SALAD

Number of Servings — 4

2 medium cucumbers, sliced
1 lge. onion, sliced
⅓ c. mayonnaise

Mix ingredients. Serve lettuce; garnish with Paprika and/or sprig of parsley.

Marjorie C. Gould, Kirkland Jr. H. S.
Kirkland, Washington

CUCUMBER MOUSSE

Number of Servings — 6-8

1 lge. unpeeled cucumber, grated
¾ c. evaporated milk
2 pkgs. low-calorie lime gelatin
½ c. boiling water
1 t. onion, grated
¼ t. salt

Chill a small mixing bowl and beaters. Chill evaporated milk in freezing compartment until ice crystals form around edge. Dissolve gelatin in boiling water. Add onion, salt and undrained cucumber. Chill until slightly thickened. Whip evaporated milk in chilled bowl until stiff. Fold gelatin mixture into whipped milk. Pour into mold and chill until firm. Unmold on bed of greens; garnish with mayonnaise.

Mrs. Eileen Roberts, Westfield H. S.
Westfield, Wisconsin

CUCUMBERS IN SOUR CREAM

Number of Servings — 3

1 medium cucumber, sliced
1 t. salt
3 T. cultured sour cream
1 t. vinegar
1 t. sugar
¼ t. dill weed

Sprinkle cucumber with salt; cover with water. Soak. Combine sour cream, vinegar, sugar and dill weed. Drain cucumber; add dressing. If dressing is too thick add a small amount of milk or cream.

Mrs. Carol S. Johnson and Miss Teresa Bauman
Central Junior H. S.
Alexandria, Minnesota

MOCK CRAB SALAD (PARSNIP)

Number of Servings — 6

3 c. raw parsnips, shredded
1½ c. celery, finely cut
1 pimento, finely cut
½ c. olives
1 t. horseradish
½ t. salt
¼ t. pepper
½ c. mayonnaise
Lettuce

Combine all ingredients; toss. Serve on lettuce.

Mrs. Mari Hurley, Central Union H. S.
El Centro, California

WINTER SALAD BOWL

Number of Servings — 2-3

½ c. raw parsnip, grated
2 T. sweet onion, chopped
¼ c. celery, chopped
4 stuffed olives, chopped
¼ t. salt
French dressing
⅓ med. head lettuce, torn in bite-size pieces
2 T. mayonnaise

Marinate parsnip, onion, celery, olives and salt in French dressing for 1-2 hours. Just before serving add lettuce. Toss lightly with mayonnaise.

Mrs. Bettie Lou Snapp, Valley H. S.
Albuquerque, New Mexico

WINTER WONDER SALAD

Number of Servings — 4

1½ c. raw parsnips, scraped and shredded
¾ c. celery, diced
¼-⅓ c. onion, minced
8-10 small stuffed olives, sliced
½ t. salt
Dash of pepper
¼ c. French dressing
¼ c. mayonnaise or salad dressing
1 small head lettuce
Green pepper or stuffed olives, sliced (garnish)

Combine parsnips, celery, onion, olives, salt and pepper. Add French dressing and mayonnaise; toss well. Arrange in lettuce nests; garnish with green pepper or stuffed olive slices.

Mrs. Zetta Forbes Robb, Napoleon Senior H. S.
Napoleon, Michigan

RAW PARSNIP SALAD

Number of Servings — 4

2-4 raw parsnips, finely grated
1/3 c. crushed pineapple
1/2 c. marshmallows
1/3 c. salad dressing
1 T. sugar
1/3 c. pineaple juice

Mix parsnips, pineapple and marshmallows. Mix salad dressing, sugar and pineapple juice. Pour dressing over the parsnip mixture; blend. Chill.

Colleen Stevenson, Ripley H. S.
Ripley, Oklahoma

PEA SALAD

Number of Servings — 6

1 medium can peas, drained
3 sweet pickles, diced
1/2 small onion, diced
1 hard cooked egg, diced (opt.)
1 raw egg
1 1/2 t. sugar
1 1/2 t. pickle vinegar
2 T. half and half cream
Dash of salt
1 T. peanut butter

Combine raw egg, sugar, vinegar, cream and salt. Cook over low heat until thickened, stirring constantly. Add peanut butter; mix. Pour cooked mixture over peas, pickles, onion and hard cooked egg. Toss lightly.

Nevaleen Joy Selmat, Wakita H. S.
Wakita, Oklahoma

GREEN PEA SALAD

Number of Servings — 6-8

1 No. 303 can green peas, drained
1 pod pimento pepper, chopped
2 hard cooked eggs, chopped
6 or 8 leaves of lettuce
2 T. butter
2 T. flour
1/4 t. salt
1/8 t. pepper
1 c. milk

Make a white sauce by melting butter in sauce pan, add flour, salt and pepper. Simmer for 1 or 2 minutes. Add milk; cook until thickened, stirring constantly. Add peas, pimento and eggs; mix well. Chill. Serve on lettuce. May be served hot, with cheese and bread crumb topping as a casserole.

Martha Berryhill, Corner H. S.
Warrior, Alabama

PEA SALAD

Number of Servings — 6

1 No. 202 can green peas, drained
1 c. medium or sharp cheese, diced
1/2 c. celery, diced
1/4 c. onion, diced
1 t. salt
4 hard coked eggs, diced
1/2 c. salad dressing

Combine all ingredients. Toss lightly.

Mrs. Fayga Parker, Cedar Springs H. S.
Cedar Springs, Michigan

PEA SALAD

Number of Servings — 4

1 c. ungraded peas, drained
4 T. sweet pickle, chopped
4 T. onion, chopped
4 T. Longhorn cheese, diced
4 T. hard cooked eggs, chopped
Salad dressing
Salt to taste

Combine all ingredients. Toss.

Mrs. Lucille L. Stewart, Lake Ville Memorial H. S.
Otisville, Michigan

PEA-PICKLE-PECAN SALAD

Number of Servings — 6

2 c. cooked English peas, drained
6 T. sweet pickles, diced
1/2 t. salt
1 c. pecans, broken
6 T. mayonnaise

Combine peas, pickles, salt and pecans. Moisten with mayonnaise. Serve on lettuce leaf.

Gussie Mae Beard, Pelican H. S.
Pelican, Louisiana

ENGLISH PEA AND CHEESE SALAD

Number of Servings — 6

1 No. 2 can English peas, drained
1 medium tomato, diced
1 c. mild Cheddar cheese, cubed
1 T. pimentos, chopped
4 T. salad dressing or mayonnaise
Dash of seasoned salt
6 lettuce leaves
Dash paprika

Combine English peas, tomato, cheese, pimentos, salad dressing or mayonnaise and seasoned salt. Toss just enough to mix lightly. Serve on lettuce leaf; garnish with paprika.

Mrs. Winnie McQueen, Santa Anna H. S.
Santa Anna, Texas

ENGLISH PEA SALAD

Number of Servings — 4

1 1-lb. can English peas, chilled
½ c. sweet pickles, drained and chopped
¼ c. pecans, chopped
2 hard cooked eggs, chopped
Mayonnaise and salt to taste

Mix ingredients. Serve on a lettuce leaf.

Mrs. J. H. Hellums, South Panola H. S.
Batesville, Mississippi

GREEN PEA SALAD

Number of Servings — 8

1 medium can green peas
3 hard cooked eggs, chopped
½ c. celery, diced
½ c. sweet pickles
½ c. onion, diced
¼ c. mayonnaise
Olive halves (garnish)
Pimento strips (garnish)

Place peas in mixing bowl and gradually add remaining ingredients stirring until well blended. Place in salad bowl and garnish with olive halves and pimento strips.

Betty Clyburn, Man H. S.
Man, West Virginia

PROSPERTY SALAD

Number of Servings — 8

2 No. 2 cans cooked dried black-eyed peas or red kidney beans, drained
1 c. salad oil
¼ c. wine vinegar
1 clove garlic
¼ c. onion, thinly sliced
½ t. salt
Freshly ground pepper to taste

Combine all ingredients. Mix thoroughly. Refrigerate. Remove garlic bud from salad after two days. For improved flavor store at least two days or as long as two weeks before serving.

Mrs. Georgia Waters Scott, Clarksville H. S.
Clarksville, Texas

POTATO SALAD

Number of Servings — 8

6 medium potatoes, cooked in jackets
1 onion, chopped
3 hard-cooked eggs, sliced
1 c. celery, chopped
¼ c. sweet pickles, chopped
1½ t. salt
1 t. celery seed
Mayonnaise

Combine all ingredients, stirring as little as possible. Serve warm or cold.

Janet Adams, Madison Central H. S.
Richmond, Kentucky

POTATO SALAD

Number of Servings — 4-6

4 c. potatoes, cooked and peeled
1-1½ t. salt
½ c. onion, thinly sliced
¼ c. celery, chopped
2 T. green pepper, chopped
3-4 hard-cooked eggs, chopped
1 c. boiled dressing or 1 c. mayonnaise plus 2 t. vinegar and ½ t. prepared mustard

Quarter potatoes then cut into ¼-inch slices. Add remaining ingredients. Chill for 4 or 5 hours.

Edna Axt, New England Public School
New England, North Dakota

POTATO SALAD

Number of Servings — 100

30 lbs. potatoes
4 doz. hard-cooked eggs, chopped
4 lge. bunches celery, chopped
2 qts. salad pickle, chopped
10 small cans pimento, chopped
6 onions, chopped
2 qts. mayonnaise
2 6-oz. jars mustard
7-8 green peppers, chopped
½ c. salt
2 T. black pepper

Peel and cube potatoes. Cook for 1 minute in pressure cooker. Cool. Combine all ingredients; mix well.

Helen Cade, Marengo County H. S.
Thomaston, Albama

POTATO-CUCUMBER SALAD

Number of Servings — 8

4 c. cooked potatoes, diced
½ cucumber, finely diced
1 small onion, chopped
¼ c. sweet peppers, diced
2 hard-cooked eggs, finely chopped
1 T. celery seed
¾ c. mayonnaise
1 T. prepared mustard
2 T. evaporated milk
1 T. vinegar
1 t. salt
½ t. pepper

Combine potatoes, cucumber, onion, peppers, eggs and celery seed. Mix remaining ingredients; add to potato mixture. Mix thoroughly. Chill 3 to 4 hours.

Mrs. Jeanette Mitchell, Pleasant Valley Jr.-Sr. H. S.
Brodheadsville, Pennsylvania

POTATO SALAD

Number of Servings — 8

6 medium new potatoes
½ c. green onion, thinly sliced
1 c. celery, chopped
2 T. celery seed
¼ lb. bacon, fried and diced
Salt and pepper to taste
¼ c. parsley, chopped
Salad dressing

Boil potatos in jackets until tender. Cool in cooking water. Peel and dice. Add bacon, bacon drippings, onions, celery, parsley and celery seed; mix. Add enough salad dressing to moisten. Salt and pepper to taste. Chill for several hours before serving.

Mrs. J. S. Elsner, Hampton H. S.
Allison Park, Pennsylvania

POTATO SALAD

Number of Servings — 8

6 medium unpeeled potatoes
3 hard-cooked eggs, chopped
½ c. pickles, chopped
2 t. salt
½ t. celery salt
½ t. garlic salt
½ t. onion salt
1 T. prepared mustard
¾ c. mayonnaise
¼ c. pickle juice

Cook unpeeled potatoes; peel while hot. Add salt, celery, garlic and onion salt. Mash with a fork. Add pickles and eggs. Combine remaining ingredients. Add to potato mixture and mix well. Refrigerate for several hours.

Maxine Gibson, Bradford County H. S.
Starke, Florida

POTATO SALAD

Number of Servings — 6

3 c. raw potatoes, diced
2 c. hot water
1½ t. salt
2 hard-cooked eggs, diced
½ c. celery, diced
½ c. sweet cucumber pickle, diced
4 T. mayonnaise
2 t. prepared mustard
¼ t. sugar
½ t. onion salt
1 medium red apple, diced
Dash of red pepper (opt.)

Boil potatoes in hot water with 1 t. salt until tender; drain. Add eggs, celery, pickle, mayonnaise, mustard, sugar, onion salt, pepper and remaining ½ t. salt. Mix well. Add apples. Serve warm or cold.

Josephine Grant, Rocky Mount Sr. H. S.
Rocky Mount, North Carolina

POTATO SALAD

Number of Servings — 4

4 medium potatoes
¾ c. salad dressing
1 t. salt
1 T. onion, finely chopped
½ c. celery, finely cut
2 hard-cooked eggs, chopped

Cook potatoes in their jackets until tender. Peel and dice. Add remaining ingredients. Chill for 3 hours before serving.

Mrs. Nancy King, Chesterfield H. S.
Chesterfield, South Carolina

POTATO SALAD

Number of Servings — 6

1½ c. cooked potatoes, cubed
4 hard-cooked eggs, chopped
1 T. sweet onion, chopped
½ c. sweet pickle, diced
2 T. pimento, chopped
¾ t. salt
Dash of white pepper
1 t. celery seed (opt.)
¾ c. mayonnaise

Combine potatoes, pickles, salt, and mayonnaise. Cover and refrigerate several hours or overnight. Add remaining ingredients. Toss lightly until well mixed.

Mrs. Nadine Martin, Vernon H. S.
Vernon, Texas

POTATO SALAD

Number of Servings — 10

6 lge. white potatoes
1 medium onion, chopped
3 hard-cooked eggs, diced
½ c. celery, chopped
3 sweet pickles, diced
3 dill pickles, diced
¼ c. green pepper, chopped
8 stuffed olives, diced
1½ t. salt
¼ t. pepper
2 t. mustard
½-¾ c. mayonnaise

Peel and cube potatoes; cook until tender. Cool. Combine all ingredients and mix with a fork.

Mrs. Beth Pittman, Whitehouse H. S.
Whitehouse, Texas

POTATO SALAD

Number of Servings — 8-10

3-4 lge. white potatoes
4 hard-cooked eggs, chopped
1 lge. onion, finely chopped
1 lge. dill pickle
1/3 c. sweet pickle relish
1 can pimento, chopped
1/2 c. celery, chopped
2 T. prepared mustard
1 t. garlic salt
1 t. black pepper
1/2 c. salad dressing

Boil potatoes in jackets until done; do not overcook. Cool. Peel and dice. Add remaining ingredients, adding eggs last to keep them from being mashed out of shape.

Mrs. Janell Samford, C. O. Wilson Jr. H. S.
Nederland, Texas

DELICIOUS POTATO SALAD

Number of Servings — 10-12

8 medium potatoes, boiled, peeled and diced
1 lge. onion, minced
8 hard-cooked eggs, chopped
3 sweet pickles, chopped
1 small can pimentos, drained and chopped
1 c. salad dressing
1 T. prepared mustard
1/2 c. plus 2 T. sugar
1 t. celery seed
Juice of 1 small can pimentos
Salt and pepper to taste

Combine potatoes, onion, eggs, pickles and pimento. Mix remaining ingredients; add to potato mixture. Chill for several hours.

Janet Oyler, Glasco H. S.
Glasco, Kansas

HAWAIIAN STYLE POTATO SALAD

6 medium potatoes
1 medium onion, minced
1/2-3/4 c. carrots, grated
4-6 hard-cooked eggs, chopped
4 T. sweet relish (heaping)
1 can solid pack tuna, drained and flaked
1/2 c. pimento, chopped
1 t. prepared mustard
2 T. parsley, minced
Black pepper to taste
Garlic
Mayonnaise to taste

Cook potatoes in water with a little garlic until done. Drain; cool and dice. Add remaining ingredients.

Mrs. Fannye Maude Franks, Caldwell, Jr. H. S.
Columbus, Mississippi

CARNIVAL POTATO SALAD

Number of Servings — 6-8

3 c. warm potatoes, cubed
1/4 c. pimento pepper, chopped
1/4 c. sour pickle, chopped
1 small onion, chopped
1/4 c. mayonnaise
1/2 t. salt
1/2 t. paprika

Combine potatoes, pimento, pickle and onion. Toss with mayonnaise, salt and paprika. Chill.

Mrs. Iris Lockey, Athens H. S.
Athens, Texas

DILLED POTATO SALAD

Number of Servings — 6

3 lge. cooked potatoes, shredded
1 t. salt
1/2 t. pepper
1/8 t. dill weed
1 T. vinegar
1/2 onion, finely minced
2 hard-cooked eggs, chopped (opt.)
2 stalks celery, finely cut
Minced fresh parsley or 1 t. dried parsley
Dash of Tabasco sauce
2 T. pimento, minced
2 heaping T. mayonnaise
2 heaping T. sour cream

Combine potatoes, salt, pepper and vinegar. Toss lightly with a fork. Add remaining ingredients; toss. Let stand until flavors are blended.

Maud R. Sharer, Columbia H. S.
White Salmon, Washington

GREEN FROSTED POTATO SALAD

Number of Servings — 9

4 lb. potatoes, cooked in jackets and diced
1/2 c. parsley, chopped
1/4 c. green pepper, chopped
1/4 c. celery tops, chopped
1/4 c. green onions, chopped
1/4 c. dill pickle, chopped
1 c. mayonnaise
1/4 c. clear French dressing
2-2 1/2 t. salt
1/2 t. pepper
1 t. dry mustard

Combine 1/4 cup parsley, green pepper, celery tops, onion and pickle. Divide mixture. Add remaining parsley to half of the mixture and potatoes to the other half. Combine mayonnaise, French dressing, salt, pepper and mustard; add to potato mixture. Mix well. Add remaining mixture. Chill.

Mrs. Marilyn Bonkrude, Waterville H. S.
Waterville, Minnesota

JEAN'S POTATO SALAD

Number of Servings — 6-8

4-6 cooked potatoes, diced
2 stalks celery, chopped
1 can pineapple tidbits, drained
2 hard-cooked eggs, chopped
1 red onion, chopped
Salt and pepper to taste
Salad dressing or sour cream

Combine ingredients with enough salad dressing or sour cream to moisten. Chill.

Mrs. Olga Masch Decker, Gunter School
Aubrey, Texas

MAIN DISH POTATO SALAD

Number of Servings — 8

3 or 4 lge. potatoes
1 medium onion, finely minced
12 red radishes, diced
1½ c. celery, diced
1 medium cucumber, diced
1 t. salt
2 t. sugar
4 hard-cooked eggs, diced
1 c. mayonnaise

Boil potatoes in their jackets. Peel and dice. Mix warm potatoes with salt, sugar, mayonnaise and eggs. Chill. Just before serving add vegetables. Toss. Add more dressing if necessary.

Esther L. Harbison, Mountain Home H. S.
Mountain Home, Arkansas

QUICK POTATO SALAD

Number of Servings — 4-6

1 envelope instant potatoes
2 hard-cooked eggs, chopped
4 T. sweet or dill pickles, cubed
2 stalks celery, chopped
1 small onion, chopped
2 T. pimento, chopped
3 T. mayonnaise
Salt and pepper

Prepare potatoes according to package directions using ¼ cup less liquid than called for. Add mayonnaise until desired consistency is reached. Add remaining ingredients. Salad will mold well if packed in an oiled container. If sour taste is desired, use vinegar as part of liquid in preparing potatoes.

Mrs. Betty G. Lawrence, Sr. H. S.
Mooresville, North Carolina

MASHED POTATO SALAD

Number of Servings — 6

3 c. hot potatoes, mashed
½ c. sweet onion, diced or 3 green onions, diced
½ c. celery, diced
4 hard-cooked eggs, diced
⅓ c. French dressing
¾ c. mayonnaise
Salt and pepper to taste
Paprika

If potatoes are cooked without salt, add salt when mashing. Do not add milk. Add onions and French dressing; mix. Chill thoroughly. About 1 hour before serving add remaining ingredients. Season to taste. Garnish with paprika. If left-over mashed potatoes are used; less mayonnaise is needed.

Norma S. Howland, Williamson Jr. Sr. H. S.
Tioga, Pennsylvania

OLIVE-POTATO SALAD

Number of Servings — 8

6 medium potatoes
2 hard-cooked eggs, chopped
1 c. stuffed olives, quartered
¼ c. celery, diced
2 T. onion, finely diced
⅓ c. thick cream
¼ c. vinegar
Salt

Boil potatoes until tender; drain and cool. Peel and cube. Add olives, eggs, celery and onion. Mix cream and vinegar; scald. Add to potato mixture; mix well. Salt to taste.

Ida Vivian Hrncir, Hallettsville H. S.
Hallettsville, Texas

PICNIC POTATO SALAD

Number of Servings — 8-10

2 T. vinegar
5½ c. cooked potatoes, sliced
1⅔ c. cucumbers, sliced
1½ c. celery, chopped
1 12-oz. can luncheon meat, cubed or ¾ lb. cooked ham, cubed
1 c. salad dressing
¾ c. green pepper, chopped
3 T. onion, minced
1 t. salt

Pour vinegar over hot potatoes. Cool. Combine all ingredients. Chill for at least 1 hour before serving.

Mrs. Jane Ferguson, La Grange H. S.
La Grange, North Carolina

POTATO SALAD-SALMON PLATE

Number of Servings — 4

3 c. potato salad
1 1-lb. can salmon, chilled
2 tomatoes, sliced
½ cucumber, sliced
4 lemon wedges
Parsley
4 lettuce leaves

Mold potato salad into 4 mounds; place each on a lettuce leaf in center of platter. Drain salmon and break into large chunks. Surround potato salad with salmon and tomato and cucumber slices. Garnish with lemon wedges and parsley.

Lois Williams, Williams H. S.
Williams, Minnesota

POTATO-TUNA-SALAD

Number of Servings — 8-10

1 can tuna, chilled
1 c. mayonnaise
3 T. mustard
1 T. lemon juice
1½ t. onion, grated
Dash of pepper
3 c. cooked potatoes, diced
1½ c. celery, diced

Combine mayonnaise, mustard, lemon juice, onion and pepper. Stir until smooth. Add potatoes and celery; mix well. Chill for several hours. Just before serving add tuna; toss with a fork.

Mrs. R. A. Moore, Breckenridge H. S.
Breckenridge, Texas

TOASTED ALMOND-POTATO SALAD

Number of Servings — 8

4 c. boiled potatoes, cubed
1-2 T. onions, finely chopped
1-2 T. pimento minced
½-1 c. celery, diced
½ c. sweet cucumber pickles, chopped
½-1 c. toasted almonds, slivered
Salt and pepper to taste
Salad dressing

Combine all ingredients. Toss with a fork. Chill.

Mrs. Norma A. Piboin, Madisonville H. S.
Madisonvile, Texas

HOT POTATO SALAD

Number of Servings — 6

6 medium potatoes, cooked and mashed
3 hard-cooked eggs, chopped
1 small onion, finely chopped
½ c. sweet pickles, chopped
¼ c. sweet pickle juice
2 T. mustard
2 T. salad dressing
Salt to taste

Combine hot mashed potatoes with all other ingredients; mix thoroughly. Serve hot.

Mrs. Floretta Brock, Laguna-Acoma Jr.-Sr. H. S.
New Laguna, New Mexico

HOT POTATO SALAD

Number of Servings — 8

3 strips bacon
1 small onion, minced
1 small green pepper, minced
1 c. mayonnaise
1 T. cider vinegar
2 T. water
1 T. Worcestershire sauce
½ t. dry mustard
3 c. cooked potatoes, sliced
3 hard-cooked eggs, chopped
½ c. celery, chopped
¼ c. dill pickle, chopped

Fry bacon until crisp; crumble. Add onion and green pepper to bacon drippings and saute until tender. Add mayonnaise, vinegar, water, Worcestershire sauce and dry mustard. Cook over very low heat for a few minutes. Remove from heat; add remaining ingredients. Toss well to coat all pieces with dressing. Sprinkle with crumbled bacon. Serve hot.

D. Ruth Morris, Ajo H. S.
Ajo, Arizona

PENNSYLVANIA DUTCH POTATO SALAD

Number of Servings — 12

10 potatoes, cooked in jackets
2 small onions, minced
1 carrot, diced
3 stalks celery, diced
18 olives, chopped
8 hard-cooked eggs, sliced
4 slices bacon, diced
1 c. sugar
4 eggs, beaten
2 heaping T. flour
1 heaping T. dry mustard
1 c. water
1 c. vinegar
1 t. salt
¼ t. pepper

Peel and dice potatoes. Combine with onions, carrot, celery, olives and hard-cooked eggs. Set aside. Fry bacon until crisp; add flour to make a paste. Combine remaining ingredients; mix well. Add to bacon-flour paste. Place over low heat; stir until thick. Pour hot mixture over potato mixture; mix lightly. Let stand in a cold place for several hours.

Mrs. Sandra Mock, Pequea Valley H. S.
Kinzers, Pennsylvania

HOT POTATO SALAD

Number of Servings — 6

½ lb. bacon, diced
3½ c. cooked potatoes, cubed
1 onion, chopped
½ t. salt
½ t. pepper
1 t. sugar
½ c. vinegar
1 egg, beaten

Cook bacon until crisp; drain. Combine potatoes, bacon and onion. Mix remaining ingredients with bacon drippings. Heat thoroughly, stirring constantly. Pour over potato mixture; mix well. Serve immediately.

Mrs. Carol McDonald, Southwest H. S.
Atascosa, Texas

FAMILY'S FAVORITE POTATO SALAD AND DRESSING

Number of Servings — 6

6 cooked potatoes, diced
¼ c. celery, chopped
¼ c. onion, chopped
¼ c. sweet pickles, chopped
2 hard-cooked eggs, chopped

Combine all ingredients in large bowl.

SALAD DRESSING:

¼ c. vinegar
¾ c. water
1 T. flour
1 T. mustard
2 T. sugar
1 egg, beaten
2 t. celery seed

Combine flour, sugar, egg and mustard. Mix vinegar, water and celery seed; add to first mixture. Cook over medium heat, stirring constantly, until thickened. Add to potato salad and toss. Serve hot or cold.

Harriet J. Harless, Logan Sr. H. S.
Logan, West Virginia

GERMAN POTATO SALAD

Number of Servings — 15

6 lge. cooked potatoes, diced
1 lge. onion, diced
6 small stalks celery, diced
1 lb. bacon
1 c. vinegar
2 T. flour
Salt and pepper to taste

Fry bacon until crisp; crumble. Add to potatoes, onion, celery and seasonings. Add vinegar to hot bacon drippings; simmer 5 minutes. Stir in flour to thicken. Pour over potato mixture. Cover; let stand in a warm place for 3 hours. Serve warm.

Ann Ross Smith, Fairfield Jr. H. S.
Richmond, Virginia

OLD-FASHIONED SKILLET SALAD

Number of Servings — 8

2 lbs. potatoes
⅓ c. salad oil
3-4 T. vinegar
1 T. garlic salt
Dash of pepper
4-6 sl. bacon
¾ c. onion, finely chopped
1 T. flour
½ t. salt
1 T. sugar
1 t. celery seed
2 T. green pepper, coarsely chopped
1 T. parsley, coarsely chopped

Cook potatoes in salted water until just tender. Drain; peel and cut into slices about ¼-inch thick. Combine oil, vinegar, garlic salt and pepper. Set aside. Fry bacon until crisp. Drain on paper towel; then crumble. Remove all except 2 tablespoons fat from the skillet. Add ½ cup of onions; saute until tender but not browned. Stir in flour, sugar, salt, celery seed and oil-vinegar mixture. Simmer until thickened. Add potatoes, remaining onions, green pepper and parsley. Stir together lightly. Garnish with crumbled bacon. Serve warm from the skillet.

Mrs. Ardery Peery, Keota H. S.
Keota, Oklahoma

PENNSYLVANIA DUTCH POTATO SALAD

Number of Servings — 10

8 potatoes
1 stalk celery, diced
2 hard-cooked eggs, sliced
1 onion, minced
1 T. parsley, minced
2 eggs, well beaten
1 c. sugar
½ c. vinegar
½ c. cold water
¼ t. dry mustard
½ t. salt
¼ t. pepper
4 sl. bacon, diced

Boil potatoes in their jackets. When soft, peel and dice. Add celery, parsley, sliced eggs and onion. Fry bacon until crisp and brown. Combine beaten eggs, sugar, mustard, salt, pepper and vinegar diluted with water. Mix well. Pour egg mixture into the hot bacon and drippings. Stir until mixture thickens, about 10 minutes. Pour over the potato mixture and mix lightly. Serve hot or cold.

Elberta Martin, Irma Marsh Jr., H. S.
Fort Worth, Texas

CREAMY POTATO SALAD

Number of Servings — 8

7 c. cooked potatoes, sliced
⅓ c. chives, chopped (opt.)
1 t. salt
⅛ t. pepper
1 T. onion, grated
1 c. garlic salad dressing
½ c. celery, chopped
½ c. cucumber, diced
½ c. sour cream
½ c. mayonnaise

Combine warm potatoes, chives, salt, pepper, onion and ½ cup garlic salad dressing. Stir well; chill. Combine celery, cucumber, sour cream and mayonnaise. Stir in the remaining garlic salad dressing. Chill. Combine mayonnaise and potato mixtures; mix well.

Mrs. Jerrard Gould, Seymour Junior H. S.
Seymour, Connecticut

DILLED POTATO SALAD

4 lge. potatoes
½ c. sour cream
½ c. mayonnaise
Salt and pepper to taste
2 T. green onion, minced
¼ c. white vinegar
½ t. dill weed
1 dash Tabasco sauce
Diced pimento and/or minced parsley for color
Hard-cooked eggs (garnish)

Cook potatoes until just barely done so they are not mushy. Shred with a shredder like hash brown potatoes. Add vinegar, salt, pepper and dill weed. Toss with forks; do not stir. Marinate an hour or longer. Add remaining ingredients and toss again being careful not to let the salad get mushy. Serve on salad greens. Top with additional dressing and hard-cooked eggs.

May M. Rorick, The Dalles Senior H. S.
The Dalles, Oregon

SOUR CREAM-POTATO SALAD

Number of Servings — 6

4-6 c. diced, cooked potatoes
Chopped or minced onion to taste
¾-1 t. celery seed
1½ t. salt
¼-½ t. pepper
3-4 hard-cooked eggs
1-1½ c. sour cream
½ c. mayonnaise
¼ c. vinegar
1 t. prepared mustard
½-¾ c. pared cucumber, diced

Combine potatoes, onions, celery seed, salt and pepper. Toss lightly. Chop egg whites and add to potato mixture. Chill. Mash egg yolks; add sour cream, mayonnaise, vinegar and mustard. Mix well. Pour dressing over potatoes; toss lightly. Let stand 20-30 minutes. Just before serving, add cucumber.

This recipe submitted by the following teachers:

Mrs. Bette D. Jenness, Linesville Conneaut Summit H. S.
Linesville, Pennsylvania

Mrs. Edith M. Newsom, McArthur H. S.
McArthur, Ohio

Peggy W. Jones, Lakeside H. S.
Lake Village, Arkansas

SOUR CREAM-POTATO SALAD

Number of Servings — 15

7 c. cooked, warm potatoes, diced
⅓ c. chives, chopped
1 t. salt
1 T. onion, grated
¼ c. salad oil
¼ c. cider vinegar
1 t. pepper
½ c. celery, chopped
½ c. cucumber, diced
¾ c. sour cream
¾ c. mayonnaise
Paprika (garnish)

Combine potatoes, chives, salt, pepper, onion, oil and vinegar. Just before serving add all remaining ingredients. Mix thoroughly. Garnish with paprika.

This recipe submitted by the following teachers:

Mrs. Wilma Adams, Lockney H. S.
Lockney, Texas

Kathryn Woods, Woodrow Wilson H. S.
Beckley, West Virginia

SOUR CREAM-POTATO SALAD

Number of Servings — 10

8 c. warm potatoes, diced
1 t. salt
⅛ t. white pepper
⅓ c. chives, chopped
1 T. onion, finely chopped
¼ c. salad oil
¼ c. cider vinegar
½ c. cucumber, diced
½ c. celery, diced
¾ c. sour cream
¾ c. mayonnaise

Combine potatoes, salt, onion, chives, pepper, oil and vinegar. Mix well; chill. Mix sour cream, mayonnaise, celery and cucumber. Chill. Just before serving combine potato mixture and mayonnaise mixture. Stir well.

Margaret Augustine, Tunkhannock Joint Schools
Tunkhannock, Pennsylvania

SOUR CREAM-POTATO SALAD

Number of Servings — 8-10

8 medium potatoes, unpeeled
1½ c. mayonnaise
1 c. sour cream
1½ t. horseradish
1 t. celery seed
½ t. salt
1 c. parsley, minced
2 medium onions, minced

Boil unpeeled potatoes in salted water until tender. Peel and slice thinly. Mix mayonnaise, sour cream, horseradish, celery seed and salt. Combine parsley and onion. On a large serving dish arrange layers of potatoes, mayonnaise-sour cream mixture and parsley-onion mixture. Repeat layers 2 or 3 times, ending with parsley-onion mixture. Cover and refrigerate for 8 hours before serving.

Novella Mae Melton, Roswell Senior H. S.
Roswell, New Mexico

POTATO SALAD WITH SOUR CREAM DRESSING

Number of Servings — 6

3 lb. potatoes, cooked in jackets and chilled
1 c. celery, diced
2 t. salt
3 T. vinegar
½ c. olives, sliced
4 hard-cooked eggs, sieved
1 pt. sour cream
2 T. vinegar
1 t. black pepper
1½ T. prepared mustard
¼ clove garlic, crushed
1 small onion, chopped

Peel potatoes; cut into ½-inch cubes. Add celery, vinegar and salt. Combine all remaining ingredients except olives. Add to potatoes; toss. Add olives.

Mrs. Martha R. Phillips, Kennett H. S.
Conway, New Hampshire

SPINACH SALAD

Number of Servings — 6-8

4 c. raw spinach, chopped
1 c. green onion, chopped
2 hard-cooked eggs, chopped
½ c. oil
½ c. vinegar
¾ c. sugar
1 t. salt

Mix oil, vinegar, sugar and salt. Pour over spinach, onions and eggs. Mix well and refrigerate an hour before serving.

Mrs. Annie May Jones, Lueders
Lueders, Texas

SPINACH SALAD

Number of Servings — 6

¼ lb. spinach, chopped
2 carrots, shredded
½ head cabbage, shredded
French dressing

Combine all ingredients. Toss. Serve on lettuce leaves.

Anita Smith, Edinburg H. S.
Edinburg, Texas

FRESH SPINACH SALAD

Number of Servings — 18

2 pkgs. fresh spinach
2 strips bacon
1 8-oz. pkg. cream cheese
1 medium onion, grated
1 8-oz. bottle French dressing
¼ c. vinegar

Fry bacon until crisp; cool and crumble. Combine cream cheese, bacon and grease; mix well. Add onion, French dressing and vinegar; stir thoroughly. Just before serving pour bacon over mixture spinach.

Mrs. Frances Baker Bishop, Sr. H. S.
Denton, Texas

FRESH SPINACH SALAD

Number of Servings — 6

1 lb. fresh spinach
4 hard-cooked eggs, chopped
8 sl. bacon, fried and crumbled
¼ c. green onions, chopped
½ c. Italian salad dressing
Salt to taste

Remove large veins from spinach and tear into small pieces. Combine spinach, eggs and bacon. Add onions; toss lightly. Just before serving add dressing and salt.

Mrs. Jane Davis, South Park Jr., H. S.
Corpus Christi, Texas

SPINACH, LETTUCE AND BACON SALAD

Number of Servings — 8

6 strips bacon, diced
4 c. raw spinach, torn in bite-size pieces
2 c. lettuce, torn in bite-size pieces
2 hard-cooked eggs, finely chopped
⅓ c. salad dressing

Fry bacon until crisp; drain. Combine spinach and lettuce; add bacon and eggs. Add salad dressing; toss lightly.

This recipe submitted by the following teachers:

Judith Robertson, Athens H. S.
Athens, Illinois

Marilyn Bersie, Alexander Ramsey Senior H. S.
St. Paul, Minnesota

RAW SPINACH SALAD

Number of Servings — 8

½ lb. spinach, shredded
1 medium onion, finely chopped
4 T. celery, diced
6-8 radishes, chopped
4 hard-cooked eggs, chopped
½ t. salt

Combine all ingredients. Toss and chill

HOT FRENCH DRESSING:
2 sl. bacon, fried crisp and chopped
4 T. bacon fat
¼ c. vinegar
1 T. sugar

Combine sugar, vinegar and bacon fat; bring to a boil. Add bacon. Pour over salad. Serve immediately.

This recipe submitted by the following teachers:

Mary Martin, Cleburne H. S.
Cleburne, Texas

Mrs. Janelle Farrell, Cleburne H. S.
Cleburne, Texas

TOSSED SPINACH AND ORANGE SALAD

Number of Servings — 6-8

French Dressing:
1 t. salt
¼ t. pepper
1 t. sugar
3 T. vinegar or lemon juice
¼ c. catsup
½ c. salad oil

Combine all ingredients. Blend or shake vigorously.

2 c. fresh spinach, cut or torn in small pieces
2 medium California oranges, sectioned
1 T. granulated sugar
Salt to taste

Combine all ingredients. Add ¼ cup of French Dressing. Toss together.

Mrs. Dorothy J. Clark, Tawas Area H. S.
Tawas City, Michigan

FROZEN TOMATO-CHEESE SALAD

Number of Servings — 6

1 c. tomato sauce
1 c. cottage cheese, drained
½ t. salt
½ t. horseradish
1 2¼-oz. can deviled ham
½ c. stuffed olives, sliced
¼-½ t. onion juice
2 T. catsup

Combine all ingredients except olives and catsup. Beat until well blended. Pour into 9-inch pie plate. Spread catsup on top; garnish with olive slices. Cover securely with aluminum foil. Freeze.

Mrs. Fred Beers Jr., Henry County H. S.
McDonough, Georgia

TOMATO AND ONION SALAD

Number of Servings — 6-8

1 garlic clove, minced
1 t. salt
1 t. sugar
¼ t. pepper
2 t. prepared mustard
¼ c. olive or salad oil
2 T. tarragon vinegar
6 firm tomatoes, sliced
1 onion, thinly sliced
Chopped parsley

Combine garlic and salt; mash with a spoon. Stir in sugar, pepper, mustard, oil and vinegar. Pour over tomato and onion slices. Sprinkle with parsley. Chill. Serve without dressing.

Mrs. Pat Ashbrook, Oldham County H. S.
LaGrange, Kentucky

TOMATOES A LA PEPPER-ONION

Tomatoes, sliced
Green pepper, finely chopped
Onion, finely chopped
French dressing

Sprinkle tomato slices with mixed onion and pepper. Sprinkle with dressing. Chill for 1 hour before serving.

Mrs. Irma B. Morley, Senior H. S.
Allegan, Michigan

TOMATO AND PEPPER SURPRISE SALAD

Number of Servings — 6

2 lge. tomatoes, diced
1 lge. bell pepper, diced
1 medium onion, diced
¼ lge. box soda crackers, crumbled
Salt and pepper to taste
2 T. (heaping) mayonnaise

Combine all ingredients. Toss lightly.

Anne G. Rollins, J. C. Lynch School
Coward, South Carolina

TOMATO PINWHEEL SALAD

2 or 3 lettuce leaves
1 medium tomato
1 cucumber, peeled, scored and sliced
1 hard-cooked egg, sliced
Mayonnaise
Grated cheese or paprika

Line a salad plate with lettuce leaves. Remove core from tomato. Slice into 6 or 8 wedges, but do not cut through to bottom of tomato. Place cucumber slices between tomato wedges to give pinwheel effect. Place cucumber and egg slices around the tomato. Fill tomato with mayonnaise. Garnish with cheese or paprika.

Mrs. Dianna Armentrout, Schertz-Cibolo H. S.
Schertz, Texas

TOMATO ROSE SALAD

Number of Servings — 1

1 firm tomato, peeled and chilled
¼ lb. cream cheese
Milk
1 hard-cooked egg yolk, strained
Salad greens
French dressing

Slightly soften cheese with milk. Form 2 rows of petals on each tomato by pressing level teaspoons of cream cheese against the side of tomato, then drawing the spoon down with a curving motion. Sprinkle center of tomato with egg. Serve on salad greens with French dressing.

Una Seeley, Superior H. S.
Superior, Montana

STUFFED TOMATO SALAD

Number of Servings — 6

6 firm tomatoes
Heart of 1 head lettuce, chopped
1 stalk celery, chopped
1 small bottle stuffed olives, chopped
1 green pepper, chopped
¼ c. mayonnaise
French dressing

Cut off stem ends of tomatoes. Scoop out the inside of the tomatoes. Combine tomato pulp, lettuce, celery, olives and green pepper. Add mayonnaise. Put mixture into tomato cups. Pour French dressing over each tomato cup.

Mrs. Lois Farrington, Mesick H. S.
Mesick, Michigan

TOMATO SURPRISE SALAD

Number of Servings — 6

6 medium tomatoes
¾ c. cucumber, diced
½ c. cooked chicken, diced
¼ c. nuts, chopped
¼ c. mayonnaise
Lettuce
Parsley
Cauliflower buds
Salt to taste

Scald tomatoes; peel and chill. Carefully scoop the inside out of the tomatoes. Remove seeds from the pulp. Chill all ingredients. Just before serving mix chicken, cucumber, tomato pulp and nuts with mayonnaise. Add salt if needed. Fill tomatoes with mixture. Arrange on lettuce leaves. Garnish with mayonnaise and decorate each tomato top with parsley and cauliflower buds. If desired tuna or ground beef may be substituted for chicken.

Mrs. Gladys W. Considine, Belgrade H. S.
Belgrade, Montana

QUICK TOMATO SLAW

Number of Servings — 6

2 c. cabbage, coarsely shredded
1 c. tomatoes, diced
¼ c. green pepper, chopped
¼ c. cucumber, sliced
1 t. salt
¼ c. salad dressing
1 T. prepared mustard

Combine salad dressing and mustard. Add remaining ingredients. Chill for 30 minutes.

Patsy K. Myers, Christian Co. H. S.
Hopkinsville, Kentucky

STUFFED TOMATO SALAD

Number of Servings — 6

6 lge. tomatoes
2 hard-cooked eggs, chopped
½ c. celery, chopped
½ c. cracker crumbs
½ c. cucumber, diced
2 T. onion, chopped
c. cottage cheese
½ t. salt
2 hard-cooked eggs, sliced
Salad greens
Paprika

Cut out stem end of tomatoes. Scoop out half of the center. Drain tomato shells; reserve remaining tomato for stuffing. Combine all ingredients except the sliced eggs, salad greens and paprika. Fill each tomato shell with the mixture. Serve on salad greens, garnished with egg slices and paprika.

Mrs. Evangelena L. Barber, Saluda H. S.
Saluda, North Carolina

BUFFET SALAD

Number of Servings — 6-8

1 small head cauliflowerlets, sliced crosswise
1 medium onion, cut in rings
½ c. stuffed olives, sliced
½-⅔ c. French dressing
1 small head lettuce, broken in pieces
¼-½ c. Bleu or Roquefort cheese, crumbled

Combine cauliflowerlets, onion, olives and French dressing. Let stand for 30 minutes. Just before serving add lettuce and cheese. Toss lightly.

This recipe submitted by the following teachers:

Mrs. Fern Gordon, Cheboygan H. S.
Cheboygan, Michigan

Geraldine Throlson, Sauk Rapids Junior H. S.
Sauk Rapids, Minnesota

CAESAR SALAD

Number of Servings — 6-8

3 or 4 cloves of garlic, diced
1 c. olive oil
2 c. crisp croutons
3 qts. salad greens
½ c. unseasoned salad oil
½ c. Parmesan cheese, grated
¼ c. Bleu cheese
1 T. Worcestershire sauce
½ t. dry mustard
Salt and pepper to taste
2 hard cooked eggs, chopped
½ c. fresh lemon juice

Combine garlic and olive oil; let stand at room temperature for several hours. Toast croutons until brown at 250°F. Combine salad greens, salad oil, Parmesan and Bleu cheese. Add Worcestershire sauce, dry mustard, salt, and pepper. Scatter eggs over greens. Pour in fresh lemon juice. Toss very thoroughly. Dip croutons into garlic-oil mixture. Add to salad. Serve while croutons are crunchy.

This recipe submitted by the following teachers:

Mrs. Mildred H. Beck, Fairhope H. S.
Fairhope, Alabama

Elsie Snellgrove, Wicksburg H. S.
Newton, Alabama

CAESAR SALAD

Number of Servings — 6-8

1 qt. croutons
½ c. oil
1 bud garlic
1 whole egg
½ c. Parmesan cheese
¼ c. lemon juice
1 t. Worcestershire sauce
1 t. salt
1 t. pepper
1 head lettuce
1 can anchovies
2 tomatoes, quartered

Mix eggs, cheese, lemon juice, Worcestershire, salt and pepper. Before serving, break lettuce and pour dressing over it. Soak oil and garlic and pour over croutons. Stir croutons into lettuce. Garnish with tomato wedges and anchovies.

Mrs. Doris C. Hodgson, Baldwin County H. S.
Bay Minette, Alabama

CAESAR SALAD

Number of Servings — 2

⅔ lb. romaine lettuce, chilled and cut in 1-inch strips
1 T. mashed anchovies
1½ oz. lemon juice
1½ oz. olive oil
2 cloves garlic, sliced
2 eggs
¼ t. white pepper
½ t. dry mustard
1 T. Worcestershire sauce
6 drops Tabasco sauce
1 c. bacon-flavored croutons
Pimento strips (opt.)

Combine 1 garlic clove and olive oil; let stand overnight. Rub wooden salad bowl with remaining garlic clove; add lettuce. Combine lemon juice and anchovies; blend well. Add garlic-oil mixture; blend. Add eggs. Blend. Pour over lettuce; toss until all leaves are covered. Add mustard, pepper, Worcestershire and Tabasco sauce; toss after each addition. Sprinkle with Parmesan cheese. Toss. Add croutons and pimento. Toss. Serve immediately in wooden salad bowls.

Marjorie B. Brice, Whiteford H. S.
Ottawa Lake, Michigan

CAESAR SALAD

Number of Servings — 6

1 clove garlic, mashed
½ c. salad oil
1 head lettuce or ½ head lettuce and 1 bunch curly endive
1 c. croutons
1 2-oz. can anchovy fillets (opt.)
3-4 tomatoes, diced
¼ c. lemon juice
1 beaten egg
½ c. Parmesan cheese, grated
¼ c. Bleu cheese finely crumbled
1 t. Worcestershire sauce
½ t. pepper
½ t. salt

Combine garlic and salad oil; let stand. Combine lettuce tomatoes and croutons, anchovies, if desired. Strain oil-garlic mixture. Pour over vegetables. Combine remaining ingredients; beat well. Pour over salad; toss lightly. Garnish with sliced tomatoes.

This recipe submitted by the following teachers:

Shirley Ann Murray, James Wood H. S.
Winchester, Virginia

Marie Jaspers, Pomeroy H. S.
Pomeroy, Washington

CAESAR SALAD

Number of Servings — 6

½ lge. head lettuce, torn in small pieces
½ medium bunch romaine, torn in small pieces
¼ c. Parmesan cheese, grated
¼ c. lemon juice
1 clove garlic, crushed
¼ c. salad oil
1 t. Worcestershire sauce
1 beaten egg
½ t. salt
¼ t. pepper
1 c. toasted bread cubes

(Continued on next page)

Combine garlic and oil; let stand 30 minutes. Combine lettuce, romaine and cheese. Strain oil-garlic mixture. Combine oil, Worcestershire sauce and lemon juice; mix well. Pour over salad. Add egg; toss until egg disappears. Add bread cubes, salt and pepper.

Mrs. Pauline Norberg, Parma H. S.
Parma, Idaho

CHEF'S SALAD

Dressing:
½ c. vinegar
1 c. salad oil
1 t. onion juice
¼ t. dry mustard
2 t. sugar
Dash of black pepper

Combine all ingredients in a bottle.

½ head lettuce, torn
½ c. spinach or endive or both
¼ c. carrots, grated
¼ c. celery, chopped
¼ c. green pepper, chopped
½ c. baked ham, chopped
¼-½ c. sharp cheese, cubed
Radishes, thinly sliced
Onion and cauliflower (opt.)

Combine all ingredients. Just before serving, toss with enough dressing to coat greens well.

Mrs. Mariguerite Crews, Lewisburg H. S.
Lewisburg, Pennsylvania

BOUQUET SALAD

Number of Servings — 8

1 head crisp lettuce
2-3 tomatoes, sliced
3 hard cooked eggs, sliced
1 small cucumber, sliced
½ green pepper, sliced
6-8 red radishes, sliced
1 carrot, cut in slivers
3 stalks celery, cut in slivers
1-2 slices Swiss cheese, cut in slivers
5 strips bacon, fried and crumbled
½ c. olives, chopped
Garlic clove
French dressing
Salt and pepper to taste

Rub wooden salad bowl with garlic clove. Toss al ingredients together. French dressing may be served separately.

Dianne J. MacPherson, Garden Spot H. S.
New Holland, Pennsylvania

CHEF'S SALAD

Number of Servings — 12

8 c. mixed greens, cut in 1-inch pieces
1 c. celery, diced
1 c. cooked ham, cut in strips
2 hard cooked eggs, finely chopped
2 T. parsley, finely chopped
4 tomatoes, cut in wedges
1 c. garlic or French dressing

Chill all ingredients. Combine greens celery, ham, eggs, parsley, and tomato wedges; toss. Add dressing; toss again.

Myrtle Stevens, Gracemont H. S.
Gracemont, Oklahoma

CHRISTMAS SALAD

Number of Servings — 16-20

1 No. 303 can small peas
1 can green string beans
1 bunch celery, finely cut
1 green pepper, finely cut
1 jar pimento, chopped
1 small onion, grated
½ t. salt
1½ c. sugar
½ c. vinegar
½ c. vegetable oil
⅓ c. water

Mix sugar, vinegar, oil and water together. Combine remaining ingredients. Pour liquid mixture over vegetables. Cover and refrigerate.

Clara E. Ander, Pipestone H. S.
Pipestone, Minnesota

DANDELION SALAD (PENNSYLVANIA DUTCH)

Number of Servings — 6

Young, tender dandelion greens
4 thick sl. bacon, cubed
½ c. salad dressing
1 egg
1 t. salt
1 T. flour
2 T. sugar
4 T. vinegar
1 c. water
2 hard-cooked eggs, sliced

Wash dandelion greens; roll in cloth and pat dry. Put into a salad bowl. Fry bacon; pour over dandelion greens. Blend salad dressing, egg, salt, flour, sugar, vinegar and water. Pour into skillet in which bacon was fried and cook until mixture boils and is quite thick. Pour hot mixture over greens; stir well. Garnish with egg slices. Serve immediately.

Mrs. Doris G. Howerten, Kutztown Area Sr. H. S.
Kutztown, Pennsylvania

CRACKER SALAD

Number of Servings — 8

2 lge. tomatoes, chopped
1 lge. bell pepper, chopped
2 stalks celery, chopped
Green onions and tops, chopped
¼ c. mayonnaise
¼ lb. crackers, crumbled

Combine vegetables; add mayonnaise. Add crackers just before serving, mix well.

Mrs. Gloria Ward, Trinidad H. S.
Trinidad, Texas

GARDEN-STYLE COTTAGE CHEESE

Number of Servings — 6

1½ c. low-calorie cottage cheese
1 c. cucumber, coarsely chopped
½ c. carrots, grated
2 green onions, chopped
1 T. lemon juice
Dash of pepper
Salad greens
Tomato wedges (garnish)

Combine all ingredients. Serve on salad greens. Garnish with tomato wedges.

Mrs. Martha Jo Bredemeyer, Lancaster H. S.
Lancaster, Texas

HAWAIIAN SALAD

Number of Servings — 4-6

2 heads romaine lettuce, sliced in 1-inch strips
2 tomatoes, peeled, and cut in eights
¼ c. green onion, chopped
½ c. Romano cheese, grated
1 lb. bacon, fried and finely chopped
1 c. croutons
2 T. imported salad oil
Salt
1 lge. clove garlic

Pour imported oil into a large wooden salad bowl; sprinkle with salt. Rub bowl firmly with garlic. Add tomatoes and lettuce. Add onions, cheese and bacon.

DRESSING:

3 oz. olive oil
Juice of 2 lemons
½ t. pepper, freshly ground
¼ t. mint, chopped
¼ t. oregano
1 coddled egg

Combine oil, lemon juice, pepper, mint and oregano. Add egg; whip vigorously. Immediately before serving, pour dressing over salad. Add croutons; toss.

Beverly Forbis, Davis H. S.
Modesto, California

GREEN AND RED SALAD

Number of Servings — 8

4 T. salad oil
1 c. wine vinegar
1 c. sugar
2 lge. cans French style green beans
1 can pimentos, chopped
1 small head cauliflower, cut in small pieces
1 c. whole almonds
Salt and pepper to taste
Rosemary to taste
Basil to taste
Bay leaf to taste

Mix oil, vinegar and sugar together. Stir until sugar dissolves. Add remaining ingredients. Refrigerate for 24 hours. Will keep for 1 week if refrigerated.

Ellen Morgan Schenck, Wilson H. S.
West Lawn, Pennsylvania

GOLDEN WEST SALAD

Number of Servings — 8

3 c. carrots, grated
6 soda crackers, rolled
3 hard cooked eggs, diced
½ t. salt
½ c. celery, chopped
3 T. lemon juice
1 T. onion juice or 1 onion, grated
¾ c. salad dressing
½ c. peanuts, ground

Combine all ingredients except salad dressing and peanuts. Make a paste with salad dressing and peanuts. Add to carrot mixture; mix lightly.

Agnes Kowitz Boulger
Bradley-Bourbonnais Community H. S.
Bradley, Illinois

GREEN GODDESS DELIGHT

Number of Servings — 8

1 No. 2½ can green peas, drained
1 No. 2½ can green beans, drained
4 stalks celery, finely chopped
1 lge. onion, finely chopped
1 c. olives, sliced
1 green pepper, finely chopped
Pimento strips (opt.)
¾ c. granulated sugar
¼ c. water
½ c. cider vinegar
½ c. salad oil

Mix beans, peas, celery, onion, olives, pepper and pimento together. Combine remaining ingredients in order given; add to pea mixture. Toss lightly.

Mrs. Gail Kvernmo, Ivanhoe Public School
Ivanhoe, Minnesota

GREEN AND ORANGE SALAD

Number of Servings — 6

1 small head lettuce
½ head curly endive
2 oranges, sectioned
1 medium grapefruit, sectioned
½ c. orange juice

Toss greens with sectioned fruit. Pour over orange juice. Serve cold.

Dee Ann R. Breuer, Cambridge H. S.
Cambridge, Minnesota

GREEN SALAD (PENNSYLVANIA DUTCH)

Number of Servings — 8

½ lb. ham, diced
1 egg. slightly beaten
3 T. ham drippings
3 T. flour
1 t. sugar
⅓ c. vinegar
½ c. water
1 t. salt
¼ t. pepper
3 hard-cooked eggs, diced
1 lb. young leaf lettuce
Dandelion greens or watercress, washed and chilled and torn or cut into pieces

Tear greens into small pieces; combine. Brown the ham over medium heat. Blend beaten egg, flour and sugar. Add vinegar, water salt and pepper. Stir into cooled ham and drippings, simmer gently until slightly thickened. Add hard-cooked eggs. Serve at once over mixed greens.

Mrs. George Rearick, Big Spring H. S.
Newville, Pennsylvania

HERB AND CHEESE SALAD

Number of Servings — 4

1 lge. head fresh green dill seed
2 T. Roquefort cheese, grated
Lettuce, torn in bite-size pieces
Celery, chopped (opt.)
Cucumber, chopped (opt.)

Shred dill seed over lettuce. Add celery or cucumber, if desired. Add dressing; toss until each lettuce leaf is covered. Add cheese.

DRESSING:

½ c. evaporated milk
3 T. sugar
1⅓ T. vinegar

Combine sugar and milk. Stir until dissolved. Add vinegar slowly, stirring constantly until thick and creamy. Pour over salad. This dressing may be made in large quantities and refrigerated for about 3 weeks.

Ora Goodrich, Coudersport Area H. S.
Coudersport, Pennsylvania

HODGE PODGE SALAD

Number of Servings — 100

6 lbs. cabbage, finely shredded
3 lbs. spinach, finely cut
2 lbs. lettuce, finely chopped
1 lb. celery, thinly sliced
1 lb. raisins, plumped
2 lbs. cheese, cubed
1 qt. bread crumbs, toasted and buttered (opt.)

Toss vegetables with dressing. Just before serving add bread crumbs if desired.

DRESSING:

2 c. vinegar
2 c. sugar
1 c. oil

Combine ingredients; mixing well.

Betty Deadman Shafer, Armada H. S.
Armada, Michigan

HOME GARDEN MARINADE

Number of Servings — 8

Radish slices
Sweet onion rings
Cucumber sticks
Tomatoes, thinly sliced
Green pepper rings
Avocado slices
Carrot curls

Arrange vegetables on a platter. Pour dressing over vegetables. Refrigerate for 1 hour.

DRESSING:

¾ c. fresh lime juice
6 T. olive oil
1 small clove garlic, crushed
1½ T. sugar
1½ t. salt
½ t. black pepper
1 t. aromatic bitters

Combine all ingredients in a covered jar or blender; mix well. Pour over vegetable p atter.

Mrs. Odell T. Lakeman, Haleyville Schools
Haleyville, Alabama

LETTUCE (A MAN'S SALAD)

1 pod garlic
1 head lettuce
Olive oil
Lemon juice
⅛ t. dry mustard
Dash of salt

Rub garlic against the side of a wooden mixing bowl. Blend ⅔ part oil, ⅓ part lemon juice, mustard and salt. Add lettuce and toss gently.

Louise Blanton, Lewisville H. S.
Lewisville, Texas

LETTUCE SALAD

Number of Servings — 6

1 head lettuce, coarsely chopped
1 onion, minced
½ c. cheese, grated
1 t. salt
2½ T. sugar
1 t. mustard
2 T. cream
2 T. vinegar
½ c. salad dressing

Mix salt, sugar, mustard and cream. Add vinegar and salad dressing; stir until smooth. Pour over lettuce, onion and cheese; mix lightly.

Mrs. Pat Meredith, Glenwood City H. S.
Glenwood City, Wisconsin

DUTCH LETTUCE

Number of Servings — 6

1 lge. head lettuce, cut in small pieces
4 green onions, chopped
3 slices bacon, diced
4 T. vinegar
4 T. sugar
1 egg
2 T. sour cream

Toss lettuce and onion together. Fry bacon; drain off most of the drippings. Combine bacon and vinegar. Cream sugar, egg and sour cream; add to bacon mixture. Cook until thick; cool slightly. Pour over lettuce and onion while warm.

Marilyn L. Gies, Eastmont Senior H. S.
East Wenatchee, Washington

HOT LETTUCE SALAD

Number of Servings — 4

4 or 5 sl. lean bacon
2 T. bacon drippings
1 T. sugar
1 T. vinegar
2 t. India relish
2 c. lettuce, torn into bite-size pieces
1 hard-cooked egg, chopped or 1 tomato, diced (opt.)

Fry bacon until very crisp. Cool and crumble. Add sugar, vinegar and India relish to bacon drippings; heat to boiling point. Combine bacon, lettuce and egg or tomato if desired. Pour hot mixture over top of bacon and lettuce; toss lightly. Serve immediately.

Mrs. Betty Thompson, Mullin H. S.
Mullin, Texas

PENNSYLVANIA DUTCH COLD LETTUCE

Number of Servings — 6

1 medium size head of lettuce, torn in small pieces
¼ c. sugar
2 T. mayonnaise
1½ T. cream or evaporated milk
¼ c. vinegar (scant)
Salt to taste

Mix sugar and mayonnaise; blend in cream or evaporated milk. Add vinegar and salt. Immediately before serving pour the dressing over lettuce. Toss so that every piece of lettuce is well-coated.

Jane E. Spangler, Shippensburg Area Senior H. S.
Shippensburg, Pennsylvania

STUFFED HEAD LETTUCE

Number of Servings — 4-6

1 solid head of lettuce, cored
1 3-oz. pkg. cream cheese
1 T. Roquefort cheese
1 T. green pepper, chopped
1 T. carrots, chopped
1 T. tomato, chopped
1 T. onoin, chopped
Salt and pepper to taste

Thoroughly mix cheeses, green pepper, carrots, tomato, onion, salt and pepper. Press into the lettuce. Wrap lettuce in a damp cloth and then in foil; let stand overnight. Cut into wedges to serve.

Mrs. Wetthalee G. Durham, Abraham Lincoln H. S.
Philadelphia, Pennsylvania

WILTED LETTUCE

Number of Servings — 4

2 c. garden lettuce, cut in bite-size pieces
2 hard-cooked eggs, diced
2 T. hot water
2 T. vinegar
4 T. vegetable oil

Mix egg and lettuce. Combine hot water, vinegar and oil. Pour over lettuce.

Mrs. Hazel Johnson, Basin H. S.
Basin, Wyoming

WILTED LETTUCE

Number of Servings — 4-6

1 head of lettuce, cut in pieces
5 strips bacon
6 T. vinegar
6 T. water
Salt and pepper
3 T. brown sugar
Hard cooked eggs, sliced (opt.)

Fry becan until crisp. Remove from pan; drain on a paper towel. Crumble bacon. Combine vinegar, water, seasonings and brown sugar with bacon drippings; heat to boiling. Add crumbled bacon. Pour over lettuce. Toss to wilt. Garnish with egg slices if desired.

Mrs. Pat Swank, Noblesville H. S.
Noblesville, Indiana

WILTED LETTUCE

Number of Servings — 4

1½ bunches leaf lettuce
¼ c. bacon drippings
1 T. vinegar
Salt and pepper to taste

Heat becan drippings until sizzling; add vinegar. Stir. Pour over lettuce; toss. Add salt and pepper.

Arrie Maxwell, Plevna H. S.
Plevna, Montana

STUFFED LETTUCE

Number of Servings — 4-5

1 lge. head lettuce
1 c. Cheddar cheese, grated
¼ c. mayonnaise or salad dressing
¼ t. curry powder
⅓ c. celery, finely cut
¼ c. cooked ham, slivered
1 pimento, diced
¼ c. parsley, snipped
French dressing

Wash and drain lettuce. Cut a 3-inch circle at core end of head. Continue cutting straight down to within ½ inch of the top of the head. Hollow out this circle as evenly as possible, reserving pieces for later use. Blend cheese with mayonnaise and curry until smooth. Stir in ham, celery, pimento, and parsley. Stuff mixture into hollowed lettuce, packing filling in firmly. Refrigerate. To serve, cut crosswise into 1-inch thick slices. Place on salad plates.

FILLING VARIATIONS:

Vegetable—Soften 1 8-oz. package cream cheese with 1 tablespoon milk; add dash of Tabasco, 1½ teaspoons horseradish, ¼ cup diced pimento, ¼ cup snipped parsley and 1 cup canned peas. Crunch—Soften 1 8-oz. package cream cheese with ¼ cup mayonnaise. Stir in ½ cup grated carrots, ½ cup grated radishes, and ¼ cup snipped chives. Fruit—Soften 1 8-oz. package cream cheese with 1 tablespoon lemon juice. Ad 2 pineapple slices cut in pieces and ½ cup broken walnuts.

Sarah Lou Cobb, Cherokee Jr., H. S.
Orlando, Florida

WILTED SALAD

Number of Servings — 6

3 or 4 scallions, chopped
4-6 sl bacon, fried
¼ c. vinegar
2 t. sugar
½ c. bacon drippings
½-1 t. salt
Coarsely ground black pepper
4-6 c. salad greens

Saute scallions in bacon drippings. Add vinegar, sugar, salt and pepper. Stir mixture until it is clear. Pour hot dressing on greens. Crumble bacon over top. Toss well.

Frances Ryan, Gaxinger H. S.
Charlotte, North Carolina

STUFFED LETTUCE

Number of Servings — 4

1 small head iceberg lettuce
½ lb. Bleu cheese
1 3-oz. pkg. cream cheese
2 T. milk
1 T. chives, chopped or green onion tops
1 whole pimento, chopped
French dressing

Hollow out center of lettuce, leaving a 1-inch shell. Beat cheese and milk together until smooth. Add chives and pimento; mix thoroughly. Fill lettuce hollow with cheese mixture. Refrigerate until cheese is firm. Just before serving, cut across the lettuce making ¾-inch slices. Serve with French dressing.

Mary S. Brisco, Calvert Sr. H. S.
Prince Frederick, Maryland

WILTED LETTUCE SALAD

Number of Servings — 4

3 sl. bacon, cut in small pieces
1 T. flour
½ c. vinegar
¾ c. water
½ t. salt
1½ T. sugar
½ lb. leaf lettuce, shredded
½ c. radishes, sliced
2 T. onion, chopped

Combine lettuce, radishes and onions; set aside. Saute bacon pieces until brown. Blend flour with drippings. Add vinegar and water and cook, stirring constantly, until slightly thickened and smooth. Stir in salt and sugar; cook 2 minutes longer. Remove from heat; add vegetables; toss lightly. Serve immediately while salad is still warm.

Mildred Callahan, Thomas Jefferson Jr. H. S.
Miami, Florida

STUFFED LETTUCE

Number of Servings — 4-6

1 solid head of lettuce, cored
2 c. American cheese, grated
¼ c. pimento, chopped
2 T. green pepper, chopped
2 t. lemon juice
1 T. sugar
Mayonnaise or salad dressing

Clean lettuce and cut out about ¼ of the inside. Place in a plastic bag and refrigerate 3 or 4 hours. Combine remaining ingredients with enough mayonnaise or salad dressing to moisten. Stuff filling into lettuce; chill. To serve, cut head into quarters.

Mrs. Doris J. Combs, Central H. S.
Woodstock, Virginia

WILTED LEAF LETTUCE

Number of Servings — 6

2 lge. bunches leaf lettuce, shredded
Salt and pepper to taste
2 t. sugar (opt.)
2 green onions, chopped
4 sl. bacon, fried and chopped
2-4 T. vinegar
2-4 T. water
1-2 hard-cooked eggs, chopped

Place lettuce into a hot bowl; add salt, pepper, sugar and onions. Combine bacon, vinegar and water; heat. Pour over lettuce and toss until wilted. Sprinkle egg over top.

This recipe submitted by the following teachers:

Jewell West, Crowder
Crowder, Oklahoma

Mrs. Clarabel Tepe, Cimarron School
Cimarron, New Mexico

Genevieve Mason, Georgetown H. S.
Georgetown, Texas

WILTED LETTUCE AND EGG SALAD

Number of Servings — 3-6

4 sl. of bacon, fried and crumbled
1 small onion, chopped
¼ c. vinegar
1 head lettuce, broken in small pieces
2-3 hard-cooked eggs, chopped
Salt and pepper to taste
Bread cubes
Garlic salt

Saute onions in bacon drippings until golden. Add vinegar; heat. Combine lettuce, eggs and bacon. Sprinkle with salt and pepper. Pour hot vinegar mixture over lettuce. Toss lightly. Cook bread cubes in butter until crisp and brown; sprinkle with garlic salt. Top lettuce mixture with bread cubes. Serve immediately.

Virginia Spencer, Sandy Ridge H. S.
Sandy Ridge, North Carolina

WESTERN WILTED SALAD

Number of Servings — 6-8

4 sl. bacon
3 T. lemon juice
1 T. sugar
1 t. salt
¼ c. onion, chopped
1 head lettuce
2-3 medium oranges, peeled and cut into pieces
6 oz. Swiss cheese, cut into thin strips

Fry bacon until crisp; remove from skillet. Stir lemon juice, sugar, salt and onion into hot bacon drippings. Heat thoroughly. Tear lettuce into pieces; rinse and drain. Place in large salad bowl. Pour hot dressing over salad greens. Crumble bacon and add with orange pieces and cheese. Toss lightly.

Louise Barton, Herren Township H. S.
Herren, Illinois

LOW-CALORIE BUTTERMILK SALAD

Number of Servings — 6-8

4 hard cooked eggs, diced
4 cucumbers, peeled and sliced
1 small onion, minced
½ head lettuce, finely cut
1 T. celery, chopped (opt.)
1 T. parsley, minced (opt.)
3 c. buttermilk
½ t. salt
¼ t. pepper
¼ t. garlic salt
1½ T. vinegar

Combine eggs, cucumbers, onions, lettuce, celery and parsley. Mix remaining ingredients; pour over egg mixture.

Mrs. Leah Jaeger, Beulah H. S.
Beulah, North Dakota

MIXED GREEN SALAD WITH BLEU CHEESE DRESSING

Number of Servings — 8

2 c. lettuce, coarsely chopped
1½ c. cabbage, coarsely chopped
¾ c. watercress, coarsely chopped
¾ c. new spinach, coarsely chopped
½ c. chives, chopped
2 T. anchovies, chopped
2 T. Bleu cheese, crumbled
⅓ c. Bleu cheese salad dressing

Combine all ingredients; toss lightly.

Barbara P. Russell, Rule H. S.
Knoxville, Tennessee

MOORE'S SALAD

Number of Servings — 4-6

1 c. lettuce, torn in small pieces
½ c. cabbage, shredded
¼ c. green pepper, diced
¼ c. pickles, chopped
1 medium tomato, cubed
1 small apple or pear, minced
¼ c. carrot, diced
¼-½ c. salad dressing
1 T. sugar
Salt to taste

Toss all ingredients.

Mrs. Maurice E. Eskridge, Tryon H. S.
Bessemer City, North Carolina

SUMMERTIME DELIGHT

Number of Servings — 4-6

2 lge. tomatoes
1 medium onion, chopped
1 medium banana pepper, chopped
½ t. salt
1 t. sugar
1 T. vinegar

Combine tomatoes, onion, and banana pepper. Add salt, sugar and vinegar. Mix.

Mrs. Ray Mofield, Benton H. S.
Benton, Kentucky

SPRING SALAD BOWL

Number of Servings — 6

1 bunch leaf lettuce, torn in bite-size pieces
½ bunch watercress
1½ c. tiny spinach leaves
24 carrot curls
4 green onions with tops, chopped
12 ripe olives, pitted
12 almonds, blanched and toasted
Italian dressing

Combine greens, carrot curls and onions. Stuff olives with almonds. Add to greens. Toss with Italian dressing.

Mrs. Verna Eberhart, Cavalier Public School
Cavalier, North Dakota

THREE WAY SALAD

Number of Servings — 6

1 head lettuce
6 carrots, chopped
1 cucumber, chopped
1 tomato, sliced
1 c. croutons or ground crackers
3 stalks celery, diced
1 small onion, chopped
¾ c. diet dressing
½ c. Cheddar cheese, grated
2 hard cooked eggs, chopped (opt.)
2 6-oz. cans de-veined shrimp (opt.)

Combine vegetables; toss lightly. Just before serving add dressing and sprinkle cheese on top.

Judith McHugh, Ankeny H. S.
Ankeny, Iowa

SPRING SALAD

4-5 slices cucumber, unpeeled
1 green onion, chopped
2 radishes, cut circular
8-10 slices carrot, cut circular
5-6 bite-size pieces lettuce, spinach or endive
2 T. French dressing
Salt to taste

Combine all ingredients; toss lightly.

Mrs. Anna Mae Gausmann, Wolf Lake H. S.
Wolf Lake, Indiana

SUMMER GARDEN SALAD

Number of Servings — 4

5 tomatoes, peeled and cut in wedges
1 small white onion, thinly sliced
2-3 medium boiled potatoes, peeled and sliced
2-3 oregano leaves, minced or ¼ t. dried oregano
½ t. salt
½ t. pepper
½ green pepper, chopped
2-3 T. salad oil

Combine all ingredients. Toss gently until all ingredients are coated. Chill before serving.

Virginia Martell, Johnston City H. S.
Johnston City, Illinois

SUNSHINE SALAD

Number of Servings — 6

1 c. cabbage, grated
1 c. carrots, grated
1 c. apples, chopped
2 T. lemon juice
2 T. orange juice
2 t. sugar
½ t. salt

Combine lemon juice, orange juice, sugar and salt. Pour over cabbage, carrots and apples; toss.

Phyllis Wack, Blue Mountain Joint School
Schuylkill Haven, Pennsylvania

TOSSED SALAD

Number of Servings — 4-5

Lettuce, cut or torn in small pieces
1 tomato, diced
1 medium cucumber, chopped
1 T. minced onion
Salt and pepper to taste
2-3 T. sour cream

Combine all ingredients except sour cream. Add enough sour cream to moisten mixture.

Mrs. Margaret Swigart, Culbertson H. S.
Culbertson, Montana

VEGETABLE SALAD BOWL

Number of Servings — 8-10

1 small head lettuce, torn into lge. pieces
1 carrot, shredded or sliced
3 tomatoes, diced
6 fresh green onions, sliced
6 radishes, sliced
¼ head raw caulifloweretes
¼-½ t. garlic powder
2 stalks celery, chopped
½ cucumber, sliced
2 T. capers
2 t. lemon juice
Corn oil
Deviled egg halves (opt.)
Shredded cheese (opt.)

Combine vegetables; sprinkle with salt and garlic powder. Toss. Add lemon juice; toss. Add desired amount of oil; Toss. Serve immediately. To make salads more interesting try these tips: Score unpared cucumbers with a fork to produce green scalloped slices and cut radishes almost through to form fans. Try rings of sweet onion in place of the fresh onions. Use a waffle cut or a ripple cut on the carrots and radishes.

Mrs. Georgia Songer, Three Oaks H. S.
Three Oaks, Michigan

ORIENTAL SALAD

Number of Servings — 2

1 hard cooked egg
1 T. light cream
¼ c. French dressing
Salt and pepper to taste
2 c. salad greens, torn in small pieces
1 T. chives chopped
3 radishes, sliced
½ cucumber, peeled and sliced
¼ c. celery, chopped
¼ c. canned water chestnuts, sliced

Mash the egg yolk with the cream; stir in French dressing. Chop the egg white. Combine salt, pepper and the greens. Add remaining ingredients. Pour dressing over salad.

Mrs. Verlyne Foster, Rolette H. S.
Rolette, North Dakota

PARSLEY-MINT SALAD

Number of Servings — 4

2 c. parsley, finely chopped
⅓ c. mint leaves, finely chopped
½ c. onion, finely chopped
⅓ c. sesame seed, toasted
2 medium tomatoes, rinsed and chilled
2 T. olive oil
4 T. lemon juice
1 T. light corn syrup
Few grains of salt
Few grains freshly ground pepper
Finely chopped lettuce (opt.)
Finely chopped cucumber, (opt.)

Combine parsley, mint, onion, lettuce and cucumber if desired. Cover tightly and chill thoroughly. Mix olive oil, lemon juice, corn syrup, salt and pepper in a jar. Cover; shake well. Refrigerate until ready to use. When ready to serve, chop tomatoes. Toss lightly with the parsley mixture. Shake dressing well; slowly pour over salad while gently turning and tossing. Use only enough dressing to lightly coat ingredients. Sprinkle sesame seed over salad; toss lightly to mix thoroughly. If desired, croutons may be substituted for sesame seed. To prepare croutons, trim crusts from 2 slices of toasted bread. Cut in ½-inch cubes. Melt 2-3 T. butter in a small skillet. Add cubes and toss until all sides are well coated with butter and are browned.

Catherine Dicks, State Supervisor,
Home Economics Education
University Park, New Mexico

RED AND WHITE SALAD

Number of Servings — 4

2 medium white turnips, grated
2 lge. beets, grated
Lettuce leaves
Low calorie French dressing

Place a mound of turnips and beets on lettuce leaves. Serve with French dressing.

Mrs. Alice L. Brooks, Strawn H. S.
Strawn, Texas

TOSSED SALAD

Number of Servings — 6

2 tomatoes, chopped
1 green pepper, chopped
1 small onion, chopped
1 carrot, chopped
1 stalk celery, chopped
1 cucumber, chopped
1 head lettuce, torn in bite-size pieces
French Dressing

Combine all ingredients. Toss.

Mrs. Edith R. Mitchell, Dickson H. S.
Dickson, Tennessee

TOSSED GREEN SALAD

Number of Servings — 6-8

1 medium head lettuce, torn in bite-size pieces
½ cucumber, sliced
1 green pepper, diced
1 c. celery, diced
Green onions, chopped
1 tomato, diced
½ to ⅓ c. Italian dressing
½ avocado, peeled and diced
½ avocado, peeled and mashed

Combine dressing and mashed avocado; mix well. Add all remaining ingredients except lettuce and tomato. Refrigerate for 2 or 3 hours. Just before serving, add lettuce and tomato. Toss lightly.

Martha Sue Purvis, Joshua H. S.
Joshua, Texas

MANDARIN ORANGE TOSSED SALAD

Number of Servings — 6-8

1 small head iceberg lettuce
1 c. carrots, shredded
½ c. celery, diced
1 c. Mandarin orange sections, drained
1 c. raisins

Break washed lettuce into bite-size pieces. Add carrots and celery. Boil raisins for 1 minute in syrup drained from oranges plus water if necessary. Drain. Add oranges and raisins to lettuce, celery and carrots; toss lightly. Serve with desired dressing.

Shelby Jean Luey, William Fleming H. S.
Roanoke, Virginia

TOSSED GREEN SALAD

Number of Servings — 6

½ head lettuce, cut in bite-size pieces
2 medium tomatoes, sliced
½ bell pepper, chopped
2 carrots, slivered
½ medium onion, chopped
5 radishes, sliced

Mix together all ingredients. Just before serving, add dressing; toss.

DRESSING:

¼ c. salad oil
¼ c. vinegar
1 t. salt

Combine all ingredients; mix well.

Mrs. Lillian King Wier, Odem H. S.
Odem, Texas

MANDARIN TOSSED SALAD

Number of Servings — 8

½ head lettuce, shredded
1 c. celery, chopped
1 T. parsley, minced
2 green onions and tops, chopped
1 can Mandarin oranges, drained
¼ c. caramelized almonds, sliced
2 T. sugar

Caramelize almonds by adding sugar and stirring over low heat until sugar melts and collects on almonds. Cool. Combine lettuce, celery, parsley, onions, oranges and almonds.

Dressing:

½ t. salt
Dash of black pepper
2 T. sugar
2 T. vinegar
¼ c. salad oil

Combine all ingredients in a jar; shake vigorously. Serve with salad.

Mrs. E. E. Tuft, Stillwater Junior H. S.
Stillwater, Minnesota

HOT VEGETABLE SALAD

Number of Servings — 4-6

1 T. cooking oil
½ head cabbage
1 bell pepper
Small bunch green onions
8-10 red radishes
4-5 carrots

Slice all vegetables into long thin strips. Put into hot oil and heat slowly until thoroughly heated. Do not saute. Vegetables should be tender yet crisp. Serve hot.

Carolyn Belanger, Tomball H. S.
Tomball, Texas

COOL VEGETABLE SALAD

Number of Servings — 10-12

2 10-oz. pkgs. frozen lima beans
2 10-oz. pkgs. frozen whole kernel corn
2 T. minced onion
½ c. pimento, diced
2 c. celery, diced
2 c. French dressing

Cook lima beans and corn separately as directed on package. Drain and cool. Mix all ingredients; chill thoroughly. Serve on crisp lettuce leaves.

Carol Katzer, Basic H. S.
Henderson, Nevada

CURRY VEGETABLE SALAD

Number of Servings — 8

1 c. rice
½ c. peas
¼ c. French dressing
¾ c. mayonnaise
¼ c. onion, minced
½ t. salt
¾ t. curry powder
½ t. dry mustard
⅛ t. pepper
½ c. cauliflowerettes
½ c. radishes, thinly sliced
½ c. celery, diced

Cook rice and peas. Toss together with French dressing. Refrigerate. Mix mayonnaise, onion, salt, curry powder, dry mustard, pepper and cauliflowerettes. Refrigerate. Just before serving, mix rice mixture and curry mixture with radishes and celery. Serve on lettuce. For additional dressing use equal parts of mayonnaise and French dressing.

Joann Parks, Chesterfield-Dover School
Wauseon, Ohio

VEGETABLE SALAD

Number of Servings — 6

Pickled Onions:
1 small can whole onions, drained
1 c. sugar
1 c. vinegar
1 t. salt
1 t. mustard seed
½ t. celery seed

Combine all ingredients except onions. Heat to a boiling point. Pour over onions. Let stand for 24 hours.

3 lge. cupped lettuce leaves
2 c. small whole carrots, cooked
1 No. 2 can whole green beans
French dressing

Marinate carrots and beans in French dressing for several hours. Drain. Place onions, carrots and beans in individual lettuce cups.

Mrs. Lena Wood, Rockford Senior H. S.
Rockford, Michigan

GREEN VEGETABLE SALAD

Number of Servings — 6-8

¾ c. raw carrots, grated
¾ c. raw cauliflower, chopped
1 c. canned peas, drained
¼ c. stuffed olives, sliced
3 T. oil
3 T. vinegar
3 T. catsup
1 t. sugar
½ t. salt

Combine vegetables. Combine remaining ingredients; pour over vegetables and let stand 1 hour before serving.

Mrs. Shirley Hansen, Abraham Lincoln H. S.
San Jose, California

WESTERN SALAD BOWL

Number of Servings — 8

2 garlic cloves, quartered
¼ c. salad oil
2 c. croutons
2 small heads lettuce, cut in bite-size pieces
½ c. Parmesan cheese, grated
¼ c. Bleu cheese, crumbled
1 t. salt
¼ t. pepper
6 T. salad oil
1 egg
3½ T. lemon juice
1 T. Worcestershire sauce

Combine garlic and ¼ cup oil; let stand several hours or overnight. Do not refrigerate. Sprinkle cheeses over lettuce; add salt, pepper and remaining oil. Drop raw egg on top. Pour lemon juice and Worcestershire sauce on egg; toss gently. Pour the garlic-oil mixture over the croutons; add to lettuce. Toss. Serve immediately.

Mrs. Ira Black, Sulphur Springs H. S.
Sulphur Springs, Texas

WILTED SALAD GREENS (PENNSYLVANIA DUTCH)

Number of Servings — 6

¼ c. onion, chopped
1 t. salt
Dash pepper
1 qt. spinach, lettuce, endive or romaine, shredded
6 sl. bacon, cut up
3 eggs
4 T. sugar
⅔ c. cream or evaporated milk
4 T. vinegar
2 hard-cooked eggs, sliced (opt.)

Fry bacon until crisp; set aside. Beat eggs and sugar; add cream and blend. Add eggs, sugar and cream to bacon and drippings. Cook over low heat, stirring constantly, until thickened. Pour over salad greens, onions, salt and pepper. Add vinegar; toss until well blended. Garnish with egg slices.

Mrs. Fern Garland, Forbes Road Joint Schools
Harrisonville, Pennsylvania

WALKING SALAD

Lettuce leaves
Peanut butter
Carrot sticks

For each serving, spread one large crisp lettuce leaf with peanut butter. Add 4 or 5 carrot sticks then roll the lettuce leaf so that the salad may be eaten from your hand, excellent for cook outs!

Martha McNatt, Beech Bluff H. S.
Beech Bluff, Tennessee

WINTER'S SUPPER SALAD

Number of Servings — 6

2 10-oz. pkgs. frozen lima beans
1 medium onion, chopped
2 stalks celery, sliced
6 sl. bacon, cut in pieces
¼ c. bacon drippings
¼ c. wine vinegar
¼ t. pepper
½ lb. salami, cut-in thin strips
1 8-oz. pkg. Swiss cheese, sliced
½ c. pitted ripe olives, halved
3 medium carrots, coarsely grated
3 sweet onion slices, separated in rings
Few romaine leaves
½ t. salt
Salad oil and vinegar

Cook frozen lima beans; drain. Place in salad bowl; add chopped onion and celery. Saute bacon until crisp. Mix ¼ cup bacon drippings with ¼ cup wine vinegar and pepper. Pour over lima beans in bowl. Add bacon; toss lightly. Arrange salami, cheese, olives and carrots in separate piles on top; place onion rings in middle. Edge salad bowl with romaine. Sprinkle salt and paprika over all. Toss lightly. Add a little oil and vinegar, if needed.

Eloise W. Hadden, Auburn H. S.
Auburn, Kentucky

WISCONSIN SALAD

Number of Servings — 4-6

7 hard-cooked eggs, chopped
½ t. horseradish
¼ t. pepper
½ c. mayonnaise
4 chilled tomatoes, peeled and sliced
Parsley sprigs
½ lb. Swiss cheese, cut in ½-inch cubes
½ t. salt
½ c. green pepper, finely chopped
½ c. sour cream
4-6 lettuce leaves

Combine horseradish, salt, pepper, sour cream and mayonnaise. Add eggs, cheese and green pepper. Chill. Just before serving put a thick slice of tomato on a lettuce leaf; cover with chilled mixture and top with another slice of tomato. Garnish with a sprig of parsley. For variety, French onion dip may be used instead of mayonnaise and sour cream.

Mrs. Vivian B. Barnes, Argyle H. S.
Argyle, Wisconsin

Macaroni, Rice & Spaghetti Salads

CUCUMBER CANOES

Number of Servings — 6

3 medium cucumbers
1 c. cooked elbow macaroni
1 12-oz. can luncheon meat, cubed
½ c. carrots, grated
¼ c. green pepper, chopped
½ c. mayonnaise
2 T. vinegar
2 T. horseradish
Salt and pepper

Cut cucumbers in half lengthwise. Scoop out pulp from each half, leaving a shell ¼-inch thick. Chop pulp and combine with macaroni, luncheon meat, carrots and green pepper. Blend mayonnaise, vinegar and horseradish. Add to meat mixture; toss lightly. Season to taste with salt and pepper. Pile salad into cucumber shells.

Mrs. Ruth Voigt, Gateway Senior H. S.
Monroeville, Pennsylvania

MACARONI SALAD

Number of Servings — 6

6 oz. shell macaroni
⅓ c. mayonnaise
1 t. Worcestershire sauce
1 t. prepared mustard
Dash of salt
Dash of pepper
½ c. celery, chopped
2 T. onion, minced
¼ c. sweet pickle, chopped
1 c. cooked ham, cubed

Cook macaroni in salted water; drain. Add mayonnaise, Worcestershire sauce, mustard, salt and pepper to hot macaroni. Mix thoroughly. Add celery, onion, sweet pickle and ham. Serve warm or chilled.

Jane Baker, Paducah H. S.
Paducah, Texas

MACARONI SALAD

Number of Servings — 6-8

3 c. cooked macaroni, drained
¾ c. ham, chopped
¾ c. chicken, chopped
¼ c. celery, diced
¼ c. onion, minced
¼ c. green pepper, chopped
1 pimento, chopped
½ c. mayonnaise
Salt and pepper to taste
2 hard-cooked eggs, chopped

Combine all ingredients except eggs. Mix well. Garnish with chopped eggs.

Judy Lennon, Achille H. S.
Achille, Oklahoma

MACARONI SALAD

Number of Servings — 6-8

1 7-oz. pkg. macaroni, cooked
1½ c. green cabbage, shredded
1½ c. Cheddar cheese, cubed
1 lge. sweet bell pepper, chopped
3 lge. tomatoes, cubed
1 small onion, chopped (opt.)
½ t. celery seed
Salt and pepper to taste
½ c. mayonnaise

Mix all ingredients. Serve on lettuce; garnish with stuffed olives and paprika if desired.

Mrs. Joalice Poehler, Reagan County H. S.
Big Lake, Texas

MACARONI SALAD

Number of Servings — 6

1 4-oz. pkg. elbow macaroni
1 lge. green pepper, chopped
4 small carrots, sliced or grated
1 small can pimento, chopped
3 stalks celery, finely cut
½ t. salt
Mayonnaise
2 hard-cooked egg yolks
¼ c. shrimp, diced ham or luncheon meat (opt.)
¼ c. cooked peas (opt.)
¼ c. cooked string beans (opt.)
¼ c. cooked butter beans (opt.)
¼ c. cheese, diced (opt.)

Cook macaroni for 15 minutes; drain and cool. Add all remaining ingredients except mayonnaise and egg yolks. Chill. Serve with combined mayonnaise and egg yolks.

Mrs. Catherine Richard, Destrehan H. S.
Destrehan, Louisiana

MACARONI SALAD

Number of Servings — 12

12 oz. shell macaroni
1 T. seasoned salt
1 t. salt
2 lge. onions, chopped
8 hard-cooked eggs, sliced
2 c. celery, chopped
½ c. pimento, sliced
1 c. green pepper, sliced
2 No. 2½ cans English peas, drained
1½ c. mayonnaise

Boil macaroni in salted water until tender. Drain; blanch with cold water and drain again. Add seasoned salt, onions, salt, eggs, celery, pimento and green pepper. Toss lightly. Add English peas; toss lightly. Gently mix in mayonnaise. Chill several hours before serving. Garnish as desired.

Mrs. Oleta M. Smith, O'Donnell H. S.
O'Donnell, Texas

MACARONI SALAD

Number of Servings — 6

1 c. uncooked shell macaroni
½ c. salad dressing
2 hard-cooked eggs, chopped
1 green pepper, chopped
1 cucumber, chopped
1 medium onion, chopped

Cook macaroni according to package directions; drain. Add remaining ingredients. Chill. Garnish with additional hard-cooked egg and green pepper.

Lois Witt, Heber Springs H. S.
Heber Springs, Arkansas

CHILLED MACARONI SALAD

Number of Servings — 6

4 c. cooked shell macaroni, chilled
4 hard-cooked eggs, chilled and chopped
¾ c. ham, diced or cubed
¾ c. cheese, cubed
¼ c. green pepper, diced
2 T. onion, diced
3 T. pickle, diced
Dash of Worcestershire sauce
½-¾ c. mayonnaise
Lettuce
Paprika
Parsley

Combine all ingredients except paprika, parsley and lettuce. Toss lightly. Spoon onto lettuce cups. Garnish with paprika and parsley. Chill before serving.

Elizabeth Overley, Gueydan H. S.
Gueydan, Louisiana

HOT OR COLD MACARONI SALAD

Number of Servings — 8

4 oz. elbow macaroni
4 strips bacon, cut in ½ inch pieces
½ c. celery, diced
¼ c. green pepper, chopped
¾ c. cucumber pickles, chopped
¼ c. onion, chopped
2 T. chili sauce
½ t. Worcestershire sauce
1 t. salt
⅛ t. pepper
1 t. sugar
¼ c. mayonnaise

Cook macaroni in boiling salted water about 12 minutes. Drain and rinse. Cook bacon bits until crisp. Fold all ingredients into the macaroni. Heat in top of double boiler. Serve hot or chill overnight before serving.

Mrs. Mary C. Williamson, Hallsboro School
Hallsboro, North Carolina

HEARTY MACARONI SALAD

Number of Servings — 6

½ c. uncooked macaroni
¼ lb. luncheon meat, cubed
½ c. canned green peas, chilled
½ c. celery, chopped
¼ lb. Cheddar cheese, cubed
1 T. onion, chopped
1 T. parsley, minced
¼ c. green pepper, chopped
Salt and pepper to taste
⅓ c. salad dressing
1 hard-cooked egg, sliced

Cook macaroni according to package directions. Toss all ingredients together except egg. Chill. Garnish with egg slices.

Mrs. Stewart Knight, Hale Center H. S.
Hale Center, Texas

MACARONI AND CHEESE SALAD

Number of Servings — 6

3 oz. cooked macaroni, drained and cooled
1 12-oz. can ham, cut in strips
1 c. Cheddar cheese, cubed
½ c. celery, cubed
¼ c. pickle relish
½ c. mayonnaise
1 T. mustard
¼ t. salt

Combine macaroni, ham, cheese, celery and relish. Blend mayonnaise, mustard and salt. Add to first mixture; toss. Chill. Serve on greens.

Betty Canada, Munford H. S.
Munford, Alabama

MACARONI-FRUIT SALAD

Number of Servings — 25-30

1 pkg. macaroni rings, cooked and drained
1 No. 303 can crushed pineapple
1 No. 303 can fruit cocktail, drained
2 T. lemon juice
2 T. flour
½ c. sugar
4 eggs, beaten
1 pkg. miniature marshmallows
1 pt. whipped cream
2 c. Mandarin oranges or desired fruit

Combine lemon juice, flour, sugar and juice drained from pineapple and fruit cocktail. Cook until thickened. Remove from heat. Add eggs and heat again. Cool slightly. Add macaroni, pineapple and fruit cocktail. Chill several hours or overnight. Just before serving add marshmallows, whipped cream and remaining fruit.

Mrs. Melba Olverson, Clark H. S.
Clark, South Dakota

MACARONI-CHICKEN SALAD BOWL

Number of Servings — 8

1 8-oz. pkg. elbow macaroni
4 c. water
½ t. salt
1 c. celery, sliced
1½ c. cooked chicken, diced
⅓ c. sweet pickle, chopped
1 T. onion, scraped
¼ c. French dressing
Mayonnaise or salad dressing

Cook macaroni in water in a 2-quart saucepan. Add salt; bring to a rapid boil. Stir; cover and boil until tender. Drain and cool. Mix celery, chicken, pickles, onion and French dressing; blend with mayonnaise or salad dressing. Mix with macaroni. Chill. Garnish with sliced sweet pickles.

Mrs. Sarah Musgrave, Rattan H. S.
Rattan, Oklahoma

MACARONI AND HAM SALAD

Number of Servings — 4

2 c. uncooked macaroni
Mayonnaise or salad dressing
1 small onion, chopped
Salt to taste
Pepper to taste
1 c. ham or cheese, diced

Cook macaroni according to package directions; drain and cool. Combine all ingredients using enough mayonnaise or salad dressing to moisten.

Phyllis Rae Horner, Severna Park H. S.
Severna Park, Maryland

MAIN DISH SALAD

Number of Servings — 4

4 oz. elbow macaroni
1 c. cooked chicken, turkey, or tuna, chopped
2 hard-cooked eggs, diced
½ c. crushed pineapple, drained
¼ c. radishes, sliced
¼ c. nuts, chopped
1 T. onion, chopped
⅓ c. mayonnaise
1½ T. pineapple juice
¼ t. celery seed
¼ t. salt
Dash of pepper

Cook macaroni as directed on package. Combine poultry or tuna, eggs, pineapple, radishes, nuts and onion. Add macaroni; toss lightly. Combine mayonnaise and pineapple juice; mix until smooth. Stir in celery seed, salt and pepper. Pour over macaroni mixture. Toss until well blended. Chill. Serve on salad greens.

Mrs. Ruth A. Blomgren, Eastern Junior H. S.
Silver Spring, Maryland

MACARONI-SHRIMP SALAD

2 c. macaroni
1 c. celery, finely chopped
¼ c. pimento
1 can shrimp
2 hard-cooked eggs, finely chopped
¼ t. paprika
½ t. salt
1 c. mayonnaise
¼ c. French dressing

Cook macaroni according to package directions; cool. Add celery, shrimp, eggs, pimento, paprika and salt. Mix mayonnaise and French dressing and add to macaroni mixture.

Mrs. Sharon Nelson, Karlstad H. S.
Karlstad, Minnesota

MACARONI-SALMON SALAD

Number of Servings — 4-6

2 c. cooked macaroni, cooled
1 c. cucumber, diced
1 8-oz. can salmon, flaked
1 T. onion, grated
1 T. parsley, minced
¾ c. mayonnaise
½ t. salt
¼ t. pepper

Combine all ingredients; toss together until blended.

Mrs. Linda J. McCraw, Gaffney Senior H. S.
Gaffney, South Carolina

MY MOTHER'S MACARONI SALAD

Number of Servings — 10

Dressing:
2 T. salad dressing or mayonnaise
1-3 T. vinegar
½ t. prepared mustard
2 t. sugar
Salt to taste

Combine all ingredients.

1½ c. macaroni
2 stalks celery, chopped or ½ t. celery seed
1 green pepper, chopped
1 cucumber, chopped
½ medium onion, chopped
2 medium tomatoes, cut in pieces
1 carrot, chopped

Cook macaroni in salted water until almost dry. Mix all ingredients with warm macaroni. Garnish as desired. Pour dressing over macaroni mixture and marinate for at least an hour before serving.

Mrs. Eileen Skaggs, Alderson H. S.
Alderson, West Virginia

SALAD SUPPER

Number of Servings — 4

1 7-oz. pkg. shell or lge. elbow macaroni
1 7-oz. can tuna, drained
1 small onion, finely chopped
2 hard-cooked eggs, sliced
1 c. celery, diced
½ c. ripe olives, sliced and pitted
2 tomatoes, quartered
Mayonnaise
Salt to taste

Cook macaroni in small amount of water. Cool. Mix all ingredients except eggs and tomatoes, adding enough mayonnaise to moisten. Garnish with eggs and tomatoes. Chill before serving.

Mrs. Joe D. Gamble, Friendswood H. S.
Friendswood, Texas

SALAD SUPREME

Number of Servings — 6

1 c. uncooked macaroni
1 c. celery, chopped
6 T. sweet pickle, chopped
3 T. pimento, chopped
6 T. green pepper, chopped
1 c. sharp cheese, diced
½ c. green peas, cooked
½ c. salad dressing

Cook macaroni according to package directions. Drain and chill for 2 hours. Add celery, pickles and pimento. Toss lightly. Add remaining ingredients; toss. Chill.

Mary Nan Fitch, Electra H. S.
Electra, Texas

VIENNA-MACARONI SALAD

Number of Servings — 6

1 8-oz. pkg. elbow macaroni
1 c. celery, chopped
1 c. sweet pickles, chopped
2 T. onion, grated
1 c. Vienna sausage, thinly sliced
1 c. mayonnaise
1 t. salt
¼ t. pepper
3 deviled eggs, halved
2 T. pickle juice
6 lettuce leaves

Cook macaroni until tender. Drain; blanch in cold water and drain again. Combine with celery, sweet pickles, onion and Vienna sausages. Blend mayonnaise with pickle juice, salt and pepper; add to macaroni mixture. Chill. Heap salad on lettuce in the center of a large serving plate. Arrange additional Vienna sausages over the top to resemble spokes. Arrange deviled egg halves around salad.

Mrs. Dorothy Sue T. Hill, Oberlin H. S.
Oberlin, Louisiana

SUMMER MACARONI SALAD

Number of Servings — 6

1 7-oz. pkg. uncooked elbow, shell or ring macaroni
1 c. Cheddar cheese, cubed
1 c. gherkins, sliced
½ c. onion, minced
½ c. mayonnaise
1 10-or 12-oz. pkg. frozen peas, cooked and drained
Salt and pepper to taste.

Cook macaroni according to package directions. Drain; rinse with cold water and drain again. Add remaining ingredients. Chill. Serve in lettuce cups.

Nelda Lowry, Caddo Mills H. S.
Caddo Mills, Texas

HOT TUNA-MACARONI TOSS

Number of Servings — 6

1 c. uncooked elbow macaroni
¼ c. Italian dressing
1 t. celery seed
¾ t. dry mustard
½ t. salt
Dash of pepper
1 6½-oz. can tuna
½ c. celery, diced
½ c. green pepper, diced
3 T. salad dressing

Cook macaroni according to package directions; drain. Mix Italian dressing and seasonings; heat just to boiling. Add macaroni, tuna, celery and green pepper. Toss lightly and heat through. Stir in salad dressing. Top with green pepper rings. Serve immediately.

Mrs. Sarah Strange Martin, Memorial Junior H. S.
Tampa, Florida

TUNA-RONI SALAD

Number of Servings — 8-10

½ c. shell macaroni
1 can tuna, flaked
1 No. 303 can English peas, drained
½ c. celery, diced
1 c. cheese, cubed
⅓ c. sweet pickles, chopped
3 pimentos, chopped
¾-1 c. salad dressing
Salt and pepper to taste
Pimento strips, paprika or hard-cooked egg wedges (garnish)

Cook macaroni in boiling salted water until tender; drain. Rinse with cold water. Combine all ingredients. Mix well. Garnish with pimento strips, paprika or egg wedges. Salad may be made the day. before serving if desired.

Mrs. Thelma Cravy, Jacksonville H. S.
Jacksonville, Texas

FAVORITE TUNA-MACARONI SALAD

Number of Servings — 8

1 6-oz. can tuna
1 c. macaroni rings
3 hard-cooked eggs, chopped
½ c. celery, chopped
1 T. onion, chopped
1 T. pickle, chopped or relish
½ c. salad dressing
2 T. evaporated milk
2 T. lemon juice or pickle juice
1 T. mayonnaise

Cook macaroni rings according to directions on package. Combine tuna, eggs, celery, onion and pickle. Add macaroni. Combine salad dressing, evaporated milk and lemon or pickle juice. Fold dressing carefully into salad mixture and chill for several hours. Just before serving add mayonnaise. Garnish with egg slices, olives and paprika.

Mrs. Esther E. Smith
Cowanesque Valley Joint School
Westfield, Pennsylvania

TUNA-CHEESE MACARONI SALAD

Number of Servings — 6

1 7 or 8 oz. pkg. macaroni, boiled
6½ oz. can tuna
1 c. Cheddar cheese, cubed
½ c. sweet pickle, chopped
¼ c. onion, minced
½ c. mayonnaise
2 T. prepared mustard
1 T. sugar
1 No. 303 can peas, drained

Drain cooked macaroni; rinse in cold water. Add tuna, cheese, pickles and onion. Mix mayonnaise, mustard and sugar. Combine the 2 mixtures. Add peas and salt to taste; mix well.

Mrs. Robert Berkner,
Community School-Lamberton
Lamberton, Minnesota

MAINLY-MACARONI SALAD

Number of Servings — 8

8 oz. salad macaroni
¼ c. green pepper, chopped
4½-oz. can olives, chopped
1 medium onion, finely chopped
¼ c. celery, chopped
3 hard-cooked eggs, sliced
Mayonnaise
Vinegar
Salt
Pepper
Paprika

Cook macaroni according to package directions; rinse. Combine next 5 ingredients, reserving some egg slices for garnish. Add mayonnaise, vinegar, salt and pepper to taste. Garnish with egg slices and paprika. Let stand several hours before serving.

Helena Tidrow Raine, Morro Bay Jr.-Sr. H. S.
Morro Bay, California

MACA-SALMON SALAD

Number of Servings — 14-18

2 c. uncooked macaroni
1 c. cheese, diced
1 c. sweet pickle, diced
1 c. celery, diced
¼ c. pimento, diced
¼ c. green pepper, minced
¼ c. onion, minced
4 c. canned salmon, drained and flaked
2 c. mayonnaise
2 T. prepared mustard
6 T. vinegar
2 heads lettuce

Cook macaroni according to directions on package; Drain. Add cheese; toss until well mixed. Cool. Add pickles, celery, pimento, green pepper and onion. Add salmon. Blend mayonnaise, mustard and vinegar. Pour over salad; chill thoroughly. At serving time, use crisp outer leaves of lettuce to line big bowls or chop plates. Cut remaining lettuce; add to salad and toss lightly.

Mrs. Ellen D. Feagan, Las Cruces High
Las Cruces, New Mexico

RICE SALAD

Number of Servings — 8

2 c. cooked rice
4 hard-cooked eggs
4 sweet pickles
1 T. onion, diced
¼ c. green pepper, diced
¼ c. celery, diced
1 t. salt
½ t. black pepper
½ c. chopped pecans (opt.)
1 T. mustard
1 T. pickle juice
½ c. salad dressing

Mix salad dressing, mustard and pickle juice. Mix with remaining ingredients. Chill.

Mrs. Dorothy Weikal Bickerstaff, Marianna H. S.
Marianna, Arkansas

RICE SALAD

Number of Servings — 8-10

1 c. rice
1 pkg. lemon gelatin
1 c. crushed pineapple
1 c. whipped cream
2 c. hot water
1 c. confectioner's sugar
½ c. walnuts, crushed
½ c. marshmallows

Cook rice until soft; drain and cool. Dissolve gelatin in hot water. Cool. Mix all ingredients; chill.

Mrs. Evelyn Johnson, Bottineau H. S.
Bottineau, North Dakota

RICE SALAD

Number of Servings — 8-12

1 c. raw rice
Paprika
4 hard-cooked eggs, chopped
½ c. celery, chopped
¼ c. onion, chopped (opt.)
½ c. sweet pickles, chopped
¼ c. green pepper, chopped
1 small can pimento, chopped (opt.)
½ c. salad dressing
Salt to taste

Cook rice according to package directions. Cool; sprinkle with paprika. Add eggs, celery, pickles, pepper, pimento, salad dressing and onion if desired. Toss lightly to mix. Salt to taste.

Mrs. Christine Weems, Hazen H. S.
Hazen, Arkansas

GELATIN-RICE SALAD

Number of Servings — 6-8

1 pkg. raspberry or lime gelatin
1 c. boiling water
1 c. whipped cream
1 small can crushed pineapple, drained
2 c. cooked rice, drained and sweetened

Dissolve gelatin in boiling water. Add rice. Chill 2 or 3 hours so rice will take up flavor of the gelatin. Blend pineapple and whipped cream into gelatin mixture. Serve on crisp lettuce.

Mrs. Patsy Stemple, Gillham H. S.
Gillham, Arkansas

GOLDEN RICE SALAD

Number of Servings — 8

2 T. salad oil
1 T. vinegar
¼ t. salt
⅛ t. pepper
¾ c. + 2 T. raw rice
½ c. + 2 T. chicken stock
½ c. ripe olives, cut in large pieces
1 hard-cooked egg, diced
¾ c. celery, chopped
2 T. dill pickle, chopped
¼ c. pimento, chopped
¼ c. green onions, chopped
¼ c. mayonnaise
1 T. prepared mustard

Cook rice in chicken stock. Blend salad oil, vinegar, salt and pepper. Pour over hot rice; mix well. Cool. Add remaining ingredients; toss lightly. Chill thoroughly.

Edna C. Hathorn, Crowley H. S.
Crowley, Louisiana

ORIENTAL SALAD

Number of Servings — 6

1 lb. bean sprouts
1¼ c. steamed rice
1 c. celery, thinly sliced
2 T. green pepper, chopped
2 small carrots, finely grated
3 green onions and tops, sliced
2 c. cooked chicken or pork, diced
½ c. toasted almonds, slivered
Salt and pepper to taste
¾ c. French dressing
Juice of ½ lemon
Soy sauce (opt.)

Cook bean sprouts in a small amount of salted water for about 3 minutes or until crisp and tender. Drain and cool. Combine bean sprouts, rice, celery, green pepper, carrots, onions, almonds and chicken or pork. Chill thoroughly. Add salt, pepper and lemon juice. Add French dressing and toss lightly. Sprinkle with soy sauce, if desired.

Mrs. Luisa Pitchford
Los Banos Elementary School
Los Banos, California

RICE AND MEAT SALAD 

Number of Servings — 6

1½ c. cooked rice, chilled
1½ c. chicken, tuna or turkey, diced
1 c. English peas
1 c. raw carrots, shredded
½ t. salt
½ c. French dressing
4 T. chili sauce (opt.)
¼ t. curry powder

Mix rice with meat and vegetables; toss lightly. Mix chili sauce, curry powder, salt and French dressing. Pour over salad and toss lightly.

Mrs. Harriet Krause, Pasadena H. S.
Pasadena, Texas

STRAWBERRY-RICE SALAD

Number of Servings — 12-15

2 pkg. strawberry gelatin
3 c. hot water
2 c. cooked rice
1 c. miniature marshmallows
1 c. crushed pineapple
1 c. whipped cream

Dissolve gelatin in hot water; cool. Add rice, marshmallows and pineapple. When mixture begins to congeal add whipped cream. Chill.

Elaine Crane, Mallard Community School
Mallard, Iowa

SEAFOOD-RICE RING

Number of Servings — 8-12

1½ c. rice
1 c. canned whole shrimp
1 c. canned or fresh crab
3 T. lemon juice
¼ c. green onions, chopped
¼ c. green pepper, chopped
½ c. stuffed olives, sliced
1 c. salad dressing
½ c. chili sauce
½ t. dry mustard
¼ t. pepper
¼ t. garlic salt
1 t. salt
1 t. Worcestershire sauce
1 T. vinegar (opt.)

Steam rice according to package directions; cool. Sprinkle seafood with lemon juice; toss with rice. Add onion, green pepper and olives. Blend remaining ingredients; add to rice mixture. Pack into a 1¾-quart ring mold. Chill for several hours or overnight before serving.

Mrs. Ireta Lyngstad, Coeur d'Alene Junior H. S.
Coeur d'Alene, Idaho

SPAGHETTI SALAD

Number of Servings — 12

1 16-oz. pkg. spaghetti
1 small head cabbage, shredded
1 small onion, minced
1 sprig celery
2 cans red kidney beans

Cook spaghetti according to package directions. Wash liquids off kidney beans; drain. Combine vegetables and macaroni.

Dressing:
3 eggs
1⅛ c. sugar
1 small jar prepared mustard
3 T. butter

Combine all ingredients. Cook until mixture thickens slightly. Cool; add to salad.

Mrs. Margaret P. Samson, Western Wayne Jointure
Lake Ariel, Pennsylvania

GEORGE RECTOR'S SPAGHETTI-CHICKEN SALAD

Number of Servings — 6

½ lb. elbow spaghetti
2 c. cooked chicken, diced
1 c. celery, chopped
1 T. onion, grated
1 t. salt
½ c. mayonnaise or salad dressing
2 T. green pepper, chopped
1 T. red pepper or pimento, minced
Hard cooked eggs (opt.)

Cook spaghetti until tender; drain and chill. Add all remaining ingredients, except eggs. Mix lightly. Serve on watercress or lettuce with Goldenrod Sauce made by rubbing hard cooked eggs through a sieve if desired.

Mrs. K. E. Sharp, Houston Junior H. S.
Borger, Texas

INEXPENSIVE SPAGHETTI-FRUIT SALAD

Number of Servings — 30-40

2 c. spaghetti, boiled and blanched
4 eggs, beaten
½ c. lemon juice
2 c. confectioner's sugar
Dash of salt
6 medium apples, diced
1 can crushed pineapple or tidbits
2 c. whipped cream, sweetened
Bananas, diced (opt.)
Nuts, chopped (opt.)
Oranges, diced (opt.)

Combine eggs, lemon juice, sugar and salt. Cook egg mixture until thick; cool. Add fruit and spaghetti. Let stand 12-24 hours. Add whipped cream.

Donna Mae Hurst, Box Elder H. S.
Brigham City, Utah

TOMATO AND SPAGHETTI SALAD

Number of Servings — 5

1 c. elbow spaghetti
1 can chicken, turkey or tuna
1 c. celery, diced
½ c. mayonnaise or undiluted Cheddar cheese soup
2 t. onion, grated
Cracked black pepper to taste
¼ t. salt
5 tomatoes, peeled
Lettuce

Cook spaghetti according to package directions. Add meat, celery, onion, salt, pepper and mayonnaise or soup to cooked spaghetti. Cut tomatoes from flower end down to the stem end into four or eight sections. Place tomato on lettuce and fill with salad.

Mrs. Gloria Hixson, Scranton H. S.
Scranton, Arkansas

Meat & Poultry Salads

ANARCTIC SALAD

Number of Servings — 8

¾ c. oil
⅛ c. cider vinegar
1 clove garlic, skewered on toothpick
½ t. soy sauce
⅛ c. lemon juice
1 t. salt
Few grains cayenne pepper
2 crushed juniper berries, threaded on toothpick
½ t. curry powder
2 c. lean roast pork, diced
1½ c. hot chicken broth or chicken bouillon cubes dissolved in water
2 T. unflavored gelatin
Juice of 1 lge. lemon
1 small head red cabbage, chilled and finely shredded

Make a marinade of oil, vinegar, lemon juice, garlic, soy sauce, salt, cayenne pepper, curry powder and juniper berries. Add meat; let stand at least 4 hours or overnight. Stir occasionally. Soak gelatin in ½ c. chicken broth; dissolve in remaining 1 cup of hot broth. Add lemon juice. Remove meat, garlic and juniper berries from marinade. Drain meat. Oil a tall mold for a "mountain". When gelatin begins to thicken, pour a small amount in the mold, turning to coat the inside of the mold with a layer of gelatin. Refrigerate mold. Keep remaining gelatin at room temperature.

Celery crescents
Capers
Green pepper
Cooked mushrooms, cooled
Cucumbers
Radish roses
Carrots
Baby lima beans
Peas
Onions

Use any desired combination of vegetables. Neatly cut them into thin, varied shapes. If desired, vegetables may be gently folded into the drained meat, or layers of vegetables, meat and gelatin may be alternated in the mold. Chill until firm.

Penguins:
8 hard-cooked eggs, halved lengthwise
32 lge. black olives, pitted
Mayonnaise
4 almonds, blanched and halved lengthwise

Remove yolks from eggs; mash and season to taste. Moisten with a little mayonnaise. Stuff eggs with yolk mixture; fit halves together firmly. Wrap each egg in waxed paper. Twist ends of paper to hold eggs firmly together. Place olives in oil so they will be shiny. Fasten olive on small end of egg for the head. Insert a piece of almond for the penguin's beak. Cut 3 olives in half lengthwise. Use 4 halves for the wings and back of the penguins, placing large ends toward the head. Use two halves for feet. Arrange finely shredded cabbage on serving platter. Unmold the gelatin "mountain" on the bed of cabbage. Arrange penguins around the mountain. Serving 1 penguin per person. Pass Russian or Thousand Island dressing.

Mrs. Jessie L. Hawks, Ripon Union H. S.
Ripon, California

CHEF'S SALAD

Number of Servings — 6

1 lge. head lettuce
¼ c. onion, minced
6 radishes, sliced
6 small tomatoes, cut in chunks
6 hard-cooked eggs, cut in wedges
1½ c. cheese strips
1½ c. boiled ham strips or any cold cut
French or Russian dressing

Tear lettuce into bite-size portions. Toss with onion radishes and tomatoes. Divide into 6 portions and pile in the center of individual salad plates. Sprinkle with a little French or Russian dressing. Arrange eggs, meat and cheese in an attractive manner over the lettuce. Sprinkle salad with dressing.

Mina F. Robinson, Perry H. S.
Perry, Kansas

COLD MEAT IN ASPIC

Number of Servings — 6

1 pkg. unflavored Gelatin
¼ c. cold water
1½ c. heated consomme, highly seasoned
½ c. cooked peas
1 c. cooked beets, sliced
1 hard-cooked egg, sliced
Ham, chicken or veal, cubed

Soften gelatin in cold water. Add to hot consomme; stir. Pour thin layer into greased pan. When gelatin thickens arrange peas, eggs and beets on top. Cover with another layer of gelatin. Cool. Mix meat with remaining gelatin mixture; pour over cooled layer. Serve on lettuce garnished with radish roses.

Mrs. Elaine Petrik, South Winneshiek Community
Calmar, Iowa

CORNED BEEF SALAD

Number of Servings — 10

2 3-oz. pkg. lemon gelatin
1 qt. hot water
4 T. vinegar
1 can corned beef, broken
2 c. celery, chopped
4 T. onion, minced
1 green pepper, finely chopped
6 hard-cooked eggs, chopped
1 c. mayonniase

Dissolve gelatin in hot water and vinegar. When partially set, fold in mayonniase and add remaining ingredients. Chill until set.

Mrs. Wilda Carr, Sr. H. S.
Holdrege, Nebraska

CORNED BEEF WITH MACARONI SALAD

Number of Servings — 8

1 pkg. lemon gelatin
1½ c. hot water
1½ c. celery, finely diced
1 c. salad dressing
1 T. onion, chopped
½ green pepper, finely chopped
3 hard-cooked eggs, chopped
1 can corned beef, shredded
2 T. vinegar
4 oz. ring macaroni

Cook macaroni according to package directions. Dissolve gelatin in hot water. Chill until slightly congealed. Gently fold in remaining ingredients. Refrigerate until firm.

Mrs. Bonnie Shaw, Clarkfield Public School
Clarkfield, Minnesota

CORNED BEEF SALAD

Number of Servings — 8

1 pkg. lemon gelatin
1¾ c. hot water
1 can-corned beef, flaked
1 c. celery, cubed
2 T. onion, diced
2 T. green pepper, chopped
1 c. mayonnaise
3 hard-cooked eggs
Parsley

Dissolve gelatin in hot water. Chill until slightly thickened. Add mayonniase, corned beef, celery, onion, green pepper, and 2 chopped eggs. Chill until set in individual molds or a ring mold. Garnish with egg slices and parsley.

Maxine Toynton, Sun Prairie Sr. H. S.
Sun Prairie, Wisconsin

CORNED BEEF SALAD

Number of Servings — 6-8

2 3-oz. pkg. lemon gelatin
3 c. hot water
1 can corned beef, minced
3 hard-cooked eggs, chopped
1 c. celery, diced
1 t. onion, chopped
1 medium green pepper, diced
3 T. pimento, diced
1 c. salad dressing

Mix gelatin and hot water; cool. Mix meat, eggs, celery, onion, pepper and pimento. Mix with salad dressing. Put in mold or bowl. Pour gelatin over all and pierce with a knife so gelatin will work through meat mixture. Chill.

Janice Hagemeister, Mott H. S.
Mott, North Dakota

MOLDED CORNED BEEF SALAD

Number of Servings — 4-6

1 box lemon gelatin
1 c. boiling water
1 c. corned beef
2 c. celery, chopped
½ onion, diced
¾ c. green pepper, chopped
1 c. mayonnaise

Dissolve gelatin in boiling water. Cool. Add corned beef, celery, onion and green pepper. Stir in mayonnaise; mix well. Pour into a large mold or individual molds. When set, serve on lettuce leaves.

Barbara Gaylor, Consultant, Michigan Department
of Public Instruction
Family Life Education
Lansing, Michigan

CRUNCHY BAKED HAM SALAD

Number of Servings — 6

3 c. cooked ham, diced
1 c. celery, diced
½ c. stuffed green olives, chopped
2 hard-cooked eggs, diced
¼ c. onion, chopped
1 T. lemon juice
1 T. prepared mustard
Dash of pepper
¾ c. mayonnaise or salad dressing
1 c. potato chips, crushed

Combine all ingredients except potato chips. Place mixture in an 8 x 2 round baking dish. Sprinkle with potato chips. Bake in 400°F. oven 20-25 minutes.

Ilene Ridgely, East Richland H. S.
Olney, Illinois

SKILLET HAM SALAD

Number of Servings — 4

¼ c. green onion, chopped
¼ c. green pepper, chopped
2 c. cooked ham, diced
1 T. fat
3 c. cooked potatoes, diced
¼ t. salt
⅛ t. pepper
¼ c. mayonnaise
½ lb. sharp American cheese, diced

Lightly brown onions, green pepper and ham in hot fat, stirring occasionally. Add potatoes, salt, pepper and mayonnaise; heat, mixing lightly. Stir in cheese; heat until it begins to melt. Garnish with additional green onions.

Joyce Bradford, Lincolnwood H. S.
Raymond, Illinois

HAM AND CABBAGE SALAD

Number of Servings — 8

1 small head cabbage, shredded
2 c. cold cooked ham, diced
1 sweet red pepper, chopped
½ onion, chopped
1 green pepper, chopped
1 c. mayonnaise
Salt to taste

Combine cabbage, ham, onions and peppers. Blend with mayonnaise. Add salt to taste.

Clara M. Dayton, Cokeville H. S.
Cokeville, Wyoming

MAIN DISH RICE AND HAM SALAD

Number of Servings — 4-6

1⅓ c. precooked rice
1½ T. dry mustard
2 T. cold water
1½ T. sugar
1½ T. wine vinegar
¼ c. vegetable oil
½ c. green pepper, chopped
1 c. cooked ham, diced
½ c. cooked peas
Parsley, chopped
Salad greens

Prepare rice as directed on package. Mix mustard, water, sugar and vinegar; gradually beat in oil. Stir lightly into warm rice. Cool; add pepper, ham and peas. Sprinkle with parsley and serve with greens.

Mrs. Jean Jordan, Spurger H. S.
Spurger, Texas

BAKED CHICKEN SALAD

Number of Servings — 4

1 c. cooked chicken, diced
1 10-oz. can cream of chicken soup
1 c. celery, diced
2 t. onion, minced
½ c. almonds, chopped
¾ c. mayonnaise
1 T. lemon juice
½ t. salt
¼ t. pepper
Parsley
2 hard-cooked eggs

Combine all ingredients except potato chips and parsley in a 1 qt. casserole. Top with potato chips; garnish with parsley. Bake in a 450°F. oven for 15 minutes. Serve with cranberry sauce.

Joan M. Kleinert, White Bear Lake H. S.
White Bear Lake, Minnesota

AVOCADO-CHICKEN-APPLE SALAD

Number of Servings — 6-8

2 lge. apples, cubed
1 ripe avocado, cubed
2 T. lemon juice
½ c. mayonnaise
¼ c. cream
1 t. onion, minced
2 c. cooked chicken, cubed
¼ c. Bleu cheese, crumbled

Sprinkle apples and avocado with lemon juice. Combine mayonnaise and cream; add onion. Toss avocado, apples, cheese and chicken with cream dressing. Serve on lettuce leaves.

Mrs. Katherine S. Hunter, Irving H. S.
Irving, Texas

BROILED CHICKEN SALAD

Number of Servings — 4

2 c. cooked chicken, diced
1½ c. celery, diced
¼ c. French dressing
½ c. mayonnaise
⅓ c. sour cream
¼ c. almonds, toasted
2 c. potato chips, crushed
1 c. cheese, grated

Marinate chicken and celery in French dressing for 1 hour. Add mayonnaise, sour cream and almonds. Place in a baking dish. Mix potato chips and cheese; sprinkle on top of the salad. Place under broiler until cheese melts.

Mrs. Johnnie T. Broome, Blackshear H. S.
Blackshear, Georgia

CHICKEN-ALMOND RING SALAD

Number of Servings — 6

2 c. chicken broth or bouillon
1 envelope unflavored gelatin
2 c. cooked chicken, diced
1 c. blanched almonds, slivered
1 small onion, finely chopped
¼ c. green pepper, chopped
1 T. pimento, chopped
½ t. salt
¼ t. pepper
1½ t. curry powder
26 Vegetable Thins, crushed
1 c. sour cream
Salad greens

Combine gelatin and broth or bouillon; heat until gelatin is dissolved. Cool. Combine all remaining ingredients except greens and Vegetable Thins. When gelatin is thick enough to mound when dropped from a spoon fold into chicken mixture. Pour into a greased 5-cup ring mold. Chill until firm. Unmold on greens. Fill center with crushed Vegetable Thins.

Mrs. Ann Davis, Trumann H. S.
Trumann, Arkansas

CHICKEN- OR TURKEY-ALMOND SALAD

Number of Servings — 8

3 c. chicken or turkey, chopped
2 c. celery, diced
1 c. almonds, chopped
½ c. pickle, chopped (opt.)
1 T. onion, finely chopped
Salt and pepper to taste
⅓ c. French dressing
¾ c. mayonnaise
Lettuce
2 hard-cooked eggs, sliced

Combine chicken or turkey, celery, almonds, pickle, onion, salt and pepper. Add French dressing. Cover and refrigerate for 2 hours. Add mayonnaise. Serve on lettuce. Garnish with egg slices.

Katharine Lee Hoover, Hyre Jr. H. S.
Akron, Ohio

CHICKEN-CRANBERRY MOLD

Number of Servings — 8

Cranberry Layer:
1 T. unflavored gelatin
¼ c. cold water
2 c. whole cranberry sauce
1 c. crushed pineapple
Lemon juice to taste
½ c. nuts, chopped (opt.)

Soften gelatin in cold water; dissolve over hot water. Add cranberry sauce, pineapple, lemon juice and nuts. Pour into a baking dish. Chill until firm.

Chicken Layer:
1 T. unflavored gelatin
¾ c. cold water
1 c. salad dressing or mayonnaise
3 T. lemon juice
¾-1 t. salt
2 c. cooked chicken, diced
½ c. celery, diced
1-2 T. parsley, chopped

Soften gelatin in ¼ cup cold water; dissolve over hot water. Blend in salad dressing or mayonnaise, remaining ½ cup cold water, lemon juice and salt. Stir in chicken, celery and parsley. Pour over firm cranberry layer. Chill until firm.

This recipe submitted by the following teachers:

Wanda M. Waddell, Walter Johnson Senior H. S.
Bethesda, Maryland

Marcia F. Swanson, Henry County H. S.
McDonough, Georgia

Mrs. Joan M. Miller, Jefferson H. S.
Jefferson, South Carolina

Mary A. Hugus, Fairless H. S.
Navarre, Ohio

Mrs. Bettie Hudson, Memorial Junior H. S.
Garland, Texas

Phyllis D. Larsen, Alameda Junior H. S.
Las Cruces, New Mexico

Mrs. Art Warwick, DeKalb H. S.
DeKalb, Texas

BUFFET CHICKEN SALAD

Number of Servings — 8

3 c. cooked chicken, diced
3 T. lemon juice
1½ c. celery, diced
1 c. pineapple tidbits
1½ c. seedless grapes or canned white grapes
½ c. pecans, broken
1 c. mayonnaise
1½ t. salt
1 t. dry mustard
Lettuce leaves or hearts

Combine chicken and lemon juice; chill for 1 hour. Add celery, pineapple, grapes and pecans. Combine mayonniase, salt and mustard; mix with chicken. Serve on lettuce leaves or toss with lettuce hearts just before serving.

Sara Phegley Chowning, Sullivan H. S.
Sullivan, Indiana

CHICKEN-CURRY SALAD

Number of Servings — 6-8

2 c. boiling water
1 pkg. dry chicken noodle soup mix
1 c. instant rice
1 c. celery, chopped
2 T. onion, chopped
1 c. chicken, chopped
1 t. curry powder
1 t. salt
½ t. dry mustard
⅛ t. pepper
¾ c. crushed pineapple
¾ c. mayonnaise

Add the soup mix and rice to boiling water. Cover and simmer until water is absorbed. Stir to fluff. Cover and set aside for 15-20 minutes. When rice mixture is cold, add all the remaining ingredients. Blend well. Cover and chill thoroughly.

Enid Hedrick, Bolsa Grande H. S.
Garden Grove, California

CHICKEN SALAD

Number of Servings — 4

1 c. cooked chicken, finely cut
1 c. celery, chopped
½ c. carrot grated
1 t. onion, grated
1 can shoe-string potatoes
¼ c. mayonnaise
¼ c. cream
Salt and pepper to taste

Combine chicken, celery, onion, carrot and potatoes. Mix mayonniase and cream, add salt and pepper. Toss with chicken mixture just before serving.

Helen Olson Beltz, Fulda H. S.
Fulda, Minnesota

CHICKEN-CREAM DELIGHT SALAD

Number of Servings — 8

1 stewing chicken
1 stalk celery
1 carrot
½ onion
1 envelope unflavored gelatin
¼ c. cold water
¾ c. hot chicken stock, highly seasoned
1 c. whipped cream
½ c. celery, finely chopped
½ green pepper, finely chopped
¼ c. stuffed olives, diced
1 T. onion juice
2 T. sweet pickle, finely chopped
1 T. lemon juice
Salt and pepper to taste
Mayonnaise
Pecans, chopped
Stuffed olives, sliced

Stew chicken with carrot, celery stalk and onion until tender. Strain and reserve ¾ cup stock. Remove celery, carrot and onion from the chicken. Remove bones from cool chicken; cut meat into bite-size pieces. Soften gelatin in cold water; add hot stock and stir until dissolved. Add onion and lemon juice. Cool until mixture begins to thicken. Beat with rotary beater until frothy. Fold in chicken, whipped cream, celery, green pepper, diced olives, pickles, salt and pepper. Turn into individual molds which have been rinsed with cold water. Chill until firm. Decorate with olive slices. Serve with mayonnaise mixed with pecans.

Mrs. Ruby C. Irvine, Coalton H. S.
Coalton, West Virginia

CHICKEN SALAD DELUXE

Number of Servings — 4-6

1⅓ c. precooked rice
1½ t. salt
1⅓ c. boiling water
⅔ c. mayonnaise
⅓ c. French dressing
⅛ t. pepper
1½ c. cooked chicken, diced
1 c. celery, diced
1 c. orange sections, drained and diced
½ c. walnuts, coarsely chopped

Combine rice, ½ teaspoon salt and boiling water; mix just enough to moisten rice. Cover and remove from heat; let stand for 5 minutes. Remove cover and cool to room temperature. Combine mayonnaise, French dressing, pepper and remaining 1 teaspoon salt; mix well. Combine chicken, celery, orange sections and walnuts; stir in mayonnaise mixture. Add rice and mix lightly. Chill for 1 hour before serving. If desired, 1 cup drained, diced pineapple or 1½ cup seeded grapes may be substituted for orange sections.

Murlene Oakley, Canton H. S.
Canton, Oklahoma

CHICKEN-FRUIT PARTY SALAD

Number of Servings — 6

2 c. cold chicken, chopped
1 c. celery, chopped
1 T. lemon juice
Salt and pepper to taste
½ c. mayonnaise
1 c. sweet green grapes or white seedless grapes, halved
1 c. pineapple, drained and chopped (opt.)
Olives
Pickles
½ c. salted almonds
Lettuce

Combine chicken, celery, lemon juice, salt, pepper, mayonnaise, grapes and pineapple, if desired. Mix thoroughly. Chill. Arrange in lettuce cups and garnish with olives, almonds and pickles.

This recipe submitted by the following teachers:

Mrs. Lucille R. Marker, Robertsdale H. S.
Robertsdale, Alabama

Opal Carpenter, Mentone H. S.
Mentone, Indiana

CHICKEN IN CHEESE SHELL

Number of Servings — 6

1½ c. sifted flour
½ t. salt
½ c. shortening
½ c. American cheese, shredded
4-5 T. cold water
1½ c. cooked or canned chicken, diced
1 9-oz. can pineapple tidbits, drained
1 c. walnuts, chopped
½ c. celery, chopped
1 c. sour cream
⅔ c. salad dressing

Combine ⅓ cup cheese and shortening. Add salt, flour and water. Bake in 8" pie pan at 450°F. for 12 minutes. Cool. Combine chicken, pineapple, nuts and celery. Blend sour cream and salad dressing; add ⅔ cup to chicken mixture. Spoon into pie shell; top with remaining sour cream mixture. Sprinkle with remaining cheese. Chill.

Mrs. Blanche Ivanish, Malta H. S.
Malta, Montana

CHICKEN SALAD

Number of Servings — 4

2 c. cooked chicken, skinned and cubed
Juice of ½ lemon or ¼ c. French Dressing
¾ c. mayonnaise or cream dressing

Sprinkle chicken with lemon juice or French dressing; let stand at least 1 hour. To each cup of chicken add ¼ to ½ cup mayonniase; mix thoroughly.

Dora G. Jones, Frankfort H. S.
Frankfort, Kansas

MOLDED CHICKEN SALAD

Number of Servings — 8-10

1 pkg. lemon gelatin
1 c. hot water
1 can cream of chicken soup
½ c. celery, chopped
¼ c. green pepper, diced
2 T. pimento, diced
1 t. onion, diced
1 c. cooked chicken, finely cut
Hard-cooked egg slices (garnish)

Dissolve gelatin in hot water. Cool. Add remaining ingredients. Chill. Garnish with egg slices. Serve on a bed of lettuce.

Mrs. Melvin Tavares, Kempton-Cabery H. S.
Kempton, Illinois

CHICKEN SALAD

Number of Servings — 8

2 c. cooked chicken, diced
1 c. celery, diced
1 T. lemon juice
Salt and pepper to taste
½ c. pineapple tidbits, quartered
Salad dressing
Sweet pickle juice
Celery salt
3-5 Mandarin orange sections
3 green grapes, left in bunch

Combine chicken, celery, lemon juice, pineapple, salt and pepper. Combine salad dressing, pickle juice and celery salt. Add enough to chicken mixture to moisten. Garnish with orange sections and grapes. Serve immediately. Salted almonds, green grapes or hard-cooked eggs may be substituted for pineapple if desired.

Mrs. James F. Massa, Winner Public School
Winner, South Dakota

CHICKEN SALAD

Number of Servings — 12

1 medium chicken, cooked
2 T. unflavored gelatin
¼ c. cold water
1½ T. lemon juice
Salt and pepper to taste
4 T. canned pimento
2 hard-cooked eggs, chopped
½ c. cooked peas
½ c. celery, finely cut
Chicken broth plus enough water to make 1 qt. liquid

Remove chicken from bones; cut into pieces. Soak gelatin in cold water. Add lemon juice to broth; heat until boiling. Remove from heat; add gelatin and remaining ingredients. Pour into a flat container so the mixture will be about 1½ inches deep. Chill.

Marguerite Holloway, Petersburg Harris H. S.
Petersburg, Illinois

CHICKEN SALAD

Number of Servings — 6

2 c. cooked chicken, cold and diced
1 c. celery, chopped into ½-inch pieces
1 T. lemon juice
Salt and pepper to taste
½ c. mayonnaise
2-3 hard-cooked eggs, diced
Parsley (opt.)
Lettuce
Olives (opt.)

Combine chicken, celery, lemon juice, salt and pepper. Toss. Add mayonnaise. Carefully fold in eggs. Chill thoroughly. Serve in lettuce cups. Garnish with olives or parsley if desired.

Mrs. Janice Strand, Lincoln H. S.
Floodwood, Minnesota

CHICKEN SALAD DELIGHT

Number of Servings — 15

1 pkg. lemon gelatin
2 c. hot chicken broth
1 c. mayonnaise
1 medium onion, grated
1½ c. cooked chicken, diced
1 c. celery, diced
1 green pepper, diced
4 hard-cooked eggs, diced
Stuffed olives, sliced

Dissolve gelatin in hot, chicken broth. Cool. Add mayonnaise and onion. Combine chicken, celery and pepper; Add to gelatin mixture. Chill. Garnish with eggs and olives.

Mrs. Meril T. Kenyon, Holyoke H. S.
Holyoke, Colorado

CHICKEN SALAD DINNER

Number of Servings — 4-6

Creamy French Dressing:
2 T. lemon juice
2 t. sugar
½ c. heavy cream
2 T. French dressing

Combine lemon juice, sugar and cream; whip until stiff. Blend in French dressing. Chill.

1½ c. cooked chicken, diced
¾ c. celery, diced
½ c. white grapes, halved or canned white cherries, drained
½ c. Creamy French Dressing
Salad greens
Ripe olive slices
Tomato wedges
Avocado slices

Combine chicken, celery and grapes or cherries. Add dressing. Serve on salad greens. Garnish with olive and avocado slices and tomato wedges.

Mrs. Mary Anne Moore, Sunnyslope H. S.
Phoenix, Arizona

CHICKEN SALAD

Number of Servings — 6-8

2 c. cold chicken, cubed
1 c. celery, diced
1 T. lemon juice
2 or 3 hard-cooked eggs, chopped
1 c. green grapes
½ c. pineapple, diced and drained
Mayonnaise to moisten
Salt and pepper to taste
Salted almonds, slivered (garnish)

Toss ingredients together; chill thoroughly. Garnish with almonds.

Mildred Christensen, Boscobel H. S.
Boscobel, Wisconsin

CHICKEN SALAD PIE

Number of Servings — 6

1 9-inch pie shell, baked and cooled
2 c. cooked chicken, chopped
¾ c. American cheese, shredded
½ c. celery, diced
½ c. crushed pineapple, drained
½ c. pecans, chopped
½ t. paprika
½ t. salt
¾ c. mayonnaise
½ c. cream
Carrots, shredded

Combine chicken, cheese, celery, pineapple, pecans, paprika, salt and ½ cup mayonnaise. Put into pie shell. Whip cream carefully by hand. Fold in remaining ¼ cup mayonnaise. Spread on pie. Garnish with carrots. Chill for 3 hours or overnight.

Mrs. Melba Smith, Grandview H. S.
Grandview, Texas

CHICKEN SALAD SUPREME

Number of Servings — 8

2½ c. cold cooked chicken, diced
1 c. celery, finely chopped
1 c. white grapes, sliced
½ c. toasted almonds, slivered
1-2 T. parsley, minced
¾-1 t. salt
½ c. whipped cream (opt.)
1 c. mayonnaise or salad dressing
Stuffed olives (garnish)
Chicken slices (garnish)
Lettuce

Combine all ingredients. Serve on lettuce. Garnish with olives and chicken slices if desired.

This recipe submitted by the following teachers:

Mrs. Grover C. Dear, Whitehaven H. S.
Memphis, Tennessee

Mrs. Dixie Black, Honey Grove H. S.
Honey Grove, Texas

Mrs. Bettye Keathley, Waco H. S.
Waco, Texas

Mary Light, King H. S.
Kingsville, Texas

CHICKEN SALAD STUFFED ROLLS

Number of Servings — 4-6

⅔ c. cooked chicken, chopped
¼ c. celery, chopped
⅛ t. salt
Pepper to taste (opt.)
2 T. pickle, chopped
3 T. mayonnaise
1 T. green pepper, chopped
1 hard-cooked egg, chopped
12 precooked rolls, unbaked

Combine all ingredients except rolls. Hollow out the rolls; stuff with salad mixture. Bake at 425°F. until rolls are hot and browned.

Agnes Dervishian, Caruthers H. S.
Caruthers, California

CHICKEN SALAD WITH RICE

Number of Servings — 6-8

⅔ c. precooked rice
1 c. water
1¼ t. salt
1 c. mayonnaise
1½ T. pimento, diced
¼ t. pepper
1½ c. cooked peas
1½ c. celery, diced
1½ c. cooked chicken, diced
Salad greens
Olives

Combine rice, water and ¼ teaspoon salt; mix until rice is moistened. Do not cover. Bring quickly to a boil while gently fluffing rice with a fork. Do not stir. Cover and remove from heat. Cool to room temperature. Mix mayonnaise, pimento, pepper and remaining salt. Add celery, peas, chicken and rice. Chill for 1 hour before serving. Place on salad greens and garnish with olives.

Nell Vaden, San Benito H. S.
San Benito, Texas

CHICKEN SOUP SALAD

Number of Servings — 6

1 envelope unflavored gelatin
¼ c. water
1 can chicken soup, heated
1 3-oz. pkg. cream cheese
Juice of 1 lemon
½ t. onion, grated
½ c. mayonnaise
1 carrot, grated
2 hard-cooked eggs, grated
½ c. celery, diced
¼ t. salt
1 c. cooked chicken, diced (opt.)

Soften gelatin in water. Pour hot chicken soup over gelatin. Cool. Mix cream cheese, mayonnaise and lemon juice. Add to gelatin mixture. Add remaining ingredients; chill.

Mrs. Evelyn Q. Webb, Columbia H. S.
Columbia, Mississippi

CHICKEN-SOUP LUNCHEON SALAD

Number of Servings — 4

1 T. unflavored gelatin
¼ c. cold water
¼ c. boiling water
1 can condensed chicken gumbo soup
½ c. salad dressing
½ c. celery, chopped
¼ c. green pepper, chopped
2 T. pimento, chopped
1 T. lemon juice
¼ t. salt
Pepper to taste
Ripe olives (garnish)
Hard-cooked eggs, sliced (garnish)
Asparagus spears (garnish)

Soften gelatin in cold water; add boiling water and stir until gelatin dissolves. Add remaining ingredients; mix well. Pour into individual molds; chill until firm. Serve on lettuce; garnish with olives, egg slices and asparagus spears.

Naomi K. Ingwalson, Chinook H. S.
Chinook, Montana

CHICKEN SALAD SUPREME

Number of Servings — 4-6

2 c. cooked chicken, cubed
2 T. green olives, cut
¾ c. celery, chopped
2 T. ripe olives, cut
2 T. mixed pickle, chopped
2 hard-cooked eggs, chopped
¾ c. mayonnaise

Combine all ingredients. Toss lightly.

Mrs. Richard P. Hempel, Lennox H. S.
Lennox, South Dakota

HOMEY CHICKEN SALAD

Number of Servings — 6-8

4-5 c. cooked or canned chicken, cubed
1 c. celery, cut at an angle
1 c. green pepper, minced
2 t. onion, grated
⅔ c. mayonnaise or cooked dressing
¼ c. light cream
1 t. salt
⅛ t. pepper
2 T. vinegar
1-2 c. pineapple chunks
Crisp greens
Cranberry or tart jelly

Combine chicken, salt, pepper, celery, green pepper, onion, pineapple and vinegar. Mix cream with mayonnaise or cooked dressing; Toss well with chicken mixture. Refrigerate. Serve on crisp greens; garnish with cranberry or tart jelly.

Mrs. Esther M. Hight, Weare H. S.
Weare, New Hampshire

CHICKEN SURPRISE

Number of Servings — 6-8

4 c. cooked chicken, diced
4 hard-cooked eggs, diced
1 c. celery, diced
¾ c. salad dressing
1 c. seedless green grapes
¾ c. almonds, slivered
1 t. lemon juice
Salt and pepper to taste

Combine chicken, eggs, celery and salad dressing. Add grapes, almonds, lemon juice, salt and pepper. Garnish as desired with tomato wedges, grapefruit or avocado sections or tiny canned shrimp.

Mrs. Jeanette Bogue, Clara City Public School
Clara City, Minnesota

CRUNCHY CHICKEN SALAD

Number of Servings — 4-6

1 c. raw carrots, shredded
¼ c. onion, minced
1 c. celery, diced
1 c. cooked chicken, diced
½ c. salad dressing, thinned with cream
1 T. pickle relish
1 can shoestring potatoes

Combine vegetables with dressing and relish. Add chicken and shoestring potatoes just before serving. If desired tuna may be substituted for chicken.

Mrs. Delores Sandbeck, Dilworth H. S.
Dilworth, Minnesota

CRANBERRY-TURKEY OR CHICKEN LOAF

Cranberry Layer:
1 envelope unflavored gelatin
1 qt. fresh cranberry sauce
½ c. walnuts, chopped
¼ c. cold water
1 9-oz. can crushed pineapple, undrained

Soften gelatin in cold water; dissolve over hot water. Break up cranberry sauce; stir in pineapple. Add walnuts. Blend in dissolved gelatin. Pour into a lightly oiled mold. Chill until firm.

Turkey or Chicken Layer:
1 envelope unflavored gelatin
½ c. mayonnaise
2 c. turkey or chicken, diced
½ c. celery
½ t. salt
¼ c. cold water
½ c. evaporated milk, undiluted
1 c. parsley, finely chopped
⅛ t. pepper
Spiced red crab apples (garnish)

Soften gelatin in cold water; dissolve over hot water. Combine mayonnaise and milk; blend in gelatin. Stir in turkey or chicken, celery, parsley, salt and pepper; blend well. Carefully spoon over cranberry layer. Chill 3 to 4 hours. Garnish with parsley and crab apples.

Miss Clyde R. Smith, Sudlersville H. S.
Sudlersville, Maryland

CURRIED CHICKEN AND GRAPE SALAD

Number of Servings — 6

3 c. cooked chicken, diced
1½ c. celery, thinly sliced
1 c. green seedless grapes
2 T. lemon juice
1¼ t. salt
¼ t. black pepper, freshly ground
1½ t. curry powder
6 T. mayonnaise
3 T. toasted almonds, slivered

Combine all ingredients; toss lightly. Chill. Serve on lettuce; garnish with almonds.

Lois Pullen, State Department of Education
Baton Rouge, Louisiana

DOUBLE DECKER SALAD

Number of Servings — 8

1 pkg. strawberry gelatin
1 c. boiling water
½ c. cold water
1 1-lb. can whole cranberry sauce
¾ c. pecans, chopped

Dissolve gelatin in boiling water; add cold water. Chill until mixture is the consistency of egg whites. Fold in cranberry sauce and pecans. Chill until firm.

1 pkg. lemon gelatin
½ c. cold water
½ c. celery, diced
¼ c. almonds, chopped
1 c. hot water
2 c. cooked chicken, diced
¼ c. mayonnaise

Dissolve gelatin in hot water; add cold water. Chill until mixture is the consistency of egg whites. Fold in remaining ingredients. Pour over firm strawberry-cranberry layer. Chill until firm.

Nina Swindler, Newbern H. S.
Newbern, Tennessee

GINGER-CREAM CHICKEN SALAD

Number of Servings — 12

6 c. cooked chicken, diced
3 c. celery, diced
3 t. salt
½ t. pepper
6 T. candied ginger, finely chopped
3 t. honey
3 c. sour cream
Paprika
Lettuce

Combine chicken, celery, salt and pepper. Chill for 2 hours. Just before serving combine honey, ginger and sour cream. Stir half of ginger mixture into chicken mixture. Spoon onto a bed of lettuce. Top with remaining ginger mixture. Sprinkle with paprika.

Mrs. Ruby Thompson King
Hahira, Georgia

FAR WEST CHICKEN SALAD

Number of Servings — 4

1 can pears
1 t. red food coloring
1 can chicken
1 c. celery, diced
½ c. walnuts, chopped
¼ c. green pepper, chopped
¼ t. salt
Dash of pepper
¼-½ c. salad dressing or mayonnaise
Salad greens
Olives

Drain pears; combine juice and food coloring. Add pears; let stand for 10 minutes. Combine chicken, celery, walnuts and green pepper. Add salt and pepper with enough salad dressing or mayonnaise to moisten ingredients. Arrange with pears on salad greens. Serve with additional salad dressing and olives.

Laura Mae Pernice, H. B. Turner Junior H. S.
Warren, Ohio

FROZEN CHICKEN SALAD

Number of Servings — 8

1½ c. cooked chicken, diced
¾ c. crushed pineapple, drained
¾ c. pecans, chopped
1 c. whipping cream
1 c. mayonnaise

Toss chicken, pineapple and nuts together. Blend whipped cream and salad dressing; fold into chicken mixture. Freeze until firm.

Myrtle Cummings, Buna H. S.
Buna, Texas

LUNCHEON OR FRUITED CHICKEN SALAD

Number of Servings — 6-8

2 c. cooked chicken or canned white meat, cubed
1 c. orange sections
¼-½ c. grapes, seeded and halved
¼-½ c. toasted or salted almonds or pecans, slivered
1-2 bananas, sliced
¾-1 c. mayonnaise or salad dressing

Chill ingredients. Combine, using enough mayonnaise to moisten. Serve on crisp lettuce or pineapple slices with watercress garnish. Salad may be garnished with whole strawberries if desired.

This recipe submitted by the following teachers:

Elizabeth Chenoweth, Consultant,
State Department of Education
Corpus Christi, Texas

Mrs. Baben J. Patricelli, Conniston Junior H. S.
West Palm Beach, Florida

HOT BAKED CHICKEN SALAD

Number of Servings — 6

2 c. chicken, chopped
2 c. celery, chopped
½ c. pecans or almonds, chopped
1 c. salad dressing or mayonnaise
½ t. salt
2 t. onion, minced (opt.)
2 T. lemon juice
½ c. cheese, grated
1 c. potato chips, crushed
2 hard-cooked eggs, chopped (opt.)

Combine chicken, celery, pecans, salad dressing, salt, lemon juice and onion. Pour into a greased casserole dish. Mix remaining ingredients. Sprinkle over casserole. Bake at 450°F. for 10 minutes.

This recipe submitted by the following teachers:

Ann Derrick, Amarillo H. S.
Amarillo, Texas

Patricia Cron, Central H. S.
Crosby, Minnesota

Mrs. Sue Duty, Halls H. S.
Knoxville, Tennessee

Miss Willie Hawkins
Lovelady, Texas

HOT CHICKEN SALAD

Number of Servings — 6

2 c. stewed chicken
1 c. celery, diced
3 hard-coked eggs, diced
½ c. mayonnaise
1 T. lemon juice
1 can cream of chicken soup
1 can water chestnuts or ⅓ c. almonds, slivered
Salt and pepper to taste
Potato chips, crushed

Mix all ingredients except potato chips. Cover with crushed potato chips. Bake at 400°F. for 20 minutes.

Margaret Hefner Peden, Hoke County H. S.
Raeford, North Carolina

HOT CHICKEN SALAD

Number of Servings — 8

2 c. cooked chicken, diced
2 c. celery, chopped
1 c. nuts
1 c. mayonnaise
3 T. onion, chopped
2 T. Worcestershire sauce
2 T. lemon juice
½ c. plain potato chips, crushed
½ c. barbecued potato chips crushed

Mix all ingredients except potato chips. Sprinkle potato chips over top. Bake for 20 minutes at 350°F.

Mrs. Myrtle G. Allen, Berkeley H. S.
Moncks Corner, South Carolina

HAWAIIAN CHICKEN SALAD

Number of Servings — 8

2½ c. cooked chicken cut in ½-inch squares
1 14-oz. can pineapple tidbits, drained
1 c. celery, cut in ½-inch pieces
3 T. salad oil
2 T. lemon juice
¼ t. salt
5 T. mayonnaise
¼ c. almonds, shredded

Combine chicken, pineapple and celery. Mix salad oil, lemon juice and salt. Marinate chicken mixture in dressing for 1 hour. Add mayonnaise; mix well. Serve on lettuce. Garnish with almonds.

Mrs. Essie Stanley, Saltillo H. S.
Saltillo, Texas

MOLDED CHICKEN OR TURKEY SALAD

Number of Servings — 8

1 pkg. lemon gelatin
1 c. boiling water
½ c. cold water
2 T. lemon juice
½ c. mayonnaise
½ t. salt
1 c. cooked chicken or turkey
½ c. Mandarin oranges or ½ c. seeded grapes
½ c. celery, finely cut
½ c. pineapple, diced

Dissolve gelatin in boiling water. Add cold water, lemon juice, mayonnaise and salt. Beat until well blended. Chill until partially set. Add remaining ingredients. Mold as desired. Chill until firm.

Mrs. Frances G. Carr, Mohawk H. S.
Bessemer, Pennsylvania

MOLDED CHICKEN SALAD

Number of Servings — 4

1 envelope unflavored gelatin
¼ c. cold chicken broth or bouillon
½ c. hot chicken stock or bouillon
¼ t. salt
1 t. lemon juice
¾ c. mayonnaise or salad dressing
1 c. cooked chicken, diced
3 T. green pepper, minced
¾ c. celery, diced

Soften gelatin in cold chicken broth in top of double boiler. Add hot stock and salt; Stir over boiling water until gelatin is dissolved. Cool. Stir in lemon juice and mayonnaise. Combine gelatin mixture with chicken, green pepper and celery. Pour into a large or 4 individual molds. Chill.

Jo Collier, Pleasant Hill Community H. S.
Pleasant Hill, Illinois

MOLDED CHICKEN SALAD

Number of Servings — 15

5-6 lb. cooked chicken, cubed
1 pkg. unflavored gelatin
¼ c. cold water
1 c. hot chicken broth
1 t. salt
1 T. Worcestershire sauce
3 hard-cooked eggs, chopped
2 c. celery, chopped
1 c. English peas
1 c. pecans, chopped
1 pt. mayonnaise

Soften gelatin in cold water; dissolve in hot broth. Add salt and Worcestershire sauce. Cool. Add remaining ingredients in order. Chill thoroughly.

Mrs. Ruth Martin, Senior H. S.
Weatherford, Texas

PRESSED CHICKEN SALAD

Number of Servings — 24

5 c. cooked chicken, chopped
1½ c. celery, chopped
6 hard-cooked eggs, chopped
1 envelope unflavored gelatin
½ c. cold water
2 c. hot chicken broth
Juice of 1 lemon
1 c. mayonnaise
1 c. pickle relish
1 t. salt

Soak gelatin in cold water; add hot broth and lemon juice. Combine remaining ingredients; mix with gelatin-broth mixture. Chill until firm.

Mrs. Rebecca McGaughy, Montevallo H. S.
Montevallo, Alabama

SUPPER MAIN DISH SALAD

Number of Servings — 6

1 pkg. lemon gelatin
1 c. boiling water
½ t. salt
1 T. onion, grated
½ c. mayonnaise
½ c. heavy cream
3 hard-cooked eggs, coarsely chopped
½ lb. pimento cheese, cubed
½ green pepper, finely cut
3 c. celery, finely cut
½ c. walnuts, broken
1 c. chicken, shrimp or tuna, cut in pieces

Mix gelatin, salt and onion in boiling water. Let stand until mixture starts to set. Mix cream and mayonnaise with electric beater. Fold into gelatin mixture. Toss remaining ingredients together and fold into the gelatin mixture. Mold as desired. Serve without dressing.

Mrs. Jessye MacKay, Pollock H. S.
Pollock, South Dakota

PARADISE SALAD

Number of Servings — 6-8

3 c. bananas, diced
½ c. crushed pineapple
1½ c. cooked chicken, chopped
¼ c. celery, chopped
¼ t. salt
½ c. pecans, chopped (opt.)
Lettuce
Olives
Mayonnaise

Combine bananas and pineapple. Add chicken, celery, salt, and pecans if desired. Add enough mayonnaise to moisten. Toss lightly. Serve on lettuce. Garnish with olives.

Mrs. Katherine Potter, Frontenac H. S.
Frontenac, Kansas

PERFECT LUNCHEON SALAD

Number of Servings — 8

1 pkg. lemon gelatin
1 c. boiling water
½ t. salt
1 T. onion, grated
½ c. mayonnaise
½ c. heavy cream
3 hard-cooked eggs, coarsely chopped
¼ lb. pimento cheese, cubed
¼ green pepper, finely chopped
3 c. celery, finely chopped
1 c. cooked chicken, diced

Dissolve gelatin in boiling water; add salt and onion. Let stand until partially set. Fold in mayonnaise and cream. Chill. Combine remaining ingredients. Fold into gelatin mixture.

Mrs. Edith Jorgensen, Bridgewater H. S.
Bridgewater, South Dakota

TALK OF THE TOWN SALAD

Number of Servings — 4

1 small head lettuce, torn
2 tomatoes, cut as desired
¼ c. celery, diced
1 4-oz. can mushrooms
⅛ c. Velveeta cheese, diced
2 T. Bleu cheese, diced
⅔ c. canned peas or French-cut beans
8 stuffed olives, sliced
½ t. onion salt
Dash of garlic salt
1½ c. chicken, crab, lobster, shrimp or combination
1 t. lemon juice (for seafood)
French dressing
Salt and pepper to taste
1 c. cooked macaroni (opt.)

Toss all ingredients together in a large salad bowl.

Annabelle Wikkerink, H. S.
Amery, Wisconsin

SILHOUETTE SALAD

Number of Servings — 4

1 envelope unflavored gelatin
1 can cream of chicken soup
1 c. cold water
1 T. lemon juice
Dash of black pepper
1 can boned chicken or turkey
½ c. celery, chopped
¼ c. green pepper, chopped
2 T. pimento, chopped
2 t. onion, grated

Soften gelatin in ½ cup cold water; dissolve over boiling water. Blend soup with remaining ½ cup cold water, lemon juice and black pepper. Stir until smooth. Add gelatin; mix thoroughly. Chill until mixture is consistency of unbeaten egg whites. Fold in chicken or turkey, celery, green pepper, pimento and onion. Pour into a 3-cup mold. Chill until firm. Each serving has 140 calories.

Mrs. Wilma B. Russell, Sterling Regional H. S.
Somerdale, New Jersey

SOUR CREAM-CHICKEN MOUSSE

Number of Servings — 8

2 envelopes unflavored gelatin
½ c. cold water
2 c. boiling water
4 chicken boullion cubes
3 T. lemon juice
1 t. dry mustard
2½ t. curry powder
1 t. onion salt
2 c. sour cream
3 c. cooked chicken, diced
1 c. celery, chopped
¼ c. green pepper, chopped
¼ c. roasted almonds, diced

Soften gelatin in cold water. Pour boiling water over boullion cubes; stir until dissolved. Add lemon juice, mustard, curry powder and onion salt. Pour boullion mixture over gelatin; stir until gelatin is dissolved. Cool for 5 minutes. Stir in sour cream; mix well. Refrigerate until mixture reaches the consistency of unbeaten egg whites. Add chicken, celery, green pepper and almonds; mix well. Chill until firm.

Evelyne Dealy, Meridian H. S.
Bellingham, Washington

SPECIAL BRIDGE CHICKEN SALAD

Number of Servings — 12

1 stewing hen
Onion slices
Salt
1 bay leaf
1 c. celery, diced
1 No. 2½ can diced pineapple
1½ c. white seedless grapes
¾ c. almonds, sliced
2 c. lettuce, chopped
Salt to taste

Cook hen with salt, onion slices and bay leaf. Remove meat from bones; skin. Cut meat into bite-size pieces. Combine all ingredients.

DRESSING:

¾ c. mayonnaise
¾ t. curry powder

Mix dressing ingredients. Add to chicken mixture. Chill. Serve on lettuce cups and garnish with stuffed olives. Note: If salad is to be prepared in advance do not add chopped lettuce until just before serving.

Mrs. Jennie June Magnuson, Woodburn H. S.
Woodburn, Oregon

HOT TURKEY OR CHICKEN SALAD

Number of Servings — 5-6

2 c. cooked turkey or chicken, chopped
2 c. celery, finely sliced
½ c. toasted almonds, chopped
½ t. salt
2 t. onion, grated
2 T. lemon juice
1 c. mayonnaise
½ c. cheese, grated
1 c. potato chips, crushed

Combine all ingredients except cheese and potato chips. Pile lightly into individual baking dishes or a casserole. Sprinkle with grated cheese and potato chips. Bake about 10 minutes at 450°F. or until mixture bubbles.

Mrs. Helene Baer Maneval, Sonora Union H. S.
Sonora, California

TURKEY SALAD SUPREME

Number of Servings — 4-6

2 c. cooked turkey, diced
2 c. celery, diced
1 c. mayonnaise or salad dressing
Salt and pepper to taste
Lemon juice to taste
Cranberry sauce (opt.)
Variations (opt.)
½ c. avocado, diced
2 T. chopped hard-cooked egg
2 T. chopped green pepper
1 t. finely grated onion
1 c. pineapple, diced
1 c. seedless white grapes
¼-½ c. toasted almonds, slivered

Combine turkey, celery and mayonniase or salad dressing. Add any desired optional ingredients except almonds. Season to taste with lemon juice, salt and pepper. Chill. Just before serving add almonds if desired. Serve on salad greens. Garnish with cranberry sauce if desired.

Janet Linse, Rice Lake H. S.
Rice Lake, Wisconsin

BAKED TURKEY SALAD

Number of Servings — 10

2 c. cooked turkey, diced
2 c. celery, diced
½ t. salt
1 T. onion, minced
½ c. nuts, chopped
1 c. mayonnaise
2 T. lemon juice
½ c. stuffed olives, sliced
½ c. Cheddar cheese, grated
1 c. potato chips, finely crushed

Combine all ingredients except cheese and potato chips. Spoon into buttered 1½-quart casserole. Combine cheese and potato chips; sprinkle over turkey mixture. Bake in 375°F. oven for 20 minutes. Serve hot.

Mary Ella Ingram, Wagram H. S.
Wagram, North Carolina

COLD TURKEY SALAD

Number of Servings — 8

1 c. turkey, chopped
1 c. lettuce, chopped
1 c. celery, chopped
½ c. pecans, chopped
½ c. salad dressing
½ c. Shedd's Old Style
Dressing
¼ c. chili sauce
½ t. salt

Combine turkey, lettuce, celery and pecans. Combine remaining ingredients; Add to turkey mixture. Serve on lettuce if desired.

Mable Elrod Allen, Joppa Community H. S.
Joppa, Illinois

TURKEY SALAD

Number of Servings — 4

2 T. vinegar
2 t. water
½ t. salt
¼ t. sugar
2½ c. cold turkey, cut into ½-inch cubes
½ c. celery, coarsely diced
½ c. Tokay grapes, halved and seeded
½ c. mayonnaise
8 or 10 sl. stuffed or ripe olives
2 hard-cooked eggs sliced
Salad greens

Combine vinegar, water, salt and sugar; drizzle over turkey. Toss lightly. Cover and refrigerate 2 to 3 hours. Chill celery and grapes. Combine turkey, celery, grapes and mayonniase; Toss lightly with a fork. Arrange on crisp greens; garnish with olives and eggs. Serve immediately.

Adaline Grissom Thomas, Jr.-Sr. H. S.
Sidney, Montana

HOT TURKEY SALAD

Number of Servings — 4

3 c. cooked turkey, cubed
1 c. sharp cheese, cubed
1 c. celery, chopped
½ c. almonds, slivered
½ c. mayonnaise
1 c. potato chips, crushed
Salt and pepper to taste

Toss together all ingredients except potato chips. Place in individual casseroles. Sprinkle potato chips over the top. Bake for 35 minutes in 325°F. oven.

Mrs. Audrey Johnson, Kickapoo Area School
Viola, Wisconsin

TURKEY SALAD

Number of Servings — 50

1 14-lb. turkey
2 qt. celery, diced
2 qt. seedless green grapes
18 hard-cooked eggs, diced
2 c. toasted almonds, slivered
Salt
Parsley
Onions, quartered
Celery, cut in large pieces
Dressing:
1 pt. whipped cream
1 qt. salad dressing
¼ c. vinegar
¼ c. sugar
Salt to taste

Clean turkey well; season with salt inside and out. Stuff with large pieces of celery, quartered onions and a little parsley. Place in a covered roaster and bake at 325°F. until meat begins to leave bones. Remove from oven; remove lid and cool. Cut into desired size pieces. Combine dressing ingredients. Mix with turkey and remaining ingredients. Chill several hours before serving.

Marie Strand, Stillwater Junior H. S.
Stillwater, Minnesota

TURKEY-ALMOND SALAD

Number of Servings — 6-8

2 c. cooked turkey, cubed
1 c. red grapes, seeded and chopped
⅓ c. celery, diced
½ c. almonds, toasted
Salad dressing

Combine turkey, grapes, celery and almonds. Add enough salad dressing to moisten. Serve on lettuce.

Ila Rea, Dayton Joint H. S.
Dayton, Pennsylvania

Seafood Salads

AVOCADOS STUFFED WITH CRAB MEAT

Number of Servings — 1

1 avocado half
½ c. crab meat
Mayonnaise
Chili sauce
Salt
Pepper
Lemon juice
Shredded lettuce
Shredded carrot
Shredded radish
Tomato strips (opt.)

Mix crab meat with a dressing made by blending equal parts of mayonnaise and chili sauce. Season to taste with salt, pepper and lemon juice. Place avocado half on bed of shredded vegetables and fill with crab mixture. Top with mayonnaise and thin strips of tomato if desired.

Shirley L. Andersen, Enterprise H. S.
Enterprise, Oregon

AVOCADO-CRAB MEAT SALAD

Number of Servings — 4

1 6½-oz. can crab meat, flaked
½ c. celery, diced
1 tomato, diced
4 stuffed olives, chopped
½ c. mayonnaise
2 avocados, halved
1 hard-cooked egg
1 t. lemon juice
Watercress

Combine crab, celery, tomato, olives and mayonnaise. Sprinkle avocado halves with lemon juice. Pile crab mixture into avocado halves. Garnish with egg and watercress.

Mrs. Pat Folland, Cory-Rawson H. S.
Rawson, Ohio

BAYLEY'S WEST INDIES SALAD

Number of Servings — 6

1 lb. fresh lump crab meat
1 medium onion, finely chopped
4 oz. salad oil
3 oz. cider vinegar
4 oz. ice water
Salt and pepper

Place half of the chopped onion in bottom of bowl. Separate crab meat lumps; place on top of onion. Spread remaining onion over crab meat. Salt and pepper to taste. Pour oil, then vinegar and lastly ice water over crab-onion. Cover and refrigerate from 2-12 hours. Toss lightly just before serving.

Grace Lunsford, Foley School
Foley, Alabama

BOWL 'EM OVER SALAD

Number of Servings — 6-8

½ c. water
¼ c. butter or margarine
½ c. flour
⅛ t. salt
½-1 t. caraway seed
2 eggs

Preheat oven to 400°F. Bring water and butter to a boil in saucepan. Immediately stir in flour, salt and caraway seed. Stir vigorously over low heat for about 1 minute until mixture leaves sides of pan and forms a ball. Remove from heat; cool about 10 minutes. Add eggs, one at a time, beating until smooth after each addition. Spread batter evenly in bottom of greased 9-inch glass pie plate. Do not spread batter up the sides of the plate. Bake 45-50 minutes. Cool slowly away from drafts. The puff will form a bowl, high on the sides and flat in the center.

Filling:
1 c. tuna or crab meat, chopped
1 c. celery, diced
1 c. lettuce hearts, broken in small pieces
1 t. lemon juice
1 t. onion, finely minced
Salt and paprika to taste
Mayonnaise

Combine all ingredients, adding mayonnaise just before serving. Fill puffs with mixture.

Mrs. Abbie Kehl, LaVega H. S.
Waco, Texas

CRAB LOUIS

Number of Servings — 4

Louis Dressing:
1 c. mayonnaise
¼ c. sour cream
¼ c. chili sauce
¼ c. green onion, chopped
1 t. lemon juice
Salt

Combine mayonnaise, sour cream, chili sauce, onion and lemon juice. Salt to taste. Chill. Makes 2 cups dressing.

1 lge. head lettuce
2-3 c. cooked crab meat, chilled
2 lge. tomatoes, cut in wedges
2 hard-cooked eggs, cut in wedges

Line 4 large plates with lettuce leaves. Shred remaining lettuce; arrange on leaves. Arrange crab meat on lettuce. Circle with tomato and egg wedges. Sprinkle with salt. Pour ¼ cup Louis Dressing over each salad. Sprinkle with paprika. Pass remaining dressing.

Betty Ann McCullough, Conneaut Lake Area H. S.
Conneaut Lake, Pennsylvania

CRAB SALAD

Number of Servings — 16

2 pkgs. lemon gelatin
2 c. boiling water
Juice of 1 lemon
Dash of salt
1 c. celery, diced
6 hard-cooked eggs, diced
1 small jar stuffed olives, sliced
1 pt. whipped cream

Dissolve gelatin in boiling water; add lemon and salt. Chill until slightly thickened. Fold in celery, eggs, olives and whipped cream. Chill firm. Serve with crab topping.

Topping:
1 pt. mayonnaise, thinned with cream
2 cans crab meat, flaked
1 sweet pickle, diced

Combine all ingredients.

Dorothy Deare O'Rear, Bellevue Sr. H. S.
Bellevue, Washington

CRAB SALAD IN ORANGE SHELLS

Number of Servings — 8

8 oranges
2 6½-oz. cans crab meat, flaked
1 c. celery, minced
1 c. orange segments, diced
1 t. onion, grated
½ c. mayonnaise

Cut blossom end off oranges and snip rind in points. Scoop out fruit. Lightly toss crab meat with celery, orange, onion and mayonnaise. Heap into orange shells. Chill thoroughly. Garnish with additional mayonnaise.

Mrs. Violet Horne, Forest Hills
Marshville, North Carolina

HOT OR COLD DEVILED CRAB SALAD

Number of Servings — 6-8

1 6½-oz. can crab meat, flaked
½ c. celery, diced
6 stuffed olives, chopped
2 hard-cooked eggs, chopped
½ c. salad dressing
½ t. Worcestershire sauce
½ t. salt
¼ t. black pepper
½ t. paprika
Avocado halves or lettuce leaves

Combine crab, celery, olives, eggs, salad dressing and seasonings. Mix well. If avocado halves are used, sprinkle them with 1 tablespoon lemon juice and chill. Fill avocado halves or lettuce leaves with crab mixture. Garnish with parsley, paprika or hard-cooked egg slices. For a hot salad omit the salad dressing and add ½ cup medium white sauce to other ingredients. Form mixture into patties; roll in cracker meal. Fry in deep fat until golden brown.

Sister M. Daniel SS.C.M., Andrean H. S.
Gary, Indiana

CAPETOWN LOBSTER SALAD

Number of Servings — 6

6 frozen lobster tails
2 cups cooked rice
1 c. mayonnaise or salad dressing
2 T. lemon juice
6 lettuce cups or other salad greens
½ t. onion salt
Dash of cayenne pepper
1 c. celery, diced
½ c. stuffed olives, sliced
Lemon slices

Boil lobster tails according to package directions. Thoroughly remove meat from shells so they will lie flat. Blend mayonnaise and lemon juice, salt and pepper. Combine with cubed lobster meat and rice. Chill. Add celery and olives at serving time. Spoon mixture into lettuce cups; arrange on platter alternately with lobster shells filled with additional dressing for serving. Garnish with lemon slices.

Jean Carolyn Leis, Buhler Rural H. S.
Buhler, Kansas

LOBSTER AND CHICKEN SALAD

Number of Servings — 4-6

1 chicken breast, cooked
½ lb. lobster meat, cooked and diced
French dressing
3 hard-cooked eggs
1 c. celery, finely chopped
1 c. mayonnaise
Salt to taste
2 T. chili sauce
1 T. chives, chopped
½ c. whipped cream
Lettuce

Cut chicken into strips. Marinate lobster and chicken in a little French dressing with chopped egg whites and celery for about an hour. Mash or sieve egg yolks and blend with mayonnaise, chili sauce, chives and salt. Fold in whipped cream. Chill. Mix chicken, lobster and dressing. Serve on lettuce.

Margaret K. Shollenberger, Rice Ave. Union H. S.
Girard, Pennsylvania

LOBSTER MOUSSE

Number of Servings — 6

1 T. unflavored gelatin
¼ c. water
¾ c. celery, minced
1½ c. canned or cooked lobster meat
⅔ c. apple, minced
¾ c. mayonnaise
3 T. lemon juice
Salt
Paprika
⅓ c. whipped cream
Watercress
Marinated cucumbers

Soak gelatin in water; dissolve over boiling water. Combine celery, lobster, apple, mayonnaise and lemon juice. Season with salt and paprika. Add gelatin; whip until mixture is stiff. Fold in cream. Place the mousse in a wet mold; chill thoroughly. Unmold on a platter, garnish with watercress and marinated cucumbers.

Gloria Shelton, Clarksville H. S.
Clarksville, Tennessee

LOBSTER SALAD

Number of Servings — 6

2 c. lobster meat, cut up
1 c. celery, finely diced
3 hard-cooked eggs, chopped
¼ t. salt
⅛ t. pepper
Mayonnaise

Combine all ingredients with enough mayonnaise to moisten. Chill. Serve on lettuce leaves.

Mrs. Genevieve Snyder, Cocalico Union Sr. H. S.
Denver, Pennsylvania

OYSTER SALAD

Number of Servings — 12

2 No. 1 cans oysters, undrained
1 medium can pimentos
8 hard-cooked eggs
4 sour pickles
4 T. margarine, melted
30 soda crackers
Salt and vinegar to taste

Grind all ingredients together; mix well. Add salt and vinegar to taste.

Mrs. Joyzelle Sauls,
Brownsville H. S.
Brownsville, Texas

BANANA-SALMON SALAD

Number of Servings — 4-5

3 ripe bananas, chopped
½ c. canned pineapple
1½ c. canned flaked salmon
¼ c. celery, diced
½ t. salt
1 T. sweet pickles, chopped
Mayonnaise

Mix bananas and pineapple; add salmon. Fold in remaining ingredients with enough mayonnaise to moisten. Garnish with lettuce and lemon slices.

Mrs. Margaret Rettke, Mason County Central H. S.
Scottville, Michigan

CRISPY SALMON SALAD

1-pound can salmon, flaked and drained
⅔ c. ripe olives, cut in large pieces
1 c. celery, sliced
1 c. lettuce, shredded
⅔ c. mayonnaise
2 T. lemon juice
1 t. onion, grated
Dash of pepper
2 c. potato chips, coarsely crushed

Remove dark skin and bones from salmon. Combine salmon, olives, celery and lettuce. Blend together mayonnaise, lemon juice, onion and pepper; add salmon mixture. Add potato chips and mix lightly just before serving.

Judy Harms, Tyler Public School
Tyler, Minnesota

SALMON SALAD MOLD

Number of Servings — 6

2 T. unflavored gelatin
½ c. cold water
⅓ c. lemon juice
2 c. flaked red salmon
1 c. salad dressing
1 c. celery, chopped
¼ c. green pepper, chopped
1 t. onion, chopped
Salt and pepper to taste

Soften gelatin in cold water; dissolve over hot water. Add lemon juice. When cold, mix lightly with remaining ingredients. Pour into lightly oiled fish mold; Chill until firm.

Alberta Ball Bickerdike, East Pike School
Milton, Illinois

SALMON SALAD

Number of Servings — 6

2 c. cooked shell macaroni
½ t. salt
2 c. salmon, flaked
4 hard-cooked eggs, diced
½ c. celery, diced
½ c. processed cheese, diced
2 medium tomatoes, diced
½ c. salad dressing

Mix macaroni, salmon, eggs; celery and cheese. Add salt, tomatoes and salad dressing; mix lightly. Chill.

Frances Watson, Lake H. S.
Millbury, Ohio

SALMON SALAD

Number of Servings — 10-12

1-pound can red salmon
Juice of ½ lemon
1 c. celery, diced
¼ c. onion, diced
¾ c. sweet cucumber pickles, diced or 1 c. fresh cucumber, diced
1 c. nuts, coarsely broken
1 c. mayonnaise
1 hard-cooked egg, diced (Opt.)
¼ c. green pepper, diced or stuffed olives, sliced (Opt.)

Remove bones and skin from salmon; drain. Break salmon into ½-inch chunks and marinate in lemon juice. Combine with remaining ingredients just before serving. Serve on bed of watercress or lettuce.

Lily Carlson, Mora Public Schools
Mora, Minnesota

SALMON SALAD

Number of Servings — 6-8

4 c. cabbage, shredded
1 1-lb. can salmon, drained
2 c. tomato chunks
⅓ c. mayonnaise

Chill cabbage, salmon and tomatoes. Add mayonnaise and toss lightly until all are combined.

Kathryn Dean, Greeneview H. S.
Jamestown, Ohio

SALMON-MACARONI SALAD

Number of Servings — 3-4

1 c. cooked macaroni
1 c. salmon, shredded
2 T. lemon juice
½ c. pickle, chopped
2 T. onion, finely chopped
Salt
Pepper
Paprika
Mayonnaise
Shredded cabbage

Cook macaroni according to package directions; rinse in cold water and drain. Combine macaroni, salmon, lemon juice, onion and pickle. Moisten with mayannaise. Season to taste and mix lightly with 2 forks. Chill. Serve on a bed of crisp, shredded cabbage.

Miss Lois Gruneberg, Layaleock Township
Jr.-Sr. H. S.
Williamsport, Pennsylvania

BRIGHT JEWEL SALAD

Number of Servings — 8

1 pkg. lemon gelatin
1 c. hot water
1 t. salt
¼ t. garlic salt
Dash of pepper
1 T. vinegar
½ c. cold water
1 c. cooked shrimp, cut in ½-inch pieces
1 avocado, diced

Dissolve gelatin in hot water. Add seasonings, vinegar and cold water. Pour into an 8-inch square pan. Chill until slightly thickened. Add shrimp and avocado pieces arranged so they will be in small cubes when cut. Chill until firm. Cut into 1-inch squares.

Salad Base:

1½ c. grapefruit sections
1 c. tomato, diced
1 c. cheese cut in thin strips (opt.)
½ c. ripe olives, sliced
¼ c. green onions, chopped
3 qt. salad greens

Combine ingredients and toss lightly. Arrange shrimp and avocado squares on top. Serve with favorite salad dressing.

Mrs. Loretta Fowler Bennett
Edgar Allan Poe Inter. School
Annandale, Virginia

CARROT AND SHRIMP SALAD

Number of Servings — 6-8

1 c. seedless raisins
1 c. celery, sliced
2 c. carrots, shredded
2 t. unflavored gelatin
1 T. cold water
1 c. cleaned shrimp, broken in pieces
1 c. mayonnaise
1 c. cottage cheese
12 stuffed olives, sliced
½ t. salt

Soak gelatin in cold water; dissolve over hot water. Mix with mayonnaise and salt. Combine shrimp, raisins, celery, carrots, olives and cheese. Carefully gold into mayonnaise mixture with forks to prevent mashing. Pour into mold or individual molds and chill. Serve with additional salad dressing.

Carolyn M. Smet, New Market H. S.
Newmarket, New Hampshire

SHRIMP SALAD

Number of Servings — 4

1 c. shrimp, chopped
1 c. celery, diced
1 c. lettuce hearts, cut in small pieces
1 t. lemon juice
1 t. onion, finely minced
Salt and paprika to taste

Mix all ingredients lightly. Chill. Just before serving, drain and toss together with mayonnaise to moisten. Serve on crisp lettuce.

Meredith Hansen, Box Elder H. S.
Brigham City, Utah

CONGEALED SHRIMP SALAD

Number of Servings — 8

1 can tomato soup
2 small pkg. cream cheese
2 T. unflavored gelatin
½ c. cold water
1 can small shrimp
2 T. onion, grated
2 T. green pepper, chopped
½ c. salad dressing

Soften gelatin in cold water. Bring soup to a boil. Dissolve cream cheese in soup. Add gelatin and stir until dissolved. Cool. Add shrimp, onion, pepper and salad dressing. Pour into individual molds or large salad mold. Chill.

Mrs. Elizabeth F. Smith,Consultant, Homemaking
State Department of Education
Big Spring, Texas

MOLDED SHRIMP SALAD

Number of Servings — 8

1 pkg. lemon gelatin
1 c. hot water
½ c. mayonnaise
1 c. coffee cream
1 small jar pimento cheese
½ c. celery, diced
¼ t. salt
2 t. green pepper, chopped
1 t. onion, minced
1 5½-oz. can shrimp, cleaned

Dissolve gelatin in hot water. Beat in mayonnaise, cream and cheese. Mix well. When gelatin mixture is cool, add the celery, salt, green pepper, onion and shrimp. Pour into a 1½-quart mold, preferably a fish or ring shape. Chill until firm.

Jean T. Rowse, J. D. Darnall Jr. H. S.
Geneseo, Illinois

MOLDED SHRIMP SALAD

Number of Servings — 8-10

1 c. shrimp, diced
1 c. celery, diced
1 c. canned peas
1 small bottle stuffed olives, minced
1 c. salad dressing
1½ envelopes unflavored gelatin
½ c. cold water
½ c. hot water
1 can condensed cream of tomato soup
1 8-oz. pkg. cream cheese, softened

Mix shrimp, celery, peas, olives and salad dressing. Chill. Soak geletin in cold water for 5 minutes; dissolve in hot water. Chill until thickened. Bring tomato soup to a boil. Remove from heat and fold in cream cheese. Mix tomato mixture into the gelatin—shrimp mixture. Chill until set.

Mrs. Marlene Gottschald, Stowe Jr. H. S.
Duluth, Minnesota

MOLDED SHRIMP SALAD

Number of Servings — 10-12

1 pkg. lemon gelatin
1 c. boiling water
½ t. salt
1 T. onion, grated
1 T. green pepper, finely chopped
3 hard cooked eggs, chopped
¼ lb. pimento cheese, cubed
1½ c. celery, thinly sliced
1 c. walnuts, chopped
1 15-oz. can shrimp, halved
½ c. mayonnaise
½ c. whipped cream

Dissolve gelatin in boiling water; cool. Fold in mayonnaise and whipped cream. Combine with other ingredients. Pour into mold and chill until firm.

Florence Burnett, Fife H. S.
Tacoma, Washington

SATURDAY LUNCH SALAD

Number of Servings — 6

2 c. cooked potatoes, diced
2 c. deveined, cooked shrimp, chopped
½ c. carrot, finely shredded
¼ c. onion, grated
¾ c. tart apple, diced
¾ c. mayonnaise
1 t. salt
½ t. pepper
2 T. prepared mustard
1 T. lemon juice

Mix all ingredients in order listed. Chill.

Mrs. Enid Beazley, Princess Anne H. S.
Virginia Beach, Virginia

MARINATED SHRIMP

Number of Servings — 8

3 c. cooked shrimp, cleaned
½ c. vinegar
¼ c. salad oil
1 t. salt
Few drops garlic juice
Dash hot pepper sauce
2 T. chives, chopped
2 T. parsley, chopped
2 T. dill pickles, chopped

Put the shrimp in a quart jar and add the vinegar, salad oil, salt, garlic juice, hot pepper sauce, chives, parsley and dill pickle. Shake jar well, and store in refrigerator. Do this a day in advance and shake jar often. The shrimp do not require a sauce. Serve with toothpicks.

Elaine Anderson, Mowat Junior H. S.
Lynn Haven, Florida

MACARONI-SHRIMP SALAD

Number of Servings — 4-6

1 7 or 8-oz. pkg. shell macaroni
1 4-6 oz. shrimp
1 c. pineapple, diced
1 c. celery, diced
½ c. sweet pickle, diced
2 T. onion, minced
½ c. mayonaise
1 T. prepared mustard
1 t. salt
Dash of pepper
1 T. pimento, diced
2 T. lemon juice

Cook macaroni in boiling salted water for 10 minutes, or until tender. Drain, and blanch with cold water; drain again. Combine all ingredients and toss thoroughly. Refrigerate until ready to serve. Garnish with greens or radish roses.

Mrs. Marguerite S. Drechsel Darnall, Mt. Empire Unified School District
Campo, California

PINEAPPLE-SHRIMP OUTRIGGER

Number of Servings — 4-6

1 lb. fresh shrimp
1 T. seafood seasoning
1 T. salt
¼ c. vinegar
¼ c. water
1 ripe pineapple
Prepared French dressing

Wash shrimp. Add seasoning, salt, vinegar and water; mix. Place in saucepan with cover. Bring to boil; simmer for 25 minutes. Drain; remove shells and devein shrimp. Cool. Cut pineapple, including crown, in half. Hollow out, leaving shell about ¼-inch thick. Remove core. Dice pineapple; mix with shrimp and marinate with enough French dressing to coat mixture. Pile mixture into pineapple outrigger. Garnish with fresh flowers.

Mrs. Rose Marie Staley Francis Scott Key H. S.
Union Bridge, Maryland

RICE AND SHRIMP SALAD

Number of Servings — 6-8

3 c. cold cooked rice
1 c. boiled shrimp
6 hard-cooked eggs
1 c. sweet or sour pickles, diced
Salt and pepper to taste
1 c. celery, diced
1 c. stuffed olives, finely chopped
Salad dressing

Combine all ingredients. Garnish with additional hard-cooked eggs.

June Wright Curtis, Hamshire-Fannett H. S.
Hamshire, Texas

SHRIMP CREME

Number of Servings — 8-10

1 pkg. lemon gelatin
1⅓ c. boiling water
1 small can shrimp
1 c. celery, diced
½ c. walnuts, chopped
½ t. onion, grated
Juice of ½ lemon
1 c. salad dressing

Dissolve gelatin in boiling water. Cool until mixture reaches the consistency of egg white. Beat with a rotary beater until double in bulk. Add remaining ingredients. Pour into an oiled mold. Chill until firm.

Mrs. Doris Smith, Dayton H. S.
Dayton, Washington

SHRIMP SALAD

Number of Servings — 12

1 can tomato soup
3 3-oz. pkg. cream cheese, softened
1 c. mayonnaise
2 pkg. lemon gelatin
1 c. boiling water
1 c. cold water
1 bunch celery, diced
½ green pepper, diced
1 T. onion, grated
2 pimentos, chopped
2 cans shrimp or 1 lb. frozen shrimp, broken

Heat tomato soup to boiling; add cream cheese and mayonnaise. Dissolve lemon gelatin in boiling water; add cold water. Add to soup mixture. Add celery, green pepper, onion, pimento and shrimp. Chill until firm.

Mrs. Mary Witt, Johnson County H. S.
Buffalo, Wyoming

SHRIMP SALAD

Number of Servings — 4

1½ pkg. lemon gelatin
2 T. vinegar
2 c. V-8 juice
2 T. onion, chopped
2 T. green pepper, chopped
2 T. celery, chopped
1 can small shrimp, de-veined

Add lemon gelatin to V-8 juice and simmer for 2-3 minutes. Add vinegar, stir and pour into bowl. Chill until slightly thickened. Add shrimp, onion, celery and green pepper.

Mrs. Richard Werblow, Chilton H. S.
Chilton, Wisconsin

SHRIMP SALAD

Number of Servings — 8

1 pkg. lemon gelatin
1¾ c. hot water
½ t. salt
2 T. lemon juice
2 T. sweet pickle, chopped
1 pimento, chopped
1 c. cleaned, canned or fresh shrimp, chopped
1 c. celery, finely diced
2 hard-cooked eggs
¼ c. mayonnaise

Dissolve gelatin in hot water. Add salt. Cool. Add remaining ingredients. Pour into well-oiled mold. Chill.

Mrs. B. Bomgardner, Sapulpa Junior H. S.
Sapulpa, Oklahoma

SHRIMP SALAD NEW ORLEANS

Number of Servings — 4

1 c. cold cooked rice
1 c. cooked shrimp, diced
¾ t. salt
1 T. lemon juice
¼ c. green pepper, slivered
1 T. onion, minced
1 T. olives, chopped
¾ c. raw cauliflower, diced
2 T. French dressing
Dash of pepper
⅓ c. mayonnaise

Toss all ingredients together. Chill. Serve on lettuce.

Mrs. Richard A. Dearing, Christiansburg H. S.
Christiansburg, Virginia

TOMATO-SHRIMP SUPPER SALAD

Number of Servings — 6-8

2 envelopes unflavored gelatin
½ c. cold water
2 1-lb. cans stewed tomatoes, cut in large pieces
2 T. vinegar
1 T. horseradish
½ t. salt
1 4½-oz. can medium shrimp, deveined
2 17-oz. cans peas, drained (opt.)
Salad greens
Cucumber slices (opt.)

Soften gelatin in cold water. Combine tomatoes, vinegar, horseradish and salt. Heat to boiling. Add gelatin; stir until dissolved. Cool. Arrange shrimp around bottom of ring mold. Carefully pour in tomato mixture. Chill for 4 hours. Unmold on greens; fill center with peas, if desired. Garnish with cucumber slices.

Mary Jane Bertrand, Blackfoot H. S.
Blackfoot, Idaho

SHRIMP STUFFED CELERY

Number of Servings — 6

2 c. shrimp, chopped
¼ c. mayonnaise
1 t. catsup
2 t. horseradish
⅛ t. monosodium glutamate
5 stalks white celery, cut in 4 pieces
Paprika
3 stuffed olives, chopped

Combine shrimp, mayonnaise, catsup, horseradish and monosodium glutamate. Stuff celery stalks with shrimp mixture. Garnish with paprika and olives.

Marguerite Robson, Flora H. S.
Flora, Louisiana

SHRIMP-TOMATO ASPIC

Number of Servings — 6

1 pkg. strawberry gelatin
1½ c. hot water
½ c. catsup
1 t. sugar
Onion, grated, to taste
Celery, diced
1 6-oz. can shrimp
Stuffed olives (Opt.)

Dissolve the gelatin in hot water. Add remaining ingredients. Chill until firm.

Mrs. Sylvia Michaud, Genesee H. S.
Genesee, Idaho

WEDDING SUPPER SALAD

Number of Servings — 20

1 6-oz. pkg. lemon gelatin
2 c. boiling water
1½ c. ice water
4 T. lemon juice
½ t. salt
½ c. or more of tiny shrimp, de-veined
1 c. mayonnaise
2 bunches red radishes
1 small sweet onion, minced
½ c. stuffed green olives, sliced
1 c. white celery, diced
1 medium head lettuce

Dissolve gelatin in boiling water; add ice water, lemon juice and salt. Chill. When quivery, but not set, beat with rotary beater until frothy. Fold in mayonnaise; add shrimp, one bunch of sliced radishes, onion, olives and celery. Pour in ring mold or individual molds. Chill until firm, stirring occasionally to prevent vegetables from sinking to bottom. Serve on lettuce. Top with mayonnaise and garnish with radish roses around the plate.

Mrs. Gladys B. Phillips, Post Falls H. S.
Post Falls, Idaho

ANTIPASTO PLATE

Number of Servings — 6

1 7-oz. can tuna, flaked
Leaf lettuce
Cheese strips
Cooked ham strips
Black and green olives
1 green pepper, cut in strips
1 red pepper, cut in strips
Radish curls
Carrot curls

Mound tuna on lettuce. Place cheese and ham strips on top of or around tuna. Add olives. Put pepper strips between cheese layer. Garnish with carrot and radish curls.

Marilee Sellman, Northridge H. S.
Dayton, Ohio

AMERICAN NICOISE SALAD

Number of Servings — 6

1 small head lettuce, shredded
2 7-oz. cans solid pack tuna, drained
1 c. cooked potatoes, sliced
1 c. cooked snap beans
3 hard-cooked eggs, quartered
3 small tomatoes, quartered
1 small red onion, thinly sliced and separated into rings
12 ripe olives, pitted

Place lettuce in large shallow bowl. Pile large pieces of tuna in center of bowl. Surround with a ring of potatoes and a ring of beans. Alternate egg and tomato quarters around beans. Garnish with onion and olives. If made ahead, cover tightly with Saran wrap and refrigerate.

Salad Dressing:
¾ t. salt
Dash of paprika
½ t. monosodium glutamate
⅓ c. lemon juice or vinegar
⅔ c. salad oil

Add the salt, paprika and monosodium glutamate to the lemon juice; stir with fork until dry ingredients are dissolved. Add oil; beat with fork until blended. Pour this dressing over salad just before serving.

Mrs. Irene Wells, Grant County Rural H. S.
Ulysses, Kansas

FORTY-NINTH STATE SALAD

Number of Servings — 4

1 c. celery, diced
¼ c. onion, finely chopped
1 can tuna or salmon
1 small can shoestring potatoes
1½ c. carrots, shredded
½ c. salad dressing

Toss together and serve as a main dish.

Mrs. Dorothy Anderson, Montrose H. S.
Montrose, South Dakota

CREAMY TUNA SALAD

Number of Servings — 4

1 envelope unflavored gelatin
½ c. cold water
1 can cream of celery soup
1 3-oz. pkg. cream cheese
1 7-oz. can flaked tuna, drained
½ c. carrots, shredded
⅓ c. celery, chopped
2 T. parsley, chopped
1 T. lemon juice

Sprinkle gelatin on cold water to soften. Place over boiling water; stir until gelatin is dissolved. Blend celery soup with cream cheese. Add gelatin and remaining ingredients. Pour into a mold. Chill.

Mrs. Florence Wiest, Wishek H. S.
Wishek, North Dakota

CONGEALED TUNA SALAD

Number of Servings — 8

1 c. white tuna
1 c. tiny English peas, drained
¼ c. pimento, diced
½ c. stuffed olives, sliced
⅓ c. pecans, chopped
⅔ c. celery, diced
½ c. salad dressing
1 pkg. lemon gelatin
2 T. lemon juice
1 c. boiling water
½ c. juice from peas or water

Dissolve gelatin in boiling water; add juice from peas and lemon juice. Refrigerate until slightly set. Fold in salad dressing; add remaining ingredients. Pour into a mold; chill until firm.

Mrs. Bill P. Edwards, Camden H. S.
Camden, Arkansas

MOLDED TUNA SALAD

Number of Servings — 4

1 envelope unflavored gelatin
¼ c. cold water
1 7-oz. white tuna, flaked
½ c. celery, chopped
½ c. green pepper, chopped
2 T. stuffed olives, chopped
¾ c. mayonnaise
½ c. salt
1 T. vinegar

Sprinkle gelatin over cold water; let stand for 5 minutes. Place bowl over boiling water until gelatin is dissolved. Cool. Add remaining ingredients. Chill.

Mrs. Emma Swett, Stevens H. S.
Claremont, New Hampshire

MOLDED TUNA SALAD

Number of Servings — 4-6

1 pkg. lime gelatin
1½ c. boiling water
1 T. vinegar
Dash of salt
½ c. celery, diced
¼ c. mayonnaise
1 c. tuna, drained and flaked
3 T. onion, minced
1 1-lb. carton cottage cheese

Dissolve gelatin in boiling water; add vinegar and salt. Let cool until slightly thickened. Combine remaining ingredients with tuna. Fold into gelatin mixture and chill until firm.

Laura Howell, Ashley Twp. H. S.
Ashley, Illinois

MAIN DISH SALAD

Number of Servings — 3-5

1 c. carrots, shredded
2 T. onion, minced
½ c. celery, diced
½ c. salad dressing
¼ t. prepared mustard
1 T. cream
1 c. chicken, tuna or salmon, diced
1 hard cooked egg, chopped (Opt.)
1 c. shoestring potatoes

Combine salad dressing, mustard and cream. Toss all ingredients together except potatoes. Chill. Just before serving, toss in shoestring potatoes.

Miss Jane Wildung, Blue Earth Public School
Blue Earth, Minnesota

MONTEREY SOUFFLE SALAD

Number of Servings — 4-6

1 pkg. lemon gelatin
1 c. hot water
½ c. cold water
2 T. lemon juice
½ c. salad dressing or mayonnaise
1 No. ½ can chunk tuna
¾ c. celery or cucumber, chopped
¼ c. stuffed olives, sliced
2 T. pimento, chopped
½ t. onion, grated
Salt to taste

Dissolve gelatin in hot water. Add cold water, lemon juice, salad dressing and salt. Blend well with rotary beater. Pour into refrigerator freezing tray. Quick-chill in freezing unit 15-20 minutes, or until firm about 1 inch from edge but soft in center. Whip with rotary beater until fluffy. Fold in remaining ingredients. Pour into 1-quart mold or individual molds. Chill until firm. Garnish with salad greens. Serve with more tuna and salad dressing, if desired.

This recipe submitted by the following teachers:

Mrs. Doris Hybl, Bell H. S.
Bell, Florida

Louise Bollinger, Newman H. S.
Sweetwater, Texas

STUFFED TOMATO WITH TUNA

Number of Servings — 6

1 can tuna, flaked
2 hard-cooked eggs, chopped
6-8 crackers, crumbled
1 t. onion, chopped
1 T. parsley, chopped
3 T. celery, chopped
2 T. mayonnaise
6 medium tomatoes

Combine all ingredients except 6 tomatoes. Cut top off tomatoes; scoop out inside. Fill each tomato with tuna mixture. Serve in lettuce cups.

Mrs. Pruda C. Prather, Carter H. S.
Carter, Kentucky

SUSAN'S TUNA SALAD

Number of Servings — 8

1 head lettuce, torn in small pieces
2-4 tomatoes, cubed
1 green pepper, diced
Salt and pepper to taste
6-8 radishes, diced
1 13-oz. can chunk tuna
2 c. bite-size cheese crackers
2 T. mayonnaise

Combine all ingredients. Chill.

Dressing:
1 clove garlic
¾ t. salt
¼ t. Worcestershire sauce
½ c. mayonnaise
1 T. vinegar

Crush garlic with salt; add remaining ingredients. Mix well. Chill. Serve with tuna mixture.

Mrs. Patricia Crouch Dabney, Wright Junior H. S.
Columbia, South Carolina

TUNA GARDEN LOAF

Number of Servings — 8

2 T. unflavored gelatin
½ c. cold water
1 can condensed cream of celery soup
¼ c. lemon juice
1 T. prepared mustard
1 t. salt
⅛ t. pepper
1 c. mayonnaise
2 7-oz. cans tuna
1 c. celery, chopped
½ c. cucumber, grated
¼ c. green pepper, chopped

Soften gelatin in cold water. Heat soup just to boiling. Add gelatin to soup; stir to dissolve. Stir in lemon juice, mustard, salt and pepper. Chill until partially set. Blend in mayonnaise. Fold in tuna, celery, cucumber and green pepper. Pour into 8½ x 4½ x 2½ inch loaf pan. Chill until firm.

Mary Elizabeth Ball, Kentwood H. S.
Grand Rapids, Michigan

TUNA LUNCHEON SALAD

Number of Servings — 6-8

1 6-oz. can chunk or grated tuna
4 hard cooked eggs, diced
4 small tomatoes, quartered
1 medium head lettuce, broken in bite size pieces
½ pkg. potato chips, crushed
Salad dressing
Salt to taste

Mix tuna, eggs, tomatoes, salt and lettuce. Moisten with enough salad dressing to hold salad together. Add potato chips. Spoon into lettuce cups. Serve with garlic toast.

Mrs. Helen R. Black, Alchesay H. S.
Whiteriver, Arizona

TASTY TUNA TREAT

Number of Servings — 15

1 pkg. lemon gelatin
1 envelope unflavored gelatin
2 c. boiling water
½ c. cold water
1 T. sugar
A few drops of green food coloring
1 c. whipped cream
1 c. salad dressing
2 c. celery, chopped
2 cans tuna fish, shredded
1 c. stuffed olives, sliced

Soak unflavored gelatin in cold water for 5 minutes. Dissolve lemon gelatin in boiling water; add softened gelatin. Stir well. Add sugar and a few drops of green coloring. Chill until nearly firm; whip with beater until fluffy. Fold in whipped cream and salad dressing, blending carefully. Fold in celery, tuna and olives. Pour into loaf pan; Chill until firm. Cut in squares and serve on crisp lettuce.

Mrs. H. W. Winifred Iverson, Riggs H. S.
Pierre, South Dakota

TUNA SALAD

Number of Servings — 8-10

1 pkg. lemon gelatin
1 c. boiling water
½ t. salt
1 T. onion, grated
½ c. whipped cream
½ c. mayonnaise
1 t. prepared mustard
1 c. celery, chopped
½ green pepper, chopped
1 c. tuna
3 hard cooked eggs
Stuffed olives (Opt.)

Dissolve gelatin in water; add salt and onion. Let set until mixture begins to thicken. Combine mayonnaise and whipped cream. Add to gelatin mixture. Add remaining ingredients.

Mrs. Grace Pylman, Independent # 1
Gary, South Dakota

TUNA OR CHICKEN MOUSSE

Number of Servings — 6

1 T. unflavored gelatin
¼ c. cold water
¼ c. pickle juice
½ c. hot water
1 7-oz. can flaked tuna or 1 7-oz. can minced chicken
¼ c. mayonnaise
1 c. celery, chopped
2 hard-cooked eggs, chopped
8 stuffed olives, sliced
8 sweet pickles, chopped
1 T. onion, minced
¼ t. salt
⅛ t. pepper

Soak gelatin in cold water. Add pickle juice and softened gelatin to hot water; heat until dissolved. Cool. Add remaining ingredients; mix thoroughly. Pour into a greased mold and refrigerate for several hours.

Letha Pearl Simpson, Sterling H. S.
Sterling, Kansas

TUNA SALAD

Number of Servings — 8

2 envelopes unflavored gelatin
½ c. cold water
1 can cream of celery soup
¼ c. lemon juice
1 T. prepared mustard
1 t. salt
Pepper to taste
1 c. mayonnaise
2 cans chunk-style tuna
1 c. celery, chopped
¼ c. green pepper, chopped
½ c. cucumber, chopped

Soak gelatin in water. Heat soup to boiling; add softened gelatin. Add lemon juice, prepared mustard, salt, and pepper; chill until partially set. Blend mayonnaise, tuna, celery, green pepper and cucumber. Pour into 2 small ring molds or 1 8-inch square pan. Garnish with hard-cooked egg slices and sliced pickled beets.

Patricia Kennett Moore, Winters Joint Union H. S.
Winters, California

TUNA SALAD

1 can tuna
½ c. celery, chopped
4 hard cooked eggs
Onion to taste
Salad dressing thinned with cream
½ can shoestring potatoes

Just before serving, combine all ingredients with enough salad dressing to moisten.

Mrs. Duane Torguson, Bristol H. S.
Bristol, South Dakota

TUNA SALAD

Number of Servings — 4

1 7-oz. can chunk style tuna
½ c. celery, diced
1 T. onion, minced
1 T. lemon juice
½ c. green pepper, chopped
¼ t. salt
Black pepper to taste
3 hard cooked eggs, quartered
2 tomatoes, chopped
¼ c. mayonnaise

Mix tuna, celery, onion, lemon juice, green pepper, salt and black pepper together. Add eggs, tomatoes and mayonnaise. Mix lightly until blended. Chill.

Miss Sybil Widvey, Medford H. S.
Medford, Wisconsin

TUNA SALAD LUAU

Number of Servings — 8

Curried Mayonnaise:
¾ c. mayonnaise
¾ t. curry powder
1 T. parsley flakes

Mix ingredients well.

1 13-oz. can tuna
1 c. pineapple chunks, drained
1 c. celery, chopped
½ c. walnuts, chopped
Curried mayonnaise
Walnut halves

Combine tuna, pineapple, celery and walnuts. Fold in curried mayonnaise. Serve on lettuce leaves garnished with whole walnuts.

Mrs. Donald Young, Greenwood H. S.
Greenwood, Arkansas

TUNA CRUNCH SALAD

Number of Servings — 6

1 7-oz. can tuna, drained
¼ c. sweet pickles, chopped
1 T. onion, minced
1 to 2 T. lemon juice
¾ c. salad dressing
1½ c. cabbage, shredded
1¼ c. potato chips, crushed

Combine tuna, pickle, onion, lemon juice and salad dressing. Cover and chill, until ready to serve. Add cabbage, and toss. Add 1 cup potato chips and toss lightly. Heap into shallow lettuce-lined bowl and sprinkle with remaining potato chips.

Miss Arlene Lenort, Maynard H. S.
Maynard, Minnesota

TUNA SALAD

Number of Servings — 6-8

1 can of tuna
½ c. cucumber, chopped
½ c. celery, chopped
1 medium ripe tomato, cut
1 small onion, finely chopped
2 hard cooked eggs, chopped
½ t. salt
1 T. mayonnaise
Lettuce or finely shredded cabbage

Combine ingredients in order; mix lightly. Serve on lettuce or cabbage.

Berdie M. Hughes, Carmi H. S.
Carmi, Illinois

TUNA-SHOESTRING POTATO SALAD

Number of Servings — 4

6 carrots, shredded
½ c. celery, diced
1 small onion, minced
1 7-oz. can tuna, drained
1 small can shoestring potatoes
1 c. cooked salad dressing
3 T. French dressing
2 T. sugar

Combine carrots, celery, onion and tuna in a bowl. In a separate bowl combine dressings and sugar. Add dressing to the salad mixture; stir until moistened. Add the shoestring potatoes just before serving.

Mrs. Sandra Ericson, Stillwater Jr. H. S.
Stillwater, Minnesota

TUNA-VEGETABLE SALAD LOAF

Number of Servings — 8

1 envelope unflavored gelatin
¼ c. cold water
¼ c. hot water
⅔ c. mayonnaise
2 t. prepared mustard
2 T. lemon juice
1 7-oz. can tuna
¾ c. celery, minced
½ c. canned peas
2 T. pimento, minced
1 t. salt
1 hard-cooked egg, chopped

Soften gelatin in cold water. Dissolve in hot water. Combine mayonnaise, mustard and lemon juice. Add dissolved gelatin. Mix tuna, celery, peas, pimento, salt and egg. Combine with gelatin mixture; pour in loaf pan and chill.

Mrs. Robbie Hanks, Ysleta H. S.
El Paso, Texas

TUNA-LETTUCE SALAD

Number of Servings — 6-8

1 can chunk tuna
1 can peas
½ c. celery, chopped
¼ c. onions, chopped
1 med. head lettuce
2-3 T. salad dressing
Dash of salt

Core and wash lettuce. Combine tuna, peas, celery and onions. Add torn lettuce. Mix with salad dressing. Salt to taste.

Mrs. Martha Wilson, Jonesville Jr. H. S.
Jonesville, Michigan

TUNA "MEAL-IN-ONE"

Number of Servings — 6

1 9¼-oz. can flaked tuna
1 No. 303 can peas, drained
3 cooked potatoes, diced
2 sweet pickles, chopped
½ medium size onion, chopped
½ c. celery, chopped
½ head lettuce, broken in small pieces
Salt to taste
Salad dressing or mayonnaise

Reserve half of the lettuce. Combine remaining lettuce with remaining ingredients. Toss lightly. Chill. Serve on reserved lettuce.

Mrs. Margaret C. Hoffman, Victory Joint School
Harrisville, Pennsylvania

SHOESTRING-TUNA SALAD

Number of Servings — 8

1 c. mayonnaise
1 T. mustard
¾ c. milk
Dash of Tabasco sauce
2 7-oz. cans tuna, drained
1½ c. celery, diced
2 4½-oz. cans shoestring potatoes

Blend mayonnaise, mustard, milk and Tabasco sauce. Add tuna and celery. Chill. Immediately before serving add the shoestring potatoes and mix just so they stick together. Serve on lettuce leaf.

Myrna E. Erickson, Cooperstown H. S.
Cooperstown, North Dakota

TUNA WALDORF SALAD

Number of Servings — 6

2 7-oz. cans tuna, drained and flaked
1 c. apples, diced
½ c. celery, chopped
1 c. nuts, chopped
½ c. mayonnaise
Lettuce

Combine all ingredients and mix lightly. Serve on lettuce.

Mrs. Ralph Earhart, Elk City H. S.
Elk City, Kansas

TUNA-TOMATO STARS

Number of Servings — 4

1 6½-oz. can chunked tuna
1 T. lemon juice
2 hardcooked eggs, chopped
¼ c. sweet pickle, chopped
¼ c. onion, chopped
2 T. green pepper, chopped
¼ t. salt
⅓ c. mayonnaise
4 medium tomatoes

Sprinkle lemon juice on tuna. Add remaining ingredients except tomato; mix gently. Chill. Cut tomatoes with stem end down (partially through) into 6 equal sections. Spread apart; sprinkle with salt. Fill with tuna salad. Top with carrot curl.

Mrs. Gerald Elliott, Crete H. S.
Crete, Nebraska

BAKED SEAFOOD SALAD

Number of Servings — 6

1 c. cooked shrimp, diced
1 c. crab meat, flaked
1 c. celery, chopped
½ c. onion, finely chopped
¼ c. green pepper, finely chopped
½ t. salt
Dash of balck pepper
1 c. salad dressing
1 c. corn flake crumbs, buttered

Combine all ingredients except corn flake crumbs. Place in casserole; sprinkle top with corn flake crumbs. Bake at 450°F. for 15 minutes.

Mrs. Esther Wasson, Bridgeton H. S.
Bridgeton, New Jersey

BAKED SEAFOOD SALAD

Number of Servings — 6

2 c. cooked crab, tuna or shrimp, diced
¾ c. green pepper, chopped
2 T. onion, finely chopped
1 c. celery, diced
¾ c. salad dressing or mayonnaise
½ t. salt
⅛ t. pepper
1 T. lemon juice
¼ c. potato chips, finely crushed
¼ c. sharp cheese, grated

Combine all ingredients except potato chips and cheese. Fill 6 individual serving shells with the mixture. Sprinkle tops with potato chips and cheese. Bake at 350°F. for 30 minutes.

Garrah Gibson, Williamsfield H. S.
Williamsfield, Illinois

HOT SEAFOOD SALAD

Number of Servings — 6-8

¼ c. butter
1 c. celery, chopped
1 green pepper, chopped
2 c. milk
3 T. butter
3 T. flour
2 c. cooked rice
¼ c. onion, chopped
1 can tuna, drained
1 can crab, drained
1 can shrimp, cleaned
1 c. mayonnaise
1 c. corn flakes, crushed
1 can cream of mushroom soup
1 can cream of celery soup

Simmer celery, onions and green pepper in ¼ cup butter in covered pan. Make white sauce of 1½ cups milk, remaining butter and flour. Add tuna, crab, shrimp, celery mixture and mayonnaise to white sauce. Pour over rice which has been spread in shallow baking dish. Cover with corn flakes. Bake 30-40 minutes at 325°F. Combine soups and remaining milk; simmer until blended. Serve over salad.

Carole A. Peterson, Cando H. S.
Cando, North Dakota

HOT CRAB MEAT SALAD

Number of Servings — 8

½ c. butter
⅔ c. sifted flour
2⅔ c. milk
2 c. flaked crab meat
1 large stalk celery, diced
⅓ green pepper, minced
Bread crumbs
1 lge. pimento, minced
⅓ c. blanched almonds, quartered
4 hard cooked eggs, cut up
2 t. salt

Make white sauce of butter, sifted flour, and milk. Cook about ten minutes. Blend in remaining ingredients. Pour into buttered baking dish. Sprinkle with buttered fine bread crumbs. Bake at 350°F. for 35 minutes. Serve hot.

Barbara Paulsen, Portola Jr.-Sr. H. S.
Portola, California

HOT CRAB SALAD

Number of Servings — 6-8

6 T. butter, melted
6 T. flour
1 t. salt
⅛ t. pepper
2½ c. milk
1 lb. crab meat
6 hard-cooked eggs, chopped
1 c. almonds, blanched and shredded
Buttered bread crumbs

Make a white sauce of butter, flour, salt, pepper and milk. Boil sauce for 1 minute, stirring constantly. Remove from heat. Add crab meat, eggs and almonds. Spread in buttered 8 x 8 pan. Cover well with buttered bread crumbs. Heat for 20 minutes in 375°F. oven. Do not let mixture boil while in oven. If desired ingredients may be mixed, refrigerated and cooked later in the day.

Mrs. Mina A. Qualley, Public School
Breckenridge, Minnesota

SUPPER SALAD

Number of Servings — 8

1 pkg. lemon gelatin
1 c. boiling water
½ c. salad dressing
½ t. salt
1 T. onion, grated
½ c. nuts
3 hard-cooked eggs, chopped
½ c. cheese, cubed
½ c. green pepper, chopped
1½ c. celery, chopped
1 can shrimp, tuna or salmon
½ c. whipped cream

Dissolve gelatin in boiling water. Chill until partially set. Add remaining ingredients, folding in whipped cream last. Chill.

Mary Ann Demuth, Todd County H. S.
Mission, South Dakota

CURRIED SEAFOOD SALAD

Number of Servings — 4-5

1⅓ c. precooked rice
½ t. salt
1⅓ c. boiling water
¾ c. mayonnaise
1½ t. lemon juice
¾ t. curry powder
1 T. onion, grated
1 c. cooked or canned shrimp, diced
1 c. celery, chopped

Combine rice, salt and water in a saucepan. Cook over low heat until rice is moistened. Cover and remove from heat. Let stand for 5 minutes. Uncover and let cool until mixture reaches room temperature. About 1 hour before serving, combine mayonnaise, lemon juice, curry powder and onion. Mix well. Combine shrimp and celery. Stir mayonnaise mixture. Add rice; mix lightly. Chill.

Variations: 1 cup cooked crab, lobster, chicken, turkey, beef or pork may be substituted for the shrimp.

This recipe submitted by the following teachers:

Marlene Cloud, North Whitfield H. S.
Dalton, Georgia

Linda R. Kelley, Sumner Junior H. S.
Sumner, Washington

FISHERMAN'S SALAD BOWL

Number of Servings — 4

1 head lettuce, broken in pieces
½ bunch romaine, broken in pieces
1 c. celery, sliced
2 T. pimento, finely chopped
½ c. lobster, chopped
1 c. shrimp, sliced
2 c. flaked salmon
1 c. crab meat
1 c. mayonnaise
¾ c. French dressing
Tomato wedges
Olives

Just before serving, combine all ingredients except tomato and olive toss. Garnish with tomato wedges and olives.

Patricia Ann Eaton, Metamora H. S.
Metamora, Illinois

SEAFOOD COCKTAIL SALAD

Number of Servings — 8-10

1 pkg. lemon gelatin
1 c. boiling water
½ c. chili sauce
2 T. horseradish, grated
1 t. Worcestershire sauce
2 drops Tabasco sauce
½ c. celery, finely cut
1 can shrimp, cleaned
1 can crab meat, flaked

Dissolve gelatin in boiling water. In a 1-cup measuring cup combine chili sauce, horseradish, Worcestershire and Tabasco. Fill remainder of cup with cold water and add to gelatin. Chill. When slightly congealed add celery, shrimp and crab meat. Chill.

Mrs. Ruth Long, Sheridan H. S.
Sheridan, Montana

OYSTER SALAD

Number of Servings — 8

Dressing:
2 eggs, well beaten
¼ c. vinegar
4 T. sugar
½ t. salt
1 t. prepared mustard
2 T. water

Mix all ingredients. Cook over hot water or low heat until mixture is consistency of soft custard. Cool.

3 cans cove oysters
12 soda crackers, crumbled
8 hard-cooked eggs, diced
1 c. sweet pickles, finely chopped
¼ t. black pepper
1 c. celery, finely cut

Mash oysters in their liquid. Add remaining ingredients; toss well. Add dressing. Chill several hours before serving.

Kathryn Davis, Community H. S.
Pinckneyville, Illinois

SEAFOOD ASPIC

Number of Servings — 6

1¾ c. tomato juice
1 pkg. lemon gelatin
¼ t. salt
1 t. lemon juice
½ t. Worcestershire sauce
3-4 drops Tabasco sauce
2 T. mayonnaise
1 c. cooked seafood, flaked
1 T. onion, chopped
¼ c. celery, finely chopped
2 T. green olives, chopped
2 hard cooked eggs

Heat tomato juice but do not boil. Dissolve gelatin in hot juice. Add salt, lemon juice, Worcestershire sauce and Tabasco. Chill until slightly thickened. Fold in mayonnaise. Fold in seafood, onion, celery, olives and eggs. Chill until firm. Serve on lettuce with garnish of parsley, ripe olives and hard cooked egg slices.

Mrs. Marian E. Henning, Marysville H. S.
Marysville, Washington.

REAL COOL FISH

Number of Servings — 6

2 1-lb. cans tuna, salmon or mackerel
1-3 c. hard-cooked eggs, chopped
1 8-oz. pkg. cream cheese
½ c. butter
2 T. lemon juice
Few drops Tabasco sauce
1 c. celery, chopped
1 c. green pepper, chopped
2 T. onion, grated
Pimento
Olives

Combine all ingredients except the pimento and olives; blend well. Pack mixture into a 6 cup fish mold. Chill for 2 or 3 hours. To unmold, unloosen edges with a sharp knife; invert mold on a serving platter; hold hot compresses to mold until mixture falls on platter. Decorate fish with thin strips of pimento for scales and tail stripes; use olive sections for eyes. Cut smiling mouth from green pepper.

This recipe submitted by the following teachers:

Sally Marnen, Moon H. S.
Coraopolis, Pennsylvania

Lona W. Capshaw, Hermitage Springs
Red Boiling Springs, Tennessee

SEAFOOD SALAD

Number of Servings — 4-6

1/3 c. catsup
1 t. unflavored gelatin
1 10 1/2-oz. can condensed tomato soup
1 T. unflavored gelatin
1/2 c. mayonnaise
1 3-oz. pkg. cream cheese
1/2 c. cream or evaporated milk
1 T. lemon juice
2 4 1/2-oz. cans shrimp or lobster, drained
1 1/2 c. celery, diced
1/4 c. green pepper, chopped
1 T. pimento, chopped

Sprinkle 1 teaspoon gelatin over catsup. Heat the catsup, stirring constantly to dissolve gelatin. Spoon the catsup into any suitable mold; place in refrigerator to congeal. Sprinkle 1 tablespoon gelatin over tomato soup; heat the soup to dissolve gelatin. Cool. Soften cream cheese with mayonnaise and cream; add lemon juice. Stir into tomato soup. Fold the shrimp or lobster, celery, green pepper and pimento into the tomato soup mixture. Pour over the congealed catsup. Chill several hours. Unmold and garnish with water cress or endive.

Mattie Finney, Vashon Island H. S.
Burton, Washington

SEAFOOD SALAD

Number of Servings — 8

1 can tomato soup
1 envelope unflavored gelatin
1/4 c. cold water
3 small pkg. cream cheese
1 medium can crab meat
1 can shrimp
Meat from one lobster
1 small onion, minced
3/4 c. celery, chopped
1 c. salad dressing or mayonnaise

Soak the gelatin in cold water. Heat the tomato soup to boiling; add the softened gelatin and cream cheese; stir until dissolved. Cool. Add remaining ingredients. Place in a mold, cover with waxed paper, and chill until firm.

Dorothy B. Tobey, Hampton Academy Jr. H. S.
Hampton, New Hampshire

SEAFOOD SALAD

Number of Servings — 6-8

1 pkg. lemon gelatin
1 c. hot water
1 jar pimento cheese
1/2 c. mayonnaise
1 c. shrimp, crab or tuna, drained
2 T. green pepper, chopped
2 T. celery, chopped
1 T. onion, chopped or grated
1 carrot, grated

Dissolve gelatin in water; chill until slightly congealed. Add remaining ingredients. Chill until firm.

Ella G. Moyer, John R. Rogers H. S.
Spokane, Washington

SEAFOOD SPECIAL

Number of Servings — 6-8

1 6-oz. pkg. lemon gelatin
2 c. hot water
Juice of 1/2 lemon
2 c. whipped cream
1/2 lb. cheese, grated
1 c. stuffed olives, chopped
6 hard cooked eggs, chopped

Dissolve gelatin in hot water; cool until slightly thickened. Whip. Combine remaining ingredients and fold into gelatin mixture. Refrigerate until firm.

Dressing:
1 c. mayonnaise
1/2 c. chili sauce
1 t. sweet relish
1 lb. crab meat or shrimp

Combine ingredients. Serve with salad.

Mrs. Jane Odell, Tempe Union H. S.
Tempe, Arizona

SHRIMP-CRAB BREAD SALAD

Number of Servings — 12

1 lge. loaf sandwich bread, sliced
Butter
1 lge. onion, finely chopped
4 hard cooked eggs, finely chopped
2 cans small shrimp, drained
1 7 1/2-oz. can crab meat
1 c. celery, finely cubed
3 c. tart mayonnaise
Cherry tomatoes
Crisp cucumbers, sliced
Salad greens

Remove crusts from bread; spread lightly with butter. Cut each slice into about 20 small cubes. Add onion and eggs. Refrigerate overnight. Add shrimp, crab meat, celery and mayonnaise. Mix well. Cover and refrigerate for 3 or 4 hours. Serve on salad greens. Garnish with cucumbers and tomatoes.

Mildred B. Goe, Wy'east H. S.
Hood River, Oregon

SEAFOOD POTPOURRI

Number of Servings — 4-6

1 can tuna, drained and flaked
1 can crab meat, flaked
1 can shrimp, deveined
2 T. French dressing
1/2 c. cucumber, diced
2 T. radishes, chopped
1 T. capers
2 T. lemon juice
1/2 c. mayonnaise
Salt and pepper to taste

Combine seafood with French dressing; chill 15 minutes. Add remaining ingredients; toss lightly. Serve in crisp lettuce cups.

Mrs. Patsy Steffensen, Lake Norden H. S.
Lake Norden, South Dakota

Foreign Salads

COLE SLAW (South Africa)

Number of Servings — 4

1 t. salt
¼ t. pepper
½ t. dry mustard
1 t. celery seed
2 T. sugar
¼ c. green pepper, chopped
1 T. red pepper or pimento, chopped
½ t. onion, grated
3 T. cooking oil
⅓ c. vinegar
3 c. cabbage, finely chopped

Combine all ingredients in order given; mix well. Cover and chill thoroughly.

Beth Ann Dugal, Wilmot H. S.
Wilmot, Arkansas

ASSYRIAN SALAD

Number of Servings — 6

1 c. Assyrian wheat or wheat germ
1 head lettuce, broken in bite-size pieces
1 lb. tomatoes, finely diced
1 small bunch parsley, finely diced
1 onion, finely diced
1 cucumber, finely diced
Juice of 2 lemons
3 T. olive oil
Salt to taste
Sugar (opt.)
Carrots (opt.)
Celery (opt.)

Cover wheat with warm water; let stand for 30 minutes. Combine vegetables; add soaked wheat. Combine remaining ingredients; pour over salad. Serve immediately.

Mrs. Alma L. Graven, Blackwell Senior H. S.
Blackwell, Oklahoma

CHINESE SALAD

Number of Servings — 8-10

1 5-oz. can noodles
1 t. garlic salt
3 T. butter, melted
1 t. curry powder
2 t. Worcestershire sauce
2 qt. salad greens
1 T. vinegar
½ c. ripe olives
2 T. salad oil

Combine noodles, garlic salt, butter, curry powder and Worcestershire sauce. Heat for 15 minutes at 200°F. Just before serving toss noodle mixture with remaining ingredients.

Joyce Tower, Braham H. S.
Braham, Minnesota

SALATA BEDINGAN (Eggplant Salad, Egypt)

Number of Servings — 4

1 eggplant, peeled and cut in ½-inch slices
2 tomatoes, sliced

Fry eggplant in butter until soft. Drain on absorbent paper. Alternate rows of eggplant and tomatoes on a platter. Serve with oil and vinegar dressing seasoned to taste.

Ruth Metaweh, Villard H. S.
Villard, Minnesota

MODIFIED FILIPINO SEAFOOD SALAD

Number of Servings — 8

1 lge. eggplant, unpeeled
¾ c. canned tuna
¾ c. canned shrimp, chopped
1 small head lettuce or cabbage, shredded
1 T. onion, finely chopped
1 t. powdered ginger root (opt.)
½ t. salt
¼ t. black pepper
Dash of cayenne pepper (opt.)
½ t. garlic powder
¼ c. salad oil
¼ c. vinegar
1 c. sharp cheese, grated

Do not peel eggplant so it will not shrink or lose moisture. Bake at 375°F. until a fork can easily be inserted. Cool and chop eggplant into small pieces. Add tuna, shrimp and lettuce or cabbage; mix well. Add onions; mix. Combine all remaining ingredients except cheese. Beat with an egg beater; pour over eggplant mixture. Garnish with cheese.

Mrs. Helen Kitchen Branson, Wilder H. S.
Wilder, Idaho

BEET SALAD (Finland)

Number of Servings — 6

1 c. cooked beets, diced
2 c. cooked potatoes, diced
¾ c. cooked carrots, diced
2 T. onion, diced
¾ c. herring or anchovies
¼ c. vinegar
Salt to taste
Lettuce
Hard-cooked egg slices

Combine all ingredients except lettuce and egg slices. Chill for 2 to 4 hours. Serve in lettuce cups; garnish with egg slices.

Mrs. Fred Lamppa, Chisholm Senior H. S.
Chisholm, Minnesota

MARINADE DE TROIX LEGAMES (France)

Number of Servings — 8

1 No. 2 can cut green beans, drained
1 No. 2 can wax beans, drained
1 No. 2 can kidney beans, washed and drained
1 onion, cut in rings
1 green pepper, cut in rings
⅓ c. salad oil
⅔ c. vinegar
¾ c. sugar
1 t. Accent
½ t. pepper
1 t. salt

Combine beans, onion and pepper. Mix remaining ingredients; add to bean mixture. Let stand for 24 hours.

Mrs. Doris C. Dunford, Flagstaff High School
Flagstaff, Arizona

SHRIMP SALAD DEAUVILLE (France)

Number of Servings — 4-6

2 c. shrimp, cooked and shelled
½ c. walnut halves
1 apple, sliced
3 hard-cooked eggs, halved
1 c. canned mushrooms, drained
1 c. iceberg lettuce, shredded
1 T. vinegar
1 t. prepared mustard
¾ t. salt
Pinch of cayenne pepper
2 T. vegetable oil
1 T. celery, minced
1 T. mayonnaise

Arrange chilled shrimp, walnuts, apple, eggs, mushrooms and lettuce in a salad bowl. Thoroughly mix remaining ingredients; pour over salad.

Gayle E. Mitchell, Quincy Jr.-Sr. H. S.
Quincy, California

HERRING AND BEET SALAD (German)

Number of Servings — 4

1 c. pickled herring, diced
3 apples, diced
5 cooked potatoes, diced
3 T. onion, minced
4 hard-cooked eggs, diced
1½ c. sour cream
3 T. mayonnaise
1 T. sugar
4 T. vinegar

Mix all ingredients. Refrigerate for at least 3 hours before serving. Serve on lettuce leaves.

Grace A. Kurz, Shannon H. S.
Shannon, Illinois

BITTA POTUFFEL (Sweet Potato Salad, Germany)

Number of Servings — 8

4 medium sweet potatoes
¼ t. salt
1 T. onions, finely chopped
2 T. vinegar
2 T. brown sugar
2 T. margarine

Cook potatoes in boiling salted water; drain and mash. Combine remaining ingredients; add to potatoes. Serve hot.

Mrs. Myrtle Wood, Rogers H. S.
Rogers, Texas

POTATO SALAD (Germany)

Number of Servings — 8-10

8 potatoes
1 stalk celery, diced
2 hard-cooked eggs, sliced
1 onion, minced
1 T. minced parsley
2 eggs, well beaten
1 c. sugar
½ c. vinegar
½ c. cold water
½ t. dry mustard
½ t. salt
¼ t. pepper
4 slices bacon, diced

Boil potatoes in jackets until soft; peel and dice. Add celery, eggs, onion and parsley. Fry bacon until crisp and lightly browned. Combine beaten eggs, sugar, mustard, salt, pepper, vinegar and water. Mix well. Pour egg mixture into hot bacon and fat; stir about 10 minutes or until mixture thickens. Pour bacon mixture over potato mixture; mix lightly. Let stand in a cold place for several hours.

Lucile S. Brown, Hartland Consolidated Schools
Hartland, Michigan

POTATO SALAD (Germany)

Number of Servings — 8

3 lb. red potatoes
3 strips bacon, diced
¼ c. onion, chopped
1 T. flour
2 t. salt
1¼ T. sugar
¼ t. black pepper
⅔ vinegar
⅓ c. water

Simmer potatoes in jackets until tender; peel and slice thin. Fry bacon until crisp; add onion and cook 1 minute. Blend in flour, salt, sugar and pepper. Stir in vinegar and water. Cook 10 minutes, stirring occasionally. Pour bacon mixture over warm potatoes. Serve warm.

Mrs. Pauline Wattner, Seagoville H. S.
Seagoville, Texas

HEISS KARTOFFEL SALAT (Hot Potato Salad)

Number of Servings — 6

6 medium potatoes, cooked and quartered
12 slices bacon, diced
1 c. onion, chopped
1 c. plus 2 T. cider vinegar
1½ t. salt
1½ T. sugar
¼ t. black pepper

Pan-broil bacon in a large skillet. Remove bacon and drippings. Return 6 tablespoons drippings to skillet. Add onions and cook until transparent, stirring occasionally. Stir in all remaining ingredients except potatoes and bacon. Pour hot dressing over combined bacon and potatoes. Toss lightly to coat.

Mrs. Violet Rhodes, Odin Com. High School
Odin, Illinois

HOT POTATO SALAD (Germany)

6 medium potatoes
6 slices bacon
¾ c. onion, thinly sliced
2 T. flour
1-2 T. sugar
1½ t. salt
½ t. celery seed
Dash of pepper
¾ c. water
½ c. vinegar

Boil potatoes in their jackets until tender. Peel and slice thin. Fry bacon until crisp; drain and crumble. Cook onion in ⅓ cup of the bacon drippings. Mix in flour, sugar, salt, celery seed and pepper. Gradually stir in water and vinegar. Bring mixture to boiling point; boil 1 minute. Pour hot dressing over the potatoes; add bacon, reserving some for garnish. Cover and let stand until ready to serve. If salad gets too cool before serving, heat over hot water. Garnish with reserved bacon bits.

Mary Ann Hribek, Giddings H. S.
Giddings, Texas

RED CABBAGE SLAW (Germany)

Number of Servings — 8

1 2-lb. head red cabbage, shredded
1 apple, diced
4 T. sugar
4 T. water
Pepper to taste
2 t. salt
6 strips bacon, diced
6-8 T. vinegar or red wine

Brown bacon in a heavy saucepan. Add cabbage, apple and water. Cover tightly; steam slowly about 1 hour. Stir often to prevent burning. Add sugar, salt, pepper and vinegar; stir. Serve warm. Will keep in refrigerator for several days.

Margaret S. Yoder, Upper Perkiomen H. S.
East Greenville, Pennsylvania

HOT SALAD (Germany)

Number of Servings — 6-7

8 strips bacon
½ c. beet or cane sugar
½ c. apple cider vinegar
⅛ t. black pepper
¾ t. celery seed
1 T. onion, grated
¼ c. green pepper, chopped
¼ c. canned pimentos, chopped
3½ c. hot cooked rice
2 hard-cooked eggs

Fry bacon until crisp. Pour off and reserve the fat as it cooks out of the bacon. Remove bacon from skillet. Return ⅓ cup of the drippings to skillet; stir in sugar, vinegar and black pepper. Cook slowly to dissolve the sugar. Add celery seed, onion, green pepper and pimentos. Add more sugar if desired. Stir in the rice. Crumble the bacon and stir in. Dice 1 egg and gently stir in. Garnish salad with slices of the remaining hard-cooked egg.

Melba Lee Moore, Harrisburg H. S.
Harrisburg, Arkansas

SENFGELEE (Mustard Relish Mold, Germany)

Number of Servings — 12

½ c. cold water
2 envelopes unflavored gelatin
6 eggs, slightly beaten
1½ c. sugar
1½ T. dry mustard
2 t. Monosodium Glutamate
1¼ t. salt
2 c. vinegar
1 1-lb. can green peas, drained
1 c. carrot, grated
1 c. celery, chopped
1 T. parsley, minced

Sprinkle gelatin evenly over water; let stand for 5 minutes. Combine sugar, mustard, monosodium glutamate and salt; add eggs. Gradually add vinegar. Cook over simmering water, stirring constantly until thick. Remove from heat. Stir in softened gelatin. Cool until mixture begins to congeal. Add peas, carrots, celery and parsley. Pour into an oiled mold. Chill until firm.

June Kreutzkampf, West Sioux Community H. S.
Hawarden, Iowa

WILTED LETTUCE SALAD (Germany)

Number of Servings — 4-6

1 hard-cooked egg, crumbled
⅓ c. Bermuda onion, minced
3 slices bacon, diced
3 T. sugar
¼ c. vinegar
1 head lettuce, torn in bite-size pieces

(Continued on next page)

Saute' bacon until crisp; remove from pan. Cool bacon fat slightly. Stir sugar and vinegar into fat. Cook until very hot. Immediately pour hot mixture over lettuce. Add egg, bacon, and onion; toss lightly. Serve immediately.

Mrs. Marcia Miller, Petoskey High School
Petoskey, Michigan

GREEK SALAD

Number of Servings — 2

4 or 5 leaves of lettuce, torn in small pieces
1 tomato, quartered
1 small onion, sliced
8 black olives
Salt and pepper to taste
1½ T. olive oil
2 T. vinegar or lemon juice

Combine lettuce, tomato and onion. Add olives, salt and pepper; toss. Just before serving, add olive oil and vinegar or lemon juice; toss.

Vivian J. Ryland, Lafargue H. S.
Effie, Louisiana

SALATA (Tossed Salad, Greece)

Number of Servings — 8

1 clove garlic
½ head lettuce, torn
½ bunch endive, torn
3 tomatoes, cut in eighths
1 cucumber, peeled and sliced
6 green onions, sliced
2 stalks celery, diced
1 green pepper, diced
2 T. fresh parsley, chopped
1 T. oregano
1 t. salt
⅛ t. pepper
Olive oil
Wine vinegar
1 cooked beet, cut shoestring style
8 sl. feta or jack cheese (Opt.)
8 ripe Greek olives
¼ c. chick peas, cooked
2 hard-cooked eggs, quartered

Rub a wooden salad bowl with garlic clove. Combine next 11 ingredients. Toss with enough oil to coat salad. Add ¼ as much vinegar as oil and toss lightly. Garnish as desired with remaining ingredients.

Niki Sitaras, Wolcott Jr. High
Warren, Michigan

DUTCH LETTUCE (Holland)

Number of Servings — 2-4

3 sl. bacon, cut in small pieces
½ T. sugar
1½ t. flour
¼ c. flour
¼ c. water
¼ c. vinegar
½ head of lettuce, torn in bite-size pieces
2 onions, chopped
½ bunch green spinach

Fry bacon pieces on medium heat until crisp and brown. Drain off all fat except 1 tablespoon. Sift 1 teaspoons flour and sugar into reserved fat and bacon pieces. Cook over low heat, stirring constantly until smooth. Combine ¼ cup flour, water and vinegar; add to bacon paste. Stir until mixture is smooth and thick. Combine lettuce, onion and spinach. Pour warm bacon dressing over lettuce.

Mrs. C. N. Davis, Felton School
Felton, Minnesota

DUTCH SLAW (Holland)

½ medium head cabbage, chopped
1 medium green pepper, chopped
1 onion, chopped
1 cucumber, chopped
2 or 3 tomatoes, chopped
½ c. vinegar
3 T. sugar
Salt to taste
Pepper to taste
Celery seed to taste

Combine cabbage, green pepper, onion, cucumber and tomatoes. Add remaining ingredients. Salad will keep for 3 or 4 days in refrigerator.

Mrs. Agnes Foster,Area Supervisor,
Home Economics Education
Hartford, Kentucky

WILTED RED CABBAGE SLAW (Holland)

Number of Servings — 4

1 lb. red cabbage, shredded
1½ c. boiling water
1½ t. salt
2 T. salad oil
2⅔ T. lemon juice
⅛ t. pepper
1 t. sugar
2 T. onion, minced
¼ c. apple, grated

Combine cabbage with boiling water and salt. Let stand 10 minutes; drain. Mix oil, lemon juice, pepper and sugar. Add cabbage mixture, onions and apple. Toss until well mixed. Chill for 30 minutes before serving.

Nancy Newman, Joliet Township H. S.
Joliet, Illinois

DUTCH SALAD (Holland)

Number of Servings — 4-6

1 small head cabbage, chopped or shredded
3 slices of bacon, diced
½ c. vinegar
¼ c. sour cream
2 T. flour
1 T. water
2 egg yolks, beaten
Salt and pepper to taste
1 hard-cooked egg, grated
4-6 radishes, sliced
Salted peanuts, chopped

Fry bacon until crisp. Remove bacon from the fat. Add vinegar, sour cream and flour to the drippings. Blend with water until smooth. Add egg yolks. Stir over low heat, until thickened. Season with salt and pepper. Pour over cabbage while still hot. Garnish with egg, radishes, peanuts and diced bacon.

Mrs. Audrey Newman, Los Banos Union H. S.
Los Banos, California

HULD'S SHRIMP SALAD (Iceland)

Number of Servings — 6

3 c. boiled shrimp
½ c. cheese, grated
1 apple, cut in strips
1 small carrot, cooked and cut in strips
⅓ c. sweet peas
5 T. mayonnaise
2 T. sour cream
4 T. carrots, grated
4 T. cauliflower
4 T. onion, chopped

Arrange ingredients separately on the same platter. Chill.

Dressing:
1-2 T. lemon juice
6 T. olive oil or salad oil
6 T. water
1½ t. honey

Combine all ingredients. Pour over shrimp platter just before serving.

Mrs. Jeannine K. Goethe, Richard Arnold Jr. H. S.
Savannah, Georgia

PACHADI (India)

1 cucumber, sliced
3 green onions, sliced
½ green pepper, sliced
1 cauliflower, sliced
1 tomato, sliced
Yoghurt or buttermilk
Salt and pepper to taste

Arrange vegetables attractively in serving dish. Cover with yoghurt or buttermilk. Season to taste.

Mrs. Frank Charles Hodge, Maury H. S.
Dandridge, Tennessee

POTATO SALAD (Italy)

Number of Servings — 6

4 lg. potatoes, cooked
1 can French-style green beans
8 small or 1 lg. onion
1 T. oregano
Salt and pepper to taste
3 tomatoes
¼ c. vegetable oil
3 T. wine vinegar

Cut potatoes, tomatoes and onion into bite-size pieces. Combine with beans and oregano. Add remaining ingredients; mix well.

Mrs. Laura F. Magro, (Gardner), Elston Jr. H. S.
Michigan City, Indiana

POTATO SALAD (Italy)

Number of Servings — 8

1 envelope Italian salad dressing mix
1 c. mayonnaise
6 c. boiled potatoes, cubed
¼ c. ripe olives, chopped
½ c. celery, thinly sliced

Combine salad dressing mix and mayonnaise. Blend in warm potatoes, celery and olives. Chill.

Mrs. Nancy Petitt Garvin, York H. S.
Yorktown, Virginia

MUSHROOM AND LIMA BEAN SALAD (Italy)

Number of Servings — 4

⅓ c. wine vinegar
3 T. olive oil or salad oil
1 clove garlic, minced
½ t. salt
¼ t. celery salt
¼ t. black pepper
1 10-oz. pkg. frozen green baby lima beans
8 fresh mushrooms or 1 4-oz. can sliced mushrooms, drained
1 lge. onion, chopped
1 T. fresh parsley, chopped or 1 t. dry parsley flakes
½ t. oregano

Combine vinegar, oil, garlic, salt, celery salt and black pepper. Blend well. Cook lima beans according to package directions; rinse with cold water and drain. Combine all ingredients. Chill for 1 to 2 hours before serving.

Pauline Gist, North Salinas H. S.
Salinas, California

EGGPLANT WITH YOGHURT SALAD (Jordan)

1 eggplant, peeled and cubed
1 box yoghurt
1 clove garlic
3 T. olive oil
Salt and pepper to taste

(Continued on next page)

Boil eggplant until tender; drain and mash. Mash garlic with salt and pepper; mix with yoghurt. Pour yoghurt mixture over eggplant; mix. Sprinkle olive oil over salad just before serving.

Mrs. Creasia Stone, Red Rock H. S.
Red Rock, Oklahoma

BEAN SPROUT SALAD (Korea)

Number of Servings — 6

2 c. canned bean sprouts, drained
1 small red sweet pepper or 1 canned pimento, chopped
2 green onions, finely chopped
2 t. prepared sesame seed
1 clove garlic, crushed
1 hard-cooked egg, thinly sliced
2 T. corn oil
1 T. vinegar
½ t. salt
¼ t. pepper
2 T. soy sauce

Combine onions, garlic, sesame seed, sweet pepper or pimento and soy sauce; pour over bean sprouts. Combine vinegar, oil, salt and pepper; add to bean sprout mixture and toss lightly. Chill. Garnish with egg slices.

Mrs. Avis E. Colgrove, Fort Lupton H. S.
Fort Lupton, Colorado

TOSSED SALAD (Lebanon)

Number of Servings — 6-8

1 lg. head lettuce, torn in bite-size pieces
4 tomatoes, chopped
3 small cucumbers, chopped
1 lg. onion, chopped
½ c. celery, chopped
½ t. pepper
1 t. salt
3 T. olive or salad oil
2 T. lemon juice

Combine all ingredients. Toss and serve immediately.

Ferial Abraham, Argyle High School
Argyle, Minnesota

TABBULI (Lebanon)

Number of Servings — 8

½ lb. Bulghour Wheat (cracked wheat)
4 fresh tomatoes, cubed or canned tomatoes
3 T. olive oil
¼ c. lemon juice
4 mint leaves, fresh or dried
Minced garlic (opt.)
6 parsley sprigs, finely chopped
½ t. salt
Lettuce leaves
1 small bunch scallions, coarsely chopped

Soak cracked wheat for 15 minutes; drain thoroughly. Combine tomatoes, garlic if desired, scallions, parsley, mint, olive oil, lemon juice and salt. Toss lightly. Add cracked wheat; toss lightly. Arrange on lettuce leaves on individual salad plates. Sprinkle olive oil over each portion.

Mrs. Annie R. Gonzales, Prescott Junior H. S.
Baton Rouge, Louisiana

TABBULI (Lebanon)

Number of Servings — 20

12 oz. Bulghour Wheat (cracked wheat)
1 lge. onion, chopped
1 lge. bunch parsley, chopped
1½ lb. tomatoes, chopped
1 5-oz. can frozen lemon juice
5 oz. salad or olive oil
Salt and pepper to taste

Wash wheat in cool water; do not soak. Add remaining ingredients in order given. Let stand at least 1 hour or overnight before serving.

Geneva Jackson, Drumright H. S.
Drumright, Oklahoma

TABBULI (Lebanon)

Number of Servings — 8-10

1 c. Bulghour Wheat (cracked wheat)
1 bunch parsley, cut in small pieces
2 tomatoes, diced
1 bunch mint leaves, cut in small pieces
1 lge. onion, minced
2 cucumbers, diced
¼ c. olive oil or salad oil
Salt and pepper to taste
6 T. lemon juice

Wash and squeeze wheat about 30 minutes before preparation so it will be soft. Combine parsley, tomatoes, mint leaves, onion, cucumbers and wheat. Combine oil, salt, pepper and lemon juice; toss with wheat mixture. Serve on lettuce leaves or fresh grape leaves. Serve as a salad or an appetizer.

Mrs. Carmen Kazen Ferris, William B. Travis H. S.
Austin, Texas

TABBULI (Lebanon)

Number of Servings — 6

1 c. fine Bulghour Wheat (cracked wheat)
3 tomatoes, diced
1 green pepper, diced
1 bunch green onions, diced
1 lge. bunch parsley, cut in small pieces
1 bunch fresh mint or 2 T. dried mint
Juice of 3 lemons
½ c. olive oil
1 t. salt
½ t. peppercorns, crushed

Cover wheat with cold water; refrigerate for 1 hour. Combine lemon juice, olive oil, peppercorns, and salt; mix well. Drain wheat and squeeze by hand. Combine wheat and vegetables. Pour oil mixture over wheat-vegetable mixture. Mix well.

Imogene Simpson, Bristow H. S.
Bristow, Oklahoma

MEDITERRANEAN SALAD

Number of Servings — 6-8

Dressing:
1/3 c. salad or olive oil
3 T. wine vinegar
1 clove garlic, crushed
1 1/2 t. salt
1/8 t. pepper

Combine all ingredients; mix well.

2 pkg. frozen mixed vegetables
1/2 c. scallions, sliced
1/2 c. raw cauliflower, finely sliced
1/2 c. stuffed olives, sliced or 1/4 c. pimento, diced

Cook mixed vegetables according to package directions. Drain and chill. Combine all ingredients and marinate in dressing for 1 hour before serving.

Joan Kettering, Garretson H. S.
Garretson, South Dakota

BEAN FIESTA (Mexico)

Number of Servings — 12

1 No. 303 can cut green beans
1 No. 303 can cut wax beans
1/2 c. sweet onion, chopped
1/2 c. salad oil
1/2 c. white vinegar
3/4 c. white sugar
1 t. salt
1 can red kidney beans, drained and rinsed
1/2 c. green pepper, chopped

Combine beans; add remaining ingredients. Cover and refrigerate for 24 hours. Salad may be kept in refrigerator for several days.

Miss Marilyn Bernd--Home Economics Teacher
Washington Junior High School
Rice Lake, Wisconsin

ENSALADA DE AQUACALE (Avocado Salad, Mexico)

Number of Servings — 6-8

1 clove garlic
1 lge. avocado, diced
2 fresh tomatoes, cubed and drained
4 radishes, chopped
1 small onion, chopped
1 small head lettuce, shredded
Salt to taste
French dressing

Rub a wooden salad bowl with garlic clove. Combine all remaining ingredients except French dressing. Chill. Add French dressing when ready to serve.

Mrs. Joseph A. Hedrick, Jr., Espanola H. S.
Espanola, New Mexico

ENSALADA DE FRIJOLE (Bean Salad, Mexico)

Number of Servings — 6-8

2 c. cooked pinto beans
1/2 c. celery, diced
3 green hot chile peppers, fresh or canned
2 medium cucumber pickles, chopped
1/2 small onion, chopped
2 T. prepared mustard
6 T. cream or evaporated milk
Salt and pepper to taste
Lettuce
Red chili powder (garnish)

Combine all ingredients except mustard and cream; mix thoroughly. Beat mustard and cream; add to bean mixture. Serve on lettuce; sprinkle with red chili powder.

Lelia Cook Greenwald, Socorro H. S.
Socorro, New Mexico

ENSALALA DE POLLO (Chicken Salad, Mexico)

Number of Servings — 4-6

1 chicken breast, boiled and cubed
2 red pimentos
1 c. tiny peas
1 c. boiled rice
1/2 c. French dressing
1 t. mustard
1 T. parsley, minced

Combine all ingredients. Chill. Serve on lettuce leaves.

Sandra K. Neese, Casa Grande Union H. S.
Casa Grande, Arizona

GUACAMOLE SALAD (Mexico)

Number of Servings — 4

2 medium avocados, peeled, seeded and mashed
2 T. onion, minced
2 T. sweet pickle relish
Dash of garlic salt
Dash of Tobasco sauce
1/8 t. chili powder
Mayonnaise
1 stalk celery, diced
1 medium tomato, diced
Lettuce

Combine avocados, onion, pickle relish and seasonings. Add enough mayonnaise to make a creamy mixture. Blend well. Add celery and tomato; mix lightly. Serve in lettuce cups or on a bed of torn lettuce.

Mrs. Annetta Bailey, Agua Dulce H. S.
Agua Dulce, Texas

GUACAMOLE SALAD (Mexico)

Number of Servings — 4

2 ripe avocados, peeled and mashed
1 small tomato, finely chopped
1 T. onion, grated
Salt to taste
Garlic salt to taste
Fried tortillas

Combine all ingredients except tortillas. To keep avocados from turning dark, leave the salad in a bowl with the avocado seeds underneath until ready to serve. Serve with tortillas.

Mrs. Emily Bierschwale, Junction H. S.
Junction, Texas

GUACAMOLE SALAD (Mexico)

Number of Servings — 4

2 lge. avocados peeled and mashed
1 lge. tomato, peeled, chopped and drained
1 lge. onion, diced
3 T. mayonnaise
1 T. salad oil
2 t. chili powder
2 t. sugar
Salt and pepper to taste
4 dashes Tabasco sauce

Mix avocados, tomato and onion. Add remaining ingredients. Serve immediately on shredded lettuce.

Mrs. Joyce Nance, Nixon H. S.
Nixon, Texas

GUACAMOLE SALAD (Mexico)

Number of Servings — 4

1 c. avocado, mashed
1 T. lemon juice
1 t. salt
1½ t. onion, grated
4 corn tortillas
4 slices fresh tomato
Ripe olives
Lettuce, shredded

Mix avocado, lemon juice, salt and onion. If desired, add either of the following to suit taste: Chopped tomato, Chili powder, Roquefort cheese, crumbled, Worcestershire sauce, Curry powder or Tabasco sauce. Heat tortillas in hot grease until crisp; fold once in the center at a 90-degree angle. Spoon avocado filling in the center of each tortilla. Serve on lettuce, garnished with tomato slices and olives.

Mrs. Hugh A. Westerman, Jr. ,Sierra Grande H. S.
Blanca, Colorado

GUACAMOLE SALAD (Mexico)

Number of Servings — 8

2 avocados, mashed
½ can tomatoes and green chilies, drained
1 medium onion, chopped
Juice of ½ lemon
2 t. mayonnaise
Salt and pepper to taste
Lettuce, shredded
Paprika

Combine all ingredients except lettuce and paprika. Mix until smooth with electric mixer. Serve on lettuce, garnished with paprika.

Mrs. Helen H. Redden, Hooper High School
Hooper, Nebraska

ORANGE SALAD (Mexico)

Number of Servings — 4-6

1 lge. head Boston lettuce
3 lge. oranges, peeled and sectioned
1 unpeeled cucumber, thinly sliced
1 small onion, thinly sliced in rings
1 green pepper, thinly sliced in rings
3 T. olive oil
1 T. wine vinegar
½ t. salt

Arrange lettuce leaves in salad bowl. Stand orange sections and cucumber slices on edge between lettuce leaves. Place onion and pepper rings on top. Combine remaining ingredients; pour over lettuce mixture. Serve cold.

Patricia Dykstra, Forest Hills H. S.
Grand Rapids, Michigan

PANAMANIAN SALAD

Grapefruit halves
Avocado, peeled and diced
Orange sections, diced
Grapefruit sections, diced
Canton ginger, finely chopped
Green pepper, minced
Cognac
Mayonnaise

Scoop meat from choice grapefruit halves. Scallop the edges. Pile diced fruits into grapefruit cups. Sprinkle with ginger and green pepper. Serve with mayonnaise flavored with minced ginger and cognac. Chill before serving. Garnish with watercress.

Mrs. Blanche Gavin Sims, Waynesboro-Central
Waynesboro, Mississippi

BEET SALAD (Poland)

4 medium beets, cooked and thinly sliced
¼ c. walnuts, ground
Juice of ½ lemon
½ t. salt
1 T. sugar
1 T. parsley, minced
1 green onion, chopped

Combine all ingredients. Toss lightly with a fork.

Alice Zanolini, Oswayo Valley Joint H. S.
Shinglehouse, Pennsylvania

RUSSIAN SALAD

Number of Servings — 6

1 head lettuce, finely shredded
3 small tomatoes, sliced
1 can English peas, drained and chilled
4 slices boiled ham, cut in strips
3 pieces cold chicken, cut in strips
2 hard-cooked eggs, chopped
1 avocado, cut in strips
Mayonnaise
Thousand Island dressing

Chill ingredients. Combine all ingredients except mayonnaise and dressing. Serve with equal amounts of mayonnaise and Thousand Island dressing.

Mrs. Fay Taylor, Ingleside H. S.
Ingleside, Texas

SCANDINAVIAN SALAD

Number of Servings — 12-16

½ c. salad oil
1 c. sugar
1 c. vinegar
2 T. water
½ t. paprika
Salt to taste
1 can green snap beans
1 can kidney beans
1 can tiny English peas
1 pkg. frozen lima beans, cooked
1 lge. onion, thinly sliced and separated into rings
1 c. celery, chopped

Combine oil, sugar, vinegar, water and paprika; blend well. Mix remaining ingredients; add dressing. Stir well. Chill for 24 hours. Stir occasionally. Will keep indefinitely if refrigerated.

Emily J. Bonds, Hillcrest H. S.
Simpsonville, South Carolina

SCANDINAVIAN SALAD

Number of Servings — 20

1 No. 303 can French style green beans, drained
1 can small green peas, drained
3 or 4 stalks celery, finely cut
1 green pepper, chopped
2 medium onions, chopped
1 small can pimento, chopped
1 c. cider vinegar
½ c. salad oil
1 c. sugar
½ t. paprika
Salt and pepper to taste

Combine all ingredients; mix well. Refrigerate for 24 hours before serving. Salad will keep for several days.

Mrs. Ferne W. Caudill, Wilkes Central H. S.
North Wilkesboro, North Carolina

SPANISH SALAD

Number of Servings — 4

½ head romaine lettuce
2 green onions, sliced
¼ c. celery, chopped
1 T. green pepper
⅛ c. cheese, sliced
¼ c. salami, sliced in 1-inch strips
¼ c. cucumbers, sliced in 1-inch strips
1 slice bacon
1 medium tomato, quartered

Fry bacon until crisp; drain and crumble. Combine all ingredients; toss lightly.

Dressing:

½ c. hot bacon drippings
¼ c. hot wine vinegar
1 t. garlic salt
¼ t. pepper
¼ c. black olives
1 hard-cooked egg, sliced

Combine bacon drippings, vinegar, garlic salt and pepper; pour over salad. Garnish with olives and egg slices.

Mrs. Penny Winchester, Munday H. S.
Munday, Texas

CHICKEN IN CURRY MAYONNAISE (Sweden)

Number of Servings — 6

2-2½ c. cooked chicken, diced
1 c. apple, peeled and diced
1 c. celery, diced
1 T. dill, chopped (opt.)
1½-2 t. curry powder
¾ c. mayonnaise
1 T. lemon juice
Pinch of sugar
½ c. whipped cream
2 hard cooked eggs, sliced
1 lge. tomato, cut in wedges

Combine chicken, apple and dill. Stir 1½ teaspoons curry powder into mayonnaise; add lemon juice and sugar. Add more curry powder, if desired. Fold in cream. Spoon curry mayonnaise over chicken mixture; toss lightly. Chill thoroughly. Garnish with egg slices and tomato wedges.

Ardis A. Williams, Yuba City H. S.
Yuba City, California

HERRING SALAD (Sweden)

Number of Servings — 6

1 8-oz. jar fillet of herring in wine sauce
1 lge. sweet onion, thinly sliced
1 tart unpeeled, red apple, cored and thinly sliced
½ c. sour cream

Remove herring from wine sauce and onions in sauce. Mix with fresh onion, apple and sour cream. Marinate 10 or 15 minutes. Serve on lettuce cups.

Ruth E. Carlson, Donovan H. S.
Donovan, Illinois

CUCUMBER SALAD (Sweden)

Number of Servings — 6

2 lg. cucumbers, peeled and thinly sliced
6 thin onion rings
⅓ c. vinegar
5 T. water
5 T. sugar
½ t. salt
Dash of pepper
Dill or parsley, chopped

Mix onion and cucumber. Combine vinegar, water, salt, sugar and pepper; mix well. Pour dressing over onion and cucumber. Chill until cucumbers are wilted. Garnish with dill or parsley.

Pat Coley, Magdalena High School
Magdalena, New Mexico

HERRING SALAD (Sweden)

Number of Servings — 6

2 lge. salt herring
2 c. canned beets, cubed
2 c. cold boiled potatoes, diced
½ c. onions, finely chopped
1 c. tart apples, peeled, cored and cubed
½ c. dill pickle, diced
½ c. English walnuts, chopped
1 c. mayonnaise
1 t. prepared mustard
Salt to taste
½ t. ground black pepper
5 T. vinegar
½ t. sugar
½ c. sour cream
Red food coloring

Soak herring in cold water for at least 5 hours. Change water every hour. Skin fillets; cut into small pieces. Combine herring, beets, potatoes, onions, apple, pickles and walnuts. Toss thoroughly. Combine remaining ingredients; add to herring mixture; toss. Let stand overnight. When ready to serve, add a mixture of additional mayonnaise and sour cream to moisten if necessary. Salad will keep 3 or 4 days if refrigerated.

Mrs. Inez K. Waechter
Anna-Jonesboro Comm. H. S.
Anna, Illinois

SWEDISH SALAD

Number of Servings — 8-10

1 No. 2½ can chunk pineapple, drained
2 small cans Mandarin oranges, drained
1 lb. green grapes
1 c. blanched almonds, slivered
¾ lb. miniature marshmallows
1 t. salt
2 T. water
2 eggs
2 T. lemon juice
½ pt. whipped cream
1 c. celery, sliced

Combine pineapple, oranges, grapes, almonds and marshmallows. Mix salt, water, eggs and lemon juice. Cook in double boiler until thick. Add to fruit mixture. Let stand for 24 hours. Just before serving, fold in whipped cream and celery.

Mrs. Sidney C. Smith, Fernandina Beach H. S.
Fernandina Beach, Florida

YALANDGI DOLMAS (Stuffed Grape Leaves, Turkey)

Number of Servings — 18

1 c. rice
3 medium onions, chopped
1 t. mint leaves, chopped
½ t. salt
¼ t. pepper
3 T. olive oil
3 doz. grape, cabbage or lettuce leaves
Juice of 1 lemon

Cook rice, onions, mint, salt, pepper and olive oil in frying pan for 15 minutes. Stir often. Wash leaves and remove midrib sections. Cover the leaves with boiling water and cook until they are slightly tender. Drain. Put 1 teaspoon of the rice mixture on each leaf. Roll leaf tightly, tucking in the ends. Place in layers in a large pan; cover with water. Add lemon juice; cover pan. Simmer until water is absorbed. If rice is not sufficiently cooked, add a little boiling water and continue cooking until it is tender.

Theresa M. Lunden, East Junior H. S.
Puyallup, Washington

★ RECIPE DIRECTORY

FIVE CUP SALAD—PAGE 114

This recipe submitted by the following teachers:

Mrs. Dorothy Ohlendorf, Bellevue Comm. School
Bellevue, Iowa
Bonnie O'Connell, Tracy H. S.
Tracy, Minnesota
Mrs. Nellis S. King, Carlin Combined
Carlin, Nevada
Carol Spiess, Winthrop H. S.
Winthrop, Minnesota
Linda C. Presidio, Capac H. S.
Capac, Michigan
Mrs. Dalthea Black, Hopewell-Loudon School
Bascom, Ohio
Katherine A. Smith, Charlestown H. S.
Charlestown, Indiana
Mrs. Wilma Christian Mitchell, Smithville H. S.
Smithville, Ohio
Wanda Frix, Mojave H. S.
Mojave, California
Mrs. Roberta Hollada, Centralia H. S.
Centralia, Illinois
Mrs. Lynn Schumacher, Lake Park H. S.
Medinah, Illinois
Janice E. Fox, Scottsburg H. S.
Scottsburg, Indiana
Linda Phillips, Knox H. S.
Knox, Indiana
Aldyne Robinson, Brewster Public School
Brewster, Minnesota
Polly Dowell, Peebles H. S.
Peebles, Ohio
Harma M. Lemon, Rudyard Twp. School
Rudyard, Michigan
Mrs. Mary K. Lands, Amanda-Clearcreek H. S.
Amanda, Ohio
Mrs. Ann Quinlan, Haines H. S.
Haines, Alaska
Mrs. Dorothy C. Daggert, Warsaw H. S.
Warsaw, Illinois
Bessie M. Sarchet, Byesville H. S.
Byesville, Ohio
Mrs. Leonese R. Hudspeth, Montrose Co. Br. H. S.
Olathe, Colorado
Phyllis Ann Barrett, Seven Mile H. S.
Seven Mile, Ohio
Mrs. Arlene Sazama, Wittenberg H. S.
Wittenberg, Wisconsin
Selma Sailors, Diller Community Schools
Diller, Nebraska
Jean H. Turk, McClain H. S.
Greenfield, Ohio
Jeanette Weiss, Sedgwick H. S.
Sedgwick, Colorado
Margaret Lott, Hanover Rural H. S.
Hanover, Kansas
Mrs. Hazel Tonseth, Lyons H. S.
Lyons, South Dakota
Maxine Barber, Alhambra H. S.
Martinez, California
Mrs. Mayme Veach, Dale H. S.
Dale, Oklahoma
Mrs. Lila Foster, Newport H. S.
Newport, Arkansas

APRICOT SALAD—PAGE 122

This recipe submitted by the following teachers:

Mrs. Lewis Vance, Jefferson-Morgan Jr.-Sr. H. S.
Jefferson, Pennsylvania
Mrs. Nedra Darrough, Aledo Community Unit 201
Aledo, Illinois
Helen Ruth McElwee, S.E. Fountain Sch. Corp.
Veedersburg, Indiana
Mrs. Betty L. Smith, Southwestern H. S.
Piasa, Illinois
Mrs. Lois Allen, Saegartown H. S.
Saegertown, Pennsylvania
Mrs. Betty Lou James, Western H. S.
Russiaville, Indiana
Mrs. John M. Hughes, Southern Area H. S.
Catawissa, Pennsylvania
Mrs. Betty Moore, Lancaster H. S.
Lancaster, Wisconsin
Mrs. Mary Meyer, Griggsville H. S.
Griggsville, Illinois
Mrs. Ruth Fowler, Peabody Public Schools
Peabody, Kansas
Mrs. Ivy C. Stacy, Wilber H. S.
Wilber, Nebraska
Kathleen Allburn, Gregory H. S.
Gregory, South Dakota
Mrs. Vada Frank, Carlinville H. S.
Carlinville, Illinois
Mildred Burris, Delta School
Delta, Ohio
Martha L. Hair, Johnsonville-New Lebanon H. S.
New Lebanon, Ohio
Mrs. Dorothy Schulz, McIntosh H. S.
McIntosh, South Dakota
Mrs. Helen Winkelman, Triopia Junior H. S.
Arenzville, Illinois
Mrs. Mary Ulrich, Equality H. S.
Equality, Illinois
Mrs. Abbie Schollmeier, Gettysburg H. S.
Gettysburg, South Dakota

BING CHERRY SALAD—PAGE 196

This recipe submitted by the following teachers:

Mrs. B. H. Canter, Oakdale H. S.
Oakdale, Louisiana
Mrs. Jacqueline T. Thurmon, Castor H. S.
Castor, Louisiana
Mrs. Wynn Bragg, Manor H. S.
Manor, Georgia
Myrna Weatherford, R. E. Lee Institute
Thomaston, Georgia
Mrs. W. P. Addy, Jr., Lakeview H. S.
Rossville, Georgia
Mrs. Richie Steger, Union Hill H. S.
Bettie, Texas
Mrs. Helen Alders, Douglass H. S.
Douglass, Texas
Mrs. Sara C. Faulkner, Clover H. S.
Clover, South Carolina
Mrs. Kathleen Joy, Franklin Jr. H. S.
Abilene, Texas
Mrs. Zelota M. Yates, Needham Broughton H. S.
Raleigh, North Carolina
Mrs. Jerry M. Cook, Live Oak H. S.
Watson, Louisiana

BING CHERRY SALAD—PAGE 197

This recipe submitted by the following teachers:

Mrs. Pauline S. Slate, Greensville County H. S.
Emporia, Virginia
Elsie H. Evans, Loris H. S.
Loris, South Carolina
Mrs. Belva Whittington, Roaring Springs H. S.
Roaring Springs, Texas
Mrs. Artie Norman, Jim Ned H. S.
Tuscola, Texas
Betty Davis, Loop H. S.
Loop, Texas
Mrs. Mary Alice Renfroe, Waynesboro-Central H.S.
Waynesboro, Mississippi
Mary Ann C. Brock, Moose Academy
Pine Apple, Alabama
Glenda R. Norwood, White Castle H. S.
Plaquemine, Louisiana
Mrs. Jeanine Williams, Meade Memorial School
Williamsport, Kentucky
Bertha Lou Thompson, Hernando H. S.
Hernando, Mississippi
Mrs. Augusta Peacock, Cleveland H. S.
Merigold, Mississippi

INDEX

Abbreviations Used in This Book

Cup	c.	Gallon	gal.
Tablespoon	T.	Large	lge.
Teaspoon	t.	Package	pkg.
Pound	lb.	Square	sq.
Ounce	oz.	Dozen	doz.
Degrees Fahrenheit	°F.	Slice	sl.
Minutes	min.	Pint	pt.
Seconds	sec.	Quart	qt.

In measuring, remember . . .

3 t. = 1 T.
2 T. = 1/8 c.
4 T. = 1/4 c.
8 T. = 1/2 c.
16 T. = 1 c.
5 T. + 1 t. = 1/3 c.
12 T. = 3/4 c.
4 oz. = 1/2 c.
8 oz. = 1 c.
16 oz. = 1 lb.
1 oz. = 2 T. fat or liquid
2 c. fat = 1 lb.
2 c. = 1 pt.

2 c. sugar = 1 lb.
5/8 c. = 1/2 c. + 2 T.
7/8 c. = 3/4 c. + 2 T.
2 2/3 c. powdered sugar = 1 lb.
2 2/3 c. brown sugar = 1 lb.
4 c. sifted flour = 1 lb.
1 lb. butter = 2 c. or 4 sticks
2 pts. = 1 qt.
1 qt. = 4 c.
A Few Grains = Less than 1/8 t.
Pinch is as much as can be taken between tip of finger and thumb.
Speck = Less than 1/8 t.

Substitutions

1 tablespoon *cornstarch* (for thickening) = 2 tablespoons flour (approximately).
1 cup sifted *all-purpose flour* = 1 cup plus 2 tablespoons sifted cake flour.
1 cup sifted *cake flour* = 1 cup minus 2 tablespoons sifted all-purpose flour.
1 teaspoon *baking powder* = 1/4 teaspoon baking soda plus 1/2 teaspoon cream of tartar.
1 cup *bottled milk* = 1/2 cup evaporated milk plus 1/2 cup water.
1 cup *sour milk* = a cup sweet milk into which 1 tablespoon vinegar or lemon juice has been stirred; or 1 cup buttermilk.
1 cup *sweet milk* = 1 cup sour milk or buttermilk plus 1/2 teaspoon baking soda.
1 cup *cream, sour, heavy* = 1/3 cup butter and 2/3 cup milk in any sour-milk recipe.
1 cup *cream, sour, thin* = 3 tablespoons butter and 3/4 cup milk in sour-milk recipe.
1 cup *molasses* = 1 cup honey.

FRP® INC

FRP creates successful connections between organizations and individuals through custom books.

Favorite Recipes Press, an imprint of FRP, Inc., located in Nashville, Tennessee, is one of the nation's best-known and most-respected cookbook companies. Favorite Recipes Press began by publishing cookbooks for its parent company, Southwestern/Great American, in 1961. FRP, Inc., is now a wholly owned subsidiary of the Southwestern/Great American family of companies, and under the Favorite Recipes Press imprint has produced hundreds of custom cookbook titles for nonprofit organizations, companies, and individuals.

Other FRP, Inc., imprints include

 BECKON BOOKS

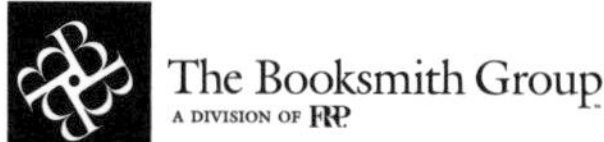

CommunityClassics®

Additional titles published by FRP, Inc., are

Recipes Worth Sharing

The Hunter's Table

More Recipes Worth Sharing

The Illustrated Encyclopedia of American Cooking

Cooking Up a Classic Christmas

Almost Homemade

The Vintner's Table

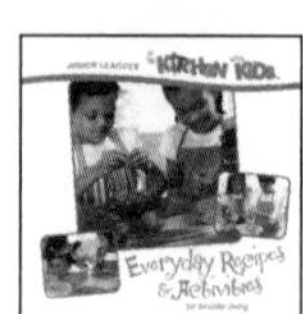
Junior Leagues In the Kitchen with Kids: Everyday Recipes & Activities for Healthy Living

To learn more about custom books, visit our Web site, www.frpbooks.com.